The Ways of the World

COMEDY AND SOCIETY

BOOKS BY ROBERT BECHTOLD HEILMAN

America in English Fiction 1760–1800 (1937)

This Great Stage: Image and Structure in King Lear (1948)

Magic in the Web: Action and Language in Othello (1956)

Tragedy and Melodrama: Versions of Experience (1968)

The Iceman, the Arsonist, and the Troubled Agent:
Tragedy and Melodrama on the Modern Stage (1973)

The Ghost on the Ramparts and Other Essays in the Humanities (1974)

The Ways of the World: Comedy and Society (1978)

The Ways of the World

Comedy and Society

BY ROBERT BECHTOLD HEILMAN

UNIVERSITY OF WASHINGTON PRESS
SEATTLE AND LONDON

Library of Congress Cataloging in Publication Data

Heilman, Robert Bechtold, 1906–
  The ways of the world.

  Includes bibliographical references and index.
   1. Comedy.   I. Title.
PN1922.H44   809.2′2′52   77-15186
ISBN 0-295-95587-2

To
Jonathan and Helen Curvin

Preface

I BEGAN regular work on this volume in 1971–72, when I was a Senior Fellow of the National Endowment for the Humanities and was on sabbatical leave from the University of Washington, and I finished the first draft in 1975–76, when I was a Guggenheim Fellow. I am most grateful to these three institutions for their generous support. The period of "regular work" had both a before and an after. The before was my pleasant stint as SAGE lecturer in 1971; my primary lecture for the eight universities in the Southeast who were my kind hosts was a sketching of some of the ideas that are developed in *The Ways of the World*. The after was the final revision; I did this in the spring of 1977 when I held the Arnold Professorship at Whitman College, an attractive appointment that allowed some time for writing, and I am happy to acknowledge the official and personal kindnesses of President Robert Skotheim. In both fellowship years I had the run of the British Library and the Marylebone Library in London, as well as the assistance of staff members at both libraries, and of course I constantly had the privileges of the University of Washington Library. I want particularly to mention the many acts of literary rescue-work by Mrs. Bernadette Gualtieri, who has the rare gift of making a request for help sound like a welcome opportunity to dig further into the reference world which she has made her own.

Between 1972 and 1976 Dr. Robert Stevick, the chairman of the Department of English at the University of Washington, kindly allowed me a format of departmental duties which permitted some continuing work on comedy. The department secretarial staff sweetly kept typewriters humming when copy was provided. The editorial staff of the University of Washington Press maintained a round-the-clock security guard against the stylistic and mental disruptiveness that the script could exhibit in its less-disciplined moods. Edith Baras is the research assistant who is an instinctive editorial critic. Dorothee Bowie managed a host of problems in ways that freed more of my time for *The Ways*.

I first started thinking about comedy in the late 1940s, when Cleanth Brooks and I were putting together *Understanding Drama*. I can no longer clearly distinguish his and my contributions to that volume, so I can only hope that I am not unconsciously shoplifting from the well-stocked intellectual store of a former collaborator and an old friend. But even if it were legally demonstrable that all of the present thoughts are wholly my own, I would still be aware of Brooks's permanent and beneficent influence on my ideas of genre. As to other critics that I have used in one way or another, D. H. Monro has done an invaluable survey of theories of comedy, Albert Cook is one of the best on the distinctions between comedy and tragedy, and Elder Olson's Aristotelianism has the fascination of a doctrinal purity that one respects even as one heretically tries to wear only parts of the seamless garment of his thought. L. J. Potts is invariably on target. I have learned from these critics as well as from others represented in the appendixes. "To learn" means at times to experience a felt congeniality of thought that somewhat mitigates the pressure for diffidence in assertion, at other times to benefit from a contributed clarification, and at still others to be aided in perceiving theoretical implications, with their combined benefits and hazards, in sharper outline. Finally, it would be churlish not to note my indebtedness to Anthony Burgess for an accurate and happy formulation of a theory that I had been coaxing from private conceptual pre-existence toward public verbal finiteness.

My wife and the dedicatees are related in more ways than one. She, of course, had to be the steady detector of verbal sound-pollution, intellectual roadside litter, dictional mud-puddles, and syntactic barbed wire. She did well in identifying such roadblocks and unpleasantnesses on the chapter-by-chapter journey, for she coude of that arte the olde daunce. She and I and the dedicatees have traveled some of the same roads. They too know the ups and downs of academic administration, a way of life that can become a costly habit, and of habitual theater-going, an addiction of which one willingly ignores the cost. Beyond that, they are not only relatives, but friends.

ROBERT B. HEILMAN

Seattle
July 1977

Contents

The Ways of the World

COMEDY AND SOCIETY

Prologue

UGÈNE Ionesco's *Foursome*, a one-acter parodying a "summit meeting" of statesmen, consists mainly of a series of 'tis-so-'taint-so exchanges between Dupont and Durand. Using the tireless verbal repetition that is a Ionesco hallmark, the two ceaselessly disagree, initially on a matter that is never defined: we hear only "Yes" and "No," "You're stubborn," and then simply "No" by both parties.[1] Martin unsuccessfully urges a more sensible communication, but even he is drawn into the melée. When a Lady enters, all three insist, "This charming lady is *my* fiancée," and in the ensuing scuffle she is half undressed and, according to the stage direction, "has also lost an arm, the other arm, a leg." She closes the play with these words to the audience: "Ladies and gentlemen, I couldn't agree with you more. All this is perfectly idiotic."

What is "idiotic," of course, is the intransigent, irreconcilable, all-or-nothing immovability, the refusal of every combatant to look at either evidence or himself. All trade verbal blows as slapstick artists trade physical blows. *Foursome* is, then, a farce. What is more, it is a farce which portrays a world of noncomedy—a world in which a defensive-aggressive-competitive rigidity cuts off all rationality and civility. Before he too becomes embroiled, Martin chides Dupont and Durand for "refusing to compromise," and Durand insists that with Dupont "no dialogue is possible. Not on his terms, they're quite unacceptable." When there can be no "compromise," and each party denounces the other's position as "unacceptable," the farce reveals the complete impossibility of the comic. Not only that, but Ionesco's jeu d'esprit becomes, as indeed farce often does, a *reductio ad absurdum* of the style of melodrama. Melodrama presents the conflict between opponents, who may in different plays appear as morally equivalent competitors (good or bad or neither) or as embodiments of virtue and vice. Combat is the thing, not concession.

But here my business is not to define "farce" and "comedy" and "melodrama," which get due treatment later on, but to sketch some relationships among them. My discussion of comedy is predictably related to my discussion of tragedy and melodrama in earlier volumes. It is impossible to explore tragedy (as the conflict within the moral nature of man) and melodrama (as the external conflict between different men and groups) without also developing some ideas about the role of comedy, or perhaps better the territory of comedy, in the wide human terrain occupied by these dramatic types. I find myself visualizing a persuasive generic map in which all drama is divided into three parts. Yet this caesarean section, in delivering triplets that have resemblances as well as individuality, should not have the air of setting up a triune divinity, a celestial final solution of the generic problem. In talking about comedy, as in talking about tragedy and melodrama, I am less propounding a "definition"—an ultimate, tight-fitting proof or demonstration slowly reached by dialectical interchange with other Tantaluses trying to grasp an always elusive generic fruit—than offering a hypothesis or using a chosen perspective or a given accent or emphasis. I would like to strike a middle ground between a relentlessly logical and limiting formula for comedy, the heroic prescription that a genre can be only thus and so (one critic is brave enough to acknowledge that his rules reduce the number of Shakespeare's comedies to five), and a lax permissiveness which despairs of discovering a basic comic form and lets the genre become endlessly capacious, a monster of and in miscegenation, a ragbag family with only a tangle of adjectives to identify all the siblings and cousins and in-laws, offspring and foster-children, when the census-taker happens in. The first camp ritually attacks the Polonius classifications; the second practices neopolonialism (and at least one critic manages to have it both ways, abusing the old categories and then realigning and recombining them in a multiple-class system supposedly different from all its predecessors). I probably lean more toward the one than toward the many, since adjectival incontinence commits one to surfaces rather than substance, to piling appellatives upon ossified underforms. Hence, without vainly trying to cast them on the rubbish-heap of worn-out goods, I seek to shy away from various standard terms, such as comedy of humors, comedy of manners, comedy of character, comedy of intrigue, romantic comedy, tragicomedy, and so on, convenient as these may be in descriptive history. Their very handiness can deflect one from the larger task: the discovery, in all of these, of a comic way of doing things that persists even as variants flourish. One tries not to dictate what comedy must be, but to perceive the kind of thing that comedy habitually does. One hypothesizes about a comic mode of dealing with experience, a comic method prior to the surface styles that first seize the eye.

The mode underlies the modal variants. Conversely, one should be able to act in the spirit of Coleridge's "esemplastic," forming (a number of things) into one. *Entia non sunt multiplicanda*, both within the realm of comedy and within the larger realm of genre. To return for a moment to my generic trilogy—tragedy, melodrama, and comedy. Without further refinements, these three cooperate, so to speak, in marking out large distinguishable areas of human experience and action: the conflict within the personality, with its echoes in the world; the conflict in the world, with the personalities defined only as they must be for this combative life; and the relations within the world that, in contrast with those pictured in Ionesco's *Foursome*, engage personalities not only in conflict but also in finding ways around it or out of it to workable solutions. Here I am not defending these very compressed accounts of three basic styles of human life but only suggesting the useful comprehensiveness of *entia* which have been prevented from multiplying. The three terms are traditional ones; since they are deeply imbedded in the habits of literary talk, it seems better to stick to them and to try to clarify them than to multiply terms while avoiding the multiplication of *entia*. One may, of course, surrender a certain tactical advantage if he fails to use freshly minted terms—I am a little tempted by "psychomachic drama," "politomachic drama," and "irenoplastic drama"—that would have the double charm of novelty and forbiddingness. But they would not notably improve the critical scene. Granted, if one uses the traditional terms he has to attempt some rehabilitation, for, as Eric Bentley has complained, they have all been debased in common usage: tragedy comes to mean anything that goes wrong, melodrama a stereotyped conflict with victory precommitted to the deserving, and comedy anything that gets a laugh. It may not be too late to try a small resistance to such loose-living populist usages. We shall see, at any rate, that not everything laughable is comic, and that not all comic experiences are laughable.

We can speak of a genre because we observe in numerous plays not only the lineaments that identify them as individuals but also certain formal traits and procedures that relate them to each other. These objective properties reflect certain persisting ways of looking at experience and move spectators to recognizable modes of aesthetic response. The observable habits of plays are rooted, then, in aspects of human nature—its attitudes, feelings, perceptions of reality, its sense of itself as manifested in the individual and in the community. When that rather sonorous term *human nature* crops up, the user may have various motives. By it I mean merely to stress the permanent in comic experience, the constants in what I have termed the comic way of doing things. It is very much of a cliché of our time, overcommitted to change as it is, that traditional forms are gone forever—as if one short century had fundamentally altered or even eliminated central activities of mind and spirit expressed in these forms. Hence, if only for the sake of balance, it should be worthwhile to look for the durable human foundations under the variations of superstructure, which, as they are produced by changing cultural fashions, are so visible that we too easily take them to be primary. In one direction this means identifying traditional elements in twentieth-century comedy, which at bottom often turns out to be less antitraditional than its deliberately surprising surfaces imply. The addiction to change, however, which makes us fancy that we have put "all that" behind us also lets us suppose that all that lies behind us is a series of changes in which one temporariness has succeeded another. One need not decry historical differentiation if one says that it has become an overtraveled route to truth. So it is well to assert that not only *entia* but also *tempora non sunt multiplicanda*. Fortunately some critics continue to resist the multiplication of times or ages and the assignment to each of a characteristic comic method only superficially related, if at all, to before and after. History is indispensable, but one can have too much of a good thing. Still, if an excess of history is misleading, there are ways away from history that are dubious too. One escape from the weight of many past times is timeliness or presentism: leaving to all pasts no role but that of resembling or confirming whatever temporary present we happen to be in. Rather than taking Shakespeare, and every other dramatist for that matter, to be our contemporary, I shall take us to be contemporaries of all of them, or, still better, all of them to be contemporaries of each other. This is the way of timelessness rather than of timeliness, of keeping in tune with the constants rather than keeping up with the calendar. That there are permanent ways of comedy may be an act of faith, but I hope to show that, in looking at plays of widely separated ages, we find in them as many elements common to the genre as traits belonging only to the individual play in its time.

All acts of faith generate theologies, and theologies in turn are notable generators of dispute that does not often lead, through surrender or self-correction by either antagonist, to unanimity. The *odium theologicum* releases vigor which makes unacceptable anything less than debate *usque ad finem*. Hence in the present essay it is better, I think, to state the basic assumption, and then see how it works in practice, than to put it through a full-dress theoretical conflict with critical structures based on other assumptions. One might undertake to argue for the "durable human foundations" as against phenomenological positions or the credo that an always altering consciousness undermines the concept of human constants. That procedure, however, would impractically extend an already long discussion; indeed it would imply another book, and a different kind of book. The most appropriate test of the basic position which I use, it seems to me, is not the logical case that can be made for it but its convincingness as an instrument for describing the generic characteristics of a considerable number of plays from different times and cultures.

Ideally we are always looking at both genre and play, and much depends on how we do it. I hope not to fall into a simple classification game: to say of a play, "This is comedy" or "This is not comedy," and to imply, "Thank heaven, that one's in the right bin" (as Kenneth Burke used to call it). If I ever seem to do this, then my execution has failed my intention. Obviously there is a risk, since generic terms have to be used. What goes on in criticism, however, should be not a baptismal rite, but rather a seeking out of the generic quality of a play, a showing that it is of such-and-such a kind rather than of some other kind, and hence that it is related to other plays in such-and-such a way. The idea of genre is a way into the play, and at the same time all the plays provide a way into genre. To speak thus, of course, is to assume that genre and play are both realities that are independent of, rather than created by, the mind that attends to them. The reality of the genre is assumed by many critics; even more so, the reality of the play. But eminent English and French critics of recent influence seem almost to deny the objectivity of the work and to see instead, in the guise of a work, only a bottomless well of possibilities to be dipped into by an infinite series of equally serviceable critical buckets actualizing a potentiality. Perhaps, however, even a critic conforming to this article of faith may unconsciously tend to evade its consequences by hoping, as he mans his windlass, to be hauling up a very big bucket, filling a water-tank which will supply a large community of reader-consumers, and leaving the well, if not dry, at least at a low level uninviting to other bucketeers. It seems an equally tenable, if less startling, assumption that the work is there, that though it does not easily yield to analysis it is still not so elusive as to gain reality only through and because of its pursuers, and that there are ways of dealing with it that identify the work rather than only the dealers.

For the most part we look at plays generally considered comic and try to see wherein they are so. We may find fresh and sound bases for received opinion about generic status. But it is well also to go outside received opinion in testing hypotheses; hence I also approach some ambiguous cases, plays that have been called by different generic names, and try to see what qualities support the use of one name rather than another, or sometimes the use of several. I look also at some plays that are offbeat or at least unexpected in this context (Gorky's *The Zykovs* is one example), for they may reveal either a certain precision or flexibility in the concept of comedy. From applying a perspective to different kinds of plays that at first may not seem accessible to it, it is only a step to applying diverse generic perspectives to one play. In my volumes on tragedy and melodrama I considered some plays usually thought of as comedies, since they had in them materials not adequately accounted for by the label most commonly used. Here I look again at several of the plays that I examined in the earlier essays. This is not, I hope, to overplay the principle of ambiguity but rather to recognize the fact that occasionally playwrights—more often, but not necessarily, modern—do apply different generic perspectives to materials that we must then observe in the same way. In *Tragedy and Melodrama*, for instance, I treated Giraudoux's *Electra* as essentially a superior melodrama which in a scene or two takes on a tragic cast, and I also mentioned in passing that it has some comic aspects; here I view *Electra* as portraying, quite remarkably, a competition between the melodramatic and comic attitudes in a situation which could go either way.

The occasional overlap of examples, then, is not inadvertent. If there is a certain duality or even plurality of modes in a given play, it is possible of course to deal with the situation by using a two-pronged term—a traditional one like "tragicomedy" or a headier one like Ionesco's "tragic farce" or some other neopolonial linking together of unlikes. I would rather avoid such condominium terms and instead look at the actual procedures, usually found in different parts of a play, which are best described by one generic term or another. It should also be more profitable to observe an actual juxtaposition of comic and noncomic than to fall back on the well-worn generalization that the tragic and comic are intimately related. This cliché, strangely enough, usually seems a sage gnomic utterance, too profound for demonstration and hence expecting, and often receiving, sober nods of approbation. However, the two may be contiguous without a merging of identity, and without either one's having to be thought a mirror-image or transvestite version of the other. Sometimes, indeed, the implied issue of relationship is entirely spurious, the result of a common tendency, when something obviously unfunny crops up in a comedy, to seek some other term for it. The apparent need for a double nomenclature or for a fusion of genres disappears if we remain open to the fact that the unfunny may be genuinely comic.

The ideal selection of plays would be an unselective inclusiveness—an ideal, unfortunately, that would engage the critic for a lifetime and discourage the reader not only by the girth of the end-product but by its depriving him of the pleasure of thinking of unmentioned plays that might support or challenge what the critic proposes. I hope only to have referred to enough plays to seem easily thorough rather than casual or overwhelming; the end to be wished is that a reader will continue on his own, whether to apply or to resist. One keeps recalling other plays that would be good examples of this or that, but he has to stop himself at some point and hope to have chosen suitable plays to illustrate points, knowing that a reader may well think of better cases. I have sought for a reasonably wide spread of plays from different periods and countries, a necessity if one believes that the comic way of doing things reflects human constants more than it does historical and cultural particularities. Plays in English come up more frequently than others, mainly because of the richness and extensiveness of the British comic tradition (and there are simply more of them than of the English translations that one wants to use for general rather than esoteric communication). I talk more about British plays than American ones; we have not been at comedy as long, and besides, with our strong commitment to change and reform, we are less at home with a genre that views human frailties and habits as more enduring than alterable. I try not to overdo recent plays, though the London theater, which has been my perennial museum case, keeps one immersed in them; in using them, I mean not to record the current scene but to seize upon their aspects that are generically representative. I refer to some plays rather frequently—not careless repetition, I hope, but evidence of the extraordinary meaningfulness of the plays.

So much has been written about comedy that no new approach will be wholly innovative. There is enough partial correspondence between my views and other views to give me some assurance as to the approach, but not so much correspondence as to render this essay gratuitous. One wants to seem neither a furioso or enfant terrible in newfangelnesse nor an honnête homme serenely trafficking in twice-told tales. To identify my own positions vis-à-vis those of predecessors, I have briefly summarized the main views of other critics, with especial attention to areas of overlap, congeniality, or shared faith; to avoid a tedious page-by-page annotation of parallels and divergencies, I have put my glossary of related opinions into appendixes arranged for convenience in comparison. If, as is inevitable, one partly repeats, one also restates and refocuses, changes emphasis and accent. For instance, I depart from the practice of some earlier essays that stick to abstractions rather than applications, and of others that theorize primarily about laughter, humor, and wit and often give plays no time, or little time, or less time than they give to witticisms, jokes, cartoons, and the style of stand-up comedians. My own concern is with the comic stage, though my views ought also to apply to comic fiction (which I mention occasionally). Some critics are interested in the characteristic styles of certain dramatists and do over-all essays on them; though I at times generalize about a dramatist, my business is the individual play rather than the playwright's *œuvre*.

In theories of comedy there is a widespread, though not universal, tendency to see the comic as negative or at least adversary in character—defending this against that, correcting this or that, chastising it or eliminating it. In my view, comedy is rather affirmative, conciliatory, less given to position-taking than to living with different positions as inevitable rather than improvable, as bearable if not always lovable, as amusing rather than contemptible, as expectably imperfect rather than destructive or fatal. There is another tendency in comic theory—to locate the comic essence somewhere outside the realm of rationality, at times on a suprarational height where mysteries invoke more than the human, but more often in subrational regions where the mysteries echo primitive ritual or the persistent dark underside of personality. I do not undertake the mythic, the archaeological, or the geological, that is, the core-borings into the seismic turmoil of psychic underlayers. The irrationalist views may contribute to rational understanding, but they are not indispensable, for the comic can be adequately, indeed profoundly, described as a mode of rational accommodation, in which drives demanding aggression are more than balanced by a communal sense leaning toward survival by adjustment. But irrationalism is in the air, and we can perhaps adapt it to our own purposes: the irrationalism of comedy is not a symbolic eruption of depths otherwise held down, but a making-do with a society that falls short of an imaginable rational order; it is an instinctive rather than rational coming to terms with subutopian actuality, without wholly losing an irrational attachment to the supra-actual.

There is a recurrent complaint that writers about comedy aren't very funny, and James Feibleman among others has argued that the critic cannot be, and should not be expected to be, a comedian. Though he is committed to making points rather than jokes, the critic is certainly not averse to any fun that may arise. What he can do is strive against pedantic heaviness. This is especially true if he has in mind an audience less of specialists (whose study is but litel on the biblical writings of each other) than of general readers in or out of academe. He will use familiar tools when they are available, and be content to go over some familiar ground, but obviously he will have his own direction or bias. In a sense his work is a primer with a slant. The slant means some key terms but not, one hopes, an oppressive private vocabulary. The critic should resist jargon, either borrowed from current fashions or cooked up by himself. Since there are key terms, there is bound to be some repetition, but at times, to resist repetition, I try to drop key terms entirely and let their meanings be implicitly present (it is possible that the discussion of some plays will seem not to be advancing the argument at all). Though the word "comedic" may help reduce ambiguity, it seems cumbersome to me; hence I stick to "comic," letting the context indicate whether it means "having the effect" or "having the structure" or "using the means" of comedy. In mentioning plays written in other languages I use English titles whenever these are familiar, unambiguous in reference, and unobtrusive. A choice of another sort governs the contents of Chapters 5 and 6, since various plays might be dealt with appropriately in either chapter or in both; hence the distinction between the two chapters is not between types of plays deemed to be different, but between chosen critical emphases. In Chapter 5 the emphasis is on the working of the comic attitude as a response to diverse materials; in Chapter 6 the emphasis is on the diverse materials themselves, the human situations that evoke the attitude. Since both Chapters 5 and 6 seek to cover the ground with a persuasive fullness, they discuss quite a few plays. Hence a reader may wish to treat either chapter as an inset reference work and, after getting the swing of things, to read on selectively, picking out the comments on plays that are of special interest.

In this kind of discussion the dates of plays are not of primary significance; only in a very broad way is chronology important. Hence the dates provided for plays at their first mention in any chapter are meant only as a convenience. If the dates of first production and first publication differ, I give the earlier; if the date of a play written in another language is doubtful, it is sometimes simplest to use the date of translation.

Though I have now let fall some rather strong hints about my view of comedy, it seems better not to try to describe it in more detail here but to let the central hypothesis be worked out step by step in the first several chapters. The title, *The Ways of the World*, gives some additional clues at the start. Here I will say only that the world is a large and often unquiet place, and that it embraces both satisfactions and disappointments, and indeed life and death. Its ways are manifold, incurably habitual, always predictable, and yet always unforeseeable. One's account of the comic way with these ways may have two kinds of impact upon those who come into contact with it. Insofar as it seems reasonably full and convincing, one's theory may, like most theories, serve a little while as a fruitful way into individual plays, and even into the vexing labyrinth of generic structure. On the other hand, one's oversights, shortcomings, and perversities will surely stimulate the life force in others humanly prone to correct, and then erect.

The critic's style may encourage one response or be a defense or even a weapon against the other. That style ought to be accessible rather than baffling, lucid rather than opaque, public rather than esoteric. In some quarters and at some times, of course, impenetrability may seem the badge of soundness, and transparency the acknowledgment of thinness of body. Jesting about two painters who had taken to lecturing and thus "explained themselves away," Oscar Wilde warned Whistler to "remain as I do, incomprehensible." He reworked the idea in Act I of *Lady Windermere's Fan*. When the Duchess of Berwick asks Darlington to "explain to me what you really mean," Darlington replies, "I think I had better not, Duchess. Nowadays to be intelligible is to be found out." The risk of intelligibility—not a bad title for an essay—should recommend itself as a goal, even to the unheroic.

CHAPTER I

Some Ways into the World of Comedy

WHEN anyone talks about tragedy in the latter part of the twentieth century, he is likely to come up with the truism that it is doomed, finished, incompatible with our present ways of thinking and feeling. If he does not opt for the truism, he feels obligated to argue against it. A writer about tragedy may be making a hopeful diagnosis, doing a biopsy, or carrying out a post-mortem. But when comedy is the subject, the situation is much clearer: rarely, if at all, does anyone argue that comedy is—or is not—dead. We all assume that comedy is alive. True, some more self-conscious writers of the form apply the narrower term *farce* to their plays, but whether they are practicing standard farce or being very modest, no one doubts that their work is in the comic domain.

What of it, then? Why the suspicion that tragedy may be on the way out, or even out of the way, and the absence of a corresponding suspicion about comedy? [1] Does the suspicion indicate an unarticulated sense that we have lost a certain force, a certain grandeur, a certain magnanimity that we take to be central in tragedy? That egalitarianism breeds no heroes? That we are victims rather than choosers? Does the absence of a suspicion that comedy is dying indicate an unspoken conception of ourselves as mistaken, muddled, traveling *nel mezzo del cammin* strewn with banana peels, meeting endless pairs of identical twins instead of identifiable individuals, misunderstanding verbal signals, beset by coincidences, jesters, messes—being and doing whatever we take to be central in comedy? Of course neither packet of self-conceptions is wholly probable. On the one hand, though we may be given to self-pity, and may be depressed by the fiercer critics of the age, we are not likely, even in the secret places of the heart, to concede that for us in this age pettiness is all. Nor, if we think that comedy is alive and is appropriate to our era, do we thereby acknowledge that a muddled life, and at best an uncertain muddling through, are the heart of modern life.

Yet asking the questions is not pointless. However people explain the widespread impression that of two major traditional genres only one is now truly alive for the creative imagination, their explanation will demand some estimate of the modern psyche and some coming to grips with the genres themselves. Only the latter is my goal. I do not try to determine why comedy should often seem to be more possible than tragedy now, but I will advance one hypothesis.

I. Solitude and Society

Put it this way: tragedy is imaginable in solitude, comedy is not. A solitary person can exist tragically, that is, beset by inner divisions that may lead to one quality of life rather than another: the religious, for instance, struggling between vocation and counterimpulse, between pure and mixed motive. There is one version of this in T. S. Eliot's Becket, another in Marlowe's Faustus. *Doctor Faustus*, indeed, is a play in which the form itself makes the point: the principal conflicts are all in Doctor Faustus' consciousness, and the more overt actions are simply executions or analogies of what goes on within. Other characters, except for Mephistophilis, exist only as reflections or shadows of Faustus. Even in tragedies in which other characters are amply developed, the central action is in the soul of the protagonist: he tends to become more and more solitary as the situation becomes more critical. But comedy and solitude are incompatible: the essence of comedy is relations with others, whether a man is laughing at them, being laughed at by them, cooperating with them, coming to terms with them, scheming against them, easily or uneasily coexisting with them. The comic mode is social; the comic stage is not the soul but the world.[2]

We may have doubts about the survival of tragedy because we know that in our day solitude is not a characteristic state. Someone may argue, in reply, that our world is beset by a feeling of "loneliness" and lack of "communication." These popular clichés, however, rarely imply the existence of a solitary state of self-awareness which nourishes the tragic; they are much more likely to be a complaint that others do not love us as they should. We likewise hear much talk about lack of privacy and of opting out of the "system." Such words represent, however, not a desire for aloneness or for an inner world of self-confrontation, but a desire, for the most part understandable enough, to substitute a smaller and more congenial society for a larger one. Thus even some of the key terms of our day do not reveal, as they might seem to do, a longing for a state of solitude that could be conducive to the tragic sensibility. We have no habit of meditation or of being alone; we seem no longer able to bear the idea of solitary confinement as a penal device; and the action of conscience, which is basic in tragic experience, often leads us, not to judge the self, but to call a press conference and to denounce the wrongdoings of others.

The point is that even in states or actions which by nature seem inner and secluded we tend to seek an outer, public, social style of expression and deportment. We instinctively move and act in the world, the domain of comedy. For us, it is the arena of power or peace, of well-being or failure, of salvation or defeat. With this spontaneous approach to value and reality, we are perhaps less likely to question the persistence of comedy as a live form in our own day. We intuit its affinity to our unspoken faith and our daily works.

The Historical Picture

Historical evidence supports the theory that a commitment to the social and societal is favorable to comedy. The last great period of comedy was the neoclassical age, when in both France and England the norms of existence were public and social, and the exemplary figure was the man of the world or in the world. Comedy began to lose its richness when the man of the world fell into disrepute and an inner light gained ascendancy over the well-lighted assembly room; when the Puritan animus narrowed cultural style in England and gave to the comic voice a hortatory intonation. Comedy all but disappeared in the Romantic period, with its faith in the private personality freed from the social norm, in the lonely wisdom unfettered by common sense, the traditional idiom of comedy. Of course within Romantic thought we can find an occasional contrary note. When Wordsworth wrote, "But in the very world, which is the world / Of all of us,—the place where, in the end, / We find our happiness, or not at all" (*The Prelude*, XI. 142–44), he might, despite the earnest prosaic style, have been writing an epigraph for an anthology of comedy. But this passage is less known than the famous Wordsworth line which epitomizes romantic antisocial feeling: "The world is too much with us" (Sonnet 33). The reductive definition of the world that follows would rule out the comic life rooted in the world, that is, in relations with others rather than with self or nature or myth. Comedy began to revive when the culture regained some faith in common sense, the group wisdom that tests the vision of the lonely seer.

Though no doubt we often echo or paraphrase Wordsworth's antiworld lines, our words rarely reflect more than a desire for a temporary change of scene. We do not divorce reality from the world; we do not put eternity in place of time, or attach ourselves to some other time than our own. So, even though we do not wholly shake off a romantic suspicion of common sense, we practice a life which permits a comic perspective.

These statements, however, assume a relationship between comedy and the world that needs explanation and clarification.

II. Protective Smiles and Multiple Laughs

In paraphrasing Meredith, J. B. Priestley throws out a far-ranging metaphor: "Comedy, we may say, is society protecting itself—with a smile." We might also say, however, that witty editorials and essays, courteous statements from public officials, and urbane conduct by the citizenry equally represent society protecting itself, with a smile. Or we might define tragedy as society protecting itself with unsmiling portrayals of the powerful human drive to limitless self-assertion. It may be that all forms of art can be construed as kinds of societal armor. If so, then Priestley's neo-Meredithian definition hinges on the phrase, "with a smile," rather than on its main predication. Be that as it may, to approach a genre as an arm of society, a sort of polite-letters security police, is to look rather at what goes on in society than at what goes on in literature. The present subject, however, is comedy as a spontaneous activity in which we express ourselves in a certain way, not because we want to move in a certain direction or serve some end, but simply because we are as we are. What do we do in comedy that makes it comedy? What does comedy do that makes it comedy? What goes on in it that makes it distinguishable from other genres? These questions partly take us in different directions and partly overlap; thus they suitably introduce a series of interrelated possibilities.

The Laughter Problem

It is tempting to think of comedy as the realm of the laughable and let it go at that. Characters often laugh, and audiences more often than not; whereas if characters in tragedy laugh, they laugh bitterly, and spectators do not laugh at all except at details by which the Elizabethans momentarily changed tone. But even if laughter does in some degree set comedy off from tragedy, it does not tell us much about comedy. We laugh at many different things—the accidental, the unexpected, the revelatory, the self-contradictory, the surprising, the shocking, the incredible, the reassuring, the fortunate, the unfortunate, the triumphant, the collapsing, the suddenly changing, the grotesque, even the horrible. But each of these terms can also call up a situation at which we do not laugh; in other words, we would need a large assembly of modifiers to specify the contexts in which an event of a given character—for instance, the revelatory—would be more or less laughable to this or that kind of participant or spectator. Then when we do laugh, we laugh in many different ways: there are the jolly laugh, the hearty laugh, the polite laugh, the nervous laugh, the exultant laugh, the belly laugh, the hollow laugh, the sneering laugh, the grin, the chortle, the chuckle, the smirk, the snicker, the titter, the smile that can be altered with a score of modifiers, the inner glow that may be reflected in only a slight change of facial line.

Other problems. Chekhov called a number of his full-length plays comedies, but any laughter that they evoke is spotty and occasional, the response to a detail rather than to the over-all reading of experience. Ionesco has declared that comedy may well produce tears. We remember Byron's "And if I laugh at any mortal thing, / 'Tis that I may not weep," and Shelley's "Our sincerest laughter / With some pain is fraught." The most that we can say for laughter is that it is a frequent symptom of the comic. Symptoms are not to be despised. Still, laughter does not so much provide a theoretical entry into the comic as translate the problem into another key. We would still have to ask what the laughable is, and that question is parallel to, rather than identical with, what the comic is.[3] We need some other way into the inner scene of comedy.

We laugh at "funny" things, but "funny" has little defining value and indeed is hardly definable. Falstaff is funny, but the pathetic is not far from the surface; the title character in Corneille's *The Liar* (1643) is funny, too, though entirely in a successful bravura of mendacity; so are the local dignitaries in Gogol's *The Inspector General* (1836), this time in improvisa-

tions that betray while seeming to save. It would be exceedingly difficult
to find a common denominator among even so few examples; the realm of
the funny is infinite. Yet we use *funny* in one sense that gives a useful clue.
We use it to mean odd, unusual, strange,* conditions that may not be
laughable at all; indeed, the phrase "That is funny" can hint danger. The
word denotes a discrepancy of some kind, and we also know that discrepancies are often, though not always, laughable (for instance, the discrepancy between what Mr. Dumby says to one person and what he says to
another in Act II of *Lady Windermere's Fan* {1892}). Here, then, we may
have a key to the nature of comedy. Before looking at this possibility,
however, we need to consider some other notions of comedy.

III. COMEDY AS PUT-DOWN

Without going into the more recondite areas of theory, we find in circulation a number of ideas of what comedy does and is.[4] A very old tradition
makes comedy corrective: it reproves, censures, chastises truancies from
good conduct. If we accept this view, however, we are dealing with
"satirical comedy" rather than "comedy" as such. In this, society may be
"protecting itself," as Priestley put it, but such self-protectiveness may
also be practiced by discontented individuals, prophets of varying stature,
special interests, missionary or salvationary groups. In protecting or advancing themselves, these usually lash out at other elements in society.
Some score society generally: one side of Brecht, for instance, or the
drama of revolt. The corrective impulse, however, is of little use; it expresses itself in too many nonartistic forms to seem a plausible root of
one art form. It seems more likely to lead into the stereotyped abusiveness
of Martial's epigrams. Once we get past Aristophanes, indeed, great
comedy is only incidentally corrective. Shakespeare is not so at all, Restoration drama is little so, even Molière is not primarily so. Sheridan is less
successful when he attempts instruction. It is a little too easy for us to fix
on specific correctibles and make them the essential subject matter of
plays. In locating topical misdeeds as the themes of Ionesco plays, for
instance, we are in danger of missing Ionesco's larger gift, a grasp of basic
types of human fallibility. It is too high a price for making Ionesco more
manageable.

While we cut comedy down to a censor with a target, we entirely beg
the question of how the corrective works, of whether satire is indeed in

---

*Cf. the title of the 1976 English play, *Funny Peculiar*, by Mike Stott. It mingles old-time farce
with new-age sexual surprise.

any way corrective. Does the liar, the boaster, the hypocrite, or the self-deceiver see himself in a satirical drama, recognize himself, accuse himself, and forthwith cease to lie, boast, simulate virtues, or kid himself? Did Athens see Aristophanes' comedies and then end the Peloponnesian War? To ask the question is to answer it. In watching the satirical playwright bastinado miscreants, the spectator may happily identify new miscreants and in this way have his vision "corrected"; but he is more likely to know the miscreants in advance, to rejoice that they are getting theirs, and thus to confirm his vision instead of correcting it. We need not deny people the gratification of seeing the odious birched (a pleasure that might have some side-advantages for society), but this should not be confused with receiving correction.

Along with the difficulties that arise if we think of comedy as essentially satirical, there is one consequence that is important in comic theory: satire cannot exist without a sense of a norm, be it parochial or cosmopolitan, temporary or transcendent, doctrinaire or humane. Later on we shall have to think about norms again.

A narrower variant of comedy as castigation is the view that the comic is latently aggressive. A smile, we often hear, is a denatured growl or snarl, but with the fang still showing; plays that laugh are ritual forms of destruction.[5] This theory of how a play functions is most applicable to satire and to farce, in which tricks and blows may be symbols of genuine hostility or sadistic longings. The practical jokers in *Twelfth Night* do let Malvolio have it, and the audience can unconsciously enjoy punitive sport; the irony of it is, however, that an accomplished actor can play Malvolio sympathetically enough to enlarge him from an obtuse target into an image of male fallibility and thus inject some discomfort into our pleasure in the antics of the sadistic tormentors. The closer to full humanity the bedevilers of others are, the less our sense of mere aggressiveness in them. If Petruchio is technically sadistic, his cracking whip is a means of liberating his victim; Benedick and Beatrice delight in inflicting verbal punishment, but ceremonially rather than committedly. Nasty tricks are the main element in *Volpone* (1606), but here we can openly enjoy the tricks if we wish, for nearly all the victims deserve what they get.

To turn to a subtler case of a possibly latent or secondary motive: in Wilde the wit may be construed as the more acute minority's punishment of or revenge on all the rest, and yet the wit constantly moves toward a gnomic perceptiveness which is less polemic than valid, for example, in *Lady Windermere's Fan*, "A cynic . . . knows the price of everything and the value of nothing" (III). In *The Way of the World* (1700) Mirabell's schemes may imply an intention to humiliate, but the dramatic evidence as a whole makes him fundamentally humane.

At most the actions of characters are ambiguous: some actions can be read as freeing aggressiveness in the spectator. But the characters are under the control of the dramatists, and what they are up to, openly or under the table, is another matter. Dramatists may use characters as bearers of a latent animus; we occasionally respond to an undermining which as it were sneaks into the formal program (disparagers of Prince Hal believe this occurs in *I Henry IV*). If we take literally Aristotle's[6] dictum that comedy presents men as worse than they are, we might indeed conclude that all writing of comedy comes out of hostility and contempt. But massive derogatoriness—reducing men to midgets—rarely occurs outside of pure farce, where it is a convention. True, Aristophanes defames Socrates, but this is a conscious affair; Aristophanes finds as many men to admire as to scorn. Molière depicts a host of follies, but he has no habit of belittlement that would eliminate the sensible characters who pull things together. Shaw ridicules all kinds of silliness, but it is silliness rather than incorrigibility, and his knack for this does not block his creation of intelligent men and women.

On the whole, indeed, comic playwrights are very generous to humanity: a few railers and rascals excepted, English comedy from the seventeenth to the nineteenth century credits the race with adequate sense. Goldsmith creates not one good-natured man but several communities of essentially good-natured men and women. Shakespeare has a stronger sense of troubled and trouble-making men, but no less faith in the influence of balanced and order-preserving men. While acknowledging both the malicious and the subhuman, *The Tempest* presents the emergence of an order founded on good judgment and self-restraint, in both the use of power to good ends and the abjuring of exceptional power. The argument for comedy as implicit aggression, however, might seem to be upheld by many works of Giraudoux and Anouilh, who often see men as petty and trivial. Yet their line is less a radical denigration of man than a combination of theatrical showmanship, psychological ingenuity that may be chic or penetrating, and an often farcical sense of men as automatons rather than choosers; they move into a somewhat special idiom rather than practice a concealed putting-down of humanity. Only a fanatic could find hidden aggressiveness in Gilbert and Sullivan, whose most outrageous lampoons never become destructive (the music itself would defeat the quest for darker tonalities).

I am trying to suggest, by some quick examples of theatrical practice in different periods, that it is not easy to experience the comic as the aggressive, punitive, or destructive in clown's dress.

The Problem of Superiority

In an affiliated view, comedy ministers to our feelings of superiority and provides the pleasures of contemptuous triumph. As a recent commentator on farce has put it, "And so we laugh the laughter of superiority, the laughter tinged with that satanic pleasure that Baudelaire saw in man's amusement at his fellow's plight."[7] This view introduces several problems. One is that, in a very special way, all generic forms permit a kind of superiority, if rarely with laughter. Whatever the depth of the empathic engagement, the spectator is not inextricably entangled in the proceedings: he is finally outside the silliness, the miscalculation, the disaster, the wretchedness that the dramatist depicts. Thus he has a freedom that dramatis personae do not have, and he has some awareness, however indistinct, of this freedom, some distant sensation of relief, with its ever so faint note of self-congratulation. Though this "superiority," the felt if not defined immunity of the vicarious participant, needs to be acknowledged, it is a response primarily to the dramatization of disabilities, which are only part of the picture. It may mean a spectator's refusing to let the whole dramatic experience get to him as it ought. On the other hand the spectator may be uncritically immersed in the dramatic flux, the likely response when the situation invites self-indulgent visions. Here there is another kind of "superiority," the kind ministered to by the fantasy of triumph. Thus the spectator of various genres may take his ease in opposite ways: he may be wholly inside a gratifying kind of action or wholly outside a distressing action.

For the most part the problem lies not in the behavior of a genre as such but in the quality of the individual work, whatever the genre.* The more

---

*Comedy is especially open to a reductive view because, however inaccurately, we tend to remember the silly, the petty, the vain people that are almost inevitably present in it. Hence it is not difficult to think that it caters to a taste for self-serving belittlement. It is equally possible, however, to let other genres, however unintentionally, provide a gratification that is not large-minded. In melodrama we may enjoy a triumph by force or wiles or, alternatively, share in beleaguered innocence; in tragedy we may experience self-pity; in the lyric, self-absorption; in utopian literature, a triumph of our social or political ideas; in biography and autobiography, self-justification; in romantic works, transcendence or escape of various kinds. A work in any generic mode can assist a leaning toward fantasy.

mature the play, the more it will inhibit fantasy by showing the conditions and cost of triumph, and the more it will inhibit withdrawal by
presenting a fullness of reality that makes it difficult to fall back on our
spectator's noninvolvement. Comedy rarely pushes us into nonparticipa-
tion; if it does, we give it a special label, "black comedy." In some
manifestations, of course, comedy may encourage our latent willingness to
feel superiority: satiric comedy can easily nourish a sense of moral elevation. (Such drama can be wholesomely deflationary only by compelling the
spectator to see the objects of satire as mirrors of himself—a kind of mirror
from which he turns away with more ease than from some mirrors.) Farce
may gratify doubly by stimulating a fantasy of immunity and by presenting a limited life that we look down on from the great height of full
humanity. When farce turns on the ignorance of the characters—in
Plautus or *Gammer Gurton's Needle* (1566) or Shakespeare or many
moderns—we in the audience are never ignorant, and we look merrily
down on those who are. An analogous comic gambit allows us an agreeable equality with, or even superiority to, exalted figures: the post-
Offenbachian reduction of old divinities into new mortals of conspicuous
frailty, as in Giraudoux's *Amphitryon 38* (1929; adapted by S. N.
Behrman, 1937) and Benn W. Levy's *The Rape of the Belt* (1960). This
mode, which has distant roots in Euripides and Plautus, has been especially popular in recent times. A derisory anthropomorphism is the aesthetic arm of an egalitarianism that rejoices in all clay feet and especially
the clay feet of tall people or of people in high places.

Yet this way of elevating many by diminishing a few is a peripheral
operation, as is the encouragement of those with some knowledge to lord
it over those who have less. In nonfarcical realms laughable ignorance or
inadequacy tends to be only an episode, as in the acting of the Pyramus
and Thisbe interlude in *A Midsummer Night's Dream*. Ignorance is hardly a
satisfying comic theme in itself; it needs to be conjoined with other
human qualities that enlarge the human scope. Mrs. Malaprop, for instance, adds pretentiousness to ignorance. If we are schoolmasterish about
her ignorance and censorious about her affectation, still in her verbal
contortions there is a joyous recklessness that turns marred sense itself into
a tour de force or even aesthetic triumph. If not precisely a lexicographic
Don Quixote, Mrs. Malaprop nevertheless shares with him a certain duality that exacts more than simple condescension. Her virtuosity in error
half-subdues our criticalness. Molière, Wilde, and Shaw aim many jests
right at the *amour-propre* of their audiences, for example, Shaw's jokes

about the English. Thus they try to make the audience feel as much needled as triumphant. If it feels needled enough, the aesthetic response may turn into activism: witness the angry disruptiveness aroused in Irish audiences by Synge and O'Casey plays.

The deeper its grasp of experience, the less comedy plays to our self-esteem. The experiences of the most interesting characters are less like triumph than like surrender or major reordering. Wilde's most "serious" characters—the "good" wives in *Lady Windermere's Fan* and *An Ideal Husband* (1895)—have to learn the lesson which is painful for all people, that is, the inadequacy of long-used rules of judgment. Honeywood in Goldsmith's *The Good-Natured Man* (1768) must learn a difficult truth, that a favorite virtue may contain an unamiable vice. In Molière's *The Misanthrope* (1666), Alceste takes us along with him in his sharp critique of social mores; then through him we have to learn that the virtuous critic may be infected with vices not unlike those he denounces. In Barrie's *Dear Brutus* (1917) we can hardly help seeing ourselves in midsummer night's dreams of alternate lives. Peter Nichols, who has made something of a specialty of illness as a comic theme (*A Day in the Death of Joe Egg* [1967] and *The National Health* [1969]), makes us come to terms with unalterable facts of life instead of being overcome by them (as in dramas of disaster) or overcoming them (as in romantic melodrama). The first-rate work does not put the spectator on top of the world; rather it puts his feet on the ground. One end of comedy is the sadder but wiser man; here *sadder* means not gloomier, but less assured, less able to leap to conclusions, or, to play with an older meaning of the word, more weighty, more solid.

There are, of course, many triumphs in comedy: the boy and girl do get around or over the obstacles and get each other, the money, or whatever. Here again the individual work may afford easy satisfactions or portray a life of discipline and quality. Ferdinand and Miranda do not fall into a gift idyl but create a relationship by delicacy, imagination, and restraint, which are not commonplace virtues (and not universally comprehensible in the 1970s, when one critic dismissed the story as an objectionable Puritan homily). Or, in a different realm, Mirabell and Millamant get each other and the money, not by lucky accident, but by great perseverance in tactical jungles, by wit and imagination, by independence of spirit coupled with a fundamental generosity. These great comedies do not minister to a love of superiority, either by central characters to whom we condescend, or by central characters whose easy ascent in the world draws us into fantasies of triumph. The greater the comic character, the less he flatters us and the more he embodies a human attainment which undermines *amour-propre* but images an admirable possibility and an available course.

The Theory of Comedy as Conservative

In one special view of comedy as put-down, what is put down is anything new: comedy as the aesthetic arm of conservatism or the status quo. There is some evidence for this: Aristophanes, for instance, exalts the old-order virtues enunciated in Aeschylus and attacks both the novelties of thought and feeling that he attributes to Euripides and the new education that he attributes to Socrates. In most post-Renaissance comedy in Europe the background is a stable existent society; even satires do not present it as disintegrating or aspire to do away with it. This society permits adequate resolutions of the personal problems in the foreground. Implicitly it embodies the norms of judgment. Comedy regularly depicts the shortcomings of outsiders, deviates, disturbers of the peace, ignorant and ill-bred men (the rustics and yokels that keep appearing from the sixteenth century on), would-be insiders who lack discrimination (e.g., Monsieur Jourdain in Molière's *Le Bourgeois Gentilhomme* {1670}), eccentrics who are social pests (the long tradition of the "humors" from Jonson on), and various individualists who by being too clever or flaunting their integrity fall short of a tolerable social style (malcontents, Puritans, plain dealers, angry men young or old). These troublesome individuals are out of line with a majority who observe the code and with whom, presumably, we identify.

But whether this deployment of characters is "conservative" depends on what is being "conserved." It is rarely, if ever, a social status quo, a current style which needs no change, that is, the usual objects of conservatism as popularly understood. It is rather the idea of the workable society, the principles that make for durable order, the urbanity by which people live with each other. If these qualities are threatened by various kinds of nonconformists who are to be pilloried, they are no less endangered by insiders who in special ways violate the style essential to ongoing social life. They fail by excess. If elegance is a mark of social accomplishment, they are too elegant: the fops who are ridiculed, for the most part good-humoredly, throughout Restoration comedy, and the dandies and their female counterparts in Molière's *Les Précieuses ridicules* (1659). If it is well to know how the world goes, one may become too knowing, like Pinchwife in Wycherley's *The Country Wife* (1675) and the whole race of jealous husbands whose failure of gentlemanly trust stirs their wives to misconduct, and Arnolphe in Molière's *The School for Wives* (1662), who plots to marry an ignorant girl as insurance against cuckold-ry, or like Joseph Surface in *The School for Scandal* (1777), who attempts too many games at once. If honor is essential in a political leader, it can become excessive, as in Hotspur. If generosity is indispensable to society, still it can sink into habitual handouts that shirk the need of discrimina-tion: the case of Honeywood in *The Good-Natured Man*. In the same play Lofty's pretentiousness and unreliability are the misfiring of ease and mastery in the world of influence and power. Honeywood's history points to financial prudence as a virtue in the world; the virtue hardens into a vice in Molière's *L'Avare* (1668). In *Ah, Wilderness!* (1933) O'Neill works from an implicit norm of bonhomie and pairs off Sid Davis, who has an al-coholic excess of it, and Lily Miller, who moves in the opposite direction toward rule-bound rigidity. Suspicious characters remind us that trust is needed in social life; but trusting becomes a destructive credulity in Orgon, the willing victim of Molière's *Tartuffe*. The play does not merely attack Tartuffe, the racketeering outsider; its central point is that he could make no headway were it not for a failure of protective common sense in the insider

Comedy, in other words, is not committed to an old order which it wants to keep closed to innovation; its conservatism, if we want to use that word, is on behalf of certain values which do not belong uniquely to a particular class or order or time but which, in whatever form, are essential in any society and may be betrayed by insiders as well as threatened by outsiders who are disenchanted or discontented or confident that they can greatly change things. Various critics have contended, then, that comedy may be either "conservative" or "revolutionary."

"Revolutionary": by sticking to surface phenomena one could make a fairly good case for comedy as an attacker, rather than a defender, of the "establishment." There is a long history of Colonel Blimps, thick-headed or unscrupulous men of the law and of the church, wrong-headed bureau-crats, unimaginative or oppressive elders to be circumvented, and I-don't-know-what-the-world-is-coming-to types, male and female. Jonson and Wycherley show little mercy to society generally; there are the ill-behaved husbands in Cibber's *The Careless Husband* (1704) and Vanbrugh's *The Provok'd Wife* (1697); there are domineering parents and other dubious senior citizens in Congreve's *Love for Love* (1695), Steele's *The Conscious Lovers* (1722), and Charles Macklin's *The Man of the World* (1781), with Sir

Anthony Absolute in Sheridan's *The Rivals* (1775) as the archetypal choleric and imperious father, innocuous finally in that his will and his son's happen to coincide. Even in Goldoni's *The Mistress of the Inn* (1753), which goes little beyond farce, the noble and plutocratic lovers are made ridiculous by the title character, Mirandolina. In G. E. Lessing's *Minna von Barnhelm* (1767) it is the government itself which is at fault, and in Duerrenmatt's *An Angel Comes to Babylon* (1953) a monarch causes trouble when he tries to improve a world by decree (*bonum fiat*). The most frequent targets of Wilde's wit are such establishment figures as the Duchess of Berwick and Lady Bracknell. In Synge's *The Playboy of the Western World* (1907) Christy Mahon is admired because he is thought to have killed his obnoxious father. Outsiders actually make a better order in Brecht's *The Caucasian Chalk Circle* (1944–45), Giraudoux's *The Madwoman of Chaillot* (1945), and Betti's *The Queen and the Rebels* (1951). Albee's *The American Dream* (1961) batters all the divinities of a culture. Somewhat the same tune is played in a different key in two early Ionesco plays, *The Bald Soprano* (1948) and *Jack, or the Submission* (1950). Beckett's *Waiting for Godot* (1952) manages to find an ultimate image for the authority or the establishment that fails those who await its pleasure.

One would make much of such plays if he believed that comedy does (as some people believe that all art must) rebel against the way things are, pointing to misdeeds in high places and wrongdoing in the seats of influence. But by focusing on quite different plays and parts of plays, one might make an equally plausible case for comedy as the scourge, not of princes, but of all manner of nonconformists, nonjurors, antinomians, oddballs, weirdos, or all those who are uncivilized rather than over-civilized or overregulatory, or fonder of prerogative than of responsibility. Two entirely opposite cases can be made; neither is all wrong, but neither is more than a half-truth. Comedy is neither pro-insider nor pro-outsider. It needs a perspective that can live with ambiguity or doubleness in comic practice. Ionesco's *Rhinoceros* (1959) offers a detached view of the ins and the outs. Looking at a society free to make choices when a new antisocial force moves into a community, the play notes the susceptibility of all ranks and types of people to even a very unattractive new fashion. The trouble cannot be attributed to either big guns or small fry as such; establishment and opposition types fail equally. But there is a faint chance that a rather ill-organized young man, more an imperfect bureaucrat than a rebel, may be the seed of survival or revival.

IV. COMEDY AS FREE SPIRIT, PLAY, SPONTANEITY, REGENERATION

In a well-ordered world the ill-organized man may be a lamentable mess; in a disordered world, a source of renewal. "Ill-organized" implies inadequately attuned to the ordering habits of a society, becoming something of a burden or joke if things are going well. But his imperfect meshing with the organized life of his world (the "system") may mean an openness to other possibilities if the system, stiff or creaky or inept or dispirited, needs revitalization. Both Ionesco and Duerrenmatt have shown interest in the rather loosely hung together individual, not taken very seriously by others, perhaps given to drink, as a potential carrier of new life.

Thus we come to another view of comedy: comedy as the affirmation of "life," as the art of the élan vital, as the embodiment of spontaneity, as akin to play. These terms, partly overlapping and partly inconsistent, all implicitly define comedy as the voice of the free spirit. It becomes a fool to the world, licensed to leap over the bounds of daily decorum and in jest and quip let fly the intuitions that are always delightful, sometimes disturbing, and implicitly therapeutic.

Comedy may play the role of the free spirit in several ways. For one thing, it may place special faith in such characters as Ionesco's Berenger and Duerrenmatt's Akki and Count Übelohe. They are distant cousins of the Shakespeare fools, the privileged pensioners whose free swinging helps keep situations open. A specialized free swinger is Falstaff, and the tendency to exalt him and to deplore judgment of him reveals, in some readers, a fascination with playing at life, making up rules along the way, bohemianizing against the usual ones. Most readers presumably think of the Falstaffian as a charmingly flamboyant weed in an otherwise well-tended garden (for those who see weeds as freedom, the garden is too well tended). It is possible, however, to imagine a whole field of Falstaffs, in rank growth threatening the vegetable and flower gardens in the area. This is the theme of John Arden's *Live like Pigs* (1958): the gypsy family who move into a housing project have vitality and gusto all right, but they make the neighborhood virtually uninhabitable by their freedom from all rules of cleanliness, decency, and orderliness. Though Arden keeps his detachment by making their rule-bound neighbors highly unattractive, as well as secretly drawn to the zestful animality of the newcomers, the play as a whole is hardly a hymn to Falstaffian free swinging. On the other hand, we can imagine a selective breeding of the Falstaffian in which the fanciful, the irresponsible, and the joy in games are divorced from the messy and the porcine. Hence we are able to relish the manifestations of it in Synge's Christy Mahon, rightly called "the playboy," and in Ibsen's Peer Gynt, in con men such as Dazzle in Dion Boucicault's *London Assurance* (1841), in tricksters from Diccon in *Gammer Gurton's Needle* (1566) to Goldsmith's Tony Lumpkin in *She Stoops to Conquer* (1773), in liars from Dorante in Corneille's *The Liar* (1643) to Young Wilding in Samuel Foote's *The Liar* (1762). Our delight in games extends to the practical jokes that are frequent in farce, but here we find a certain ambiguity: the practical joke may be the spirit of play in action, or it may involve a conscious scheming in which spontaneity no longer has much part. There is the difference between the "Puckish" tricks in *A Midsummer Night's Dream* and the punitive ones against Malvolio in *Twelfth Night* and the ruthless one-upmanship of Iachimo in *Cymbeline*. That is, once the trick goes beyond an innocuous upsetting of business-as-usual and is less an end than a means to an end, the tone is no longer that of spontaneity and free play. When Myrrhine in Aristophanes' *Lysistrata* (411 B.C.) is tantalizing her husband Cinesias with a sexual yes-and-no, her "playing games" is not effervescent vitality in action, nor a source of the sadistic pleasure that Hobbesian critics think comedy offers, but an ingenious technique of antiwar propaganda: it assumes both our delight in the strip-tease and our approval of the social end. Horner's pretended impotence in Wycherley's *Country Wife* is not disinterested game-playing; the high-spirited sexuality creates one mood, and the plotting to deceive husbands and get their wives creates another. The latter mood wholly dominates Machiavelli's *Mandragola* (1518?) in which everyone plays a "game" which is really a fancy scheme to assist adultery.

So there is a sharp contrast between gleeful play outside the rules and "play" that is really scheming within the rules. The same contrast of styles may appear in criticism of the world of rules. Criticism is still playful in Falstaff. He has a flair for parody, and his apt miming is in effect a Fool's spontaneous critique of the "system." The critique is a form of fun, and we are happy spectators of the game, not social critics. It is utterly different with Manly in Wycherley's *The Plain Dealer* (1676); his style is forthright polemics, Falstaffian exuberance replaced by an injured man's indignation. What was free play in Falstaff is now earnest, tense combat. Similarly in Wycherley's source, Molière's *Misanthrope* (1666): Alceste, the critic of society, is a man of principle, which curtails liberty and is not friendly to mere play. He calls for a satiric partisanship, which excludes the fun of an open and unexpected world. We move still further away from such a world when Manly and Alceste shrink into the ranters in John Osborne's plays and lesser imitations of them, whose abuse of everyone in sight, sometimes witty but always humorless, has an imprisoning effect.

Freedom as End and as Theme

A comic play is most like play, which has its own rules, when it is farcical. The essence of farce is immunity to real-life rules: certain events do physical damage, cause emotional anguish, and offend good sense. A mad romp by an audience at a farce is a liberating case of "Let's pretend." But the more substantial the characters, the less the freedom from the hazards of life: Hotspur is killed and Falstaff cast off; Tartuffe nearly wrecks a world before the world, with its rex ex machina, recovers its grip on things. With all the wits since the Renaissance we do have an intellectual romp, but we are reminded of all the imperfections that feed wit rather than led to play games outside them; and wit suggests cool, disciplined thrusts rather than a spontaneous gushing forth of unchanneled vitality.

We might argue, on the other hand, that in getting beneath the surface of things, the more incisive comedy confers on us the freedom of new insights, and thus loosens the bonds of custom and cliché. In *The Misanthrope*, for example, Molière shows the self-interest and self-love that may be powerful in a man of integrity. In *The White Liars* (1968) Peter Shaffer presents "givers" as oppressors of "takers." In *The Way of the World* Congreve detects the affinity between types that seem wholly opposed, the fop and the rustic. Wilde characteristically treats foppishness as an inverted wisdom, or as shrewdness modestly pretending to be frivolity. Perhaps such aperçus give us a sense of cutting loose with new knowledge; or on the other hand, in giving us a firmer sense of how the world goes, of implications that we have missed, and of the risks in the virtues of ourselves and others, they may inhibit us with a new understanding that means a burden as well as a release.

The comic spirit may comment on freedom as a theme. Offhand we might expect of comedy a simple confirmation of freedom. Certainly Jonson's humor-ridden people, Molière's neurotics, and Ionesco's creatures of habit lead the life of prisoners; in such contexts we know exactly what life receives the blessing of the comic muse. But in other, and sometimes subtler, contexts, the picture is not so clear. When John Tanner surrenders to the Life Force as embodied in Ann Whitefield in

Shaw's *Man and Superman* (1901–3), it is not at all certain that his lost freedom is better than his new chains. Shakespeare's Benedick and Beatrice give up their favorite form of free speech and accept a yoke that has certain advantages. In Shaw's *Pygmalion* (1912) Henry Higgins takes away Eliza Doolittle's freedom of speech—her native woodnotes wild—without seeming to oppress her. Or we might say that he substitutes better chains for inferior ones, a tough discipline for a bad habit. Clearly we are moving into a realm of ambiguities and paradoxes, where the ringing affirmations of the free and the brave are not possible. There is a similar situation in *The Taming of the Shrew*: Petruchio mercilessly deprives Kate of her freedom, and if we say that what he deprives her of is not really freedom, then we again fall back on an ambiguity. The artist Dubedat in Shaw's *The Doctor's Dilemma* (1906) has total freedom from the mores of society, but it is a mixed blessing; if it is helpful to his art, it makes him so obnoxious that the doctor who might save his life finds it easier not to do so. The title character in Christopher Hampton's *The Philanthropist* (1970) is unwilling to impose his views on others; he allows them so much freedom that in matters of joint concern his apparent indifference angers them. That is, some desire to limit the freedom of others is one way of indicating to others that they matter. Hampton's play is an acute critique of that modern figure, "the permissive man."

In general, then, if some comedies appear to espouse spontaneity and the free spirit almost unconditionally, others reflect the advantages that lie in such curtailments of freedom as discipline. If some comedies provide a vacation from the ordinary "rules" of life, others give us a better grasp of the rules. And if the comic imagination is an avenue to knowledge, that knowledge may, as we usually assume, be freeing; but our enlarged sense of hazards and disabilities, which are an inevitable part of total truth, may be constraining. The situation is indeed ambiguous.

Life Goes On: Continuity

Taken in the broadest sense, the concept of comedy as the voice of the élan vital, of spontaneity and "life," leads us into two other views. One is that comedy is an "episode"; the other is that comedy has to do with regeneration. To say that comedy is "episodic" is to make a contrast between comedy and tragedy. The tragic experience is total; it exhausts a life, there is no room for anything else, and a sequel is improbable, perhaps unimaginable. Comic experience, however, has the quality of a single event in a life; it does not finish off the participants, or their capacity for feeling and thought and interacting. Presumably they could go on into other experiences that are similar or even more taxing. Clearly this is true of many characters, especially the younger ones for whom a crisis has meant no devastating call upon reserves of strength. Charles Surface and Maria in Sheridan's *The School for Scandal* are good examples, and they can well stand for the large number of those fit for many other "episodes." Still, it is not certain that this type offers us a true modal differentiation. For one thing, even a tragic figure may endure a terrible catastrophe and yet go on to live through other profound experiences, for example, Oedipus. One might argue, of course, that these experiences are not really new, but only the logical completion of the first. Still, there is Orestes, who lived through a destructive tragic ordeal and yet retained the vitality to undergo and survive subsequent crises. But though tragic life itself can permit something to come after, what is more to our purpose is the comic experience in which so much goes on that it appears to be a life rather than an episode. By the time Molière's "misanthrope" has cut himself off from social life and the life of love, he has acquired a degree of self-knowledge that is all but shattering. Possibly other experiences of comparable depth are imaginable for him, but as the play ends, he has the air of one who has passed a central divide after which there will be a descent into a postclimactic flatness. Some of the doctors in Shaw's *The Doctor's Dilemma* have come up against an experience that has permanently changed the scenery for them; it has been, if not a "life," at least more than an episode. Most of the major actors in Jonson's *Volpone* will not again resume life at the old stand, all ready for new engagements.

The view that comic experience is a temporary "episode," in sum, sheds some light on, but is not a reliable criterion of, generic identity. However, the idea that after the central comic encounter "life goes on" is useful: it leads us into the problem of what life goes on not only after comic action but also after tragic action. For tragedy does not lead simply to cessation; only some kinds of disaster terminate in a blank. What survives in tragedy is the human quality by which a man acknowledges the power of good and evil as realities in himself; he understands moral consequences rather than cynically reduces nemesis to bad luck or a bad system; the tragic continuity, which is not a victim of mortality, is essentially spiritual. What survives in comedy is the human quality by which man acknowledges the nature of life in the immediate world; he understands the claims of others and the limits in himself rather than romantically mistakes both as symbols of an oppression that he must rebel against or escape from into utopia or solitude; the comic continuity, which depends upon a nonsentimental mutuality, is essentially social. The manners that we can hardly dissociate from comedy—specialized in, but not an exclusive property of, comedy of manners—symbolize concessions to others, curbings of the native aggressiveness that is inimical to social existence.

Birth and Rebirth

The simplest form of "continuity" is that of physical life. In this last phase of the comedy-life equation, comedy is the voice of birth or re-birth,[8] the rite of spring, the celebration of fertility and reproduction, be it slapdash bedroom farce or the grave betrothal of Ferdinand and Miranda, the bringing forth of heirs or brave new worlds. This theory obliterates the distinction in the old joke of "Sex for recreation, not procreation." It takes us way back to ancient practices rooted in myths: the Dionysiac revels with their celebration of the "life force" in literal ways that in the 1970s broke out again very self-assertively. The historical sequence can be put thus: phallic effigies carried in processions were re-duced, in another age, to codpieces at one remove from the pure phallic idea; codpieces in turn surrendered to verbal jests of varying candor; by Shaw's time both the bawdy joke and the double entendre had given way to lectures on the life force that hardly seemed sexual at all. Whether a post-Shavian fling with nudity and obscenity on the stage means a return to an old hearty animality or a neo-Aristophanic lustiness, or is only a flash of self-conscious naughtiness, a nose-thumbing at post-Renaissance proprie-ties, or a decline of the too sophisticated into the too simple—this is not yet altogether clear. (It would be a nice paradox if an overpopulated world were to cheer itself by a deep plunge into fertility rites: the life force as death-wish.) At any rate, while sex fashions in the theater veer inconsistently toward bold bawdry or sly innuendo or equivocation or silence about the bodily or an effort to ally it with other values, it is a truism that plays since Menander have kept bringing lovers together in amiable wedlock or bedlock. The events that imply reproduction are rarer in tragedy (in *Lear* there is a lust-begotten destructive rivalry) or satirical drama; they end in failure in the drama of disaster (*Romeo and Juliet*); and they may have an incidental role in melodrama. But when boy meets girl, or soul mates soul, and hope abounds—this seems a standard fare in comedy.

The critical problem is whether it is indispensable to and indivisible from the comic; whether the ultimate comic theme is renewal of life, whether a happy pairing of the sexes can imply other values than a state of good repair in the life force. Chekhov, for instance, applied the term *comedy* to various full-length plays, but he has almost no touch of successful young love (the best-working love is the not-quite-humdrum arrangement of the middle-aged Irina and Trigorin in *The Sea Gull* [1896]); for him the rarest tune is the spring song. This is true, too, of Turgenev's *A Month in the Country* (1850) and, though it is rather a special case, of Gogol's *The Inspector General* (1836). In a good deal of Molière the amatory arrangements are secondary to problems of affectation, rackets, and personality disorders; almost the same thing may be said of Ben Jonson. Insofar as love is a theme in Anouilh's comedies, it takes us mostly into fantastic games and plots, and farcical and ironic confusions, as in *Thieves' Carnival* (1938), *Ring round the Moon* (1947), and *The Waltz of the Toreadors* (1952). Bedroom farce habitually employs two extremes that are equidistant from procreative love: the obstacles to casual lust (one could never conceive of conception as a result), and the frenetic flight from accidental bedfellowship (the Plautine and Puritan versions of nonmarital sex).

But comedy departs most subtly from the myth of spring when center stage is indeed given to the rapprochement of young lovers, and yet this action seems more than a celebration of the life force and a promise of a fertile future, more than a biological event, less a case of love makes the world go on for another generation than of love as one ingredient in a tolerable life for the present generation. In *The Way of the World* there are as many disappointed lovers as fulfilled ones; the former have to make do with friendship, or financial adequacy, or imperfect but manageable situations, or with the bare avoidance of disaster. The context is one of coming to terms with reality. Mirabell and Millamant, far from taking an automatic ride on a surge of the life force, think, plan, bargain with each other and with the society in which they will live, make concessions, face conflicting claims, and, in a word, unite feeling and good sense in arriving at a complex modus vivendi that is more than a symbolic declaration that "life goes on" or a new refrain in a universal spring song. Though the situation is formally less elaborate, there is a similar tone of new understanding and general adjustment in Hugo von Hofmannsthal's *The Difficult Man* (1921).

There is no need of a fuller census of comedies in which the new-life theme is or is not central and defining. The sampling on both sides indicates that, as with other proposed definitions of comedy, the situation is ambiguous. In brief, the celebration of ongoing life is a mode of comedy rather than the soul of comedy.

V. ABSURDITY, THE RIDICULOUS, DISCREPANCY

For a time it would have been fashionable to equate the comic and the "absurd." But the absurd became an undergraduate cliché ordinarily implying that the user has either a solemn burden to be borne or an up-to-date knowingness about reality. When a loose popular sense dribbles out of a technical philosophic sense, the problem of definition is greater than usual. Furthermore, of literary works usually taken to reflect absurdity, many are tragic or melodramatic; much of the so-called theater of cruelty and violence it would be hard to squeeze into the confines of even a generous definition of comedy. Again, the state of affairs called absurd is commonly felt to be a product of our times; hence there would be a clash between the term and my operating principle that the comic mode embodies certain nontemporal staples. Of course, Martin Esslin, the only begetter of the absurd theater, likes to find antecedent parallels and even roots and thus to expand absurd drama into an almost universal affair. One might, then, either treat the absurd as essentially a recent development with a built-in tendency to create an empire by annexing as much of the past as possible (by no means an unprecedented style in literary study); or treat the absurd as only a recent manifestation of an old tradition.

As for the second tack, Esslin gives us a clue with his remark that "absurd" originally meant "'out of harmony,' in a musical context."[9] "Out of harmony" we immediately recognize as a very old theme in drama. Individuals may be out of harmony with others or with the way things are, or, more frequently perhaps, things may be out of harmony with our expectations or heart's desire. We sometimes distinguish ourselves from other ages by claiming a special burden of "metaphysical anguish"; the self-esteem of a period may manifest itself in a sense of unusual burdens as well as of unusual attainments.[10] It is doubtful, though, whether the sense of universal discord in Strindberg, O'Neill, Genet, and Beckett is any greater than that in *King Lear* or *Troilus and Cressida*. So, even when we seem to define ourselves in a vision of disharmony, we are probably—granted many dramaturgic innovations—doing only new variations on a well-established tradition.[11] I am not, however, taking an antiabsurd position but rather using the popular term as a way into an issue for which I find other terms more useful.

In comedy there is a constant awareness of the discordant. In Plato's definition the "ridiculous" embodies the particular disharmony between the image of self and the reality of self. A man thinks himself handsomer or wiser or better than he is, and we are amused by his self-ignorance. Plato adds the significant point that such a person has no power to undertake revenge if his misconception is brought to light. This is important for generic distinctions: if the man whose self-image is undermined can retaliate, the resulting generic form is the melodrama of revenge. Likewise, the ruling out of revenge would eliminate the severe self-punishment inflicted by Oedipus when he came to see that he was less wise and immaculate than he had supposed. In talking about the ridiculous, then, Plato has in effect distinguished a comic mode from both the melodramatic and the tragic treatments of the situation that develops from a misconception of the self. [12]

Comedy makes wide use of the Platonic ridiculous, that is, the illusion of distinction that is innocuous when maintained or deflated. To take the last case first: a representative comic character whom everyone is on to but himself is "Monsewer" in Brendan Behan's *The Hostage* (1960). A sponger in a brothel, he has fortified himself against the facts by taking refuge in a total life-governing fantasy that he is a military commander on active duty. (In Meredith's *The Egoist* Willoughby Patterne does not even have to be balmy to stay enclosed and almost invulnerable in the illusion of himself as the "pattern" of gentlemanly virtues.) In Molière's *Le Malade imaginaire* (1673) the title character is never quite brought out of the protective fortress of hypochondria which everyone else sees through. But in Restoration drama many confidently knowing fathers and husbands learn the truth; those self-conscious men of integrity, Alceste in Molière's *Misanthrope* and Sir Robert in Wilde's *An Ideal Husband*, have to see themselves more clearly; in *The School for Scandal* Joseph Surface's confidence in his ability to juggle several schemes at the same time is shattered; Goldsmith's Honeywood finds that the good nature on which he prides himself is a way of ducking judgments that he ought to make; Shakespeare's Malvolio fancies himself as an object of love; and Synge's Christy Mahon, if his father can be trusted, has been addicted to a mirror.

Types of Incongruity

In addition to these discrepancies between self-estimate and fact, dramatists also exploit a discrepancy between two characters whom we view at the same time, between a character and the situation or role in which he finds himself, between one element of his make-up and another. For such disharmonies the best-known term is incongruity, and up to a point it is useful in delineating the comic situation. The incongruous has been employed in a wide range of ways from the obvious to the subtle.[13] There are the comic-sheet versions of physically unmatched pairs—long and short, fat and thin—the Mutt-and-Jeff idiom. It actually appears, though under a novel stylistic cover, in Pozzo and Lucky in Beckett's *Waiting for Godot*. The idiom is turned upside down in the pairs who look identical, the twins that sprang from Plautus into a new life in the Renaissance. There is the incongruity of temperament and role, as in the terrified duelists in *Twelfth Night* and *The Rivals*. There is the incongruity of unmatched emotions, as in the medley of unreciprocated loves in *A Midsummer Night's Dream* and scores of less fanciful successors. There is the incongruity of scheme and results, as in Congreve's *Love for Love*, when foppish Tattle, the expositor of fashionable love to rustic Miss Prue and the suitor of the heroine Angelica, finds himself married to Mrs. Frail, the tart. There is the very large realm of incongruity of pretension and actuality, as in the Politic Would-Be's in *Volpone*, Lofty in *The Good-Natured Man*, the long race of *milites gloriosi* from Plautus to Udall's *Ralph Roister Doister* (1553), Bobadill in Jonson's *Every Man in His Humour* (1598), Captain Brazen in Farquhar's *The Recruiting Officer* (1706)—a type turned upside down in Bluntschli in Shaw's *Arms and the Man* (1894) and saved from traditional exposure by innocuous madness, as we have already seen, in Monsewer of Behan's *Hostage*. Here we are coming to incongruities within the personality, and these, of course, may be handled in different styles and tones. The man whose emotions and ideals do not quite match is neatly portrayed in Ferrovius in Shaw's *Androcles and the Lion* (1911–12), the earnest convert to Christianity who finds humility and forbearance hard going, and in Britannicus in Shaw's *Caesar and Cleopatra* (1899), the Englishman of culture who easily turns into enthusiastic warrior. S. N. Behrman's *The Second Man* (1927) catches skillfully the clash between the spontaneous emotion and the critical spirit that suspects it. In Julia Shuttlethwaite in *The Cocktail Party* (1949) T. S. Eliot combines two incongruous personalities—gossipy busybody and apparently supernatural agent—to enforce a thoughtfulness that theater-goers are not prone to.

  The dramatist may use incongruities within character to evoke amusing or eye-opening surprise, to cause shock, or to explore human tensions of disturbing magnitude. He can surprise in styles that range from the farcical to the somber comedy of disappointed love (Mrs. Marwood in *The*

Way of the World) or that combine the two (notably in Chekhov). A variety of farcical effects, bordering on comedy of character, may derive from ineptitudes that lead to slip-up, downfall, or loss of dignity; we see this in Trofimov and Yepikhodov in *The Cherry Orchard* (1904). Beyond the more mechanized discords in Georges Feydeau, there is an ultimate of farcical possibility in Roger Vitrac's *Victor, ou les enfants au pouvoir* (1928), which includes not only rational, adultlike children (Victor, aged nine, is seven feet tall), but also a beautiful and charming woman, very much a lady, discomfited by an untamable explosive flatulence which, like a stammer or tic, may break out on any occasion. One must say "ne plus ultra" of Vitrac's symbol for the relentless physical disabilities that are incongruous with the accepted styles of civilized life. Such farce gains meaning: incongruity hinges often upon the idea of a compelling norm from which we would not willingly defect.

But alas for what looks like one of the more persuasive accounts of comedy, "incongruous" also describes accurately the strong competing forces that may tear man apart or destroy him. Richard II wanted to be king but lacked the stamina for it; Macbeth wanted to be king but lacked a legitimate opportunity; Phaedra was not cynical about vice but could not control a passion for her foster son; Eddie Carbone, in Arthur Miller's *A View from the Bridge* (1955), had an eye for the supposed vices of others but did not know he had a passion for his niece. In other words, the incongruous may be the material of tragedy as well as comedy; furthermore, as often in O'Neill, there are the inner incongruities that lead to drama of disaster. Indeed, if one is aware of all that the incongruous implies, he may plausibly see it extending outward toward the essential conflict in which all drama originates. On the other hand, there is a sharply contrasting problem: comic situations can work themselves out in some other way than the resolution of the incongruous: vis-à-vis both the world and each other, Mirabell and Millamant are not burdened with inconsistencies that create problems, but rather discover the resources for a relationship of unusual quality. Again with those rather different lovers, Ferdinand and Miranda, what takes place is essentially a spontaneous development of a natural harmony. Again, one mode of incongruity is the paradox, and paradoxes may have a depth which is hardly the province of comic life—for instance, "I could not love thee, dear, so much / Loved I not honor more," and "He who would gain his life must lose it." We see finally that, while on the one hand there may be comedies which do not rely centrally on incongruity, on the other hand the concept of the incongruous is so insistently present in all kinds of dramatic and rhetorical situations that it does not provide a primary way into comedy.

By now it is plain that the center of the incongruous (as of the ridiculous and the "absurd") is the ironic. No one doubts that there is comic irony, or needs to be reminded that there is tragic irony. But since we need the qualifying adjectives, the noun itself will not take us into serious generic distinctions. Not that we shall not find the concept of the ironic, or the incongruous, helpful.

VI. THE THREE BASIC TYPES AND THEIR AMBIGUITIES

The ways of defining or explaining the comic surveyed in the preceding sections have more of ambiguity than of authority, for what each asserts is true only of some comedies, or is true also of noncomic writing, or is even contradicted by some comedies. This means not that the theories are useless, but that their usefulness varies with occasions. At different times we shall come back to one or another for corroborative or illustrative service. If a theory of comedy is comprehensive enough, it will embrace these alternative approaches and the insights that they make available.

The various hypotheses that we have glanced at—ten or a dozen altogether—really fall into three major types. One large school of opinion sees comedy as censor. It is "corrective" or satirical; it looks mainly at the flaws of men, concentrating, as some see it, on outsiders, but, as others see it, on insiders; on the whole it takes a dim view of men, seeing them as "worse than they are"; it may be punitive and lacerating. Hence, for authors and audience, it is covertly aggressive and possibly revengeful; it gives the id a vicarious fling. Through it we frown, look down, on weaker vessels; it springs from, and gratifies, a sense of superiority.

Another school sees comedy as liberator, the voice and hence also the promoter of spontaneity, play, the free spirit, "life." Through it we cut loose, abandon responsibility, indulge gusto and zest, express the élan vital, live on, ever ready for more living. Recreation makes for re-creation, continuity: the life force surges ahead. We celebrate fertility, sing spring songs, are born again.

In one way these two main theoretical lines may seem partly congruent. Insofar as vitality not only signifies continuity but breeds superiority, and health requires not only freedom but the restriction of hostile forces, comedy as censor and comedy as liberator may seem to be different manifestations of the same spirit: another version of the paradox of destroyer and preserver. But such an attempt at reconciliation runs into serious difficulty because of different conceptions of what freedom is and what the hostile forces are, of what should be destroyed and what preserved. Hence in some quarters comedy will remain the voice of order, in others a mode of dissent and protest. The doubleness of our thought about it reflects the inherent ambiguities of the form, and these demand a more inclusive view.

This might seem to be provided by the third broad way of looking at comedy: the theory that its material is the disharmonies or discrepancies of existence, or, in the term most used, the incongruities. But here we face a major difficulty, as we have seen: the key terms also denote disruptive or destructive tensions that are axiomatically the province of other genres, that is, melodrama and tragedy. If, however, we add a qualification and say "pragmatically resolvable incongruities," we at least exclude the disastrous and the tragic. Unfortunately this is too cumbersome a term to work with regularly. But initially it helps clear the ground. We can identify the nonfatal incongruities between characters or within character, between opinion and fact, between image and actuality, between expectation and outcome. Still there remain the nonfatal but perhaps unresolvable incongruities between postures—attitudes, ideas—each of which claims a validity not easily denied. These may compel the historian of the incongruous to come to rest on the ambiguous.

Comedy as a day of judgment, comedy as a declaration of independence, comedy as the ironic observer of contradictions in human style and circumstance: though each is inconclusive and even leads to different conclusions, still at times we shall see more of them. They will be most helpful when they are used within a more inclusive view of the comic realm. Let us seek that.

CHAPTER 2

The World as Comic Realm

AN INDIRECT clue to comic attitude is offered by a 1970s study of twentieth-century British drama. The author of the work remarkably assesses the action of Wilde's *The Importance of Being Earnest* (1895) thus: an "obsessed society has triumphed over a set of potentially imaginative, rebellious youths." As if aware that this account turns the youths into victims that in the drama they show no sign whatever of being, the author goes on to lay the blame on them: "Algernon and Jack are typical of those who lack the will and self-knowledge to either find social confirmation outside their society or to initiate significant reforms." [1] We need not long exclaim over this singular misreading. Its utility, however, lies in the fact that it misreads a genre, or, more precisely, complains that the play does not belong to another genre than that which the dramatist has elected to use. This critic would like it better if Wilde had written a romantic melodrama—a form that Wilde lamentably did venture into at times—instead of a comedy. The critic wants the heroes to take either of two romantic options, that is, become either solitaries or reformers, instead of living gaily, ingeniously, and ironically within the social order that is their natural habitat. They should give up their fancifulness and their humor, develop an inner voice or an ideological system that would denounce actuality, and opt unsmilingly for retreat or revolution.

But these are not comic styles of action. For one thing, comedy and solitude, as we have already noted, are not compatible, and reformism creates a good-vs.-evil conflict that has to end in exhaustion or disaster, which no one has ever associated with comedy, or in the kind of public triumph where the comic possibility is undermined by self-congratulation in the winners. What is basic in Algernon and Jack, on the contrary, is the spirit of play, the tactical agility, and, still more important, the acceptance of the price tag and the sense that this is the way things are. The standards of conduct are not those of the private vision* or of the minority cause; they are those of the public scene in which people act, imperfect and mutable as the operating rules of society characteristically are. The unspoken sense of the general state of affairs is not that things could be better but rather that things could be worse. Yet the way things are is not mistaken for an ideal to be preserved at any cost (the melodrama of the beleaguered stronghold) any more than it is mistaken for a fraud to be debunked (the melodrama of satirical or utopian assault). Things as they are are simply the conveniences of life, inseparable from their accompanying inconveniences. Though one lives with them, comfortably for the most part but of course grumblingly, one is not taken in by them; one is clear-sighted, not starry-eyed or ferret-eyed. Half the wit of Congreve and Wilde (and most of that of Shaw, though he is a special case, further beyond the comic center toward the satirical extreme) embodies their awareness of the human shortcomings that make the official standards often seem inappropriate, inconsistent, obscure, and even hypocritical. The awareness is a jesting one. It rarely proposes amendment, alternatives, or avoidance. It works from the implicit assumption that the kind of defects evident in the present society would, human nature being what it is, appear in any other society.

I. Comedies on Comic Life

Passages in a number of comedies formulate, more or less explicitly, the standards and attitudes of comic life; the independent repetition of terms by different playwrights points toward a common thematic center. In *Lady Windermere's Fan* (1892) Lord Darlington has to double as romantic

---

*Lest this seem hasty, I want to anticipate a later qualification: in comedy, the private norm may be added to the public standard, not as a repudiation or displacement of it (as with the romantic sensibility), but as an additional personal responsibility for those capable and desirous of undertaking it. Mirabell and Millamant do not flee from, castigate, or try to change the world, which they expect to live in and enjoy; they simply adopt, for themselves, a code more taxing than that of their associates.

lover and as jester, and in both roles he invokes the same source of the judgments that are to be reckoned with. Darlington is at his best of course when, as a Wilde persona, he turns upside down the standard forms of self-praise and self-importance. He pretends to be bad and frivolous: "If you pretend to be good, the world takes you very seriously. If you pretend to be bad, it doesn't." Not to be taken seriously is desirable, for "the world takes seriously" "All the dull people one can think of . . ." (I).[2] He is less acting a part when, alluding to Mrs. Erlynne, he speaks of "women who have committed what the world calls a fault" (I). How much authority is conceded to "the world" as arbiter appears when Darlington is trying to persuade Lady Windermere to elope with him: "I won't tell you that the world matters nothing, or the world's voice, or the voice of society. They matter a great deal. They matter far too much." As lover, he must argue that to take him as a lover is morally superior to "some false, shallow, degrading existence that the world in its hypocrisy demands" (II)—almost the sole note of romantic antiworldliness in the play. It is dramatically countered by the fact that Mrs. Erlynne would be happy to win back a spot "in the world." She has encountered "the horrible laughter of the world, a thing more tragic than all the tears the world has ever shed" (III), painfully maudlin terms characteristic of the rhetoric of dissuasion with which Mrs. Erlynne counters Darlington's sales-pitch to Lady Windermere (and of Wilde's stylistic decline when he attempts the passionate). Mrs. Erlynne is much more real when, making another of her successful financial demands upon Lord Windermere, she gaily asks him, ". . . don't you think the world an intensely amusing place? I do!" (II). Here she is the voice of comedy. And, of all the unlikely things to happen in the play, Lady Windermere herself, magically rescued from priggish rigidity, becomes a still better voice of the comic spirit: "There is the same world for all of us, and good and evil, sin and innocence, go through it hand in hand" (IV).

Boucicault and Goldsmith

When Darlington, not yet over the border into his lover's polemic against the world, refuses to say "that the world matters nothing," his refusal is in line with a sturdy tradition in comedy. If we go back fifty years before Wilde, we find in Dion Boucicault's *London Assurance* (1841) a key avowal by Sir Harcourt Courtly, the traditional fop who in this play has imagined himself a successful seducer of another man's wife. When he discovers that Lady Gay Spanker has only been pretending a willingness to elope with him, Sir Harcourt comes to with a shock of self-understanding: "Have I deceived myself?—Have I turned all my senses inwards—looking toward self—always self?—and has the world been ever laughing at me? Well, if they have, I will revert the joke . . ." (V). That is, he will confess and repent. The point is that he does not resent, belittle, deny, or counterattack the world, but accepts it as censor and judge; it is not conscience or principle or some private imperative that moves him, but the awareness of the world as laughing observer, as voice of common sense, that stirs his resolve to be wiser.

Let us go back another seventy-five years to Oliver Goldsmith's *The Good-Natured Man* (1768): here we have a different kind of self-deceiver but a similar experience of self-recognition. Rather than attempting a special grab as Sir Harcourt does, Honeywood tries to buy general favor; unfortunately, his campaign to please all by presents to all leaves him broke and hence impotent and ridiculous. Others try unsuccessfully to bring this home to him. Honeywood is not really touched until he is called "contemptible to the world"; he then speaks an aside which is a turning-point in the action: "Ha! 'contemptible to the world!' That reaches me" (V). That is, he gives up a mistaken standard for a true one, bowing to a norm of good sense that will automatically win the approval of the world of rational observers. There is, in other words, a reliable public voice*—one that does not press for perfection or an ideal, but exhibits a sound grasp of actuality.

Congreve

Another backward move in time takes us to 1700. In Congreve's *Way of the World*, as we might expect, the world evokes a wider range of judgments. Marwood, whose emotional intensities are beyond the reach of good sense, inveighs against "the whole treacherous world" (II). Lady Wishfort, an all-but-farcical Marwood, alludes to the "bad world" and indeed proposes the ultimate romantic therapy: "Dear Marwood, let us leave the world, and retire by ourselves and be shepherdesses" (V). Such

*There is an interesting contrast between *The Good-Natured Man* and *The School for Scandal*. This starts with the fact that Goldsmith's Honeywood, the generous prodigal, is really revived in Sheridan's Charles Surface. But Sheridan, at once more sentimental and more satirical (and less comic) than Goldsmith, introduces no standard of good sense in the world by which Charles could also experience Honeywood's liberation. Instead, Sheridan justifies Charles by the standard of the "good heart"; the only other available standard in the play is that of "people of fashion," who are made the objects of satire. In this satirical ploy Sheridan enlarges a minor strain in Congreve. *The Way of the World* jests amiably at "the fashion" as represented in the fops Witwoud and Petulant; Witwoud's rustic half-brother, Sir Wilfull, sums up bluntly, "The fashion's a fool; and you're a fop, dear brother" (III).

anti-world-ism is the idiom of disappointment in people whom the world does not satisfy. When an apparently similar reaching for salvation is voiced by a wholly unsentimental character, it undergoes a subtle change; thus Fainall to his mistress Marwood, ". . . we'll retire somewhere, anywhere, to another world" (II). "To another world": not a pastoral retreat, but a society hopefully without the frustrating entanglements of the present one. Beneath the fantasy of leaving an unsatisfying world there lurks an unformed sense of not having satisfied the world. This standard is expressed overtly by Witwoud when he says of Petulant, his fellow-fop, "And if he had but any judgment in the world, he would not be altogether contemptible" (I). That both are fops does not undermine the point of view: neither is a fool; and no one proposes an alternative norm.

The sense of the world as arbiter undergoes certain modifications when we move from these casual remarks to the title-theme of the play and the circumstances in which it is used in the text. Thrice it is spoken by Fainall, whose reality-sense is virtually as good as Mirabell's. Once he tells Marwood that he has a "heart of proof, and something of a constitution [i.e., is "tough enough"] to bustle through the ways of wedlock and this world" (II). They are, then, taxing ways. As to wedlock: he married for money only, and now he finds that he is a cuckold. He comments with wry irony: ". . . all in the way of the world" (III)—a sardonic consolation perhaps, but less a rancorous judgment than a reminder to keep his emotions in line with the facts of life. When his and Marwood's affair, and their efforts to blackmail Lady Wishfort, are at the point of being betrayed, Fainall exclaims, "If it must all come out, why let 'em know it; 'tis but the way of the world" (V). It is hardly a condemnation of the world, but it could be a cynical self-defense: all are corrupt, and that includes us.

Yet it is subtler than that, I think: it is more like an assertion that we are not special cases but, admirably or not, in line with general patterns of conduct. We cannot be outcasts because we are in the swim. In no sense does the play as a whole condemn the swim. Life is competitive, and in the competition few Congreve characters behave ideally. On the other hand, if the general style is flawed, still society is by no means so irre-claimable that some authoritative character has to say of it—as the title character in Duerrenmatt's *Romulus the Great* says of the Roman Em-pire—that it ought to be destroyed. On the contrary. Fainall's at-tempted snatch is eventually foiled by the fact that his wife had previously deeded her whole estate in trust to Mirabell when he was her lover; hence in no way can it be conveyed to Fainall. Of this device Mirabell says, ". . . 'tis the way of the world, sir, of the widows of the world" (V). The way of the world includes, then, not only many kinds of self-seeking, but a sensible prudence, particularly in self-protection.[3] We should note that Mrs. Fainall's prudence embodies the risk of putting herself totally in Mirabell's power; significantly, the final action in the play is not Mirabell's embracing Millamant, but Mirabell's returning the deed to Mrs. Fainall. In the way of the world, then, one not only protects oneself but identifies trustworthy aides in one's protective measures; in the way of the world one finds reliability and generosity as well as tough-fibered self-seeking. The way things are is not necessarily a source of disillusionment or hopelessness; sometimes it may hurt, it always demands that one be wary, but it may offer comfort or security or at least a bearable modus vivendi.

T. S. Eliot

T. S. Eliot defines the way of the world more formally. In *The Family Reunion* (1939) he has little good to say of it, but a decade later, in *The Cocktail Party* (1949), he exhibits a much wider range of sympathies and makes a good case for the world. Sir Henry Harcourt-Reilly tells Celia Coplestone that there are two roads to well-being, and he comments, "Neither way is better. / Both ways are necessary" (II). Theologically they are the negative way—that of the spirit, of the saint, perhaps of martyrdom—and the affirmative way, that of ordinary life in the world. Celia chooses the former, Edward and Lavinia Chamberlayne are by nature meant for the latter, in which the cocktail party (a secular communion) is a central symbol. Eliot pictures the way of the world with illuminating fullness by defining it from two perspectives. After their family-therapy session with Reilly, Edward Chamberlayne says to Lavinia, ". . . we must make the best of a bad job. / That is what he means" (II). It is an excellent unsentimental way of describing a life that is workable but unideal, and it might describe the solution for many a character in tough-minded comedy. Eliot is a little worried about its toughness, however, and modifies it slightly in Reilly's reply, though the revisionist impulse is held in check by a certain syntactic density. Reilly says, in effect, that this rather chilling phrase will fade in memory when they realize that "the best of a bad job is all any of us make of it." Then, assessing this "human condition" for Celia, Reilly defines it, and its merit, in more detail. Those who make do with it

> may remember
> The vision they have had, but they cease to regret it,
> Maintain themselves by the common routine,
> Learn to avoid excessive expectation,
> Become tolerant of themselves and others. . . .

They do the usual "giving and taking," they "do not repine," they are "contented" with daily routines; parents make out though they do not understand each other or their children.

This is the common-sense post-Romantic coming to terms with things as they are. Eliot might be consciously defining a central motif of the comic tradition: the resolution of incongruities between the self-image and the way the world goes. Both in this underlying action and in the surface details of their life—comfort, cocktails, conversation, and occasional wit—the Chamberlaynes represent the comic mode, and Eliot is formally contrasting it with that other mode which Celia elects and which, with its spiritual tension, borders upon the tragic. Though his heart is with Celia's negative way, Eliot is at pains to justify the Chamberlaynes' way. Reilly tells Celia, "In a world of lunacy, / Violence, stupidity, greed . . . it is a good life" (II). Lunacy, violence, stupidity, greed: though they may lead to tragedy, they are normally the substance of melodrama and of sharp satire. They are inalienable in life and in art, and, in remembering them, we avoid rendering facile the adjustment to circumstances—to human and hence social actuality—that occupies so large a role in the comic mode.

The Paradoxical World: Heterogeneous and Normative

The comic mode is social, I noted in my opening chapter; the comic stage is the world.[4] In exploring this hypothesis, we have been looking at the words and actions by which quite a few comedies define men's sense of the world. Their views are numerous, and it may not be possible to find total unity among the variations that crop up. Still, one thing is clear: though at times men and women criticize the world because it is imperfect and brings disappointments, they never want to do away with it, they do not expect to change it, and though when they suffer reversals they may propose to flee it, they almost never do so. At worst it is the lesser of the evils that may have to be put up with. But it is less an evil than a mixture of good and evil; it may be grasping, nonmoral, and hypocritical, but it is also prudent, regular, dependable, and even capable of decency. It is likely to be routine, unspectacular, unconcerned, unfriendly to great ambition, unflattering. It is the sum of the way things are because we are as we are. It is what we make do with, its familiar surfaces little enhanced by the glint of illusion. To live with it is to recognize actuality, to settle for its medley of the gratifying, the bearable, the upsetting, the grievous, and occasionally the inimical.

Yet paradoxically the world that sums up man's heterogeneity as a social being acts also as an arbiter whose voice elicits respect, even if the respect is grudged. Accommodating oneself to actuality includes heeding a judgment that appears valid. We see that everything is present in the world, but we cannot say that everything goes; diversity includes a sensed norm. What is expected may not be loved, and what is tolerated need not go unjudged. Of all the things that go into it, society has some idea of which ones better serve its coherence and continuity. Thus it resists the tendency of its inherent inclusiveness to generate an uncentered medley bound to disintegrate. The fullness of the world includes rational discrimination;[5] in the way things are there is a measure of good sense, the bar both against everything goes and against its opposite, nothing goes (the recurrent purist revolt against fullness). Goldsmith's world includes benevolence, naïveté, machination, self-serving, pretentiousness, sponging, and diverse follies, and no one supposes that these are going to disappear; but it is also the "world" that brings home to Honeywood the silliness of his self-deceptions and their undermining of the good ends he has believed himself to be serving.

II. A Formulation

I have been trying to summarize the diversities of the world as we have seen it consistently displayed and viewed in several representative comedies from three centuries: the world as here cometh everyman, as average sensual man, and as the man of sense. I have proposed a way of reconciling the competing tendencies of the world—the tendency to be an inevitably unpurified welter of human possibilities, and the tendency to be an influential, though nonlegislative, consensus of what is better and what is worse. The sense of comedy that I have been describing has never, so far as I know, been expressed better or more compactly than in some apparently unmediated words by Anthony Burgess: "Comedy has a meaning in terms of—not of content, but effects: elation, *acceptance of the world, of the fundamental disparateness of all the elements of the world* [italics added]. The test is, it makes one, if not laugh, at least consider laughing. One feels one can push on."[6] In the limitation imposed in his first sentence ("not of content") Burgess, I feel, does an injustice to the truly wide applicability of his own definition: surely it describes what goes on in comedies as well as what goes on in those who experience the comedies. The audience accept what the drama accepts, that is, what the characters accept with the approval, or without the express disapproval, of the dramatist (this assumes that he is an adequate artist with imaginative spread and is not merely the spokesman for some dogma or the manipulator of familiar routines). The dramatis personae in Congreve and Wilde may jest about, rail at, and throw barbs at the world, but no one ever denies the world; the fact that the drama does not reject, however much it needles and upbraids, the world, is one means of reconciling the audience to the world while keeping them wholly free of illusions about it. The characters feel they can "push on"—though failing in this or that project, though making do with less than they hoped for (cured of "excessive expectation"), though embarrassed, even humiliated; for them, and hence for us, shortcomings are not irremediable, and reality is mingled enough to provide ways of living with, or compensations in, or counters to, or continuities beyond, apparent defeat.

"Elation"—what this word of Burgess introduces, I believe, is the view of comedy as free spirit, as zestful, as liberating, as recreating play. Yet the elation is not isolated from the ways of the world; it is not a kicking against the traces or a debunking of false idols. It accompanies the acceptance of the world: it is, perhaps, the joy of finding an accommodation with things, of knowing more without letting the knowledge become a burden and a justification for sad disillusionment. As for laughter, Burgess delimits it enough to reduce the problems inherent in simply thinking of the comic as that which is laughable. Here, laughter accompanies the acceptance of the world; it is not, then, the laughter of condescension or of triumph, but the good spirits of coming to terms with actuality, the well-being which makes it natural to push on, or, to put it negatively, the release from single-track dejection or resentment at the way things are.[7] Laughter, too, accompanies the acceptance of "the fundamental disparateness of all the elements of the world"; that is, a cutting loose from the doctrinaire singleness to which we are all prone at times, a finding of balance amid the contrarieties that are indifferent alike to the blueprints of logic and of expectation. We can see this as a fundamental charitableness,* and the laughter, then, as the signal of a good humor that masters the frustrating condition and the thwarting surprise. Or we can see the disparateness as the ground of all the incongruities often proposed as the genesis of the laughable and the comic.

Burgess' view of the comic, then, embraces two of the views we surveyed in Chapter 1—comedy as the spirit of ongoing life, and comedy as the sense of the incongruous that always keeps trespassing on the ordered design which we instinctively expect to find in existence (or with which we hope to rectify it). Burgess' phrases, however, do not allow for the view of comedy as corrector, as censor, as whiplash in the hands of an angry man looking down with scorn on a defective humanity. Burgess is implicitly separating comedy from satire. This separation is essential, though even as we make it we have also to remember that in practice the forms may overlap or intersect.[8]

Some Comedies on the Comic Role

In defining comedy as the acceptance of the world, Burgess puts into epigrammatic form an idea that crops up elsewhere in different but not discordant formulations.[9] Frank Hauser says of the Edmund Kean in the Dumas-Sartre drama, "Like the non-actors in the play . . . he has to make his peace with things as they are. *Kean*, after all, is a comedy."[10] "Things as they are" is a way of defining "the world" that we have already used. Half a century earlier, in *The Doctor's Dilemma* (1906), Shaw made a comparable, though indirect, contribution to the defining of comedy. Though Shaw flamboyantly subtitled the play "a Tragedy," it is conspicuously a comedy of the obdurate refusal of human nature to make it easier for people who have to make value judgments: Shaw's doctors would be much more comfortable if an artistically gifted patient, Dubedat, were also a decent human being. Sir Patrick Cullen sums it up for Sir Colenso Ridgeon, faced with a choice between tubercular patients whom he could presumably save: "The world isnt [*sic*] going to be made simple for you, my lad: you must take it as it is" (II). In Burgess' terms, Sir Colenso has

---

*Kurt J. Fickert argues, in *To Heaven and Back: The New Morality in the Plays of Friedrich Dürrenmatt* (Lexington: University Press of Kentucky, 1972), that for Duerrenmatt the key to morality is "a willingness to allow consideration for others, confraternity, love, to be the sole basis for action" (p. 10). This is relevant here because in his theoretical observations on genre Duerrenmatt thinks of tragedy as belonging to the past and assigns to comedy a significant role as an order-producing form. If, then, in practicing comedy he is asserting the fundamental value of *caritas*, he conceives of comedy in a way analogous to that of the present essay.

to "accept" the "disparateness" of the world that embraces different standards of value (as do the audience who have to empathize with him in his dilemma: he is forced to choose between the artist-scoundrel and the ungifted good man when he cannot save both).

To return to more recent times, we find an apposite speech, and one of great intellectual vivacity, in Max Frisch's *Don Juan, or the Love of Geometry* (1953; rev., 1962). The Bishop is speaking to Don Juan in Act V:

> God punishes man by creating him as he is, not as he ought to be, and the atonement for all that we have done in our pride and obstinacy is to learn to live, as we grow mature, with the knowledge: There is no solution! We must live with the necessity of our unfulfilled longing—as creatures of a creation that does not conform to our geometry—we must learn to live without cursing—for as long as we curse our fate, even the happiness we *might* have is only a purgatory.[11]

"Man as he is"—the world again (and with an amusing side-glance at Aristotle); "live with the knowledge," "live with the necessity," "live without cursing"—again, "accept"; "there is no solution," "a creation that does not conform to our geometry"—as effective translations of "disparateness" as one could wish, since the disparateness of which men are most conscious is that between their own designs and preconceptions and the circumstances that do not heed their plans. This homily on accommodation to actuality is not a casual purple passage but a thematic statement of an over-all action in which Don Juan has to get used to an antigeometrical, or at least nongeometrical, world, specifically, to the ordinariness of married life, a prosaic inferno quite in contrast to the romantic spectacularities of the myth.

The general notions of "the world" and of "acceptance" are clear enough. We can, however, go somewhat further with the implications of each. To take a closer look at the world will lead to some distinctions between comedy and tragedy; to examine acceptance more fully will take us into the distinctions between comedy and melodrama. A picture of the relationships among the three—the common grounds in each of three possible pairings, and the corresponding oppositions—will be the background for a more detailed look at the operations of comedy.

III. COMIC VS. TRAGIC REALMS

Balzac both defined the realm of comedy and revealed the inclusiveness of comedy when he called his immense novelistic panorama "La Comédie humaine": not the divine comedy, this, but the total picture of the way things go in this world. Yet despite its inclusiveness Balzac's phrase does some cutting back that will help us make distinctions: it eliminates, for instance, the transcendent and the eschatological, either of which may have a literal or a symbolic role in tragedy. The comic embrace of the world is in contrast with the rejection of it in the Book of Common Prayer, which identifies antispiritual life in familiar trinitarian terms: "the world, the flesh, and the devil." ("The world" invariably means "this world," not "the other world.") In this formulation the world—secular life—is really narrower than it is in comedy, for by definition it includes only the unworthy bound to be lost; in comedy, however much may be lost, there are always immanent possibilities of salvation—for instance, by personal or institutional good sense. If we go behind the Prayer Book into scriptural sources, we find in Matthew and Mark the familiar overt distinction between the world and other realities: in Mark's phrasing, "What shall it profit a man, if he shall gain the whole world, and lose his own soul?" Someone might be inclined to rephrase, "If he succeeds in comedy but loses in tragedy." Actually, however, "gain the whole world" is hardly what characters in comedy are up to; they may endeavor to snatch a little more of it than is their due—Malvolio of love, Hotspur of glory, Alceste of power, Jack Tanner of freedom—but graspingness is not the only form of error. In *She Stoops to Conquer* Marlow has to be tricked into taking a willing girl, and Hastings through an excess of anxiety might well lose his girl; their error would be not gaining an available world. One may err in the world by being recessive as well as by being aggressive, loose-handed as well as strong-armed. Gaining the whole world better describes the ambition of a Faustus or a Macbeth, and losing his soul the fate of either; such a pursuit and such a stake are the heart of tragedy.

Mark's metaphor speaks of the world as a totality (coveted by the mistaken, fled by the true). If, by way of instructive anticlimax, we throw Mark into juxtaposition with a mistress of Louis XIV, we get a different extreme. In W. S. Landor's *Imaginary Conversations* there is an ironic dialogue between the Duchess de Fontanges and Bishop Bossuet, who is to be her confessor. "Do you hate the world, mademoiselle?" he asks, and she replies, "A good deal of it: all Picardy for example, and all Sologne: nothing is uglier—and, oh my life! what frightful men and women!" To the Duchess the world is the unpleasant parts of familiar territory, a smallish space for comic purposes, and, what is more, she rejects it. While Mark describes a tragic relationship to the world, the Duchess enacts a satirical one. But this unconscious satirist is herself viewed comically: the Conversation does not approve or disapprove her rejection, but lets it stand as a piece of ingenuous literalness charmingly deployed against a metaphor so conventionalized as to have become a rather faded concrete universal.

Here I am not defining the rejection of the world—that issue is related to "acceptance," the major point of the next chapter—but looking at some of the ways of defining the world implicit in rejective statements. The realm of the human comedy is obviously something between the vast complex of material, secular, godless existences whose essence is spiritual peril ("the world" in Christian terms), and parochial areas too restricted to be representative (Picardy and Sologne). Again, it is something between the corrupt and depraved condition which appears to call for an Inquisition, a Terror, a Flood, or an Inferno, and the life of spiritual struggle in which guilt may be the penalty for the courses that an individual does pursue or needs or is driven to pursue. The life of spiritual struggle is what Eliot dramatizes in Celia in *The Cocktail Party*, and what he balances against it is not an opposite extreme of callousness and vice, but rather that middling life, neither diabolical nor saintly, in which the ordinary Chamberlaynes find a social adjustment to their circumstances and their natures. Eliot's comedy, then, is about comic and tragic modes; that is, in employing the comic mode—the discovery of working personal relationships in the world—he uniquely transcends the mode by presenting another option in which the vital decisions lead into a nonworldly mode of action. Comedy characteristically ignores this option.[12]

The Inner World as Tragic Stage

All the world's a comic stage, we might say. The tragic stage is the inner one in which the conflict is between elements in the personality or in the mind or the psyche of the protagonist.* It would be wrong to think

---

*For various definitions of the relationships between tragedy and comedy see Appendix 8. Discussing Eliot's *Confidential Clerk*, Bonamy Dobrée makes some observations relevant to the distinction which I have proposed: "Comedy deals with the relation of people to each other in society, or with their place in society, with their interactions in a social milieu; tragedy deals with the relation of man to God—or whatever name he may be called by. . . . But whereas the moral of comedy is usually 'Fit yourself into society,' here it is 'Follow the indication that God has given you of the sort of life you ought to lead, the sort of person you ought to be.' [*The Confidential Clerk*] is, in fact, as some have called it, 'a religious farce'" ("*The Confidential Clerk*," *Sewanee Review*, 62 [1954]: 128–29).

However, Benn W. Levy's skillful *The Devil: A Religious Comedy* (London: Martin Secker, 1930) seems on the face of it to merge the two areas. In this modern reinterpretation of the Faust myth, several English people—artists, writers, an actress, a clergyman—play Faust to the Mephistopheles of the Rev. Nicholas Lucy (Old Nick, Lucifer), who seems able to gratify their various publicly expressed desires for passion, success, fame, etc. Each person can choose between gratifying his desire at a known price such as Faust paid (here, dishonesty, infidelity, etc.) and living more honorably but less glamorously (as Macbeth too might have done). But Nicholas Lucy, the tempter with mysterious

of Celia as an achieved tragic figure; rather, she receives the kind of portrayal that characteristically occurs in the realm of tragedy. When Reilly says of his patients that "usually they think that someone else is to blame," Celia replies, "I at least have no one to blame but myself." Later she says that she has a "sense of sin," of "failure / Towards someone, or something, outside of myself" (II). That is, she takes responsibility for what she does; she has the capacity for self-judgment. Yet, as we come to see, Celia has not really committed the tragic act that has a catastrophic outcome; like Becket in *Murder in the Cathedral* and Harry in *The Family Reunion*, Celia has a fear and a consciousness of wrong action greater than her capacity for it. The complete tragic hero is likely to fall into action first and come into an awareness of truth later. But the time relationship between action and knowledge is not a constant; either may precede, or they may coincide; when knowledge comes is less important than the capacity for knowledge, knowledge of self and of the deed done. Knowledge means judgment, and judgment reflects the felt moral standard which, in acting, one has ignored or thought to circumvent or forced into a temporary subsurface oblivion where it cannot determine conduct. Conduct comes from one source of energy, judgment from another. A person acts from bounding ambition, delusions of invulnerability, unmanageable passion, a conviction that seems to take precedence over all other guides to action—all the outbreaks of self into the active arrogance for which the traditional term is *hubris*. Yet he knows, or comes to know, or is able to know, the nature of what he has done and to place himself as the doer. His conflict is between need, passion, drive, will, or illusion on the one hand, and, on the other, whatever sense of right or principle or obligation or authority would have a restraining effect or impel one to a different mode of conduct. Faustus and Macbeth both know what they are up to when they embark on their grand enterprises; Oedipus comes to see what he has been up to in the past.

For the opposite poles of influence upon divided man a convenient pair of terms is *impulse* and *imperative*; *impulse* as the whole range of self-aggrandizing forces and motives, *imperative* as the range of sanctions—

power, is strictly a Goethean Mephistopheles who "seeks the bad but works the good": these Fausts opt for a decent mediocrity instead of paying the huge price for an imagined power and glory (we are not sure, finally, whether Lucy is an ironically disguised divine agent who succeeds, or a demonic figure who fails, in his assignment). In generic terms, the crucial actions take place in the inner arena of tragedy, but the nature of the final action is comic: the characters accept an imperfect world. Hence "religious comedy": a supramundane agent helps define destiny as an accommodation to the actual. Cf. Harcourt-Reilly and the Chamberlaynes in *The Cocktail Party*.

religious, traditional, community—that, acting through conscience, both morally restrain and morally commit. The terms indicate tendencies rather than absolutes, and the opposites can even move toward each other. Further, there can be a paradoxical conflict of two imperatives that seem equally valid. Orestes cannot avenge his father without killing his mother, and Hamlet's situation is fascinatingly similar; Antigone, of course, is the archetypal figure caught in a conflict of imperatives, the familial and the civic (some critics tend to diminish the stature of the drama by treating the civic imperative as no more than callous arbitrariness by Creon). Two protagonists in modern dramas of political life agonize in similar conflicts. In Arthur Koestler's *Darkness at Noon* (1941; dramatized by Sidney Kingsley, 1951) Rubashov is caught between loyalty to the Party as it actually exists and loyalty to the ideals that created it; in Carl Zuckmayer's *The Devil's General* (1946) General Harras is loyal to Germany at war, though this also leads to collaboration with the Nazi regime that he detests.

This hasty survey of the modes of tragic action is meant only to make concrete the generalization that I have introduced several times—that the essential action of tragedy occurs on an inner stage: everything flows from the conflict in the divided personality.[13] If Macbeth did not know what he was up to, or Lear was incapable of finding out, they would be less significant personalities, and the plays about them would be relatively unsubtle, and quite untragic, dramas of aggression and disaster. This does not mean that the inner struggle is sealed within a private chamber that shuts off all possibilities of outer resonance. Only in Marlowe's *Doctor Faustus* is the conflict so internalized that it has no tangible impact on the society in which the hero lives. In most tragedies, indeed, the hero is a principal figure in a realm or community that is vitally marked by his private choices—the Thebes of Oedipus, the Britain of Lear, the Scotland of Macbeth; the tragedy of the hero is the disaster of the state. But the dramas do not focus our attention upon the disaster as such; the disasters function as the public echoes of the crucial private acts. There is plenty of action in the public world, but the restoration of well-being to the political realms is secondary to the resolution of the conflict within the personality of the political head.

The World as Comic: Implications

Tragedy is not our business, however, and it enters the discussion only temporarily to help establish and clarify the limits of the comic realm. To say that comedy is of the world, then, is to say that it is of this world, not of the other, or some other, world; that it is not of that inner domain in which the human being struggles among diverse impulses and imperatives. Not that comedy forbids a confronting of self: a new opening up of common sense may make a character criticize his earlier lack of it, as is true of both Honeywood and Lofty in *The Good-Natured Man*. Mandryka in Hugo von Hofmannsthal's *Arabella* (1928; 1933) can exclaim, "Fool, fool that I am! / How should she ever pardon me for this, / unable as I am to pardon myself for it?" (III). In Peter Nichols' *A Day in the Death of Joe Egg* (1967) the wife, Sheila, can say, "It was my fault. I've been asking too much," and the husband, Bri, can acknowledge his immaturity (II). But three comments are in order here. First, such passages are less moral judgments than acknowledgments of tactical errors or practical missteps; second, they are incidents of the dramatic movement rather than the resolution of long struggles; third, the comic tone can survive even the ill-temper of a man who clings to his grievances rather than acknowledges his part in them, for example, Malvolio's final exit line in *Twelfth Night*, "I'll be reveng'd on the whole pack of you" (V.i.386).

For comic character there is one very important implication in viewing "the world" as primarily the realm of relationships with others, as the actual working out of situations by participants who face each other with difficulties and differences to adjust, cross-purposes to reconcile, clashing interests and intentions to be mediated. In these relationships the characters cannot be significantly troubled by inner splits, which simply by being present would have to take the drama off in a different direction. Unlike the tragic figure, the comic figure is to all intents and purposes undivided; that is, he is not caught in a basic cross-fire of desires and values that makes the primary demand upon his psychic energy and hence upon ours. Not that he is really free of uncertainties, inconsistencies, and alternatives: to take several almost too clear-cut examples, Mrs. Erlynne has to choose between pressing on with her campaign to re-enter society and repressing her daughter's intended exit from it, and Sir Colenso Ridgeon has to choose which of two patients he will try to save. But the choices are not between a right and a wrong; hubris is not a key element; and the choosing itself is not an agonizing affair which would have to become central in the drama. Each chooser acts, finally, as if there were only one real course, and he pursues it, not dividedly, but with "wholeness."

The comic choice characteristically turns on what is suitable, sensible, feasible; it does not often forget the convenient and the pragmatic. To Peachum and Lockit in Gay's *The Beggar's Opera* (1728) there is only one course to pursue with Macheath, however that course may impinge upon the tender hearts of their daughters; and vis-à-vis the daughters, Macheath strives for a comic both-and rather than a romantic either-or. In Synge's *Playboy of the Western World* (1907) Pegeen Mike fluctuates in her attitude to the playboy; the drama is based not on her struggle, however, but on the thoroughness of her pursuit, and then of her disenchantment with him, and finally of her sense of loss. Those somewhat similar trainers of women, Petruchio and Henry Higgins, could imaginably be split between the disciplinarian and the humanitarian, or between the professional and the man, but in fact there is no such split even when there is every *a priori* reason for us to expect one. Thus the comic management of the situation. In Petruchio, of course, the dual functions are integrated in a seamless garment of personality; in that sense his wholeness is more complex than that of Henry Higgins, in whom the trainer becomes virtually the whole man. Indeed, Petruchio provides a good, almost too good, pattern of the comic personality. If he were tragic, he would be split between loving and a need to dominate; as it is, temporary domination is the means of securing two independences that make possible a genuine mutuality. Likewise Congreve's Mirabell acts as a man of fashion, as a devoted lover, and as an independent man; the comic achievement is the integration of all elements in action rather than the domination of one element in the self which leads to the rebound of another neglected one, as in tragedy.

In the world, then, people meet each other as whole or as-if whole;[14] either their wholeness is actual, or it is secured as a comic necessity by the ignoring of any element from which an anticomic dividedness might spring. (Aristophanes, for instance, does not let Lysistrata, an opponent of war, be troubled by any suspicion that people are inalienably warlike, for her having such a fear would inevitably reorder the drama into a conflict of fact and desire, or ideal and actual.) The wholeness, whether intrinsic or pragmatic, is essential to a drama of relationships that are to lead neither to failure nor to an impasse; a person acting for only a part of himself would establish relationships of an abortive, unbalanced, or distorted kind that could scarcely produce even a temporary, not to mention a permanent, accommodation of moot issues or of adversaries. Ibsen's men— Solness and Rosmer, for instance—tend to remedy unsatisfying lives by taking up with alluring demonic women, but the relationship corresponds to only part of their unintegrated natures and hence leads to disaster. These men, that is, are not conceived comically.

So much for these various ways of outlining, circumscribing, and giving substance to "the world" which is the scene of comedy: an immediate world—solid, populated, representative—where the conflicts are not between impulses and imperatives that are elements of the psyche, but between individuals who are elements of society; where public events, whether political or social or familial, are primary, and not, as in tragedy, the aftermath of private moral actions; where the issue is not an individual's coming to spiritual terms with himself but his coming to working terms with other persons or groups of persons; where the individual may not have to engage in self-criticism at all but where, if he does, it takes the form "I have been foolish" or "I have made a practical mistake" rather than "I have been morally at fault"; where the actors are characterized, not by the dividedness of tragedy, but by an essential or working wholeness that equips them for all the tactics, bargaining, and even scheming that are the expectable currency of dealings in a scene where men and the shape of things are something less than perfect and yet not hostile to betterment for, or achievement by, those equipped for it. Comic action is outer, public, relational, social, comprising all the modes of intercourse in which accommodation—the end-product of struggling, jockeying, compromising, giving as well as taking—is made possible by the relative equality, instead of the excessive strength or weakness, of those concerned.

IV. The World and Its Forms

The Human Comedy of Balzac embraced many aspects of the world, or alternatively, many worlds. Balzac saw a threefold division of his materials: "studies of manners," "studies of philosophy," and "studies of marriage"; and "manners," in turn, included "private life," "provincial life," "Parisian life," "country life," "political life," and "military life." This division is a convenient clue to the diversity of scenes within "the world," a diversity likewise figured in the numerousness of characters always brought to mind by the name of Balzac.* Diversity of scenes makes possible, too, a diversity of ways of symbolizing the world. In its literal dimen-

---

*The diversity of the world is described in hostile terms by Deeley in Harold Pinter's *Old Times* (New York: Grove Press, 1971), pp. 40–41. Deeley says that his work involves dealings "with people all over the globe," and he adds, "I use the word globe because the word world possesses emotional political sociological and psychological pretensions and resonances which I prefer as a matter of choice to do without. . . ."

sion each symbolic representation of it may be extensive or confined, but its essential largeness or smallness will depend less on its surface spread than on its representative depth. In *Tartuffe* (1664), for instance, the world of the family exhibits a greater range and substance than does the international world in Robert Sherwood's *Idiot's Delight* (1936).

The family, of course, is one of the very common forms of the world that comedy examines: it opens up various dramatic options, with conflicts between generations or sexes or other groupings, and with different kinds of intrusions by, or extensions into, the life outside it. In Peter Nichols' *A Day in the Death of Joe Egg* the world is almost exclusively that of the parents of a spastic child; another man and wife with contrasting attitudes are introduced to establish the wider dimensions of the foreground household scene. In Eugene O'Neill's *Ah, Wilderness!* (1933) the family world is a more "normal" one and a more varied one, at least in the sense that its life is not illness-oriented; here an adolescent love affair leads to the introduction of other people, so that we see the family in the larger setting of local society. The family, in its limited sense or in the larger sense of a miscellaneous group of relatives, associates, and servants, is always the Chekhov world, but Chekhov repeatedly gives a special twist to the situation: this is the tension between the immediate provincial world and the distant one of Moscow or Paris that seems to those not there to embrace a magically glamorous reality. Or a visitor from outside may cause turmoil in the family world, as in Turgenev's *A Month in the Country* (1850).

The bridge between the family world and other scenes is most frequently love; there are many different versions of this, as we see in *Much Ado about Nothing* (1598–99), Goldsmith's *She Stoops to Conquer* (1773), Shaw's *Arms and the Man* (1894), and Hofmannsthal's *The Difficult Man* (1921). The family world is joined with the world of politics in Aristophanes' *Lysistrata* (411 B.C.) and in O'Casey's *Juno and the Paycock* (1924) and *The Plough and the Stars* (1926), and with that of the economic community in Brecht's *The Good Person of Setzuan* (1938–40). Here the world moves toward "society," as it does in Ibsen's *A Doll's House* (1879) and *An Enemy of the People* (1882), in all these plays, of course, with different emphases and the resultant complications of tone. The world is a given local "society" in Behan's *The Hostage* (1960) and in Gogol's *The Inspector General* (1836). In Gogol's comedy, however, the members of society whom we see belong predominantly to the local upper crust or at least the ruling bureaucracy; hence we are well on the way toward the

"Society" which is the world of Restoration comedy, of Wilde, and of dozens of writers of comedy from George Colman, Sr., and Hugh Kelly (not to mention Royall Tyler and William Dunlap) in the eighteenth century to Noel Coward and T. S. Eliot in the twentieth.

Society appears as a world of especial urban sophistication in Henry Becque's *La Parisienne* (1885), of the money-centered well-to-do in Jonson's *Volpone* (1606), and of final earthly glory, court life, most conspicuously in a half-dozen Shakespeare comedies such as *A Midsummer Night's Dream* (1595–96) and *As You Like It* (1599). It may be concentrated in a place like a hostelry which is a natural meeting-ground for all kinds of people; we see this in plays from Carlo Goldoni's *The Mistress of the Inn* (1753) to Vicki Baum's *Grand Hotel* (1930) and Philip Barry's *Hotel Universe* (1930), where a physical place represents a less material realm, and to William Inge's *Bus Stop* (1955) and Lanford Wilson's *The Hot l Baltimore* (1973) (which, a late-comer in an old tradition, surprisingly won prizes). The world may be that of the theater, as in Buckingham's *The Rehearsal* (1671), Sheridan's *The Critic* (1779), and many modern plays; of sport, as in David Storey's *The Changing Room* (1971); of the academic mind, as in Chekhov's *Uncle Vanya* (1899) and such recent plays as Simon Gray's *Butley* (1971) and Tom Stoppard's *Jumpers* (1972); of medicine (a recurrent theme in Molière), as in Arthur Schnitzler's *Professor Bernhardi* (1912) and many other plays of the sick such as Dale Wasserman's dramatization of Ken Kesey's *One Flew over the Cuckoo's Nest* (1963) and Peter Nichols' *The National Health* (1969); of an international scene, as in Shakespeare's *Troilus and Cressida* (ca. 1600) and Christopher Fry's *The Dark Is Light Enough* (1954). While "the world" is predominantly social in the broadest possible sense of that word, it can occasionally take on a different character. It can become biological, in the sense that maintaining or intensifying "life" takes priority over finding a modus vivendi among others; we find this whenever Shaw is pushing the "life force" theme, in such plays as Alejandro Casona's *Suicide Prohibited in Spring Time* (1937), and in the Lawrentian plays of Tennessee Williams such as *The Rose Tattoo* (1950). The world of ideas is Shaw's principal arena (one after another, critics keep discovering that in Shaw the actors play ideas rather than people), as it is for Duerrenmatt, Frisch, and Ionesco. In these we move toward or into a world beyond time and place that is perhaps best exemplified in Samuel Beckett's *Waiting for Godot* (1952)—a cosmic world that stretches the borders of comedy to the utmost.

Examples of this kind could continue indefinitely, but they would then seem, as they may seem even now, to constitute a list that keeps on going without going anywhere. These titles and descriptive phrases are simply an endeavor to identify solidly the world, that working reality of men and women that lies somewhere between utopian visions and frightening nightmares, between the idyllic and the unbearable, between the celestial and the infernal, and is influenced, for the most part only peripherally, by both. The concept of the world—the arena of the comic—should not remain vague, though it is bound to be multifold. The world manifests itself in a number of ways—as Society or the Good Society or society or societies with common bonds or as the political entity or as the natural community (family, liaison, sex for begetting or forgetting). Here people compete or maneuver for position or possession, for authority or advantage, for the girl or the game, for the man or the money, for a comfortable or a colorful style; they experience conflict *and* community; they survive by finding some timely resolution of the eternal tension between theory, longing, and program within, and the wayward, elusive, and intractable out there.[15]

This summation may evoke several questions. One might ask: are not all these worlds, all these scenes in which the world manifests itself, also the scenes of tragedy? Or again: does not this sketch of the forms of the world dissolve into a list of themes that might appear equally in different genres? A brief note on each of these inquiries will end the present chapter.

Macbeth *versus* Prince Hal

Naturally tragedy and comedy may coinhabit a given human territory or share a given landscape—family, community, state, or some other order. They may even do this at the same time, as we know from occasional plays that combine modes. But it may be worth saying once again—and this is clearly a reiteration—that the outer world reflects or feels the impact of tragic action but is the primary field and norm of comic action. Tragic man acts in his world as a consequence of, or as an expression of, primary actions in an inner moral realm of felt divisions; comic man either feels no divisions or has them disciplined to a pragmatic wholeness as he takes his primary actions in the outer world.

If we use an example from the drama of political action, we can see the generic contrast unmistakably in the differences between *Macbeth* and *I* and *II Henry IV*. In *Macbeth* the focus is on the struggle between Macbeth's desire for the throne and his knowledge that those steps to it which are temptingly at hand will not do, and then between his sense of achieved possession and the anxiety and guilt inseparable from possession. Of the inwardness of this conflict, of its taking place out of this world, there is no better evidence than the Ghost that appears to Macbeth alone. Prince Hal is likewise headed for a throne, and as a candidate he too has moral disabilities, or at least what appear to his royal father to be moral disabilities. He is drawn by some elements in his nature to an unkingly life with roisterers and rogues, and a dramatist might with such materials transform Hal into a figure of tragic dividedness. But even to suggest this possibility will seem strained, so little is Hal a divided man; he does no acting on the inner stage where Macbeth does all his essential acting. If there are inconsistencies in his outer conduct, they hardly come out of true discords of nature; with a part of himself Hal can enjoy playing unprincelike games without ever letting that part hurt or disfigure the king-to-be. He has either actual or pragmatic wholeness, as Shakespeare lets us know with an early explicitness and thoroughness (*I Henry IV*, I.ii.218 ff.) that cause some readers to raise eyebrows at what they take to be Hal's cool calculatingness. Hal's self-explicatory soliloquy is technically striking: by its nature the voice of inner turmoil, the soliloquy here is the means of dispelling our expectation of an inner turmoil that could be disruptive. That is, Hal is acting entirely in the world; what is more, he is even acting rather complexly by responding variously to disparate elements of the world. The things that he appears to forget he does not reject, and he rejects unprincely things only when he has to. Thus he approaches the world with more flexibility than either Hotspur or Falstaff, who are equally undivided characters but who cannot go beyond their single-track styles—the gestures of honor, and the jests that subvert honor—and who hence, however attractive either mode may be in a suitable context, are satisfactorily attuned to the world only as long as a single trait can serve in place of a variously responsive personality. Hal can consort with rascals, play practical jokes, and be reliable in a military crisis; parody his father but respect him; parody Hotspur, listen quietly to a rather tedious lecture on his "vile participation" and his inferiority to Hotspur, promise to show up well against Hotspur, and then deliver. Finally, after some further indulgences with his lowbrow friends, he can rebuke himself and hastily make off for serious work (*II Henry IV*, II.iv.390–95). There is no inner struggle here; the course is clear; and there is no problem in following it. Hal and the torn Macbeth exhibit almost classically the comic and tragic styles in politics—the sense of the world and its ways, and the inner conflict between hubris that would conquer the world, and moral consciousness that undermines the glory of conquest.

The other hypothetical question was this: does not an outline of the ways in which the world manifests itself dwindle into a list of themes—family, the town, the professions—open to various genres? Aristotle, for instance, spoke of the family as a natural site of tragic actions; Faustus is the professor as tragic hero. But if the family or the profession or the society is the concrete manifestation of the world that is the locus of comedy, the hallmark of comic style is denoted by another term that we have formally introduced but not yet examined: the term *accept*. To it we now turn.

CHAPTER 3

Attitudes to the World:
Flight, Challenge, Conciliation

"ACCEPTANCE of the world" may seem, to one kind of mind, to state an obvious condition of life; to another kind of mind, to state an unbearable way of life. Perhaps we should ascribe these responses to moods rather than kinds of mind. But whether it originates in mood or mind, neither response is conducive to the production or the relish of comedy. Yet hesitancy over the word *accept*—the supposition that it tells us nothing new, or the fear that it demands too much—may reflect uncertainty about the implications of the word. Hence these are worth some attention. Since *accept* denotes a certain attitude, we can help define that attitude by sketching briefly some of the available attitudes to the world and of the literary forms that give imaginative expression to these attitudes.

I. ESCAPE, COMBAT, REJECTION

We can live with the world, that is, discover a mean between excessive expectations and total submissiveness. But there are numerous other attitudes that we can fall into. Many are rejective. We can leave the world or opt out of it; we can regard it as an oppressive force that tries to reduce us

to servitude or impotence, or at least as a hostile force that will make
things hard for us as individuals; we can be puzzled by it, troubled by its
nature, unsure whether we form it or it forms us, whether we see it as it is
or see it as our own beings dictate; we can think that it is none too sharp
and be tempted to play games with it, to make it pay much for little, to
diddle it; we can censure, condemn, denounce, punish, rail at, or sneer at
it; we can try to change, reform, reorder, revolutionize, utopianize it, and
this ordinarily means compelling it to remake itself in terms of some
preconception that determines our view of it; we can assail it, storm it,
take it over, intent upon a conquest of whatever kind is congenial to us;
or, on the other hand, we can gladly surrender to it, asking only for
instructions and mandates so that we may conform to whatever the world
in which we live and its more agile managers have in mind for us. In
practice, different options may overlap or coalesce in ways that create
complex styles of response to the world. But though it may be incomplete
or oversimplified, the list should provide a working picture of alternative
attitudes that will help illuminate comic acceptance.

Opting Out

Leave, withdraw, opt out: for a retreat, a convent or commune, or
solitude. Provided the seeker of separation succeeds in actually divesting
himself of the world and does not only set it up elsewhere in miniature or
under bylaws apparently more congenial or more amenable to heart's
desire, he moves into the realm of the single speaker. The matching
literary form is the lyric: the private voice, though of course the user of it
tends to hope for a public audience. Every Walden Pond is equipped with
at least a metaphorical loud-speaker. But the audience, if there is one,
only listens; there is no interplay, no dialogue, and hence no drama. Yet it
is interesting to see an occasional effort to reduce drama itself to a lyric
denial of its own nature. I do not mean the drama with intercalary lyrics,
from the Elizabethans to Brecht, or *Pippa Passes*, in which there is a
quasi-dramatic accretion around a lyric nucleus, but the form attractive to
Beckett in which the dialogue shrinks into, or is concentrated into,
monologue (approaching a Browning effect from the opposite side). It is
most obvious in *Krapp's Last Tape* (1958), but *Happy Days* (1961) might as
well do without its second character, who is little more than a prop. Such
solitude is a symbol of the speaker's nonrelatedness or of his living in
formulae that substitute for a free relatedness (as in Ionesco occasionally).
The speaker's words, then, are a commentary on what happens or has hap-

pened rather than a participation in, or a contribution to, what happens.* Perhaps Krapp and Winnie "accept" what is there, but their acceptance is ex post facto quietude or nonresistance rather than the activity of coming to terms with. It is a quite different thing when Congreve's Lady Wishfort, feeling that she can't come to terms with the world, or that it will grossly disregard her terms, proposes to leave the world and be a shepherdess. This is not an anticomic flight but a comic self-misunderstanding. Lady Wishfort has no talent for solitude, as she betrays by the shepherdess image: for her, as for many, the pastoral means merely finding a new backdrop and costume supposed to give full play and power to the benign constituents of an actual world and to one's own will. On the other hand, Jimmy Porter and Alison end John Osborne's *Look Back in Anger* (1956) by discovering that what they are fitted for is a withdrawn life in a playpen: a lyric duet, with only themselves as audience.

Another opting out is hardly distinguishable from being squeezed out: that drifting toward an exit which is dictated by one's own weakness vis-à-vis the going world, or by the conviction of an oppressiveness or inflexibility or nonnegotiability in the world. Here nonacceptance is less a conscious choice than a failure of will or of the talent for the reciprocal life of human society. Hence the drama of a disaster rooted in debility, such as Maxim Gorky's *The Lower Depths* (1902) and O'Neill's *The Iceman Cometh* (1946). Though it might be argued that in these plays the world manifests itself in a social island which is in effect a microcosm, this will hardly do. We are too aware of the recessive and retrogressive to conceive of either the Gorky or the O'Neill hostelry as a ghetto Brook Farm rather than the sick ward that it is, and it is clear that from Harry Hope's island there can never be, as there can be from Prospero's, a return to the mainland world; we might call it a hypocosm (in contrast with the actual microcosm in such a world as that of Brendan Behan's *The Hostage* [1960]).

Defeat and Puzzlement

But if there is some ambiguity in these situations—is the world too big and strong for some good men, or are some men too weak to meet the world on ordinary terms?—there is a clear-cut relationship, in another class of noncomic dramas, between strength and indifference or ruthless-

---

*There is a somewhat similar effect in Vladimir Mayakovsky's *The Bedbug* (1929), in which fantastic characters and actions hardly become human beings and deeds, but are rather analogous to the images and other verbal components of a lyric, that is, contributors to thematic and tonal identity.

ness without, and weakness or vulnerability within. In these, the perspective is that of individuals to whom the world is essentially a manifestation of hostile or destructive power. This sense of things appears in naturalistic drama such as, to mention familiar examples, Henry Becque's *The Vultures* (1882) (in Zola's *Theresa Raquin* [1873] the ruthless destroy themselves), Eugène Brieux's *The Red Robe* (1900), and Gerhart Hauptmann's *Before Sunrise* (1889) and *The Weavers* (1892). If the world is primarily or wholly a seamy place—in contrast to the considerable but not invincible seaminess of, say, Shakespeare's "dark comedies"—then acceptance would require a diminution of being that would lead to a cynical rather than a comic tone. If the world is viewed in terms of its seamy side, of its blind processes (of nature or society), or of its unscrupulous holders of power, part of the stress is upon its victims, and victims, as well as their portrayers, are in no sense accepters. There is an immense theater of victims from the victims of revenge, such as the title character in John Webster's *The Duchess of Malfi* (1614), to those of nature, as in John M. Synge's *Riders to the Sea* (1904), those of society, as in Ibsen's *An Enemy of the People* (1882) and Friedrich Duerrenmatt's *The Visit* (1956), and those of political oppression from *Richard III* and Lope de Vega's *The Sheep Well* (ca. 1614) to Lillian Hellman's *Watch on the Rhine* (1941) and Kaj Munk's *Niels Ebbesen* (1940).

One may, then, experience the world as a force that diminishes him, weighs heavily upon him, enslaves him, does him in. This oppressiveness may appear also in a psychological or metaphysical form. In the latter the hostile or burdensome force is not an impersonal process or a personal tyranny but a resistant meaning; the world is not peremptory but ambiguous, not punitive but elusive; our problem is less peonage than puzzlement. We find something of a transition from one type of world to the other in Luigi Pirandello's *The Rules of the Game* (1918), in which Gala forces his wife's lover Guido to carry on, though badly overmatched, in a duel in which Gala's wife Silia had thought that Gala himself would meet death. On the face of it, the strong man practices a novel kind of tyranny on a weaker one, and we may admire one and pity the other, or both. More than that, however, we undergo a certain disquieting wonderment at the world of motives that actuate this trio; the dramatist alters, without providing guideposts, an expectable assessment of the triangular roles. The wife is less pleased by her lover than annoyed by her husband's apparent indifference; his apparent indifference masks a subtle and ruthless revengefulness; and the lover accepts a suicidal role through an obligation casuistically foisted upon him. We keep inquiring, What really goes on here?

Obviously I am straining *The Rules of the Game* somewhat to make a transition to the drama in which the pain of defeat by the world is replaced by the problem of defining the world. Does it exist as an object, or is it created by the subjective viewer? The theme, of course, is one to which Pirandello returns repeatedly. A title of his, as it happens, is a reminder of one of the earliest European dramas to query the nature of reality: Pirandello's *Sogno (ma forse no)* (*Dream [But Perhaps Not]*, 1929) carries us back to Pedro Calderón's *La vida es sueño* (*Life Is a Dream*, ca. 1638). Though dream plays do not always question the nature of reality,* the substitution of ambiguity for firm reality is a familiar stage procedure. Harold Pinter does this repeatedly. *The Birthday Party* (1958) introduces an ominously jocose gangster pair in whom we detect "the system" rather than professional racketeers preying upon it. But masking a reality in the style of its countertype is rather an ironic gambit than a fundamental questioning of reality such as Pinter achieves in *Old Times* (1971): here our only clues to a past which three people discuss, and on which the present appears to depend, are sharply contradictory recollections in which valid memories, hazy memories, mistaken memories, and deliberately distorting memories, many of these used as shield or weapon in an ongoing duel, are only partly distinguishable, if at all.

Another version of the cosmic puzzle turns on the confounding of theatrical and nontheatrical reality, exploited in a range of moods from ironic laughter at naïveté in Beaumont and Fletcher's *The Knight of the Burning Pestle* (1607) to sophisticated interplay in Pirandello's *Six Characters in Search of an Author* (1921). Of all the ways of dealing inconclusively with the world as mystery, the one most in danger of becoming a cliché is that of juxtaposing the apparently mad and the apparently sane and raising doubts as to which manages a better grasp of truth. Shakespeare first turned the theme into central paradoxes in *King Lear* (1606), and Ibsen introduced the modern clinical approach with the madhouse scenes in *Peer Gynt* (1867). Pirandello does it best in *Henry IV* (1922), Duerrenmatt uses it ingeniously in *The Physicists* (1962), and there is a touch of it in the Wasserman-Kesey *One Flew over the Cuckoo's Nest* (1963).

*A run-through of any index of plays will reveal the popularity of *dream, dreamer*, and *dreaming* in titles. Very few raise psychological or epistemological questions; one is Henri-René Lenormand's *Time Is a Dream* (1913–18). In August Strindberg's *A Dream Play* (1901) a dream mediates reality; in Elmer Rice's *Dream Girl* (1945) dream has to be distinguished from reality.

Con and Conquer

Any kind of moving away from the world, clearly, is not accepting it. Yet there are also kinds of moving toward the world that are different from accepting it. For instance, instead of taking it to be inscrutable, man can regard it as credulous and ready to be taken; instead of its power to wound him, he can see only its vulnerability; in this view, the basic human unit of the world is simply the one-born-every-minute. The genre that embodies this attitude is the picaresque, which invites sympathy for and delight in the rogue, the trickster, the con man. The genre exploits human ingenuity and banishes human fragility and vulnerability from sight; the fragile and the victimized have to stay offstage, as if nonexistent. Falstaff has something of the picaro, but, though charming, is neither energetic nor successful enough; Tartuffe the slick gamesman becomes sinister racketeer, for we can see him inflicting real damage on the community. Volpone and Mosca come closer to the picaro because of their zestful virtuosity and the equal scheming and noninnocence of most of their victims. It is Hlestakov in Gogol's *The Inspector General* (1836), however, who is a better picaro than any of these; forced into the role of profiteering rogue by the self-defensive bribery of the town officials, he is an agile fraud, easily identified with because of his zany opportunism and because his victims, petty rascals asking to be bilked, can claim no sympathy. The picaro takes on a still more charismatic quality* in the title character of Frank Wedekind's *The Marquis of Keith* (1900) and in Krank, the central character of John Arden's *The Waters of Babylon* (1957).

Again, one can move toward the world by substituting, for the trickery of the picaro, the power of the conqueror; instead of accepting the world, one makes it accept oneself. One is strong rather than sly, and moves against weakness rather than credulity. The literary form is the melodrama of conquest: Marlowe's *Tamburlaine* is the pre-eminent example. The melodrama of conquest may naturally slide into the melodrama of liberation from the conqueror, as in *Richard III*. The drama may present simply a melancholy view of how power works—economic power in Brecht's *St. Joan of the Stockyards* (1929–30), the power of a political faction in his

---

*In taking on charismatic traits the picaro can become a highly ambiguous figure, from one perspective pure con man, from another a spiritual prop or deliverer. The term "picaresque saint" (see R. W. B. Lewis, *The Picaresque Saint* [Philadelphia: Lippincott, 1959]) suggests the duality. This duality appears in Tennessee Williams' *The Milk Train Doesn't Stop Here Anymore* (Chris Flanders) and in the Wasserman-Kesey *One Flew over the Cuckoo's Nest* (McMurphy). See Theodore Ziolkowski, *Fictional Transfigurations of Jesus* (Princeton, N.J.: Princeton University Press, 1972), pp. 225 ff., 266 and n.

Private Life of the Master Race (1935–38). Or it may view ironically the efforts of certain kinds of individuals to impose a private will or doctrine upon the world—from Shakespeare's *Coriolanus* (1608–9) to Mississippi and St. Claude in Duerrenmatt's *The Marriage of Mr. Mississippi* (1952)— or the efforts to maximize royal power by commanding the introduction of utopian conditions, as in Dorothy Sayers' *The Devil to Pay* (1939) and Duerrenmatt's *An Angel Comes to Babylon* (1953). Numerous plays picture, too, a subtler quest for power, that of people who work not through the instruments of position but through the devices of personality such as obsessions and neuroses employed as subtle means of control. Here we find the jealous people of Restoration comedy, the humors of Jonson and Shadwell, certain neurotic figures in Molière, notably the title characters in *L'Avare* (1668) and *Le Malade imaginaire* (1673).

In the last half dozen plays, as my use of the word *power* suggests, the melodrama that records the modes of conquest really merges with or gives way to other types. Insofar as the urgent seeker of power moves toward disaster and comes into some awareness of himself, the play moves toward tragedy. Insofar as the seeker of power is viewed ironically as annoying rather than injurious, as more mistaken than malicious, or comes around to a better adjustment to the world, the move is toward comedy. Insofar as the seeker of power is the object of attack, censure, or scorn, the move is toward satire. We come, then, to the satirical attitude to the world.

Scourge and Reject

Though on theoretical grounds comedy and satire are anything but identical, in practice they are often found together, and talk about them often reveals a tendency not to distinguish them.[1] Presumably this is because the link between them, though accidental, may seem indivisible and essential. That link is laughter: we laugh at what is ridiculed as well as at incongruities of situation and personal style that do not invite censure or contempt. This inclusive spread of the laughable makes it natural for the drama of demonstrably comic tone to include satirical barbs. In Dylan Thomas' *Under Milk Wood* (1953), where the humor is always brushing against the pathos of frustration, one object of satire is the super-cleanly Mrs. Ogmore-Pritchard, who says, "And before you let the sun in, mind it wipes its shoes." In incongruity there is a range where the satirical and the comic material are not readily distinguishable; nevertheless there is a dividing line, and it lies between the incongruity found in a person whose apparent benevolence is accompanied by a drive or calculation that can be noxious, and the incongruity which is no more than the expectable, unconscious, and relatively innocent inconsistencies of human nature. When the situation is clear-cut, the difference is that between Tartuffe, a rascal, and M. Jourdain, the bourgeois gentleman who is confused about status symbols. Or, in abstract terms, the difference is between the sneer at what is contemptible and perhaps dangerous, and the amiable smile that in part registers the embarrassment of kinship. It is natural for the two to be present in the same play when the victims of the aggressive hypocrite (or jealous man or power-seeker, whichever is the immediate embodiment of the community disrupter) are seen, not in pathetic defenselessness like Celia in *Volpone*, but in a contributory self-deceptiveness that may come out of moral vanity: thus Molière's stage is shared by the satirized Tartuffe and the mainly comic Orgon.

We have said enough now to recall the great spectrum of possibilities included under "laughter" and the consequent difficulty of using laughter as a reliable criterion of genre (as surveyed in Chapter 1).[2] We can approach the present problem differently by noting the great tonal range that is possible within the realm of satire—the familiar spectrum with Juvenal at one extreme and Horace at the other. Satire may be relentless and holocaustic; the closer it is to invective—as in *A Modest Proposal* and in Parts III and IV of *Gulliver's Travels*—the less likely it is to produce laughter, in any common sense, as a symptom, and the more complete its alienation from comic acceptance. William Wycherley's *The Plain Dealer* (1676) has an almost Swiftian animus against the world, so much so that Fidelia's devotion to the bitter Manly seems almost a sentimental effect. When Aristophanes lampoons Cleon in *The Knights* (424 B.C.) and Socrates in *The Clouds* (423 B.C.), the "old comedy" hardly wavers in its satiric direction. Ibsen's middle-period problem plays concentrate so earnestly on certain social defects that, without falling into despair, they nevertheless make little move toward the comic. Philip Massinger in *A New Way to Pay Old Debts* (1621–25) and Ben Jonson in *Every Man Out of His Humour* (1599) and *The Alchemist* (1610) are sharply satirical, but in these plays the tone moves in considerably from an extreme of the harsh or savage: in Massinger, Sir Giles Overreach is finally defeated, and in Jonson the greedy and pretentious have some ability to come to self-recognition. In Goldsmith's *She Stoops to Conquer* (1773) the move away from severity in satire is a long one: in many characters the qualities that invite ridicule are minor neuroses or innocent foibles rather than idiosyncrasies that front for basic self-seeking. To finish this sketch of examples, another glance at *Tartuffe*: Tartuffe's credulous devotee, Orgon, I have called "mainly comic." To be more precise, the treatment of him is ambivalent. As a man stubborn in his faith and blind to the consequences of his actions, he can be a cause of disaster in several lives; he is dangerous, then, and an object of satire. Yet at the same time he is neither crudely self-seeking nor malicious; he has a kind of vulnerability—the vulnerability of the moral idealist—which stirs us to a sense of kinship rather than to contempt; through him we smile uncomfortably at ourselves rather than point the finger of scorn at another, as we do with Tartuffe. Thus, comic as well as satirized, Orgon illustrates one way in which comedy and satire may come together, as they do most easily at the Horatian end of the scale.

I have wanted to go enough into the concurrence or coalescence of the satiric and the comic to avoid the imputation of ignoring this possibility. However, whatever partial affinity they may have for each other in a practice that tends to leap over generic borders, the satiric and the comic are not likely to be confused at the theoretical level. In the view that we are gradually working out here, the comic attitude is one of acceptance; satire, on the other hand, is rejective. It takes and demands an adversary stance; it separates the observer and the observed; it looks down on and points censoriously at others. It makes us draw away from others rather than see ourselves reflected in them. We think, not "There but for the grace of God go I," but "Thank heaven I am not as they"—be it crass, crooked, dangerous, dirty, fanatic, grasping, hypocritical, ignorant, ill-bred, pretentious, sadistic, scheming, slippery, uncouth, or unkind.

The satirical mode is the most familiar voice in a set of rejective attitudes that themselves have a wide range. They extend from the jesting, the mocking, the condescending, the contemptuous, and the derisive, to the censorious, the abusive, the punitive, the revengeful, and the destructive; from finding the world laughable or lamentable to finding it untrustworthy and unforgivable; from finding it regrettable to judging it intolerable. The verbal expressions of these attitudes may range from jokes to jeremiads, from sturdy hammerstrokes to sick humor, from the ritually splenetic to the tirelessly vilifying. They may be found in youth prey to a premature disgust or in aged philosophers discovering the delights (not to mention the profits, tangible or intangible) of cosmic nausée. Disillusionment afflicts the idealistic or animates the ill. Detection of vice makes half the news on air or paper; ideologists point out how grossly things fail to square with their blueprints; self-styled iconoclasts crunch to powder the clay feet of other people's *lares* and *penates*; viperine essays make a living for writers trying to make a generation uncomfortable over the grossness of things. The one-time scourges of princes now debunk politicians, scarify the bourgeoisie, and expose "dreams." Described thus, these rejective styles seem like tedious bad habits, but it is the persistence and humorless earnestness of such rejectors that lead to cynicism, a lust for panaceas, and periodic outbreaks of the nihilistic spirit. Satire joins with comedy to produce Orwell's *1984*, and there is much praise of D. H. Lawrence's nose for its infallible detection of a "death" that, believed to pervade the world, evoked Lawrence's diatribes and prescriptions.

Rant and Tirade

Some of the attitudes in the rejective spectrum dominate whole plays, and some are dramatized in individual characters whose vitality springs from intense feeling. Shakespeare more than once portrays, not without sympathy, the extremely vocal lambaster of mankind, most notably in Apeimantus and Timon himself in *Timon of Athens*. (The railer can have a minor role; the best example is the Fool in *Lear*, the honest commentator who is reduced, in Thersites of *Troilus and Cressida*, to a mechanical virtuoso cynic and word-thug.) Bosola in Webster's *The Duchess of Malfi* is a notable railer,* evidently meant to evoke the sympathy that accrues to the denunciatory man of truth, and yet rendered ambiguous by his use, conscious or not, of railing to palliate his dark actions as the agent of others' evil. A similarly ambiguous combination of self-righteous railing and a suspect motive appears in Vendice in Tourneur's *The Revenger's Tragedy* (1607): Vendice's other motive is an obsessive sadistic pleasure in torturing the evildoers whose vice he denounces. The title character of George Chapman's *Bussy D'Ambois* (1604) is again an unfettered denouncer: in him the accompanying element is a hubris of integrity that would lead to tragedy were it not for his unshaken sense of moral triumph.

---

*Bosola's "Oh this gloomy world!" (V.v) echoes, or is echoed in, other Elizabethan and Jacobean works. The most vehement parallel appears in Hieronimo's line in Kyd's *Spanish Tragedy* (1592): "Oh world, no world, but mass of public wrongs" (III.ii.3), an appropriate complaint in a melodrama of disaster (yet "no world" implies that a world, if indeed it is a world, is an acceptable place). Less vehement, but no more hopeful, is "This world uncertain is" in Thomas Nashe's (d. 1601) "A Litany in Time of Plague." "A Mad World, My Masters" was apparently irresistible, appearing in a work by John Taylor (1580–1653) and as the title of a dialogue by Nicholas Breton (1545?–1626?), and best known as the title of Thomas Middleton's satirical drama (1608). This mode of rejection reaches a fantastic extreme in Robert Owen's (1771–1858) "All the world is queer save thee and me, and even thou art a little queer," a metaphor for a certain personality so apt that it has gone on into independent anecdotal life in various formulations. Middleton's title was distantly reflected in the title of an inferior 1960s film; the film title repeated the word *mad* four times.

The subtlest of all the treatments of the railer at social vice is in the title character of Molière's *The Misanthrope* (1666): Alceste's denunciations, whatever their accuracy, are also, as the drama makes clear, expressions of his own egotism. All the subtlety disappears when Wycherley rewrites Molière's play as *The Plain Dealer* and provides no dramatic challenge to Manly's snarling self-righteousness.* The mode here really goes back to John Marston's *The Malcontent* (1604): the railer is right, and the plot carries him from nearly ruined victim of usurpation to victorious restoration to rulership. Though *The Malcontent* is sometimes called a comedy, it illustrates the basically melodramatic structure of all plays of the type except *The Misanthrope*: the plays are essentially sympathetic with the railer, becoming melodramas of triumph if he wins out, and melodramas of defeat if he goes down.

The verbal sniper and machine-gunner has had at least a minor vogue in the twentieth century. The tirade (literally a rifle volley; once a long speech or "flight") or rant is of course a constant in Shaw, but his characters differ from the earlier malcontents in that, giving up intensity, bitterness, and malice, they gleefully express amusement at folly (inconsistency, excessive consistency, habituality, calm faith in cliché) rather than indignation at vice. Shaw is the lettered and sophisticated version of the candidate for office whose stock-in-trade is vituperation, practiced and admired as an art-form; I have heard an audience at such an aesthetic exhibit cry out in happy praise, "Pour it on 'em, Bill." Naturally this is not quite fair to Shaw, but it does help distinguish both him and the candidate from the other type, the sour, resentful, often self-righteous denouncer that we have seen in Renaissance drama and that has been partly revived in our day by John Osborne. Jimmy Porter of *Look Back in Anger* (1956) is of course the star addict of invective who rejects the world and finally opts out of it. He appears also under other names and guises in *Epitaph for George Dillon* (1958; written earlier with Anthony Creighton), *Inadmissible Evidence* (1964), *Time Present* (1968), and *West of Suez* (1971), where the chief loud-mouth is an obnoxious drop-out. This type of criminal manqué, quick on the trigger with his emotional weaponry, surfaces again in Simon Gray's *Butley* (1971). The popularity of such plays attests to a certain anticomic animus in the play-conscious public; they respond

---

*Many critics have detected the moral flaw in Manly. Such rants against the world are to be distinguished from the rants of "heroic drama" (Davenant, Dryden, etc.), where magniloquent rodomontade was meant to establish great-mindedness. This style, of course, was put into comic perspective by *The Rehearsal* (1671) of Buckingham and others, and by Fielding's *The Tragedy of Tragedies; or the Life and Death of Tom Thumb the Great* (1731).

to that passion in the playwright which confers central vitality upon the ranting characters; the latter liberate fantasies of the triumphant hero mowing down clods in all directions.* Yet we also realize that this won't quite do, and railers ancient and modern have most of them had to go down some convenient drain or other. Creators and consumers of the big savage voice sense that here is a prima donna who wants to dominate the stage of life all the time, and everyone sees in time that you can't have an opera with a prima donna alone.

Virtually all the cathartic exercises of power-love end in failure, a failure that restores the essential world of human reciprocity. The literal conqueror ends up in the grave (though his progress toward it is sometimes discouragingly slow), the picaro in the clink (we always have to know about this at the start, so hesitant are we to give empathic freedom to the rogue within), the ranting denouncer in some doghouse or playpen or solitary cell, the natural sanitarium for the ego more and more out of touch with the world. In literary terms, a melodrama of triumph in which there are victims has to undergo a therapeutic transformation into a melodrama of defeat.

Yet there is a way of treating the denouncer that renders him amenable to the comic mode. We find this in Peter Nichols' handling of Bri, the sharp-tongued male shrew in *A Day in the Death of Joe Egg* (1967). Bri's wife, Sheila, a woman of keen intuition, sees that a tirade may in effect be a tantrum. Bri "throws a tantrum" to make her act as he wishes: "He thinks he's only got to cry to get what he wants" (I). Through her analysis of Bri we perceive that a tirade often aspires to be a magic compulsion of others, a threatened curse or excommunication, a strategy of an ego giving a moral front to a power-play. Thus we look at the denouncer in perspective, whereas in most such plays his vitality seems to authenticate his railing. The presence of this perspective changes the tone to the comic; we now accept the railer as a fact of life rather than are forced into a partisan role with or against him. It is what we find again in Nichols' *The National*

---

*The fantasy appears in the male protagonist in Joyce's *Exiles* (1915). Richard Rowan's sense of superiority to the world, though not translated into tirades, is not undercut by the drama as a whole. The melodrama of conquest operates in intellectual terms, only slightly complicated by the masochistic elements in Rowan. Turn the self-centered introvert Rowan into the self-centered extrovert, and the result is Sheridan Whiteside in George S. Kaufman and Moss Hart's *The Man Who Came to Dinner* (1939). Actually this melodrama of triumph is more complex than it may appear on the surface. The domestic Tamburlaine, routinely spearing everyone in sight, becomes a sort of Jonsonian "humor," close to the farcical mechanicalness that renders blows innocuous; like Tartuffe, he gains differing responses; and if we are invited to share in his tyranny, we also feel ricocheting spears, counter spears, and the fury of his victims. Thus a comic perspective inhibits the monopathic (i.e., single-valued) response characteristic of a primarily melodramatic situation.

Health (1969), in which the tirades against the evils of the world are delivered by a terminally ill man named Mackie. But other hospital patients have contrasting attitudes to life, and in this context Mackie's denunciations seem only like outbursts of bad temper. Again, if the tirade is shown as overkill, we see it in perspective. In sum: the less the play is committed to the ranter, the further it is from the castigating mode, and hence the larger its comic potential.* *The Misanthrope* is the archetypal example of this distance and of its impact on tone.

Punish, Revenge, Destroy

The vituperators who represent one form of rejection of the world may, in their merciless flogging of it, act punitively, revengefully, or even destructively. Or characters may punish, seek revenge, or attempt to destroy without tirades and rants, that is, through direct action or through attitudes revealed in ordinary dialogue. Here again an author (or a play) may portray hostility or vindictiveness with a sympathy that resembles commitment. Or, though detached, he may record hostility and vindictiveness as such powerful realities that in the resultant world, despite the copresence of palliative forces, comic acceptance is not easily a tenable style. Here we may seem back at the Juvenalian end of the satirical spectrum, and there is indeed some overlap; but now I mean rather to comment on works that seem to go beyond pillory, stocks, and whipping post to the chopping block or butcher shop. In the former the victim gets it in the neck, or in the face, or in the rear for not living up to community standards that presumably are within his powers; in the latter he is a wholly obnoxious or hopeless case. In the former the victim receives scorn and jeers or even blows, but he lives on, hypothetically chastened, improved; in the latter, the victim is done in, as if by feuding enemy, mob, gang, merciless court, bitter or cynical annihilator—whatever form the punitive, revengeful, or destroying spirit may take. However, there is a considerable range of possibilities between the theoretical poles, and people might reasonably disagree on whether the style of a given play is that of the whipping post or the chopping block.

---

*In Christopher Hampton's *The Philanthropist* (1970) the novelist Braham is an often witty debunker of chic clichés, and thus approaches the denouncer type. But Hampton lets us see in him both malice and a perverse candor that is self-defensive; thus the play is taken away from him even in the one scene that he controls, and the general comic perspective is not lost. In *Ivanov* (1887) Chekhov does an interesting variation on the tirade-type: Ivanov's long speeches interminably record the defects, not of the world, but of himself (he even jeers at himself for playing Hamlet). Even with the change of theme, however, there is the same basic egotism which prefers monologue to dialogue.

The dividing line is most likely to be uncertain when the dramatic picture is of a society rather than of individuals. In *Troilus and Cressida*, for instance, does Shakespeare chastise an erring society or metaphorically destroy it by presenting it as unfit to exist? Does the final crowning of Lucius really save the world of *Titus Andronicus* from the dramatic condemnation of it by episodes that cumulatively declare it a place of unmitigated savagery? The anguish out of which Strindberg wrote often created—revengefully, perhaps?—a world that, despite occasional notes of grace, hardly seems bearable: the world of the marriage plays, of *A Dream Play* (1901) and *The Ghost Sonata* (1907). The bad-dream vision of the world is even more harrowing in such earlier plays of Strindberg's follower, Arthur Adamov, as *La Grande et la Petite Manœuvre* (1950) and *Ping Pong* (1955). A dehumanized life is the theme of Elmer Rice's *The Adding Machine* (1923); the mechanical language, a major symbol, anticipates the style of such Ionesco plays as *The Bald Soprano* (1948) and *Jack, or the Submission* (1950). A nauseated disgust presides over the begetting of Alfred Jarry's Ubu plays, especially the best-known *King Ubu* (1896). Edward Albee's *The American Dream* (1961), arising in part, as we know, from the disgusts of the dramatist's early family life, is virtually a dramatic execution of a society not fit to live.* We cannot, however, establish a firm border line between satirical plays which, fierce as they may be, still include some hope and thus escape the tone of the slaughterhouse, and plays in which the apparently satirical, animated by disgust or despair, becomes savagely punitive and finally destructive. Of the plays mentioned above, some tend in one direction, some in the other; many have a virulence that distinguishes them from, let us say, the strongly critical but by no means hopeless plays of Ibsen's middle period. All, it is clear, approach the world with something other than acceptance.

In some of the plays we at least surmise a revengeful dramatist, or one whose spirit is tinctured with the punitive. That spirit goes on a tear in Arthur Kopit's *Oh Dad, Poor Dad, Mamma's Hung You in the Closet and I'm Feelin' So Sad* (1960)—a madly peerless end-form of the mother-flogging motif that has its share in *Hamlet* and is the source of satire, but not despair, in Sidney Howard's *The Silver Cord* (1926). If such a dramatist is himself the punitive-revengeful man, other dramatists reveal a profound

---

*These terms could almost be applied to John Osborne's *West of Suez* (1971), and some readers perceive in John Arden's *Live like Pigs* (1958) only the clash of two equally unpalatable ways of life. Roger Vitrac's *Victor* (1928) is a pre-Ionesco fantasy of family life, its mercilessness partly undercut, however, by some remarkable farcical effects.

understanding of him. Friedrich Duerrenmatt, who rarely can forget the revengefulness abroad in the world, presents, in *The Visit*, a full picture of the deranged community and the deranging individual, revengeful or destructive or both. The town of Güllen, impoverished and desperate, is suddenly proffered economic grace: an immense bequest from a former resident, now a fabulously wealthy woman. All the town has to do is kill a leading citizen whom the benefactress wants punished for seducing and traducing her many years before. Duerrenmatt sees the town as intending, but finally unable, to resist the bribe; he sees it, further, as not only carrying out a quasi-judicial murder but as deceiving itself about its motives and its way of life as it turns, with public ceremonial and self-congratulation, to an expected new prosperity. Thus the disordered community. On the other hand Duerrenmatt sees both the cynicism and the vindictiveness of Claire Zachanassian, who has risen from victimhood to unlimited power, and who gets total revenge both on the man who betrayed her and on the town that cast her out. She is the most striking modern successor of a long line of uncomic revengers that extends from Medea, Electra, and Phaedra as presented by the Greek dramatists to their re-creations by Corneille and Racine in the seventeenth century, and of course to the even richer flourishing of revengers, predominantly male, in sixteenth- and seventeenth-century English drama—from Kyd's Hieronimo to Webster's Duke Ferdinand and Cardinal to Shirley's Cardinal.

The ultimate revengers are those whose revenge stems less from outer cause than from inner need. There is something of the born revenger in Vendice in Tourneur's *The Revenger's Tragedy*, though the machinations of the Duke and his family do provide Vendice with some justification for the exercise of his exceptional retaliatory gifts. The finest of all congenital revengers is of course Iago, satanically driven to destroy a world that is a rebuke to his own spiritual inferiority. The Iago strain surfaces periodically, not always in expectable places. In *The Borderers* (1795–96) Wordsworth makes a quite remarkable analysis of the Iago type in Oswald, who tricks Marmaduke, a border Robin Hood, into thinking an innocent old man (the father of the girl he loves) evil and hence causing his death. Oswald had been similarly victimized, and in that sense he has a motive; his revenge, however, is not against his deceivers but against an innocent young man who reminds him of himself before he had acted against his original innocent victim. So what actuates him is the true Iago spirit: vindictiveness against the possessor of what he himself does not have. Oswald's *invidia* is the true heart of revenge, and this could hardly operate more classically than by transforming innocence into fellow-criminality. Yet Wordsworth complicates his revenger with a quality peculiarly modern: Oswald declares that crime has liberated him from "slavery" to the prejudices of little men, and he puts this in terms that nicely serve our purposes here. On turning, Oswald says,

> . . . to contemplate
> The World's opinions and her usages,
> I seemed a Being who had passed alone
> Into a region of futurity,
> Whose natural element was freedom.
>
> [IV.165–69]

He invites Marmaduke, now also fallen and free, "Let us be fellow-labourers, then, to enlarge / Man's intellectual empire" (IV.205–6). That is, he has rejected the world as petty and beneath him; he has triumphed over it and even purports to serve mankind; but, as one kind of twentieth-century writer would not be able to do, Wordsworth makes clear that Oswald has really been a destroyer.*

*At the same time the treatment of Marmaduke is tragic: for him the central arena is the inner one of conscience which Oswald has tried desperately to wipe out. Traditional in the treatment of Marmaduke, Wordsworth seems almost predictive in the treatment of Oswald, who, in part reflecting Wordsworth's growing skepticism of the French Revolution, foreshadows certain twentieth-century styles. Oswald expresses his preference for an herb which, "Strong to destroy, is also strong to heal" (I.47)—an early hint of the therapeutic effect sometimes attributed to destruction by latter-day improvers (quotations are from the text of *The Borderers* in *The Complete Poetical Works of Wordsworth*, ed. A. J. George, Cambridge Edition [Boston: Houghton Mifflin, 1904], pp. 33–70). Oswald's recipe for controlling Marmaduke is exactly the professional revolutionary's recipe for converting the innocent into followers: ". . . a few swelling phrases, and a flash / Of truth, enough to dazzle and to blind" (II.13–14). He praises "The wholesome ministry of pain and evil" (II.69); he lauds "passion" as against "proof," "the spiritless shape of Fact," and "the idol, Demonstration" (III.14, 23, 24). And two speeches of his would serve for all those who, rejecting comic acceptance, believe that their moral sense is superior to that of the community. He praises the border "tracts, that own / No law but what each man makes for himself; / Here justice has indeed a field of triumph" (II.46–48), and insists that

> . . . they who would be just must seek the rule
> By diving for it into their own bosoms.
> To-day you have thrown off a tyranny
> That lives but in the torpid acquiescence
> Of our emasculated souls, the tyranny
> Of the world's masters, with the musty rules
> By which they uphold their craft from age to age:
> You have obeyed the only law that sense
> Submits to recognise; the immediate law,
> From the clear light of circumstances, flashed
> Upon an independent Intellect.
>
> [III.352–62]

Oswald's repeated scorn for "the world"—here on the familiar ground that he has an exceptionalness that justifies crime—illustrates very well one of the noncomic styles.

Oswald wants to disguise envious destructiveness as a special privilege of merit: the aristocratic version of the animus against the world (Byronism carried over the border from contempt to crime). Under the influence of egalitarianism it is expectable that this spirit will be embodied in vulgar men such as Schmitz and Eisenring in Max Frisch's *The Firebugs* (1958), one of the best portrayals of the destructive spirit in modern dress. Schmitz and Eisenring's pitch is not privilege but being underprivileged, and they employ every cliché of deficiency in a special way: not as a reason for getting even, but as a blind to confuse their victims and to arouse in them a feeling of guilt that will inhibit an indispensable self-protectiveness. These sinister boors are exercising a congenital destructiveness, burning down house after house "for," in the words of another character, "the pure joy of it."[3] That is, they are spontaneous in a world-hate that, like Iago's, is the recompense for defective being.*

There are many punitive-revengeful-destructive types in modern drama. They attract Pirandello and Camus; Medea is repeatedly born again, and Electra has been a subject not only for O'Neill, but for Benito Pérez Galdós, Hugo von Hofmannsthal, Karl Vollmoeller, Robinson Jeffers, Gerhart Hauptmann, and Jean Giraudoux, whose treatment of her is so germane to a discussion of comic form that it will come up for special attention a little later. Friedrich Duerrenmatt presents the revenger-destroyer type, for which he has a sharp eye, in a very complex way in Mr. Mississippi and St. Claude in *The Marriage of Mr. Mississippi* (1952): under the skin of both these opposed political idealists Duerrenmatt detects a subtle revengefulness of spirit, whether congenital or bred in their gutter background. They are always punishing a world that, for the most part unknowingly, they hate. But, like some chastisements outside the theater, the ones they inflict are unacknowledged ingredients in formal programs of quite different tone: they are running reform schools for the world. They are a Schmitz and Eisenring whose weapon is not arson but millennialism. They are, respectively, Mosaic and Marxist ideologues with fierce programs for universal rehabilitation by universal slavery.

Reform and Transform

Hence they provide a transition to the last of the rejective attitudes which we are surveying: the proposal to reform or transform an imperfect

---

*Louis Simpson puts it amusingly in his autobiography: ". . . young women from Brooklyn with warts, whose politics were purely revenge" (*North of Jamaica* [New York: Harper and Row, 1972], p. 269).

world. The spelling out of what is better is not a frequent exercise in drama. Not that there is not plenty of the hortatory, the admonitory, and even the minatory (pollution will get you if you don't watch out); but advisories and homilies mostly concern general attitudes: be less warlike, less prejudiced; be more tolerant, more just, and so on. The stage is little given to grand designs. Utopian specification is largely the business of tracts and fictions, perhaps because blueprinting and constructing an ideal take more space and time than a play can afford. Besides, diagramed utopias may be appalling in their serene rigidities,[4] since paradises are always more difficult than hells to represent successfully. Negations are more spontaneous than affirmations; dramas tend to condemn better than they save. Brecht was much better at dramatizations of present iniquity than at eschatological realizations of his political doctrine. He proposed less than he disposed, as he did skillfully in St. Joan of the Stockyards (1929–30), Roundheads and Peakheads: Rich and Rich Make Good Company (1932–34), and The Private Life of the Master Race (1935–38). The stage does better with dystopias than utopias.

The implied incompatibility between the utopian theme and the comic theater may seem contradicted by Aristophanes' The Birds (414 B.C.) and Lysistrata (411 B.C.). They may indeed be among the exceptions, which at best are very few. Lysistrata, however, accepts as much as it transforms; its men and women remain humanly flawed while showing a capacity for improvement—in one way at least, for the moment at least—that comedy rarely grants to everyman. In The Birds Nephelococcygia (Cloudcuckoo-land) is a fantasy, so that, unlike the Republic Plato describes, it less constructs a new world than it ridicules the actual one; add this to the satire of various human types, and its main cast becomes rejective rather than transforming. Fantasy is almost the standard theatrical dress of the uto-pian impulse. We see this in Brecht's The Caucasian Chalk Circle (1944–45), in which the judgeship of Azdak brings to the court a Solomonic ingenuity and hence a rare ideality in judgments that are at times uproar-ious. We can see it even more sharply in the contemporary Madwoman of Chaillot (1945) of Jean Giraudoux, whose main characters design a crazy plot to eliminate sinners and install in power the joyful and the just. Using old motifs—folkish wisdom and the sanity of the mad, respec-tively—both dramatists create fairy tales, wish-fulfillments for out-siders who dream of taking over institutions and purifying them.[5] In such plays the satirical animus leads on to romantic purgation of the world, with final gratifications of a melodramatic rather than a comic sort.

The transformationist theme is contained within the comic fold only when an acceptance of imperfection furnishes an independent perspective on the utopian instinct. J. M. Barrie uses this perspective in both *The Admirable Crichton* (1902) and *Dear Brutus* (1917). The former portrays a utopia 'of talent but sees that it is relative rather than absolute, bound to be succeeded by a comfortable nonutopia of habit after the temporary crisis that evokes universal voluntary submission to sheer talent. *Dear Brutus* conjures up a fantastic fulfillment of a half dozen personal utopianizing dreams, the temporary alternative life enabling the dreamer to spot his illusions and thus to adjust to an unchanging self that would make an imagined utopia ironically much like the actuality that stirs him to dreams. Again, Frisch's *Biography* (1967) records the difficulties of re-forming a life even when rational hindsight is fantastically given freedom and power to make it over.[6]

Drama deals most vigorously with the utopian theme when it looks detachedly at millennialists who tend to be enforcers of ideals, upon themselves and upon others. Ibsen's interest in the theme extended over several decades—from the portrait of the fanatical absolutist in *Brand* (1866) to the merciless man of principle in *The Wild Duck* (1884) who in the name of the "ideal" destroys a family's working accommodation to their world. Gregers Werle is singularly revived in Hickey,[7] the mad reformer in O'Neill's *The Iceman Cometh*. And so we come back to our starting-point, the rival doctrinaire would-be saviors of the world in Duerrenmatt's *The Marriage of Mr. Mississippi*. In such plays the tone and form push toward the tragic, the expectable destiny of one "born to set it right." A certain intransigence in things as they are, or of people as they are, reveals the hopeful transformer as vainly utopian or essentially hubristic. Hence the incompatibility between the comic and the reformist or transformist sensibility. The incompatibility was first voiced by Aristophanes or at least by Bdelycleon, who is the voice of authority in *The Wasps* (422 B.C.): "The cure of a disease [litigiousness], so inveterate and so widespread in Athens, is a difficult task and of too great importance for the scope of Comedy."[8] Or, in G. Wilson Knight's more recent formulation, "A moralistic comedy is a contradiction in terms."[9]

Underacceptance and Overacceptance

Bdelycleon and Knight implicitly distinguish the comic from the satirical, which attacks though it may not "cure a disease." Satire is the central and most frequent of the rejective attitudes that can intensify to

destructive malice or beget transformationist dreams. All the attitudes to
the world that we have been describing thus far may be brought together
under the blanket term "underacceptance," a neutral term that may signify either appropriate or inappropriate attitudes. This will immediately
suggest its opposite, "overacceptance," the way of life which, like the
satirical, has some affiliation with, and yet has to be distinguished from,
the central comic style. On the one hand we punish the world, on the
other we collaborate with it; on the one hand, condescension or con-
tumely, and on the other, cooperation and collusion; on the one hand,
triumph, of whatever kind, over the existent order, and, on the other,
submission as the groundwork for subsistence, survival, and ultimately
success within the existent order. The programmatic versus the pragmatic;
the doctrinaire versus the expedient; the fanatic versus the fleshly; the
utopian versus the cynical; the rejective versus the overly hospitable. I am
trying, not to make these oppositions schematic, but, by various rephras-
ings in terms that are contiguous rather than synonymous, or connota-
tively divergent rather than precisely antonymous, to suggest two broad
attitudinal styles that are roughly contrasting rather than tightly logical
alternatives. We see both patterns—the transformationist and the
collusionist—in wide use in the popular theater: all kinds of reform plays
and all kinds of success plays; throw-the-rascals-out plots and local-boy-
makes-good plots.

Another way of putting the matter is to distinguish between those who
want to impose unconditional surrender and those who are quite ready to
submit to it. This sounds as if, in dramatic terms, we are talking about
melodramas of triumph and melodramas of defeat. But "melodrama of
defeat" has the wrong connotation when the protagonists willingly take
on whatever yoke or fall into whatever pattern circumstances or men
impose upon them, or buy whatever goods are tossed on their porches or
dropped into their mailboxes, or even go out of their way to discover such
yokes or patterns or goods as ways with or into the world. They are not
victims but what might be called overadjusters. Theirs is the broad realm
of what has variously been called cynical comedy, "gray comedy," "dark
comedy," and "black comedy," or, in Henry Becque's striking term,
"*comédies rosses*," that is, "beastly" or "nasty" comedies. In all such phrases
the noun *comedy* implies acceptance, but the adjective, which is always the
key element, challenges the noun, implying that acceptance is a too easy
and uncomplicated response, that for whatever one gets, the price is too
high (too high, that is, for fully sentient human beings). Hence "overac-

ceptance," a certain sprawling excess of the comic spirit, either a compliance with and a docility toward whatever comes up, or a positive outreach toward any handles at all to marginal or central insidership in a wholly unjudged world, local or larger. We do what we have to do to get on, to get in, to make out, to go up, to beat the game, to save our skins, to top out, to keep from going under, dropping out, getting axed, losing our shirts, taking the rap. We learn the rules, the score, the price, the odds, the percentages, the bargains, the trade-ins, the insurance rates; we learn about fall guys, guys on the make, con men, city hall; we learn about getting something on someone else, about people who know something, people who have something, people who have something on us or on others; we identify clay feet, Achilles heels, the well heeled, soft touches, hard heads, thick skins, thin stories.

Such activities identify the norms of "black comedy," which is the most convenient of the terms for the class. A remarkable example of the form is Joe Orton's *Entertaining Mr. Sloane* (1964), which looks at two murders, not as moral wrongs that should be suffered for or avenged, but as tactical mistakes that make the doer of them vulnerable. The doer is a young man who is in the power of a brother and sister because they know what he has done. They are presumably about twice his age; the sister is a nymphomaniac, and the brother a homosexual; both find the young man irresistible, and their competing for him creates a parody of traditional triangles. While their power over him is their power to hang him, he has a certain power too—a sexual attractiveness that drives both of them panting into the strategies of lust. In the Jacobean theater this would lead to lies, treachery, demonic vengefulness, and a total blood bath. But not here, for everyone sensibly acknowledges the rational advantages of sharing. The young man will live with the sister for six months and then with the brother for six months (with visiting rights to ease the half-year dry spells for the sibling on sabbatical).

This provides an excellent symbolization of the spirit of hyperacceptance that goes beyond the centrally comic into the blackly comic: such acceptance rules out all elements of human personality that would oppose the solution arrived at. The three characters like it, and the dramatist does not introduce alternative standards that, by making us aware of an ampler moral world, would imply a critique of the tricornered accommodation. In that sense the play "accepts" a more limited world than would be satisfactory to characters of fuller humanity.

The distinction between accepting and overaccepting is put hortatorily in Francis Quarles's *Emblemes* (1635): "Be wisely worldly, be not worldly wise" (Book 2, Poem 2, l. 46).

The Five Types

So much, then, for the context of possible attitudes to the world which help place and identify comic acceptance. Though for expository convenience I have used eight subheadings, there is some overlap, and the various attitudes fall logically into five main types. The first is withdrawal, flight, or defeat of whatever kind: one may choose the solitary life that finds its voice, if any, in the lyric or monologue; one may be too weak to cope, or be victimized, or thrown into a brown study by the puzzling ambiguities of the men and things around him. In one way or another the world gets man down or takes him, whether he runs, fails, suffers, or is metaphysically perplexed. His experience is a melodrama of defeat. In the opposite camp (the second category) are those who take the world or take it over— the hit-and-run rogues or picaros, the conquerors and possessors of power (military, political, financial), and the indirect manipulators who can convert their own weakness or illness or obsession into an instrument for the control of others. Insofar as we are invited to be sympathetic with the take-over types, the mode is the melodrama of triumph. But the exercise of power, direct or indirect, also arouses antipathy or censure, and so we move into a third attitude, which expresses itself in the satirical mode. In it the central style is that of hostility and rejection, which may reveal themselves either in the dramatist's concentration upon what is blameworthy or in his disillusionment with the world as a whole; this is the realm of snigger and sneer, denunciation and diatribe. It generates the familiar melodrama of right, actual or self-proclaimed, against wrong, real or imagined; the range is from earnest or caustic complaint to disgust or a desire to wound or even annihilate. Idealism, envy, maladjustment may make men condemnatory, punitive, revengeful, or even totally destructive. If, however, they combine the rejective with the plastic turn of mind, men will fall into the fourth attitude, the transformationist, whether this appear in limited reformism, revolutionary utopianism, or millennialist fantasies. The fifth attitude can be contrasted with the ultrarejective styles: if we think of these as underaccepting, the final posture is overacceptance—that noncritical collusion with a manifestly confining or stultifying actuality that is at the heart of black comedy.

In sum, men are not accepting the world when they are fleeing it or flogging it, falling behind it or getting ahead of it, going down the drain or over the top; when they are compelled to lay their heads on the block or find their heads confused by the apparent illogic of things; when their game is trick or triumph, con or conquer; when they are trampling upon the world, spitting upon it, being sickened by it, getting even with it, exposing it, cleaning it up, or wiping it out; when they are totally renovating the house of life or building a completely new one (possibly from the ground up, but often from an aerial paradigm downward); or on the other hand are content to make out in any unventilated room, close-quartered tenement, unelastic attic, or unlighted doghouse where they may be received by those inclined, and not unable, to effect cooperation.

Nonacceptance, of course, may be admirable or something else. Various forms of nonacceptance are necessary to the welfare of the world (as the proponent of comedy should remind himself). But we have seen that, while nonacceptance may be defensible or indispensable disapproval, it may also denote self-esteem, self-magnification, and self-advancement, or inner disorder translating itself into a public-health measure.

II. ASPECTS OF ACCEPTANCE

The definition of black comedy as overacceptance should make clear that acceptance itself does not mean, to repeat a phrase used earlier, unconditional surrender. By now, on the contrary, it should be apparent that acceptance means something between conquering the world and being defeated by it, something between an unrelenting criticalness and a genial universal abdication of judgment, something between "I will accept no world that does not conform to my rules for goodness and justice" and "I will accept any world that is presented to me; just let me know what the going rules are." Men avoid extremes by keeping a certain benign pressure upon themselves; they protect themselves against an excess of the critical and attacking spirit by keeping in mind the inevitable imperfections of humanity and of the societies it somewhat haphazardly puts together; and they protect themselves against an uncritical adaptation to imperfection by keeping in mind the melioristic designs that humanity continues to turn out because it can imagine less imperfect states. Men need to maintain a tension between the idea and unregulated actuality, to find a comic mean between ascetic utopianism and gross cynicism. To seek this mean is rather like maintaining a state of peace: it implies compromise, adjustment, yielding. This is not always easy, for it requires forgoing the excitement of combat, feud, polemic (the essential Osborne stance), the self-reassuring sense of being at one with good and at war with evil. That is, our idea of the good life is modified by our sense of reality, of an insistent, unprogramed movement of people and things that cannot be much changed. In a slightly different image, one cannot play Prometheus and maintain the comic style (romantic lovers of Prometheus necessarily lacked—or lack—a comic sense).

We might say that black comedy means the acceptance of the unacceptable. The objectively unacceptable is not the domain of comedy; hence, when the objectively unacceptable is permitted under some conditions to enlarge its valid domain, it constricts the life of comedy. "Is permitted to enlarge": that is, men let it hypertrophy or even encourage this expansion. The undue enlargement of the unacceptable accompanies every kind of puritanism, the spirit of which is the refusal to accept anything that does not wholly conform to *a priori* theory. Despite recent changes usually taken to represent depuritanization, America could be described as a Puritan country which has never had a genuine 1660. Hence it is not surprising that the American comic tradition is not a strong one, for this tradition cannot find nourishment in habitual dissentism, reformism, and legislationism, with hysteria always just around the corner. Dissenters and reformers, however socially useful and needful they may be on occasion, have to be earnest, nonironic, nonaccepting, and therefore noncomic if not actually anticomic; they are likely to think comedy trivial or even undesirable because it does not aid transformationist activities. I do not mean that America does not occasionally practice acceptance, despite itself, nor that it never writes comedies, but the fact is that our theatrical talent is rather on the tragic side, for tragedy, like reform, invokes conscience (though in tragedy conscience observes the defects of the self rather than those of other people and the world). The American comic tradition is very slender compared with that of England and France and even that of Russia, whose theatrical history is scarcely longer than our own. In Europe we are thought to be especially gifted in musical comedy, and this surely is no coincidence, for the generic statement of musical comedy is that good finally triumphs.

Modes of Nonacceptance

The understanding of comedy requires the distinguishing, not so much between the objectively unacceptable and the demonstrably acceptable, as between the apparently unacceptable and the apparently acceptable. Problems lie in the gray territory, the middle ground with shifting shades, the interpretable. Clear absolutes lead only to truisms; to say that comedy accepts the acceptable is to say nothing at all. Let us approach the central issue by distinguishing among the three modes of that nonacceptance of the world which is noncomic or anticomic: obligatory, obsessive, and optional.

Obligatory nonacceptance is the response to unmistakable evil and vice when they seem to control the world and hence force us into an adversary role. Unarguable examples: Richard III, Macbeth, the Nazis. When the world is in such hands, comedy is impossible; the political and the literary style both have to be the melodrama of opposition to evil men. We can say of Gloucester that in attempting to get on with the post-Lear regime in Britain he undertook to substitute a mode of comic acceptance for the melodramatic style of resistance that was required by the political reality; he was too late in recognizing the objectively unacceptable.

Obsessive nonacceptance is the antipode of obligatory nonacceptance: the types have in common the element of compulsion, but in the obsessed the compulsion is psychological rather than moral, private and idiosyncratic rather than communal or traditional. Obsessive nonacceptance appears in a very wide range of characters, all of whom proscribe or inhibit comic life. It appears, for instance, in habitual criminals. It appears in the malicious or troubled whose main weapon is the tongue and who exist only by denigration, which may take the form of neighborhood sniping and snidery. It appears in the professional dissenter, who feels real only when he rises to a point of order, detects incompetence and malfeasance, and opposes official policy or the lack of it; he equally laments the hollowness of the past, decries the abysses of the status quo, or warns against the pitfalls of change. (He is the secular inheritor of the spirit identified by Burke, "the dissidence of dissent, and the protestantism of the Protestant religion," then picked up as a motto by the *Nonconformist*, and finally mourned by Arnold as the antithesis of sweetness and light. Irving Howe's *Dissent* is a more self-conscious inheritor of the protestant way with a flawed world.) Obsessive nonacceptance may appear, finally, in the innocuous eccentric who has to do everything differently, but who, by definition, is content with difference and wishes only to be seen by others and not to push them around. His willingness to let others pursue their noneccentricity opens a door, of course, to the realm where comedy is possible. A nonaccepter for himself, he accepts what others choose for themselves.

A still wider door is opened by the third class of nonaccepters, that is, the optionals. These have a choice; they fall midway between the obsessive nonaccepters who are in a continuous melodrama of opposition, and the total accepters who play roles in black comedy. Presumably optionals distinguish between what cannot be borne and what must be borne, between what it is necessary to oppose, and what it is expedient, or bearable, or more comfortable, or even wiser to accept: between, in a word, greater and lesser evils, or between inevitabilities that cannot be countenanced (murder, for instance) and those that can or have to be lived with (greediness, for instance). Presumably optionals distinguish between changing times, between circumstances that render a type of conduct odious and those that render it a subject for tolerant irony: profit-making seems a different thing in wartime and in peacetime; Tartuffe's pretended virtue is vicious, and Lady Wishfort's is venial, because his would damage others, while hers reflects only upon the lady herself. Presumably optionals can distinguish, not only among different claims that come from without, but among worse and better styles in themselves. This self-judgment is nicely illustrated by Perpetua Reedbeck in Christopher Fry's *Venus Observed* (1950). Perpetua once belonged to an American student outfit named the Society for the Desecration of Ancient and Modern Monumental Errors (in creating this outfit Fry was two decades ahead of the times). In it, she learned to use a gun. She says of it, "We destroyed, or tried to destroy, whatever we loathed / As bad" (I):[10] the ultimate activism of the professional dissenter, who enlarges personal need or taste into a universal moral judgment. Sent to jail, Perpetua had time to reflect:

> And there I knew it was all no use.
> The more we destroyed, the worse the bad sprang up.

This is an acute recognition: that pure destructiveness seems to fertilize the objects of destruction. Then Perpetua takes the next and harder step: "And I thought and thought, What can I do for the world?" And she comes to the hard conclusion: "You must make good, before you break the bad." Note that it is "the world" with which she is concerned, and with some appropriate style to it, not with the exercise of some private craving. She sees that the avenue to usefulness in the world is not the quick trigger but the slow reordering of the self. In generic terms, she is escaping from the seductions of self-righteousness and millennialism that make one kind of melodrama, and discovering the comic spirit. (And a judgment against the self, since it may be made in comic or tragic terms, is one concrete link between comedy and tragedy, whose often asserted consanguinity is almost always left unhelpfully vague.)[11] That spirit puts into practice an implicit acceptance even of kinds of conduct and situation that ideally one might wish done away with.

The Style of Acceptance

The optional nonaccepter, then, knows or finds out when to oppose, protest, or reject, and when to adjust with an amiable sense that all is not lost. Acceptance is a perception of the world as a livable middle ground that is not celestial but is not infernal either. If the hellish potential, always present, shows symptoms of becoming hyperkinetic, the flexible observer will opt for an appropriate rejective mode. But he refrains from the simplistic rejections that tend to rise in us daily because of our common humanity, with its always lively sense of shortcomings in others, and its addiction to censure. In choosing fittingly between acceptance and rejection, a person is not simply voting yes or no, or putting situations into one bin or another: the more perceptive he is, the more he goes beyond pat and mechanical divisions into an awareness of qualifications that may alter the first-glance picture. Here we get into that complex interplay of world and observer in which the world is neither wholly independent of the observer nor wholly his creation; he modifies it, and it modifies him. This interplay can relax that uncritical commitment to the real which yields to any historical actuality as to a dictator's fiat, or it can mitigate that fanatical clinging to the idea which leads to automatic, doctrinaire decisions on what must be rejected. The world educates the observer, but the personality of the observer is also at work, attending especially to what I have called the gray area, a pepper-and-salt medley, the dark partly redeemed by the intermingling of light, the light never distilled into artificial purity through separation from the dark spotting in the human and historical substance. In international politics, where the comic spirit is the alternative to the crusading spirit (that conjoining of power and idea essential for conquest, and sought by all who would conquer), acceptance means both refraining from the effort to impose one's own rightness, and enduring, apostatic though it seem, deviations from the courses charted by the gospel of one's own faith.

Comedy is the style of survival when nonacceptance is reasonably optional, that is, neither compelled by troubles without nor compulsive through troubles within. Finding accommodation with the different is the indispensable style. The mode is in part concessive; we see things—actions, situations, attitudes—not in the light of an absolute, but in the light of time, of relations, of possibility.* The procedure is antidestructive; it may be civilizing. We detect in the seen a quality once not discerned, or grant it a status or role once not conceded. Here is a shorthand description of this by no means simple process: to find the acceptability of, or acceptable areas in, what is or once was or seemed unacceptable. (Cf. the earlier shorthand definition of black comedy: "the acceptance of the unacceptable.") We modify moral prescriptions, we get on with fashions that once put us off; as lambs, we risk lying down with lions. Wilde's Lady Windermere comes to see that her idea of human goodness is faulty and that in fact the "fallen woman," Mrs. Erlynne, is a "good" woman; and Wilde understands that her new acceptance, though assisted by an improbable coincidence, is the central comic action. Chekhov applies the term *comedy* to portrayals of lives where, along with some making out and getting on, there is much of disappointment, frustration, failure to cope; he does not shed or invite tears, fall into complaint, or declare man unfortunate and the world absurd. In this sense the playwright, as well as his play, accepts equally the frequent life in which much falls short of expectation. He practiced, long before it was formulated, the rule voiced by T. S. Eliot's Harcourt-Reilly, "Learn to avoid excessive expectation." If acceptance means taking what comes, it may also mean the maintenance of a life-shaping expectation despite the nonarrival of the apparently promised: in Beckett's *Waiting for Godot* expectation is a way of life, that is, the rejection of despair when an expected meeting, possibly a theophany, fails to materialize.

*This issue is presented dramatically in an episode in Chapter 31 of George Gissing's *New Grub Street* (1891). Reardon, a struggling writer, has a grievance against his wife, who is worried and bitter about their poverty. Reardon clings to his grievance obsessively, masochistically, and self-destructively. When his wife comes into money, he takes pleasure in refusing the occasion to seek a rapprochement to which she appears not averse. His good friend Biffen, equally poverty-stricken but better adjusted to the facts of life, tells him that "we have both of us too little practicality. The art of living is the art of compromise. We have no right to foster sensibilities, and conduct ourselves as if the world allowed of ideal relations; it leads to misery for others as well as ourselves. Genial coarseness is what it behoves men like you and me to cultivate. Your reply to your wife's last letter was preposterous. You ought to have gone to her of your own accord as soon as ever you heard she was rich; she would have thanked you for such common-sense disregard of delicacies. Let there be an end of this nonsense, I implore you!" (*New Grub Street*, ed. Bernard Bergonzi [Baltimore: Penguin Books, 1968], pp. 476–77). Gissing's sympathies seem to be with Reardon; hence the thread of irony in Biffen's exhortation. Still, Gissing fully imagines the common-sense comic view that is opposed to the melodrama in which Reardon wants to persist.

Acceptance versus Nonacceptability

What we come to accept is not the objectively unacceptable. Rather we retranslate the unpalatable and the undesirable that we would like to postpone, forget, ignore, or deny. There is such an experience as the "comic discovery of the fraudulent, the inauthentic, the illusionary, the hypocritical, the merely perspectival." [12] Comedy has learned to deal with illness and death, which we generally associate with sentimental, melo-dramatic, and tragic tones, or else with the slender mode of sick humor, with its wry treatment of the disastrous or fatal as casual, annoying, or inopportune.* Comedy rather treats illness and death, not as trivial or as unmentionable, nor as mournful or shocking, but as standard, inevitable, and much like all discomforts and disadvantages. When Dr. Patrick Cullen in Shaw's *Doctor's Dilemma* uses the expression, "When you've killed as many people as I have" (IV), his words seem not shockingly callous but ironically accepting: we are invited, not to be indignant or sardonic, but to smile dryly at this fact of medical life. (Compare Goethe's Faust, who, on being praised for his medical skill, bursts into anguished outcries over the victims killed by his malpractice: "Poison to thousands I myself did give; / They withered away—yet I must live / To hear the barefaced murderers blest.") [13] Peter Nichols has an exceptional flair for depicting the acceptance of illness. In *A Day in the Death of Joe Egg* his theme is not the pathos of a spastic child, but the ironies in the parents' endeavoring to come to terms with the situation; in *The National Health* the scene is a hospital ward in which being ill, going down hill, and dying are seen, not as pathetic or lamentable disasters, but in ironic contrast with hopes, with personalities, with hospital routines, with illusions, and with soap-opera views of these events. This acceptance of transitoriness appears in other ways in Kaufman and Hart's *You Can't Take It with You* (1936) and in Bernard Kops's *The Dream of Peter Mann* (1960).

Acceptance of the world may mean acceptance of second best, that is, making do with something less than a total good that one is capable of

---

*There is a skillful use of sick humor in Christopher Hampton's *The Philanthropist*, in which a young playwright inadvertently commits suicide in a spectacularly messy way that illustrates verbatim a theatrical effect in the play he has just been reading to others. In a *New York Times* review of a baseball film Jim Bouton provides another good illustration of sick humor: trying to make clear the kind of style that baseball players use among themselves, Bouton suggests that if a player were dying of leukemia, his teammates would probably call him "Luke" (September 30, 1973, Section 2, p. 12). Cf. "Fatso" or "Shorty": the pattern is the ironic analogy between terminal disease and innocuous deviation.

imagining.* In *Lady Windermere's Fan* Mrs. Erlynne wants to re-enter society, but she accepts, instead, her daughter's safety there and her own marriage to the amiable but not very bright Lord Augustus. In Henry Becque's *La Parisienne* (1885) a husband and two lovers accept shares in Clotilde as sex corporation, so to speak; how much each one suspects or knows we do not know, but at least none of them complains or demands total ownership. In *The Way of the World* virtually all the lovers accept situations less ideal than they seek or imagine: some fail wholly; Fainall may or may not keep his mistress, and he may continue with his wife for the economic benefits; Mirabell and Millamant themselves accept conditions that impose limits on their own freedom of action. In Congreve's *Love for Love* (1695) Tattle is paid off for his vanities and pretenses by finding himself married to Frail, a promiscuous woman—a punishment for both; yet the satirical impact is blunted, and the event turned comic, by the newlyweds' treating their union, not as an unbearable affliction, but as an ironic embarrassment that can be borne.

We have become so fond of Falstaff that we forget the strenuous imaginative efforts on his behalf: Shakespeare entices us into applauding, for its entertainment value, a personality that, given much play in affairs, would render a world chaotic; and he does it so well that he makes some readers sentimentally unwilling to accept the ultimate rejection of Falstaff that has to be made in a full-scale world. In *The Taming of the Shrew* Kate accepts a subordination that on the face of it greatly reduces her long freedom of abuse and tantrum; here, of course, her acceptance of second best is paradoxical, for Petruchio's nominal mastery is benevolent compared with the masochistic willfulness that had enslaved her before.

Perhaps the best of all dramatizations of the second-best principle is the treatment of Eliante and Philinte in Molière's *Misanthrope*: though their eyes are fixed primarily on greater stars in the firmament of love, they are willing to find in each other a workable actuality that can compensate for

---

*We might also call this the acceptance of inequity—not inequity in a legal or moral sense that would require remedial action of an appropriate kind, but inequity as a built-in fact of life: in the sense that some people are stronger, healthier, better organized, wiser, or simply luckier than others. Capricious distribution of merits and advantages is one of the ways of the world; the ordinary tendency in comedy is to see a rough equivalence between what one gets and, in the broadest sense, what one is. This is one of the ways of defining the disparateness of the world that comedy accepts. Hence egalitarianism has to be without the sense of humor—the sense of incongruity—that we associate with comedy. Its hallmark is the earnest nonacceptance of anything less than total equality: unable to acknowledge diversity of talent and adaptability, it is compelled to associate advantage with malfeasance, render mechanical and invariable the influx of good things, lament and lash instead of laugh, and endeavor to store the wheel of fortune in the museum of antiquities.

an unfulfilled dream. As Philinte puts it to Eliante, "In short, should you be cheated of Alceste, / I'd be most happy to be second best."[14] This urbanity in accepting an amatory realignment appears in a moral readjustment in *The Tempest*. In giving up his use of magic, Prospero accepts what we might legitimately call second best in a political power-world; again, at one point he offers forgiveness, and at another Alonso asks for it—in either case an acceptance of something less than ordinary pride normally drives man to. Further, while the audience sees a final world in which much has been rectified, various miscreants have not been permanently disposed of; all who have plotted still survive, so that we accept a world in which the forces that may subvert order are not romantically eliminated. In *Cymbeline*, too, the world is not really purged of human elements that cause trouble and injury; these are, so to speak, accepted as inevitable. But a number of individuals are able to relax or give up the resentment and revengefulness stirred up by injurious deeds; they exhibit forbearance or forgiveness or magnanimity when they might feel recalcitrant or retaliatory. Posthumus blames himself rather than Iachimo, Lucius asks that Fidele be saved, Belarius and Cymbeline rise above recriminations, Imogen is forgiving, Cymbeline acknowledges that he owes tribute to Rome. That is, they do not dismiss imperfect conduct as "unacceptable," that key word of nations and persons committed to an adversary role. In this quasi acceptance they in effect defuse the potential explosiveness of a situation. And that is one way of describing the action of the comic spirit.

III. DRAMATIC MODES: SHARED ELEMENTS AND CONTRASTS

Before entering into this examination of comic "acceptance," we were exploring the notion of "the world" as the arena of comedy (chap. 2). The world, we saw, is the sum of social actions and public actions; it means interplay between and among people, between the individual and the group, within groups, between groups; it is realized in the community, in its just claims upon the individual; in its indispensability, which takes precedence over its imperfections, artificialities, or inflexibilities; in a *sens commun* or common sense—rather than personal intuitions, private dreams, utopian visions, or mystical insights—that articulates the norms in terms of which men adjust, associate, fraternize, and come together instead of falling or flying apart. We also noted an alternative scene and drama—inner, personal, private; the divisions that plague all sentient men, concentrated within a representative individual; the tensions in which he faces himself, or in which one part of himself collides with another; the conflicts between impulses, between impulse and imperative, or between imperatives. This is in the tragic realm, where men are inwardly torn between the absolutes of passion and obligation, where their hubris violates and endangers community, and where they serve the continuity of order by undergoing self-recognition and self-judgment. It is a quite different life from that of accommodation to the world—by adjustment, or by compromise, or by living with it. In comedy what is at stake is the world, a livable kind of society; in tragedy, what is at stake is the soul, or the quality of man's moral or spiritual life.

Tragedy and Comedy: Common Ground

Yet the forms have in common a putting up with elements that are less than ideal. In comedy man puts up with the imperfections of the world or recognizes the imperfections in himself that make him a nuisance in the world; in tragedy man recognizes the flaws that make him crave triumphs incompatible with the moral ordering of mankind. The bond between tragedy and comedy is that in both, man accepts the way things are— either in the private domain of the self or in the public domain of the world (or in that underlying domain of human nature which issues in the diversity of the world). This bond, though it in no way diminishes the gap between the two domains of action, nevertheless opens the way to a distinction between what we might call the realm of tragedy-and-comedy and the realm of melodrama. For in melodrama the central action or style is almost never one of acceptance (the exception is the rather rare situation in which defective personalities accept defeat, as in *The Iceman Cometh*); on the contrary the melodramatic note is one of protest, resistance, challenge, opposition, combat, war. The way in which we laughingly define the conflict in "popular melodrama" as between "good guys" and "bad guys" actually expresses the basic situation. Either one side is combating a genuine wrong, or, if what goes on is a bare conflict for power, each side instinctively conceives of itself, or tactically defines itself, as the good guy and hence translates the opponents into bad guys (we do this unconsciously in athletic competitions).

There is, of course, always a bad guy of some sort to deal with. In tragedy, the bad guy is within; in melodrama, he is the external adversary that one is lined up against; in comedy, he turns out to be not so bad after all or else lives on peripherally, a steady ingredient in life but not a serious danger that demands combative action and makes comic life impossible. Bad guys, we might note, are a very desirable, and perhaps necessary, dish in the diet of life. They alone give man a sense of clear-cut outlines, of unambiguous issues, of singleness of purpose and wholeness of being. Hence the human addiction to war, rarely taken account of by those who war against war. "We flee," said Marquis Childs just after World War II, "from the complexities of peace to the terrible simplicity of war." [15] It was just at the start of World War II that Thornton Wilder's *The Skin of Our Teeth* (1942) framed the same perception in reverse terms, those of difficult return instead of easing flight. After the war Mr. Antrobus exclaims to his son Henry, the paranoid Cain-figure: "I wish I were back at war still, because it's easier to fight you than to live with you. War's a pleasure—do you hear me?—War's a pleasure compared to what faces us now: trying to build up a peacetime with you in the middle of it" (III). Childs and Wilder picture the negative attractions of war as a relief from the difficulties of peace; more recently John Sisk, in a brilliant survey, has analyzed the positive attractions of war to mankind; in his terms "war fictions" minister to our "hunger for the kind of violent clarification of terms and agonistic purity that characterize melodrama."* War, of course, is the *Ultima Thule* of melodrama; the "complexities of peace"—the contradictions in the self and in the world—are the stuff of tragedy and comedy. These tax dramatist and audience more. Hence dramatists may thin out the texture of both forms, in tragedy by making hard insights seem easy, in comedy by reliance on stereotyped situations and characters that render the complexities of peace simpler than they are.

Tragedy and Melodrama: Common Ground

If tragedy and comedy have in common an accepting recognition of actuality in different keys, tragedy and melodrama do have in common

---

*John P. Sisk, "War Fictions," *Commentary*, 56 (August 1973): 60. Sisk's whole article is relevant to my own discussion, for Sisk surveys many views on the attractiveness of war to humanity generally, and analyzes acutely the psychological and moral values of war to the participant. He notes the warlike attitudes and methods that often characterize the opponents of war. "In the minds of men war is structured like fiction, usually melodrama . . ." (p. 59). ". . . war fiction, dependent . . . on extreme agonistic situations, . . . gets its characters into the right kind of trouble" (p. 60). ". . . the tendency of war . . . is to enclose its public within a melodramatic fiction of war in which the alternatives are total victory or total defeat . . ." (p. 61). Conflict over the Vietnam war created a "melodrama, . . . in the intensity of which the anti-military party often became extremely warlike, and of necessity then practiced both the virtues and the vices of the military-minded" (p. 65). In noting the ultimate relationship of war and melodrama, Sisk portrays vividly that basic attitude to the world which is incompatible with comic acceptance.

one psychological constituent: the basic assumption that initiates action. In both, the protagonist hopes to triumph over the way things are. The tragic hero, beset by an impulse or adhering to an imperative not tenable with impunity, contests the moral order or one of the injunctions that issue from it, whether because, in pride of power, he wants to, or, in pride of judgment, feels he has to. Things out there remain the way they are, and through the sentience that makes him tragic, the protagonist comes into a fuller view of himself and of things. For the protagonist in melodrama, the way things are is less a moral order than it is the status quo, the distribution of power, the current arrangements, the going public style. As combatant, the melodramatic hero may seek triumph of various kinds: power for its own sake, the redistribution of power toward whatever end, the defeat of evil or simply of antagonists. Whereas tragedy records the ultimate firmness of things as they are (that is, in the order that the hero wants to ignore or even deny), melodrama may record everything from stonewall resistance by, to the breaching and crumbling of, things, depending on the distribution of power and luck; the protagonist may triumph or be defeated or come in somewhere between these two extremes. And whereas tragedy is concerned finally with the self-revaluation of the hero, melodrama is not; triumph leads to self-congratulation rather than self-inspection, and if defeat leads to inward inquiry (inquiry after defeat usually takes the form of an investigation by someone else, that is, a new melodrama of good and evil), any flaw that the hero may acknowledge is not in moral vision but in tactical judgment.

Melodrama and Comedy: Common Ground

So, while I began the preceding point by identifying a common element in tragedy and melodrama, I worked around to a notation of the essential differences between them. To repeat, tragedy is centered in the conflict within, melodrama in external conflict with other agents or forces. The tragic scene is the soul, the melodramatic scene is the world. This, of course, is exactly the distinction which I made earlier between tragedy and comedy. Melodrama and comedy, then, share a large common ground: they are both ways of meeting the world—the many-sided, inconsistent, imperfect world, occasionally gratifying or fulfilling, often frustrating, and perhaps still more often seeming punishably unregenerate. Melodrama would do something about it, comedy would strive for ways of coming to terms with it. Melodrama would take arms, comedy accept.

Melodrama is for victory or defeat, comedy for compromise. We compromise only with what we accept, and we compromise only when we can see what has to be accepted.

If we may use *humanity* as a temporary synonym for *world*, Joseph Conrad's words to H. G. Wells are much to the present point: "The difference between us is fundamental. You don't care for humanity but think they are to be improved. I love humanity but know they are not." [16] Wells is the voice of melodrama, Conrad of both tragedy and comedy.

CHAPTER 4

Melodrama and Comedy:
Rival Claimants to the World

I F "DON'T CARE FOR" and "improve" are taken as interlocking metaphors for related attitudes to the world, then the melodrama which
we have described is an embodiment of the spirit of Wells as Conrad
defined it. We have spoken of adversary roles and of the melodrama of
opposition, of the melodrama of railing and of satirical melodrama and
revenge melodrama; of the melodrama of conquest and liberation, the
melodrama of triumph and defeat. Clearly all these styles of action are in
the world and with respect to the world; they are ways of dealing with an
immediate society or with society generally. Unless one gives up or gives
out, one gives it to the world by ridicule or censure or reform or rude
power. On the other hand, to practice the comic mode, to accept, is in
some sense to "love"—a risky word, these days—what is there and not to
long for or expect much betterment. Cherishing what is decent and generous comes, we suppose, easily, but it does mean having the ability and
taking the pains to spot the decent and generous; with it goes a willingness to acknowledge, without bitterness, that the world will not much
diminish its capacity to be devious, calculating, parochial, shortsighted,
combative, phobia-prone, and so on.

I. MODES OF INTERPLAY

With their common materials and arena—the great medley of relationships which we call the world—melodrama and comedy inevitably have different kinds of interplay. Both styles, as we have seen, may inhabit the same drama. Tartuffe, a buccaneer of piety, hopes to take the world; Orgon naïvely aspires to spiritual betterment. The play satirizes Tartuffe but for the most part views Orgon comically. It might lash about in all directions instead of taking Orgon's gullibility as a frequent human attribute, troublesome but still more ridiculous than shameful or denounceable. The frequent mixture of satire and comedy in drama is the best evidence that the rejective and the accepting can appear together. A dramatist may waver between the two attitudes, drawn toward both condemnation and amused tolerance.

But when I speak of interplay, I am thinking of a larger scene: one can conceive of a dramatist or an age or a culture as more hospitable to the melodramatic or to the comic spirit or as wavering between them. In despair over the Peloponnesian War, Aristophanes is dominantly a satirist; yet his work is modified by so strong a sense of the ludicrous that his indictments, though not undercut, are continually infiltrated by his jests. If one could list all American plays whose theme is the world, it is likely that those proposing to "do something about it" (from frowning to castigating to replacing) would outnumber by three to one those implicitly taking its imperfections as inevitable, endurable, and more amusing than upsetting. Thornton Wilder stands out as the twentieth-century writer who, without falling into sentimentality, characteristically adopts the tone of comic acceptance. He has few companions.

After the Restoration

In his turn from humor to despair Mark Twain is widely felt, it appears, to have graduated, reformed, gained stature. Our tendency to value his disgust more highly than his detached sense of ironic discord reflects the odd confluence of the puritan and the romantic in American culture. To say this is to look back, of course, to our cultural antecedents. In England the Restoration was the great period in which the comic dominated the theater. Though some critics have detected in Restoration drama a strong tinge of what I have called overacceptance, by and large its strong sense of human frailty, for the most part tolerant enough, coexisted with a certain faith in human virtues—especially generosity and magnanimity—that

render the world tolerable and prevent acceptance of it from being taste-
less or callous. Although the Puritanism which by its excesses had helped
produce the Restoration never died, afterwards it continued its course—
its antiworldliness—in a much subtler style and hence with more enduring effect. The Christian repudiation of the world had become the Puritan
transformation of the world, exported to America for a history that is still
going strong, but in England foiled in 1660; foiled, however, only in its
direct political utopianism, with its psychic energy not depleted but
redirected to a private achievement that eventuated in economic and hence
other power in the world. The impact of that power on literature is a
historical truism; in the theater it greatly diminished comic acceptance.

From 1700 on, the history of drama is a record of the struggle of
comedy against that instinct to improve the world which, just like
twentieth-century political ideologies, strove to convert the theater into a
podium from which to enunciate doctrine. The comic style suffered from
other pressures too. Doctrinaire sentimentalism valued right feeling and
contrasted it with wrong feeling or unfeelingness in the world (the culti-
vation of feeling was analogous to Puritan self-searching and Quaker
looking for the Inner Light). Hence the concept of the *belle âme*, a mode of
perfection that could counterbalance a naughty world. Rousseau went to
greatest lengths, secularizing Christian repudiation of the world by making the world the very begetter of corruption; primitivism is incompatible
with the comic, for it is a refuge from or a cudgel for worldly error. It is
astonishing that, despite the pressure of these influences, eighteenth-
century drama retained as much of the comic spirit as it did. If one looks
at drama from Cibber to Sheridan in the light of the truism that sentimental drama was taking over the stage,[1] he is surprised to find how much of
comic effect there is even in the work of Hugh Kelly, Richard Cumber-
land, and the Colmans, conventionally treated as exemplars of the new
development. But if one uses the perspective of Restoration comedy, he is
struck by the incursions of praise for good conduct and feeling, often very
narrowly conceived, and of censure for their opposite; that is, by the
melodramatic impulse to divide the world into good and evil and to
support reformist courses.

In the age of two revolutions a number of literary titles reveal the
nonaccepting spirit. If we take two Bunyan characters—Christian and Mr.
Worldly Wiseman—and imagine them transformed by the eighteenth-
century impulses that I have been sketching, we can see them emerging as
the title characters in two novels by Henry Mackenzie, who, as the "Scot-

tish Addison," was much esteemed in his day. The two novels are *The Man of Feeling* (1771) and *The Man of the World* (1773). In the former, Bunyan's hardy pilgrim, guided by doctrine but capable of error "in the wilderness of this world," has shrunk into the infallible hero of sensibility, his unerring tender feeling so strained by the vicissitudes of existence that he cannot survive. Mr. Worldly Wiseman, in his chipper but erring assurance almost a traditional comic figure, is darkened into the title villain of *The Man of the World*, an evil seducer who barely escapes incest. Amid such interpretations of "the world" as a den of iniquity, Charles Macklin's *The Man of the World* (London, 1781) is a pleasant throwback to an older order: Sir Pertinax Macsycophant, a marrying father not unlike Sir Anthony Absolute in Sheridan's *Rivals* (1775), is money-mad but manageable, so that neither he nor romantic youth is badly served. But in the main the world has changed from laughable to reprehensible—callous, gross, cruel. Elizabeth Inchbald entitled a play attacking prison conditions *Such Things Are* (1787). When the paper-maker Robert Bage turned novelist in his fifties, he fell into the romantic primitivism that was having a long run. His *Man as He Is* (1792) registered some of the characteristic disgust at the world; then he wrote a balancing work, *Hermsprong, or Man as He Is Not* (1796). Hermsprong, reared by American Indians who exist in Edenic innocence, acquires all of the forest virtues, including a talent for incisive criticism of man as he is in Europe. Bage might have borrowed his subtitle from a much larger figure, William Godwin, who in 1794 provided *The Adventures of Caleb Williams* with a sardonic subtitle, *or Things as They Are*.

It is no accident that the longest low period in English comedy coincides with the dominance of a spirit variously sentimental, romantic, and reformist that views the world as a mass of wrongs to be put down rather than a medley of human errors to be put up with, as a subject for derision and disgust rather than disinterested and ironic observation. On occasion the two attitudes may coexist spontaneously. In Thomas Morton's *Speed the Plough* (1798), for instance, Dame Ashfield's excessive fear of "Mrs. Grundy" (who thus, though she never appears, materializes as a figure in English mythology) gives a genuinely comic reflection of uncritical fear of the world as censor. On the other hand the play contains an evil baronet and a belatedly good baronet (the world is bettered), and one line of action preaches the nobility of rustic labor. That is, along with amused observation there is an insistence on what won't do and on what men ought to do. This sense of mission—of wrongdoing to oppose, solutions to propose,

lists to enter—that began in the eighteenth-century theater almost dominated that of the nineteenth. Victorian earnestness, intent on improvement, created a drama that for many decades gave center stage to melodrama both in its narrow conventional meaning and in the much broader
meaning which we give it here.[2] But history is not my business. This brief
note on familiar historical matters is here simply because in the Romantic
period, as in its immediately preceding and following times, we see a
one-sided phase of the struggle to possess the stage by the opposite attitudes to the world, the melodramatic and the comic.

Post-Romantic Comic Comeback

Poets' phrases let us sense an atmosphere conducive to one kind of
theatrical tone or the other. When Byron's Childe Harold says, "I have
not loved the world, nor the world me" * (echoed in Emerson's "Goodbye, proud world! . . . / Thou are not my friend, and I'm not thine"),
his words sum up perfectly the romantic antipathy which leads to a
castigating or reformist style. Just about the same time Coleridge was
giving a rather Childe Harold complexion to Ordonio in *Remorse* (1813; a
revision of *Osorio*, 1797): "All men seemed mad to him! / . . . In this
world / He found no fit companion" (IV.i). The "self-diagnosis," as
G. W. Knight says, is "Byronic."[3] Again, Byron speaks of growing "aged
in this world of woe"; Emily Brontë asks, "How could I seek the empty
world again?"; and Whitman invokes the cleansing of "this soiled world."

On the other hand, when Longfellow can say, in "Michael Angelo,"
"You would attain to the divine perfection, / And yet not turn your back
upon the world," he records a duality natural to high comedy. Tennyson's "And this wise world of ours is mainly right" ("Geraint and Enid,"
900) is made applicable only in a limited context, but at that the phrase
and the sentiment are unimaginable in the Romantics. In such a sense
Browning is antiromantic: witness his "The world and its ways have a
certain worth" ("The Statue and the Bust," 138) and "This world's no

---

*Byron's antithesis raises another question: the relationship between accepting and being accepted.
Being, or simply feeling, rejected by the world is one source of the rejective attitude; the unwilling
outsider has a keen eye for the vices of insiders. Yet here again there is more than one possibility. If
resentment at nonacceptance by the world leads to hostility to the world, fear of nonacceptance may
lead to exaggerated acquiescence; a Grundyism with a strong emotional component was expressed,
long before Morton's *Speed the Plough*, in Thomson's *Seasons*: "For still the world prevail'd, and its
dread laugh, / Which scarce the firm philosopher can scorn." At such extremes the comic is foreclosed. In the middle, as we saw in *London Assurance*, a sense that the world considers one foolish may
lead to self-judgment in the comic vein. Or the desire to belong to even the most transient of worlds
may be presented with tolerant irony, as in a line in Cibber's *Love's Last Shift* (1696): "As soon be out of
the world as out of the fashion."

blot for us, / Nor blank; it means intensely, and means good: / To find its meaning is my meat and drink" ("Fra Lippo Lippi," 313–15). These are faint and scattered symptoms of a rebound that rehabilitates the world— not totally redeems it, but rescues it from seeming fit only for flight and hostility. It begins to become positively attractive in Frederick Locker-Lampson's "The Jester's Plea": "The world's as ugly, ay, as sin, / And almost as delightful." Thus the comic attitude begins to revive. That attitude is wonderfully and madly rephrased in the song in Brendan Behan's *The Hostage* (1960), "There's no place on earth like the world" (I). The song ends by glimpsing a terminal holocaust with wry-to-sick humor rather than horrified indignation: "The South and the North Poles they are parted, / Perhaps it is all for the best, / Till the H-bomb will bring them together— / And there we will let matters rest." Though the song gets a little ahead of the picture, it indicates how far the imagination could depart from the mirthless distress about the world that so largely influenced literature from 1750 to 1850. This distress was rooted in phases of English character succinctly outlined by George Meredith.*

Meredith also phrased the comic attitude neatly in *The Egoist* (1879). Miss Middleton asks Vernon Whitford, "You have not an evil opinion of the world?" He replies, "One might as well have an evil opinion of a river: here it's muddy, there it's clear; one day troubled, another at rest. We have to treat it with common sense" (chap. 8). From evil opinion to common sense: it is the movement from aversion and retreat, which find chief expression in lyric and melodramatic forms, to the coming to terms with complex actuality that makes comedy possible. In common sense we may see various possibilities: it can range from an undisturbed awareness of things as they are to a dry notation of contradictions in our habitual ways to a witty reversal of expectation and custom or fresh viewing of appearance and reality. Such attitudes to the world make possible and

*The English have, he says, "a sentimental objection to face the study of the actual world. They take up disdain of it, when its truths appear humiliating: . . . They approve of Satire, because, like the beak of the vulture, it smells of carrion, which they are not. But of Comedy they have a shivering dread, . . ." They "excel in satire," since "the national disposition is for hard-hitting, with a moral purpose to sanction it; . . ." The quotations are from *An Essay on Comedy* (New York: Scribner, 1897), pp. 20–21, 72. His observations are equally applicable to America.

When the English temper, as Meredith defines it, appears in satirical or romantic fiction, "the world" gets short shrift. In George Gissing's *New Grub Street* (1891) Jasper Milvain, the calculating young literary journalist who coolly outlines the route to success, says, "Wait till I show that I have helped myself, and hands will be stretched to me from every side. 'Tis the way of the world" (chap. 28; ed. Bernard Bergonzi [Baltimore: Penguin Books, 1968], p. 421). In Conrad's *Victory* (1915) it is the demonic marauder, Jones, who says, "It's the way of the world—gorge and disgorge!" (pt. IV, chap. 11 [Anchor Book; Garden City, N.Y.: Doubleday, 1957], p. 316).

appear in the revival of comedy that began in the 1890s, when the plays of
Shaw and Wilde essentially accepted an imperfect but going world, erring
rather than corrupt, unclear about virtue and vice but meaning to keep the
former in the saddle, and more given to self-deception than to trickery or
injury. Not that Shaw and Wilde made a total break with Ibsen problem
plays, devoted to questions and exposure, but that they added to Ibsen
melodrama a sense that folly and mistakes live on and are open to contemplation as well as efforts at elimination. They could put a finger on folly
without taking up a flail. Writers that accept the world are always in the
world and see it as it is; they do not overvalue it any more than they
undervalue it. Their comic strength is being unillusioned without becoming disillusioned.

Since the Romantics were by nature anticomic, it is fitting that Shaw is
consistently antiromantic—for instance in *Arms and the Man* (1894), *The
Devil's Disciple* (1897), *Candida* (1897), and *Caesar and Cleopatra* (1899).
Arms and the Man is consciously anti-idealistic; here, as in the other plays,
the practical and the self-serving work out best for everyone, and noble
thoughts and postures, far from being a bludgeon against an actual world,
turn out to belong only to foolish role-playing. Shaw charmingly calls *The
Devil's Disciple* a "melodrama," but there are no good guys and bad guys;
those who might belong to either category all turn out to be more complex than everybody, including themselves, had supposed, and thus act, if
only from blind instinct, to the general advantage. Shelley would not see
himself flattered in Marchbanks in *Candida*, where a wife chooses an
unglamorous life suited to her nature rather than follows a romantic
script. *Caesar and Cleopatra* avoids patriotic indignation and moral
homilies on international relations. In general, what works for Shaw
characters is often what would be deplored and attacked by the melodramatic imagination. In Wilde, those who adopt triviality as a role are
usually the most perceptive; those who take high-toned roles learn, if they
are lucky, to use the soft pedal and the quiet voice of a less elevated
attitude.

II. The Single Career: T. S. Eliot

The movement from one mode to another, or the shifting commitment,
or the conflict, direct or implicit, between two generic modes, that is, two
attitudes to the world, may also be found in the creative life of a dramatist
and may indeed become the formal subject of a play. The one person
whose career, as far as I know, exemplifies both situations is T. S. Eliot.

Eliot could write comedy only when he became able or willing to accept the world. *The Cocktail Party* (1949) is the turning point; in *The Confidential Clerk* (1953) and *The Elder Statesman* (1958) he transposed his interpretations of experience into comic terms. *Murder in the Cathedral* (1935) and *The Family Reunion* (1939), of course, aspire to the tragic, but both reveal in Eliot an antiworld (i.e., anticomic) bias.

The essential action of *Murder in the Cathedral* is Becket's resistance to the wiles of the world—of pleasure, of sharing royal power, of sharing baronial power, of using martyrdom itself as an instrument of power in the world. This situation offers no options; sainthood is the embrace of another world, and that is by definition a rejection of this world. If Becket yielded to the blandishments of this world, his exquisite awareness of meanings would make him a tragic figure; and he has to have this tragic potential to make the drama the generally effective morality play that it is. Otherwise we would have simply the triumph of a good man against the pressure of a bad world. In portraying the rejected world Eliot fortunately does not fall into romantic disparagement and denunciation. The tempters are devious, but they are permitted to make cases that could be effective with lesser men than Thomas; the churchmen who want to save Thomas from what they see as rashness may not understand him but are themselves understandable and able to evoke sympathy; the murderers are satirized, but with a brilliant Shavian perceptiveness that turns this quartet, who might be cliché bad guys (hatchet men of a sinister power), into striking symbols of universal human knavery utilizing demagogic clichés in self-defense.

When Eliot rewrites the Orestes story in *The Family Reunion*, he is doing another version of the Becket story, as if compulsively gripped by the myth of the potential saint who must find his vocation by rejecting the voices of the world. But in the second play Eliot runs into a problem not latent in the raw materials of *Murder in the Cathedral*. In *The Family Reunion* the world is represented, not by familiar human temptations, by well-meaning churchmen, by assassins who sound remarkably like popular editorialists, but by an immediate family who Eliot mistakenly feels have to deserve Harry's rejection of them. So Eliot turns on them and makes their unlovableness excessive; though he might get away with this as a familiar kind of comic exaggeration, he makes the serious mistake of having Harry openly reject them in terms that fall little short of openly declaring his own spiritual superiority. Thus the quasi-tragic hero (he has never really committed an act which would bring about the downfall of a good man) at times degenerates into the prig, as Eliot was to acknowledge with admirable candor in *Poetry and Drama* (1951). Fortunately, however, Eliot was really of two minds about the world. If some personal disgust or moralist's aversion pressed him to trivialize the Monchensey family as a whole, still some imaginative outreach or saving compassion, perhaps unconscious, led him to modify the role of Lady Monchensey, who at first seems destined only for another furious mother-lashing, and to make her understandable and growingly sympathetic. The effect, as Eliot himself later saw, was that she partly stole the stage from the intended hero. This failure of integration signalized the presence, in Eliot, of a more complex view of reality than he was formally using. He was learning that one might opt for the saintly or religious life without repudiating the world as wholly stupid and corrupt (and indeed that an acceptable Christian life need not require flight from the world).

He was discovering, in generic terms, that he was not only a pro-tagonist of the spirit and a satirist of human failure but also the owner of a comic sense, and thus he was becoming a more spacious dramatist. He was getting ready for *The Cocktail Party*, in which he would not only give rein to his comic view of human activity, but would implicitly reject the more solemn single-track commitments of the earlier plays. Eliot now asserts the validity of the world and its ways. *The Cocktail Party*, as we saw in Chapter 2, really makes a case both for the life in the world and for the life out of it, and thus for two generic modes. In accepting duality, Eliot focuses, to paraphrase Arnold, on "the eternal *not ourselves* that makes for" right choices of life. Hence the hero is Harcourt-Reilly, who with his aides leads different individuals to awareness of their talents for a worldly or nonworldly life. In his approval of both choices Eliot gets over a hump and moves away from his original narrow position. His acceptance of the world prepares him for his last two plays, in which the discovery of vocation and the discovery of self are actions in a world marked by human limitations but still bearable and even offering satisfying courses of action.*

---

*Eliot's choice of materials is mildly illuminating. Euripides' *Alcestis*, the "source" of *The Cocktail Party*, has, so to speak, a double duality that probably would not have appealed at all to the earlier Eliot: the duality of the divine and the human on the one hand, and on the other of the romantic and the near-tragic. (Besides, the rehabilitation of Admetus by Euripides provides a model for the rehabilitation of the Chamberlayne life by the more tolerant Eliot.) Euripides' *Ion* and 'Sophocles' *Oedipus at Colonus* lack the dualities of *Alcestis*; hence they are fitted for translation into the dominantly social terms of *The Confidential Clerk* and *The Elder Statesman*.

In Chapter 3 I observed that withdrawal from the world leads to the lyric voice. There is perhaps less of this tendency than one might expect in *Murder in the Cathedral*. But in *The Family Reunion*,

III. THE SINGLE PLAY

The interplay between the melodramatic and the comic attitudes to the world, an interplay which can become an outright competition for the stage, appears not only in the history of a period or in the individual dramatist's career, but also in single plays. Here the attitudes compete for the lives enacted, and the dramatist observes characters as in their impulses and choices they gravitate toward one or the other, toward concession or enforcement. Characters rarely think about genre, but life draws them toward what we identify as one generic style or the other. The conflict of genres within or between characters animates a number of excellent plays.

Molière's "Misanthrope"

How one is to take the world is the central issue of Molière's *Misanthrope*. Most of the characters go along with the world in an uncritical way, probably too much so, though Molière in no way pushes this point; they are formed by fashion, and they do whatever fashion permits or approves, from fawning to backbiting. To an extent, Molière views attacks on this modus vivendi as self-serving; also-rans make severe judgments, and pique takes on the voice of principle. The best exemplar of this conversion is Arsinoë "the prude," who, unsought by men, is very censorious of the world. The woman of the world who especially stirs Arsinoë to moralizing is Célimène the coquette, besieged by men, and therefore given to treating most of them with an insouciance that seems to them unscrupulous and even sadistic. The flytings between Arsinoë and Célimène are keen battles of wit; Molière reveals his hand by giving Célimène all the better of it in the duels between the scourge and the flirt. Their conflict, however, is structurally secondary; the central one is between Alceste, the title character, and nearly everyone else except Arsinoë. Alceste comes closer than Arsinoë to seeming a true voice of principle; at least his egotism is so much subtler than hers that his criticism of the world achieves a partial air of disinterestedness. So he makes a few points that are surely meant to have some validity despite his humorless intemperateness:[4] he inveighs against a code in which much depends on flattery, insincerity, conventional exchange, and so on. Yet Molière limits Alceste's authority both by revealing

when Harry attempts to describe the new life that he will undertake, and in *The Cocktail Party*, when others describe the saintly life of Celia, we get evocative imagery rather than full dramatic embodiment. Robert Colby compares Celia with Colby Simpkins, the central character in *The Confidential Clerk*, and calls the latter "the one character of the play who remains a lyric poem." This is in "Orpheus in the Counting House: *The Confidential Clerk*," *PMLA*, 72 (1957): 801.

his self-admiration and by making the objects of his criticism into rather harmless game-playing worldlings instead of worthy targets for opprobrium. The voice that speaks for the world is Philinte, Alceste's quite tolerant but not uncritical friend:

> Good sense views all extremes with detestation,
> And bids us to be noble in moderation.
> The rigid virtues of the ancient days
> Are not for us; they jar with all our ways
> And ask of us too lofty a perfection.
> Wise men *accept* their times without objection,
> And there's no greater folly, if you ask me,
> Than trying to *reform* society.
> Like you, I see each day a hundred and one
> Unhandsome deeds that might be better done,
> But still, for all the faults that meet my view,
> I'm never known to storm and rave like you.[5]

Philinte may not be critical enough of the world, and he may dismiss ancient virtues too blithely, but he makes a reasonable case for that adjustment to things as they are, for the "good sense" and the "moderation" that make comedy possible. For obvious reasons I have italicized his words *accept* and *reform*: they embody the conflicting ideas of the play and the contrasting attitudes that create different kinds of plays. ("Reform society" translates *corriger le monde*—a phrase that comes a shade closer to my term for one melodramatic mode.) Philinte not merely says *accept* but applies acceptance in his conduct; aside from accepting "second best," as we noted in Chapter 3, and accepting the ways of the world around him, he accepts Alceste, the man whose basic style he complains of more than once. He likes Alceste and keeps talking to him. He enacts as well as articulates the comic style; he refrains from rejecting the very rejecter of whom the complete rejection would be easy and understandable but would alter the over-all tone of magnanimity. In being up to a rather difficult action, Philinte reminds us that the comic style is not always easy: tolerance is exacting. Granted, Molière cooperates by keeping Alceste within the bounds of the bearable; his censoriousness is too lacking in calculation and power to make it dictatorial and hence insufferable. It is still a long distance from him to Robespierre. Compulsive reformism in Alceste does not mean compulsory reform for all others, as it might if Molière saw him as the troubled man needing to trouble others, the relentless neurotic whose own complaint issues in complaints about others, and for whom it is only a step from complaint to command. Thus the anticomic man himself can be seen in comic perspective.

Ibsen's "Wild Duck"

In *The Wild Duck* (1884) Ibsen transposes *The Misanthrope* into a domestic key. Here Ibsen comes sharply out of the "problem play" phase in which he looked at the world, symbolized in community or family, through Alceste's eyes and detected falsities, pretensions, and the inadequacy of conventions. In *The Wild Duck* he does an about-face and looks keenly at the Alceste-figure, doubtless with a considerable sense of there-go-I. He alters Molière's rather Platonic critic by giving him power over others; he alters the world by substituting, for a fashionable and witty society and its conventions, an ordinary Norwegian family (the Ekdals), middle class or lower, and the conventions which it has developed for coming to terms with things as they are. Old Ekdal is happy as a hunter in a "forest" which is no more than a stage-setting in an attic; his son Hjalmar likewise enjoys the hunting and cherishes illusions about himself as inventor, loving father, sacrificing husband, and hard worker; Hjalmar is happily supported by his wife Gina, who shares his conviction that he is an extraordinary person, who has all but forgotten her earlier life as mistress of well-to-do Håkon Werle, and who lives untroubled by not being sure whether the father of Hedvig, aged fourteen, is Hjalmar or Werle. In the Ekdals, Ibsen dramatizes a life that satisfies all who live it; in its medley of easy-going, self-deceptive refraining from hard questions, adjusting to circumstances, living with present dreams instead of suffering from unrealizable visions, it embodies in a fresh way the accommodation to reality that belongs to the comic mode. It even has a theorist, Dr. Relling, who defends "life illusions" as a human necessity.

The Alceste of the piece is Gregers Werle, old Håkon's son, a father-hater turned apostle of "the ideal." He inflicts upon the Ekdals what I have called "compulsory reform," that is, a plunge into a new "ideal" life founded upon a set of bedrock truths which, however unpalatable, are to replace the family's comfortably working half-truths and illusions.* Gregers himself enlightens Hjalmar about the family facts of life and pressures

---

*A number of Ibsen heroes act against the world. Rosmer in *Rosmersholm* wants to reform it, at least in spirit. Dr. Stockmann's self-comforting observation in *An Enemy of the People* exalts the individual over the world: "The strongest man in the world is he who stands most alone" (V). Ibsen, of course, looks at these characters, as he does at Hjalmar, with some detachment. On the other hand, if James Hurt is right, the creation of characters with a deep distrust of or aversion to the world is natural to Ibsen's imagination. Writing about *Catiline*, Hurt remarks, "'Vague foreshadowings' of Ibsen's later plays are found not only in the separate motifs of Catiline's dream . . . but also in the character of the dreamer. The dreamer, like Catiline himself and like Ibsen's later protagonists, perceives the world as a threatening place, 'a vaulted chamber, black as any grave.'" The quotation is from Hurt's *Catiline's Dream: An Essay on Ibsen's Plays* (Urbana: University of Illinois Press, 1972), p. 21.

him into attempting a new illusion-free existence. But Gregers' melo-drama of reform turns into a melodrama of disaster: under the manifold strains of the new situation the daughter Hedvig commits suicide, and, however the parents may manage to survive, they will have something far less than the old adequate way of life.

In surveying the conflict of the two modes of life Ibsen carries his play to the borders of another genre. At the end Gregers does some questioning of his advocacy of the "ideal." Could he take this far enough to understand the power-motif in his own reformism, and to acknowledge that it re-sulted in evil, he would have the lineaments of a tragic hero. But Ibsen does not attribute that magnitude to his melodramatic hero.

Büchner's "Danton's Death"

Alceste and Gregers Werle are "men of principle" or "men of integrity" who assume that they have achieved a moral life; hence they need not struggle to adhere to a code of conduct. Rather they seek to establish, as the authority of their societies, a code whose validity they take for granted. Such men become variously idealists, reformers, patriots, revolu-tionaries. They have mixed motives, they are necessary to the world, and they find it hard to stop in time. Though the melodrama that they enact is, as a spur to a society, a good thing, still we have too much of a good thing if it eliminates the comic variety of ongoing life. Drama has recur-rently dealt with the tendency, in activists of principle and integrity, to pursue unrelentingly single-track courses, to make life single-valued, and to let the power which is a means become an end. Alceste has no real power, Gregers Werle has moral power in a small world; but let such a man have power in a public domain, and he develops the Robespierre syndrome, that is, the total freedom from limits assumed to be the privilege of incorruptibility. We get this extreme in Georg Büchner's *Danton's Death*, written in 1835, shortly after Ibsen's birth, but not produced until 1902, shortly before his death. Oddly enough, Büchner allows Robespierre a moment's troubled reflection about his own motives (I.vi), but does not develop a character of tragic conflict. Instead he makes Robespierre rigid and self-righteous enough to proceed with the Terror and through it to dispose of his revolutionary associates who want to move in a more humanistic direction. Thus we see the ultimate dictatorial extreme of the Alceste personality.

But Büchner is still more to our purpose here in that, within a revolu-tionary movement which might seem to permit no options, his play shows two ways of viewing life. The melodramatic way is unmistakable: Robespierre's Terror as the enforcer of the cause. On the other hand we could say that Danton, Desmoulins, Lacroix, and others represent the "comedy of revolution." Unfortunately this phrase may have the disadvantage of paradox (the tendency to evoke resistance) without its corresponding advantage (the power to convey new insight). Revolution is obviously an archetypal form of political melodrama. Nevertheless, when the revolutionaries whom Robespierre opposes speak of the life they seek for France, they name rights, happiness, hedonism. In this there is the acceptance of a world that includes laissez faire and the pleasure-principle—in a way, a common man's world of Restoration drama—that could not be countenanced by the state of Spartan virtue dictated by Robespierre puritanism.

Wilde's "Lady Windermere's Fan"

The relentless Robespierre enforcer may also be female. Wilde's Lady Windermere is the conventional insider with very little give; Giraudoux's Electra is driven by an ultimate passion to make a moral rule negate every other consideration that may bear on public policy. Giraudoux sets up a formal confrontation of alternatives, making us reflect on which imperfect choice is the lesser evil. Wilde employs a familiar social conflict, not so much challenging the conventional solutions as using a difference in moral views for repeated conflicts along the way. *Lady Windermere's Fan* (1892) turns on Lady Windermere's attitude to the social outcast, Mrs. Erlynne, who deserted husband and child for a lover twenty years earlier and now wants to re-enter London society (in one of Wilde's gimmicky coincidences she is the mother of Lady Windermere, who doesn't know this). Lady Windermere opposes Mrs. Erlynne's comeback, just as she opposes Lord Darlington's making love to herself. She tells him, "I have something of the Puritan in me. . . . [My aunt] taught me what the world is forgetting, the difference that there is between what is right and what is wrong. *She* allowed of no compromise. *I* allow of none" (I). (Cf. the aphorism of Ibsen's Brand, "Compromise is the way of Satan!" [V].) Darlington opposes this rigidity by arguing that "good people do a great deal of harm in this world. Certainly the greatest harm they do is that they make badness of such extraordinary importance. It is absurd to divide people into good and bad. People are either charming or tedious." Though Darlington's social-aesthetic code might be as rigorous as Lady Windermere's moral dualism, still in his rejection of her mechanical-moral exclusivism he is the voice of comedy. He is more definitely that voice in the dialogue that follows his subsequent question: ". . . do you think seriously that women who have committed what the world calls a fault should never be forgiven?"

> LADY W.: I think they should never be forgiven.
> LORD D.: And men? Do you think that there should be the same laws for men as there are for women?
> LADY W.: Certainly!
> LORD D.: I think life too complex a thing to be settled by these hard-and-fast rules.
> LADY W.: If we had "these hard-and-fast rules," we should find life much more simple.
> LORD D.: You allow of no exceptions?
> LADY W.: None!
> LORD D.: Ah, what a fascinating Puritan you are, Lady Windermere!
>
> [I]

Lady Windermere's "never" and "no exceptions" are the Alcestian condemnation taken into the social establishment and directed, not against prevailing fashion, but against moral outsiders; Darlington's "too complex" and his demur against "hard-and-fast rules," if they go less far than Philinte's noncriticism of "unhandsome deeds that might be better done," still are on the side of comic tolerance. So are his witty observations on the flaws and pretensions of the world, which he spots and pinks like a fencer rather than damns like a censor. But Darlington is also fated to be the would-be lover of Lady Windermere, and in this role he solemnly spouts romantic clichés that come out of a much simpler view of life than what he says as a worldling.

Lady Windermere's theoretical black-and-white positions burst into stage-worn clichés when she thinks that her husband is playing around with Mrs. Erlynne, and most of what she says and does from then on becomes an extended cliché of offended wifehood. Lord Windermere, knowing that Mrs. Erlynne is his wife's mother, now picks up Darlington's life-is-complex line, making the best case he can in arguing to his wife that Mrs. Erlynne deserves her understanding and help toward her present goal, "a happier, a surer life than she has had" (I). But this clash of attitudes, instead of being followed through as an important theme, is replaced by a contrived reversal that in its theatricality pushes the theme out of sight. Lady Windermere, rashly deciding to elope with Lord Darlington and then rescued from this potential disaster by her self-sacrificing mother (incognita, of course), now decides that Mrs. Erlynne is "a very good woman" (IV). Thus, on a basis of extraordinary evidence, more overwhelming than is ever available to mortals making a decision, she accepts at least one person whom she had thought to be unforgivable. Whether she accepts any more of the world is questionable. Still the one change is some gain. Unfortunately for the comic spirit, Lord Windermere, turned raging moralist by scanty and unassessed evidence, shifts to his wife's former position and belabors Mrs. Erlynne with flooding clichés of offended virtue. So we are back where we started, with a much too symmetrical exchange of positions by the accepter and the rejecter.

Though at his best he writes fine comedy, Wilde is saying here that in human conduct generally, the attitudes which underlie comedy have pretty hard going against the widespread melodramatic habits of rule-bound judgment and chastisement. Furthermore, by giving his play a dual structure of plot, Wilde himself enacts the conflict between the melodramatic and the comic views. He does not kid the melodramatic plot, which, if we desire, we can believe forčed upon him by the times. He does not conspicuously withhold essential sympathy from the black-and-white morality espoused passionately by Lady Windermere and at least formally by everyone else; from their conviction that the errant must be punished; from Lady Windermere's mechanical conclusion that, as a "good" woman victimized by the faithlessness of a "bad" husband, she has no choice but romantic flight from vice (which does not exist) and elopement with a "good" lover (without any passion for him, of course, since this would lead into complexities of emotional life that are foreign to Wilde's imagination). Wilde is momentarily less conventional in seeing that Lady Windermere cannot face the music, the facts, or herself, and so he turns to a "rescue" of her by Mrs. Erlynne. But this is an indoors tea-table version of a thousand adventurous rescues in popular theater. Both women think and feel only in terms of melodrama. The language is hackneyed, full of theatrical hyperbole and cliché images; Mrs. Erlynne, bent on rescuing a runaway daughter, can only think of such phrases as these: "Oh! You are on the brink of ruin, you are on the brink of a hideous precipice" (III).

On the other hand Wilde produces a fine comic body of action—carried on by Darlington as observer of the world rather than lover, by the Duchess of Berwick, by various witty young men, and of course by Mrs. Erlynne when she views the social scene rather than labors as a marriage-saving mother. All speak with a tonic wit, often about individuals but more often about types of people and of action in the world. Darlington's "little vanity" is to "pretend to be worse [than other men]" because "nowadays so many conceited people go about Society pretending to be good, that I think it shows rather a sweet and modest disposition to pretend to be bad." The Duchess of Berwick insists that all men are bad, reports that her "susceptible" husband constantly causes her to fire maids or pass them on to other members of the family, and summarizes, ". . . wicked women get our husbands away from us, but they always come back, slightly damaged, of course" (I). Mrs. Erlynne prophesies political success for a young man because he "thinks like a Tory, and talks like a Radical," and generalizes "that there are just as many fools in society as there used to be" (II). All observers see that the world is inconsistent, unintelligent, untrue, or otherwise defective; everyone is clear-eyed, but no one believes that such flaws must be fled or cured. Things are as they are, those in the world propose to stay there, and Mrs. Erlynne is eager to get back into it.

Satire is constantly surprised and always displeased; the comic writer is never surprised and rarely displeased. Satire views with alarm or disgust, comedy with tolerant amusement. In *Lady Windermere's Fan* there is no surprise, displeasure, or alarm; what stimulates us is not the detection of concealed or unrecognized ill-doing, but the fresh and acute picturing of the known ways of the world. Yet I can hear a stock response of this sort: "Wilde is satirizing the hypocrisies of society." *Hypocrisy* is a word that comes too easily into the mouths of social and literary critics, who by using it may unconsciously practice a little self-flattery. The word is applicable only to the unmistakable discrepancy between a conspicuously claimed virtue and the conscious utilization of the virtue, or the deliberate violation of it, in activities that mean profit for the violator and disadvantage or damage for others. True hypocrisy requires a Iago ingredient. What should never be mistaken for it is that inconsistency between ideal and action which is the spontaneous product of human fallibility or which occurs when average sensual man, with an eye on what seems essential to community welfare, preaches higher standards than he is up to day by day. (To modernize this: a 1970s moralist might demand, for social well-being, a sexual promiscuity which his own taste and talents might not equip him for.) These are the inevitable human shortcomings that comedy takes in its stride, forgoing the indignation and other emotions that enable the committed censor to feel secure in his own rightminded-ness. The satirist would flail, among the supporters of the moral order in the Windermere world, the Duchess of Berwick, the quickfooted and heavyhanded marrying mother, and Lady Plymdale and Dumby, who are having an affair. Wilde's comedy accepts them as part of the infinite variety of an actual nonutopian world.* Comedy does not mistake foibles for evil, or failure for vice.

It is a pity, then, that Wilde cannot let the Windermeres wholly accept an actual world. Lady Windermere might learn, and live with, the fact that the outcast Mrs. Erlynne is her mother (and that that explains all those Windermere checks to her, which in Act I make Lady Windermere distraught and which in Act IV she singularly forgets about), and Lord Windermere might learn, and live with, the fact that his wife tried to elope with Lord Darlington, was hiding in his flat, and was saved from public disgrace only by Mrs. Erlynne's letting herself be discovered. But here Wilde is stuck with his melodramatic consciousness and so denies to his characters that acceptance of self-diminishing fact which would enlarge them as characters. He opts for ignorance on both sides, so that husband and wife can both cling to an incomplete knowledge of things as they are. Wilde uses Mrs. Erlynne to enforce this blissful but humanly limiting ignorance—an assignment as surprising as it is unfair, since she knows more of the facts of life than anyone else but is now forbidden to use that knowledge, and, what is worse, to recognize it as essential to moral growth. In making her priggish and anticomic, Wilde presumably was

---

*The range of acceptance is still wider in Somerset Maugham's *The Circle* (1920), which might be a rewrite of *Lady Windermere's Fan* a quarter of a century later in post–World War I atmosphere. Again a young woman is considering an elopement which would be a second-generation repeat—this time of a flight by the mother-in-law rather than the mother. Maugham raises almost no question of right and wrong; the dramatic issue is whether husband or lover can do a cleverer job of persuading the young lady, and whether she would have a more gratifying life with a conventional husband in England or with a romantic lover on an exciting Malayan frontier. So the concern is pragmatic (comedy) rather than moral (melodrama or tragedy). But Maugham does not want to play serious ball even on his chosen comic field. He weights the game heavily against the husband by making him into a prissy house-beautiful type, so that on personal grounds Elizabeth, the young wife, hardly has a choice to make. Maugham does appear to toughen up the choice by introducing the senior runaway lovers, Lady Kitty and Lord Porteous, whose trivial and quarrelsome style is hardly an advertisement for extramarital romance. Maugham is at his best in imagining the mutual vindictiveness created by the disappointments of a life-for-romance-only. The old lovers might well frighten off Elizabeth and her romantic Teddy. But Maugham doesn't stick to his guns. For one thing, he tells us that the earlier elopers were basically frivolous people, as the present would-be elopers are not. Worse, he doesn't honor the commitment that he makes to serious issues of personality when he perceives the old pair's vindictiveness (and Kitty's infidelities to her lover). He handles crucial moments with farcical gags, such as silly errors at bridge, or Porteous' losing his dentures; he even makes the empty and cynical old pair turn sentimental. Like Wilde, Maugham is split between two theatrical modes; while Wilde veers between comic and melodramatic writer, Maugham is half the comic writer who can go deep enough to hurt, and half the mere entertainer who will do anything to reassure and tickle his audience. He prefers to surrender his real issues of character to farcical, sentimental, and romantic effects: at the end the young lovers fly joyously off to an oriental Eden, cheered by their messy predecessors, and the comic tone maintained only by the irony of the old cuckold's thinking that the rhetorical tricks he has taught to his son have saved the latter's marriage.

governed, perhaps compelled, by some moral preconception that has dated badly. It may be that whenever drama relies on the irrational persistence of a certain melodramatic attitude, in the face of available alternatives, it is because the dramatist is caught within a contemporary ethos that he cannot escape.

On the other hand, Giraudoux bases a major action of his *Electra* on "the irrational persistence of a melodramatic attitude." He treats this persistence as a permanent feature of the human scene, and he makes it the object of dramatic attention. Wilde not only presents characters with different attitudes (the rigid and the flexible) but himself comes in on different wave-lengths that are comparable to the two attitudes, apparently unaware of the duality in his own perspective. Giraudoux, however, maintains a single firm perspective on a world facing a critical choice between two attitudes that always exist in the world—the melodramatic and the comic.

Giraudoux's "Electra"

Ingeniously discovering a new representativeness in a myth dramatized by three Greek and various modern dramatists, Giraudoux makes his *Electra* (1937) a revealing study of two fundamental approaches to the world.* One party puts "justice" before survival, the other goes for survival but accepts it as a mixed bag which no one could think of simplistically as "virtue triumphant" (compare the similarly tough-bitten understanding of survival in Act III of Wilder's *Skin of Our Teeth*). Though the survival issue is introduced rather late in the play, still it affords a dramatically effective test of values by extending their conflict into the public domain (just as Aeschylus extends the significance of the Orestes story by making the outcome crucial for Athenian prehistory). Giraudoux climactically focuses on the division between two patterns of life in Argos, a duality symbolized in an early description of the palace as "laughing and crying at the same time" (I.i).[6]

---

*Giraudoux is a sort of highbrow Maugham (see preceding note): he has much of the entertainer in him but uses subtler methods to appeal to a less naïve audience. He does not duck serious issues or work to reassure his audience; far from it. But the pyrotechnics of images, paradoxes, and even conundrums that come pouring out of his imagination are distracting, and hence the actional and thematic flow may elude the audience. For example, the immensely clever transformation of the Furies into flippant and knowing young girls who grow throughout the play and finally become replicas of Electra is a brilliant attention-seizing fantasia that virtually takes off on its own, fascinating enough to deflect questions as to its function and meaning. At various times characters fall into lengthy Shavian lectures that explore peripheral subjects or toy with images in a purple-passage style. Electra's relentless pursuit of her mother Clytemnestra, and the resultant flytings between them, take on a showpiece quality.

Clytemnestra is Queen; Aegisthus is Regent; Agamemnon is commonly supposed to have died of a fall in his bath. The Clytemnestra-Aegisthus affair is discreet enough so that Electra, suspicious as she is, does not know of it. Indeed Aegisthus carries on with various women, including Agatha Theocathocles, the young wife of the older President of the Council. Agatha also has several lovers, and is much attracted to Orestes when he arrives as a "Stranger." So we have on one side the official life, the social swim, strong on scheming and short on nobility, a conventional candidate for a satirical flogging if the dramatist wants to set things up that way. On the other side is Electra, hating her mother, sure that something is rotten in the Argive Denmark, and bent on exposing it and taking arms against it. She gets Orestes on her side, and when they turn their fire on their mother, Clytemnestra exclaims, "What kind of children are you, turning our meeting into a melodrama?" (II.iv). Though Clytemnestra may mean the word only in a belittling sense, it is still quite accurate technically, for Electra is ever the prosecutor, the self-assured voice of right hunting down wrong. In terms of the myth and of the immediate situation as Giraudoux has developed it, Electra is of course "right," but Giraudoux fascinatingly presents her as something less than an admirable girl on a white horse. He examines the heroine-with-a-cause rather than simply sides with her.

Although we see her primarily through the eyes of those in the establishment, we are not invited to take adverse comments on Electra as inaccurate because they are self-serving. She is acknowledged to be "the most beautiful girl in Argos" and "intelligence personified" and to have an "especially good memory," but the President of the Council calls her "the kind of woman that makes trouble." She stands for "justice, generosity, duty," but then we run square into a paradox: ". . . it's by justice, generosity, duty, and not by egoism and easy-going ways, that the state, individuals, and the best families are ruined."* The phrase "the best families" may seem to shrink the paradox into a joke against class defensiveness, but the President goes on with an explanation that confirms the paradox and reduces the mere joke: "Because those three virtues have in common the one element fatal to humanity—implacability. Happiness is never the lot of implacable people." So it is that "every evening" Electra "spreads her net for everything that without her would have abandoned this pleasant, agreeable earth—remorse, confessions, old blood stains, rust, bones of murdered men, a mass of accusations." He adds, "A horri-

---

*Giraudoux was anticipating the later witticism of a university president much troubled by irreconcilable faculty members: "The more I see of men of principle, the less I think of principle."

ble country, one where because of an avenger of wrongs, ghosts walk, dead men, half asleep,—where no allowance is ever made for human weakness, or perjury, where a ghost and an avenger constantly threaten." He alludes to "the most dangerous enemy in the world, . . . Electra's ally, uncompromising justice" (cf. Lady Windermere's "*She* allowed of no compromise. *I* allow of none"). The President's various descriptions record, it is clear, a richly ambiguous situation: without someone like Electra, crime might go undiscovered and unpunished; with her, the punishment may destroy not only the criminals but the whole community. Justice-seeking may become obsessive, maniac. Electra makes all the dead, whatever their role in life, cry out together, "Oh, Heavens! here's Electra! And we were so peaceful." The President can even polish off his exposition with a wonderful piece of fantasy. In a garden Electra's "justice and memory," which "means hatred," will affect even the flowers: the fuchsias and the geraniums will "show their knavery and ingratitude" (I.ii).

Aegisthus, the Regent, invokes a great theological image to define the problem of Electra: man must preserve human affairs from intervention by the gods, who always mess things up unpredictably, causing disaster to good and evil peoples alike. So, he says, "I wage merciless war against all who signal to the gods"—in the present situation, Electra alone. To minimize the trouble that she can cause, he's planning to marry her to a gardener, member of "a lowly family, unseen by the gods," since "In a third-class zone the most implacable fate will do only third-class harm" (I.iii)—a striking hierarchical view of things. Aegisthus' scheme leads into various complications, including some bedroom farce; it fails.

Electra "loves" Agamemnon, "marries" Orestes, and lives principally on an energizing hatred of Clytemnestra and Aegisthus; her destiny is to "follow the trail" (I.viii). The Beggar, who acts as a chorus, closes Act I with a long soliloquy that characterizes Electra thus:

She's unadulterated truth, . . . So if she kills . . . all happiness and peace around her, it's because she's right. . . . [She's] the guardian of truth; she has to go after it whether or not the world bursts and cracks down to its foundations, . . . [Will not she and Orestes] bring to life, for the world and for ages to come, a crime already forgotten, the punishment of which will be a worse crime? [I.xiii]

His words describe excellently an extreme form of the life of melodrama. Electra herself pictures this life in somewhat nobler terms. Women, she says, give men "a hatred of injustice and a scorn for small joys" (II.iii). This defensiveness is matched by Clytemnestra's attack: "All the evil in the world is caused by the so-called pure people trying to dig up secrets and bring them to light" (II.iv), and she adjures her daughter, "Stop acting like a judge, Electra" (II.v).

At this point Giraudoux makes his remarkably original addition to the myth: Argos is threatened by attacking Corinthians, who are already at the gates of the city. Giraudoux thus enriches the traditional melodrama of revenge by giving a public dimension to the family feud. The problem now is not only, what happens to the family? but also, what happens to the world? What form of action is to be taken in the world? Giraudoux makes us consider alternatives that illustrate precisely the two contrasting attitudes to the world represented in the different literary genres (this illustration of two contrasting attitudes is analogous to what Eliot does in *The Cocktail Party*).

The choice that Giraudoux sets up for Argos is a central and meaningful one. On the one hand, of course, there is the Electra way: traditional revenge—the cause of "right," "truth," and "justice"—takes precedence over every other consideration. On the other hand there is the survival of Argos, and we now learn that Aegisthus has all the makings of a leader who can save the state ("Fine for Greece!" wryly remarks the choral Beggar, "But not so gay for the family" [II.vii]). To gain public acceptance, and be politically effective, Aegisthus must marry Queen Clytemnestra, and he is ready to do this and take over. He is masterful; the Guards are "joyfully getting ready to fight"; he calls Argos "a country I swear to save," and we believe that he can.

But Electra sternly advances the idealist view: "No one should save his fatherland with impure hands." They clash vigorously. Aegisthus: "Is there anyone in the world who can take from us the right to save our city?" Electra: "Save our city from hypocrisy, from corruption? There are thousands. The purest, the handsomest, the youngest is here, in this courtyard" (II.vii) (she means Orestes). The debate goes on at length, with undiminished vigor. Aegisthus: "And you sacrifice your family and your country to a dream." Electra argues that his line is, "If you lie and let other people lie, you'll have a prosperous country. If you hide your crimes, your country will be victorious." Aegisthus: "And you dare call this justice, that makes you burn your city, damn your family, you dare call this the justice of the gods?" Electra: "A magnificent repentance for a crime is the gods' verdict on your case. I don't accept it." Aegisthus: "Electra's justice consists in re-examining every sin, making every act irreparable?" Not so, says she; it's "when the crime is an assault on human dignity, infects a nation, corrupts its loyalty, then—no pardon is possi-

ble." Aegisthus: "I must save the city and Greece." Electra: "That's a
small duty. I'm saving their soul." (She is a Gregers Werle translated from
private to public life.) While she is obdurate, Aegisthus makes concessions and promises. He has the spirit of compromise: ". . . as soon as
Argos is saved, the guilty, if there are any, shall disappear, . . . I can
kill you. Yesterday I should have killed you. Instead of that I promise, as
soon as the enemy is repulsed, to step down from the throne and place
Orestes on it. . . . First let me save the city." But in this discussion of
priorities, Electra even stops talking about "truth first"; all she wants now
is to know why Clytemnestra hated Agamemnon, and to see Clytemnestra
punished (II.viii).

Orestes kills Clytemnestra and Aegisthus as they stand on a "marble
balcony, calming the rioters" (II.ix). The Furies now take up the Aegisthus role.

SECOND FURY: Satisfied, Electra? The city's dying.

ELECTRA: I'm satisfied. I know now that it will be born again.

THIRD FURY: And the people killing each other in the streets, will they be born again?
The Corinthians have started the attack, and it's a massacre.

FIRST FURY: Your pride has brought you to this, Electra. You have nothing left,
nothing.

ELECTRA: I have my conscience, I have Orestes, I have justice, I have everything.

[II.x]

As the Furies continue to hack away at these elements in her triumph, she
is finally reduced to "I have justice, I have everything." Argos is devastated,
finished.*

*Such a finale is actually amenable to comic treatment, as in Friedrich Duerrenmatt's *Romulus the
Great: An Historical Comedy without Historical Basis* (1949). Here the Electra role, that of the virtuous
destroyer of a state, is taken by the title character, who is using the Emperor's throne to assist in
finishing off the Roman Empire because he thinks it corrupt enough to deserve only destruction. But
while Electra is tense, rigid, and savage, Romulus is relaxed, ironic, and urbane; Electra has a cause,
but Romulus is a detached assistant of the inevitable. He is accepting, so to speak, the biological way
of the world: disease leads to death, and one should cooperate rather than interfere. That is, he engages
in a complex act of acceptance while others fall into simplistic roles in endeavoring to prolong the life
of the doomed Empire. There is a remarkable similarity in the foreign affairs of Giraudoux's Argos and
Duerrenmatt's Rome: the former is attacked by the Corinthians, the latter by the Teutons. But the
resemblance ends there, as the two dramatists focus their equally complex views differently. The
Corinthians are sworn to a simple total massacre of the Argives; the complexity lies in the area of
choice by the Argive leadership. In Duerrenmatt's play the complexity is found in the attacking
Teutons, who, instead of being simply a destructive "enemy," include both "friends" and "enemies."
Their leader Odoaker is a civilized man like Romulus; he points out that the real enemy of both of
them is his nephew Theodoric, a Spartan militaristic type whose dream is world conquest. He is
another version of the Electra-figure, this time found outside the threatened state rather than within
it. But Theodoric and his melodramatic view are much more peripheral than Electra and her passion.
Thus the public disaster appears mainly in a comic perspective: the tone is created largely by an ironic
observer capable of accepting events that would puzzle or antagonize people with more standardized
points of view.

Giraudoux balances out the rival positions with great detachment; he misses none of the ambiguity on both sides. Aegisthus seems an excellent leader in a crisis, and it is hard not to assent to his desire to save the city; on the other hand, he is guilty of murder in the past and promiscuity in the present. We are always aware, then, of the possible self-interest in all his moves, even in the valiant effort to persuade Electra that fighting off the Corinthians is the most compelling priority. Electra makes an undeniable case for "truth" and "justice" and against the corruptness of the city, but at the same time we are aware of implacable revengefulness in her, of the mother-hating, of the strange father-loving and brother-loving (Giraudoux partly repeats what O'Neill had already done in *Mourning Becomes Electra* [1931]). Hence he has set up an extraordinary difficulty of choice and has effectively illustrated the absence of perfect choices. He can actually make his readers' sympathies fluctuate as he lets each side, first one and then the other, put its best foot forward. Thus Giraudoux himself exemplifies the comic view of life: he accepts everything that he finds on both sides, that is, presents it as understandable and inevitable rather than as chargeable and changeable. The play exacts both a rueful smile at things as they are and some sadness that the comic view is powerless in a crisis.

Electra is worth special attention because of its splendidly full portrayal of the melodramatic and comic attitudes competing in and for their common ground, the world. On the one hand there is the rejective, punitive, revengeful way of looking at the world; the idea of truth and justice cannot tolerate the mixed actuality of life. On the other there is the instinct for continuity; the world is to be saved, painfully imperfect though it is, and claims of the absolute are to be postponed; this program postulates at least a temporary acceptance of the way things are.*

*There is a sharply different contrast of the melodramatic and the comic attitudes in Mark Medoff's prize-winning *When You Comin' Back, Red Ryder?* (1973). Here again we have a confrontation between an implacable person and an ordinary community, this one symbolized in a small ham-and-egg place beside a highway gas station (cf. Inge's *Bus Stop* [1955]). Here, however, the implacable person is not a woman of principle but a hippie dope-smuggler who holds up the customers to get some ready cash. But this is more than an ordinary melodrama of crime. The hold-up—and apparent getaway—are accomplished very quickly at the end as if this were a necessary but incidental routine for the invading hippie, Teddy. His chief need is to terrorize, humiliate, and even destroy others; like Giraudoux's Electra, he is a total revenger, though we never know what sickness or failure he is revenging. A jaunty, self-confident, abrasive intimacy that he immediately inflicts on all is the first sign of a hatred for the world. He has demonic skill in finding people's weak spots and thus the best ways of terrifying or blackmailing them into actions revolting or hateful to them. In giving them commands, he apes the style of a mad film director. All the time he is tongue-lashing his victims with belittlements, taunts, revilements, exposures of supposed inner dark spots; he is a skillful stylist in savagery, bounding from standard vulgarities and obscenities and gross sarcasms to a quasi-intellectual vilifica-

The President of the Council, who has in him touches both of the early Gloucester and of Polonius, who is cuckolded by his young wife, but who still is not a stupid man, remarks, "Life can be pleasant." He asserts its inevitable constituents: "Take any group of human beings at random, each will have the same percentage of crime, lies, vice and adultery." Given this premise, why is it, he asks, "that in one group life slips by softly, conventionally, the dead are forgotten, the living get on well together, while in another there's hell to pay?" He replies, "It's simply that in the latter there's a woman who makes trouble." Theocathocles' farcically simple analysis of "hell" is countered by Orestes (still anonymous), "That means there's a conscience in the second group," and this introduces an antiphonal exchange between them. Theocathocles interprets "conscience" in a different way: "A conscience, you say? If criminals don't forget their sins, if the conquered don't forget their defeats, if there are curses, quarrels, hatreds, the fault is not with humanity's conscience, which always tends toward compromise and forgetfulness, it lies with ten or fifteen women who make trouble." Orestes picks it up: "I agree with you. Those ten or fifteen women save the world from egoism." No, answers Theocathocles, "They save it from happiness," and he goes on into the argument that I have already quoted—that the women's virtues always add up to "implacability" (I.ii).

This early argument outlines, then, the concepts which in the subsequent action are shown in conflict: the combat stance, the memory of wrongs, and implacability, and, opposite them, "compromise and forgetfulness"—a phrase which admirably defines the comic spirit. Electra never wavers in her punitive intransigence; when he sees that he cannot persuade her to even temporary forgetfulness, Aegisthus tries valiantly for compromise, willing, unless we attribute to him an improbable duplicity,

---

tion that draws on the going vocabularies in fields of learning dipped into in college or in reading. Like Iago, he has an inexhaustible welling up of motiveless malignity; like Richard III, he is mad to humiliate and rich in the necessary resourcefulness, drivenness, and ruthlessness. He belongs partly to the long line of scourging ranters from Bosola to Butley, but to verbal malice he adds an executive talent by which he compels people not only to hear his contempt but to act out the shames that he assigns to them.

    Medoff has not only put together an effective melodrama of evil but has defined that evil as a determined, barbarous violation of the norms of conduct which make human community possible. In generic terms we see, not the struggle of a comic spirit—good sense, compromise, an acceptance of the disparate—to preserve itself against an all-or-nothing world, as in Giraudoux, but a normal order of life unable to sustain itself against compulsive demonic reductivism. On the other hand, the mad humiliator is active only for several hours; after that, the ordinary routines begin struggling back into activity. Though injured, the community is not destroyed; it survives the demonic visitor better than it does the home-grown absolutist of justice, Electra.

to take great risks. In thus dramatizing these counter attitudes, the uncompromising and the compromising, Giraudoux carries each mode out to a logical extreme. Proponents of either mode have to face all of its implications because there is no intermediate stopping point at which one can have only the advantages of "justice" or "compromise." "Justice" here entails an immense community cost; saving the "soul" is as hard on bodies, individual and social, as a witch-hunt or an inquisition. "Compromise and forgetfulness": survival means giving up something of "justice" and forgetting a murder in the past and sexual irregularities in past and present. Survival includes everybody. In an actual nonmythic world, Noah's Ark is a vast unselective Ship of Fools.

Furthermore, President Theocathocles offers key words for the end-developments of each style: he sets up an opposition of "implacability" and "happiness." The former, as we have seen, leads to the "ruin" of "the state, individuals, and the best families." By play's end, of course, we have seen that ruin. On the other hand, while he is all for happiness, Theocathocles does not define it in terms that make it look like an easy and obvious choice: "A happy family makes a surrender. A happy epoch demands unanimous capitulation" (I.ii). "Surrender" is ambiguous: it could mean "compromise," or tactical concessions, or an unconditional giving up that would leave one defenseless. "Unanimous capitulation" seems inevitably to imply an absolute giving in to all hostile forces. So we may ask whether Theocathocles is the voice of stern truth or of corruption, whether "compromise" and "forgetfulness," indispensable as they are, do not themselves need to be checked by some greater authority lest they lead only to cynical skin-saving.

We can approach this issue in another way by focusing on the built-in risks of either option. Electra's victory lets us see that to live a melodrama of good and evil is to run the risk of total destruction. Theocathocles' doctrine of happiness, on the other hand, lets us see that to live a comedy of adjustment is to run the risk of living black comedy, that acceptance as a style risks accepting the unacceptable. To lead us to such inferences is to communicate deeply and unsentimentally about generic modes. In actual existence, extreme cases that require grossly unpalatable choices are rare; in art, it is good to have extreme cases that tell us where our available styles may lead if we are forced outside the bounds that we always hope are there to free us from absolute courses.

Character Types

To trace the line of descent from Alceste through Robespierre, Gregers Werle, and the Windermeres to Electra is to see not only different versions of the hero of melodrama but also the persistence, through different ages, of the basic attitudes which create this human type. It never dies. The type, or the spirit which animates it, may dominate a drama and determine the tone and course of the action. In the plays at which we have looked, however, the melodramatic view is regularly brought into contrast or conflict with the comic view: the issue is always which view, through its proponents, is to determine the direction and quality of the immediate world, be it family or class or state. Are those with *a priori* rules and ideals to manage it, chastise it, reform it, or destroy it? Or will it be allowed to live on through the influence of those who can accept— that is, come to terms with, put up with, tolerate—its inconsistencies and imperfections? In every action in which the rigid enforcer of principle is able to exercise power—Robespierre, Gregers Werle, Electra—the immediate result is disaster (whatever hope for the distant future may be proposed). But when the would-be enforcer does not have power, the more flexible people, those at home with the ways of the world, keep things going and make possible the continuance of a manageable life and the comic tone. The Windermeres and Mrs. Erlynne have their good moments, and Philinte is a model of the tolerant man. Even Alceste comes to a self-estimate that diminishes a rectitude once bent on dictating to the world.

These plays that turn on contrasts between ways of life throw the comic mode into relief; they take us, in our discussion of comedy, from theory into an especially revealing practice.

CHAPTER 5

Make Jokes, Not War

"MAKE LOVE, not war" is a sometime slogan of social revisionists, who may range from lovable to very warlike, and who seem not always to grasp the complexities of either love or war. But whatever their styles, their slogan happens to be one way of differentiating between the genres that depend respectively on accommodation and on opposition. Yet "love" comes a little too easily into the mouth, and has been cheapened; if we give it an adequate meaning, it demands more than "accept" implies. Let us emend, then, to "Make jokes, not war." If we translate this imperative into a simply descriptive statement, it is a compact summation of the difference between the comic and the melodramatic styles. Hence on, of course, the latter will appear only incidentally for illustrative purposes.

I. JEST AND DISCONTENT: COUNTER STYLES

"Make jokes" is more meaningful than it may at first seem: without acceptance there is no joking. We do not joke with someone we do not accept, whom we place beyond a serious barrier of either irrational dislike or rational judgment. When we do not accept someone, we do not make jokes about him in his presence, and any joke that we may make when he is absent is less comic than caustic, and thus is rejective. We certainly do not make jokes about ourselves in the presence of someone we do not accept; unless intended to disarm, such a joke would breach the self-defensiveness that accompanies nonacceptance. Defense goes with combat; fighting and laughing are rarely compatible; what we laugh about we do not fight about. Jokes and laughter imply community: the acceptance not only of others but of oneself as sharing both in the protection which membership affords and in the vulnerability whence many jokes emerge. The joke displaces adversary feeling or brings it into a larger synthesis. When the black coach of a professional sports team says of a new talented white player whom he is introducing to the press, "Next week I'll only call him 'Boy,'" he cleverly reverses old racial positions, but, more than that, he puts an ironic sense in the place of unironic resentment; he accepts the once enemy class by tying them with himself in a joke.

The idea of "accept" is also conveyed by a number of other terms, some of which I have already used. To "accept" may be to accommodate (to), to acknowledge (the claims of), to adapt to, to adjust to, to bear with, to become reconciled, to come to terms with, to compromise, to conform, to fall into line, to *laisser faire*, to let live, to live with (it), to make do, to make out with, to put up with, to settle out of court (as opposed to a fight to the end), to stand (it; for it), to tolerate, to use common sense or good sense, to work things out. Obviously these are not exact synonyms, but the connotative extensions beyond precise overlap suggest the ample spread of the responsiveness that creates the comic realm and of the alternatives to objection, discontent, opposition. Some of the terms (e.g., "adjust to," "conform") may raise the hackles of people nurtured on a strenuous and assertive individualism, since the further one goes with individualism, the less one's tolerance of a world that has other members. Some of the synonyms (e.g., "fall into line," "put up with") also remind us that comic situations may slide toward black comedy; we have to recall the implication of the survival option in Giraudoux's *Electra*, that we can't have comedy without the risk of overacceptance (just as we can't dissent, oppose, and otherwise reject without the risk of eliminating comedy and moving toward war of one kind or another). Yet the whole vocabulary of acceptance, which restricts the styles of total freedom, in no way glorifies subservience or shortchanges dignity. Rather this vocabulary signifies an acknowledgment of the claims and rights of others, erring and flawed though the others may be, and our kinship with them. The best outer symbol of this acknowledgment is good manners, which are really the implicit standard of comedy of manners. In the civilized world the central virtue is urbanity, and urbanity, far from being a superficial polish, the artifices that conceal the self, or a labored subordination of honesty to decorum (as it is sometimes taken to be in egalitarian and neoprimitive circles), is the gracious conceding of place or position or priority or privilege to others. Such a style, indispensable to social life, is akin to the acceptance that makes comedy possible. The springs of comedy and of a bearable life in the world are all but identical.

The dramatist who accepts the world accepts characters who fall short of perfection: they do not become loathsome or unbearable, and they do not need to be fled from or flogged. Liars may become charming (Falstaff, the title character in Corneille's *The Liar*), pretentious ignoramuses a source of amusement (the Politic Would-Be's, Mrs. Malaprop), rascals entertaining (Snake in *The School for Scandal*), thieves romantic adventurers (Anouilh's *Thieves' Carnival*, 1938), whores jolly companions (from the Gay and Brecht versions of *The Beggar's Opera* to Behan's *The Hostage*). Obviously the withholding of judgment can become sentimental if it mechanically reverses the usual attitudes or automatically finds golden hearts in all unlikely places, as in Saroyan's *The Time of Your Life* (1939). But comedy tolerates actuality rather than softens it. It may tolerate by revealing actuality as more of a mixed bag than it initially seems. In *The School for Scandal*, for instance, Sheridan satirizes the gossips: they lie, backbite, cheat, plot seductions. Yet at the same time he gives them so much wit and imagination that we cannot simply reject them; along with partial rejection goes the partial acceptance that always flows to talent, and thus the comic has cut into the merely satiric. Restoration fops are repeatedly granted a hopefulness, innocuousness, and even charm that draws us in as much as their pretentiousness and snobbery may repel. In Chekhov's *Cherry Orchard* (1904) Lyubov Ranevsky's charm is accompanied by a fecklessness and general disorderliness of existence that are facts of life, not objects of finger-pointing or invitations to eyebrow-lifting. Comedy copes with significant infusions of human unhappiness by treating it not as due to removable causes or unjust or guilty actions but as in the nature of things. For original sin it substitutes original vulnerability. There are the bitter frustration of Marwood in *The Way of the World*, the series of troubled hearts in Turgenev's *A Month in the Country*, the sadness and even suffering that are always a thread, if not more, in the fabric of Chekhov's comedies. If the comic writer deals with characters who inveigh against the shortcomings of human experience or who have fail-proof plans for altering the ways of the world, he sees such characters in perspective. Here the archetype is Molière's Alceste in *The Misanthrope*. He is a severe critic of the world, and not by any means an inaccurate one, but he does not become the author's voice or the voice of the play, for his criticisms are obsessive, total, and unceasing. On the other hand, he does not become a freak but remains a voice: Philinte and Eliante like him throughout, and thus, speaking for the reasonableness that dominates the play, they declare, as it were, the ration of acceptableness in the total nonaccepter. This is the ultimate urbanity of the comic mode, its largest undertaking in its characteristic embrace of reality.

Strindberg's "Easter"

Strindberg's comic notes are few and far between; though some of the "redemption" plays alter his most familiar tone, he rarely finds an acceptable world or portrays a mood of acceptance. In *Easter* (1901), however, he reverses himself: his paranoid voice, if not muted, is much reduced, its irreconcilability challenged by dramatic elements of greater authority. Elis Heyst is censorious and resentful; his father was jailed for financial misdealings, his younger sister is in a mental asylum, his best student fails an examination, his girl-friend seems to be carrying on with his best friend; his sister leaves the hospital and is charged with theft, and the expected visit of Lindkvist, their father's chief creditor, threatens a final disaster. In addition, Elis learns from his mother that she could have been legally charged along with his father, and that what "brought [his] father down" was not the malice of others but "Pride—as it always does" (III).[1] Although Elis' taut readiness to accuse an apparently hostile world is partly justified, it is also in his own nature; if Strindberg were to make this voice his own, as temperamentally he might do, the play would have an abrasive melodramatic tone. But Strindberg presents Elis in a context of others who can better live with the facts of life. He helps them, of course, by making the facts better than they seem at first, as comedy may do: the placing of the final actions on Easter Sunday intimates a secular resurrection. Strindberg attributes several difficulties to misunderstanding—the accusation of theft, the apparent infidelity of Elis' girl-friend, and the expected denunciation by the creditor Lindkvist. Lindkvist, it turns out, comes not to complete the ruin of the family, but to show mercy, for he remembers* a kindness done him long ago by the senior Heyst who later

---

*There is a nice contrast between Lindkvist and Giraudoux's Electra: the latter's "good memory" embraces only wrongs, whereas Lindkvist's focuses on an early good deed done to him rather than the later wrong. And while Electra wants only "justice," i.e., the punishment of wrongdoers, Lindkvist,

defrauded him. The kindness may be a Dickensian surprise, but still Strindberg sticks to drama of character instead of undermining it with sentimental event. He portrays Lindkvist not only as merciful but also as ironist and critic; Lindkvist wants to shock the suspicious and resentful Elis out of his stiff-necked righteous indignation: "I would force out your pride and your malice" (III).

He may or may not succeed. But for once Strindberg gives his stage to a disciplining and reordering of anticomic forces, and to the human styles that make social life possible: Lindkvist forgives, Mrs. Heyst faces two truths (the source of her husband's debacle, and her own involvement in it), and Eleanora comes back from illness with a sweetness and spontaneity that help restore others. The world is altered, not by the removal of difficulties, for the major ones remain, but by human attitudes that are versions of acceptance.

Chekhov's "Ivanov"

For contrast: Chekhov's early full-length play *Ivanov* (1887), which significantly he called "drama" instead of "comedy," his standard term for his major plays.[2] In *Ivanov* his characters do not decently find an accommodation with the life about them; they live by excesses and deficiencies that register or increase discontent. Some people have a vigor that goes into pure calculation, others have not the vigor to calculate when they should. Some hoard, lend, and invest; one man plans a matrimonial deal between title and cash; others gamble. A tough moral predator is Dr. Lvov, who anticipates Giraudoux's Electra: a self-conscious voice of "conscience," "honesty," and "duty," he keeps attacking others. Count Shabelsky alludes to his "wooden sincerity" and "merciless honesty" (II), and Sasha Lebedev, aged twenty, tells him decisively, "And no matter what acts of violence or cruelty or meanness you may commit, you'll still

who could exact such justice, chooses a different course: "So you see, there is a charity that contradicts the law and supersedes it—and that is mercy" (III). These opposite styles are responsible for crucial differences of tone. Further, while Electra is indifferent to everything but justice, Lindkvist is aware that if he exacted "justice"—getting back all he has lost—he would seem harsh and would antagonize "public opinion." Such sensitivity to community feeling, which is quite different from Grundyism, is one ingredient in comic life. In putting mercy above justice, Lindkvist naturally reminds us of *The Merchant of Venice*: the others expect him to be a Shylock, but he turns out to have a Portia within his own make-up. Without a Shylock, *Easter* goes less far than *The Merchant* in portraying the total human world. Still, *Easter* moves in that direction when Lindkvist says, "But the human heart is unfathomable—a mixture of gold and dross. Peter was a faithless friend, but he was a friend none the less" (III). A similar speech by Lindkvist is really a gloss on comic acceptance: "In the great crises of life, we must take each other with all our faults and weaknesses—swallow each other whole, as it were" (III).

think of yourself as an extraordinarily honest and progressive man" (IV).[3] In portraying skillfully the sheer aggressor for whom principle is an unconscious façade, Chekhov does not employ the comic method that Molière used with Alceste; Chekhov does not modify Lvov's self-righteous rigidity with any touch of the humanity that makes Alceste partly acceptable to his peers. Like Lvov, Sasha Lebedev lacks the basic adjustability which the comic view sees in people afflicted with preconceptions or single-trackism. Having fallen in love, real or imaginary, with the older and directionless Ivanov because she "understands" him and hopes to "cure" him, Sasha actually comes to realize that "something is wrong . . . wrong, wrong, wrong" (IV) in the relationship but cannot give it up.

Opposite those who energize unrewardingly are those who can't cope and take to drink or witty disparagement of others or early death. At age thirty-five the title character falls into an undefined malaise which calls to mind such traditional terms as *acedia* or spiritual dryness or loss of faith or despair; romantic terms like life-weariness or self-irony or Carlyle's Everlasting No; pathological terms like melancholia, hypochondria, nervous exhaustion, guilt neurosis, self-hatred; and colloquial terms like washout, griper, whiner, and man who feels sorry for himself.[4] Yet Chekhov makes some use of the diversity of perspective that comedy often applies to hard cases. We hesitate among three views: Ivanov's idea that he is the dying ember of a fiery quixotic individualist, the view of some that he is a fine man who has got off the track, or the opinion of others that he is a racketeer behind a plausible façade (ironically, it is the Tartuffian Lvov who calls Ivanov a "Tartuffe" {I and III}). Further, Borkin thrice calls Ivanov a "comedian," and Ivanov tells Sasha that they must end a "senseless comedy" (IV).

But such intimations of the somber comedy that was soon to become Chekhov's forte do not produce a comic effect here, for we have almost no human beings capable of a workable life in the world. Their insufficiency shows—it is Chekhov's shrewdest insight—in a boredom that is endemic. A shade more of general acquiescence in this insufficient life, and the air would be that of black comedy. In a new twist of the ennui theme, however, Ivanov feels that he is "boring everyone to death" and shoots himself at the threshold of marriage, and Shabelsky rejects a marriage of convenience (IV); such retreats from profitable arrangements (both wives would have money) prevent the cynicism of black comedy. But when death is the only escape from boredom, the life depicted is not hospitable to comic effect. *Ivanov* is really a melodrama of failure, a rather mild upper-crust anticipation of Gorky's *Lower Depths* (1902) and O'Neill's *Iceman Cometh* (1946).

II. ILLNESS AND COMEDY

Since Chekhov's Ivanov has a kind of illness, and since his wife is dying of tuberculosis, their situation might seem intrinsically closed to comic treatment. But illness, as we noted briefly in Chapter 3, can receive acceptance of a sort that need be neither sentimental nor heroic nor despairing; we see how in Peter Nichols' *A Day in the Death of Joe Egg* (1967) and *The National Health* (1969). In both, Nichols starts with the disease and death which are persistent facts of life and looks at them as they lead to problems in social life, that is, the relations among those affected. His basic method is to show the ironic diversity of responses, no one of which—resentment, despair, stoicism, sacrificial devotion, heroism—is permitted to dominate and thus create one of the noncomic tones which the subject might lead us to expect. When people find different ways of dealing with a situation, these differences deny that the subject must inspire a certain response.

In *A Day in the Death of Joe Egg* Nichols chooses a situation which would seem *a priori* unamenable to comic treatment: a husband and wife, Bri and Sheila, confront the fact that their ten-year-old daughter Josephine (Joe for short) is a spastic and epileptic—a permanent invalid, hardly human.* This suggests nothing but a case-history, a melodrama of triumph or disaster. Nichols strongly rejects the case-history, the unique circumstance dear to Sunday journalism. Quite early he has Sheila say, "Watching somebody as limited as Joe over ten years, I've begun to feel she's only one kind of cripple. Everybody's damaged in some way. There's a limit to what we can do" (I).[5] Sheila may be consoling herself, seeking courage through a sense of ordinariness in her experience, but she is not simply giving a lecture outside the drama. Though the adult characters are not

---

*In Lloyd Gold's *A Grave Undertaking* (1974) the action also centers on a young daughter, perhaps twelve or thirteen, who is incurably ill (bad heart) and on her devoted father's effort to come to terms with this. The fact that the girl dies and that the father lets his undertaking business go to pot makes the pun in the title work several ways. The pun has the lead-off role in a series of jokes that run through the play. But the essential note of comedy is due less to the jokes themselves, help as they may, than to the underlying ironic situation: the father translates his devotion to the girl both into a blunt style of command and rebuke (they often use familiar profanities and vulgarities) that may puzzle observers, and into an insistence on life-as-usual (i.e., a birthday party on schedule) that can seem callous or reckless. Thus he "lives with" it. Though the old theme of the dying young girl is a likely source of sentimentality, Gold avoids it until the end, when a young priest who has become attached to the girl inveighs against death as a "dirty joke."

exactly cripples, still they reveal limitations, inflexibilities, and a need for the kind of attentiveness that Joe has to have. But Joe becomes meaningful in a deeper way: she is the intractability of experience in the world, the unchosen fact of life, the inherent imperfection of things. Nichols daringly uses incurable illness to define the reality which demands great efforts of man and yet proscribes hopes for major change; he also sees that men, or some men, make out. They enact a comedy as long as they are acting pragmatically rather than making ultimate moral choices, as long as they are not figures of pure suffering or defeat, as long as they do not leap to a facile triumph. Comic acceptance lies somewhere between wretchedness and glory. And in that wide space, too, lies a spectrum of options which gives Nichols his central approach to his theme. We are ironically diverse in our ways of living with what we have to live with, and then we live with this diversity too.

Bri's mother Grace blames Sheila: Joe's illness is due to Sheila's nonvirginity at marriage or else to an epileptic strain in her family—a fine picture of irrational cause-hunting. Pamela Underwood, a family friend, simply wants to get away from Joe, for she can stand nothing "N.P.A.," that is, "Non-Physically Attractive" (II). Pamela's husband Freddie is difficult in an opposite way: a do-gooder, he well-meaningly lavishes platitudinous advice upon Bri and Sheila. Bri brilliantly parodies medical men who offer routine recommendations and pedantic explanations, and a swinging Anglican vicar who drives Sheila to prescribe "no more parables" and who proposes his "Laying On Of Hands bit" (I).

Bri's mimings belong to the defensive games—ironic cracks, zany images, sardonic fantasies—which, as Sheila says, "help him live with [Joe]." Sheila feels guilty on grounds no more rational than her mother-in-law's, and she does penance by especial attentiveness to Joe. But she is a naturally affectionate person who, as Bri puts it, "embraces all living things" (II), and who keeps many pets (hedge against sentimentality: fleas from cats make everybody itch at some time or other). The ironic price of goodness: Sheila's wide-ranging affections ("She liked whate'er / She looked on, and her looks went everywhere") and her devotion to Joe make Bri feel slighted, so that his witty, often outrageous, games, defensive in origin, become also aggressive, intended to needle her and make her notice him ("Showing off to get attention" [II], Sheila and Freddie agree). With a role-playing at times dazzling he tries to force a reorientation of the world toward himself.

Furthermore, Bri challenges the facts of life with an ultimate wild strategy that he brilliantly defends to the others before his not quite concealed use of it—a do-it-yourself euthanasia that almost works. Joe lives, as she has to; did she not, we would have either a utopian "final solution" wholly outside comedy, or a melodramatic situation in which the formalities of justice would replace the improvisations of adjustment. Yet Nichols daringly stretches comic boundaries to accommodate what we might think hopelessly outside them—not only incurable disease, but an effort to end a hopeless life. Bri's action is treated not as a sin or crime but as a step that ordinary man thinks of; we are not to judge in terms of good and evil but to see how things work out. Things don't work; Bri's strength is words, not deeds. The command "Thou shalt not kill" is put into the mouth of Freddie, the unimaginative, well-meaning sideline coach; as usual, points are scored against him by the agile master of paradox Bri, who characteristically adopts a "mad laugh." The efforts to save a Joe who may be dying take us into rescue melodrama, but here Nichols protects his tone by injecting farce—the messy explosion of the "ginger-beer plant," the efforts to eject flea-ridden cats, and some mother-in-law routines. Such turns declare life wry rather than unbearable.

What is insoluble need not be disastrous; the way is still open for a persistent trial-and-error, the ordinary-life surrogate for heroics; multiple extemporizations by the parents show a lively quest for accommodations. We are not invited to judge the extemporizations as better or worse. We understand Bri's final flight, if flight it is, as the inevitable last move of the ironist* whose detachment is now complete and of the verbal magician whose one daring venture in exorcism has encountered a possession not amenable to instant therapy. In the comic view his opting out is less a moral failing than a fact of life.

"Sick Comedy"

When Freddie Underwood decries "the whole fallacy of the sick joke" (II), we attach "fallacy" to the humorless "squaresville" in Freddie: to conventional people certain topics demand euphemisms and hushed voices and are not open to jest. "Sick joke" and "sick humor" are terms that we

---

*Nichols is keenly aware that irony means a detachment that may imply other modes of separation from the action. In *The National Health* Barnet, the ironic *raisonneur*, is more observer than participant, and is even capable of minor racketeering. In time the ironic observer such as Bri in *Joe Egg* may be expected to move on to an observation post wholly outside the battle lines. There is only a hair's breadth between the ironic way of life and irresponsibility. Jane Austen made that clear in her treatment of Mr. Bennet in *Pride and Prejudice*.

use with some ambiguity or some overlap of meanings. Basically "sick" does no more than identify subject matter, that is, illness and death. Nichols does more with the "sick" in *The National Health* than in *Joe Egg*; the action of the former takes place in a hospital ward where more patients die than recover. Recovery, however, is not a victorious or glorious thing, and death is not a sad or solemn or lamentable thing, but each is "just one of those things"—episodes, like conversations or meals or working days, to be seen in a context of plans, personalities, official attitudes and methods, institutional procedures, and good or bad luck. We are not mournful, indignant, or overawed; we see that mortality itself is subject to the same mischances, discordances, good humor and bad humor, good sense and nonsense as is ordinary life. Hence it can bear as much of occasional irreverence as education, marriage, and other central experiences which may work out well or not so well. In that sense we might call such plays "sick comedy," the stage version of an old tradition of irony and jest which surfaces in any anthology of light verse and has indeed created at least one anthology of "sick verse."[6]

One problem of the term "sick comedy," however, is that "sick" may connote an attitude as well as denote a subject. In *Joe Egg*, as we saw, Bri's "sick jokes" are understood by Sheila as helping him "live with" the problem; hence we may consider his wit health-giving. Yet to Freddie there is something of disorder in Bri's wit, and though we dismiss Freddie, we know that his interpretation would be thought sound by almost as many people as would think it cranky. While from one angle the "sick" seems protective, from another it may seem a gratification of a suspect sort. When "sick" alludes not to what the joke is about, but to the jokester or consumer of the joke, it implies a forbidden or unhealthy pleasure, one beyond the limits of the "normal." There are some fairly self-evident cases of this: the sinister geniality of psychopaths in horror stories, or the sadistic jests of the title character in Camus's *Caligula* (1945). Charles Addams catches this kind of response in *New Yorker* cartoons of characters who, looking disturbed or malevolent, find pleasure in frightening, nauseating, or injuring others, and thus in implying that a sly or deadpan habitual infliction of outrages is in the way of life of all of us.* We need not go into the intricacies of the artist's own psychological

---

*As far as I know, the earliest allusion to this kind of effect is in the "Author's Preface" to Henry Fielding's *Joseph Andrews* (1742). Fielding explains that "The Ridiculous," which he declares is the proper material of comedy, has been "wonderfully . . . mistaken, even by Writers who have profess'd it," and he goes on to ask, ". . . to what but such a Mistake, can we attribute the many Attempts to ridicule the blackest Villanies; and what is yet worse, the most dreadful Calamities? What could

role in such art, but we can make some guesses about the psychological satisfactions of the consumer. Perhaps he simply experiences a catharsis of certain instincts, the old vicarious exercise of impulses to be out of line, troublesome, nasty, harmful: achieving health by letting the sick spot in the self have an innocuous fling. Perhaps, on the other hand, he sterilizes the unwelcome or repellent by meeting it in a comic aspect to which he can respond by laughter instead of by the incredulity and horror evoked by actual experience. Or through sick humor one may vaccinate oneself against a dangerous infection by the emotions (terror, despair, panic) welling up from the experience in its raw, precomic form.

When the dramatist's use of his medium—be this the situation* itself or a jesting attitude or a witty comment—derives laughter from what ordinarily evokes horror or pity (a horror and a pity essential to the maintenance of community), we unconsciously conclude: laughter means comedy. But behind this simple equation lies a deeper significance. To make jokes about the repellent, the frightening, or the pitiable is to grant them acceptance; as we observed earlier, jokes are symptomatic of acceptability or acceptedness. To be repelled, to be frightened, even to pity, is to draw away from, to set up a barrier. One becomes rejective, and his posture is melodramatic. And while pity traditionally signifies kinship, that is, shared vulnerability, still it can be exercised only by those outside the situations eliciting pity. However, we need not push this argument too hard. We look at modes of warding off only to clarify the concept of "sick humor" as one mode of the acceptance that identifies comedy. To laugh at something is to take it to oneself rather than to declare it alien, unthinkable, unmentionable, unacknowledgeable, unacceptable, or exclusively terrible. To take it to oneself, even by transposing it into a key different from the common one, is to grow.

In *Joe Egg*, Bri tries to accept his crippled daughter by ironic wit; when this fails, he has left only more drastic methods of dealing with an unchangeable life—eradication and escape. We in turn accept all his modes, that is, accommodate ourselves to them not as desirable or admirable, but as authentic and understandable, as exemplifying the kind of tactics,

exceed the Absurdity of an Author, who should write *the Comedy of Nero, with the merry Incident of ripping up his Mother's Belly*; or what would give a greater Shock to Humanity, than an Attempt to expose the Miseries of Poverty and Distress to Ridicule? And yet, the Reader will not want much Learning to suggest such Instances to himself." Clearly, sick comedy is not altogether a recent affair.

*A single episode can exploit the accidental ludicrousness of a situation intrinsically more painful than funny. In Nichols' *National Health* a bedridden hospital patient, because of a misunderstood request, has to endure a long perch on an unsought and unneeded bedpan.

fallibility, and inadequacy that permit the smile suitable for "one of us" and do not invite the disgust or indignation required by a willed assault on the norms.

Corpses as Comic Material

Death is an occasion for something other than grief and mourning (Cordelia, Lear) or general relief (Macbeth, Richard III) or shock (Polonius, Prince Arthur) in various plays, mostly modern. There is something "modern" in the scene in which Falstaff pretends to be dead, stabs the already dead Hotspur, and then claims to have killed him (V.iv). We might call this the first "sick comedy," inviting, with a daring hardly to be appreciated in determinedly postheroic days, acceptance of the self-serving pseudoheroic as a style not requiring even ritual disparagement.

The ways in which the living may try to deal with or make use of a corpse can thus enter into, or at least approach, the comic realm. Corpses may indeed be literal or symbolic. In Edward Albee's *All Over* (1971) an old man is dying (in an on-stage bed), and the play consists of the talk of those waiting for the end: the wife, mistress, son, daughter, best friend, doctor, and nurse. But in place of hushed tones and a solemn air there is a sharp-toned, often harsh exchange of recollections, antipathies, and mutual judgments. A nasty candor, ironic abuse, self-pity, cutting observations that reflect or point to emptiness in life replace the expectable proprieties and pieties. Albee is of course bent on digging out the human realities that lie beneath the usual decorous routines of the "last hour," and we might argue that he is frankly accepting the passions that underlie our traditional solemnities. Yet "accept" is only partly right, for a certain unease hangs over. The relentless family infighting that is an Albee trade-mark seems, despite frequent bright wit, less the product of a disinterested perceptiveness than of plain hostility; the vitality of the play lies less in aesthetic skill than in the dramatist's animus, his governing need to exhibit men and women as essentially knife-wielding and knife-deserving. He is more displeased than amused; indeed he often seems revengeful, sardonically gratified. That is, a play that might have achieved the wry acceptance that belongs to sick comedy (which includes death comedy) takes on, instead, the rejective hue of satire.

When the corpse is symbolic, the tone may be ironic or satiric. In Eugène Ionesco's *Amédée, or How to Get Rid of It* (1954), we soon spot the corpse as the visible presence of something dead in the bickering marriage of a middle-aged pair, Amédée, a would-be writer, and Madeleine, a nagger. The corpse is expressionistic too; it may belong to someone Amédée may have killed, it works out from the couple's bedroom, and, in Ionesco's most brilliant stroke, it is steadily growing, expanding into the couple's living room and day by day leaving them less space to subsist in. Here the over-all style is that of comedy rather than of satire.* Though neither Amédée nor Madeleine is lovable, we are not so much invited to excommunicate them as to experience the uncomfortable laugh of fellowship in their recognizable ineptitude in dealing with a strange intruder in the domestic dust. At one of Ionesco's moments of keen insight, Amédée carefully marks out the growth of the corpse since the day before: the human addiction to measurement instead of understanding. But surprisingly enough in Ionesco, the comedy takes a fantastic-romantic turn, substituting rescue for acceptance: having resisted various efforts at disposal, the corpse finally becomes airborne and, like a great kite or glider, carries Amédée up and away, presumably to a happier, more creative life. Perhaps Ionesco thought of Shelley's West Wind, destroyer and preserver, or of Tennyson's "rise on stepping-stones / Of their dead selves to higher things."

The real corpse used for the sick-comic effect is produced, with striking theatricality, in the opening scene of Christopher Hampton's *The Philanthropist* (1970). John, a hopeful young dramatist, reads his script to two university lecturers, Don and Philip. The play has a shock ending: the protagonist, putting a revolver in his mouth and pulling the trigger, blows out his brains, and the producers are directed to "use some quaint device to cover [the wall behind him] with great gobs of brain and bright blood" (i). Illustrating the procedure, John succeeds in blowing out his own brains ("a grotesque accident," Don calls it [ii]), and, says Hampton's stage-direction, "By some quaint device, gobs of brain and bright blood appear on the whitewashed wall" (i). The shock of death is instantly replaced by the surprise of the splattered wall and of the astonishing coincidence: these are farcical in effect, and we giggle instead of feeling horrified. Hampton continues to develop the sick-joke effect with skill. Up to now he has ingeniously adopted the method of bluntly canceling out the "normal" response to the distressful by making another

---

*In *Oh Dad, Poor Dad, Mamma's Hung You in the Closet and I'm Feelin' So Sad* (1960) Arthur Kopit uses the symbolic corpse satirically. When the corpse first pops out of the closet, it is the unruly object that is a staple of farce (the unclosable suitcase, the immovable zipper, the umbrella that can't be kept up or down). But we soon see that it functions symbolically; the domineering wife and mother is a life-destroying force who is to be rejected. Kopit calls the play a "tragifarce"; since the main characters are a victimizer and her victims, "melofarce" would be more accurate.

response irresistible. Now he alters the method by having characters try to adhere to the "normal" response but fail. They talk, "a few days later," about the mess that had to be cleaned up, including a Picasso print that had to be thrown away; Don remarks that Philip has "managed to get [John] off the wall," he speaks of John's play as "far too cerebral," and Philip quotes his girl-friend Celia's remark that the late playwright was "ludicrously absent-minded." Titillated by the accidental puns, Don laughs, checks himself severely ("No, it was a terrible thing to happen, really"), then "tries to look solemn, but is suddenly overcome by helpless laughter" (ii). Here, the sick humor works more complexly than through an arbitrary reduction of full human responsiveness to death; the little tug-of-war between Don's sense of sick humor and his sense of what is fitting enables us to feel that decent responsiveness has not been callously lost but is temporarily neutralized by a farcical event coming close to the banana-peel routine. We take the event to be "one of those things" rather than a sobering disaster, but without shutting off the sympathetic con-science about whose well-being sick jokes can arouse our subliminal con-cern.* The sick is an episode in an action that encompasses a larger world; thus we see that the sick is a part of the whole that in comedy we accept.

A "live" corpse is a major stage property in Joe Orton's *Loot* (1966); it inevitably affords some sick comedy in a multilayered drama built up from farce, black comedy, and seething satire, the last strong enough to give the final and lingering flavor. The action takes place on the funeral day of Mrs. McLeavy. Her son Hal and his friend Dennis, the assistant undertaker, have robbed a bank and have a hundred thousand pounds that they want to hide in the coffin. So they stow Hal's mother's body on its head in the wardrobe (a glass eye drops out of it in the process—again the unruly object of farce), and we have a skeleton in the closet.† The nurse who has attended the deceased (and, we learn later, has murdered her) discovers the body, screams appropriately, and then, for a cut of the swag, joins the robbers. In a parody of a strip-tease she undresses the corpse, tossing out

---

*Hampton uses the double-track approach in an analogous way when he has Braham, the commer-cially successful novelist, say," . . . of course I'm sorry thousands of Indians starve to death every year, but I mean that's their problem, isn't it, if they will go in for all this injudicious fucking" (iii). Here he sets off the audience's sense of sick humor, that is, its willingness to see, in an event which can traditionally appeal only to sympathy, not the moving and distressful, but the incongruous. (Cf. Fielding's comment on p. 134n.) But if the audience feels any guilt about laughing, it can hastily recall that the wisecrack is made by an obnoxious character. Thus the audience can have it both ways.

†Likewise, apparently, in Tom Stoppard's *Jumpers* (1972). Here again a farcical object is used to a satirical end: a police agent finds good reasons for not inquiring further into the corpse's presence in the closet.

the dentures which might identify it, and then swaddles it in a mattress-cover. When a detective arrives and takes the late Mom for a mummy, the nurse explains, "It's not a mummy. It's a dummy. I used to sew my dresses on it" (I).[7] From here on, a series of jocular and sometimes melodramatic effects turns on the interplay between those who know, and those who don't, that the "dummy" is a corpse. Insofar as the traditional attitudes to the dead are displaced by the treatment of the corpse as if it were a casual object, tell-tale or disposable or even utilizable, the effect is that of sick comedy.* But here we see unmistakably that pure sick comedy must be disinterested, providing only a momentary freedom from customary feelings and unaccusingly letting people simplify existence for an hour by reducing sick or dead bodies to objects that can evoke many responses, including laughter. The knock-about treatment of the corpse in *Loot*, however, is not really a free experience in a special aesthetic mode. For Orton carefully attributes to two of the looting trio a pretense to appropriate feelings (here, Catholic piety and filial piety); the stress is on the discrepancy between verbal protest and actional profit-seeking. So potential Falstaffs become Tartuffes, and sick-comedy elements yield ground under the heavy pressure of black comedy and satire.

Neurosis as Theme

Sick comedy works, to use another formulation, by securing our willing acceptance of a limited or nominally perverse response such as laughter at disease or death. A related but different kind of play takes as its material a limited or a nonwhole response by key characters. This is a large subject, for men have many ways of responding to experience with only a part of the human equipment available to them, of letting a single impulse or emotion determine an over-all style of action in the world. Such nonwholeness can range from ordinary mistakes to habitual deviancies, from folly to neurosis.

Molière had a lasting interest in neurotic characters, witness the title of an early play, *Sganarelle, ou le cocu imaginaire* (1660), and of his last play, *Le Malade imaginaire* (1673). The troubled personalities that invent their own miseries are of course easy to laugh at, for they permit us to think our own difficulties more genuine (a lesser neurotic personality appears in Faulk-

---

*It is only a step to "gallows humor," well exemplified in Brendan Behan's *The Quare Fellow* (1954), the action of which takes place in a prison. An occupant of death-row (who does not appear) is much talked about by the others: some comments reflect the pathos of death, but many jest, as if being executed were an experience on the order of going to the dentist or the store.

land, the fearful and suspicious lover in Sheridan's *The Rivals* [1775]).
Their illnesses lack the deep roots or the irreversibility that begets true
sick comedy. Yet Molière finds moral significance in the self-troubled
character by showing that he uses his disability for self-service or power.
This is of course most evident in the actions of Harpagon in *L'Avare*
(1668). But avarice is less likely to be felt as a disability than hypochondria, which always claims the benefits of true illness. Thus Argan, the
imaginary invalid, is determined to marry his daughter to a medical man
just to have a doctor in the house. Then Molière ingeniously shows this
would-be victimizer Argan as the victim of the doctors, whom Molière
frequently ridicules. Argan's double role complicates the audience's response; it interferes with the simple feeling for the victim that pushes a
play toward the satirical realm. But the chief element that helps preserve a
comic tone against the satirical tendency—this is true of various Molière
plays—is the role of the common-sense characters frequently present.
They finally prevent the operations of the neurotic and self-deluded
characters from getting out of hand and doing real damage. By such
dramatic means these characters are accepted as a part, if not a very lovable
part, of the world rather than set up as simple objects of condemnation.

Take away the common-sense influence and let the sick person call the
tune, and the comic, if it still persists, takes on a gray tone. In Natalia
Ginzburg's *The Advertisement* (1968) the Molière neurotic is Teresa, whose
life is endless talking about her troubles.[8] She hires listeners instead of
nurses; at the beginning of the play her advertisement for a roomer-
companion is answered by Elena, at the end by Giovanna. Teresa's husband Lorenzo had fled earlier; the volume of self-centered talk drives Elena
away; when Elena and Lorenzo fall in love, Teresa threatens suicide,
succeeds instead in shooting Elena, and promptly telephones Lorenzo,
calling passionately for the help that she somehow exacts from others. We
do not know whether Giovanna's arrival at this point will save Lorenzo, if
he cannot save himself, from disastrous reinvolvement. Only the fact that
the victims are not constantly on stage keeps the play from being simply a
satire of the merciless wielder of "sick power." Instead the dramatist
attempts the difficult feat of "accepting" what we would rather reject, that
is, an extreme form of the self-absorption which is fairly common in
human experience. The return of Lorenzo into a what-can-you-do-about-it
bondage to Teresa would give us black comedy. Insofar as this does not
happen, "gray" seems the right descriptive term.

Madness as Theme

When we move from the off-center personality that still functions in "normal" life to what is considered "abnormal," we open up a vast range of effects, from the melodramatic exploitation of madness in numerous Renaissance plays (Kyd's *Spanish Tragedy*, Webster's *Duchess of Malfi*) through a large realm of sick jokes and humor to modern stage applications that include the satirical documentary, the translation of ordinary life into madhouse idiom (ultimately exploited in Peter Weiss's *Marat/ Sade* [1964]), and the paradox that has become a cliché, namely, that the mad are saner than the sane (as in Giraudoux's romantic *Madwoman of Chaillot* [1945]). The Wasserman-Kesey *One Flew over the Cuckoo's Nest* (1963), where the scene is a mental hospital, is mainly a satire of therapeutic discipline which becomes a dictatorship, equating wellness with the cooperative spirit and using shock treatment and lobotomy as threats against patients who shrink from the humiliations of group therapy or show any independence of spirit. Thus Kesey symbolically satirizes a larger social world that uses coercive methods against individualists difficult to cope with. At the same time there are genuine comic effects, again of a microcosmic sort: individuals adjust to their imperfect selves and their imperfect life in a good-humored way. There is also room for some sick humor: jokes based on the different kinds of illness that patients suffer from. There is no room at all for loony-bin jokes in *Marat/ Sade*, which we might call sick melodrama (it translates "a tale / Told by an idiot" into dramatic lines read by schizophrenics), nor in Pirandello's *Henry IV* (1922), where the action, which takes place in a private madhouse, reflects inner intensities that approach the tragic.

In *The Physicists* (1962), which Duerrenmatt calls a "comedy," the madhouse is hardly a madhouse at all, but partly an intellectual sanctuary, partly a microcosm; it goes the old who-is-really-mad paradox one better by turning the head psychiatrist, a hunchbacked virgin, into a financial entrepreneur* who aims at world-wide domination and hence is called

---

*The satire of the psychiatrist that is prominent in the Kesey-Wasserman and the Duerrenmatt plays of the early 1960s appears also in Joe Orton's *What the Butler Saw* (1969) and Tom Stoppard's *Jumpers* (1972). In such plays the psychiatrist is a racketeer, economic or psychological or both. He inherits the traits ascribed to medical men in satirical episodes in Plautus and regularly in European drama and fiction (e.g., Fielding's *Joseph Andrews* [1742]) from the Renaissance through the eighteenth century (and as late as George Eliot's *Middlemarch* [1871–72]). Ignorance, pedantry, and pretentiousness were the traditional equipment of satirized doctors; in psychiatrists it is pedantry, power, and profits. In Saul Bellow's *The Last Analysis* (1965) a professional comedian works at do-it-yourself analysis, and we follow him through ludicrous enactments of womb and infancy and early

"mad" by the physicist-inmates—a diagnosis permitted to remain ambiguous. When the three physicists murder their nurses, who love them, the effect is not that of frenzied melodrama or of sick comedy; the murders are so clearly symbolic acts that they elicit only a cerebral intake of the meaning (scientific dedication forecloses a full personal life). Insofar as what goes on in the institution is an intensification or an absolutizing of the life outside the walls, *The Physicists* might be a derivative of the Cairo madhouse scene in Act IV of Ibsen's *Peer Gynt* (1867): here all the inmates exemplify the ultimate development of that concern with the "self" that has been a central principle of Peer's life. The style is often that of perennial loony-bin jokes, but instead of reassuring the "normal" joker of his own mental health, they picture the pathological end of the line toward which his own way of life leads.

In Ted Tiller's *Count Dracula* (1971) we are again in an asylum, though now the central action is a melodrama of evil and its victims. Still this melodrama is modified in two ways: one is to add substance by means of psychological and even mythological amplifications,* and the other is to introduce comic materials such as often go with mystery plots. The head of the place, Dr. Arthur Seward, at times drifts amusingly into the prissy

childhood experiences that are supposed to help him define himself and thus aid the public. This seems like an ultimate parody of analytical method. Yet Bellow declares that the play "is not simply a spoof of Freudian psychology"; he calls the comedian "the artist who is forced to be his own theoretician." We do give some sympathy to the comedian because he is surrounded by relatives and friends who want to make a financial good thing of him and his scheme to educate himself and the public. The final effect, however, is one of ambiguity, for the direction is uncertain. Another remark of Bellow's indicates a comic intention: the "real subject," he says, "is the mind's comical struggle for survival in an environment of Ideas—its fascination with metaphors, and the peculiarly literal and solemn manner in which Americans dedicate themselves to programs, fancies, or brainstorms." Here is the humorous understanding that Bellow characteristically displays. But the details of the action tend less to draw on our sympathetic acceptance than to elicit the rejectiveness of the satirical mode. The quotations are from the "Author's Note" and the "Cast of Characters," *The Last Analysis* (Compass Book; New York: Viking Press, 1966), pp. vii–ix.

*Count Dracula is in various ways given a Satanic cast, so that the vampirism, though it is very much present as a physical fact, gains significance as a symbolic activity. Like Satan, the Count is an envious figure who wants to increase his empire by seducing human beings to his way of life. He has great powers, but these are circumscribed by the efficacy of Christian symbols; the demonology is like that employed by Goethe in *Faust I*. (Some of this, of course, appears in the source, Bram Stoker's novel *Dracula* [1897], and in an earlier stage version by Hamilton Deane and John L. Balderston [1927].) Again, Nina, the victim in Tiller's version, fluctuates between two worlds; the mere victim is enlarged into an infected person who alternately loves and resists the new evil. Thus psychologically she resembles the near-addictee or the split personality, and morally the tragic protagonist. Finally, another inmate of the asylum, Renfield, is also a victim of Dracula and plays a kind of Ariel to Dracula's demonic Prospero. Such echoes fill out the simple melodrama, making it partly exemplify the Aristotelian idea of the "probable impossible"—"probable" in that various imaginative appeals assist the outsize suspension of disbelief required by the literal events.

or pedantic. But what is more to our purpose here is the dramatist's invention of a sister for Dr. Seward: in a generally innocuous dottiness Sybil provides an old form of sick comedy. Tiller toughens up the script, however, by making her aberrations include an admiration for a new neighbor, Count Dracula; thus she helps establish him socially in the community which he then demonically attacks. Sybil's continuing unreliability augments the difficulties of combating the vampire: a mild sick comedy helps complicate melodrama.

If she gets much sicker, Sybil becomes Martha and Abby Brewster in Joseph O. Kesselring's *Arsenic and Old Lace* (1941)—amiable and cheery lovers of humanity whose do-goodism takes the form of welcoming lonely old men, painlessly poisoning them, and burying them in the cellar, where the bodies of a dozen beneficiaries now rest. In this charitable work the sisters are aided by an insane nephew, and the situation is fantastically enlarged when two more mad persons—another nephew, Jonathan, and a friend with whom he has just escaped from an asylum—arrive on the scene, bringing along another body to dispose of. Trying to deal with this situation is the sisters' sane nephew Mortimer, who finally succeeds and whose high moment is his discovery that he is not a blood relation of the Brewsters, so that he cries out gleefully, "I'm a bastard." It is surely an ultimate of sick comedy—and some time before it would become voguish—to use as simultaneous fodder madness, murder, and corpse-disposal, since two of these seem sinister and the third either sinister or, as a reminder of what humanity wants to forget, so unappetizing as to require cosmetic solemnification. Various methods make the aesthetic product sick comedy rather than melodrama of terror. For one thing, the multiple madness is almost like an epidemic of measles, a passing general affliction rather than a dreadful danger to an individual. In multiple murders there is something mechanical that tends to deaden ordinary responses. We sympathize less easily with mass victims than with the single neighborhood victim (despite our usual feeling that wide incidence makes evil seem more dreadful than a single act does). Still more important, we neither know nor see any individual victim: hence, as in popular mystery comedies, murder is more of an abstract problem than a concrete reality which stirs our humanity. (Here there is a parallel with the working of picaresque art, in which we sympathize with the rogue because we see his agile wit rather than his victims' pain; such an indulgence in roguery or in laughter at mad murders does not seem dangerous because those whom we do not cast out, as we have to think we should, do get immured in the end—rogue in jail, lunatics in the asylum.) Further, the victims are all old men, a class with whom the smallest number of the audience will empathize. Still further, their absence has apparently been noticed by no one, as if they had not really existed. Hence the elimination of them is rather a hypothesis for theatrical purposes than an act which makes moral outrage inevitable. Again, the failure of anyone to miss them is the kind of improbability that we find in a dream, and such a hint of a dream subtly diminishes the reality of what has happened. Finally, the victims not only did not suffer but rather, we are told, were freed from suffering. (And whether they have been deprived of a right or of choice is not permitted to come up.) Nor are the murderers given hateful styles that would evoke fear and detestation; if they are a kind of ultimate form of erring do-gooders who in the actual life around us would be trying, still we perceive in them no sign of malice. In their estimate of their victims as beneficiaries they are not rationalizing a hostility of their own. They come off as a fantastic incarnation of good intentions.

"Comic Faith"

All this is an effort to get at the reasons for the successful functioning, as material for comedy, of a private euthanasia factory which would not seem altogether laughable in the actual world. We see in operation a "comic faith" analogous to Coleridge's "poetic faith": we practice a special kind of "willing suspension of disbelief." The conditions that I have just described make possible a willing suspension of dismay, disgust, disquiet, distress, disturbance—all the expectable reactions to the given facts if these appeared bare, untransmuted by their aesthetic dress. This suspension is the mode of acceptance that characterizes sick comedy generally. To exercise it with respect to poisoners is obviously a holiday from the responsibility to reject it which is felt in life outside the theater. On the other hand, the acceptance of illness, dying, and the dead in sick comedy—a larger experience than the acceptance of psychopathic conduct—may indeed be imagined, not to be a freedom from the ordinary demands and habits of experience, but to have a salubrious carry-over into the ordinary nontheatrical world. We may guess that sick humor helps restore a balance by diminishing the stature of what has come to assume excessive importance with us. Apply this principle to the Middle Ages, and we see that its sick humor consisted in outrageous jests that trivialized the devil and the priesthood, who had the keys to an eternity that was then of transcendent importance. Our sick humor concerns the secularized modern variants of these two great forces: the devil is now death, and the priesthood is the medical profession. Our sick comedy may be said to encourage· adjustment to nature by taking a whack at excessive fear of death and excessive reliance on agents of a presumptively available immortality.

If we can do this, how much greater should be our ability to adjust to the irritations, frustrations, disappointments, cross-purposes, and irrationalities faced in the wider world of "nonsick" comedy.

III. EGO AND IDENTITY: THE ACCEPTABILITY OF DIMINUTION

Adjustment to mortality, the hidden component in the experience of sick comedy, is a modification of the egoism that schemes for immortality—immortality, of course, of the intramundane sort permitted by post-Enlightenment habits of mind. Immortality is an ultimate symbol of human expansiveness; it images the infinite acquisitions desired for and appropriate to the self that the individual detects within. These acquisitions symbolize an identity which is a precious possession; it is a center of stability, and any shaking of it is uncomfortable. It is given to outward movement and annexation; thus it runs into many of the expansive identities that compose a world. Adjustment is necessary, and comedy records some of its modes.

Jonson's "Epicoene"

In Ben Jonson's *Epicoene, or, The Silent Woman* (1609) Morose is half an anticipation of a Molière neurotic and half a modern man driven wild by noise. He is understandable enough in this, as well as in his impractical dream of creating a world that will minister to a monomaniac love of quiet: he not only has a servant, Mute, who communicates only by sign language, but he resolves to marry a dumb wife. As a second profit he will beget an heir and thus disinherit a nephew, Sir Dauphine Eugenie, who with his friends, Morose feels, has shown lack of respect for his uncle. Thus Morose will impose his identity, as a noise-hater and ridicule-revenger, upon his world. Obviously he could be called "sick," yet his sickness manifests itself in a representative kind of comic hubris. He lacks power to be the oppressive figure that would demand satire; his intended victims are always a step ahead of him, and he becomes the overreacher overreached. When Epicoene, the mousy, almost voiceless girl that he marries, turns into a loud-mouthed shrew with a gang of noisy friends, Morose madly craves divorce, giving up his plans both for a domestic utopia and for fiscal triumph over his nephew. In seeking grounds for divorce he undergoes various public humiliations: he admits impotence ("I am no man, ladies") and is ridiculed, hears other men say that they have slept with Epicoene ("Marry a whore, and so much noise"), and in despair promises everything to Sir Dauphine, if the latter can help his uncle break the hideous marriage: "That, and anything beside. Make thine own conditions. My whole estate is thine; manage it, I will become thy ward" (V.iv). He signs a property agreement that Sir Dauphine presents to him and then, gaining his freedom through Sir Dauphine, suffers an ultimate humiliation: his "wife" Epicoene is actually a boy trained for this role. Morose has really adjusted to a world in which other people also have interests; instead of making others pay his price, he has paid a price necessary to secure as much as can be had of a resistant world. Further, the nephew's conduct makes an important contribution to the comic tone. Sir Dauphine has his uncle over the barrel and yet remains aware of what is necessary to the uncle's life: he demands not the whole estate, as technically he could, but only a third of it. Although neither character is exactly urbane (Sir Dauphine says to Morose, "I care not how soon [your funeral will] come"), both apply a sense of reality which includes concessions to the other.

Shaffer's "The White Liars"

To change the terms slightly, Morose has accepted a diminution of the identity that seemed indispensable to his ego. The ego-identity issue occurs in different comic formulations. One of the most ingenious of these appears in Peter Shaffer's *The White Liars* (1968), which looks ironically at several people who try to get on in their worlds by adopting, or endeavoring to confer on others, identities thought to be advantageous. Pop singer Tom, apparently a crude, harsh-accented son of a poor miner, is actually middle-class but had to fake a laboring-class origin to succeed in pop music. Then Shaffer deepens the comedy by going on from the irony of socioeconomic pressure to the irony of psychological pressure on Tom: Frank is sure that Tom must have a history of poverty and suffering, and Tom gratifies him with a very particularized biography that conforms to Frank's expectations. In Tom's account of things, Frank and his girl Sue "made me up";[9] they were driven by the "crazy want in someone for an image to turn him on"; for them, the turning-on image was that of the "Prole . . . the last repository of instinct"; in his own view, Tom was chained by their clichés, "a prisoner of somebody else's dream." This sounds like self-pity, and Tom like the victim of a strange psychological tyranny. Fortunately this melodramatic possibility yields in turn to a richer interpretation: Tom, we learn, had been less a victim of than a collaborator with his jailers. Partly the fake identity had seemed professionally advantageous, but the subtler reason is this: "I liked it all too much. Much too much." In the end he does not deceive himself but grasps a much more complex truth than we had expected. On the one hand the play accepts the world's desire to see people in certain roles, and the willingness of people to play the roles. On the other, it says that the players accept not only the roles but eventually the hard fact that the roles may not be altogether good for them.

The Tom story is very effectively balanced against the stories of Frank and of Sophie the fortune-teller, both of whom have claimed identities nobler than their real ones (the "Great Gatsby" motif). Frank, an assistant in a Chelsea boutique, presents himself as an impresario who has created "The White Liars," Tom's singing group. Sophie, it turns out, is not the "Baroness Lemberg" that she purports to be but, as she acknowledges, "just a Jewish girl called Weinberg." Five years earlier, what is more, Sophie had tried to persuade a younger lover, Vassi, a Greek grocer's son, that he was a "gentleman," a scion, perhaps illegitimate, of "real nobility." She wanted him to conform to her preconception of human values, just as Frank and Sue wanted Tom to conform to theirs. Sophie's ennoblement program didn't work. Again, the play simply records the ways in which personalities act; it does not blame or spank.

Shaffer rather neatly plays against each other two opposing techniques of self-improvement. Sophie sees in Vassi an "aristocrat" of the old order; Frank and Sue consider Tom "a natural aristocrat" (i.e., the "working class is the last repository of instinct": D. H. Lawrence aristocracy). Shaffer balances a traditional snobbery against a modern inverted snobbery; one promotes a man by social ascent, the other by social descent. Both changes of identity are wrong—not morally deceptive but pragmatically unreliable. Shaffer goes on to explore still another idea of superiority by class. Sophie proposes this one: ". . . the world is divided only into Givers and Takers, . . . The Givers are the world's aristocrats. . . .

The Takers are the peasants, emotional peasants. . . . And we [Givers]
. . . are the innocents of this earth. Over and over again its victims."*
Sophie is not only enunciating the theory but interpreting it to her own
advantage. Shaffer counters her touch of self-pity by having Tom apply
her theory against her: "Because that's what it's really like with your
beautiful Givers. They give you your role" (i.e., Frank and Sue's pro-
letarianization of him, and Sophie's attempted aristocratization of Vassi).
There is excellent irony in Tom's definition of the Giver as a taker-away of
true identity, but the further irony is that Tom is as defensive as Sophie,
since he did not fight off those who gave him a role. So his words, shrewd
as they are, do not state a whole truth: a chain reaction of various half-
truths colliding one with another is one ingenious way of maintaining a
comic perspective.

Yet we are not dismissed with a barrage of ricocheting half-truths. The
final point is that people become more aware of the hazardousness of
assuming or assigning roles for gratification or profit, and more capable of
accepting a less grand but more substantial identity. Tom can say he's
glad that in time Frank did break up the identity-game that they both
relished. Sophie comes to see that as "just . . . Weinberg" she might
have held on to Vassi. Though their games belong to the ways of the
world, all three finally accept a world to be encountered without benefit of
games. Actual identity, though unexciting, is the best policy.

Shaw's "Arms and the Man"

Up to a point *The White Liars* could be taken as a nonmilitary version of
a much earlier play—Shaw's *Arms and the Man* (1894). In Shaw we see all
persons but one striving to maintain an aristocratic pattern of identity;
they try to adhere to preconceptions of the nature of reality. In the world
of Shaffer's play a pop singer has to be a "prole," and a prole is the true
aristocrat; in the world Shaw depicts, soldiers have to be heroic and
chivalric figures, men and women knights and ladies. But while Shaffer
simply observes that such preconceptions do not work very well in practice, Shaw wants to establish the wrongness of the preconceptions. In

---

*The concept of Givers and Takers as fundamental human types is also utilized in Tom Gallacher's
Mr. Joyce Is Leaving Paris (1971), in which another character attacks Joyce as only a Taker. Though the
key words are used only once, the implied dualism is fairly central: it is as a human being that Joyce is
a Taker, but we are to see this as counterbalanced by a creativity that gives to others. Gallacher's play
does not really transmute biography into comedy; but insofar as it is comic, it is of the mature kind
that maintains a sense of double-track actuality.

Shaffer, the role of noblemen is a source of temporary gratification rather than of true advantage; in Shaw, the nobilities of love and war, as they are voiced by true believers, are contrary to the facts of life. As hero or as lover in the grand style, Shaw's aristocrat is trying to ride a kite to the moon; if he is lucky (and Shaw believes that most characters are savable and so lets them have enough luck), he will land on some quite bearable spot on the earth instead of getting killed or disappearing into space.

Major Sergius Saranoff, a Balkan cavalry officer in the romantic tradition, gets credit for leading a "gallant" charge that is tactically foolish, but he is lucky and escapes getting killed only because the enemy haven't got the munitions they should have. In love, too, he is noble and soulful; thus he is quite in tune with Raina Petkoff, another major's daughter, who has equally operatic ideas of love and war. They believe that they have "found the higher love" (II), though it is hard for them to maintain what Bluntschli calls the "noble attitude" and "thrilling voice" (III). But Sergius is lucky again: after various convolutions of attitudinizing, he contentedly settles for the intelligent, rather grumpy maid Louka, who is ready to go up in the world. The beau geste and the dream of glory are out of touch with military (and sexual) reality; war means rather the humdrum keeping on hand of food, getting scared, saving oneself in any unheroic way one can, and making half-a-loaf peace arrangements. This antiromantic concept of war belongs to Bluntschli, the shrewd, matter-of-fact Swiss hotel-man who has been an unheroic professional soldier in the enemy's army (and who keeps a supply of chocolate in his cartridge belt: hence *The Chocolate Soldier*). Such an identity is distasteful to Raina, yet in time she comes around to accept him as lover. He is intelligent enough to make some romantic gestures to please her, and she has a fund of good sense beneath the layers of romantic-chivalric attitudes that had seemed her true identity. So the cavalryman accepts the housemaid, the major's daughter accepts the well-organized, businesslike realist who is in trade, and Major Petkoff accepts the fact that his troops are "far more frightened" of his wife than of himself (III). Another dramatist might manage this revisionism of attitudes to war and self in a different tone: the characters would engage in wailing and gnashing of teeth, complain bitterly that they had been bamboozled and betrayed (by someone who is to be blamed for it), and mourn harshly that glory and heroism are dead or else always had been illusory. This familiar modern style is a long way from the Shavian. In Shaw, no one screams angrily at the newly discovered actualities:

gracefully or with decreasing discomfort, people trade in the previously unexamined ideas and identities for a working arrangement with things as they are, in *Arms and the Man* with the ways of the world of war.

Wilde's "The Importance of Being Earnest"

Wilde's *The Importance of Being Earnest* (1895) is not at all a farce, as it is often called: it is a fantasy, with satirical notes in a central action that is almost a definition of comedy. By now Wilde has completely escaped from the vacillation between two tones that afflicted the earlier *Lady Winder-mere's Fan*. The problem of identity, which there led him into melodrama, here becomes the source of dramatic games and jests.[10] The satirical elements give a certain tang to, but do not really violate, the comic tone.

Lady Bracknell stands for rules, conventions, the money standard—frequent butts of satire. But in her hands they seem inapplicable rather than harsh or false, sources of striking gestures rather than faulty and inflexible imperatives; they become her idiom rather than oppressive wrong values. In effect she parodies what she nominally stands for, constantly enunciating dogma, but lightfootedly readjusting it to suit her purposes; her formulae we may question, may be annoyed by, but are not gravely troubled by. Her hyperbolic style lets us see her views with detachment rather than compels us to feel them dangerous or contemptible. Here is how she expresses the standard of "good birth" when she hears that Jack Worthing, the suitor of her niece Gwendolen Fairfax, was a foundling left in "an ordinary hand-bag. . . . In the cloak-room at Victoria Station": "To be born, or at any rate bred, in a hand-bag, whether it had handles or not, seems to me to display a contempt for the ordinary decencies of family life that reminds one of the worst excesses of the French Revolution" (I). It would take a pretty earnest social consciousness to read this as deplorable snobbishness and lack of sympathy for the unfortunate; rather it comically exaggerates our tendency, when expressing some conviction or passion, to yoke unlike things together in a kinship taken for granted by, but evident only to, us who declare it. Lady Bracknell believes in her power to forbid or veto, but she agrees to the engagements that the two couples have worked out—a surrender of the rules to the life force as Shavian as is Miss Prism's successful pursuit of Canon Chasuble.

When Jack Worthing turns out to be a nephew of Lady Bracknell, Wilde is playing an old literary game—parodying the look-who's-who plot of romance by suddenly identifying someone whose disappearance was not noted when it happened a long time ago (Fielding uses this device in *Joseph Andrews*, as does Jane Austen in her juvenilia). The game is to trivialize, and thus accept, what might not seem trivializable (much as in sick comedy). This is just what happens in Wilde's central comic routine: Jack Worthing and Algernon Moncrieff both plan to be baptized "Ernest" because their girls, Gwendolen Fairfax and Cecily Cardew, can love only someone named "Ernest" (as Gwendolen puts it to Jack in terms that extraordinarily anticipate the 1970s, "Ernest . . . produces vibrations," while "Jack . . . produces absolutely no vibrations" [I]). Here Wilde turns the usual effect of symbolization upside down: ordinarily symbols tend to enlarge and solemnify, but in this symbolization, as so often in the style of his witty young men, Wilde trivializes. Two girls' wanting to marry an "Ernest" may indeed, as is often supposed, be Wilde's having some fun with Victorian "earnestness," but he is doing more than tossing out a topical quip. To trivialize is to accept, as we have noted: Wilde's name-game fantastically sums up all the irrationalities—the choices or preferences incomprehensible to others—that are at the heart of love affairs, and, besides that, the ironic similarities among the irrationalities of different individuals, whom one might expect to make unique demands. Jack and Algernon do not doubt, deplore, or try to lead their darlings to higher things: with their scheme for baptismal accommodation —as if they were repairing their bicycles or having new photographs made—they wonderfully accept Ernestophilia as an inescapable aspect of the way things are in the world of love. ". . . my ideal has always been to love some one of the name of Ernest" (I) is, as the young men—and their creator—wisely see, a perfect summation of universal romantic feeling.

Though Wilde trips it on a very light fantastic toe, what goes on here is not unlike the accommodations that are at the heart of *The Way of the World*. Wilde's range is narrower; he does not admit lasting frustrations, and even transitory anguish is excluded by the idiom. And yet the trivializing symbol does not render trivial the reality that is trivially expressed. After all, the young lovers lie to each other, the young ladies can sharpen knives for each other or for the young men as joint enemy, and like Lady Bracknell they shift ground with changing circumstances. In the ways of this world there are both will and feeling, though the air of a fencing match may disguise some genuine dueling. To speak thus, of course, is not to attribute a high seriousness to the play, but to reaffirm that a chosen frivolity of manner does not exclude feelings that could be dealt with in a highly serious way. Wilde's great feat of mediating the conventional by the unexpected appears, too, in a lovely detail. Instead of practicing a modest ladylike reserve, Gwendolen tells Jack that he has "always had an irresistible fascination" for her, assures him, before he has proposed, that she is "fully determined to accept" him, and then complains, "How long you have been about it! I am afraid you have had very little experience in how to propose" (I)—as if proposing were like helping a lady on with her jacket. It is not unlike Congreve's translation of feeling into wit.

"Iolanthe" and Versions of the Identity Motif

The purely fanciful adjustment to the facts of life is managed with the same fine playfulness in Gilbert and Sullivan's *Iolanthe* (1882), in which human habits and ways are transposed into the practices and rules of the Fairies' kingdom. The perennial human opposition to inappropriate marriage is made into a very firm law: any Fairy who marries a mortal is sentenced to death. Thus the spirit of the Duchess of Berwick and Lady Bracknell and other such matrimonial managers operates through legal proviso instead of private pressure and footwork. But when it turns out that not only Iolanthe but nearly all the other Fairies are married to mortals, the law is blithely changed to require that "every fairy shall die who don't marry a mortal" (II). The pattern is that of romantic comedy: the social order finds a way of accepting the ways of the world in love. Or in more general terms: comic flexibility may mean adjusting conduct to the rules, or adjusting the rules to conduct, depending on which way of the world is better attuned to human realities.*

Iolanthe makes two uses of the identity theme that occurs widely in comedy. The central action depicts the acceptance of a previously unap-

---

*Iolanthe materials are a take-off point for another comment or two on generic matters. One difference between comedy and tragedy is that the former has to do with "rules," the latter with "imperatives." Rules are adjustable; imperatives are not. Rules are the fashions, conventions, decencies, norms, and common sense that undergird social life. They are time-bound and hence alterable, though this is more likely to be true of detailed regulations than of the general attitudes which they express and which are likely to be very persistent ("good manners" is an ever-present and indispensable concept, though the specific actions regarded as good manners change). But once a principle or standard is felt to be humanly essential—say, the canons against assassination of people or character—then the trespass of them is not negotiable, that is, susceptible of comic mediation, but takes us into the noncompromising realms of melodrama and tragedy. One of the details in *Iolanthe*— and there are similar tonal devices all through Gilbert and Sullivan—bears on the distinction between the comic and satiric to which we allude periodically. In Parliament the half-mortal Fairy Strephon introduces a bill making the House of Lords open to competitive examination: satire against the intelligence of the Lords. But when one peer says, "I've a great respect for brains; I often wish I had some myself" (II), the tone becomes that of ironic comedy. The peer charmingly manages to treat brains, not as a *sine qua non*, but as an adornment which, like good looks, one might be thankful for, but the absence of which would not be disastrous. His good-natured acceptance of reality sheathes the knife of satire.

preciated element in the identity of Fairies—their tendency to love mortal men; so they abandon their ethnic separatism, once thought to be of the essence. The new openness to a larger world (plus the fascinating inclination to make a law of the new outgoingness, and thus—most humanly—to render inflexible the product of flexibility) is triggered by the straightening out of various literal identities.

The plain who's-who motif is ancient and ubiquitous: mistaken identity is a central element in farce of all times. Two people may be confused because they look alike, as in *Menaechmi* and *The Comedy of Errors*. Most frequently someone errs, is deceived, or is misled by a coincidence, as repeatedly in Georges Feydeau and Ben Travers. We begin to move across the border from farce to comedy in such a play as Gogol's *The Inspector General*, when a mistake in identity is not an accident but the product of a frame of mind that drives people to the misinterpretation of perfectly clear evidence. Here we are watching the spontaneous action of personalities that, though limited, bring into play a good deal of human nature. Almost unintentionally Gogol's Hlestakov takes on, for pleasure and profit, an identity wrongly attributed to him in a town in which he is briefly a visitor. When a character acts with more deliberateness in using or imposing an identity, the result is the comedies which introduce fundamental problems of personalities vis-à-vis society. Jonson's Morose wants the world to serve his identity as noise-hater and ridicule-revenger; his effort to enforce this acceptance of him leads finally to his own acceptance of a less ample identity. He gives up much, and even his successful adversary takes much less than he might. In Shaffer's *White Liars* people adopt identities that they think are required, or endeavor to impose admired identities upon others; in time they all accept the fact that these are more perilous than profitable, or more tempting than workable. Shaw's army people discover and accept actual identities quite at variance with the heroic and romantic types that they had thought themselves to belong to. Wilde's Jack and Algy are ready to accept the Ernest-hood that sums up all irrational romantic cravings, and *Iolanthe* makes a joyful game of adjustment to things as they are.

IV. COMIC ACTION IN DIFFERENT WORLDS

Pirandello's *Naked* (1922; *Vestire gl'ignudi*, "To Clothe the Naked") gradually reveals the misrepresentations by which Ersilia Drei, a young woman who thinks of herself as "naked" (I.1494; II.650; III.809), endeavors unsuccessfully to secure "a decent dress to die in" (III.821).[11]

She wants, that is, to conceal the sordid facts of her life in a conventionally romantic tale that, given wide journalistic circulation, will be generally accepted in Rome as she commits suicide. A Pirandello-figure, the novelist Ludovico Nota, speaks with delight of the unfolding true story of Ersilia as "this comedy of a lie discovered" (III.491–92). But there is "comedy" neither in the revelatory actions that the novelist observes, nor in the larger action in which he participates by treating Ersilia's history as material for fiction* or for analytical comment. In saying that these matters are not comic, I allude not to a tone generally tense and dark— after all, Chekhov can introduce considerable bleakness into comedy—but to the fact that the dominant mood of author and characters is nonacceptance. The flight from one's own reality is an O'Neill theme, but while O'Neill pictures the illusion that the individual himself needs, Pirandello focuses on the illusion about oneself that the individual wants others to have: Ersilia would like Nota's proposed novel about her to present her cosmetically. True, she acknowledges her lies and their purpose, and her last words are that she has "died naked" (III.853). But here the truthfulness of death is combined with a despair so bitter that it undermines what is potentially tragic; this cannot survive the tone of utter failure and the pathetic, which is the product of Ersilia's plea for understanding. Ersilia has had too much to despair about—a sexual history and an apparent role in an infant's death—to make possible an accommodation with herself or with the world. All the others involved with her are indignant either at what she has said or at what she has done, since either her nakedness or her assumed finery seems to them to damage them. The tearing away of her "beautiful dress" is of course their work, but in a larger way it is also attributed to a "world" (symbolized in a street which is abominably noisy and in which an old man is killed in an accident) which thus, in an almost romantic style, is made hostile and even destructive rather than acceptable.

Naked is useful, then, for contrast. If the post–World War I Italian world, as interpreted by Pirandello, inhibits acceptancy, we can neverthe-

---

*Nota feels that he is freed from "the facts" (III.535–50) and that he can "make a farce out of it" (III.504–5) or find "a way to put an ending on a comedy" (III.528–29). This sense of mastery over his materials is directly countered in Raymond Queneau's *The Flight of Icarus*, trans. Barbara Wright (New York: New Directions, 1973). In this fiction in the form of dramatic dialogues, the independence of characters from their creators' intentions is symbolized in Icarus' bodily escape from a novelist's work in progress and subsequent pursuit of adventures of his own (including some with other such escapees). But in the end Icarus has to accept a world, for him the world of mythic definition: his destiny, even in independence, is a fall from high place. Thus he and his re-creator reach a final accommodation.

less find acceptancy, even in the face of difficulty, in a number of different worlds—of the theater, of the nineteenth-century English upper class, of a twentieth-century Irish lower class, of twentieth-century Russian classlessness, of provincial Ireland at the turn of the last century.

When Jean-Paul Sartre rewrote Alexandre Dumas's *Kean* (1836; Dumas's subtitle, "Disorder and Genius," defines his subject) in 1953, he showed either a knowledge of, or an affinity with, Pirandello.[12] "Who is Edmund? What is he?" is a persisting motif in Sartre's re-do. Is Kean, because he is an actor, nobody? Or is his reality what he is as a man outside the theater? Even offstage he is usually living in a role of some sort. All this could lead into an agonizing riddle for Kean and for the audience too, but long before such an extreme materializes, Sartre serenely parts company with Pirandello: Kean makes do with an inevitable sense of duality in himself as actor and man. At the same time he works his way peaceably out of amorous entanglements, and gets ready instead to marry the determined daughter of a moneybags and to go to America. Thus the historical Kean who, competitive and megalomaniac, gave a melodramatic hue to almost every real-life situation, is under the molding of two dramatic imaginations reconstituted as a man of amiable good sense adapting himself to the world as he finds it.

Kataev's "Squaring the Circle"

If we jump from an English scene, as envisaged by two sharply different Frenchmen a century apart, to an early post-Revolutionary Russia as envisaged by a contemporary Russian, we find the same amiable good sense in ultimate control. V. P. Kataev's *Squaring the Circle* (1928; a product of a temporary "thaw" in ideological life) laughs at problems that occur in the wake of the Revolution without, of course, laughing at the Revolution itself. It accepts not only the world of the Revolution but also the imperfection of human arrangements that persists even in a world purified by revolution. A historical housing shortage in Moscow is the starting-point: two newly wed couples have to share the room formerly occupied only by the two young men before they acquired wives. But the discomforts attaching to spatial shortage are only a surface theme; the real problem is the mismating in both couples. A politically serious man is married to a domestic, all-feminine, baby-talk girl, and an earthy, hedonistic man is married to an ideological, nonhousekeeping woman. In time the needed interchange of spouses takes place. But Kataev knows that such realignments are not easily accomplished, and he carefully traces all the steps necessary to human beings as they slowly and even guiltily acknowledge mistakes and edge toward rectifications that, grounded on emotions as they have to be, nevertheless will seem to conform to the doctrines by which they want to live.

All parties, indeed, have to accept getting married in the first place, since marriage itself has been defined, in their world, as a "bourgeois" prejudice; the two men's confessions of having fallen into matrimony are made with embarrassment and hence the traditional misunderstandings and delays of farce. Then all have to accept that the marriages are not so "durable" as they thought. (Ironically the food-and-fun husband sees his as "durable" because of "class consciousness, a common political platform, labor solidarity." As for "love"—no, it's "a social prejudice! A lot of banana oil, rotten idealism" [I].)[13] Both couples fight; each fight brings forth allegations of "drowning in this petty bourgeois swamp" or accusations of "bourgeois tricks" (II). Kataev picks up admirably the human habit of translating felt discord into charges of unprincipled conduct— here made in political clichés. The less political couple discover some congeniality and go to the zoo, but wonder what the "book on Communist Ethics" would say. The left-behind pair drift into an embrace but immediately fear that they are being "incorrect" or "unethical" or out of line with "Communist family morality" and resolve to "surrender our personal well-being in the interest of general social well-being" (II). Everyone, indeed, thinks that his own defection will be the ruin of his spouse; both girls take off; the husbands are pleased but promptly quarrel, each accusing the other of bad husbandly conduct, and each screaming "bourgeois," "renegade," and "opportunist" at the other; the girls come back and break into tears and sobs. The deus ex machina is Flavius, the sensible party organizer, who assures them that remarriage "can't hurt the Revolution" and that tears "can't hurt the Revolution" and that he will take "the trouble of divorcing and remarrying you properly." When Abram asks if this is "ethical," Flavius replies, "Abramchik, don't be an overclever parrot," and he commands the new couples, "Love one another and don't play the fool. It can't hurt the Revolution" (III). At the final curtain the radio blares forth various propagandistic phrases; one of these is "Love, superstition and other bourgeois prejudices" *—a charming final irony.

*The gradual acceptance of pleasurable experience by the doctrinaire spirit is a central motif in Jacques Deval's comedy *Tovarich* (1933), adapted by Robert Sherwood in 1936 and made into a musical comedy in 1963.

The couples have no difficulty about accepting the Communist ordering of the world. What they have also to accept is that they can misinterpret doctrine, themselves and their needs, and even the needs of their spouses. And the Party itself can accept what members and followers think may be unacceptable. The recognition of reality and the flexible adjusting to it are in the best comic tradition.

Wilde's "An Ideal Husband"

In upper-class England of the 1890s things are not dissimilar: there is a code, though not a political one, and the principals must come to terms with a violation of it and thus with themselves as not quite the persons they had assumed themselves to be. Yet in Wilde's *An Ideal Husband* (1895) neither the code nor the deviant conduct is open to interpretation, and the rectified image of the "ideal husband" with which the husband and wife must live includes a dark spot rather than reflects an altered light. Like *Lady Windermere's Fan* (1892), of which it is a less time-bound reincarnation,* *An Ideal Husband* has a fund of the melodramatic in its basic structure: a successful young English politician, Sir Robert Chiltern, once sold a state secret for money. Mrs. Cheveley, an old schoolmate of Sir Robert's wife, has this information in a letter, and she will reveal it unless he withholds his opposition to a shady investment scheme that she has a finger in. So he must fear being publicly disgraced and being unmasked to his idealizing wife, who takes him for an almost divinely pure statesman. Mrs. Cheveley is a lively villain: she is half a Becky Sharp harassing a goody-goody Amelia Sedley (Lady Chiltern) whom she can't stand, and half a demonic figure faintly anticipating Duerrenmatt's Claire Zachanassian. She gleefully drops the bad news into Lady Chiltern's lap, and the wife is utterly disillusioned about her "ideal husband." Fortunately Mrs. Cheveley, although demonic, is not grand enough to be invulnerable: Sir

---

*In each play there is a happy, virtuous, well-bred, well-to-do couple (the Windermeres and the Chilterns) whose Edenic existence is threatened by a serpentine visitor (Mrs. Erlynne and Mrs. Cheveley); she introduces a malodorous past that has in some way to be dealt with or lived with. Mrs. Erlynne, of course, feels that she has served enough time for her "error" and wants merely to get back into society's heaven; Mrs. Cheveley, however, has the Iago streak and wants to disturb a harmony that arouses her resentment. Lord Darlington urges Lady Windermere to be more generous in her judgments of the fallen; likewise Lord Goring to Lady Chiltern. (A big gain is the transformation of Darlington from straight romantic lover into Goring, witty and worldly suitor.) In the film of *An Ideal Husband* the defeated Mrs. Cheveley, instead of simply disappearing from an altered and wiser Eden, gains a husband: this might have been inspired by the treatment of Mrs. Erlynne in *Lady Windermere's Fan*. It is in accord with the comic spirit which, acknowledging the survival of the Mrs. Cheveleys, can let even the foiled trouble-maker have something to go on with—if not the pastry of revenge, at least a few crumbs from the tray of plainer nourishment.

Robert's best friend Lord Goring has the goods on her—knowledge of a jewel theft she had carried out—and thus gets the incriminating letter from her.

This mish-mash of concealed misconduct in the past, threatened exposure in the present, a disillusioned wife, and a rescuing white knight would seem, on the face of it, to contain negligible comic possibility. Yet the comic tone is firmer than that which struggles to maintain its footing in *Lady Windermere's Fan*. For one thing the white knight, Lord Goring, is the very witty, pretendedly frivolous Wildian young man (a prototype of Dorothy Sayers' Lord Peter Wimsey). He argues amusingly with his angry-old-man father, and cleverly courts Sir Robert's sister; as in the best comedy of manners, all their feelings are translated into an ironic, witty idiom. More fundamentally, Lord Goring is the voice of that unaffected good sense which combines moral acuity with tactical judgment. Without ever falling into a high-tone manner—his wisdom comes through as the spin-off of playful repartee—he advises Sir Robert to let his wife know the facts, and Lady Chiltern to moderate her judgment of her husband, to let him know of an unwise letter of her own, and to rescind her ruling that Sir Robert penitentially abstain from the political life for which he has gifts. Goring is really the voice of the comic spirit, and he prevails: the result is acceptance of a mixed world by both parties. Lady Chiltern climbs down off her high moral horse, and Sir Robert, who has been successful for so long that he has almost forgotten he isn't a god, learns to go on feet of clay as well as the spotless wings of the dove. More important, both know all the relevant facts: thus *An Ideal Husband* improves on the morality of ignorance that weakens *Lady Windermere's Fan*.

Behan's "The Hostage"

The Irish playwrights who stick to domestic scenes manage acceptance in different ways. In Brendan Behan's *The Hostage* (1960) there are no hidden blots to surface and mar present securities; everything is out in the open. Surprises come only from moods, shifts, details of speech and conduct. Here, in the old *Grand Hotel* convention, the world is a Dublin combination of rooming-house, pub, and brothel ("brockel" is one in-house term for it), and everybody is here—several virtually middle-class characters, several homosexuals (a black and an ex-priest, "Princess Grace"), several whores, Monsewer (a loony Englishman who has turned Irish patriot, plays the bagpipes, and imagines himself a military leader), some ne'er-do-wells, and a maid Teresa, an innocent country girl. Squabbles, bickerings, occasional insults do not seriously affect the fundamental style of general good-humored live and let live. The title character, an English soldier named Leslie Williams, who is to be killed if the British forces kill an Irish prisoner of theirs, is virtually a member of the club, consistently treated with geniality and sympathy. His death, apparently an accident during a police raid, is a source of pathos, but this in turn is modified by fantasy when the corpse sings the last of the dozen songs that create a musical-comedy air in a world at war. They join with an ironic sense to cut off the partisanship that begets melodrama. Almost nothing makes for war rather than jokes.

The risk to comic effect is that we may condescend to characters whom we could think lacking in human fullness. This is often a risk in comedy, though it is actualized only in farce. Behan's creations do lack one quality—the habitual aggressiveness which would make the comic way untenable. Otherwise his community indeed embodies a wide spread of human traits: illusions, prejudices, clashing codes, changing emotions, a lyric impulse, irritability mitigated by forgetfulness or a put-up-with-it spirit, and various types of naïveté in contrast with an ironic turn of mind that brakes the intensity of feeling begotten by fanatic loyalties. Still the representativeness is enacted on a field so small and enclosed that we may seem to have—I repeat terms used early in Chapter 3—less a microcosm than a hypocosm, a world too limited to exact sympathy. But if we compare the Dublin place run by Pat, the one-legged "laughing boy," with Harry Hope's New York sanctuary in still another play from an Irish imagination, *The Iceman Cometh*, we see a large difference. In O'Neill, retreat, incompetence for life, self-deception; against this, in Behan, confidence, humor, toughness of spirit, a vitality that comes through in bawdiness, jest, the feeling for song and dance. Hence, for us, comic engagement rather than a looking down from the heights.

Synge's "Playboy of the Western World"

If we go back half a century, cross Ireland westward to the "wild coast of Mayo," moving from urban "brockel" to rural seaside "shebeen" or pub, we come across a similar range of personalities—from the naïve to the knowing, from the spontaneous to the calculating, the extremes sometimes merging contradictorily—and a working community in which daily discords are all absorbed into the local way of life. In Synge's *The Playboy of the Western World* (1907), however, there is a real outsider: Christy Mahon comes from afar into a County Mayo village to excite longings and stir people at deeper levels usually not active in day-to-day life. The twenty-four-hour crisis—a remarkable feat of compression by the dramatist—turns on no political or societal problems, but unpretentiously goes to the heart of never wholly resolvable human desires and needs, and Synge is correspondingly closer to comic greatness than Behan. Christy Mahon is the mysterious visitant who sets people together by the ears or stands the local world on its head. He is potentially a demonic disturber or a new divinity. Thus Synge starts with an ancient archetype of community experience.

By reporting that he has murdered his father, whom he describes as a cruel and oppressive monster, Christy becomes a local idol. Patricide works with something of mythic force; kill the old king or priest or god and introduce a new and more vital order. Christy is an exciting medley of Hercules and potential Don Juan, fascinating to the women and hence subtly alarming to the men. As a hero he represents a break-through, daring, and the greatest liberty of all, that which recklessly subverts (the goal of all Ibsen characters who deride, or yearn to override, the "sickly conscience"). Again, what goes on can be described in terms of Mann's dualism: the bohemian has charmed the bourgeois almost out of its usual caution and safety regulations. Christy is the liberating artist; there are various references to his poetic speech. Yet he himself does not wholly understand what psychic currents he has set up; pleasurably surprised at the warmth of his reception, he keeps repeating the murder story rather mechanically—tediously to some—like a comedian with a sure-fire gag.

The hero has to be tested by further experience. It looks as if Christy will be done for when his supposedly dead father, furious over the filial blow on his still-bandaged head, shows up. For a while, though, he is held off by the Widow Quin ("about 30"). The one calmly pragmatic person in the community, she sees a good thing in Christy; she would gladly snatch him as a husband from Pegeen Mike, the lively, sharp-tongued, emotional young woman whom he really wants, and, failing the snatch, the widow is willing to help him for her own pecuniary advantage (with her balance and her sense of reality, she could be almost a Molière restabilizer of a situation). Her attitude really establishes Christy for us as more than a flash in the pan. We now see the naturalization of the hero—on the one hand the reduction of mystery in a packed Act III, on the other his earning of a more substantial local status: he wins various events in a local Olympic games. We infer that hitting his father, though Christy is still frightened of him, was itself a liberating experience that

made it possible for him to discover latent abilities: this is the old myth of
the late-developing hero who has been overlong oafish or inept. Christy's
triumph ("such poet's talking, and such bravery of heart" [III]) completes
his conquest of Pegeen Mike, who throws over her local swain Shawn
Keogh ("a scarecrow, with no savagery or fine words in him at all"), and
even wins her father's approval of a quick marriage to "a daring fellow"
who "split his father's middle with a single clout." Re-enter the father,
unsplit and contemptuous: Pegeen Mike, who embodies a community's
fickleness, turns against Christy; desperate to recover lost ground, Christy
again lays his father out with a "loy" (spade). Shock: the whole community turns against its erstwhile hero; only Widow Quin and a girl try to
help him escape a new animosity—that of Pegeen Mike and all the
men—which threatens him with hanging for his brutal crime. Resurrected a second time, his father rescues Christy: now in high spirits—
Christy feeling himself a new masterful man, and his father delighted by
his son's new manhood—they go off, declaring the local air uninhabitable, ridiculing Mayo, and anticipating a lively future elsewhere.

Synge's comedy achieves magnitude by giving play to some deeper
human motives that stir up a community and could even shatter it.
Beneath the villagers' attraction to the hero and to the spirit of romantic
adventure which he embodies, Synge spots a strong inclination to violence
("savagery") and disorder, matters to which comic acceptance does not
often extend. Synge's genius, however, is to present this anarchic,
primitivistic passion in terms of the villagers' response to a deed marvel-
ously conceived for its ambiguity and hence double utility. The father-
"murder" happens twice, and Synge's big stroke is that the two events
seem wholly different to the local audience. The first violent act is distant
and narrated instead of present and actual. The villagers' admiration is
called forth by a tale, a work of imagination; the exciting, envied breach
of piety, of a fundamental bond of community, is a symbolic one. The
catharsis is literary; the id roars, but there is no price. Then Synge
brilliantly replaces the symbolic "murder" by a literal, present, public
one, and the "clever, fearless" hero becomes a scoundrel worthy of hanging. Symbol and imagination are permitted what the actual is not; literary
life has no limits, but literal life has to be limited. Synge now shows the
community doing what it cannot fail to do, however unheroic and craven
it may look as it condemns its once glorious hero. Pegeen Mike voices the
issue: ". . . there's a great gap between a gallous [great, noble] story and
a dirty deed" (III). "Story" and "deed": a fine summation of one of the

dualisms that belong to the ways of the world. Back the town moves to the superego; to propriety and property, which, tame though they be, reaffirm stability; the bohemians go merrily on the way, and the bourgeois rules take over again, as they have to, even though they cause the sad sense of diminishment that always accompanies the resumption of ordinary life after a romantic escapade, a plunge into the forbidden, an imaginative adventure into new, gratifying, and frightening experience. The traveling minstrels depart, glory yields to safety, the spirit of bugle and drum to the humdrum.

The world that Synge leads us into is rich in meaning. The bohemians are outside the community and yet they, too, constitute a community with dynamics that hold for the village itself. The young hero finds himself, and the old order rejoices that he has done so, accepting the new possessor of manhood as a welcome companion. The new man establishes himself by a kind of initiation: demonstrating the ability, not to bear pain, but to inflict it; practicing, not the unconscious cruelty of child-hood, but the conscious ruthlessness that at the right times must coexist with pity if the adult world is not to go sentimental. The old order cries out at being hit, but it also sees the blow as a symbolic act; its absence would be worse than its presence. To the village the hero is a paradoxical fellow: he is liberating, but he is dangerous, an implicit critic of the nonheroic on which daily life depends. The community loves him but also fears and hates him; it enacts the perennial enthronement-followed-by-dethronement by which the sociopolitical body gratifies itself, that successive exercise of reverence for a hero and righteous indignation against him by which the public assures itself of its possession of opposite virtues— looking up to and looking down upon. At a different level the community knows what art may do and life may not. Let the libertinism embraced in art break out in the village square, and the villagers combine fear, right judgment, and self-righteousness in one confused, ambivalent, but vigorous response.

Yet, while he sees what the common feeling is, Synge does not make the village too homogeneous. It does what it cannot help doing, but it has a healthful diversity. Even after the second "murder" of Mahon, Sr., the Widow Quin and Sara Tansey are with Christy, wanting to save him from the mob; some women have an instinctual fidelity to the hero, a daring that answers to daring, a spontaneous affinity for the Juan in the strong man who pushes aside the code. Another energy besides that of convention and commandment is still active. We may wonder that Pegeen Mike is with the men, but we should not. She is essentially a nonsubversive child of the village, but, with her strong and quick feeling, she is a jump ahead of the community in its characteristic actions, either embracing the new hero or fearing and repudiating him. Yet Synge does not limit her to that, either, for he makes her also capable of the fine line that closes the play: "I've lost the only Playboy of the Western World." She does not disparage him to keep her self-image untarnished, or blame the community as if she were its victim. She acknowledges both that she has suffered a loss, and that the losing was hers. Instead of falling into sour grapes or recrimination or stoical nonexpression, she cries out with the pain of loss.

It has been said that the cry of anguish goes outside the bounds of comedy. On the contrary, it is the identifying mark of the sturdiest comedy that strains at conventional limits to include an unexpected range of the ways of the world. Comedy includes pain; it characteristically accepts pain as fact. To clarify: its business is not the pain of guilt, which is tragic, or the pain of hopeless suffering, which creates the drama of disaster, or of the stifling or barely salable life, which is the material of black comedy. It is not the pain from which there is no escape and for which there is no remedy. It is simply the pain of things as they are and for the most part have to be; most frequently it is the pain of getting only what one is up to. The gently ironic notation of that pain is the apex of Synge's drama, which, without finger-pointing or side-taking, has genially accepted the ambiguous interplay between generations, between the hero and society, between different voices in society, between the symbolic and the literal forms of subversive action, between the realm of imagination with its libertine leaping and bounding, and the realm of workaday living with its inevitable walking and even trudging.

V. Tests of Acceptance:
The Unmalleable, the Unflattering, the Unpalatable

The world may set up various difficulties for those who desire, or have, to come to terms with it. It may offer less than they would like, or other things than they would like, or more of the distasteful than they would like. It may refuse to yield, to make compliments, to undergo cosmetic modifications, even to negotiate. So men and women have to effect some change of view or feelings or self-image, to rebalance the old cargo of motives and attitudes. On the other hand the difficulty of this reordering cannot be excessive, that is, unbearable to actors or audience; if it is, the tone will be something other than comic. What characters undergo must seem, in whatever terms, fitting and ameliorative, beneficial to themselves and also, though perhaps only negatively, to the immediate society.

Middleton's "A Trick to Catch the Old One"

A situation very difficult to put up with is that in which Walkadine Hoard finds himself in Thomas Middleton's *A Trick to Catch the Old One* (ca. 1607): his new wife turns out to be the former mistress of Theodorus Witgood. This past doubly pains Hoard, for Witgood is notorious as "a rioter, a wastethrift, a brothel-master" (I.iii.41) and is, besides, the nephew of Hoard's enemy and financial rival, Pecunius Lucre.[14] Furthermore, the marriage is the result of an elaborate plot by which Witgood takes care of his mistress, cons both his rapacious uncle and Hoard, and solves his own money problems. Hoard might seem to be, then, only another victim in a world in which a harsh *caveat emptor* is the prime morality. But Hoard is not an innocent victim; from the start he has been the greedy antagonist of Lucre, bitter because Lucre once beat him to the draw in cozening a third party, and living for a chance to get even. Hence, when Witgood shows up with a reputedly wealthy "Widow Medler" as fiancée (the role that Witgood has got his girl to play), Hoard sees a chance to pick up her money and to triumph over both Witgood and his uncle Lucre, who is delighted by his nephew's rich match. So Hoard goes for the "widow" himself and gets her, paying all of Witgood's debts so that Witgood will sign a release from an alleged "pre-contract" with the girl. It is Hoard's lust for revenge and new riches that makes him take the bait and get hooked by the courtesan. He rejoices: "In this one chance shines a twice happy fate; / I both deject my foe and raise my state" (II.ii.93–94). Married, he is tickled by victory; he thinks with glee of how this "will so vex my adversary Lucre [that] he will . . . hang himself presently" (IV.iv.26–31). So hubris has a characteristic comedown: Hoard has a glorious, triumphant wedding party—and then he learns who his wife is.

Middleton is very careful to preserve the comic tone against the satiric, the bitter, and the black that could easily take over. For one thing, Hoard has "asked for it"; no trap had been set for him; he had gone into action because he had believed a rumor about the widow's wealth, and he cannot challenge her reminder, "I told you I had nothing" (V.ii.125; cf. III.i.260), words which he had really chosen not to hear. On learning the truth, he might well burst into violence and inaugurate a Jacobean shambles, but instead he begins to look at things pragmatically: "I must embrace shame, to be rid of shame! / Concealed disgrace prevents a public name" (V.ii.179–80), and he closes the play with a wry judgment on himself: "Who seem most crafty prove ofttimes most fools" (V.ii.232). The effect is that of an ironic reversal, of a new adaptation to reality, rather than of bitter defeat or a nasty new stock-piling of resentment: peace instead of a feud.

Middleton has the others refrain from triumph and try to make defeat bearable for Hoard. The "covetous uncle" (I.i.80) Lucre gets in a laugh or two, but his triumph is small, for he was equally taken in by the rich-widow hoax and, gratified by the vision of more money in the family (if Witgood married the widow), he had restored to Witgood some funds that he had snatched from him. Witgood goes out of his way to reassure Hoard about his new wife: "Excepting but myself, I dare swear she's a virgin" (V.ii.185–86), and, instead of gloating over his successful game, criticizes his debauchery and declares himself "reclaimed" (V.ii.230). The courtesan, who has sounded rather decent throughout, has already averred that she is "reclaimed" (V.ii.213). The risk of sentimentality is reduced by the lively couplets in which both of them catalogue the naughty activities now abjured.

Middleton has a Jonsonian sense of men's money-madness, and he can plunge into direct satire—for instance, of Witgood's creditors and of such usurers as Gulf and Dampit, the latter a crook turned drunkard. The courtesan complains, "the world is so deceitful" (III.i.248), and Wit-good's confederate, the inn host, remarks with glee when Hoard schemes to snatch the widow, "What gulls there are a this side the world" (III.i.180). And à propos of people's dashing to help those with money, the widow comments, " 'Tis right the world" (I.i.120)—"just the way of the world." Yet these commentators on the world do not despair of it. There are other harsh facts too: a half dozen times, as used by and of Lucre and Hoard, the word "conscience" means "consciousness of profit or ad-vantage" or even of "successful cozenage." [15] Middleton does not take this to be the full story, however; twice Witgood says it's been on his "con-science . . . to see [the courtesan] well bestowed" (III.i.147–49; V.ii.182–83), and the widow can regret Witgood's having "burdened my conscience" with another sleight against Hoard (IV.iv.233–34). So some people are not limited to indifference or rapacity but can have the true "conscience" and the kinds of concern that make social life possible. Middleton anticipates Congreve, not in the richness of the human world depicted, but in seeing, in the ways of the world, not only the grasping schemes that declare the author unsentimental and hard-bitten, but also the good sense and the impulse to good behavior that make the world, on balance, acceptable.

Christopher Fry and the Comic Theme

More than once Christopher Fry explores the issue of acceptance. In *Venus Observed* (1950), as we saw in Chapter 3, Perpetua Reedbeck learns that she can aid the world, not by trying to whip away its vices, but by being a better person herself. Likewise her brother, a sort of one-man vice squad (someone calls him a "conscience-nudging, / Parent-pesting, guilt-corroded child" [III]), is jarred into some reconsideration of his own ethical certitudes.[16] Other characters likewise come to acceptance of possible imperfections in the world and in the self.*

Fry tests the comic spirit in the toughest possible context by choosing an actual war as the setting for *The Dark Is Light Enough* (1954)†—the unsuccessful Hungarian revolt against Austria (i.e., the Habsburg Empire) in 1848–49. In this world, where partisanship seems inescapable, the Countess Rosmarin Ostenburg conducts a kind of open house at her place near border and battlefront. She first gives sanctuary to Richard Gettner, a renegade, against pursuing Hungarians, and then to a Hungarian officer against pursuing Austrians. These acts are not cost-free sentimental gestures but run all the risks that arise in wartime; they put the Countess and household and guests in double jeopardy. Besides, the renegade Gettner was the first husband of the Countess' daughter Gelda,

---

*The Duke of Altair, fifty, puts up with the peculations of his agent, Herbert Reedbeck, as a possible route to the heart of Reedbeck's daughter Perpetua, twenty-five, while Perpetua, thinking to save her father, tries to accept and even reciprocate the Duke's love. But sounder feeling and sense eventually take over: Perpetua gravitates toward the Duke's son, and the Duke resolves to marry a former flame (who has set his astronomical observatory afire as a lesson to him) nearer to his own age. Before her and two other old loves the Duke has dangled himself as matrimonial bait; the two nonwinners survive comfortably with life as it is—one with a husband, the other as handy woman to those who want a listener and a comforter. Thus "Venus" has been "observed," and though there have been some moments of madness, they have catalyzed a beneficial adaptivity in which everyone settles for the possible instead of driving on in disastrous rivalries.

†This title comes from a passage by J.-H. Fabre which, altering it slightly, Fry uses as an epigraph. Fabre's words are "Nocturnal darkness is light enough for this night-flier" (see Jean-Henri Fabre, *Marvels of the Insect World*, ed. and trans. Percy F. Bicknell [New York and London: Appleton-Century, 1938], p. 44). "This night-flier" is the male peacock-butterfly; Fabre describes the mysterious arrival, under difficult conditions, of numerous males in the house where there is a female ready for fertilization. Fry's application of the image is a little puzzling. While various men do arrive at the residence of a countess who is very much the center of things, she is aged, ailing, and at death's door. She does things for the men rather than they for her; one might well call her the "fertilizing" agent. Fry may wish to suggest that even the darkness of war does not defeat the human instinct for essential things.

and taking him in not only gives him another chance at Gelda but threatens the life of Gelda's second husband, Count Peter Zichy, an Austrian official held hostage by the Hungarians. What is more, Gettner is unattractive—vain, self-centered, whining, ungentlemanly: the born moral outsider who is the sternest test of charitableness. Though he repels the others, the Countess never flags in her tolerance of him; and just as she stirs others to be at their best, so in the end she apparently elicits from him a surprising decency and courage.

If the Countess is not exactly making jokes instead of war, she is exhibiting openness instead of partisan feeling; she has accepted the world in its diversity instead of only in its congeniality. In aiding fugitives from both sides, she has symbolically denied the unilateral virtue that is assumed in melodrama. Neither doctrinaire nor sentimental, she sums up her attitude well when Gettner, trying like others to understand her attitude to him, asks her what he has "meant" to her. She replies, "Simply what any life may mean" (III).[17] "Any life" is not deflating; rather it means "every life." That is, all lives are to be received rather than rejected. The Countess speaks as an author of comedy might.

Fry has said that if characters are not qualified for tragedy, they are not the materials of comedy; he alludes to "all their divisions and perplexities."[18] The efforts at self-understanding which result from a sense of dividedness appear in several characters in *The Dark Is Light Enough*, and most interestingly in the Countess' daughter Gelda. When her former husband, the unattractive Gettner, approaches her with masterful assurance and insists that she still loves him, she seems, puzzlingly, somewhat drawn to him. Later she explains this to Zichy, her present husband:

> It may have been right,
> That first instinct, to put out with a lifeboat
> For Richard, but on to it scrambled
> Such a crew of pirates, my curiosity,
> My pride, my ambition to succeed
> Where I failed before, my longing to discover
> What conversions could be made by love,
> We all began to sink.   [III]

Here is a rare perception of mixed motives, above all a realization that one may derive love for an unlovable being from the dream of saving him by love. One's own mistakes are part of the world that one accepts—mistakes that could lead to tragedy but do not do so because one comes to terms with reality instead of trying to impose one's will, or one's dreams, on it.

Goldsmith's "The Good-Natured Man"

Gelda's experience is much like the one undergone by three characters, and most notably Honeywood the title character, in Oliver Goldsmith's underappreciated *The Good-Natured Man* (1768), which, despite obvious shortcomings,* excellently embodies the comic spirit. Honeywood shares the stage with Lofty, who lets on that he knows important people and has influence, and Croaker, who chronically expects disaster. Though Lofty is almost a caricature, still beneath his absurdities we detect the true lineaments of the name-dropper and self-deceiver, and behind them even some capability of enlightenment. Croaker could be only a "humor," a black-bile man, but his abiding fear of a Jesuit take-over of England images brightly the xenophobic monomanias of all ages. Besides, Croaker is a long-suffering and ironic husband, a would-be dictatorial father of his son, an affectionate father of his daughter, a somewhat ironic self-observer, a confused man, and finally a forgiving man who can live amiably with actuality. Goldsmith cuts back farce and satire by investing potential stereotypes with a degree of humanity that enables them to embrace eccentricities without becoming mere eccentrics. Thus in Honeywood, whose monomania is a foolish give-away habit, he finds a resurrectible good sense.

Lofty, Croaker, and Honeywood compete for the stage. Goldsmith's imagination is unifying, however, for in analogous ways the three suffer from a distorting sense of reality. Lofty thinks that people are more gullible than they are, Croaker that they are more conspiratorial and threatening, and Honeywood that, treated with endless generosity and kindness, they will respond more generously and kindly than they do. Thus the three exhibit, respectively, cynicism, paranoia, and sentimentality—three kinds of unbalance that constitute a great threat to the human community. But also the three men are responsive to the qualities that make the community possible—the clearheadedness and emotional stability of Honeywood's man Jarvis, of his admirer Miss Richland, and especially of his uncle Sir William. When various pressures lead them all to

---

*The action line, afflicted with complicated plottings that survive from the seventeenth century, is somewhat blurred; the exposition is often murky; the amorous intrigues work out almost too neatly; and the hero tends to lose stage to several "character" types and to the Leontine-Olivia elopement plot.

†A deus ex machina, Sir William seems to some critics to make things too easy. But fortunately his line is not free salvation for the erring but compulsory education aimed at self-knowledge: he plans to "involve [Honeywood] in a fictitious distress, before he has plunged himself into real calamity" (I). Thus he is a solid mentor, in illuminating contrast within the fixer-uncle of a decade later, Sir Oliver

see themselves more clearly, *The Good-Natured Man* moves into the realm of high comedy.

Forced to live with a muddlement contrary to his once-clear view of things and with matrimonial arrangements contrary to his plans, Croaker comments with gentle irony on the relative equanimity that replaces his persistent anxiety: "There's the advantage of fretting away our misfortunes beforehand; we never feel them when they come" (V). Shown up as a fraud, Lofty too looks at himself in a new perspective and thus contributes to the comic spirit; he sees that he "cuts but a very poor figure," resolves on "reformation," and reveals his latest lies. To head off the sentimental effect that is always a risk of reform, Goldsmith keeps Lofty partly ironic: "I now begin to find that the man who first invented the art of speaking truth was a much cunninger fellow than I thought him" (V).

Goldsmith's ability to construe men as capable of sensible self-understanding is most conspicuous in his treatment of Honeywood, so sentimentally addicted to largesse that he becomes a dupe, goes broke by handouts, and so finally lacks the means to practice his theory that "universal benevolence is the first law of nature" (IV). What he has to learn is that a useful life in the community depends upon balancing benevolence with rational self-interest; otherwise givers go from being used to being useless, and takers from beneficiaries to sponges. Honeywood comes to spot and renounce his own folly: "How have I sunk by too great an assiduity to please! How have I overtaxed all my abilities, lest the approbation of a single fool should escape me! . . . I now too plainly perceive my . . . vanity, in attempting to please all by fearing to offend any; my meanness, in approving folly lest fools should disapprove" (V). Honeywood's sense of failure exists vis-à-vis an actual world, viewed not as the voice of fashionable triviality and prejudice, nor as the embodiment of moral imperatives, but as the residence of a good sense that makes for personal and general survival. That is what comes through to Honeywood when he learns with chagrin that he is "contemptible to the world" (V).

There is nothing simplistic about this comic movement; Honeywood's

in Sheridan's *School for Scandal* (1777). There are several external resemblances between the uncles: both return unannounced from abroad, with a partial anonymity that permits others, with ironic effect, to reveal themselves unknowingly to the new arrivals. But Sheridan's uncle is sentimentally conceived, as Goldsmith's is not: Sir Oliver rescues a nephew by a handout instead of an instructional experience, mistakes (along with his creator) for a crowning virtue what Sir William (along with his creator) has perceived to be at best ambiguous (i.e., handouts of money), and his judgment of his nephew's quality is based on an irrelevancy and on naïve self-esteem rather than good sense, which he lacks. Goldsmith deflated a chic sentimentalism even before Sheridan swallowed it whole.

troubles come not from vice but from a mismanaged virtue. Nor is Honeywood a topical figure only: Goldsmith's revolt against the good-heart sentimentalism of his day (which Tom Jones finally rejected but which Sheridan would uncritically endorse in Charles Surface) creates a credible image of the mechanical or professional do-gooder of all times. Goldsmith raises a penetrating theoretical question: does Honeywood suffer from faulty doctrine or emotional disorder? Honeywood's well-balanced man Jarvis attributes the follies to "philosophy"; Sir William, loyal to philosophy, argues that Honeywood's "good nature arises rather from his fears of offending the importunate" (I), and accuses his nephew of seeking applause (using a praying-on-street-corners style), lacking courage, letting charity become injustice, benevolence weakness, and friendship credulity (V). Sir William acutely diagnoses the Honeywood type: "They who pretend most to this universal benevolence, are either deceivers, or dupes: men who desire to cover their private ill-nature by a pretended regard for all; or men who, reasoning themselves into false feelings, are more earnest in pursuit of splendid, than of useful virtues" (III). Goldsmith has caught both the exhibitionistic façade and the emotional basement of an apparently admirable structure of principled conduct.

The Good-Natured Man, then, is in a small domain of comedies in which original thought is active and the critical mind examines widely held preconceptions, not to dissolve them as a nihilist would do, or to stand them on their heads as a romantic or a professional shock-peddler would do, but to push a half-truth toward wholeness by seeing the dual nature of accepted virtues. In these terms the play achieves much more than it has been given credit for. The shortcoming is that Honeywood gains insight more through verbal lessons and devoted instructions* than through pure dramatic experience.

---

*Philip, the Honeywood type of protagonist in Christopher Hampton's *The Philanthropist* (1970), has no such battery of instructors and helpers, and so he is pretty much empty-handed at the end (he loses his girl, instead of being rescued by her). Philip has to face, not an instructional crisis arranged for his own good, but substantial difficulties arising from his own compulsions. Along with this difference, however, there is a significant resemblance between the two characters. Philip is a give-away artist too: what he hands out indiscriminately is not money but good will and approval. Like Honeywood, he is morbidly afraid of arousing resentment and hostility. As he says to his girl Celia, who leaves him only because he is wishy-washy, ". . . the basic feature of my character is an anxiety to please people and to do what they want, which leads to, that is, which amounts to a passion, and which is, in fact, so advanced that I can only describe it as . . . terror" (sc. v in *The Philanthropist* [London: Faber and Faber, 1970]). Honeywood and Philip both descend from Timon: the link is an excessive dependence on others' good will and therefore the purchasing of it with whatever currency is provided by the times and by one's own nature.

Goldsmith's "She Stoops to Conquer"

She Stoops to Conquer (1773) makes less use of ideas, but it continues to exploit Goldsmith's spirited antisentimentalism. It relies, not on explication, but entirely on the laughter aroused by vivacious personalities whom Goldsmith spontaneously imagines in their responses to puzzling or trying situations. The trickster Tony Lumpkin leads Marlow and Hastings to believe that the Hardcastle country house is an inn, and his mother to believe that a carriage-run around the neighborhood has been a hazardous trip to a distant sinister spot. There is much farcical confusion, yet Goldsmith makes the individuals seem not mere robots in farce, but human beings trying to understand or acting understandably. Marlow tries nonfarcically to use his head when the "innkeeper" behaves inexplicably, and he manages to guess at the truth though it does not seem tenable: "How's this! Sure I have not mistaken the house!" (IV). As a dupe, Tony's mother (Mrs. Hardcastle) is a farcical source of laughter, but surely she exacts a less easy response, an uncomfortable fellow-feeling: we too could well misread such planted evidence.

Two wise women help transform the farcical into the comic. Marlow likes Kate Hardcastle but can get on with it only because he takes her for a barmaid. His "humor" is that he is at ease only with maids and tarts, and is frightened speechless by nice girls. Taken literally, this is an idiosyncrasy hardly interesting, but symbolically it works well enough, representing all the neurotic fears of facing situations that are not inherently unfaceable (the same aesthetic method would appear in the girls' Ernestophilia in *The Importance of Being Earnest*: symbolize a familiar human experience in an attitude or response that seems freakish or trivializing—really a fine mode of understatement). Instead of complaining, riding Marlow, or lecturing him, Kate continues in her public role as barmaid, charming in humor, knowingness, and assumed naïveté; while nominally playing a trick or game, she is taking him as he comes and thus enabling him to discover that he is not really limited to barmaids for friendship and love. By humoring his humor, she is being therapeutic. Indeed her action is analogous to the comic process generally: acceptance modifies a deviancy (if it has not become outright psychological or moral illness) and thus it helps effect a better adjustment to reality.

Goldsmith's other wise woman is Kate's cousin Neville: her lover Hastings also has a problem, a sentimental romanticism so poorly attuned to the world that she has to be the voice of reasonableness. He wants to elope without her jewels: "Perish the baubles! Your person is all I desire" (II). Neville is for "patience" and "prudence": "In the moment of passion fortune may be despised, but it ever produces a lasting repentance" (V.ii). Neville sees the world much as Mirabell and Millamant do; through her, good sense triumphs, and the couple get the money as well as each other. Yet happily Goldsmith does not let her dwindle into an allegory of prudence; she can be merry and quippish, can romp with Tony in lively games of pretended affection, can be ironic about love and its obstacles.

Goldsmith is a master in imagining in people an amiability which smiles at, that is, adjusts to, the way things are. Mrs. Hardcastle is finally gracious as an unsuccessful marrying mother. Marlow moves from arrogance as a guest at the "inn" to willing self-criticism: "My stupidity saw every thing the wrong way" (IV). Kate is Goldsmith's masterpiece, bringing Marlow along superficially by a barmaid's easy flirtatiousness, but more deeply by good temper, irony, sense of the ridiculous. If she is not quite the urgent fencer or urban epigrammatist that Millamant is, still she is a wit. Her description of Marlow in the role of "professed admirer"— "Said some civil things of my face, talked much of his want of merit, and the greatness of mine; mentioned his heart, gave a short tragedy speech, and ended with pretended rapture" (V.i)—nicely reveals wit as not only an elegant adornment of comic action but also a meaningful participant in it. If comedy often regards convention as an integral part of the world that is accepted, still wit may identify foibles in the way of the world: though deviants may fall laughably short of indispensable convention, convention itself may fall short of the truth indispensable in the way of the world.

Hofmannsthal's "The Difficult Man"

There is a most interesting variant of the Kate-Marlow relationship in Hugo von Hofmannsthal's The Difficult Man (1921), substantial as a comedy and mildly reminiscent of The Way of the World, which Hofmannsthal knew. Though Hofmannsthal uses more satire than Congreve does, he presents an essentially good-humored, urbane world, one in which much scheming precedes the working-out of the central relationship between the lovers. Hans Karl Bühl, the title character, is partly in the Mirabell tradition. He is a social figure with charm for both men and women; men tend to depend on him,* women fall in love with him and thus become jealous and spiteful, and he may have been something of a rake. While Mirabell is a controlling force in his world, however, other people try to control, or at least manage, Hans Karl. He does not cope well. He seems unclear about where he is going; he feels different claims and does not reconcile them, or choose among them firmly: he slips into philosophic, gnomic, or hypothetical talk in tactical situations, and thus puzzles or misleads others. He seems elusive and hard to pin down,[19] and in this he is less a Congreve than a Goldsmith character. While Goldsmith's Marlow is abashed only by well-bred women, Hans Karl is insecure or at least indecisive in all sorts of circumstances. He needs a tactful bringing along and bringing out, and in a somewhat larger game Helen Altenwyl plays Kate Hardcastle to his Marlow.

But Hofmannsthal's situation is a richer one, for we see Hans Karl's hesitancies and "shilly-shallyings" in a context of vast self-assurance in several managerial types. Two women dominate successive scenes with Hans Karl, loquaciously telling him what to do, while his views are only implied in laconic statements (I.iii, vi), and then two men conduct parallel scenes with him (I.viii, x, xii)—Baron Neuhoff, the "Northerner," that is, German, and Hans Karl's nephew Stani. Baron Neuhoff, who believes that his "strength" and "the force of my will" are irresistible "in a weak-willed world," is so unsubtle that his judgment of Hans Karl— "boneless equivocal creature" (II.xiii)—really stigmatizes himself and in effect praises the man he disparages. Stani repeatedly flatters himself on the decisiveness that he believes gets results and wins admiration (I.xvi); he works by "categories" and by decisions that must be "instantaneous"; and as to "complications," he "refuse[s] to admit them" (I.viii). These self-assured, single-track men are no closer to reality than Hans Karl with his burdensome sense of the puzzling and the irresolvable. As writers of comedy often do, Hofmannsthal portrays a world needing a balance between the extremes to which human nature is inclined. The others have too little critical awareness of both self and actuality; Hans Karl has too much. They underestimate the doubleness of things; he overestimates

*The number of suppliants is greatly reduced from that in Molière's *Les Fâcheux* (1661), which can be thought of as the ultimate point of origin for *The Difficult Man* (with Hofmannsthal's *Die Lästigen* [1916] as an intermediate stage). Hofmannsthal transforms Molière farce and satire into high comedy. The importunate are both less numerous and more fully developed; their victim becomes the substantial central character; and the woman he loves, in Molière a walk-on, has an important role.

it.* They systematically miss the boat because they think there is only one, while Hans Karl sees too many boats to make a choice.

Though characters with simplistic positions are always in the human picture, the world depends on those who can move toward a mean. Hans Karl can do this, but like many he needs the initial steering of someone who serves a mean by withholding the adverse judgment easily elicited by an extreme. Helen Altenwyl sees through the layers of self-doubt that make Hans Karl speak and act ambiguously, perceives his quality and his feelings, and finds words for the proposal that he has not quite worked up to. She is not just the warmhearted dea ex machina that Goldsmith and Fielding both call on at times (Sheridan donates a rescuing uncle), but is the subtler aide who brings the man to a better awareness of what he wants and what he is up to (in both senses). Hence the effect is not sentimental; Hans Karl is not a passive recipient of emotional charities and other goodies but is an active participant in the process of self-discovery. Thus he becomes capable of responsible love instead of retreat, uncertainty, and vague do-goodism. He remains capable of self-censure without being self-destructive. His final adjustment to reality ironically reverses that of many comic figures: instead of overcoming a distorting vanity, he must shake off a debilitating self-disparagement; he must deal, not with belittlement by others, but with their tendency to magnify his worth.

VI. Ways of, and Ways with, the World

Accepting the world—adjusting to it, making do with it—takes many

---

*Hofmannsthal's method is close to that of Jane Austen, who uses excesses of a virtue to establish the value of an apparent deficiency. In *Sense and Sensibility* Marianne is deficient in rational control; but in the John Dashwoods rational control has grown into unfeeling calculation, so that, in contrast with their chilly materialism, Marianne's emotionality has an admirable core of spontaneous feeling. In *Pride and Prejudice* Elizabeth Bennet's "prejudice" shows her lack of ironic detachment; but her father's excess of ironic detachment helps us see, even in her animus against Darcy, a strength of feeling and principle which makes her the responsible person that her father is not. Thus the self-confident oversimplifications of others make Hans Karl's unsureness and scrupulosity look the more reliable. If his qualities were in contrast only with achieved balance and taste, he might seem only an incurable Prufrock.

Hofmannsthal's sense of these opposite extremes is nicely imaged in the description of the clown Furlani, whom Hans Karl admires: "He plays his role: the man who wants to understand everybody and help everybody and yet brings everything into the utmost confusion. He makes the silliest blunders, . . . and yet he does it with such elegance, such discretion, that one realizes how much he respects himself and everything in the world." Other circus entertainers calculate, concentrate, "following a purposeful line . . . till they have achieved their purpose. . . . But he apparently has no purpose of his own at all—he only enters into the purposes of others. He wants to join in everything the others are doing, he's so full of good will, he's so fascinated by every single bit of their performance . . ." (II.i). That is, all the world's a circus, divided between the self-conscious programmatic personalities and the charming, well-meaning, bumbling participators who mess things up but remain admirable. This is only a part of the play, of course.

forms. Writers of comedy characteristically present a world that is both
actual and bearable; its inevitable shortcomings do not make it intolerable. Some people are harder to take than others, but they can be lived
with; if they were vicious and incurably selfish, they would not belong to
comedy. People who misconceive the world can achieve a saner or better-
balanced view of things as they are. Some are more sensible or more
tolerant or have a better eye for the facts than others. But even those who
fall into "excessive expectation" are capable of coming around, of adding
an iota or two of rationality to their estimate of actuality and probability.
When people seem incurable or unredeemable, the dramatist may fall into
despair or lash out with a satirical voice, which occasionally does a duet
with the comic voice; on the other hand he may imagine characters who
neither flee nor defame the world, who live with it and in it, and who yet
fashion a private standard that demands more of them than the world
does. Here the exemplars are Mirabell and Millamant, who by not being
easy on themselves unsentimentally perform the special feat of making the
world easier to accept.

Sometimes dramatists reverse habitual attitudes. In *Easter* Strindberg's
characteristic animus against the world yields to a temporary faith that in
it there can be enough good judgment—and good luck—to render it
quite livable, a refutation of its paranoidal observers. But Chekhov, who
ordinarily sees human beings surviving the disappointment and frustration that crop up almost as irrationally as do achievement and well-being,
presents in *Ivanov* an uncomic view of a society in which most men and
women are sadly maladjusted to the life around them. We might dispose
of them by calling them "ill" and hence wholly unamenable to comic
treatment. Yet Peter Nichols has skillfully practiced the comedy of illness: in *A Day in the Death of Joe Egg* and *The National Health* his method is
a detached panorama of the ways in which we endeavor to live with
physical states that can't be much changed. "Sick humor"—as distinguished from a sick gratification by suffering (e.g., sadism)—is a way of
living with what we dread. Death itself may be a subject for comedy; as
such it does not call for solemnity, but is simply another event in the
nature of things, one which can evoke annoyance, indifference, or irony.
As Ridgeon says in *The Doctor's Dilemma*, "Life does not cease to be funny
when people die any more than it ceases to be serious when people laugh"
(V). The dead or their bodies may be a starting-point for satire, whether of
the immediate survivors or a larger world, as in Albee's *All Over*; or for
farce and satire as in Orton's *Loot*; or for genuine comic effect as in

Ionesco's *Amédée* or Hampton's *Philanthropist*. Madness may be, not a source of dread or pity, but an ironic improvement on sanity or simply one of those things, a neutral state that can invite a host of responses. So in *Arsenic and Old Lace*, which jests about a private euthanasia factory, we have a kind of ultimate sick comedy using a variety of devices to translate death and the devil into manageable terms.

If we can deal with not being alive and well, as some comedies assure us we can, it seems possible to accept many other reductions of identity. Jonson's Morose agrees to a serious cutback in what he can do, be, and have; nearly all the major characters in Shaffer's *White Liars* learn the ultimate impracticability of identities contrived to gratify; in *Arms and the Man* everybody but one man who already knows the world has to give up a romantic or heroic identity heretofore taken to be in the very nature of things. On the other hand, the two male leads in *The Importance of Being Earnest* are happy to accept a nominal identity required by the girls they love: in trying to become "Ernest" they enact—through Wilde's characteristic use of the "trivializing symbol"—a coming to terms with all the irrationalities of the amatory world. Edmund Kean, as interpreted by Dumas and then reinterpreted by Sartre, not only finds a way to live in a not wholly acquiescent world, but accepts finally the evasiveness of his own identity. In contrast: Ersilia in Pirandello's *Naked* cannot accept herself and her history; her romantic escapism leads only to noncomic disaster.

The young Communists in Kataev's *Squaring the Circle* accept the world as defined by the Party, and the Party in turn accepts the conduct which they themselves thought to be out of line: an urbanity not often cohabiting with ideology. In Behan's *Hostage* members of different social groups and hostile nationalities get on amiably; there are almost no rigidities to render difficult a very mixed world that might be all combat. The husband and wife in Wilde's *Ideal Husband* make peace with a less flattering new life in which a long-buried misdeed is resurrected as a troubling live fact. Synge's *Playboy* takes us into a several-tiered life in which varieties of self-acceptance are mingled with different styles of greeting new shocks to a world of reassuring custom. The village is charmed by a romantic visitor from afar but finds him more palatable as a mythic rebel than as a literal head-breaker before their eyes: while they accept their limiting order by rejecting the man newly finding an unruly strength, the heroine acknowledges that her falling in with their play-safe denial of him has meant a sad setback: "I've lost the only Playboy." The counter recognition is that of

Middleton's *Hoard*: instead of losing a love, he finds that he has gained another man's ex-mistress as wife. Synge's saddened girl and Middleton's shaken man both live. In two plays Christopher Fry depicts three modes of acceptance: the Duke of *Venus Observed*, and others, settle for lives and loves less glamorous than their imaginations are wont to design, and the young woman with a mission decides that it lies in improving herself by degrees rather than the world by force; the Countess of *The Dark Is Light Enough*, embodying an essential graciousness that is the ultimate achievement of the comic spirit, accepts as guests not only men from both sides in a war, but, in one of these, a man whose social and moral style puts a strain on all who are with him.

Acceptance may mean a good-tempered adjustment to the inevitable. Yet the withholding of the rejective spirit may go beyond the concessive and become therapeutic. Fry's Countess, accepting the unpalatable Gettner, draws out of him at least a moment's decency and courage. At a lesser level of personality, sensible girls in Goldsmith's *She Stoops to Conquer* play along or deal gently with their lovers' oddities or preconceptions and thus steer the young men away from second-rate solutions. In *The Good-Natured Man* Miss Richland recognizes the underlying soundness in a man whose doctrinal obsession and need to be liked have almost ruined him. She helps him in a process undergone by three major characters in this play, as well as by the two central male characters in *She Stoops*: identifying and finding compatible a world quite different from what they had supposed it to be. Again in Hofmannsthal's *The Difficult Man* a shrewd woman identifies, and helps develop, the potential balance and adequacy in a man whose unclear direction and indecisiveness might have inspired only amused rejection. Hans Karl slowly learns that response to the world which is half way between a drift into defeat and the illusion of mastery by forceful nonhesitancy.

These are among the diverse ways in which comic life manages its characteristic action of finding accommodation with the ways of the world and of the diverse individuals who constitute it. To say that the comic mode is to make jokes, not war, means that it gives up the spirit of combat and rejection and reform and sets up instead a sense of kinship with what is there, even with error; an affinity that means tolerance or persuasion rather than denial, teasing instead of flagellation, good temper rather than censure, good manners rather than enforcement, and an ironic sense of the deviant that might invite either the belly laugh or, better, the rueful delayed smile that registers an unvoiced "There go I."

CHAPTER 6

Infinite Variety

THE COMIC style of finding accommodation with the ways of the world does not imply the acceptance of anything and everything that unpredictable life serves up to us. It may serve up abuse, dishonesty, malice, sadism, treachery; one may be the victim of human unregenerateness or of disasters inflicted by a careless human hand or a nonhuman cataclysm. Blows of this kind evoke grief, anger, rebellion, bitterness. These noncomic responses are inevitable. Yet we have to remember the Jewish humor that extraordinarily manages to treat hostility, irrationality, and injustice as if they were of the ways of the world that receive comic placement. Such jesting may be heroic, stoic, therapeutic; a resistance movement, at least against despair, of the subtlest kind; an incredible civil triumph over evil.

Ordinary comic practice does not call for heroism in either participants or audience. It does, however, exact something more than the quick routine responses of ordinary intercourse. "Acceptance" is meaningful only if it implies difficulty and effort. One could define no literary genre whatever by saying that it has to do with the acceptance of payments, rewards, accolades, honors, gifts, legacies; of what is due or of the keys of the city; in general, of what is earned, what is gratifying, and what comes through grace. On the other hand, as we have noted, one is not called on to accept indecency, grossness, hatefulness, cruelty. The "difficult" that requires intellectual or moral effort in "acceptance" must lie, it appears, between what it would be foolish or perverse not to accept, and what it would be impossible to accept.

I. DISPARATENESS AS KEY

We need an identification of that middle ground. Fortunately we already have it: it is a basic element in the definition of comedy explored since Chapter 2. In that brief formula the now familiar phrase "acceptance of the world" is followed by these words: "of the fundamental disparateness of all the elements in the world." *Disparateness* is a quite useful word. It is of course akin to the *incongruity* family (*discordancy, discrepancy, inconsistency, contradictoriness, inappropriateness*) which has had such a big run among theorists of laughter and comedy since Kant and Schopenhauer. But incongruity theories tend to deal mainly with jokes and witticisms; they do not look often or regularly at comic drama. Furthermore, they tend to imply a static combination of unlike elements that is risible in itself, or to describe an arbitrary juxtaposition of the discordant (as in gag-making, cartoons, and mock-heroic method). *Disparateness* has an advantage in that it is a virtual newcomer[1] in the vocabulary of laughter/comedy theorists: thus it tends to prevent conventional associations and, as new, to be appropriate to a partly new enterprise—the identifying of the characteristic actions of stage comedy.

Besides not being shopworn, *disparateness* is a desirably neutral, dispassionate term. We would hardly apply it to the passionate inner conflicts of tragedy (the struggles between imperative and impulse, or between irreconcilable motives). Nor would we apply it to the outer or worldly conflicts of melodrama (the gross discords between men of aggressive, violent action—thievery, fraudulence, murder, conquest, oppression—and those who defend legal and moral order), in other words, to the elements of a situation involving axiomatic unacceptability. Further, *disparateness* would never seem the right term for such an obvious discord as that between Tartuffe's public style and his private actuality, that is, for the kinds of deviant conduct which would have to evoke scorn or censure. Thus in using *disparateness* to identify comic materials, we incidentally protect comedy against the reductive view that it is "corrective," against the pressure to make it satirical, particularly against the wide desire to find the world guilty of hypocrisy and to make the punishment of hypocrisy the first order of literary business. The trouble with that desire is this:

if we can simplify troublesome discords into hypocrisy, and thus enjoy the pleasure of accusing willful deceivers, we ignore the vast comic field of what we might call natural or spontaneous hypocrisy, that is, the inevitable, unintended, and often unconscious disparity between ideals quite genuinely held to, and the conduct of people who in their humanity drift away from those ideals. In sum: since *disparateness* is not a term likely to be applied to tragic and melodramatic materials, or to the realm of willed misconduct that calls for satire, the use of it automatically closes off large areas of noncomic materials and thus decreases the natural fuzziness of the borders between comedy and these contiguous realms.

Disparateness alludes not only to all kinds of troublesome dualities but to the immense heterogeneity of the world: to the infinite variety which may make an individual irresistibly charming and which may be the goal of everyman on a holiday, but which in ordinary life can be irritating or maddening because it defeats the longing for sameness and oneness that unofficially governs most of our relations with others. Hence, with *disparate* in mind, we can think of comedy as a kind of negotiator between homogeneity and heterogeneity. In homogeneity—as fact, as faith, as object of desire—lie the standards of judgment by which we identify the -out-of-line, the eccentric: all those departures from the norms which in some theories are the sole business of comedy. But acceptance of the disparate means also a great concession to heterogeneity, that is, letting live, with dispassionateness or even sympathy, all those unlikenesses and even divergencies that may be an affront to preferred patterns. In its difficulty infinite variety demands the effort that makes acceptance meaningful. Comedy tolerates what ideology takes arms against.

Par, Uniformity, Problems

Disparateness has another advantage: it suggests not only difference and variety, but downright inequity. In comedy, inequity—of endowment or achievement—is a fact of life; hence compromise, hence make-do. *Disparate* suggests "not par." This may mean "not up to par": not so good a citizen as might be, and yet to be borne with. Or "under par" in scoring, that is, exceptional; the comic range includes the extraordinary person, the Millamant or the Meredithian woman. Not up to par: further from an imaginable ideal; under par, closer to it. In general, "not par" is not coming up to or not being held down by a given standard, not identical with a mean. People are not of the same height or weight or color or race or strength or health or intelligence or point of view; we note this lack of uniformity, we may jest about it, but we do not reject people because of their divergencies. Par is the expectable; some men surpass, some fall short of, expectation. *Disparateness* defines, not an artificial collocation designed by a comic writer according to a recipe for laughter and allied responses, but a persistent state of human affairs. In our humanity, we differ from each other in candor, veracity, reliability, consistency, amiability, charitableness, thoughtfulness, urbanity, cooperativeness, responsiveness to the *sens commun*.

In our humanity, also, we are not comfortable with all these variations, for we inconsistently crave uniformity as much as we tend to diverge from it. Besides, we desire to know the world; hence not only feeling, the craving for order, but also the intellectual quest leads us to uniformitize. Then we run into intransigent materials. We postulate a knowable uniformity of character and conduct—witness the clichés of motive-classification that represent the layman's use of depth psychology—and promptly run into constant inconstancies and regular irregularities. These unrulinesses are disturbing. We may apply such denigratory labels as "hypocrisy" to them or even try to suppress them, for every society recurrently itches for compulsory uniformity. Or some men go for the opposite of compulsion, that is, a sentimental, nonjudgmental "tolerance" which waives all general standards as inapplicable or valueless (the respectable form of despair over multiple discrepancies). But this is not the comic acceptance, which derives vitality from a certain resistance, from a sense of difficulty. For example, we accept the erring because there go we, but it is hard because we resist the identity. Again, though we accept what Molière's Alceste, Ibsen's Gregers Werle, and Giraudoux's Electra wanted to eliminate from the world—polite lies, illusions, survival before total justice—still we have some residual sympathy with the pure standards that their impure executive hands would make into dictatorial absolutes. Hence the difficulty that prevents acceptance from being effortless and commonplace. The difficulty, as we have seen, does not mean that the disparateness includes noxious or destructive elements, since these would require a rejective style. Rather, what is accepted, lived with, may initially seem obnoxious or noxious; then it turns out to be, if not totally innocuous, at least bearable. Thus a learning process is going on, often both on the stage and in the theater. We learn, perhaps with initial dismay, that things are neither intolerable nor much changeable, and that we may be partners in the deviations that our rule-making side would put down. If we were not learning, if full awareness were prior to the experience, what we call acceptance might be only self-defense. The characteristic comic movement is from a lesser to a greater awareness of worldly reality, and of how we share in it.

To canvass a representative spread of dramatists' ways of approaching disparateness, we will look first at a mixed group of plays that have some thematic resemblances, then proceed historically, touching a few high spots from Attic to Restoration periods, and finally note some special cases that lead up to the ultimate form of disparateness, multiplicity.

Politician, Artist, Doctor

Three familiar ways of life—the political, the theatrical, the medical—provide exemplary comic materials.

The politician John Shand, a "Scotsman on the make" in J. M. Barrie's *What Every Woman Knows* (1908), has illusions about the magnitude of his oratorical talents. We soon see that his success depends largely upon his wife Maggie's clever additions to his scripts. His egotism also takes him into an affair with a woman of title whom he believes better suited than Maggie to be the consort of the man of destiny he thinks he is. In this ignorance and self-love he might be simply an object of satire. But Barrie does not really satirize the disparateness between his vanity and the human facts; he presents John not as a callous schemer but as an ingenuous self-deceiver with a bare ability eventually to be undeceived, not as a threat to the community but as an ordinary male with a standard case of *amour-propre*. Barrie's treatment of the sexes is rather Meredithian. Maggie recovers John Shand both for herself and for good sense by great patience, intelligence, and risk-taking. In this there is nothing of the sentimental often imputed to Barrie: Maggie's victory is not a soft handout by a warm-hearted author but a plausible accomplishment by the exceptional character included in the disparateness observed by comedy.

The play of "Pyramus and Thisby" in *A Midsummer Night's Dream* never lets us forget the principle of disparateness. There are the malapropisms and the famous descriptive phrases—"most lamentable comedy" (I.ii. 11–12), "rehearse most obscenely" (110–11), the "tedious brief scene" and the "tragical mirth" (V.i.56, 57).[2] Then there are the crowding discrepancies between the humble-life cast and courtly audience, between the lives of the actors ("Hard-handed men that work" [V.i.72]) and the mythic lives enacted, between the venturesomeness and the talents of the actors, between their inability to portray character and their fear that their portrayals may affright the audience. Thus the inept and ludicrous might become only an object of derision. We do relish the witticisms of the noble audience, but we feel them a little ungraciously superior too; hence we somewhat draw away from the commentators. That is, the whole tone of things works against mere rejection of the incompetent actors. What works for them is their good will and good nature, their earnestness and lack of self-consciousness, their nontedious brevity, their equal freedom from vanity and embarrassment, and their fundamental simplicity which unconsciously parodies theatrical artifice. We are drawn into sympathy with a project that runs counter to standard expectations of dramatic entertainment.

To go back from the inset play in *A Midsummer Night's Dream* to Aristophanes' *The Frogs* (405 B.C.) is to move to a comedy essentially concerned with dramatic criticism—the famous case of Aeschylus vs. Euripides. This conflict comes on, however, only after extensive farcical actions by Dionysus (frights, arguments, jockeyings with his servant Xanthias). Nor does farce die out when Aeschylus and Euripides enter and each attacks the other and praises himself. Name-calling and insult keep much of the literary conflict at a game-playing level ("pompous portmantologist," "cripple puppeteer").[3] Dionysus, of course, having heard the debate, reverses the attitude that brought him to Hades and votes for Aeschylus. This, plus Aristophanes' dislike of Euripides' antitraditionalism, might well have led to a sharp satire of Euripides. But the contest is essentially in the comic vein,* with both competitors making points. Doubtless, Aristophanes considered Aeschylus the better moral

---

*In Aristophanes the satire that might be in total control may at any time yield ground to the comic. This sharing of the stage is very evident in *Lysistrata* (411 B.C.). Though *Lysistrata* is one of Aristophanes' continuing attacks on Athens' war with Sparta, the serious critique of war and the satire of the male vanity that contributes to war-proneness are mingled with an easy laughing awareness of the habits, penchants, and instincts of women which almost wreck Lysistrata's antimilitary campaigning. Aristophanes might be satirically attacking women for unpunctuality, engrossment in household routines, love of adornment and fashion, and of course the sexuality that could break the sex-strike as an antiwar move. But such traits appear only as a source of amusing inconsistency. Always Aristophanes exploits discrepancies: between the seriousness of the antiwar effort and the women's trivial excuses for dropping out, between the solemnity of their oath and its being sworn on a wineskin, between the ribaldry of both men and women in the battle of the Acropolis and the momentous issues at stake, between the constant slapstick and the very serious arguments that Lysistrata makes to the magistrate ("What of us then, / who ever in vain for our children must weep / Borne but to perish afar and in vain?"), between the strip-tease style of Myrrhine to her husband Cinesias and its political objective, between the sex-jokes and the political issues at the peace conference. Anger at the evil of war is always implicitly present, but it is almost dissolved in the dominant air of the disparateness of all the elements of life—the physical realities, the human flaws, and the saner international politics—that in their inevitable contradictions might present a hopeless situation but somehow can be accommodated in a workable way of life. The quotations are from the translation by Jack Lindsay in *The Complete Plays of Aristophanes*, ed. Moses Hadas (New York: Bantam Books, 1962), pp. 299, 307.

guide and the more sublime poet, and Euripides open to charges of
sentimentality and of diverting youth from traditional virtues to wise-acre
quibbling about important issues. Yet he also lets Euripides spoof Aeschylus' reliance on nonspeaking or little-speaking characters and his
obscure, heavy-worded style. In their often stichomythic flyting the two
sound like modern close-readers as they quote lines from their plays, one
challenging, the other defending.[4] The final decisive test—the weighing
of given lines which each submits for competition in the scales—is a
charming fantasy not calculated seriously to glorify Aeschylus and deflate
Euripides. Before being forced to make a final choice, Dionysus speaks of
the difficulty of judging, since both dramatists are his friends, and
"Neither / Would I have my enemy." He goes on, "One I think clever,
the other delights me," and "One speaks cleverly, / The other clearly."
Though he loses the first-place prize, Euripides clearly survives as a talented dramatic poet. The play almost gives up partisanship to accept
disparateness, just as it mingles much farce with the exploration of a
serious literary difference.

Like *The Frogs*, Shaw's *The Doctor's Dilemma* (1906) depicts diversity in
the world. It presents half a dozen medical doctors who have blind faith in
their different panaceas. Up to a point Shaw satirizes the whole profession
for substituting private quasi-scientific passions for a truly scientific uni-
versality. Yet the satirical impetus,* though present, is subordinate to
the ironic observation of divergencies—among the diagnostic and
therapeutic methods, between the confidence and the success of each
practitioner, and even between the conventionally expectable and the
actual attitude of a physician when his treatment fails: not remorse but
technical puzzlement. Worldly as most of these men are, they are generally naïve rather than calculating, hopeful rather than cynical. The tone is
less that of the-way-things-are-is-awful than of this-is-the-way-things-are.
Sir Patrick Cullen, almost the Shavian overvoice in this world, sums up
neatly: "A blackguard's a blackguard; an honest man's an honest man; and
neither of them will ever be at a loss for a religion or a morality to prove
that their ways are the right ways. It's the same with nations, the same
with professions, the same all the world over and always will be" (IV).

The theme of the ways of the world, managed generally through a

*Shaw's satire is most evident in the treatment of the reporter, a "young man who is disabled for
ordinary business pursuits by a congenital erroneousness which renders him incapable of describing
accurately anything he sees, or understanding or reporting accurately anything he hears" and who "has
perforce become a journalist" because journalism is "the only employment in which these defects do
not matter" (IV). The description is justified in the ensuing dialogue.

wide-angled lens focused on multiple medical figures, is treated specifically through the dualism of bohemian and bourgeois (or artist and citizen, which Shaw doubtless observed in several late Ibsen plays). As citizens, the doctors judge others by a code of reliability and honor. Hence, though charmed by the artist's wife Jennifer Dubedat, they detest her husband Louis, who in loyalty to art scorns the conventions of financial and sexual conduct and defends himself by impudent paradox. We see disparate ways of life: if we are to have both society and art, we live with unreconciled fidelities. (To make the most uncompromising case for artistic independence from social codes, Shaw lets Dubedat become a brazen liar and scrounger; then, to rescue him in human terms, Shaw makes his wife Jennifer into a modern Griselda, not only selfless and understanding, but aggressive in helping and promoting him.) When conflicting values are felt, a choice is agonizingly difficult: the newly knighted Colenso Ridgeon, who can take on only one more tuberculosis patient, has to choose between Dubedat and Dr. Blenkinsop, a money-poor, decent physician. Ridgeon loathes Dubedat but tries hard to be detached: "I'm not at all convinced that the world wouldnt be a better place if everybody behaved as Dubedat does than it is now that everybody behaves as Blenkinsop does." Sir Patrick makes a silencing reply: "Then why dont *you* behave as Dubedat does?" (II). Ridgeon saves Blenkinsop, but the play does not assert that his choice is good or bad.

Indeed, Shaw has gone on to another ambivalence, that of motives. Ridgeon is strongly attracted to Jennifer Dubedat and believes that she is attracted to him. Hence his saving Blenkinsop represents complex motives, and doubtless he oversimplifies when he tells Jennifer that he "killed" Dubedat "because I was in love with you" (V). Though this confession could trigger emotional melodrama, Shaw uses it only for a comic development: they argue about the nature of his act. Ridgeon thinks he has saved Jennifer from disillusionment with her "scoundrel . . . rascal . . . blackguard" of a husband, while Jennifer insists not only that Dubedat was her "King of Men" (the title of her biography of him) but even that Ridgeon could not have had any real influence on his living or dying. Another unresolved issue: doubleness again. Further, Ridgeon's letting Dubedat die is treated, not as a moral act, but as a practical choice in the world, as good or bad strategy. Jennifer's first reaction to Ridgeon's confession is utter astonishment that an "elderly" man ("twenty years older than I am") could be "in love," and Ridgeon, becoming virtually the self-judging comic hero, exclaims, "Dubedat:

thou art avenged!" As a further shock, Ridgeon suddenly learns from Jennifer that she has remarried, and again he is driven to a self-placing exclamation: "Then I have committed a purely disinterested murder!" Ridgeon is not satirized for secret vice disguised as a neutral professional option; rather he is treated ironically as a man who has illusions about himself—an example of the Platonic ludicrous—and has placed his bet badly. Besides, a man who can define a failure (loss of a love confidently counted on) as an inadvertent virtue ("purely disinterested murder") has a wit that fortifies him against a rejective satirical attitude. And when Shaw makes us see in pragmatic terms an action that seems *a priori* to demand a moral judgment, he applies the principle of disparateness with unique ingenuity.

II. DISPARATENESS: SUBJECTS AND OBJECTS

The four plays above illustrate two frequent types of disparateness—that of subject and object, and that of object and object. In the former, someone thinks, believes, plans, or schemes in a certain way, and actuality or outcome differs from his conception of it. In the latter, two or more different or contradictory ways of life coexist; they are more or less permanent, and no final judgment is made between or among them. Barrie's John Shand and Shakespeare's cast of "Pyramus and Thisby" have definite views of how they are performing on their stages (subject), but their sense of things is not in accord with actuality (object). Aristophanes' Aeschylus and Euripides, however, practice different dramatic modes neither of which is wholly glorified or excommunicated (object and object); likewise with the bourgeois and artistic ways of life that Shaw throws into contrast, and the half-dozen rival sure-fire therapies. In such plays, as in Behan's *Hostage* and Synge's *Playboy*,* we are invited to accept a diversity of styles in the world. None has final authority; ironic disparity rules.

The subject-object and object-object disparities do not exhaust the possibilities of comic structure. Zealous reduction of categories will not reduce the infinite variety. But these two patterns are a useful reference-point, though by no means a standard invariably to be applied.

---

*Most of the plays examined in Chapter 5 illustrate these categories. Subject and object: in *Epicoene* a utopian project, in *The White Liars* aspirations cloaked in assumed identities, in *Arms and the Man* preconceptions, and in *The Inspector General* a psychological readiness to misinterpret—all are out of line with reality. In *The Good-Natured Man* and *Squaring the Circle* characters misapply doctrines (subjective deviations), but the doctrines, far from being private illusions, have public existence (objects), though not always in tune with an actual state of affairs. *The Importance of Being Earnest* and Nichols' comedies of illness use conventions and different individual styles of action as discordant objective entities.

Aristophanes

There is an instructive contrast between Aristophanes' *The Clouds* (423 B.C.) and his *Thesmophoriazusae* (411 B.C.). The earlier play is satiric, the later essentially comic. *The Clouds* attacks the "New Education" that it attributes to Socrates and that is remarkably familiar to us today—its scientism (as we would call it), its exclusive concern with practical ends, and its antitraditionalism, which makes possible sophistries to justify acts of passion and dishonest self-serving conduct. Strepsiades wants to experience this education, marketed at Socrates' "Think-shop," in order to be able to evade his creditors (Strepsiades anticipates George Eliot's Mr. Tulliver, who wants his son Tom to be educated, that is, to be able "to wrap things up in words as aren't actionable"). He first learns that Zeus is nonexistent, that "Vortex" is "King in his place," and that the divine trinity is now composed of "Chaos, Clouds, Tongue," but he cannot follow the pedantries and preposterous notions that Aristophanes attributes to Socrates, who throws him out.[5] Strepsiades' son Pheidippides, who spends all the family money on race horses, refers to the faculty as "such loonies," but proves a better learner of "Knavery omnipotent" from Socrates and passes on to Strepsiades the techniques for logically overwhelming creditors. But then Pheidippides beats up his father and uses the new education to justify the beating; Strepsiades in a rage sets the Think-shop afire.

Since *The Clouds* includes a hit at Euripides—the father scorns him, the slick son reveres him—we might expect more anti-Euripidism in a play that turns on a clash between Athenian women and Euripides. In *Thesmophoriazusae*—"Women Celebrating the Thesmophoria," an October festival honoring Demeter and Persephone, "the twain-Home-givers"— the women denounce Euripides for having defamed them in his plays.[6] Yet Aristophanes acts mainly as a detached observer, anticipating the ambivalent *Frogs* (405 B.C.); if anything, there is still less of hostility to Euripides.*

*There are some satirical jests—for instance, those about Euripides' style, Agathon's style, and his effeminacy. Other elements are the hilarious farce in connection with Mnesilochus' being disguised as a woman, and the archetypal rescue melodrama when Euripides tries to aid Mnesilochus, captured by the women. The aid is fantastic and highbrow: Mnesilochus and Euripides re-enact, unsuccessfully of course, rescue scenes from various Euripides plays. The final peace treaty between Euripides and the women takes care of everything but a Scythian guard, who seems to act autonomously. In a musical-comedy device a dancing girl brought in by Euripides seduces the guard, Mnesilochus runs off, and the Scythian ends the play by beginning what looks like a farcical chase. The semiliterate Scythian provides considerable ethnic and dialect farce in a pattern that was to hold until the antihumorous spirit of all causes, infecting many pressure groups after mid twentieth century, brought about a cessation, probably temporary, of activity in this mode.

The women charge that Euripides "insults us all" by his portraits of women, harms them with his atheism, and so on. Mnesilochus, who appears at the festival disguised as a woman to defend his younger kinsman Euripides, replies that "we women" are really worse than Euripides has portrayed us. Aristophanes lets us see case-making and inconsistencies on both sides: the woman who said Euripides' atheism is ruining her chaplet business has to dash off to fill a special order, and another woman's "baby" turns out to be a wine-flask. On the other hand the Chorus makes some good attacks on men, on their inconsistent attitudes to women and their general inferiority. Women are more honest, for men's "purses [are] distended with cash they have filched from the state"; women are superior in domestic economy (perhaps an echo of a passage in *Lysistrata*, Aristophanes' immediately preceding play); as the mothers of heroes, women should not "remain unhonored." On the other hand, in a touch of magnanimity or at least ritual propriety, the Chorus specifically denies, as it enters "the holy festival hours," "That the garland will be flecked / With abuse of mortal men; such a thought is incorrect."

Aristophanes lets us feel that much is to be said on both sides. This prepares for the final solution by which Euripides secures the release of old Mnesilochus, whom the women have taken captive. Euripides proposes:

> Ladies, I offer terms. If well and truly
> Your honorable sex befriend me now,
> I won't abuse your honorable sex
> From this time forth forever. . . .
> That poor old man there, he's my poor old cousin.
> Let him go free, and nevermore will I
> Traduce your worthy sex; . . .

The Chorus replies, "We take your terms, . . ." This kind of accommodation is a basic comic action; different claims are accepted because neither can be wholly denied. Here the disparateness is between two objects; these are different perspectives which can be very much at odds but neither of which is dismissed. The holders of both perspectives make some good points but are partly vulnerable; neither can wholly triumph, but neither is so vulnerable as to force the dramatist into satire.

Plautus and Terence

In *Aulularia* (*The Pot of Gold*) Plautus (254–184 B.C.) goes beyond the intervening Menander and the following Terence both in expanding the farcical that is one half of the Aristophanic tradition and in adding to farce some touches of a comic sense of character.* Plautus' basic offering is a fast-paced parade of farcical staples: accidents, accusations, bawlings out, beatings, brawlings, coincidences, double entendres, misconceptions, suspicions, threats, and, above all, remarkable overhearings and nonseeings of the very visible (including a pregnancy that has gone nine months without anyone's noticing it). On the other hand, Plautus manages several departures from the formulae of farce. An uncle and nephew, Megadorus and Lyconides, are suitors for the same girl, but the uncle, instead of being the usual nasty January character, is not only a decent fellow but a sage observer of worldly follies.[7] More important, however, Plautus' treatment of Euclio (the source of Molière's miser) makes an interesting move from the satirical toward the comic: Euclio is out-of-line but still is representative; he departs from a norm, yet his trouble is a normalcy gone haywire. A poor man, he finds a pot of gold, and it affects him badly: it makes him watchful, fearful, suspicious, and generally miserable. The abuse and blows that he lavishes on whoever is vulnerable are old farcical routines, but his smelling of plots everywhere and of course in the most innocent actions goes beyond the puppetry of stinginess farce and becomes ironically human: self-protectiveness backfires and makes the world ever less safe. Euclio has no real power to injure others (in fact, it may be that in the missing fifth act he turns out routinely benevolent), but his neurotic fearfulness and self-punitive anxiety make him misinterpret everybody. Plautus thus manages a representative disparateness of subject and object.

*Despite the good repute of the Menandrine fragments, *Dyscolus*, the one surviving complete play by Menander (ca. 342–292 B.C.), does not have in it much more than routine mishaps, misunderstandings, quick angers, flytings, beatings, and triumphs in which the participants are hardly more than puppets. The title character Cnemon—the "grouch" or "misanthrope"—is routinely satirized, and a ducking in a well helps him to a mechanical reform. We scent a touch of character when his reform is followed by a relapse, but this seems contrived—only an occasion for sadistic persuaders to bring Cnemon back into line (i.e., make him attend his daughter's wedding). Once, however, he is allowed a moment of the humanizing complexity that would appear in Molière's misanthrope. Cnemon makes an apparently sound criticism of a well-to-do family's preparations for a religious festival: "Now there's religion for you! Bring a lot / of bedding and a barrelful of wine. The hypocrites! / They think it's God they're honoring. It really is themselves." This insight in a professional grouch moves him an iota toward comic status. The quotation is from *Menander's Dyscolus*, ed. and trans. Warren E. Blake, Philological Monographs No. 24 (American Philological Association, 1966), lines 446–48.

As for Terence's *Phormio*, commented on after *Aulularia*, it depends mainly on the ingenious intrigues of a clever slave Geta and a tricky parasite Phormio to help young men get or stay married despite parental opposition. Phormio was a model for Molière's Scapin and a forerunner of Jonson's Mosca. One girl turns out to be the destined bride of the young man—a forerunner of the Horace-Agnès plot in Molière's *The School for Wives* and the Absolute-Languish affair in Sheridan's *The Rivals*. The machinery is predominantly farcical.

Euclio suffers from an acute case of nonclinical paranoia (all readers are struck by the fine fantasy of his bludgeoning a rooster which, scratching near the hidden gold, seems to Euclio an agent of cooks bent on robbery). Thus he is a pre-Jonson Jonsonian humor all but humanized. Insofar as he is understood and recognized rather than merely derided, we may say that he evokes comic acceptance.

Praised as Terence (ca. 190–159 B.C.) usually is for his plotting, for his enlargement of emotional life, and for his reduction of Plautine brawling, only two brief episodes in his *Phormio* (161 B.C.) involve a comic sense of disparateness. Demipho, a distressed parent, seeks help of three "advisers": they speak to him in such safely generalized and jargonish ways that he has to conclude, "I'm much more bewildered than before."[8] Again, Phaedria, who has not yet raised money to buy the slave girl Pamphila he dotes on, envies Antipho, who has already married his sweetheart Phanium; but Antipho, who fears paternal anger and hates to be "suffering this everlasting anxiety," envies the freedom of unmarried Phaedria. As Phaedria puts it to Antipho, "Other men are wretched because they haven't got the object of their love, but you're unhappy because you've got too much of it" (II.15 ff.). This kind of leap to the comic observation of divergent attitudes—the disparateness of objects—is a happy shift from the whirling of plot machinery that for the most part treats human nature as an automatic stimulus-and-response system.

"The Second Shepherds' Play"

The comic possibilities of medieval drama are nowhere better actualized than in the Wakefield *Second Shepherds' Play* (ca. 1425–50), which is so familiar that what it achieves may be obscured by what we all know about it. We all know about its bold juxtaposition of the farcical (all the details of the sheep-stealing and sheep-hiding action) and the straightforwardly and tenderly devout (the shepherds' visit to the newborn Christ child). We know that the former is a parody of the latter, with an imaginative reversal of the central event: the climactic birth of the divine-human child in animal quarters preceded by the "birth" of an animal in a human bed, the miracle secularized as a rogue's temporary deception of honest men. Beneath the jests and the worship and the translation of sacred into profane lies a great exercise in the acceptance of the disparate—of the two vast areas of reality that are often at odds, religious myth and the secular world (again the two objects). Here there is none of the Christian rejection of the world (which we noted in chap. 2) as unregenerate or hostile to the spirit; rather, in its practice of daily tasks and pursuit of subsistence and survival, the world is granted a liveliness and immediacy which would prevent even a very doctrinaire "believer" from decrying it. In fact, the shepherds are able both to carry on their daily life as if it were a final reality, and then to transcend it when mystery calls—the Angel's summons to Bethlehem.

The length of the first part of the play—about 630 out of some 750 lines—might seem to declare earthly life the important thing and eternal life worth no more than brief ritual attention. But this possible implication of proportion is resisted by position: the Christ story has the final climactic placement. Besides, it is climactic in spirit: there is nothing flat and routine about the visit to the stable, for the naturalness and unpretentious reverence of the shepherds give the scene a great vitality. Again, the parodic birth scene might seem to devalue the biblical story. But if the dramatist's bias were antimythic, he would handle the birth scene differently. If the stolen animal were a calf or a pig, for instance, the grotesqueness might indeed diminish the Christ-child story. But Mak's wife's "newborn" is a lamb: a lesser lamb of God as it were, to be sacrificed that Mak and kin may live—the playful jesting with a mystery that is possible when spontaneous faith has not stiffened into humorless institutional defensiveness or been eroded away by time. The shepherds' secular life is subtly validated by the way in which it is taken over into a fine ritual in the stable: the shepherds' presents to the Christ child all come from nonsacred spheres—a bob of cherries, a bird, a tennis ball. Thus the secular and the redeemed merge.

The shepherds' existence has a vivifying inner disparateness rather than a desultory homogeneity. The first shepherd mourns the hard weather and the economic problems of his class; the second complains about married life (as does Mak later); these two suspect the honesty of the third and younger shepherd, another sufferer from the weather. The three constitute an in-group of solid citizens, in contrast with poor but agile and tricky Mak; yet Mak, the outsider-rogue, gains the acceptance owed to the lively, entertaining, imaginative special personality, parasitic though he may be. Mak is picaro, gamesman, actor—an earlier and less sophisticated Falstaff, doomed to eventual ritual chastisement, but meanwhile the energetic and refreshing disturber of routines that have to be maintained, routines that we accept but enjoy seeing shaken. To leap recklessly into anachronism, the "Wakefield master" has managed to portray the confrontation of bourgeois and bohemian and to give each his due. The disparateness of objects distantly foreshadows that in Synge's *Playboy*.

III. SHAKESPEARE: THREE TREATMENTS OF LOVE

Shakespeare makes three somewhat different applications of the comic principle in three plays on love and its counterforces—*Love's Labour's Lost* (ca. 1593–94), *Much Ado about Nothing* (1598–99), and *Measure for Measure* (1604). While all three rely partly on the farcical effects of Shakespeare's earliest years,* all move quickly into a less simple comic level. *Love's Labour's Lost* employs primarily the disparateness between subject and object—between what the men think they can do and what they actually do, and between a sense of easy triumph and the greater difficulty of actual achievement. In *Much Ado* the same comic procedure appears: what Benedick and Beatrice take to be their convictions have less impact than other forces upon their vital actions. But *Much Ado* shadows the scene with the graver discrepancy between Hero's actual virtue and Don John's slander of her, between the fact and the misconception of it caused by false witness. This situation is intensified in *Measure for Measure*: while Don John gratifies himself by getting sexual misconduct charged to Hero, Angelo and Claudio try to blackmail Isabella into sexual misconduct, Angelo to gratify himself, and Claudio to save himself from Angelo. When a false charge of illicit sex is replaced by pressure for illicit sex, comedy obviously takes on a more difficult assignment.

"Love's Labour's Lost"

While charting four parallel love affairs, *Love's Labour's Lost* also jests at malapropism, pretentious language (historically, euphuism), pedantic language, Petrarchan sonneteering. Yet these departures from a norm of effective speech are not savaged. The aspiring stylists are innocuous; they lack the power that would call for satire (in a classroom, Holofernes would more likely be a butt than a tyrant). Besides, the language of the lovers themselves is so infected with puns, verbal tricks, quibbles (as Johnson called them), that the lines of the lesser characters seem fantastic variants

---

*In *Love's Labour's Lost* there are the mechanical quickness of the pairings of lovers, the misdeliverings of love letters, and the verbal sleight-of-hand. In *Much Ado* there are the automatic belief in the flimsy case against Hero, the role of drunken babbling and lucky overhearing in the solution, and the mental and verbal habits of the police. In *Measure for Measure* there are the simplicities of Elbow and Froth, the wisecracks of low-life characters, the automatic rascalities of Lucio (the "Fantastic"), and the gallows humor of Abhorson, Pompey, and Barnardine.

on the verbal high jinks of the lovers rather than censurable follies. When Holofernes says to Dull, "Thou hast spoken no word all this while," Dull's reply, "Nor understood none neither, sir" (V.i.156–57), is less a proof of his dullness than a plain man's comeuppance to a gaudy-worded man, and hence a parallel to the games by which the women deflate the lovers' fancy styles. Yet the women also leap and spring in the tireless verbal gymnastics—the homonymic sallies, the onomastic tours de force, the stichomythic fencing, the high-spirited logomachy.

The four-ply central action turns, of course, on the defeat of the male quartet's initial vows to spend three womanless years as "fellow-scholars," "living in philosophy," and seeking "study's god-like recompence" (I.i.17, 32, 58). The men are not foolishly ignorant of worldly alternatives, whose skillful voice is Biron (Berowne). On the one hand Biron laments "barren tasks, too hard to keep, / Not to see ladies, study, fast, not sleep" (47–48); he gaily portrays the delights of love and then concludes that he has "for barbarism spoke more / Than for that angel, knowledge, you can say" (112–13). So from the beginning there is an awareness of and a tension between disparate values available to man. The King of Navarre, the leader of the scholars, tries to accommodate both values when the Princess of France, of course accompanied by three ladies, arrives on an important mission. If the visitors are excluded from the court by the men's vows, they may at least reside on the grounds—a solution in the spirit of comedy. It is not long, of course, before the hopeful scholars backslide and become hopeful lovers. We might say that they are satirized for having attempted a preposterous program of self-improvement, or, on the other hand, that with some self-recognition they have perceived the folly of a one-dimensional life and in the new commitment to love have found a better over-all adjustment to the world.

These readings are plausible enough. Yet both have the same weakness: the men's monastic-academic regimen is false and is set up only to be knocked down. But this is too easy an operation; it assumes the quick, mechanical responses of farce, absolutizes the value of young love, denies that of study, and thus trivializes the play. To settle for so simple a reading is not to see that Shakespeare very carefully guards against triviality; he is entirely clear-headed about the fast-paced apostasy. He makes Biron jest about "men forsworn" (IV.iii.385), the Princess of France speak of the men's sudden change of direction as "wit turn'd fool" (V.ii.71), and Rosaline remark ironically, "The blood of youth burns not with such excess / As gravity's revolt to wantonness" (V.ii.73–74). Hence the ridicule of the men for half of the long Act V, scene ii, combine as it does sexual play with a savoring of power, is also a chastisement of turncoats who in effect change "I could not love thee, dear, so much, / Loved I not honor more," to "I could not love thee, dear, so much, / Loved I my studies still." The ladies sense that fickleness may be transferable from one realm to another, and they demonstrate this in a playful symbolism when by wearing masks they betray the men into declarations to the wrong women. The men take identities for granted because they are in haste, and haste is not compatible with truth. So there is seriousness as well as playfulness in various statements by the Princess: "Nor God, nor I, delights in perjur'd men"; "So much I hate a breaking cause to be / Of heavenly oaths, vow'd with integrity"; "Your oath once broke, you force not to forswear" (346, 355–56, 440). And Biron acknowledges, "Thus pour the stars down plagues for perjury," and "Now, to our perjury to add more terror, / We are again forsworn, in will and error" (394, 470–71).

The men's fault, of course, is the breaking of a vow rather than of a specific vow to a period of solitary study. But the comic way of entertaining different values is present too. The young men do not make a foolish mistake in seeking an intellectual retreat, for their plan answers to a constant and important part of human nature; rather they absolutize study and endeavor to pursue it with a rigor that puts too much strain on the rest of their human nature. Still, when they break down, they want not to be "forsworn," as Biron says they are. The King commands Biron to "prove / Our loving lawful, and our faith not torn" (IV.iii.284–85), and Biron responds with an eighty-line exaltation of women in which the key statement is "They are the books, the arts, the academes, / That show, contain, and nourish all the world" (352–53). Biron really anticipates Sir Richard Steele's famous praise of Lady Elizabeth Hastings: "To love her was a liberal education." * In loving the women the four exanchorites will serve the very ends of their monastic triennium and thus hold to the spirit of their oath.

This delightful praise says in effect that a true value may be served in an easy way. But Biron says this, not Shakespeare. The larger drama reasserts the value and the not-easy discipline that it demands, for in the final action the men accept a regimen not unlike that of the triennium. When the death of the Princess' father is reported and she prepares to leave, the

---

*Steele's apothegm was wittily recast by Oscar Wilde. In Act III of *Lady Windermere's Fan* Cecil Graham says, "The world is perfectly packed with good women. To know them is a middle-class education."

young men are once again in haste, and their sentiment is voiced by the King: "Now, at the latest minute of the hour, / Grant us your loves" (V.2.797–98). The Princess denies his request promptly, though not unkindly, and gives him a year to think it over and see if he will then renew an "offer made in heat of blood," for "Your oath I will not trust" (810, 804). Not only a year, but—here is the key point—a year to be spent in "some forlorn and naked hermitage, / Remote from all the pleasures of the world" (805–6). The three ladies prescribe the same year's delay for their lovers. Rosaline adjures Biron to discipline his "gibing spirit" (868) and "idle scorns" (875), and specifies how he shall spend the time:

> Visit the speechless sick and still converse
> With groaning wretches; and your task shall be,
> With all the fierce endeavour of your wit
> To enforce the pained impotent to smile.
>
> [861–64]

As Biron puts it, he is to "jest a twelvemonth in a hospital" (881). It is one year instead of three, but it is a period out of the world, conditions perhaps monastic, the men undergoing a discipline such as they had fled. The value of their original commitment is in effect restored, and the disparateness of the ways in the world is recognized. The men's breaking their vows was a "dear guiltiness" (801), but still a guiltiness; love does not instantly wipe out all other loyalties.

"Much Ado about Nothing"

Much Ado complicates the drama of love by presenting not only those who misunderstand themselves (continuing, with variations, the subject-object disparity of *Love's Labour's Lost* and *The Taming of the Shrew*) but also one man who in congenital resentfulness creates dangerous misunderstandings. Thus it uses a larger canvas of the diversities that beset the ease we crave. Don John first tries to make Claudio suspicious of Don Pedro (who is to woo Hero for Claudio) and, when that gambit fails, stages a scene in which a mock-Hero entertains a lover and which, seen by Pedro and Claudio, leads Claudio, supported by Pedro, to reject Hero publicly. John's evil will is a grave new element in comedy; he anticipates the envy and malice of Iago, and hence the play might well move into melodrama or tragedy. The problem is how comedy can "accept" evil and remain comedy. It does this when it sees evil as what we might call a fact of life rather than as a destructive aberration which must draw all emotional energy into conflict against it.

Compare Don John and Iago: Don John does not plan a thorough and remorseless campaign but gambles all on one trick. He has to use an agent, the agent is caught by the police, and Don John runs. There is no follow-through; short-term evil is discoverable in time. Discoverability-in-time is essential, but the mode of discovery also contributes to tone. Shakespeare reduces the melodramatic possibility by using farcical devices: drunken blabbing by Don John's agent Borachio, and malapropistic police who improbably capture the wrongdoer, hold on to him, and extract a confession. As if in penance for these lucky events, Shakespeare introduces an unlucky event with a little more basis in character: the governor Leonato, Hero's father, is bored by the long-windedness of Dogberry and Verges as they report on their prisoner and cuts them off before they provide the information that could prevent the near-disaster.

But if good luck and farce fend off the noncomic, the affirmative contribution to comic tone is the essential good sense of some of those allied with Hero. A charge of infidelity is an occasion on which good sense is rare. Don Pedro and Claudio roar with the voice of "honor." Honor, be it self-aggrandizing or self-obligating, has no affiliations with good sense, which also is absent in Leonato's credulity and high-sounding self-pity. But Shakespeare has all three brandish words instead of weapons; thus others can still use their heads even amidst the swirling rhetoric of those about them who have lost theirs. Benedick is the first to use his head; introducing a theme that occupied Shakespeare from the early comedies into the late tragedies,[9] he urges Leonato to "be patient" (IV.i.145), a behest echoed by the Friar (256). Beatrice affirms that Hero "is belied" (148); the Friar argues calmly and persuasively that Hero lies "guiltless here / Under some biting error" (171–72) and insists, "There is some strange misprision in the princes" (187); Benedick rightly suspects that "The practice of it lives in John the Bastard" (190), is sure that Hero "is wrong'd" (261), and, faced with Beatrice's demand that he "kill Claudio" (291), does not easily undertake a mission which could turn the affair bloody. The best headwork is shown by the Friar, who proposes that Hero be reported dead and spells out the psychological advantages of the ploy: "Change slander to remorse" (213). In effect, they live with the imputation instead of taking fatal arms against it; this practical good sense allows time for truth to come out and so prevents a noncomic conclusion.*

*It is significant that Don John all but disappears from the play; only at the end do we hear that he is "ta'en" and will be brought back to face the music. But the play makes nothing dramatically of the punishment of Don John; it is as if his conduct were less an evil to be dealt with severely than "one of those things."

Benedick and Beatrice's hesitancy to believe evil of Hero is ironically related to their hesitancy to believe good of each other: the skepticism is much the same. Their initial skepticism of love helps generate the witty skirmishing that, since it both opens and, with a change of mood, closes the play (I.i; V.iv), surrounds the more conventional Hero-Claudio plot and has a greater influence on the over-all tone. But the skepticism which is advantageous in one situation is inadequate in another; that is, between lovers good sense needs to be supplemented by another element also conducive to comic effect. Understanding as Beatrice and Benedick are, they do not understand themselves fully—that is, their need for a yoke of feeling as well as for independence of thought, their need to accept the ways of the world as well as make witty sallies against them. Their independent criticalness is not devalued; rather it has to be joined with an unlike mode of response. Their ironic surrender of what had seemed like ultimate rationality to them is brought about ironically: they learn the truth about themselves through the plotting of others less gifted than they, and to the pleasure of dueling they add the desire to reciprocate (each uses the verb *requite*) which enables people to live with each other. Furthermore, the plotting that brings together Benedick and Beatrice resembles the plotting that temporarily separates Claudio and Hero: stories that subordinate pure fact to an end in view. That is, people may plot to make a match or unmake it; in comedy, plotting is neutral and can be used to hide truth from those who should know it or to reveal truth to those who have to learn it.

"Measure for Measure"

While we sometimes hear of the "tragic" elements in *Measure for Measure*, in fact the events that appear to fall outside the ordinary domain of comedy belong mainly to melodrama. The central actions of Angelo and Isabella do not turn on the inner dividedness that begets tragic action. The emotions of the characters are rooted in the pressure of external situations, which are meant to keep the audience in constant suspense about outcomes.* Equally melodramatic is the basic conflict of tyrant

---

*Angelo puts up very little fight when lustful feelings supplant judicial ones, and the discomfort of his later ruminations, which are quickly over, turns more on practical dangers than moral issues (IV.iv.23–37). When he is caught, his self-judgments do seem tragic, but they are too brief and pat to be truly so. Isabella is so committed to chastity that she feels almost no counterpressure in her brother's plea for a sexual concession that will save his life. These are some of the crucial situations inviting suspense over outcomes: the first and second meetings between Isabella and Angelo, the interview between Isabella and Claudio, the Duke's return as general savior. The focus is less on the process than on the end-results—a perennial theatrical mode.

and victims—Angelo as utterly rigid enforcer, as merciless would-be seducer of Isabella (II.iv), as wholly treacherous bargainer (he orders the death of Claudio after the midnight sexual encounter guaranteed to save him). This externalized conflict is happily resolved by an externalized agency: the disguised Duke is the most ingenious and theatrical deus ex machina—in this case a savior from Act II on instead of a last-minute preventer of injustice—before modern secret agents. The problem is how such materials, which seem bound to produce another generic mode, can be assimilated within the comic form. The problem is made no easier when the villain, foiled, seems actually to be rewarded—by regaining life, freedom from the burden of murderer, and a bride who blesses him in her joy of having him (as well as permitting him the pleasure of restitution).

The "happy ending" which we associate with comedy seems a little too happy. What goes on here, however, is at bottom an "acceptance" of Angelo: when he is brought into the rather crowded fold of happy marriages, his evil will, most narrowly saved from evil results, is in effect treated, not as an intolerable deviancy, but as a recognizable human possibility to be lived with. The man of inflexible principle takes on a new humanity, though not a lovable one, as lustful man; in him, the principle of hard-nosed justice is paradoxically converted into the principle of satisfying desire and saving oneself by any means. We may resist, but we are encouraged not to reject Angelo as an inadmissible moral alien. When Isabella pleads for Angelo, she "forgives" him, and forgiveness implies some degree of forgivability. What she forgives is a "bad intent" that did not ripen into action but "perish'd by the way" (V.i.456–58). So we are to accept evil will and kinds of self-serving that are at least unpalatable.

This tendency of the play is more overt in the treatment of Claudio. His willingness, indeed eagerness, to have his sister Isabella prefer her adultery to his death is not *a priori* "acceptable," but Shakespeare works hard to reduce our critical distance from Claudio by writing for him the most moving pleas to her and descriptions of the horrors of death (III.i.118 ff.). When, utterly rejected by Isabella—who is here as harsh an enforcer of her rule of chastity as is Angelo of the law against fornication—Claudio can say sadly, "Let me ask my sister pardon" (173), his self-judgment adds strength to the question which the earlier part of the scene implicitly asks the audience, "Can you believe that in the same situation you would have acted far differently?" On the other hand, his sister, in rejecting him, falls into a highly unattractive style, so hotly rule-enforcing and so chillily unsympathetic as to transform love of virtue into self-love. Thus Isabella and Claudio, as well as Angelo, test our ability to acknowledge unpalatable conduct as belonging to, rather than violating the nature of, ordinary humanity. In addition we have to see that the way of life of Lucio, a Falstaff become urbanized and slick, and the views of life of Overdone and Pompey are not going to be sharply contradicted by ongoing Viennese life.

Here, then, is a quite emphatic disparateness between what the action of the play accepts and what men are ordinarily inclined to acknowledge as acceptable; the plot threatens certain preconceptions that are important to our self-belief. Hence *Measure for Measure* has always imposed some burdens on its public, and the burden has been handled by various expedients. One is the idea that the play has somehow gone awry, perhaps fallen into "cynicism," a charge that lets us substitute regret for consent. A more literary adjustment is to see the play as moving toward or into a subcategory, "dark comedy" or "black comedy" (the technical differentia of which is the acceptance of what we characteristically take to be unacceptable). There is another possibility: we could regard *Measure for Measure* as moving toward the embracing and unillusioned sense of humanity that produced the great comedies of the Restoration. One detail points in this direction: Lucio's fate, "Marrying a punk" (V.i.528), is like that of Tattle in Congreve's *Love for Love*.

IV. MOLIÈRE AND WYCHERLEY

To move from *Measure for Measure* to partly analogous plays by Molière (*The School for Wives*) and Wycherley (*The Country Wife*) is to shift from a man's scheme to gratify his lust to men's schemes for preventing the gratification of lust by women supposed to lack all immunity to it. Both later dramatists look at the male theory that ignorance/innocence is the ultimate chastity belt. But the two plays handle the defeat of the illusion in quite different ways. To go from *Measure for Measure* to *The School for Wives* (1662) is to find a more familiar playing with theatrical counters and hence a reduced call on the comic imagination. Then to move on to *The Country Wife* (1675) is to find a less reassuring view of how the world goes and a comedy almost as taxing as *Measure for Measure*.*

Molière's "The School for Wives"

The School for Wives uses much farcical material, including "farcical

---

*Wycherley can greatly reduce Molière's demands on our imagination. *The Plain Dealer*, revising *The Misanthrope*, thins down a complex protagonist into a self-righteous denouncer of vice and so deserts the comic spirit. Many critics have observed the inferiority of *The Plain Dealer* to *The Misanthrope*.

irony," and of course it satirizes Arnolphe, the know-it-all middle-aged schemer who seeks to guarantee a cuckoldry-free marriage by acquiring a young, subservient, and doltish bride.* Yet even such a callous calculator is not entirely a butt of satire, for Molière takes several steps that almost bring him within the fold as a comic figure. Arnolphe is not only the crafty self-server but at times also the man of feeling genuinely moved by the charms of the young lady (a development partly sentimentalized in Sheridan's treatment of Sir Peter Teazle's love in *The School for Scandal*). In a sort of oh-my-ducats-oh-my-daughter soliloquy, Arnolphe alternates between revengeful scheming and an admission of genuine attraction to Agnès: "The loss of her entails a double hell: / My honor suffers, and my love as well," and amidst self-pity and resentment he can admit, "In spite of all, I love her to distraction!" Fearing that he may lose her, he prays for "Such patient strength as some poor men display." [10] At such moments he looks less like an impugnable "humor" and more like a full human being given to understandable procedural errors.

Again, Arnolphe's efforts to bring Agnès up as stupidly obedient do no damage; Agnès is never a sad victim whose presence would create a harsh satire of Arnolphe. On the contrary, there is a charming irony: the slave-education foisted on Agnès has somehow created, or at least not hindered the development of, an attractively free and direct woman, one whose spontaneous feeling enables her to recognize and respond to the honest affection of Horace and, more than that, to defuse all of Arnolphe's selfish arguments and go right to the heart of the matter. Though she resents his efforts to keep her ignorant, her "born yesterday" sort of wise naïveté raises the nice issue of whether some other education, less restrictive in intent, might really have been better for her. The ironic working-out of wrong intentions—which reveals the disparateness of subjective plans and objective events—obviously does not make the intender "acceptable," but it diminishes the need for a noncomic rejective action against him.

In a sideline action of some intellectual appeal Molière presents a clash

---

*"Farcical irony" depends upon ignorance prearranged by the author rather than mistakes of judgment. Horace does not know that Arnolphe wants to marry his ward Agnès; so Horace, who loves Agnès, makes Arnolphe his confidant and asks his help. None of these principals knows that Agnès is the daughter of Enrique, who decides to marry her to a friend's son who no one knows is Horace. So Arnolphe, who does not know who Horace's girl is, favors a marriage that confounds his own plans, and Horace bucks a marriage that is just what he wants (the idea of the secret sweetheart as the designated bride goes back, of course, to Roman farce).

Interestingly enough, the satirized Arnolphe is something of a satirist himself. He sneers at cuckolds and plans to triumph over them brilliantly by bringing up Agnès without the training of brains which he is sure is the main source of infidelity in wives. So he doubly illustrates the Hobbesian doctrine of laughter as superiority; he laughs thus at husbands, and we laugh thus at him.

of attitudes which has a bearing on generic form. Arnolphe sneers at cuckolds and is sure he can prevent being cuckolded: his style is that of a hero of melodrama. Arguing against him is his friend Chrysalde, Agnès' uncle, the voice of good sense often heard in Molière plays. Chrysalde's ground is not moral but practical: man cannot prevent misfortune and misconduct, and he does better to live with what happens. "Fate gives men horns, and fate can't be withstood; / To fret about such matters does no good" (I.i). Molière protects Chrysalde against a charge of cynicism by making him say that he also "may condemn / Loose wives, and husbands who put up with them" and will not "endure the wrongs which some weak men endure" (I.i). Later Chrysalde tries again to persuade Arnolphe that his obsessive fear of cuckoldry only causes needless anguish, insisting that, if this misfortune should occur, "to a man of sense, / There's nothing crushing in such accidents," and "It can be lived with, if one has the wit / To take it calmly, and make the best of it." He speaks, as comedy often does, for "A middle way that's favored by the wise," since it's "wiser to avoid extremes." One extreme is indignant public outcry: "They vent their grievances with savage fury, / Calling the whole world to be judge and jury." The other extreme is to be too complaisant, as are "husbands who permit / Such scandal, and who take a pride in it," and who are excessively friendly to "their wives' latest gallants," thus "offending / Society, which properly resents / Displays of laxity and impudence" (IV.viii).

These two extremes correspond exactly to generic forms: to take violent arms against misconduct is the way of melodrama, and to welcome misconduct is the way of black comedy. The middle way is that of comedy: putting up with the unpredictable events that interfere with an imaginable perfection of life. I think that the play asks us to take cuckoldry less as a literal event than as a strong symbol of the disparity between what may happen and what we would ideally like. But if Chrysalde's program seems to invite a tolerance of what some readers find intolerable,* then it is needful to repeat what has been said before: that to practice the acceptance of disparateness which creates comedy is always to risk the overacceptance which creates black comedy. Boundaries waver.

Wycherley's "The Country Wife"

In Molière, however, cuckoldry is only a feared possibility. Wycherley actualizes it. His Arnolphe and Agnès are Pinchwife and Mrs. Margery

---

*For example, Richard Wilbur, the brilliant translator, regards Chrysalde's "discourses about cuckoldry . . . both as frequently dubious 'reasoning' and as bear-baiting" (Introduction, p. xiii).

Pinchwife: the cuckoldry-preventer and his innocent rural bride. The Pinchwifes are visiting in London, where everything conspires to defeat a husband plotting to preserve his wife's virtue. His strongest antagonist, as in Molière, is the feeling of the girl herself. But whereas Agnès' ingenuous feelings make her respond to a charming and honest young man, Mrs. Pinchwife's draw her to the city's professional cuckold-maker, Horner (his name is allegorical, as are various other elements in a play more devoted to making points wittily than to ordering the plot), and stimulate her ingenuity in reciprocating his moves and initiating others of her own. Meanwhile Horner, having spread a rumor that he is sexually incompetent, becomes the lover of Lady Fidget (Sir Jasper's wife), Mrs. Dainty Fidget (his sister), and Mrs. Squeamish, whom their menfolk are happy to entrust to so innocuous a male companion. Threatened disasters are staved off; at the end the men, temporarily undeceived about Horner, are comfortably redeceived. Adultery goes on, and ignorance is bliss.

This state of affairs has troubled later readers, who have responded variously: *The Country Wife* is immoral, it is purely cynical, it is a bitter satire, it plays a game unrelated to life, it records life in a distant era to which it is not cricket to apply the moral rules of later times. Yet several qualities keep the play from yielding patiently to such single-minded descriptions. It has too much vivacity—in wit, in thought, in the depiction of various human tendencies—to survive merely as a cool camera or hot whiplash of its times; in it surely, as in Aristophanes with the necessary differences, there are comic ways of doing things that take it beyond the period piece. Insofar as it is satirical, it is not time-bound: the lustful women, who identify virtue with not being found out in their affairs, are satirized for their hypocrisy—a perennial theme in satire. ". . . women of honour . . . are only chary of their reputations, not their persons," says Horner (I), who interestingly enough is the chief scorner in the cast, and who continues to play lively variations on the theme that honor is a protective mask only. Horner is committed to seeing things as they are, to undermining all pretenses. To make a seducer a satirist is ingenious, but still Horner as satirist is suspect: he is less the disinterested voice of truth than a man who needs to prove a doctrine for his own sense of triumph. Besides, hypocrisy tends to become less a vice in itself than the occasional style of a widespread self-interest. While for many self-interest means quick sexual gratification, for Sir Jasper Fidget it means escaping from his wife and having freedom for other pursuits, for Pinchwife the negative triumph of personal freedom from an endemic cuckoldry, and for Sparkish a pride in himself as the nonjealous man of fashion. However, these various desires and vanities, create discomfort and anxiety though they do, still are not really injurious to anyone; hence the actions do not demand the sympathy for victims that would lead to a substantial satirical effect.

Does *The Country Wife*, then, simply portray a group of people so content with immediate and one-dimensional satisfactions, with petty games and petty egotisms, that the tone is cynical? Some of this tone is of course there, and yet there are also elements that work against it, for instance, the Harcourt-Alithea-Sparkish triangle. Alithea (Truth) falls in love with Harcourt but feels bound to Sparkish, her fiancé, by her honor and by her respect for his freedom from jealousy. Her "honor" clearly is not the kind that Horner debunks; it means obligation. Sparkish's absence of jealousy appears a genuine virtue in contrast with Pinchwife's obsessive fear of cuckoldry. Harcourt uses various intrigues to get Alithea or at least to prevent her marriage to Sparkish; his object is not the liaison that most of the others seek, but marriage. Since Alithea is firm in her loyalty, it takes some typical clever-servant machinations by her maid Lucy, who sees that Sparkish is inferior to Harcourt, to create a situation in which nonjealous Sparkish becomes jealous after all. Harcourt then takes over, and his marriage to Alithea seems likely. Though Wycherley underplays this action, as if doing penance for the sentimentality of the Fidelia-Manly affair in *The Plain Dealer*, it is clear that this world does not exclude a love which is more than transient sex. As a matter of fact, when Mrs. Pinchwife escapes from her husband's arms into Horner's, she believes—in an irony almost pathetic—not that she is providing and receiving sexual service, but finding a better husband.

The continual lively wit helps undercut the cynical tendency. Harcourt's simile opens up the facts in two worlds: "I see all women are like these of the Exchange; who to enhance the price of their commodities, report to their fond customers offers which were never made 'em" (III.ii). When Pinchwife complains, "I could never keep a whore to myself," Horner retorts, "So, then you only married to keep a whore to yourself" (I). Though the worldlings may act as if commonplace sex were all, they talk as if clearsightedness in all matters were more important than sex. Characters seeking both to be unillusioned and to speak well do not argue a despairing playwright. Nor does a mind which has an active sense of paradox: for the most part, the treatment of Sparkish involves a fresh look at the apparent virtue of nonjealousy. Carried to a logical extreme, nonjealousy can become a tedious affectation, a failure of legitimate concern, and finally a rejection of good sense. It is a fine moment when Alithea, shocked by Sparkish's blindness to a rival's actions, exclaims, "Invincible stupidity!" (IV.i).* Such bounciness of observation resists a tone of cynical despair.

The Country Wife achieves a comic tone by observing the types of amatory behavior without making them deplorable or injurious. As the Harcourt-Alithea affair shows, Wycherley can imagine a more grown-up alternative to a lowest-common-denominator sexuality, but he does not make Harcourt and Alithea either censure the others or propose to leave the world.† On the other hand, Wycherley does not picture the sex intriguers as home free in an untroubled life of pleasure. Horner's mistresses are not happy to find themselves constituting a harem instead of each one's luxuriating in an exclusive love-nest, and Margery Pinchwife's not yet cured habit of truth-telling may at any time give the whole show away. Horner too must pay a price for his pleasure. If his scheme is to work, he cannot acknowledge the truth to any man; so he must endure endless jesting about his "impotence," and his lines that close the play are more than a clever jingle: "But he who aims by women to be priz'd, / First by the men, you see, must be despis'd." Profits have their penalties,

---

*For a while the reader suspects that Wycherley is anticipating the brilliant reversal of Molière's *Misanthrope* in Christopher Hampton's *The Philanthropist* (1970): Hampton turns Alceste, Molière's watchful and censorious lover, into Philip, a lover so mild and permissive that his girl doubts his love and his fitness for her. Likewise Wycherley seems on the way to showing Sparkish defeated by the very virtue which he and his girl make into an absolute. So we sense a falling off when Wycherley retreats from this possible paradox to conventional actions: Sparkish breaks with Alithea in a fit of standardized jealousy. It is not unreasonable to suppose that Alceste, the model for Manly in *The Plain Dealer*, was still present in Wycherley's imagination. Pinchwife's couplet at the end of *The Country Wife*—"For my own sake fain would I all believe; / Cuckolds, like lovers, should themselves deceive"—is psychologically very close to Alceste's plea to Célimène, "Pretend, pretend, that you are just and true, / And I shall make myself believe in you" (IV.iii in the Wilbur translation of *The Misanthrope*).

†Both, indeed, implicitly accept "the world" as normative. Alithea feels that if she jilted Sparkish, her "reputation would suffer in the world"; Harcourt retorts that if she does marry Sparkish, her "reputation suffers in the world," for Sparkish is "contemptible to all the world" (II). To her, that is, the world provides a code of honorable conduct; to him, the world is the voice of good sense. In comedy generally, either meaning may come to the fore. People who know that they are vulnerable tend, not to deny the world, but to impute unamiable motives to it. Lady Fidget: "'Tis a nasty world" (II); "'tis a wicked, censorious world" (IV.iii); and women must "deceive the world" (V.iv). They have a sense that there are regulatory voices which, though used unkindly, may not be ignored; this is quite different from the cynic's sense that everything goes, and reputation does not matter. There is a charming irony when Sparkish unconsciously gives the world divine status: his favorite oath, which he uses in every act after Act I, is "by the world." Likewise Horner asserts that "bigots in honour . . . fear the eye of the world more than the eye of Heaven" (IV.iii); that is to say, of course, that the rules are those of comedy, not of tragedy. In no other play is the word *world* more frequently used: repeatedly in emphatic statements ("best in the world," etc.) and in value statements ("not for the world," etc.).

not in moral retribution, but in the practical difficulties of managing the ways of the world for special gains.

We can profitably read Horner as a picaro, as a con man in the world of sex. His brightness surely gives him the attractiveness that the rogue must have if he is not to shrink into the simple bad guy. The basic rule of picaresque art is that the picaro's victims remain offstage or else deserve what happens to them; thus sympathy is not deflected to them. In *The Country Wife* the "victims" are present, that is, the two husbands, Sir Jasper Fidget and Pinchwife. They only too obviously ask for what happens to them, and in opposite ways that reveal a neat structure of thought. Pinchwife is the traditional older husband who by lies, tricks, locks, and rustication hopes to keep his young wife entirely to himself; and Sir Jasper is the remarkably modern figure, the "business" man (he uses the word repeatedly) who wants to get rid of his wife and in addition have the pleasure of laughing at the "eunuch" to whom he commits her.

What we tend to expect is that Horner, having excessively gratified himself by acting as an agent of retribution on foolish people, will eventually experience a retribution of his own. This always happens in picaresque: the picaro lands in jail. The picaresque range is narrow, and in time it makes us feel the constrictions of a life which by definition excludes most of a full humanity. Hence we need the final restoration of the values, symbolized in punishment for rascality, from which we have been on a holiday. It is this restoration that is largely missing at the end of *The Country Wife*. The full values are of course hinted at positively in the Harcourt-Alithea affair, and negatively in the practical difficulties of the transgressors, but we do not see the latter brought to book in any substantial way. Some rackets do go on, we know, the world being what it is. Still we feel restricted within a way of life that gives only minimal play to human forces that we believe would be active. In *The Country Wife*, then, we move from the feeling of limitation characteristic of the picaresque to the feeling of limitation characteristic of black comedy. To say this is to give one account of the modal complexity of the play.

V. PRECONCEPTION, IDÉE FIXE, EXPECTATION

In the highly selective historical sketch of comedies from Aristophanes to Wycherley we have seen different utilizations of the disparateness between subject and object. I will resume a thematic approach to glance at some other versions of the disproportion between preconception (*idée fixe* or general expectation) and actuality. Though drama has not dealt with the theme as brilliantly as *Tristram Shandy* does, nevertheless dramatists are frequently attracted to it. They use it very effectively in plays about the theater.

Echoes are always interesting. In Goldsmith's *The Good-Natured Man*, as we have seen, a stabilizing force in Croaker's life is the gloomy *idée fixe* that England will be overrun by the Jesuits. Croaker is resurrected in Harry, the caretaker in David Storey's *The Changing Room* (1971), who expects a Russian takeover of England and attributes all evils, including the bad weather, to the Russians.* The theme gets a much broader base when an *idée fixe* overtakes a whole community and renders it impervious to the meaning of plain evidence before its eyes. This is what happens in Gogol's *The Inspector General* (1836). The guilt of small-town officeholders who cheat makes them sure that an impecunious transient is an inspecting official from Moscow, and that every naïve action of his is a diabolically clever effort to deceive them. In the irrationalities produced by their awareness of their misdeeds the human defensiveness is so recognizable, farcical though it is in detail, that it is difficult not to have an embarrassed fellow-feeling with the troubled local souls. Hence, despite a poignant detail or two, the play is scarcely the satire that some critics have called it. The disparateness between the officials' misdeeds and expectable community behavior hardly leads to a strong desire to see the erring punished; rather in their misconduct there is a representative kind of imperfection of which a satisfactory penalty is the anxiety suffered by the imperfect.

In various plots of this type the initiating preconception may be cured or may persist like a chronic ailment, but in either case it comes within a pale of human tendency that evokes more amusement than moral judgment.

Theater about Theater

Plays about plays may exploit the contrast between expectation and theatrical practice, between theatrical convention and the actuality that it transforms, and between different conceptions of theatricality.

Pirandello's *Six Characters in Search of an Author* (1921) is of course the

*In both plays these special cases are set off against larger but less conspicuous preconceptions. In Goldsmith: Honeywood's conviction that universal benevolence is always beneficial. In Storey: the rugby-bound thought and talk of the principal characters. As we saw, there is an induced misconception in Goldsmith's *She Stoops to Conquer* and in Middleton's *A Trick to Catch the Old One*. In Shaw preconception is a frequent point of departure—romantic ideas in *Arms and the Man*, the panaceas in *The Doctor's Dilemma*, and resistance to women in *Man and Superman*.

most striking drama of the conflict between the "transitory and fleeting illusion" of the stage and "immutable reality." The latter is claimed by participants in a bitter family situation who, half-created by a dramatist, are seeking a complete theatrical interpretation and yet who find in the theatrical way of doing things a falsification of the true drama that they see in their relationships. In this dramatization of the creative process, as Pirandello defined it, the artist tangles futilely with the intransigency of the semiraw material of his imagination. The family situation intensifies into disaster even as the theater people are trying to adapt it to their sense of things, and the theater director flees. Hence Pirandello may appear to be straining things when he applies the term *comedy* to a portrayal of the apparently unresolvable incompatibility between the theater and the complex tensions of pretheatrical half-life. Yet it is not inaccurate, I think, to say that he "accepts" both the theatrical practice and the imaginative life that are at variance with each other. The practice is the "object"; the six characters are the "subject" in the sense that the material seeking an outer stage form has a built-in conception of itself. The happy ending is that Pirandello has completed a successful theatrical work; thus he has effected an adjustment between form and material, even though his material is the assertion that the form is impossible. His art triumphs over his concept.

The subtlety of locating the subjective preconception in the material-as-a-whole rather than in someone's mind is unique. A distant ancestor of *Six Characters*, Beaumont's *The Knight of the Burning Pestle* (1607), turns on the difference between some laymen's conception of the theater and the style of the professional theater. George, a London grocer, and his wife Nell attend a performance of *The London Merchant*, a romantic comedy, and respond in a number of ways: demand a stage fare that will show respect for "citizens,"[11] treat the play as reality, criticize the author's sense of reality, and even devise some episodes to be presented on the stage by apprentices, with apprentice Rafe in the lead part of quixotic hero. So we have not only the contrast between the lay mind at the theater and the theatrical mind as it is exhibited in *The London Merchant*—a wonderfully merry and perceptive drama in itself (relaxed versus up-tight characters, the lively independent son versus his mother's-boy brother)—but some different motives in the lay mind itself: George and Nell do in time have Rafe enact a pro-grocer episode, but for the most part they have him in romantic roles that reflect Beaumont's knowledge of Cervantes. The performance of Rafe and his companions in the knightly episodes resembles that of the Pyramus-and-Thisbe cast in *A Midsummer Night's Dream*—

inept, but lively and essentially charming. Rafe's drama shares the stage
with *The London Merchant*, and the disjointed total presentation is constantly interrupted by George and Nell. But there are no hard feelings;
the good-natured side-by-side bumping along of unintegrated elements
constitutes almost a textbook demonstration of the comic acceptance of
the disparate. Most plays about the theater are more partisan.*

Peter Nichols' *The National Health* (1969) juxtaposes a popular
television-cinema version of hospital life with the real thing. In one scene
that illustrates Nichols' crackling theatricality, we see in forestage pan-
tomime a glorious T.V. transplant operation, which is made virtually a
religious experience but also has a father-son rapprochement and black-
white and youth-age romances attached to it. At the same time, at the
opposite side and to the rear, we see an unspectacular and unsuccessful
effort to remedy a cardiac arrest in a patient whom the audience has become
well acquainted with. Thus the popular heart's-desire hospital story
chic-ly romanticizes and sentimentalizes medical experience. Beside its
stereotyped conflicts and happy endings, we see actual ward patients with
injuries, disabilities, and diseases, some dying; doctors mechanical and
ironic; an overworked female intern falling asleep on a patient dying of
cancer; and spiritual consolation provided by a mad old lady pussyfoot-
ing in to deliver evangelical pamphlets, and a black chaplain confused
about patients' identities and chuckling about his labors.

This contrast may suggest a bitterly satirical play: human suffering
ignored in trivial art and badly treated in actual life. Fortunately Nichols
avoids that cliché. On the one hand, the romantic-sentimental serial is not
presented as an injurious saccharine lie; rather we are to relish the discrepancy between the seen actuality and the popular-art version which, humanity being what it is, is also a fact of life. Nichols' parodic skill makes
the "corny" cinema story a delight in itself rather than a revolting falsification. Then, in presenting the real-life patients, Nichols quickly introduces another disparateness—that between expected tone and his own way
of doing things. Disease and death are ordinarily managed with solemn
slowness, but Nichols sets a fast pace, hurrying from case to case as if they
were ingredients in a farce. He never lets death seem unnecessary or
unjust, as one brand of modern sentimentality often makes it; rather it is

---

*Buckingham's *Rehearsal* (1671) satirizes heroic tragedy; Sheridan's *The Critic* (1779), sentimental
drama, theatrical styles, critics. Rostand's *Cyrano de Bergerac* (1897) proceeds in another way: Cyrano
attacks the neoclassical theater of the seventeenth century by literally breaking up a performance, and
then substitutes for it, in effect, a romantic theater in which he is the main actor. All three plays act as
partisans, not as amiably detached recorders.

just something that happens. Nichols abstains from indignation and blame; we are not to feel that the hospital staff—impersonal, hurried, routinized in its procedures, overworked, given to sick jokes—is reprehensible. The patients have a certain bluntness or irony that implies a kind of mastery of the situation. The only serious complainer is a terminally ill cancer patient, but he is not allowed to evoke sympathy. When he dies, the jaunty orderly Barnet beautifully violates the rule of *de mortuis nil nisi bonum*; in a parodic eulogy Barnet says, "I'm sure I speak for all those who knew him in life when I say that he will be remembered as an evil-tempered, physically repulsive old man" (II.ii).[12] Hardian complaints about the universe are not in order; the central note is not the sadness of it all, but the incongruity of it all. Someone complains, not about pain, but about the slowness of an ambulance; Parkinson's law and Parkinson's disease are confused; a bottle may contain urine or contraband whiskey; amid the ailing, a patient may trap a nurse into a little sex play. If a patient has "no time for religion," he is "always [classified as] C. of E."; there are jokes about the audience's not liking to see the dead. Barnet ends the play with fine wit: "It's a funny old world we live in and you're lucky to get out of it alive" (II.ix). Barnet is often the scornful mocker, but he is balanced by Ash, the apparently incurable ulcer-patient who is the continual helper of men, rarely successful; these two are disguised descendants of the traditional fool and the saint. In them we simply see two ways of making do with the world, embodiments of the disparateness that comedy embraces.

Expectations in the Audience

Nichols' *National Health* leads us in one direction toward comedies in which one of the disparate elements is an expectable attitude in the audience. A solemn subject that we usually ignore or treat gravely, death becomes for Nichols a source of dramatic jokes as if it were on a par with a sprained ankle sustained in skiing. By way of contrast, a gratifying subject—a fundamental virtue that we admire, such as good nature, generosity, laissez faire—becomes for Brecht and Christopher Hampton, if not a flaw in its possessors, at least a source of trouble to them. Not that *The Good Person of Setzuan* (1938–40) and *The Philanthropist* (1970) wholly deny the virtue, but that they detect its unrecognized implications and unforeseen practical consequences; the audience has to live with an unexpected duality. Brecht's heroine Shen Te, the "good person," means to be and naturally is good-hearted and charitable, but her virtue stimulates vice in others: they become callous spongers. Hampton's Philip has a generosity of spirit which makes other less generous people turn on him because they take his unaggressive agreeableness as an ironic ploy or as lack of affection. A lesser reversal: a character casually dismisses, as if it were a trivial lunch-counter meeting, a sexual adventure. Of a night spent with a man she doesn't even like, the heroine Celia says, "I just suddenly felt like it" (v).

Virtually the same words are used by Jean, the wife in the Dutch dramatist Hugo Claus's *Friday* (1969; as it appears in the somewhat shortened English version by Christopher Logue); she ran into her husband's friend Eric at a funeral (a nice variant of the folk formula of sex in the cemetery), and this led on to other things and a child. Husband George was absent at the time: serving a jail sentence for incest with his daughter. So there we have a triangle, or quadrangle, that could produce a Jacobean slaughter, yet Claus works everything out peacefully: the lover leaves (though promising support for his illegitimate child), and husband and wife resume married life. The method is to treat traditional sins, not as evil acts, but matter-of-factly as foibles, as slips that sneak up on people, and hence as forgivable and forgettable. The characters are not emotionless, but they often convert feeling into irony: George underplays conventional husbandly feeling by complaining that Eric has "watered" his wife rather than his garden, which is grievously full of weeds. With regard to the incest—one incident only, not a habit—Eric looks at George jocosely, almost admiringly, as if he had pulled off an unusually original larceny. Since the girl is "randy" and unselective, Eric theorizes merrily: "If you can go with niggers, what's wrong with your own father?"—as if the issue were social democracy. Such trivializing of taboos could be merely shocking, or fall into farce or black comedy, but these risks are foreclosed by the principals' sensible and generally good-natured return to lives within the code. Behind the surface of unexpected events, indeed, lies an almost Shavian* comedy of ideas: the ancient question of whether

---

*There are Shavian elements in Stanley Houghton's bright *Hindle Wakes* (1912), which also exploits the difference between expectations and a fresh common-sense solution. Fanny Hawthorn has spent a weekend with her father's boss's son, Alan Jeffcote, and the parents determine that the two must marry; this solution is even approved by Alan's fiancée, Beatrice Farrar. But it is Fanny who won't have it: the weekend meant nothing to her. Her version of "I just felt like it" is "You were just someone to have a bit of fun with. You were an amusement—a lark." Alan, expressing shock, is the Shavian conventional Englishman: "It sounds so jolly immoral. I never thought of a girl looking on a chap just like that!" Fanny carries it further: "You're not good enough for me. . . . My husband, if ever I have one, will be a man, not a fellow who'll throw over his girl at his father's bidding!" She concludes ironically: "Then it looks as if I'm asked to wed him to turn him into an honest man?" (III). This turn of events satisfies virtually everybody except Fanny's marrying mother, who in her defeat

a good life results from obeying the rules or from a certain quality of heart and mind. Claus really accepts both, though he does not scream for the rules or slobber over the personal quality.

A dramatist can refuse the expected solemnities to war as well as to sex: Robert Sherwood does this in *Idiot's Delight* (1936) and Shaw does it in *Geneva* (1938; rev. 1940, 1945). Sherwood is not lighthearted about war, of course, but until a bomb falls at the end, it appears more an offstage irrationality than a concrete brutality, more a mistake like speeding than a disease like cancer. Indeed it seems to assist a love affair, and artists, scientists, and other human classes respond to it by a turn to national loyalties—a shrinkage of their lives perhaps, but a mode of adjustment to imperfect reality; a kind of faith in a world rather than a bald passion to survive. A reader expecting a crashing antiwar sermon would be disappointed in the generally ironic view. In *Geneva*, on the other hand, Shaw makes a target of nationalist feeling; for him it is neither a form of loyalty, as it is for Sherwood, nor an outright evil, but rather an *idée fixe* which, like other obsessions, is harmful to those whom it actuates. Though the plot has to do with the outbreak of World War II, the partisanship that one might expect at such a time does not appear: the nations represented at the International Court are not really divided into the good and the bad, but all lack the good sense requisite for a rational world order. They all automatically lapse into habitual forms of apparent self-interest that are really self-injurious. Even the dictators are less evil men than they are laughably inflated pretenders. The expected opposition of good and bad is transposed into the unexpected key of ironic disparateness: notions of profit (subject) are at variance with actual advantage (object).

The New Broom

One of the romantic prescriptions for an imperfect sociopolitical world is a new broom: the coming into power of outsiders—a theme handled fantastically, as we have seen, in Giraudoux's *The Madwoman of Chaillot* (1945), where virtue has a final triumph, and less fantastically in Brecht's *The Caucasian Chalk Circle* (1944–45), where the shrewd judgeship of Azdak, a clownish village figure, is only temporary.

becomes as bitter as an unsuccessful lover in Restoration comedy—another case of an unhappiness that mature comedy successfully includes.

The difference between actual event and expectable pattern is neatly exploited in Act IV of Chekhov's *The Sea Gull* when Polina urges Treplev, the young writer, to be "a little kinder" to Polina's married daughter Masha, who is in love with him. She adds, "She's a nice little thing" (Constance Garnett's translation; Dunnigan's version reads, "She's a good girl"). Thus Polina reverses the role of the mother trying to protect her daughter against nonmatrimonial sex.

Carl Zuckmayer's *The Captain of Köpenick* (1931) brilliantly alters the reformist script: the new broom is a bold and ingenious picaro. A permanent underdog, Wilhelm Voigt, forty-six, gets an army captain's uniform, bones up on military orders and procedures, and thus is able to take control of the town of Köpenick, jail the officials, and make off with the town funds. Before this exploit, Voigt was the victim of bureaucracies that, handling all cases in a mechanical, rule-bound way, fail to make a rational response to any individual situation. Voigt's difficulties constitute a satire of "the system." But the system is more a Gilbert-and-Sullivan affair than it is the work of hard or self-seeking or malicious men. The "other side," in Zuckmayer's own words, is not "simply castigated but represented with an attempt at justice"; he wanted to avoid the "nasty aftertaste that a one-sided view, or propaganda, always inspires."[13] A recent adapter has called the play a "gentle satire," and Zuckmayer himself sought "the tone of a comedy."[14] This is to say that we are invited not so much to detest the bureaucrats as to see ourselves in all officials (and citizens) who act and think primarily in terms of "the rules" and who take the easy way of applying them routinely. But we also have the quite different response of empathizing with the worm that turns; Voigt is not crushed by his misfortunes, but through durability and dry wit transcends his victimhood. His masterful browbeating, jailing, and robbing of the town officials make a fine comedy of contrast between the true state of affairs and the pseudo truth installed by paraphernalia and ritual (Voigt's uniform and mastery of commands). The Mayor says that "there's something magical about a uniform" (vii); in Voigt's words, "Well, any child knows that here in Germany one can do anything one likes if one has a uniform," and the Kaiser himself is "proud" of the "discipline" which produced obedience to Voigt's commands (xvi).[15]

The disparate facts here are that formal procedures are essential, but that they may lead to fantastically wrong results. The officials, going by formulae, fall into a self-deception reminiscent of the self-deception of the officials in Gogol's great comedy. Indeed Thomas Mann calls Zuckmayer's play "the best comedy in world literature since Gogol's *The Inspector General*."[16] Voigt's control of the town ends soon, as it has to, and with fine comic effect: not an oppressive retaliation of authority against Voigt, but the picaro's turning himself in and enjoying a last wonderfully gleeful laugh at the "incredible" success of his exploit. The play does not excoriate official misdeeds but laughs at errors and misconceptions in an order that seems highly rational to itself.

VI. Disparateness in Attitudes and Identities

Although the subject/object and object/object modes of disparateness may not often appear in unmixed form, still in most comedies one mode or the other tends to dominate. The plays in the preceding section, for instance, are mostly on the subject/object side, whereas those to which we now come (two by Chekhov, one by Hofmannsthal, one by Gorky) rely mainly on disparateness among objects, be these ways of life or analyses of character. And to focus on plays that contemplate disparate objects is to move toward the ultimate material of comedy, the multiplicity theme (Section VII).

"The Three Sisters"

Chekhov is virtually characterized by his sense of human discordancies; thus even in farce he may sketch diverse impulses that could develop quite unfarcically.* *The Three Sisters* (1901), however, is so far from the slapstick gaiety of the earlier farces that some critics think it not even comic. Since so many hopes and desires go down the drain, it would be easy to describe *The Three Sisters* as a melodrama of defeat. But it is that kind of somber comedy in which the materials really strain against the bounds of genre but do not finally break out. Though the disasters may seem incompatible with the comic, still the play maintains a subtle sense of the disparate that is something other than the mere defeat of the deserving by hostile events. This is apparent in Chekhov's treatment of four conspicuous thematic ideas.

Following the lead of Tuzenbach and Vershinin, the Prozorov girls cling to a utopian vision of a good and happy life that will be realized in two or three hundred years. Second is the work theme, voiced especially by Tuzenbach and Irina: the praise of work—whether programmatic (route to the great future), penitential, therapeutic, or simply autotelic—as a source of advantages such as fifty years later would be ascribed to leisure. (No one pays much attention to Vershinin's accurate qualification of this simplistic faith: "If . . . we could add culture to the love of work, and love of work to culture" [IV]—a notable marriage of

---

*In *The Proposal: A Farce in One Act* (1888–89), for instance, Natasha Chubukov and Ivan Lomov want to get married but can't help being vehemently disputatious in such matters as who owns Oxpen Field or who owns the better dog. (Natasha's father has to trick them into an engagement.) There is a double disparateness between objects: between the couple's opposed views, and between the matrimonial hope and other emotions felt by each. In S. N. Behrman's *The Second Man* (1927) the disparateness is between love and a skeptical spirit which the hero identifies as a "second man" within, a "cynical, odious person" (II.i).

Arnold's Hellenism and Hebraism.)[17] Still larger is the dream theme, whether dreaming is an obligation, as Vershinin makes it (like work an avenue to the expected future utopia), or a spontaneous picturing of a more nearly ideal existence. Finally, the one great symbol of a shining and exciting life is Moscow (a recurrent symbol in Chekhov), at once a re-membered Eden and a land of heart's desire, an enticement to all, summed up in Irina's call to Olga: ". . . only let us go to Moscow! I implore you, let us go! There's nothing in the world better than Moscow! Let us go! Olya! Let us go!" (III).

No one ever does anything about it; the ideal and action are separate compartments; "work" and "dream" are divorced. Vershinin calls our attention to this disparateness with a question: "A Russian is peculiarly given to an exalted way of thinking, but tell me, why is it that in life he falls so short?" (II). Chekhov is recording the eternal discrepancy between human program and performance, but he is also giving it a special twist. When Irina says that she will marry Tuzenbach, though she does not love him, she goes on to a remarkable confession: "I have never in my life been in love. Oh, how I have dreamed of love, dreamed of it for a long time now, day and night, but my soul is like a fine piano that is locked, and the key lost" (IV). It is consistent with the play as a whole to suppose that she has never been in love, not because of some unique disability, but because she has romantically pictured an ideal love which actuality could never approximate—exactly as a Russian "falls short" because his "exalted way of thinking" is out of tune with possibility. Thus nobody gets to Moscow because it is a never-never land; the pilgrims do indeed lack drive, but Moscow isn't really there either. Chekhov has given us new symbols for the comedy of illusion and reality—Moscow and the provincial city, the latter an image of the ordinary life that men must come to terms with. But he stops short of the final comic action in which the principals get hold of the good sense that helps correct faulty vision. More subtly than that, he leaves it to us to see over their heads in this central issue. They may feel stifled, trapped, finished, but surely we are to remember that most of their lives are ahead of them. They speak as if they were closer to fifty than to thirty;* here the essentially comic disparateness is between

*Irina is not yet twenty-four when she says that she is "moving away from the real, beautiful life . . . into some sort of abyss" (III). Her strong emotion may dim our perception of the irony, which is quite like that in Jane Austen's *Sense and Sensibility* when Marianne Dashwood, aged seventeen, declares with authority, "A woman of seven and twenty . . . can never hope to feel or inspire affection again . . ." (chap. 8).

the length of life, with all its possibilities (object), and the intensity of feeling that makes a passing moment seem a final one (subject).

"The Cherry Orchard"

Chekhov's least ambiguous employment of the comic principle appears in *The Cherry Orchard* (1904), in which he underscores his comic intent by using little farcical happenings: the idealist student Trofimov falls downstairs, and Lopakhin accidentally receives Varya's blow intended for Yepikhodov (III). The central business of the play is the balanced, sympathetic presentation of two ways of life: the old order and the new order. Nonpartisan, Chekhov simply says, "There they are." He observes admirable qualities without becoming a cheerleader for them; he observes shortcomings without regretting or blaming. The old estate-owners, Mme. Lyubov Ranevsky and her brother Gayev, and their friend Semyonov-Pishchik have lost touch with the practicalities of land-management and with economic necessity; Lyubov, the central character, has in effect become a Parisian and an absentee landlord, and is emotionally tied to a worthless lover in Paris. She wants to save the estate, with its beautiful orchard, but, like the men, is hardly up to any action more definite than hoping for a miracle. She could be made the object of sharp satire; she could be shown as self-indulgent, foolish, idle, irresponsible, a betrayer of people and loyalties. (In fact, on the old-order side the only people who seem to have their feet on the ground are an adoptive daughter Varya and the eighty-seven-year-old servant Firs, who at the final curtain is symbolically left alone in the country house, flat on his back.) But there is no satire. The gestures of the older men, especially the sentimentalities of Gayev and his addiction to spread-eagle rhetoric, are both laughable and pitiable. Lyubov is simply a human being who, not by moral indifference or perversity, but rather by a generous impracticality has fallen into a hopeful, thoughtless life and hence lost a grip on the ways of keeping an estate which is dear to her. In fact, she is made an extraordinarily attractive person—full of spontaneous feeling, attachment to the place, liking for many other people, often wise about them and even at times about herself, alternately gay and tearfully nostalgic, winning without effort the attention and affection of others. She has remarkable charm; what remains in her possession is all the social and aesthetic grace of an order no longer capable of managing the land productively.

On the other side there is the nouveau arrivé Lopakhin, up from peasantry and indeed slavery, hard working, knowing how to do things, seeing what has to be done, finally triumphing: he buys the beautiful cherry orchard which is for everyone the heart of the estate, and will cut down the trees and replace them with a housing project. Nor is he unlikable; his wonder at, and his enthusiasm for, his glorious achievement have their own kind of attractiveness. Yet he is the agent of a plain utility that succeeds loveliness. And the potential marriage between him and Varya never works out; somehow he is incapable of the purely emotional investment. In effect he is all business; what he can do is recondition and modernize the holdings of a system that has worn out. His new order is inevitable; yet we feel the loss of all the charm, the warmer feeling, the grace of the dying order.

Chekhov's sympathetic presentation of the old and the new involves a fine symbolic use of the cherry orchard. For those of the old order it is a permanent and a beautiful thing, irresistible in its power over the feelings. Once, however, the cherries were a major source of income; that is, the orchard symbolized a social order with two indispensable countervalues —beauty and utility, grace and productiveness, aesthetic and economic adequacy. Then "they" forgot the process of drying the cherries and taking them to market (I); the economic base disappeared, and the aesthetic alone remained, the complement in nature of Lyubov's charm, an occasional blessing on her visits from an alien urban world. Blossoms but no roots, so to speak: the trees go down, houses go up. Chekhov gives each its due: the old beauty, the new economic life. Thus he provides an especially fine drama of the disparateness between object and object. Different styles of life are not clearly defined as better or worse; their value is that in their inconsistency they are inevitable expressions of different tendencies within human nature.

Comedy of Identity: "The Difficult Man"

Comedy may turn on conflicting views of someone's identity. Here, of course, we may have errors of purely physical origin (as with the twins in *Menaechmi* and *Comedy of Errors*) or artificially brought about (as by disguise in Renaissance and occasionally in later drama). Moral disguises lead to a more profound comedy: Tartuffe does not fool everybody, but he succeeds with the most important man in the world of the play (who even in being taken in exhibits a capacity for faith that is essential to the world). Those around Tartuffe do not agree on what his identity is. Again, interpretations of identity may turn not on observers' credulity or acuity but on their attending to this or that aspect of the person observed and getting incomplete pictures. In such a play perspectivism is an amusing object in itself, not, as in Pirandello, an evidence of perceptual insecurity or of the inherent elusiveness of reality. In Goldsmith's *She Stoops to Conquer*, Tony Lumpkin, the trickster who is a prime mover of events, seems a different person to his doting mother, to his fellow jesters at the inn, to the Miss Neville to whom his mother wants to marry him, and to the lovers at different times as he is gamesome or helpful. To Tony, in turn, Miss Neville is a shrew; to Hastings, an angel. To Hardcastle and his daughter Kate, Marlow seems two different people. His way with servants, suitable to them, drives Hardcastle frantic. Hardcastle complains of their drunkenness; Marlow says Hardcastle ought to be glad they are drinking so much and running up the bill (and this, incidentally, raises drunkenness, a traditional business of farce, to the comic level).

Hofmannsthal's *The Difficult Man* (1921) bases much of its dramatic life on misunderstandings and misjudgments of the main character. These are not the mistakes of gulls and nitwits, nor the product of an unknowable world whose apparent truth is no more than a dustbin of subjectivities or the foamy wake of solipsisms that pass in the night, but errors rooted in human nature. Hofmannsthal's comedy attributes inaccurate judgments and expectations to habits and desires that modify what men see. Ironically, Hans Karl, the "difficult man," contributes to others' wrong impressions of himself by his very fear of being misunderstood. He rails against "the odious confusions that a man exposes himself to when he mixes with people" (III.x), he wants "to be spared the usual misunderstandings" (x), he is convinced that it's impossible to "open one's mouth without causing the most ineradicable confusion" (xiii).[18] So he tends to hold back from social occasions ("a twisted tangle of misunderstandings" [I.iii]) and to be hesitant or reserved in conversation. Such efforts to reduce the misconceptions that abound in life lead associates to puzzled uncertainties and erring certainties about him.

Vincent, a new footman, thinks that Hans Karl will be easy to manage, and then finds himself fired within a day. Crescence, Hans Karl's sister, a loquacious, good-natured, scatterbrained matchmaker and fix-it, tries to push him into what she sees as right actions and then rebukes him for being "erratic" (I.iii) and for "shilly-shallying" (III.xii). She never hesitates to define a role for him, and she complains that "one never knows where one is" with him (I.xvi, xviii). Antoinette, Countess Hechingen, who would like to extend a brief affair with Hans Karl, says to him,

". . . at this moment I know as little how I stand with you as if there had never been anything between us," though a little later she claims, "I usually do understand you well enough" (II.x). Helen Altenwyl declares that "it's impossible to plumb [Hans Karl's] words to the bottom . . .—he belongs only to himself—nobody knows him" (II.xiii). The comic fact is that Antoinette does not understand him, and Helen does. Crescence's son Stani assures his uncle Hans Karl, "I know you through and through" (I.xvi), but totally misunderstands Hans Karl's key relationships with Antoinette and Helen. Stani calls Hans Karl an "idealist" whose "thoughts fly off to the absolute, to some ideal of perfection" (I.xvi); but Edine Merenberg, the culture-lover, regrets that Hans Karl has never met anyone "who could have instilled a bit of idealism into him" (II.vi). Stani sees in him an elegant, effortless power (I.viii); such a man is of course an "egotist" (x). But to Neuhoff, the heavy-handed German, Hans Karl is an "absolute, arrogant nonentity" or "unlimited triviality" (II.ii); Antoinette calls Hans Karl and Stani "Monsters of selfishness and utterly without delicacy," and, fearful of losing Hans Karl, terms him "frightening," "charming and at the same time so monstrously vain and selfish and heartless!", "A cynic, an egoist, a devil . . ." (II.x). A real Hans Karl who is none of these things, or has some such elements in him along with many others, is dramatically defined in time. The point is less that the disparate judgments are wrong* or stupid (only Neuhoff is stupid) than that their shortcomings reflect personalities which, combining certain feelings with limited points of view, we are to see as understandable phases of human reality.

Gorky's "The Zykovs"

Hofmannsthal portrays a complex individual whom others size up variously. If the focus is shifted from these diverse identifications to diverse identities that reveal themselves in general styles of meeting the world, the result could be a play like Maxim Gorky's *The Zykovs* (1914). Antipa Zykov, a self-made lumber merchant of fifty, aggressive, roughshod,

---

*The irony of contradictory characterizations is matched by events at variance with expectations and predictions. Various people think that Hans Karl can restore his ex-mistress Antoinette to contented wifehood, but his effort leads only to Antoinette's sharp, delightful resistance: ". . . you want to palm me off on my husband" (II.x). Crescence and Stani both think that Hans Karl can persuade Helen to marry Stani; Hans Karl's effort to bring this about only leads to his getting engaged to Helen himself (an old type of action, of course). Despite the fact that both Antoinette and Helen love Hans Karl, Stani infers that Hans Karl has enraged Antoinette by letting her know "that she's lost me [Stani] forever" (III.vii) and that Antoinette in revenge has blackened his name with Helen. More incomplete perspectives.

overbearing, has little faith in others: "I don't like people" (I).[19] But, paradoxically attracted by his mild son Mikhail's fiancée, Pavla Tselovanyeva, a convent-bred girl who keeps agitating for "love" and "kindness," Antipa snatches and weds her. This complementary marriage is a fiasco; yet Gorky presents less a clash of unlike temperaments than a Chekhovian management of perspectives on ways of confronting reality—a far cry from an imaginable melodrama of strength ruining or being tamed by gentleness, or a romance of continual battling relished by both. Pavla is attracted by Antipa's strength, but she is fragile, neurotically fearful, not up to facing anything difficult, and yet difficult to take in her constant preaching about goodness. Antipa, marrying in a sudden quest for "joy in something good" (I), finds no joy, is upset, and even neglects his business; he is almost a husband killed by kindness, that is, troubled and somehow done in by the nunnery sentiments of Pavla, who, as Mikhail puts it, "still lives as if she were playing with dolls" (III). He loses strength, and she gentleness; both fall into self-pity and recrimination. Antipa calls her "meek little viper," and her reply, "beat me," is an indictment (IV). She accuses him of lacking "pity or love for anybody," and he retorts, "To listen to you kindhearted people, every kind of work is a sin against something" (IV). Lest we take sides against the hard man, Gorky has the wise woman of the play, Antipa's sister Sophia, say, "You talk a lot about love, Pavla, but you don't know how to love" (IV).

The third style is Sophia's—a middling one; Antipa calls her "neither kind nor cruel" (I). She gets Antipa to free Pavla, and he tells Pavla, "Go your own way" (IV); thus the good sense of the comic domain may be a brake on total disaster. A sentimental dramatist might make Sophia a pain-free ever-wise maternal figure, but Gorky understands the strain she feels in continually trying to lead emotional people to act with some restraint. As she says, "You have to pay a stiff price for happiness" (IV). Yet her sense of reality is not despairing; she can go on looking for "good men" and believing that in general "life is a blessing and people are good" (IV)—by no means a sentimental view in a manifestly clear-eyed observer. A fourth style of life is that of Antipa's son Mikhail, who does not work like his father, or fight for his girl against his father; he remains amiable, noncompetitive, jesting (he can even define Pavla as "playing too—at simplicity, kindness—" {I}); he drinks too, and at one point, half-pursued by Pavla and abused by his jealous father, he manages to wound himself with a gun. Alarums, outcry, panic. It is actually Mikhail himself who tries to quiet things down: "Hold on, Father, don't excite yourself.

There's nothing really terrible in all this—it's more funny than anything—" (IV). When "funny," which reflects the sense of disparateness, even laughable disparateness, can be attributed to a person who might fall into recrimination or self-pity, the dramatist himself reveals a spacious comic imagination. Thus he works out a varied pattern of ways in the world (objects). None of the four styles leads to triumph, but each will do for its possessor, much as it leaves out. The result is a rather somber comedy in the Chekhov vein.*

For additional evidence on the ironic sense of diversity in attitudes, I will return briefly to the Peter Nichols plays on disease and death. *Joe Egg* observes a half-dozen styles of confronting permanent illness in a child. One parent is overly devoted, the other takes refuge in irony and fantasy; one friend offers do-gooder platitudes, another can't even look at the patient; a grandparent seeking causes falls into pseudo science, and a clergyman falls into self-parodying routines. We do not judge the styles; we relish their piquant disparity. *The National Health* gets its life from the diversity of attitudes among hospital patients: persistent optimism or good cheer, a strong gaiety, an energizing irony, complaint and denunciation, bluntness to or sharp criticalness of bed-neighbors, suspicion, illusion, indignation about small matters. It is not that the styles are better or worse, but that they are different; a rapid kaleidoscopic display of options allows little time for pathos; pity is not excluded, but the pitiable is inseparable from the ludicrous. The discomfort or even pain of a stretcher patient is less significant than the exacerbation of it by a stretcher-bearer's constant coughing, or a man's death than the delay in resuscitatory efforts

*Gorky and Chekhov were friends. Gorky's *Enemies* (1906) partly drifts away from a class melodrama (good workers versus evil managers and owners) to a Chekhovian employment of various perspectives. On the owner-manager side there are not only the put-them-down-by-force types, but also Zakhar Bardin, a good-natured person who wants to talk things over reasonably with the workers (he falls afoul of both sides); his brother Yakov, an ironist and alcoholic, who finds the workers more likable than the others do; Yakov's wife Tatyana, an actress who is indecisive about classes; Zakhar's niece Nadya, a bespectacled teen-ager who rather vocally hates evil and loves good. This diversity partly rescues the play from the simplicity of its basic conflict. As Alexander Block said, "Gorky is bigger than he wants to be and than he always wanted to be, because his intuition is deeper than his intellect: . . ." This is quoted by Alexander Bakshy in "The Theater of Maxim Gorky," in *Seven Plays of Maxim Gorky*, trans. Alexander Bakshy in collaboration with Paul S. Nathan (New Haven, Conn.: Yale University Press, 1945), p. 12.

The more recent theater often uses the Chekhovian juxtaposition of alternatives that displaces the linear plot, or at least obscures it. Alan Bennett's *Getting On* (1971) is pseudo-Chekhovian. It assembles its scenes about a middle-aged M.P. who feels vaguely dissatisfied with things; his younger wife who carries on with a hippie living in the house; the husband's friend who is carrying on homosexually with the hippie; the hippie who walks out and lacerates several hearts; the M.P.'s son who reciprocates his father's disgust. At different times nearly all break into rants; they are less characters than they are stereotypes representing various habits and attitudes of the day.

because no one can find a wrench to open an oxygen tank (and the orderly says, in effect, "s.n.a.f.u.").

Death, then, as well as ordinary life, and indeed every kind of relationship that life embraces, evokes many ways of accommodation to the reality at hand. These beget comedy.

VII. MULTIPLICITY: THE ULTIMATE DISPARATENESS

In metaphysics it was the one and the many, always foes; in comedy it is the two and the many, always akin. Initially "disparateness" suggests a pair of opposing elements, be they subject and object, or object and object. Aristophanes spells out the dissimilar virtues of Aeschylus and Euripides; the Wakefield master values the farcical and the sacred versions of the miracle; Shakespeare celebrates the love centered in straightforward romantic feeling and that which filters feeling through the competitive exercise of wits, and he maintains some of the claims of the studious and disciplined life against its potent rival, amorous life; Chekhov images the charms of the doomed old order as well as the limitations of the inevitable new order.

But then in Wycherley's *Country Wife* this doubleness is, if not actually redoubled, at least repeated in neighboring thematic panels: there are the instinctively jealous and the determinedly nonjealous men; the worldly men who resist or flee marriage, and the worldly couple who desire marriage; the men who flaunt their virility, and the man who by denying his gains it a more populous playground. So in this play we begin to cross over from the two to the many, or from disparateness as duality to disparateness as multiplicity, from disparateness "between" to disparateness "among" objects. With disparateness the inner pressure is inevitably toward multiplicity; to have a sense of different options is to discover more options, to move toward the human situation as described by Hegio in Terence's *Phormio*. Asked for advice by a disobeyed father, Hegio rejects the single solution: ". . . this is the way of it; many men of many minds, many birds of many kinds; each man has his own point of view" (III. 268–70). [20] We have already moved close to "many men" and "many minds" in noting the divergent ideas of identity in *She Stoops to Conquer* and *The Difficult Man*, the quartet of basic styles in *The Zykovs*, and the multiple attitudes to illness and death in the Peter Nichols plays.

"The fullness of the world includes rational discrimination," I remarked in Chapter 2; "in the way things are there is a measure of good sense, the bar against both everything goes and nothing goes." The implicit middle ground between "everything goes" and "nothing goes" is that many things go. "Go": that is, occur, work more or less; are not *a priori* obnoxious or evil; have some kind of pragmatic utility, greater or lesser; are the natural expressions of different personalities interacting with people and events; if not always innovative or creative, are essentially innocuous; may not approximate a definable ideal, but in their excess or deficiency are not destructive; may mark either an intrinsically satisfactory modus vivendi or at least some sort of muddling through, or alternatively a failure so rooted in personality that we do not regard it as a wrong thing or a summons to punitive or ameliorative action. The observer of the many things is not primarily a judge of them, yet he does see them in a public situation where they illustrate or interpret each other. They coexist, not in a doctrinally established hierarchy, but as hypothetical equals, their ultimate rank, if any, to be determined by what, and whom, they are good for.

L. J. Potts says something applicable here: he insists, "The pattern we want in comedy is . . . a grouping of characters rather than a march of events," and he amplifies this conception in a striking contrast: "There are at least two kinds of plot: the tragic plot, in *time*, and the comic plot, in *space*." [21] The "grouping of characters" I take to mean a placing of them that will make us aware of the patterns of significance that they form, of the ways in which they are alike and different, and in which they serve as variations on a theme. Their role is not only to work out a situation but also to represent possibilities of being and style. Potts does not bother to protect himself with some qualifications that he might advantageously make, for many comedies do maintain a "march of events" and do function "in time." Nevertheless the concept of "plots in time" and "plots in space" is an arresting one, and if exceptions are needed for the sake of precision, the contrast is essentially right. The "plot in space" effectively images the multiplicity pattern. The multiple elements do not so much follow each other (though there is always an observable succession of events, however makeshift) as they lie, or move, side by side. They are like roughly parallel lines, or they show alternative courses to some common goal; we shift our attention from one to another and are aware of each as a part of a pattern of options. To set up a paradigm of the situation: six different characters may seek popularity or money or status or sex by the different devices or ideas that their personalities make available to them; or else they just live, not consciously seeking, as their natures demand.

We are invited less to see the results, the arrivals (though we do not ignore these), than to watch the different styles of procedure or to be aware of the different objects sought (or, for that matter, spurned). The issue is not entirely what one actor does now, then does next, and then does later, as what all are more or less doing at the same time. The endings are less outcomes of the doing than parts of the doing.

The ideal formal ground for the multiplicity aesthetic or the "plot in space" is the novel, since its dimensions can be virtually unlimited. One need only think of *Pride and Prejudice, Middlemarch*, and *Point Counter Point* to realize that the multiplicity novel is neither a rare form nor a specifically modern form. Indeed the multiplicity form in the novel, as in the comic drama, exists long before there is theory for it.* However, certain plays of the kind are self-conscious enough: the fairly large crop of

*This theoretical issue is overtly present in *Point Counter Point* (1928) by Aldous Huxley, who in the text regularly discusses the concept of "multiplicity." His large cast of characters contains men and women who exemplify diverse attitudes to politics (fascism, communism, rationalism, indifferentism), to religion (atheism, scientism, naïve emotionalism, ritualism, aestheticism), to sex (the working marriage, the affair, adultery, promiscuity, seduction, misogyny), to art and literature (the philosophic practitioner, the genius, the entrepreneur), and so on. Huxley shifts rapidly ("modulates," as he puts it in a controlling musical metaphor)—sometimes more than once on a page—from one mode of life to another. We perceive that each of these represents needs and choices rooted in different aspects of human nature. Some episodes are farcical, some somber, but in the mass they embody a comic contemplation of the disparateness of the world.

Without a trace of theorizing, Jane Austen fully anticipates *Point Counter Point* in *Pride and Prejudice*: she instinctively juxtaposes multiple versions of attitudes and experience. *Pride*, which initially appears to be unambiguous, we gradually see used by people in a dozen different ways, ranging from the self-regard that issues in vanity and arrogance to the self-regard that issues in a sense of obligation to certain standards of conduct. When Lydia runs away with Wickham, Austen focuses entirely not on this breach of sexual propriety but on the diverse attitudes to it: the joyful censoriousness of the community, Mrs. Bennet's simple hope for a marriage that will save all, Mr. Bennet's irony and irresponsibility, Darcy's contrasting responsibility, Collins' heavy moralizing, Mary's truisms, the elopers' bland insensitivity to anything but their own feeling of achievement, and finally, when to almost everyone's satisfaction the pair are married, the sharply ambivalent response of Elizabeth Bennet—the acknowledgment that though this conventional patching-up seems mandatory, it still is a dubious, unpromising way out. Further, this affair itself is one element in the over-all multiplicity structure of the novel: it is one of six relationships that develop the marriage theme as diversely as has ever been done in English fiction. The Gardiners represent a working marriage of fundamentally congenial people; the elder Bennets a working marriage of very unlike people whose original bond was sex alone. Against the background of these established marriages we see the gradual working out of four others that are the termini of the various narrative lines of the novel: the shotgun wedding of Lydia and Wickham, the *mariage de convenance* of Charlotte Lucas and Mr. Collins, the easy spontaneous relationship of two agreeable uncomplicated people, Jane Bennet and Bingley, and, overshadowing all of these, the difficult discovery of each other, and of course of themselves, by Elizabeth and Darcy, the two more complex people whose strong feelings and independent minds naturally create misunderstandings and resentments. Again we have the great comedy of diverse possibilities which we know are qualitatively different but which in the main we understand as the products of circumstances and of human capabilities that cannot be much altered. In that sense the marriages are equal in validity if not in value.

There is a comparable multiplicity of ideas and relationships in *Middlemarch*.

twentieth-century plays in what we may call "the Grand Hotel style," *
in which the dramatist's basic act is the choice of a scene that automatically brings together a large number of people and thus guarantees
ready-made contrasts. Some earlier dramas, however, do not start out
either with a scene bound to produce a many-sided configuration of
characters or with a theory of diversity but move spontaneously into
multiplicity as an expression of their own sense of disparateness.

Chekhov's *The Sea Gull* (1896), Turgenev's *A Month in the Country*
(1850), and Congreve's *The Way of the World* (1700) all present multiple
versions of love—that central experience in comedy in which enough is
always the same to convince some observers that all comedy is the same,
that is, a fertility rite, but in which enough is different to produce
innumerable variants of the sex story in a vast range of tones that are
frequently unheeded. What we may hear extends from the simplest tin-
tinnabulation of wedding bells to the routine clang of dinner bells, from a
sigh or a cry to a paean or a knell, from a reveille to a taps, from an "all
aboard" to an "end of the line," from cheers to arraignments, from battle
cries to murmurs of peace with more or less honor, from a rare resounding
certainty for a hot pursuer to a more frequent dusty answer to the soul.

The earliest of these plays is the most complex; hence we can profitably
proceed by reverse chronology.

Chekhov's "The Sea Gull"

The Sea Gull applies the multiplicity approach to the art theme as well
as to the love theme. Treplev, the apprentice writer, wants to innovate; he
has enough talent to gain the appreciation of Dr. Dorn, but not patience
enough to listen to Dorn's sound criticism of his work. Trigorin, the
successful popular writer, seems a hack to Treplev, but can torture himself
with an almost Hamletian self-searching over his ceaseless and obsessive
work. Treplev's girl, Nina Zarechnaya, comes from a well-to-do conventional family but is glamorized by the stage; she has small talent and
wretched experiences, but at the end may be painfully winning a faint
toehold in the theater. Irina, Treplev's mother, a successful actress, dis-
likes his work but charms him and everyone else: in successive scenes in
Act III we see her brilliantly play the sister, the mother, and the mistress,

---

*There is a special version of this in Arnold Wesker's *The Kitchen* (1959), where a very large staff of
workers, many of whom come from different countries, dramatize multiplicity. But the tendency of
the play is to lament rather than to accept; weltschmerz, aggression, and disaster are more frequent
than adjustment; and the owner-manager has a strong resemblance to the capitalist villain of cliché
leftist writing. Hence the tone is more on the melodramatic side.

and thus resist plaints and pleas by her brother, son, and lover. None of these artists, aspiring or successful, is made an exemplar as person or professional; we simply observe the different styles of the life in art, each with its greater or less adjustment to the way the world goes.

Chekhov portrays more numerous versions of the sex relationship: the long-time open liaison, in effect a marriage (Trigorin and Irina); the sub-rosa extramatrimonial affair (Madam Shamrayev and Dr. Dorn), he content with this, she anguishing over the inadequacy and subterfuge; a wife's longing for another man who does not respond (Madam Shamrayev's daughter Masha and Treplev); the affair of the romantic young lovers (Treplev and Nina), broken up when she falls for an older man; the brief passionate affair (Trigorin and Nina), the man essentially self-serving and soon out of it, the girl caught in an enduring infatuation. These relationships are for the most part parallel, but still the participants form a singular ironic series: Medvedenko, suitor and later husband, is in love with Masha, who is in love with Treplev, who is in love with Nina, who is in love with Trigorin, who is never really detached from Irina, who loves her role as powerful charming center of the scene.* This is not a bitter documentary of endemic frustration but a neutral view of the frequent hiatus between desire and fulfillment, of the different kinds of amatory relationship, and of the varying degrees of satisfactoriness in these relationships. The problems are not moral ones but ones of making out; Chekhov does not mourn, blame, or judge. He simply uses the comic method of accepting the disparateness of the world. The comedy is often somber, granted; yet it by no means lacks the wit and jests and, in its characters, the share of amiability and good sense—the eye for facts—that are the more evident signs of the comic mode.

Turgenev's "A Month in the Country"

There are resemblances between *The Sea Gull* and *A Month in the Country*: the scene is a rural estate, various hearts yearn in directions from which there is little or no reply (subjective feelings and objective actualities again), glamorous possibilities of Moscow origin are succeeded by

---

*This situation is quite different from the temporary and readjustable mismatings in *A Midsummer Night's Dream* and from the mechanical sequence of pairings and repairings in the ten duet-scenes of *Reigen* (1900) by Chekhov's contemporary and fellow physician-dramatist Arthur Schnitzler. In Shakespeare the unrequited passion is a momentary aberration; in Schnitzler, every passion is both requited, and momentary, as if he had read *The Sea Gull* and converted the nonrequitals into a series of quick beddings-down: Medvedenko-Masha, then Masha-Treplev, then Treplev-Nina, and so on. Schnitzler converts the permanently unsatisfied desires in Chekhov into successive cases of instant satiety, the plot in space into the plot in time.

make-do arrangements. But Turgenev includes no shock like that of Treplev's suicide, though he does admit an intensity of feeling that could lead to a tragic structure. Both dramatists present a series of sexual relationships, but, while Chekhov portrays more or less permanent situations, Turgenev depicts the lightning-storm disturbances in an otherwise placid country scene when a charming young man from Moscow comes for a month's stay. This is the old mythic event of the alien visitor who stands the local community on its head (as in the later *Playboy of the Western World*).

The visitor is Beliayev, twenty-one, the summer tutor of Kolya, ten, son of the well-to-do landowner Islayev. Islayev's wife Natalya, twenty-nine, has a lover of some four years' standing, Rakitin. In the offing there is a possible *mariage de convenance* between the loquacious and humorous Dr. Shpigelsky and Lizaveta Bogdanovna, an Islayev companion pushing forty. There is a familiar ludicrousness as Shpigelsky tries to aid Bolshintsov, an oafish farmer of forty-eight, in his suit for the hand of Vera, the Islayev ward aged seventeen. Matvey, the Islayev manservant, is angling for the hand of the maid Katya, who seems also to enjoy the passes of Schaaf, the German tutor (a traditional almost farcical pedagogue). Actual or possible pairings everywhere. Enter Beliayev, the attractive Moscow university student, lively, zestful, an enthusiastic leader of others in sports, rather shy, and an erotic catalyst *malgré lui*. Katya the maid gets a crush on him; Vera falls in love with him and thus sets up her first taste of unhappiness; and Natalya, husband and lover notwithstanding, is infatuated with him.

Natalya, jealous, becomes nasty to the younger Vera, Rakitin bitterly resents losing his position as favorite, Islayev fears infidelity by his wife. The dramatic centering of Natalya, with the intensity of the emotions that she feels and begets, lets us imagine what *The Way of the World* would be like if Marwood were the main character. Along with sensuality Natalya has in her something of "heddism"—that not wholly defined yearning in which a superstructure of romantic idealism rests on a hidden base of power-love that can be voracious or destructive. Somewhat the spoiled child too, and sure of the attentiveness and even subservience of others, Natalya never anticipates the cost of letting passion take over. She can be indifferent to the suffering Rakitin, can wheedle secrets from Vera and try to steer her away from Beliayev. She can pretend, plot, and then confess and throw herself on the mercy of the court, enjoying the theatricality of this and hoping to appease her victims. To Beliayev she can acknowledge her infatuation and, taking an enormous gamble, virtually invite him to her bed.

Yet she has just enough awareness of what she is doing, and inability to stop doing it, to have the dividedness of the tragic personality. She is a potential Phaedra. And Beliayev, her Hippolytus, partly reciprocates Natalya's sexual excitement—but just enough to be frightened rather than cooperative. Here the play fascinatingly balances on a border line between tragedy and comedy. In tragedy, the choice is irresistibly for the out-of-bounds, come what may; in comedy, the choice is for the safer and less glamorous course. Beliayev has some concern for the unhappiness he has unwittingly caused, but above all his fear of the hangover outweighs his susceptibility to the proffered intoxication. He edges away. And since he can, and does, retreat to Moscow, he is invulnerable to revenge by the rejected Phaedra: the elimination of a potentially tragic or melodramatic outcome.

So the summer storm dies away. Yet it leaves marks. His idyl ended, Rakitin resentfully departs with Beliayev, sardonically remarking, "Nice position mine! Glorious, it certainly is! Really it's positively refreshing. And what a farewell after four years of love!" (V).[22] Vera, the charming teen-ager, not loved by Beliayev, and fearing Natalya's feline hostility, escapes by marrying the unromantic older Bolshintsov, at whose suit she had once laughed incredulously. Islayev has known suspicion of his wife for the first time (an ironic tardiness in him). Natalya, having given up Rakitin and failed to acquire Beliayev in his stead, is in much distress. After all the lightning things look drab. Yet Natalya still has a devoted husband. Beliayev has escaped a potential disaster. Rakitin may have a good time in Moscow. We are by no means sure that Vera cannot make do with Bolshintsov, and in time she may have a Rakitin of her own. Shpigelsky, happy with the three horses he has got for brokering the Bolshintsov-Vera affair, talks on in his merry or jocose style, and his marriage with Lizaveta Bogdanovna seems likely to come off. In these multiple developments we are not forced to think anyone irretrievably lost; rather we see the various compromises that are the fare of all but the wisest or luckiest. Thus the "essence of the play" is, as Michael Redgrave has said, "comic and anti-romantic."[23] The note of misunderstanding which repeatedly contributes amusement during the play is important in the closing scene. Islayev and his mother are both confused by all the goings-on, especially the goings-away. As Islayev puts it, "I understand nothing. . . . All fluttering off in different directions like a lot of partridges, and all because they're honourable men. . . . And all at once on the same day" (V). There is a touch of farce in this. The pace prevents the held focus on failure or grief that the dramatist uses when he does not treat the situation as comic.

Congreve's "The Way of the World"

While Turgenev's play is sometimes thought to be noncomic, no one tries to alter the traditional classification of *The Way of the World* (though commentators are often tempted to see in it a "tragic" coloring). What is not always seen, however, is that it is one of the earliest and greatest plays to view the world generously in its multiplicity (and in the years when society was becoming averse to such generosity and was beginning to demand of literature and the theater a more simplistic and indeed censorious view). Congreve extraordinarily manages to smile in many directions without sneering or disparaging, and yet never to let understanding drift into a permissiveness that is really value-dismissive. He sees that sexual relationships take as many forms as circumstances and the personalities of lovers make possible; he also sees that some personalities move toward an exemplary relationship which, simply by existing and without in any faint way being pushed toward such a role by the author, becomes an implicit commentary on all the others. In setting a permanent example for the treatment of love in terms of multiplicity, Congreve has an ampler view than is possible to most of his successors: his characters are more conscious of social and fiscal realities than would be possible after Romantic feeling swept Europe. Mirabell and Millamant want to live in the world, be adequately endowed, and have a marriage in which a sense of form and dignity will strengthen the substance; they do not make passionate feeling a sole value, think of running away to some Arcadia, or plan an off-limits affair. They do not, that is, seek a solution in either nonworldly or exclusively worldly terms. The Fainalls represent the *mariage de convenance*, his concern money, hers a husband in case she should become pregnant (an arrangement not disparaged in the play; in the closing lines Mirabell does not "toy" with Millamant but rather expresses the hope that, with property restored to Mrs. Fainall, the Fainalls may "live easily together"). The Mirabell–Mrs. Fainall relationship is the friendship that survives an affair. Fainall and Mrs. Marwood struggle in an extramatrimonial liaison beset by difficulties; one of these is that Marwood can't get over a passion for Mirabell—a case of unrequited love. The servants Waitwell and Foible represent a practical arrangement different from that of the Fainalls.

When Mirabell jestingly complains, ". . . you think you were married for your own recreation, and not for my conveniency," Waitwell replies, ". . . we have indeed been solacing in lawful delights; but still with an eye to business, sir" (II): sex in a context of assigned tasks. Mrs. Fainall's mother Lady Wishfort has not only financial power but a live sexual interest which, in her desire to "save decorums," she translates into romantic platitudes that make her an easy mark for the pseudo protestations of Waitwell in an intrigue engineered by Mirabell. Millamant is so fashionable a belle that even fops and a rustic seek, or are encouraged to seek, her hand.

These are the ways of the world in love—all seen as in the nature of things, none regretted or inveighed against or for that matter formally exalted. Multiplicity means multiobjectivity: variety with a kind of equivalence. The ways are observed as more or less workable, more or less comfortable, more or less costly or taxing. Some are doomed to failure, and there is nothing that can be done about it. If these were at the center, the result would be a romantic drama of disaster, but when they are seen in the full context of possibilities, they stay within the realm of comedy; indeed, by pushing comedy beyond its ordinary bounds, they enlarge and enrich it. Lady Wishfort's ill-concealed eagerness for sex is ludicrous, but in its futility—both in her naïve striving for propriety and in the impossibility of a successful outcome—it approaches the pathetic. So we have a complication of tone that works against the possibility of stereotyping. Still stronger in impact is Marwood's bitter resentment at Mirabell: she has to disguise this other love and jealousy from her lover Fainall, and she gambles everything on a plot to infuriate Lady Wishfort against Mrs. Fainall, Millamant, and Mirabell, partly in the hope of getting Lady Wishfort's money for Fainall, but primarily to spite the lovers whose happiness prevents hers. There is something of the Medea in her. So along with her recklessness and revengefulness goes a capacity for suffering. She can tell Fainall that "it is not yet too late . . . to loathe, detest, abhor mankind, myself, and the whole treacherous world" (II), and when her plotting is exposed to Lady Wishfort, she can cry out, "Oh, my shame!" (V)—remarkable lines in a play where most feelings are translated into the language of wit. When the vindictiveness against nearly all the others is paired with Marwood's anguished judgment of herself, we have indeed a moment of tragic feeling. But it is a moment; it does not become a major segment of the action. It is a very spacious kind of comedy that can include such intensity of feeling.

The number of women who love or have loved Mirabell is matched by the number of men who pursue Millamant. The famous "bargaining scene" between Mirabell and Millamant in Act IV gains some of its effectiveness by being juxtaposed with a series of other love-makings: here there is a multiplicity of revelatory styles. The act opens with Lady Wishfort's nervously arranging the coynesses that will most impress "Sir Rowland" (Waitwell), who is coming to ask her hand. But her rustic nephew Sir Wilfull, whom she has ordered to propose to Millamant, is getting drunk to face this ordeal. Then comes the central Mirabell-Millamant scene. After it the two fops, Witwoud (Sir Wilfull's half-brother) and Petulant, enter drunk, and Petulant makes a quick mechanical proposal to Millamant. The drunken fop is followed by the drunken rustic Sir Wilfull: "But if you have a mind to be married, say the word, . . . Wilfull will do't." (Congreve not only makes the opposing types, rustic and fop, good-natured and occasionally sensible or witty, but he paradoxically discovers their likenesses; having proposed, Petulant cries, "I'll go to bed to my maid," and Sir Wilfull, "Where are the wenches?") Then come the flowery protestations of "Sir Rowland" to Lady Wishfort, who nearly overwhelms him with her denials of "sinister appetite," "lethargy of continence," and "prone [ness] to any iteration of nuptials" (after which Waitwell assures his wife that he will "have no appetite to iteration of nuptials this eight-and-forty hours"). So in this act we have seen the key proposal, one that brings into play both deep feeling and sharp intelligence, as a center: on one side of it, dutiful or fashionable proposals and on the other the rhetoric of romantic tradition well simulated in a mock proposal. Among these styles practiced in the world, one is humanly superior, and it marks a way of life that has advantages over some of the other relationships surveyed in Congreve's tolerant panoramic vision.

Opening Out and Closing In

Two counterpressures are always at work in the world: the pressure to widen the scene or open it out, and the pressure to narrow it down, to close it off. Here I allude not to public formal actions such as those which encourage a wider tolerance (e.g., desegregation) or try to repress actions deemed bad (e.g., "Prohibition"), but to much less evident pressures—emotional, psychological, credal. In the 1960s and 1970s, for instance, there was a much greater openness to nonrational phenomena as possible bearers of truth and value than there had been some decades earlier—an

"opening out." On the other hand, a "closing in": the popular applications of Freudian psychology or Marxian dialectic that crowd the air are
almost invariably reductive: they tend to refer all kinds of phenomena to a
lowest common denominator, to an easily manageable simplicity. (Every
age has such counterimpulses: in the eighteenth century one opening-out
form was humanitarianism, and one closing-in form was the shrinking of
sex to the unmentionable.)

Such impulses affect comic form. The tendency to find a single most
desirable option created, in the eighteenth century, sentimental comedy:
the good heart became an exclusive value, and hence an easy divider of the
good and the bad. In our own day the simplifying reductive tendency, the
quest for the lowest common denominator, results in the limited form
which we call black comedy.

But I introduce the comparison only as a way into the more important
point: that the multiplicity form is one aesthetic evidence of the impulse
to expand the scene, to open it out. The form says, in effect, that we do
not expect one pattern of life to be equally open to or obligatory upon
everyone; hence we do not condemn alternatives but live with different
forms of living. The multiplicity form opens the stage to a wide range of
characters; it permits the introduction of various eccentrics without falling
into a doctrinaire contrast of the deviant and the normal. Comedy from
Ben Jonson to Congreve tended to use large casts, and that century
produced the widest range of "characters" on the comic stage. Finally, and
most important, the wide range of characters makes it easy and natural to
introduce, without obtrusive emphases, those individuals who embody a
way of life that makes fullest use of the human potential. The dramatist
does not formally set them up as an ideal; rather they are spontaneously
and inevitably produced by a wide-ranging, inclusive imagination. And
simply by their presence they put a kind of pressure on the world—the
world to which they belong and the world of us who observe them—not to
fall below its full capabilities; they are never reformers, but by their
presence they may assist a world not to be too easy on itself.

Some time back we were observing that "the world" is paradoxically
both a medley of diverse options and a normative voice that is audible to
those who will hear. In one sense, the world collectively embodies a norm
of good sense which may not be wholly embodied in any one person. In
another sense, the "medley of diverse options," when it is broadly enough
conceived, has to include the individual of talent or wisdom or a beneficent style that makes itself felt. This individual is not pushed downstage

as an exemplar; he is not a speaker for a code, but simply *is*, the unself-conscious enacter of an option which has to recommend itself. The dispa-rate, that is to say, includes not merely the ordinary, the average, the neutrally differing, and the less adequate, but also the excellent, which may be exceptional but need not be the untransmittable possession of the few.

Two forms of excellence, neither spectacular but both valuable in and to the world, characteristically manifest themselves in comedy. One excel-lence takes a negative form: the rejection of wrong ideas and attitudes, and the making-do with a less illusioned view of oneself. We have seen various kinds of self-recognition in Goldsmith's two plays (especially by Hon-eywood in *The Good-Natured Man*), in Boucicault's *London Assurance*, in Hofmannsthal's *Arabella*, in Eliot's *Cocktail Party* (the Chamberlaynes), in Fry's *The Dark Is Light Enough*, in Shaffer's *The White Liars*, in Nichols' *A Day in the Death of Joe Egg*.* One of the most illustrative of such experi-ences is that of Perpetua Reedbeck in Fry's *Venus Observed* (noted in chap. 3). She gives up reform-by-destruction as futile, ponders what she can do "for the world," and concludes, "You must make good, before you break the bad" (I). In recognizing her error—the millennializing which is the antithesis of comic acceptance—she does more than act negatively: she also voices the affirmative excellence which is exhibited in comedy—enacting a certain quality of life. To *be* "good" is to *do* something for the world.

This second mode of excellence—exemplification of a durable value—is especially characteristic of the multiplicity pattern, for this pattern in-evitably includes the individuals who serve the world simply by exhibit-ing a certain quality that is admirable in itself. It is characteristic of multiplicity works not only to survey various options dispassionately but also, without using a moral pointer, to imagine one option in which a man and a woman achieve an especially mature and adequate way of life. In Huxley's *Point Counter Point* the Rampions, with a relationship marked by both strong feeling and lively thinking, have a better basis for living than those who go mainly by ideological dogmas of the left or right, sentimentality, sexuality alone, habit, vanity, intellectual dominance, and so on. In *Pride and Prejudice* Elizabeth and Darcy bring the fullest

*There is an interesting bit of repentant self-knowledge by Strepsiades late in Aristophanes' *Clouds*: "Alas for my delusion! Mad indeed I was when for Socrates' sake / I cast out the gods. Dear Hermes, be not angry with me, / Do not crush me, pardon the glib silliness I spoke." But this comic episode is subordinate to the satire of Socrates.

natures into play as they gradually recognize their suitability for each other; both have strong preconceptions that lead to mutual censoriousness and misjudgment, and each must mature by correcting himself and re-valuing the other. In contrast with the other pairings, which result from simple design or uncomplicated feelings, the relationship of Elizabeth and Darcy is an *earned* one: thus they reveal a human capacity that bodes well for the world. They like the world and are going to live in it, though they will not form themselves on the easiest pattern that it makes available.

Mirabell and Millamant

This brings us back to Mirabell and Millamant and a scene which we passed over lightly before—the "bargaining scene" which is the symbolic center of their relationship. Like Elizabeth and Darcy, they are going to be very much of the world, but they also seek terms that will improve on the most obvious ways of that world. From the beginning they have engaged in spirited battles of wit, and their exchanges nearly always embody a very active play of ideas. When they argue whether a woman's beauty is a thing-in-itself to which lovers respond, or is only a creation of the lovers, they very brightly rehearse an old philosophical question. Mirabell is annoyed at her taking "a course [i.e., medical treatment] of fools," and she objects to being "reprimanded" and "instructed" and to his "violent and inflexible wise face." He feels tossed about by her "whirlwind ways," and comments to himself, "To know this, and yet continue to be in love, is to be made wise from the dictates of reason, and yet persevere to play the fool by the force of instinct" (II). So there is continual evidence that they are exceptional people, skilled in playful but acute criticisms, and yet self-knowing too.

Hence we are ready for the engagement scene, in which they try to define a marriage style that will avoid the usual sentimentalities and vulgarities, and in which each in turn, despite his independence, is will-ing to let the other "speak and spare not" in defining what they shall do and not do. Above all, it is not a humorless marriage-counselor type of blue-printing; the jesting style never flags, and occasional sexual jokes are another hedge against solemnity. Every point is both a critical thrust at bad matrimonial behavior but also a pledge to avoid it. We need not summarize the terms here. They prescribe a dignity and reserve of style for both (no "nauseous cant" of trite endearments in public; "Let us be as strange as if we had been married a great while, and as well-bred as if we were not married at all") and independence for the wife: "To have my closet inviolate," that is, to have a room of her own that he cannot enter without permission. She in turn will do without a female confidante, masked adventures, tight lacing during pregnancy, private drinking, and so on—a notable abstinence from fashionable ways. Her unsentimental acceptance of him is "I think—I'll endure you," though she can tell Mrs. Fainall that "if Mirabell should not make a good husband, I am a lost thing, for I find I love him violently" (IV). She rejects the clichés of emotion, but the emotion itself is there, leaping forth in rare moments to reveal the firm foundation beneath verbal games in which very bright minds, governed by taste and imagination, reject the foolish and the false.

But whatever the foolish and false elements in the world, it is in the world that Mirabell and Millamant will live. They do not ape Molière's Alceste, who would "seek some spot unpeopled and apart / Where I'll be free to have an honest heart" (V.viii). In these lines Alceste, who can do better on occasion, is the voice of romantic escapism; elsewhere he is the voice of all who blame and scourge the world, of the satirists, the uto-pians, the ideologues, of all those who take for granted their own posses-sion of the virtues in which they see the world sadly lacking. What is extraordinary in Mirabell and Millamant is the way in which they reverse this anticomic style: they see the world clearly, but they do not deny it, abjure it, or even claim superiority to it. What they really do is this: instead of demanding, like censors, that the world find a higher style than it customarily displays, they *impose higher expectations upon themselves*. That is the heart of the second excellence which the comic imagination discerns as a human possibility in the many-sided world.

In accepting the world in all its disparateness, then—in its multiplicity of ways that may be foolish or sensible, conventional or contriving, shrewd or dream-driven—comedy also accepts the ability and desire of some men and women to see into or through themselves and to understand and, whether they formally define it or not, to engage in a way of life that exacts more of them than do the ordinary routines in which most people live. Thus its characteristically genial view of multiplicity is not valueless, for the many include the few who live easily with the rest but also unself-consciously practice an *ought* amid all the varieties of the *is*. Nor is the acceptance of many ways cynical, for comedy does not assert that all are equal in value (or lack of value). What it does assert is that every way has its own validity—its appropriate utility for the personalities to which, in their greater or lesser resources, it corresponds. But comedy goes on from acknowledging validities to discovering value when it portrays the few who untheatrically prefer a demanding imperative to an easy custom. They do not announce it, any more than the dramatist does; we simply see them acting it out. And that acting out of the ought, simply by being there, puts a quiet, uninsistent pressure upon the world in which it occurs—and indeed upon the larger world represented by the audience observing the stage world. The action of the special comic heroes, unpreached but visible, makes it harder for other men to be as easy on themselves as they can be when they look only at the less wise.* The rare possessors of these excellences in the world are not always present; what they stand for may be only implied. When they are present, we see them as parts of the infinite variety of the comic scene—a variety accepted unquarrelsomely, jestingly, often urbanely. There go all of us. There, too, may go a Mirabell and a Millamant, forming and exhibiting a life that makes special demands on them. They may have the impact that the better achievement sometimes has.

*Perhaps in that sense comedy might be thought to have the function long attributed to it and traditionally called "corrective." I use the term hesitantly, and I immediately hasten to repeat that the comic correctiveness, if we are to use the term, does not proceed by the satiric flagellation of the uncorrected, but operates only through the unpretentious enactment of a corrected way of life that, being perceived, might stir some sharper perception of what is possible. And yet even so circumspect a statement might suggest the formal exemplum, which is entirely outside the domain of comedy. Whatever might be thought corrective is only one element in the arsenal of comic materials; its presence might not even be felt, and at best it would be uninsistent, not raising its voice above the choral amplitude of presented life.

Epilogue

To accept the ways of the world means often to come to terms with a wayward world; to come to terms is less to affix an easy seal of approval than to contemplate the habitual and indeed incurable ironies of life in the world; the laughter that we often associate with this observing of waywardness implies something of good nature, some awareness that deviancy is "normal," some recognition that we ourselves participate in disparateness, that we move in the imperfect scene as well as behold it from the gazebo. So our way with the ways of the world is somewhat mixed: it is mostly unjudging, it ought to be ungrudging, it cannot be unbudging.

Disparateness

"Waywardness": since it does not let us off the hook too easily, it sums up fittingly all the modes of disparateness that comedy accepts. In the broadest sense comedy observes the discrepancy between imaginable or stated ideals and human actuality: we laud truthfulness, but we are imperfectly truthful. The "ideal" can dwindle from the Platonic idea to a party platform or a private preoccupation; the concept not realized in action may be a philosophic notion, a dogma, a doctrine, an expectation, a preconception. Goldsmith's Honeywood tries to live out a theory of benevolence (as does Shakespeare's Timon, who is more vague and self-deceptive about it), but his handouts exhaust his means, and, people being what they are, elicit no gratitude or reciprocity. Beckett's Didi and Gogo cherish expectations that the event does not fulfill; it is wrong to read as bitter or absurd an outcome that is a uniquely brilliant symbolization of commonplace experience. The Gods in Brecht's *Good Person of Setzuan* expect more "good" people than they find, and the good person they approve finds that her generosity only spoils her beneficiaries. Molière's M. Jourdain embodies an unusual doubleness: he reveres gentlemanliness but understands it so poorly that, while apparently helping him upward, the world only parodies his aspirations. M. Jourdain, who is so foggy about the ideal that he can be put upon by pranksters, is the opposite of the idealist who is so sure about the good that he wants to put it over on the world by law. In the comic vision of disparateness, the risk of program is making all life programmatic, but fuzziness in program means vulnerability to jest and plot; doctrine begets the doctrinaire, but its absence means a confused course.

The preconception that disregards the many-stranded texture of actuality may be a piece of naïveté, a mistake, an illusion, an *idée fixe*, a monomania. The prejudgment that ignores the way the world goes may be neither harmful nor prophetic,* but simply foolish or vexing. An errant egotism may make a person suspicious, grasping, interfering, controlling, possessive, sponging, self-important, pretentious, or rude. Such a person is comic if he is more annoying than dangerous, more expectable than shocking, more a frail everyman than a censurable wrongdoer. Fops, rustics, malaprops, fixers such as Austen's Emma, overreachers in Jacobean and Restoration comedy, doctrinaires in Aristophanes, and the neurotics, schemers, and self-righteous in Molière—in most of them there is more of human fallibility than of inadmissible vice. But if comedy bears with the erring, it also bears with the special individuals who do better than most of us do most of the time—by holding to standards that exact more of them than the world does. Comedy escapes that discomfort with superiority which, as Margaret Kennedy has observed, makes us want to apply the term "realistic" only to obviously inferior conduct.[1]

In noticing the discrepancy between idea and fact, I have at times edged

---

*The more the idea-ridden man becomes intense, intransigent, and power-seeking, the more he demands the rejective style of satire. If he throws others into a struggle for survival, the result is melodrama. If he is an aggressor but is capable of moral awareness, the form can be tragic. Or if he is treated as a lonely prophet—he is right, and the world wrong—the mode is romantic.

into the contiguous realm of inconsistency within personalities or between personalities and the norms of this world. Along with the self-image that is palpably erroneous (as with Malvolio), there is the self-image that can be but is not sustained. Thus in *Twelfth Night* and Sheridan's *Rivals* characters who are drawn into duels reveal a disquietude and fearfulness never admitted in the noncomic treatment of heroes (or, for that matter, of nonheroes, as in R. C. Sherriff's *Journey's End* [1928]). Likewise Sheridan's Sir Peter Teazle in *The School for Scandal* is sure he is a very reasonable man, but he is charmingly self-deceptive: "I am, myself, the sweetest-tempered man alive, and hate a teasing temper; and so I tell her [Lady Teazle] a hundred times a day" (I.ii), and "I'll not bear her presuming to keep her temper" (III.i). Men and women make commitments and then find them hard to live up to: Aristophanes' women swear off sex to make men swear off war, but Lysistrata needs great moral force to foil their schemes to evade their oath. Shaw's John Tanner believes in freedom generally, including his own from female wiles, but he is captured by Ann Whitefield. Henry Fielding repeatedly makes a character assert a value and then face the test of experience: in *Joseph Andrews* good Parson Adams first lectures Joseph against despair when his girl Fanny is apparently kidnaped by a rapist, and then, when his own son is reported drowned, goes completely to pieces. An individual may nourish an intention or a plan and then have it undercut by surprising motives and forces: thus Shakespeare's Benedick and Beatrice. "Life," as Robert Balzer has said, "is what happens to you while you're making other plans."[2] "Life" may be accidents, which create the reversals of farce, or another part of oneself. Hence a comeuppance that may be deflating or neutral or even ameliorative. Whatever her misery, Shakespeare's Kate doubtless relishes the sheer power of a shrew's tantrums; then she learns her capacity for gratifications of a quite different sort.

An individual "protests" that he is or does so and so; then his conduct betrays his protestation. "Protest" ties in admirably with "protests too much"; thus we distinguish the spontaneous inconsistency from the planned deception. To "protest" is to assert honestly, if mistakenly; to "protest too much" is hypocrisy, which, as Fielding put it, is the pretense to virtues that are the opposite of one's actual vices. This is the Tartuffian, of course, which demands satire.

The individual may depart from the "norms" which many critics see as one pole in comic disparateness. Jealous husbands and lovers in Restoration comedy fall away from a standard of good sense; familiar human emotions deflect them, not from moral conduct, but from a pragmatically sounder style established by experience. Misers and prodigals likewise fail in sense: one lets prudence shrink into tightfistedness, the other mistakes prudence for parsimony (or imprudence for benevolence). Comedy may juxtapose a deviation from a norm with a dramatized norm: Molière's egoistic critic Alceste is countered by Philinte and Eliante with their active moderation (whereas Osborne drifts over into melodrama because his impossible Alcestes have a roaring energy to which there is rarely an effective counterweight of good sense). Or a dramatist may juxtapose a too-much and a too-little: in terms of social history, fops and rustics; in folk terms, the Mutt-and-Jeff principle; in terms of theory, the Aristotelian concept of excesses and deficiencies. In *Pride and Prejudice* Mrs. Bennet has too little sense, whereas Mr. Bennet, we may say, has too much; Mr. Collins is strong on rules and short on charm, while Wickham is short on rules and long on charm. In Nichols' *The National Health* there are the sentimentality of the television show and the cynicism of Barnet. Restoration drama more than once balances the naïve girl against the oversophisticated schemer; in turn it may be her practical eye against his egotistic blind spot.

Inconsistency may not require a norm; the artist may simply present different attitudes or styles each of which can claim some validity or utility. In Trollope's *The Warden* Harding displays the Christian spirit as conscience, Grantly turns it into institutional combativeness. Different personalities make different choices; the emphasis is less on better or worse than on variety of response, perhaps infinite variety. The point of *A Day in the Death of Joe Egg* is the diversity of adjustments to a child's incurable illness; the author lets us judge the modes of response if we will, but his objective is variety rather than judgment. If variety becomes absolute and no judgment is even possible, the end result is a Pirandellian relativism.

When the author uses the Mutt-and-Jeff principle, the easily visible physical terms may be symbolic. Mutt and Jeff, for instance, are reduced commonplace descendants of Don Quixote and Sancho Panza. Cervantes' characters, observes György Lukács, "have something mask-like about them: the one is tall and the other short, the one thin, the other fat; and the existence of each, being of such a kind, is absolute and excludes its opposite from the start."[3] Hence Don Quixote and Sancho Panza illustrate the disparateness, not only between subjective visions and an objective world (the Don's experience), but also between objective entities or modes of being. As comic writer, Cervantes appreciates both sides, whereas a romantic would idealize Quixote, and an anti-idealist, Sancho.

Hence, as critics such as Monro and Rodway argue, comedy can be either "conservative" or "radical." Yet it need be neither, and it is safest to avoid both these terms, since they imply a sociopolitical direction which is more often absent than present, and invoke loyalties and biases that can obscure our insight into comic processes. Let us try a different formulation: insofar as the comic sense of disparateness invokes a norm, that norm may be better exemplified by the representatives of "the system" or by individuals not wholly identified with it (and yet not revolutionary in posture). Still better: a durable norm is rooted in the coalescence of complementary values. Don Quixote is, so to speak, an "outsider," one who is neither romanticized nor satirized: his flaw is that he misses the thrust of ordinary reality, but on the other hand he embodies a spirit that is indispensable if ordinary reality itself is not to fall below human potential and become grossly material. Sancho is in tune with actuality, with majorities, and in that sense is an "insider"; his way of seeing is also indispensable, and yet its obvious deficiency is that it imprisons men within the commonplace. The system and its would-be physician are both justified partially; the comic embraces both states, the "is" and the "can be." In Jane Austen everybody is within the system; all deviations are excesses or deficiencies of the qualities needed for its health (good sense, good manners, good feeling); the critiques of the order envisage not its replacement but its living up to the rules for well-being. Austen's superior characters, much like those in Restoration drama, improve on going styles by finding the human resources for a code that will be more demanding and more gratifying than the commonplace routines. In Shakespearian comedy, as often noted, resolutions involve a general reintegration within the social framework (the festive, as C. L. Barber calls it, implies an ordering and healing rite), yet at times the guiding voice comes from outside. Prospero might be content forever with his Edenic isle, but he elects, finally, to use it as a base for a rectification of order in the larger world: he gives up both the romantic scene and the romantic instrument that he has used restoratively. The "norm" has survived in an outside spot; then it returns to the inside, though with no guarantee that it will be invulnerable. "Reconciliation" is never free from risk.

In Kataev's *Squaring the Circle* no one questions the rules of the order, and hence there may seem to be no possibility of disparateness. But in

Kataev's skillful handling, the needed inconsistency is between the way the rules work and the way the adherents think they work. The young couples feel that their new loves are unacceptable deviancies; then the system turns out to have an accommodating flexibility rather than a condemning rigidity. The play reinterprets the norm, much as a brief brilliant episode late in *The School for Scandal* does. In the final confrontation Snake is expected to save the sinners by a profitable perjury, but his evidence wrecks them. He explains apologetically to Lady Sneerwell, "I beg your ladyship ten thousand pardons: you paid me extremely liberally for the lie in question; but I unfortunately have been offered double to speak the truth" (V.iii). If he had said something like "I cannot tell a lie," comic disparateness would give way to a simplistic victory of truth over falsehood. Happily the effect turns instead on a jest about values. If ideally men believe that honesty is an obligation and hence its own "reward," in practice they often translate the idea downward into the proverb quoted by various figures from Cervantes to Washington, "Honesty is the best policy." Snake's action "interprets" this "norm": honesty not only succeeds (the end of policy), but pays off, that is, may be bought, even from a rascal. The disparateness is that of venality and veracity as fellow-travelers, of dubious means and good ends.

Mirabell and Millamant, as we have seen, reinterpret the norm in a different way: they make harder (above normal) rules for themselves but get on with those who take easier ways. Thus, though "deviants," they are not romanticized into lonely prophets. They know what the world is, they do not try to change it, and they will live in it.

Acceptance

The varieties of disparateness—the waywardnesses of the world—that comedy accepts are matched by the styles of acceptance. On occasion comedy celebrates superiority and the especially well done—an acceptance that avoids banality because it does not mean rejecting the nonsuperior and the not-well-done. More often comedy applauds good sense or common sense, the balance that combines survival with the surrender of first choices or of very desirable ends seen finally as unattainable. To accept is to see what is possible, probable, or inevitable and yet, though these may not be wholly desirable or admirable, to make do. To accept is to see that what will be can be manageable and even satisfying; to find the disappointing and the imperfect understandable, and yet not to extend understanding into the forgiveness of the unforgivable (the vicious and destructive). It does not mistake the frustrating and the disturbing for the insufferable. Acceptance of apparent disaster—illness or even death—is the heart of sick comedy, which greets the hostilities of nature with jest or fantasy or even the outrageous rather than with stiff-lipped stoicism. To accept is to grant that life ordinarily gives people what their talents and their use of them permit, even though what comes to people like ourselves may fall below desire. To accept is to join Conrad in loving humanity while knowing that it cannot be improved. It frequently means being content with half a loaf, even while recognizing that the gifted may earn, or the lucky may find in their hands, more than half a loaf, and the less talented or fortunate, a belated slice or two (in melodrama the quest is for the whole loaf, or against the loaf-holder, or in behalf of those with crumbs only). The comic view means, as Eliot's Harcourt-Reilly puts it, avoiding "excessive expectation." It means being at ease with the mixed bag. In Giraudoux's *Electra* President Theocathocles inferentially attributes a comic sense to humanity when he says that its inclination is always toward "compromise and forgetfulness." In a perceptive essay on *The Merchant of Venice* J. A. Bryant, Jr., argues that Shakespeare's plays continually ask us "to accept substitutes until a true king be by," for present action "correcting whatever is obviously in need of correction and continuing to hope that the rest will in good time either correct itself or prove the critics wrong." Bryant continues, "Such acceptance Shakespearean comedy regularly requires of us in lieu of the poetic justice and other kinds of distortion that we are sometimes tempted to impose upon it. This is the bittersweet truth that we all too often fail to penetrate to as the vision of harmony blinds us; but the bittersweet is there, and only an acceptance of both parts of that compound can make the plays truly satisfying, as they stand, without reduction." [4] It is well said.

In nonliterary life the chief analogue of comedy is the society committed to the acceptance of the disparate (in America, rigid opponents of integration, both white and black, want to live in a melodrama of opposition). British pre-eminence in comedy reflects a society with a strong gift for compromise and a strong sense of the constant imperfect ways of the world. (Bossuet's "perfidious Albion" voices the craving for absolute determinations, like Captain Ahab's.) The psychotherapy that seeks acceptance rather than conversion is analogous to the comic, as are most educational processes, since they embrace disparate expectations and objectives and enact compromises rather than ideal codes (and are capable of farcical pratfalls).[5] The analogy between the literary and the societal is excellently put by Thomas Mann in a comment on politics: "Politics has been called the 'art of the possible,' and it actually is a realm akin to art insofar as, like art, it occupies a creatively mediating position between the spirit and life, the idea and reality, the desirable and the necessary, conscience and deed, morality and power. It embraces much that is hard, necessary, amoral, much of expediency and concession to facts, much of human weakness and much of the vulgar."[6] Mann describes compactly "the world," as the Countess puts it in Fry's *The Dark Is Light Enough*, "where bad and good eat at the same table" (I), and where, to go a step further with Anaïs Nin, there is "the great uneven flow of life with its necessary disorder and ugliness."[7]

Now for two final amplifications of the idea of acceptance: first, the fact that it can embrace other ways of accounting for comic experience; and second, the kinds of antagonism to acceptance which would render comedy impossible.

At the end of Chapter 1, I remarked that certain traditional accounts of comedy which were ambiguous in themselves nevertheless could be useful if seen in the light of a more inclusive description of comic action such as I think mine is. For instance, the incongruity theory is good up to a point, but it implies, first, the comic value of a static situation instead of locating the comic in the acceptance of the situation, and, second, a temporary discord rather than a disparateness in the nature of things, reparable in some details perhaps, but on the whole to be lived with. Likewise the ambivalence theory is most meaningful if it applies not simply to the doubleness of a situation but rather to our making do with the doubleness. The view that comic laughter gushes forth from a sense of superiority embodies a series of possibilities. For instance, comedy deals frequently with complacent or scheming people who believe themselves superior to others; they meet with setbacks and comedowns, and possibly we enjoy a triumph over them. But so simple a pleasure is afforded less by comedy than by farce, which depicts a confusion inferior to our own clarity. Above the farce level, we are rather asked to look at the nontriumphant and say "There go I." At least we are made aware of the difficulties for the sense of the superiority as it struggles with a resistant world, and we may identify with the good sense that ordinarily makes do with much less than the sense of superiority seeks. The greater the comedy, the more it discourages simplistic responses such as triumph. Instead it produces the sense of well-being conferred by adequate art; it makes us aware of a complex actuality in which we participate too much to be looking down on it from a safe pedestal.

Two other familiar theories of comedy contradict each other: the ancient view that comedy is corrective, and the more recent product of Bergson romanticism, that comedy is the voice of freedom, spontaneity, "life," a voice that is antimechanistic and antiauthoritarian and may espouse phallic revivalism. In the one view comedy chastises, in the other it glorifies, deviancy. However, the corrective work is satirical rather than comic; it opposes rather than accepts. Even the corrective action is only within the play; the spectator is less likely to see himself among the castigated than to relish the castigation of others. The problem with the freedom-spontaneity theory is that it rejects the norm instead of accepting it as an inevitable pole in the disparateness of the world, and thus makes comedy not an ironic contemplator but an evangelist for anarchy. But we can make some use of each position if we see both in relation to the comic acceptance of disparateness. We can construe the acceptance as "corrective" if we understand that by it the reader, just as in his reception of all mature art, is imaginatively modifying a prior view which does not adequately embrace the reality he is confronting. We can construe the acceptance as "liberating" if we understand that its impact upon his imagination helps free him from too rigid ideas of what the world is or must be. In such a sense, too, the acceptance of the disparate embraces Elder Olson's theory of the comic katastasis, the relaxation of concern (though without adopting Olson's unfortunately trivializing view that we relax when the cause of concern is shown to be not serious).

To see the comic as a ferule is, ironically, to make cause with all those combat positions that would proscribe comedy by treating acceptance as a form of acquiescence in what should be punished or eliminated. Inflexible rules for the good are anticomic, as is any utopian dreaming which treats defections from the ideal as intolerable errors rather than expectable shortcomings. Edward Shils's essay "Ideology and Civility" is relevant: it defines "civility" as "the virtue of the citizen,"[8] that is, "compromise and reasonableness, prudent self-restraint, and responsibility" (p. 57). Civility "requires a partial transcendence of partisanship [the melodramatic stance] as well as an empathic appreciation of the other parties within the circle. . . . Above all, civil politics require an understanding of the complexity of virtue, that no virtue stands alone, that every virtuous act costs something in terms of other virtuous acts, that virtues are intertwined with evils, and that no theoretical system of a hierarchy of virtues is ever realizable in practice" (pp. 61–62). Sociopolitical "civility" is, then, the acceptance of disparateness which in aesthetic terms produces comedy.

The major antagonist of civility, in Shils's view, is the "unbridgeable dualism of ideological politics which makes the most radical and uncompromising distinction between good and evil, left and right, national and unnational, American and un-American. Admixtures are intolerable . . ." (p. 44). "The ideological outlook is preoccupied with the evil of the world as it exists; it believes in the immiscibility of good and evil. It distinguishes sharply between the children of light and the children of darkness" (p. 51). One of the rigid and prescriptive ideologies is Marxism, with "its sheer unresponsiveness to the multiplicity of life itself" (p. 46)—the very multiplicity which I have proposed as the ultimate theme of comedy. Another antagonist of civility is "the millenarian tradition which is the oldest source of the ideological outlook" and which is "an ever-present potentiality in Christian teaching and experience" (p. 50),* and another is romanticism, which "views any existing order as repugnant because it mediates, compromises, and deforms the ideal" (p. 57). Shils's theoretical analysis corresponds exactly with the historical fact that the Romantic period was profoundly noncomic. All the pressures toward uniformity that Shils describes represent impulses that in aesthetic terms produce the melodramatic form—that form which, as we observed in Chapter 4, is constantly trying to snatch the world from the comic spirit. As long as we can call names, can see witches, can find villains rather than mistake-making, difference-prone people, we cannot compromise, we can demand the whole loaf, we can crusade—in a word, enjoy all the simple stimuli of melodrama rather than the more exacting pleasures of comedy. The other face of the passion to extirpate vice is the melioristic monomania: men of good will will to impose their good on men (Prohibition in the 1920s or compulsory seatbelts in the 1970s). Virtue-by-law, the reformists' melodrama, has occasionally a mild advantage on some melodrama: it can

---

*There is of course a Christian comic spirit; it can accept the disparateness of a world not in accord with doctrine. It began to appear in the miracle plays; another form of it is in C. S. Lewis' *Screwtape Letters*, and it crops up in T. S. Eliot's later plays. The religious may lead to the millenarian or to a forbearing contemplation of an actuality that could be wished better. One form of the disparateness of the world has as its poles the religious and the secular, or, to alter the terms, doctrine and performance, idea and history, the indispensable and the inevitable, the true way and waywardness. The better the dramatist, the more he embraces this basic duality (e.g., Shakespeare, Molière). And perhaps the steady stream of Irish comic writers may mean, not only a high incidence of genius, but the nourishing of that genius in a culture where one feels the church as a massive influence and has at the same time an extraordinary sense of human waywardness.

become the subject of comedy once men can see the disparateness between the sensible-possible and the utopian fiat. *Iolanthe* carries the "We need a law" mentality to a parodic ultimate.

Conspicuously anticomic is the egalitarian sensibility: a mania for homogeneity translates every disparateness into a curable inequity. To the egalitarian, a norm is not a reference-point defined by common sense through experience, but an oppressive middling state with which all must be brought into conformity. To the egalitarian, Mutt and Jeff are not independent symbols of eternal disparateness but victims in need of re-habilitation by institutional action. One must wear ballet slippers and the other elevator shoes; one must stoop and one must stretch (cosmetic traction); or doses of hormones will salvage both from differentness and push them toward indistinguishability. And as for Don Quixote and Sancho Panza, the egalitarian cannot say, "There goes everyman," and see him divided, much as in the morality plays, into alternative poten-tialities. Instead, each will be given a special diet, the Don will be packed off into group therapy, and Sancho pushed into night-school courses in the humanities. The dogma of absolute equality (as distinct from well-understood equalities in law, opportunity, and the like) always works against quality; it strengthens the pressure of the lowest common de-nominator against distinction. While antielitism, the trendy populism of the 1970s, appears to be a protest against inequitable privilege, it is at heart a rejection of the disparateness which manifests itself in superior taste or manners or perception (in literary terms, a resentment at or disbelief in the achievement of a Mirabell and a Millamant); it may also be a Tartuffian façade for those planning to be the power elite come the next apocalypse. Antielitism is a cousin of that solemn antiethnicism which pursues equality by rejecting ethnic and national comedy; it mistakes a sense of disparateness for a sense of superiority, that inferior man's self-defensiveness which will alas exist eternally to spark venomous jokes and which will of course gain in underground strength if a society cuts off the legitimate comedy of ethnic disparateness. If we are fortunate, Elmer Blistein is right when, opposing the proscriptive measures of well-meaning ethnic organizations, he declares that dialect humor has only "hibernated" and that we will "once again listen to [it] with easy enjoy-ment."[9]

In sum, the acceptance which makes comedy possible has as opponents all the ideological constrainers of the world, the enforcers of whatever coloration (Puritans, radicals, millenarians), and the egalitarians, all those for whom the disparate is desperate, and whose law is to make a law and not a play. All these partisan proclaimers of the nonnegotiable fall into two main anticomic types: the enforcers of the utopian, and the enforcers of the average. They would subject all daily life to the compulsion of first principles. But the world which we accept is the over-all medley of the casual, the heedless; the inconsistent, the inexplicable (the uneven distribution of talent and luck), the fallible, the illusive, and even the scheming—a mixed actuality which somehow evades first principles, not really to defy or deny them, but to forget them or limit their applicability, and thus exhibits whole, impure humanity in action.

If we do not call upon the numerous terms of nonacceptance—regret, disapprove, dislike, sorrow over, censure, can't stand, can't bear to look, flee from, feel disgust, feel sickened by, become indignant, protest, rebel, reject, retreat, despair, stoically endure—we manage an attunement to the disparateness of reality that produces its own mode of satisfaction. Conventionally we take laughter to be a symptom of that satisfaction, but laughter, as we have seen, is too many-sided and polysemous* to be a cornerstone of theory. At most it gives clues. There is a range from the antipathetic laugh to the sympathetic laugh, from the recognition of others to the recognition of oneself. There is a range from the belly-laugh (at the disparateness of the hurrying confusion that borders on chaos without getting too far from innocuousness) to the smile (at the disparateness that takes us a little closer to basic discords in which we share) or further to the steady recognition—smile more subdued or perhaps turned inward into a contemplative mood not cheerless but partly tinged with sadness—of those discrepancies that border on pain and yet do not call for remedy or do not admit of it. "Sadness" should not connote urgent distress or grief or sorrow, but rather the sobering awareness of the disappointments that always lurk in the wings, ready to diminish the lightness of some lives while others go on in the good cheer accompanying a sense of movement in a right direction (a combination of moods that we can observe in Chekhov and Turgenev, in Congreve and Synge). That is, the comic satisfaction or well-being may issue in merriment of different de-

*Alan Ayckbourn's *Absent Friends* (1975), a farce edging toward comedy, provides almost a glossary of theatrical laughter; in few plays do so many characters laugh so much or so variously. They laugh from high spirits, from animal energy, from confidence in insight, from uncertainty, from embarrassment, from the desire to simulate an unfelt hospitality or warmth; laughter expresses surprise, good intention, annoyance, the need to break a silence when words cannot be found, the desire to confer upon a party the gaiety which the situation itself does not encourage. The comic effect lies in the disparateness between the motives of these laughers and the more homogeneous expectations of laughter that the spectators have.

grees or in a more subdued sense of concord. The well-being may spring from two related kinds of gratification. One of these may be thought of as an increment of wisdom: the profitable pleasure of seeing anew, or seeing better, how the world goes, of grasping its disparateness in a way that makes us unillusioned but not disillusioned. We have a better sense both of human frailty and of human capacity; in the sense of the disparate, disappointed expectations are offset by unexpected betterments. In much comedy the saving element in a heterogeneous or discordant world is the capacity of some men to achieve a style that makes for balance and harmony. Hence the other sense of well-being that comes from observing such men acting, if only for a time, sensibly, understandingly, knowingly in the world: we feel ordered, with delight or a susurrus of contentment, by the imaginative experience of well-ordered conduct.*

The Impact of Comedy

We have gradually edged over from the meaning of "accept" to the impact of that central ingredient in the comic experience. Anthony Burgess, whose terms I have found so apposite, uses the word "elation" and adds, "The test is, it makes one, if not laugh, at least consider laughing. One feels one can push on." [10] "Elation" denotes the sense of gratification that I have been describing but also adds to it the excitement created by the dramatic tensions. "Consider laughing" places us neatly on the appropriate border between overt hilarity and the subtler sense of well-being that may appear in an actual smile or remain, so to speak, an inner smile. "Can push on"—not stoic fortitude, surely, not cold resolution and the steely will, but rather a perception of the bearable and occasionally the better-than-bearable, a pragmatic at-one-ness with a mixed reality, a consciousness that despair would be a neurotic excess and the utopian vision a delusion, a bearing with a middling—perhaps muddling—way of the world in which the lamentable and the frustrating, inalienable as they are, will not always defeat a persisting, if at times

*Such an account calls to mind a recent tendency to attribute a "redemptive" action to comedy and hence to hint at elements which would make the adjective "divine" transferable from Dante's unique work to a genus, or large areas of it, secular in scope. This tendency leads to accolades and the hushed reverential tones once reserved for tragedy, and often to a downgrading of tragedy and an upgrading of comedy as the ultimate voice of human possibility. But such better-and-worse classifications are beside the point, for comedy and tragedy have indispensable, noninterchangeable, and noncomparable functions. Comedy's function is reconciliation with the world that will not do the best we can imagine, tragedy's is reconciliation with a self that will not bow to the imperatives that it acknowledges; comedy means the acceptance of the world, and tragedy, the judgment of the self; comedy, the discovery of one's pragmatic follies, and tragedy, of one's moral flaws.

muted, good sense, and in which the inferior in human inclinations will on occasion find itself, briefly perhaps but cheeringly, overmatched by the superior style of being that now and then emerges from latency into overt activity.

Whether the response of the moment implies an effect beyond the moment is an interesting question. Bummidge, the ambiguous protagonist of Saul Bellow's *The Last Analysis*, believes that the comedy he hopes to make available to the public will have a therapeutic effect. J. A. Bryant suggests that the "perception of the quality of Shakespeare's comic achievement [i.e., the "acceptance" of the mixed or "bittersweet truth"] can . . . bring the force of his plays from scene to audience as a power in people's lives. . . . If we . . . escape confrontation with the challenges of normal daily existence, we may continue to stand in self-absorption with Antonio in a world where absolute perfection remains a hypothetical possibility. If like most people we must expect daily disappointments, mediocre wine and rain in the afternoon, then the implicit injunction in this play may be of some relevance to us."[11] I back off a little from "injunction," even if "implicit," since it implies a lessoning. Our concern is rather with the residue in sensibility, and hence in behavior, of a certain kind of imaginative experience (an area of difference between Plato and Aristotle), with the possible carry-over from the drama to the ways in the world, temporary or ongoing, of the audience. Two critics come at this from their views of the contrasting impacts of tragedy and comedy. While "the tragic character as well as the audience is essentially primitive," Elmer Blistein argues, "the comic character is essentially civil."[12] Allan Rodway partly echoes, partly contradicts: "In one word, good comedy tends to be civilising; good tragedy, exalting."[13] The split in theories about tragedy—one seeing a drop to depths, the other a soaring to heights—makes still more impressive the closeness of the two positions on comedy, a closeness signalized in the key words *civil* and *civilizing*. Hence *civility*, which, as we noted earlier, Edward Shils defines as "the virtue of the citizen." Having said this, Shils pauses for a strange demur that takes something away from his case. He laments, "Civility has meant more than good manners, and it is an impoverishment of our vocabulary as well as a sign of the impoverishment of our thought on political matters that this word has been allowed to dwindle to the point where it has come to refer to good manners in face-to-face relationships."[14] "Dwindle"? Surely not. For the very qualities that Shils rightly attributes to civil society— "compromise and reasonableness, prudent self-restraint, and responsibility," "transcendence of partisanship," "appreciation of the other parties"—are not entities that can be divorced from the style in which they are manifested. These virtues become evident in and are symbolized in good manners. Bad manners declare the absence of the virtues; good manners declare their active presence. The old term "comedy of manners"—which I have largely avoided, along with its fellows, in the hope of dispensing with qualifications that obscure the concept or multiply it out of utility—is the bridge between societal well-being and comic practice. In one sense "manners" means conduct that reveals character; in another it connotes good manners. The further away from its farcical underlayers it gets, the more comedy invokes both these meanings. Characters act significantly, and good manners signify a general civility which is the foundation of a livable society.[15]

Critics testify regularly to the influence of comedy and the comic perspective. The commentaries, though their orbits vary, all revolve about a common center which is the interrelationship of comedy, civility, manners, and acceptance. Words of connotative affinity recur: "accommodation," "politeness," "consideration," "fellowship," "balance wheel," "tie of sympathy," "protection against perverse tendencies," "values have meaning."* They are in accord with other words that I have used: attunement, adjustment, concession, coming to terms with, flexibility. All of these become meaningful only in relation to a disparateness of which the absence would render the key terms otiose. Comedy, in treating

---

*Ronald Peacock interprets Meredith thus: ". . . comedy merely reinforces a movement towards balanced and refined living that has already begun" (*The Poet in the Theatre* [New York: Harcourt, Brace, 1946], p. 151). Marie Collins Swabey echoes the implications of "refined" but makes her subject "comic insight," which, she avers, "expressing the common sense of the group, operates to refine men's characters through encouraging accommodation, politeness, consideration of others, and self-control. It makes for a spirit of fellowship, for uniting and pulling together, for discretion and good manners in social dealings" (*Comic Laughter: A Philosophical Essay* [New Haven and London: Yale University Press, 1961], p. 35). Swabey adds less hopefully that "contradictions or distortions [may] inhere in our natures beyond redemption" (p. 36), which is to say, in effect, that when human nature is fully engaged, tragic action is inevitable. Over a century ago Ralph Waldo Emerson, perhaps surprisingly, praised the "perception of the Comic" as a "balance-wheel in our metaphysical structure," as an "essential element in a fine character," one that will be found "wherever the intellect is constructive" and the "absence" of which will be felt "as a defect in the noblest and most oracular soul"; as "a tie of sympathy with other men, a pledge of sanity, and a protection from those perverse tendencies and gloomy insanities in which fine intellects sometimes lose themselves" (from "The Comic" [1843], reprinted in *Theories of Comedy*, ed. Paul Lauter [Anchor Book; Garden City, N.Y.: Doubleday and Co., 1964], p. 380). Elder Olson says of "the values of life" that "anyone who laughs, anyone who is moved in any way by the comic, proclaims them. So long as there is the absurd, therefore, there cannot really be the Absurd [an admirable deflation of a chic term imprecise enough to have become an undergraduate cliché]; and so long as comedy and the comic are possible, so long will life and its values have meaning" (*The Theory of Comedy* [Bloomington and London: Indiana University Press, 1968], p. 128).

the disparateness as bearable, as ingestible, asserts that social order is imaginable and so possible. How much comedy, a theatrical artifact, enhances the possibility or supports the actuality, is conjectural and a bit elusive. We can imagine the comic stage to be a product as well as a producer. Ronald Peacock voices the theoretical complexity when he asserts "the obvious paradox of comedy that it is both a symptom and an agent of civilization." [16]

"Civilization" has to be a "civilized" order, that is, consenting and disciplined, not an ideologically enforced homogeneity which cuts off all differences by direct action and hence could not have comedy as a symptom. The disparateness observed in comedy comes out of spontaneity, and the genial observation of it cannot take place without freedom. Yet freedom is not so much the opposite of ideological compulsion as it is a mean; out on the other side of it there can be a vulgar libertinism in which disparateness no longer means the human variabilities contained within an order but is a chaotic absolute, a denial of all norms. When everybody accepts everything, what was once civility declines into a vanishing of judgment and taste. One may wonder—hopefully without seeming only a ghostly voice from the past—whether an endemic permissiveness, the unlimited legitimatization of ancient improprieties, the unrestrictedness of the pornographic, the spread of black comedy are not constituents of an anticivility as powerful as millenarian enforcement of a simplistic totalitarian standard. It is less that these everything-goes phenomena are too "low," as they were once called, than that they are too easy. Ruthless institutional compulsion forces life into a strait jacket; infinite acceptingness lets it collapse into shapelessness. In this ultimate egalitarianism there does paradoxically emerge a controlling voice: that of an ochlocratic lowest-common-denominatorism. What it will not tolerate, born though it be of the everything-goes dogma, is the disparateness which suggests a higher level of conduct, an elevation of taste and being, the conjoining of freedom and discipline in a true civility. Mass-culture antidisparateness would foreclose comedy as a voice but would demand entertainments of an essentially mechanical type, which would require no one to be receptive to diversity.*

These inconclusive speculations may help clarify the hypothesis of com-

---

*Along with this drift away from a center there appears, in many parts of the political worlds of the 1970s, an analogous separatism of a very insistent sort. The result is a combative, self-exalting disparateness as hostile to the comic as the total indiscriminateness of a life which mistakes all limits for oppressions.

edy as a symptom of civilization. On the other hand, the view that comedy is an agent of civilization—that is, of civilized life, of civility in an order—raises the immense problem of the impact of art on individuals and society. Peacock offers a tempting solution when he says that comedy, like tragedy, is a "constituent of civilized consciousness as distinct from practical civilized behaviour."[17] One may wonder whether this inviting theoretical distinction makes, finally, a tenable pragmatic separation, whether the consciousness which defines the individual is static rather than dynamic, whether it can create a subject for a portrait who is not also an agent in the world. Once again we come back to the Platonic-Aristotelian disagreement on the impact of aesthetic experience. Perhaps we can have it both ways. It is possible that the catharsis—or katastasis, as Olson terms the comic variety—occurs but is not wholly terminal, that the aesthetic exercise leaves some trace, that the person who has undergone it is different from the person who has not, that the elimination of the emotion evoked means not its traceless vanishing but a minutely altered responsiveness that reduces the limitations inherent in a nonexperience of comedy. This possibility would permit the assumption that an experiencing of comedy, the more so if it were habitual, could be thought of as cathartic and yet also as contributing to the civility which is the ground of a beneficent continuing society. Yeats alludes to "the sense of comedy [that] John Eglinton called 'the social cement of our civilization.'"[18]

We cannot, at any rate, fail to see the analogy between the life of comedy and the life of civil society. Civil society does not treat the disparate in the world as a mere object of scorn or polemic or as an inequity requiring sociopolitical therapy. Thus it manifests the sensibility from which comedy springs; and the presence of that sensibility, in literature or in the theater, is at least conceivable as a nutrient or catalyst of civility. In the comic and in the civil there is an easy acknowledgment of differentness and inconsistency which may extend from merry laughter to the genial or subdued smile and to the tolerant ironic sense that may be grave but is never bitter. One at least imagines a kinship with the erring rather than views them with alarm. In the imperfections of the world one senses the expectable jests of circumstance rather than the blows of hostile fate. The good manners implicit in comedy and inseparable from civility are not gratuitous routines but the symbolic rites both of a concessiveness to others and of a restraint of the will always ready to break out in a grasping and competitive style. All these forms of a nonsentimental sympathy are an acceptance of the inalienable disparateness which exists because the world does contain others as well as ourselves. The ultimate tolerance, however, has to bear not only with neutral otherness and the flawed social style but with that excellence of being which may be rare but which is also a saving fact of life. In a singular mixture of amusement and forbearance and even discipline, in bearing with errancy and coming to terms with others whose main problem is that they are others, and in being of the world but not always adopting the easiest styles that it admits—in such attitudes and actions lies the graciousness that echoes the best of, accepts most of, and may a little soften all of, the ways of the world.

Appendixes

APPENDIX 1. A BRIEF SURVEY OF SELECTED STUDIES OF COMEDY

Appendix 1 contains briefly annotated lists of works that have something to say about comedy. Appendix 1.A sketches the contents of various twentieth-century works. Appendix 1.B notes some earlier sources often referred to. Appendix 1.C indicates the contents of several anthologies in the field.

1.A. *Twentieth-Century Works*

This appendix contains brief notes on the main premises or directions of other books on comedy. It is not all-inclusive; it spends more time on later than on earlier books; omissions may be due to flaws of judgment or alertness. In using this means of referring to other commentators, I have three purposes: (1) to make due acknowledgment of the work of fellow students whose views I may repeat or depart from; (2) to avoid a continuous registry of other views in a thicket of footnotes that can encumber the pages of the text and be more distracting than helpful; and (3) to make available for the reader, if he is interested in this matter, a quick prefatory survey of the continual theorizing about comedy, with its marked tendency toward both diversity and duplication. Here it may be timely to recall the Samuel Johnson aphorism ruefully quoted by more than one of these practitioners, that "comedy has been particularly unpropitious to definers."

In endeavoring to provide a hasty glimpse of the key positions of each writer, I have used a combination of descriptive notes, paraphrase, and direct quotation. Some critics tend to encapsulate their central ideas in relatively brief quotable passages; with others it seems better to rely on summary. Granted the soundness of my reading of the texts, limitations of space hinder an adequate representation of a critic's thought in its fullness, its shadings, and its variations from the work of others with which it has affinities.

In this appendix each work is identified fully; when these works are mentioned in later appendixes, they are referred to only by author, title, and date. In all appendixes the works are listed in chronological order.

Allardyce Nicoll, *An Introduction to Dramatic Theory* (New York: Brentano's [1931]). Nicoll gives a full, systematic discussion of tragedy, comedy, and related, intermediate, and subordinate types. Concerning the "laughable," he sums up, "we have found, first, that there are three cardinal reasons for an object's being ludicrous—degradation, incongruity, automatism; and alongside of these a number of subsidiary causes, such as the sense of liberation; second, that the objects of laughter are unconscious of their ridiculousness; and, third, that there are two species of the risible, wit and humour, which lie apart from the rest in being conscious and, in the case of humour, sympathetic" (p. 160).

Elizabeth Drew, *Discovering Drama* (New York: W. W. Norton, 1937). This book has a chapter on comedy (pp. 137–72). Drew is chary of general theory and prefers to deal with comedy by classification: "comedies which are *critical* in spirit and those which are not." Critical comedies may practice *"explicit* criticism, which exposes definite follies or abuses to contempt and ridicule, and *implicit*, which is the natural result of revealing human nature as it is. . . . On the other side are all those comedies which are definitely an escape from reality, and intend to be so" (p. 148).

James Feibleman, *In Praise of Comedy: A Study in Its Theory and Practice* (New York: Macmillan, 1939). Feibleman insists on the "logical structure of comedy" and on an "objective basis for comedy," both of which he sees as threatened by the "subjective postulate of nominalism," the dominant metaphysics since the late Middle Ages (p. 121). He mentions "the derogation of what-is in favour of what-ought-to-be, which certainly gives rise to comedy" (p. 146) as the "generalized comical situation" which "must be logical in its nature" (p. 167). "Thus comedy tends to ignore the values of actuality, and points chiefly to its limitations" (p. 176). Comedy is a "constant reminder of the existence of the logical order as the perfect goal of actuality . . ." (p. 178). *"Comedy*, then, *consists in the indirect affirmation of the ideal logical order by means of the derogation of the limited orders of actuality"* (pp. 178–79). Comedy "is in sympathy with the revolutionary struggle for something better and again for something still better" (p. 214). It "calls for the girding up of loins and the pressing ever forward toward fresh values and original organizations, demanding new victories and new achievements for the human race" (p. 215). "Now, the comedian, like logic itself, has no use for compromises. He is an absolutist, a dealer in extremes, . . . comedy tends to have some political significance. . . . there is a recognizable tendency for comedy to arise from the oppressed classes and also from those whose sympathies go out to the oppressed" (p. 222). (Feibleman refers to even fewer plays than that later philosophic critic, Marie Swabey.)

L. J. Potts, *Comedy* (London: Hutchinson's University Library, 1948). Potts provides an orderly and discerning exposition, in general utility hardly superseded by numerous successors. (The main exception is that he is weak on tragedy when he uses it for contrast and alludes to no plays later than Shaw's.) Comedy "depends on the eye of the beholder, not on the character of the object he has in view, [for] nothing in nature is categorically comic . . ." (p. 45). Comedy is "an expression of the natural modesty of man, mixing with his kind, and defending them and himself against megalomania, egoism, misanthropy, and the other forces of disintegration inside human nature" (p. 114). "The general effect of comedy is to relax tension of feeling . . ." (p. 33). "But all comic writers must have a norm in view" (p. 47). "Perhaps the subject matter of comedy might be defined as 'curable or man-ageable faults or maladjustments'" (p. 49). "The pattern we want in comedy is . . . a grouping of characters rather than a march of events" (p. 130). He finds this best illustrated in *Don Quixote* and *The Way of the World* (pp. 130–31). He discusses both novels and plays.

Albert Cook, *The Dark Voyage and the Golden Mean: A Philosophy of Comedy* (Cambridge, Mass.: Harvard University Press, 1949). Cook approaches comedy in the light of a funda-mental dualism of human attitudes that, in literary art, is expressed in the tragic and comic modes (hence there will be further notes on his position in Appendix 8). His basic "antinomic symbols" are the "probable" and the "wonderful." Associated with the "prob-able" are the social, the predictable, the classical; the mean, totem, sex, Burke's "beauti-ful." On the "wonderful" side are the individual, the artist, the imaginative, the extreme, the nonpredictable, the symbolic; taboo, death, Burke's "sublime" (p. 28). The former is the realm of the comic, the latter the realm of the tragic. "Usually in probable comedy the pattern is: abnormality of the pariah, his expulsion by normal society, the joy of society. In serene comedy of wonderful-as-probable (or vice versa), the pattern becomes: expulsion of the searcher . . . , his experience in the wonderful, his self-rehabilitation with new knowledge into control of society" (p. 175).

D. H. Monro, *Argument of Laughter* (1951; rpt., Notre Dame, Ind.: University of Notre Dame Press, 1963). Monro follows Feibleman, whom he criticizes, and precedes Swabey and Olson in the small fraternity of "philosophic" critics, that is, those who erect positions with systematic logic. He is unusually detached, noting both pros and cons in describing the systems and views of others. Like other philosophic critics, he says little about drama; his study of laughter relies primarily on jokes, witticisms, cartoons, and so on. He seeks "the common element in laughable situations" (p. 19). In Chapter 2 he surveys "non-humorous laughter"; in Chapter 3 he describes "ten classes" of humor (p. 40); in Chapters 4 to 7 he explicates these classes. In Chapters 8 to 18, he surveys existent theories of humor, which he classifies into four central types; he evaluates each theory by noting how many of his ten classes it will account for, and in most of them he finds a mixed utility. A central value of his work is his classification of theories of humor into four main types, as follows: (1) Superiority Theories, as in Hobbes and Bain (chaps. 8 and 9), and derivatives of them, as in Bergson, Feibleman, and McDougall (chaps. 10 and 11); (2) Incongruity Theories, as in Kant, Schopenhauer, Spencer, and Eastman (chaps. 12 and 13); (3) Release from Restraint Theories, as in L. W. Kline, Freud, and J. C. Gregory (chaps. 14, 15, and 16); and (4) Ambivalence Theories, as in J. Y. T. Greig and V. K. K. Menon (chaps. 17 and 18). The laughter of ambivalence occurs when "we find opposite emotions struggling in us for mastery" (p. 210). In Chapter 19, entitled "The Inappropriate," Monro himself opts for a theory based on "the linking of disparates: the importing into one sphere, of ideas which belong in another" (p. 238), which he admits is "an incongruity theory . . . not very different from Schopenhauer's" (p. 254). He composes an excellent summarizing section (pp. 248–52). One of his best points, one not often made, is that "humour may be either conservative or radical in its effects" (p. 243).

Paul Goodman, *The Structure of Literature* (Chicago: University of Chicago Press, 1954). Committed to "inductive formal analysis" (p. 22), Goodman elaborates a special vocabu-lary (he provides a glossary), partly illustrated in this central defining passage, where he proposes to "explore the relation between a base character and his action. This is 'comic' when the intrigue can be reversed or even be deflated (come to nothing), and still the character is not destroyed; . . . It will be seen at once that a character of comedy has two aspects: that which is destroyed and that which survives in, let us say, 'normalcy.' Most of the possibilities of this comic relation occur in *The Alchemist*" (p. 82). On this general basis he describes six types of comic action or situation, ending with "6. A completely deflatable trait is a Buffoon. Mostly this would occur in passing" (p. 84). He affirms that "among English plays Ben Jonson's are the purest comic actions, as pure deflation, and *The Alchemist* is the most fully worked out . . ." (p. 82).

Marie Collins Swabey, *Comic Laughter: A Philosophical Essay* (New Haven, Conn., and London: Yale University Press, 1961). Like Feibleman, Swabey opposes all nonlogical, nonrational explanations of the comic—various biological, sociological, and psychological (with especial reference to the unconscious) accounts. "What is genuinely funny in words, character, or situation must have a logical point, drift, nub, or pertinence and yield some insight into values. . . . in the laughter of comic insight we achieve a logical moment of truth; . . . we detect an incongruence as cancelled by an underlying congruence. We gain an inkling, as it were, of the hang of things, sometimes even a hint of cosmic beneficence. In short, perception of the ludicrous helps us to comprehend both ourselves and the world . . ." (p. v). She claims that "the perception of the comic . . . requires logical and metaphysical comprehension, a normative intellectual insight which grasps what is worthy of laughter . . ." (p. 13). We must recognize "the roots of the comic in the autonomy of reason" (p. 39). Comedy does not have to do with "utter foolishness, pure silliness, senselessness. The ludicrous encounter must yield not blindness but an insight. Awareness of the comic requires an intellectual process . . ." (p. 16). The comic is "the presence of an incongruity, contradiction, or absurdity that is humanly relevant without being oppressively grave or momentous" (p. 28). "Basically, perception of the comic requires . . . a sense of consonance in dissonance, concord in discord, that is, congruence in incongruence" (p. 115). While Swabey's logical comedy finds harmony beneath disharmony, Feibleman's logical comedy finds a disharmony which calls for reform or revolution.

G. S. Amur, *The Concept of Comedy: A Re-Statement* (Karnatak University Research Series, no. 4; Dharwar: Karnatak University, 1963). Amur stresses "joy," "harmony," Schopenhauer's "continued assertion of the will [to live]," Hegel's "infinite geniality and confidence . . . capable of rising superior to its own contradiction" (pp. 6, 13, 14) as elements in "the Spirit of Comedy." He stresses "the happy frame of mind," an "ardent belief in the value of man and of human life," the joy "of being alive and of being able to feel and to think," and "the essential goodness of man and the inherent benevolence of the natural order" (pp. 14, 16, 19, 21). Comedy depends on our having "a firm grasp" of "the Norm" (p. 24). One summary statement, in reduced form, is this: "1. a spirit of hope and faith . . . ; 2. a spirit of ardent joy in man and the natural order; 3. a spirit of amusement and laughter . . . ; 4. a spirit of creation and fertility . . . ; 5. a spirit of morality [which is tolerant but firm]; 6. a spirit of good nature and kindliness . . . ; 7. a spirit of invention and imagination . . ." (p. 36). Another summary: "1. . . . a spirit which continually asserts our will to live . . . ; 2. a spirit of relaxation and reassurance . . . ; 3. the . . . appeal . . . of joy and manifold relaxation . . ." (p. 151). Sample judgments reflecting these criteria: *A Month in the Country* is tragic (pp. 4–5), *The Country Wife* is "immoral" (pp. 32–33), *The Three Sisters* is tragic (p. 104), and *The Cherry Orchard* leans in that direction (pp. 155 ff.).

Eric Bentley, *The Life of the Drama* (New York: Atheneum, 1964). Bentley is especially concerned with the relations between farce and comedy. "Aggression is common to farce and comedy, but, while in farce it is mere retaliation, in comedy it is might backed by the conviction of right. In comedy, the anger of farce is backed by the conscience" (p. 296). He distinguishes the various tones possible in comic disapproval (p. 297), noting "the bitterness and sadness that so readily come to the surface in comedy . . ." (p. 298). The basic "comic dialectic" lies in the "dynamic contrast . . . between a frivolous manner and a grim meaning" (p. 312). One kind of comedy keeps pushing toward "what is horrible"; the other presents "an effect of enchantment in the shape of an apparent realization of our fondest hopes—that is, our hopes for love and happiness" (p. 313). Again, "one [kind] moves toward unresolved discord, one [kind] moves just as irresistibly toward complete concord . . ." (p. 314).

Elmer M. Blistein, *Comedy in Action* (Durham, N.C.: Duke University Press, 1964). Blistein shies away from theory but tries to describe certain aspects of comedy in terms of how it works on the audience. Comedy is "a respectable art form that creates and fosters an attitude toward life that is vigorous, corrective, and penetrating" (p. 20). Again he alludes to "the clear-eyed vision and the multi-faceted sanity which is comedy in action" (p. 130). He discusses "the drive for respectability" in comedy (pp. 5 ff.), the comic butt (pp. 21 ff.), cruelty and comedy (pp. 42 ff.), and the role of love and sex in comedy (pp. 77 ff.).

Cyrus Hoy, *The Hyacinth Room: An Investigation into the Nature of Comedy, Tragedy, and Tragicomedy* (New York: Alfred A. Knopf, 1964). Hoy is committed to an incongruity theory and to the analogies between tragedy and comedy; his work will be noted under those headings. He stresses the discrepancy between deed and intention (p. 5), the protagonists' "lack of self-knowledge" (p. 6). "When [the issue] is joined in comedy, discordant elements are reconciled in a spirit of wise tolerance" (p. 8). Man's "duality makes him an incongruous figure" (p. 21).

Bernard N. Schilling, *The Comic Spirit: Boccaccio to Thomas Mann* (Detroit: Wayne State University Press, 1965). Schilling is concerned more with describing various individual works than with constructing a theory. However, viewing various human incongruities, the observer "may think of himself as sharing like other men in the weakness that his intelligence perceives, and so end in a mood of tolerance—his laughter tempered by sympathy" (p. 11). Comedy "invites a certain discernment, an ability to see man as incongruously different from what he should be . . ." (p. 17).

Nelvin Vos, *The Drama of Comedy: Victim and Victor* (Richmond, Va.: John Knox Press, 1966). Vos defines comedy in the light of Christian belief and doctrine. He argues that "the structure of dramatic comedy and the structure of Christ's passionate action bear an analogical relation to each other . . ." (p. 7). "The structure of comedy also arises out of an effort to close the gap between the finite and the infinite and, here, the comedy lies in the protagonist's final realization of the disappearance of the chasm between the two" (p. 13). Vos argues that three types of comedy correspond to the "interpretation . . . of Christ as the Victim," to the interpretation of "Christ as Victor," and to the interpretation of "Christ as the *Victim-Victor*" (p. 15). There is some lack of clarity in these categories, and one is tempted to suggest that they would apply equally well to tragedy. The "Victor" type is roughly all happy-ending plays; Vos uses Thornton Wilder for his principal discussion (pp. 32 ff.). The "Victim" type appears in Jonson, Molière, Chekhov, and all absurd drama; Vos selects Ionesco for special treatment (pp. 53 ff.). The "Victim-Victor" type includes *Measure for Measure* and the plays of T. S. Eliot and Christopher Fry, who is discussed in detail (pp. 82 ff.).

Walter Kerr, *Tragedy and Comedy* (New York: Simon and Schuster, 1967). Kerr is able to call upon a very wide range of materials for his generic study, and he writes with a great deal of vitality and zest. He is naturally metaphorical. As his title indicates, he is especially concerned with relationships, and his main ideas will be noted under that heading. In general he regards tragedy and comedy as distinguishable, but hardly separable in a study of genre. However, comedy "points to the thousand ways in which the admittedly free man is not free" (p. 146). "That a creature capable of transcending himself should at the same time be incapable of controlling himself is hilarious" (p. 145). The effect is comic "when we are most preoccupied with man's physical limitations" (pp. 148–49). "Our original incongruity—that of infinitely flexible talents harnessed to a fixed, inferior appetite—still stands, shaking its sides and also shaking its head" (p. 220).

Elder Olson, *The Theory of Comedy* (Bloomington and London: Indiana University Press, 1968). Olson's "business here is . . . to construct an Aristotelian theory of comedy" (p. 48). One of various summaries: "Comedy is the imitation of a worthless action, complete and of a certain magnitude, in language with pleasing accessories differing from part to part, enacted, not narrated, effecting a *katastasis* of concern through the absurd" (pp. 46–47). Katastasis (relaxation) of concern is effected "by exhibiting an apparent absurdity in the grounds of concern" (p. 61). To produce the "laughter emotion" (p. 11) we need a concurrence of three factors: "(1) a certain *kind of object*, (2) a certain *frame of mind* in us, (3) the *grounds* on which we feel" (p. 12; cf. p. 61). He defines in detail "the agent," the "ridiculous" and the "ludicrous," the "laughter emotion" (pp. 15 ff.). ". . . the comic is not so much a question of laughter as of the restoration of the mind to a certain condition . . . a pleasant, or rather a euphoric condition of freedom from desires and emotions which move men to action, and one in which we [are] inclined to take nothing seriously and to be gay about everything" (p. 25). Since "comedy takes the worth away," comedy is "an imitation of valueless action . . ." (p. 36). These dicta tend, in application, to limit comedy to the farcical; thus Olson acknowledges that when we use the theory to consider Shakespeare, "We are left, then, with only five comedies in our sense of the word: *Merry Wives of Windsor, The Comedy of Errors, Love's Labour's Lost, A Midsummer Night's Dream,* and *The Taming of the Shrew*" (p. 89).

J. L. Styan, *The Dark Comedy: The Development of Modern Comic Tragedy* (2d ed.; Cambridge: Cambridge University Press, 1968). Styan questions the utility of traditional genres in dealing with twentieth-century drama, and even of the variants of these secured by adjectival qualifications of the two original modes. "It is time to call a halt to the Polonius-like mobilization of genres and sub-genres" (p. 2). But he is committed to the idea of mixed modes, and he briefly traces different versions of "tragicomedy" to the present day and sees it eventuating in a modern form for which he uses two contrasting terms that appear in his title as synonyms, "dark comedy" and "comic tragedy." This does rather resemble the "mobilization of genres and sub-genres." Starting with aspects of Ibsen, Strindberg, and Chekhov, he goes on to comment on about a dozen twentieth-century dramatists (chaps. 2, 3, and 4).

A. N. Kaul, *The Action of English Comedy: Studies in the Encounter of Abstraction and*

Experience from Shakespeare to Shaw (New Haven, Conn., and London: Yale University Press, 1970). Kaul's title tells the story. Discussing both plays and novels by English authors, he employs a basic conception of "plot"—the encounter of abstractions (preconceptions, dated ideas, illusions, *a priori* theories) and experience (facts, actuality, circumstances, reality). Deriving from Schopenhauer (pp. 39 ff.), he opposes laughter theories of comedy because such theory "invalidates the whole idea of comic *action*" (p. 16).

William G. McCollom, *The Divine Average: A View of Comedy* (Cleveland and London: Press of Case Western Reserve University, 1971). McCollom's title is revelatory. *"Comedy is an amusing, relatively discontinuous action concerning success and failure in social relations and culminating in a judgment whereby the 'divine average' triumphs over the exceptional or peculiar. The movements toward success and failure are arranged in a pattern of inevitability and chance: the freedom of the will is not stressed. The total work, therefore, presents life as a product of natural law and erratic fortune"* (p. 7). The comic vision "either penetrates to a new and vivid justification of common sense and 'public policy' or affirms this consensus while intimating ways in which it may be reinterpreted and transcended" (p. 7). "If the play is very successful, it will not only testify to but extend the wisdom of the race. On the other hand, [the writer] may develop an ambiguous, almost inscrutable work of art, one that will allow the audience only a very qualified self-congratulation" (p. 18). In its solutions, "comedy chooses not between the wicked and the just or even the foolish and the wise, but among the foolish, and its election lights on the healthy, the normal, the 'divine average' of foolishness" (p. 19). McCollom welcomes the multiplication of generic forms to bring concepts into line with actual practice; he distinguishes four types of tragicomedy (pp. 45–46). He sees three main types of comic structure: (1) "chance," (2) "plan" or "intrigue," and (3) a form in which plot "gives way to broader and more varied concepts of design" (pp. 54, 64). "The comic hero is insecurely poised between his excellence and his absurdity" (p. 82). "One way of understanding comic characters is to divide them into the festive and the cautionary" (p. 88). He insists that "to describe Chekhov's major work as comedy is perverse" (p. 44).

W. Moelwyn Merchant, *Comedy* (The Critical Idiom, no. 21; London: Methuen, 1972). Merchant is more diffident about definition than all other writers on the comic. He hopes to "avoid the dilemmas into which more general *a priori* theories of comedy have so regularly fallen" (p. ix). He is fascinated by modal variants, cross types, generic overlap, the indistinguishability of pure types, the "inevitable intersection of comedy and tragedy" (p. 12; cf. pp. 40, 49, 52). In effect he despairs of doing what the title of his book seems to commit him to. His one effort to identify comedy is this: ". . . here we may attempt a modest definition of comedy as the permanent possibility of a happy resolution" (p. 50). He is interested in the relation between ritual and comedy (pp. 53 ff.), and his final chapter, "Conclusion: The Metaphysics of Comedy," intimates, without explicit formulation, a metaphysical or theological dimension in comedy, a generic tendency to move toward the realm of the *Divine Comedy* (pp. 79–81).

Robert Bernard Martin, *The Triumph of Wit: A Study of Victorian Comic Theory* (Oxford: Clarendon Press, 1974). Many ideas about comedy naturally enter into this "attempt to document the change of comic theory in the Victorian period, from a belief in amiable, sentimental humour to an acceptance of intellect as the basis of comedy" (p. vii). Martin "deals with the inherited beliefs of the Victorians about comedy; with the conflicting theories of superiority and incongruity as the sources of comedy; with the opposition of humour and wit; . . . and with the conflicting claims of the Imagination and Fancy. Throughout the Victorian era there is a gradual shift towards the acceptance of incongruity and wit as the essence of comedy" (p. viii). In general, "comedy during the reign of Queen Victoria changed from sentimental comedy to the comedy of wit and paradox" (p. 3). Martin finds a "change of interest in comedy from personality to idea, from humour to wit" (p. 3).

Allan Rodway, *English Comedy: Its Role and Nature from Chaucer to the Present Day* (Berkeley and Los Angeles: University of California Press, 1975). Like Kaul in 1970, Rodway limits himself to the English scene, and his basic procedure is historical, for he feels that most English comedies are "wholly dependent on specifically contemporary issues" and that it is necessary "to relate comic literature of all kinds to the life of its time" (p. ix). He uses an extensive critical apparatus and terminology. He objects to treating comedy "as if it needed no distinction from farce and divertisement," forms which "leave the meaning out" (pp. 11, 32). In most periods English comedy "was used to advance competing viewpoints" (p. 13); it "'places' men and manners against certain standards, and these inevitably tend to vary according to period needs" (pp. 14–15). He calls many comedies "mithridatic," that is, "covertly *inuring* us to the faults of society and self" (p. 21). Comedy may be "conserving" or "innovating" (p. 27). It may be at once "conserving" and "restraining" or "innovating" and "releasing" (p. 30). The following statement sums up the system and provides most of the terms by which he classifies English comic works (poems, fictions, plays, etc.): "*Comedy, farce* and *divertisement* are to be taken as MODES; *Satire, humour, cynicism* and *celebration* as MOODS; *Irony, invective, parody, incongruity, slapstick, nonsense* and *wit* as METHODS" (p. 33). The "mode may be altered by alterations of mood and methods . . ." (p. 34). "All the methods listed are no more than tools, which could be used in tragedy as well as comedy" (p. 35).

1.B. *Older Sources*

Many critics refer to Immanuel Kant, *Critique of Judgment* (1790), Book II (and especially *Critique of Aesthetic Judgment*, trans. J. C. Meredith [Oxford: Clarendon Press, 1911], pp. 199 ff.); Arthur Schopenhauer, *The World as Will and Idea* (1819), trans. R. B. Haldane and J. Kemp (London, 1883; rpt., New York: Humanities Press, 1964), Book I, chap. 13 and elsewhere (see entry in Appendix 1.C below); Søren Kierkegaard, *Concluding Unscientific Postscript* (1840), trans. David F. Swenson and W. Lowrie (Princeton, N.J.: Princeton University Press, 1941), pp. 450 ff. (see entry under Hoy in Appendix 8); George Meredith, *On the Idea of Comedy and of the Uses of the Comic Spirit* (1877; New York: C. Scribner's Sons, 1897); Henri Louis Bergson, *Laughter* (1900); and Sigmund Freud, *Wit and Its Relation to the Unconscious* (1905), trans. A. A. Brill (New York: Moffat, Yard, 1916).

1.C. *Anthologies*

Three anthologies are especially useful.

1. Wylie Sypher, ed., *Comedy* (Anchor Book; Garden City, N.Y.: Doubleday, 1956), contains the essays by Meredith (pp. 3-57) and Bergson (pp. 61–190) and the editor's "The Meanings of Comedy" (pp. 193–255). Meredith and Bergson are too well known to justify summarizing here.

Meredith, however, makes some points related to views used in the present volume. *Acceptance* (cf. Appendix 2): "And to love comedy you must know the real world, and know men and women well enough not to expect too much of them . . ." (p. 24). ". . . the mind accepts them [certain Molière characters] because they are clear interpretations of certain chapters of the Book lying open before us all" (p. 51). *Laughter* (cf. Appendix 5): Meredith was ahead of the pack in distinguishing kinds of laughers ("agelasts" or non-laughers; "misogelasts" or laughter-haters; "hypergelasts" or overlaughers) (p. 4), and in distinguishing kinds of laughter ("derisive laughter . . . thwarts the comic idea. . . . the test of true comedy is that it shall awaken thoughtful laughter") (p. 47). *Satire and comedy* (cf. Appendix 6): "The laughter of satire is a blow in the back or the face. The laughter of comedy is impersonal and of unrivaled politeness, nearer a smile . . ." (p. 47). Molière's Alceste has "qualities which constitute the satirist" (p. 23). The English prefer satire, since "The national disposition is for hard-hitting, with a moral purpose to sanction it; . . . But the comic is a different spirit" (p. 42). *The world* (cf. Appendix 9): Sentimental people dislike comedy, which "enfolds them with the wretched host of the world" (p. 14). Molière's Célimène has "perspicacious, clear eyes for the world, and a very distinct knowledge that she belongs to the world, and is most at home in it" (p. 21).

Bergson also stresses the "social" as the comic sphere (pp. 62–65), but his statement "Comedy . . . begins, in fact, with what might be called *a growing callousness to social life*" (p. 147) is equally applicable to melodrama and tragedy.

Sypher's concluding essay is a very inclusive survey of ideas about, theories of, meanings of, and relationships of comedy. He draws on depth psychologists, anthropologists, classicists, philosophers, art critics, and artists themselves. Section I, "Our New Sense of the Comic," deals with absurdist and existentialist thought, the unconscious, the new sense of comic range, and various theories of laughter and efforts to define comedy. Section II, "The Ancient Rites of Comedy," has reference to both comedy and tragedy and notes some modern cases where ritual interpretations work (cf. C. L. Barber). Section III, "The Guises of the Comic Hero," treats Falstaff and Socrates as counter types, discusses versions of the Fool (cf. Enid Welsford), and makes some comparisons of tragic and comic heroes (Hamlet as Puck). Section IV, "The Social Meanings of Comedy," discusses comic ambivalence as evidenced in a wide range of social functions ("rebellion and defense"), and surveys different comic programs in Shakespeare.

2. Paul Lauter, ed., *Theories of Comedy* (Anchor Book; Garden City, N.Y.: Doubleday, 1964), is especially valuable for its numerous selections from older theorists—classical, medieval, Renaissance, neoclassical, nineteenth century, and modern (for more recent critics it is superseded by the Corrigan volume noted in the following entry); eight critics appear in both volumes. Lauter provides a convenient introduction to Schopenhauer by assembling the relevant passages on the theory of incongruity that is much alluded to (pp. 355–71). An oft-quoted passage is this: ". . . the source of the ludicrous is always the . . . unexpected subsumption of an object under a conception which in some respects is different from it . . ." (p. 359).

Interesting, too, is R. W. Emerson's incongruity theory in his essay "The Comic" (1843). Man's Reason grasps "the Whole," and so his imagination expects "the perfection of truth or goodness," but then "the facts that occur when actual men enter do not make good this anticipation . . ." (p. 379). "The comedy is in the intellect's perception of discrepancy" (p. 380). He sees as profoundly comic the contrast between "some pure idealist [who] goes up and down among the institutions of society" and "a man who knows the world, and who, sympathizing with the philosopher's scrutiny, sympathizes also with the confusion and indignation of the detected, skulking institutions" (p. 379).

3. Robert W. Corrigan, ed., *Comedy: Meaning and Form* (San Francisco: Chandler, 1965), contains some thirty selections (either independent essays or chapters from books), virtually all of them from the period since World War II. Notable exceptions are pieces by Molière, Charles Baudelaire, Meredith, Bergson, Freud, Vsevolod Meyerhold, Gustave Lanson, and George Santayana. Six essays are studies of individual plays, playwrights, or periods; five others are on farce or satire; three are on psychological matters. Of the fifteen selections dealing with the "Spirit," "Form," "Characteristics," or "Nature" of comedy, several are noticed elsewhere in these appendixes: the chapters from the books by Potts and Styan in Appendix 1.A, the essay by Fry in Appendix 8, and the essay by Sypher above in this section.

APPENDIX 2. "ACCEPTANCE" IN COMIC THEORY

The idea that comic experience involves some kind of "acceptance"—whether of the world, of society, of the mores of the age, of the way things go, of human limitations, of "life"—appears often in treatments of comedy. Almost invariably, however, the idea is mentioned *en passant*; as an aspect of comedy, it has a subordinate position; it is alluded to but does not elicit direct or extended critical attention. The following quotations indicate some variations on the idea of comic acceptance as it appears implicitly or explicitly in different expositions.

Nicoll, *An Introduction to Dramatic Theory* (1931): "Pure comedy largely grows out of the acceptance of social conventions and the presentation in an amusing form of any variations from the normal custom" (p. 175).

Drew, *Discovering Drama* (1937): "Comedy may, and frequently does, challenge the workings of a particular social order, . . . but its solutions are nevertheless within the limits of a social order. Its motto is 'Reason can find a way.' The conclusions of comedy imply the acceptance of the terms on which human life has got to be lived" (p. 170).

Feibleman, *In Praise of Comedy* (1939), rather remarkably accepts the idea of acceptance but translates it into nonacceptance. "It is the final difficulty of human life which comedy accepts because it cannot change, . . . comedy, then, is perforce mostly preoccupied with limitations, . . . And having to deal with these things, it is compelled psychologically to accept them. Thus psychologically comedy is not felt as criticism but as an acceptance, an acceptance of the comic aspects of actuality" (p. 189). But through this comic "recognition of the insuperable defects of actuality," "we become reconciled to the unimportance of limitations, and realize that we can surmount them. . . . Laughter is thus a release of a sort from the limitations of the human lot, a recognition . . . that obstacles in the path of improvement are not impossible obstacles . . ." (p. 191). From this he proceeds to this conclusion: "Comedy is negative; it is a criticism of limitations and an unwillingness to accept them" (p. 199). He has already called comedy a "continual rebellion and a refusal, even when faced with the inability to change conditions, to accept the compromises meted out by actuality" (p. 192).

Potts, *Comedy* (1948): "Comedy accepts life and human nature: sometimes with a light heart, as in *A Midsummer Night's Dream*, sometimes rather sadly as in *Don Quixote*, but always with the good sense that comes from clear vision and understanding" (p. 155).

Cook, *The Dark Voyage and the Golden Mean* (1949): "But basically comedy is approval, not disapproval, of present society; it is conservative, not liberal, however much the socialist Feibleman would like it to be" (p. 49). "From the social and probable point of view, one must accept the ways of the majority as they are, or one is doomed to failure" (p. 109). "The conservativism of comedy is reflected in the comedy of Gilbert, which accepts without question, while it twits them, the social classes of Victorian England" (p. 117).

Swabey, *Comic Laughter* (1961): "Presupposed . . . is a certain rough realism, a knowledge of the uses and wonts of society that does not expect too much of mankind" (p. 33). "What Molière seems gayly to be saying [in *The Misanthrope*] is that since it is natural for man to live in society, it is an absurd violation of his nature to reject his fellows and the human community" (p. 139). Comedy "usually involves acceptance of the generally received frame of values . . ." (p. 186). Though comic laughter may have a corrective function, "along with this goes . . . a fresh conviction of the camaraderie of truth, a renewal of hope, of springtime in life, which despite all reverses finds the world good, reason in its heaven, and man eager to fare forth on new adventures" (p. 247).

Amur, *The Concept of Comedy* (1963): The Spirit of Comedy "delights in discovering the limitations of human life on earth and, instead of being overwhelmed by this knowledge, uses it as a means of power and, by the voluntary acceptance of these limitations as also by the attainment of a fuller perspective of life, makes human existence not only bearable but positively pleasant" (p. 15). He rephrases, ". . . the joy of grateful acceptance of life" (p. 17). Comedy has not "the object of condemning life, but of expressing it and making it acceptable" (pp. 20–21).

Blistein, *Comedy in Action* (1964): "But Alfred Doolittle can adjust, even Lady Wishfort and Mrs. Malaprop are able to adjust, to a change in circumstances. Destruction is not for them because they are flexible. The spirit of compromise, the ability to see the human situation from more than one point of view, is the mark of the comic character . . ." (p. 19).

Hoy, *The Hyacinth Room* (1964): "Comedy implies, then, an acceptance of life, which implies as well an acceptance of man. And to accept man, one must be prepared to forgive the weakness, the treachery, the downright depravity which, in spite of man's best intentions, are inherent in his behavior. To accept and to forgive, one must be, above everything else, clear-sighted about what man is . . ." (pp. 17–18). Comedy is "realistic" but also "compassionate in its forgiveness and its acceptance of human failings . . ." (p. 18).

Schilling, *The Comic Spirit* (1965): "If the comic spirit is humane, calling forth a sense of the richness of life, willing participation in it, an acceptance of the full responsibility of being human, it also invites a certain discernment, an ability to see man as incongruously different from what he should be . . ." (p. 17).

Vos, *The Drama of Comedy* (1966): The comic protagonist "accepts every condition of his finitude" (p. 13). "What moves the comic protagonist is his acceptance of self-renunciation, and the inevitably comic result is self-preservation. . . . The comic protagonist's acceptance of his own finitude is the unique 'act' of comedy . . ." (p. 14).

Kerr, *Tragedy and Comedy* (1967): "Comedy is a tolerable form, then, and is even thought to be a 'happy' form, because man is able to accept his limitations philosophically" (p. 189). Molière's Alceste "abhors . . . the comic attitude toward life," which "accepts limitation, supposing it to be inevitable . . ." (pp. 257–58).

Kaul, *The Action of English Comedy* (1970): "New Comedy is not interested in social conflict, in the necessity or even the possibility of social change. It takes the existing world for granted and addresses itself to the unusual private case . . ." (p. 22). Much comedy "takes happily for granted the basic social and economic structure of the existing world" (p. 23).

McCollom, *The Divine Average* (1971): "The tone of Aristophanes, so difficult for us to grasp today, embraces brutal attack and benign acceptance" (p. 12).

Rodway, *English Comedy* (1975), alludes to "the social mode of comedy, its unheroic adaptability, and its wariness about rigid philosophy . . ." (p. 23). His term *celebration* (one of the "moods" of comedy) indicates that " 'comedy' is not being implicitly equated with 'humorous satire'" (p. 37). Comedy is noncorrective. "Hence the prevailing climate of [a writer's] comedy may be that of the 'celebration' of inescapably unideal common humanity, despite squalls of satire and bright periods of humour" (p. 37). (He suggests that a possible synonym for "celebratory" might be "festive," though he rejects it as "too gay" [p. 37n; cf. C. L. Barber's *Shakespeare's Festive Comedy: A Study of Dramatic Form in Its Relation to Social Custom*, 1959].) Writers of "great comedy" "relish the absurd at the same time as they expose it, have a good deal of charity for the failings of human nature and appreciate the need for variety in the world. Thus, though they place what is laughable by some implicit norm of sanity and balance, they also seem to accept it as a concomitant of human nature—and none of them thinks human nature itself can be much changed, though it may be amended somewhat" (p. 37).

APPENDIX 3. THE ARISTOTELIAN TRADITION

The Aristotelian tradition is too extensive even to sketch here; these are only a few random notes. Lane Cooper's *An Aristotelian Theory of Comedy* (New York: Harcourt, Brace, 1922), though it appears to be virtually forgotten now, is still useful. Its bibliography (pp. xv–xxi), which covers the field broadly up to 1922, is excellent. Cooper brings together numerous Greek materials, mainly Aristotelian but some also Platonic, bearing on the subject of comedy (pp. 1–165), and then presents "The *Poetics* of Aristotle Applied to Comedy" (pp. 166–223).

Cooper provides a translation of the post-Aristotelian *Tractatus Coislinianus* (pp. 224–26) and discusses this brief work at length (pp. 1–15, 227–86). There is a shorter, but helpful, discussion of the *Tractatus* in J. W. H. Atkins, *Literary Criticism in Antiquity: A Sketch of Its Development* (1934; rpt., 2 vols.; London: Methuen, 1952) 2:138–43.

The *Tractatus* periodically pops up in recent criticism, e.g., Northrop Frye, *Anatomy of Criticism* (Princeton, N.J.: Princeton University Press, 1957), p. 166, Cf. Kaul, *The Action of English Comedy*, p. 14. Some other recent applications of Aristotelian ideas:

Feibleman, *In Praise of Comedy* (1939), treats Plato and Aristotle together as spokesmen for a realistic theory of comedy (pp. 74 ff.) and often alludes to Aristotle in discussions of later theorists.

Goodman, *The Structure of Literature* (1954): "This book is a collection of inductive formal analyses of classical poems. They are arranged according to an abstract theory of genres borrowed from Aristotle . . ." (p. 24). Discussing *Philoctetes*, Goodman remarks, "The error of the *Poetics* is to put in the foreground the complex plot . . ." (p. 50). On comic plots, he makes a passing reference to Aristotle (p. 80). In the following statement the Aristotelian flavor is evident (the general subject is Beginnings, Middles, and Endings): "The deflation of the comic intrigue is the beginning of the ending. The humors are destroyed. The incidents of the ending comprise the salvaging of what survives in normalcy" (p. 91).

Swabey, *Comic Laughter* (1961), sketches an Aristotelian view of comedy by proceeding from remarks and hints in the *Poetics* (pp. 133–38).

Olson, *The Theory of Comedy* (1968), says that the author of the *Tractatus Coislinianus* "did not quite understand it [Aristotle's *Poetics*] or its function . . ." (p. 45). We cannot "discuss comedy by simple adaptations of what Aristotle says about tragedy. That is what got the author of the *Coislinian Tractate* into difficulty" (p. 49). For key statements on Olson's professedly Aristotelian theory, see Appendix 1. Olson works out a logical structure of great precision and complexity. In the course of this he does some enlightening explicatory readings of various parts of the *Poetics*. Treating comedy as an "imitation" with its "four causes" (pp. 27 ff.), he argues for a katastasis instead of catharsis (pp. 16, 36 ff.). Chapter 3, "The Poetics of Comedy (II)," follows through with systematic parallels to Aristotle (pp. 45 ff.).

APPENDIX 4. INCONGRUITY AND ITS VARIATIONS

Any reader in the field of comic theory will be struck by the recurrent appearance of the idea of incongruity as a source of the laughable, the ludicrous, the comic. Here are some versions of incongruity.

Nicoll, *An Introduction to Dramatic Theory* (1931), characteristically accepts multiple sources for comic effects. He devotes an extended discussion to incongruity as a source (pp. 155 ff.).

Drew, *Discovering Drama* (1937), lists among the virtues of comedy "the power to create ironic situation" (p. 114), especially "the difference between the conception of his own personality as held by the hero, and the reality as perceived by the audience" (p. 145).

Potts, *Comedy* (1948), discusses incongruity as a significant element in comedy, noting several kinds of it. He praises Shaw's "perception of this duality in human nature" (p. 25).

Potts speaks of "the paradox by which extreme fastidious refinement exists in us side by side with the vulgarest fleshly processes and propensities," of "the fundamental human inconsistency between the ideal and the reality," and of the comic utilization of "every variety of clash between contrasting ideas and temperaments" (p. 26).

Monro, *Argument of Laughter* (1951), not only discusses the "Incongruity Theories" of his predecessors (pp. 147–75), but advances a version of the incongruity theory in his own endeavor to elaborate a synthesis of different views of humor that he has discussed (pp. 235–56). His key is "the linking of disparates"; the idea is "to obtrude these disparities suddenly" (p. 238). One frequent element in such disparities is the "stereotypes and conventions" by which "much of our thinking really is controlled" (p. 239). Notably, when "something is represented as clashing with a particular system of values," either "the system of values exposes the inadequacy of the discordant element, or . . . the system itself is exposed." That is, "humour may be either conservative or radical in its effects" (p. 243).

Swabey, *Comic Laughter* (1961), uses the idea of the incongruous but insists on "an incongruity that makes sense" (p. 15), one that "requires an intellectual process" (p. 16). In her anti-Freudian view, wit "turns upon the intellect's recognition of sense in apparent nonsense and rejection of an absurdity in the light of consistency as a standard" (p. 70). She opposes Kant's idea of the perception of the incongruous as an aesthetic, nonlogical experience (pp. 104 ff.). She offers a catalogue of various kinds of incongruity (pp. 110 ff.). She explains Schopenhauer's definition of incongruity (p. 164), a definition to which various moderns allude, but argues against it that "comedy, especially in its higher forms, does penetrate behind appearances to noumena," and that "by grasping the noumenal order under the Idea of truth . . . we lay hold of the laughable in comedy" (p. 170).

Hoy, *The Hyacinth Room* (1964), says outright that "incongruity is of the essence of comedy. . . . The discrepancy between the noble intention and the ignoble deed points directly to the most glaring incongruity in the human condition . . ." (p. 5), and "the ironic disparity between the ideal and the reality" may appear in different genres; likewise the "sense of all such contradictions, disparities, and anomalies . . ." (p. 7). The "crucial fact about man is his dual nature. His duality makes him an incongruous figure, and if there were nothing incongruous in the human condition, there would be nothing to dramatize" (pp. 21–22).

Kerr, *Tragedy and Comedy* (1967), entitles his Chapter 8, "The Comic Incongruity." He refers to "the one incongruity upon which all other incongruities rest. That a being so entirely free should be so little free is absurd" (p. 145). He plays different variations upon this theme (see the entry in Appendix 1), but still it is a relatively small part of his total discussion.

Olson, *The Theory of Comedy* (1968), is one of a very small number of critics who point out that what we designate by "incongruity" and cognate terms may appear equally in noncomic situations (p. 10).

Styan, *The Dark Comedy* (1968), also notes that "incongruity is not necessarily laughable" (p. 43). "For Hazlitt the essence of the laughable was 'the incongruous,' a distinction between 'what things are and what they ought to be'" (p. 40).

Kaul, *The Action of English Comedy* (1970), pursues one particular mode of incongruity, that which appears in "a conflict between abstraction and experience" (p. 2). He attributes to Schopenhauer's *The World as Will and Idea* the "best philosophical analysis of the clash between abstraction and experience, in terms of the effect of incongruity and laughter" (p. 39) and discusses this at length (pp. 39 ff.).

Martin, *The Triumph of Wit* (1974), discovers in Victorian thought "a gradual shift from belief in superiority as the source of the risible, to an acceptance of its basis being in various forms of the incongruous . . ." (p. 17). The idea appears throughout the book but is dealt with especially in Chapter 2 (pp. 17–24).

Appendix 5. Laughter as Measure

Some treatments regard the comic and the laughable as identical; some discuss laughter without paying much attention to comedy; some analyze comedy without paying much attention to laughter; there are different views of priority and dependency. Various modern critics quote from a passage in Ben Jonson's *Timber*: "Nor is the moving of laughter always the end of comedy. . . . This is truly leaping from the Stage to the Tumbrell again, reducing all wit to the original Dungcart."

Nicoll, *An Introduction to Dramatic Theory* (1931), discusses at some length the varieties of the laughable, has some reservations about Bergson, and anticipates Olson in introducing the mood of the laugher as an element in the situation which produces laughter (pp. 131 ff.).

Feibleman, *In Praise of Comedy* (1939), is vigorously opposed to theories of laughter that derive from qualities of the laugher (the subject) rather than from qualities of the laughable (the object). Through the rise of nominalism "the logic of comedy was transformed into the psychology of laughter" (p. 121). Likewise, "Physiology has little to offer as yet in the way of the analysis of laughter . . ." (p. 161). He insists that "certainly there is something which occasions the laughter, something in the nature of a generalized comical situation . . ." (p. 167). "Laughter is the result of the sudden recognition of the wide difference between what is and what ought to be . . . [and] is thus a release of a sort from the limitations of the human lot . . ." (p. 191).

Potts, *Comedy* (1948), asserts that "to identify laughter with comedy is to begin at the wrong end." He notes that we laugh at many different things, and that there are many kinds of laughter. "Moreover it is very doubtful whether the end of comedy is to produce laughter. Many of the greatest comedies have a rather sobering effect . . ." (p. 19).

Monro, *Argument of Laughter* (1951), is concerned with all kinds of "laughable situations." These are humorous situations, and he divides them into ten classes. He also disposes of "Non-Humorous Laughter," that is, laughter produced by such causes as tickling, laughing gas, nervousness, relief after strain, "laughing it off," joy, play, make-believe, and contests, saying that he wants to "get them out of the way" (p. 33) before going on to a discussion of humor.

Swabey, *Comic Laughter* (1961), distinguishes, as her title indicates, among kinds of laughter (pp. 1–2, 7)—the comic and the noncomic. "Comic Laughter" must involve insight, perception, understanding: ". . . in the laughter of comic insight we achieve a logical moment of truth; . . . we detect an incongruence as cancelled by an underlying congruence" (p. v). ". . . only when [laughter actions] ensue from mentation are they genuinely to be labelled as comic" (p. 3). What is needed is a "perception of contrariety and absurdity" (p. 3), "a certain inconsistency or absurdity in its referent" (p. 4). ". . . the perception of the comic . . . requires a logical and metaphysical comprehension, a normative intellectual insight which grasps what is worthy of laughter . . ." (p. 13). Chapter 10, "The Genesis of Laughter," rejects "regressive" and "infantile" sources, that is, the physiological and the somatic (Spencer and Darwin), because they are antirational (pp. 199 ff.), and the "superiority laughter" of Hobbes and Alexander Bain (pp. 212 ff.), and challenges the views of Freud and Bergson as too restrictive (pp. 213 ff., 222 ff.).

Amur, *The Concept of Comedy* (1963), says that "to equate the effect of Comedy with laughter is . . . narrow and unrealistic" (pp. 4 ff.). He opposes the view that "our experience of Comedy is a sort of malicious and derogatory laughter" (pp. 17–18), for "the earth never ceases to be a source of joy" (p. 18). Again he protests against the view that comedy "provokes laughter" (p. 22). Later he returns to summarize a number of opinions on the nature and function of laughter (pp. 122 ff.), but this time not so much to rule out laughter as to make it acceptable by introducing suitable qualifications (pp. 123–25). He is feeling his way toward the position formally articulated by Swabey.

Blistein, *Comedy in Action* (1964), comments on laughter in connection with the "cruel" in comedy: "Perhaps, then, we may offer the theory that we laugh at cruelty if the pain that results from it is limited . . ." (p. 62). Perhaps by such laughter "we are able to purge ourselves of the latent sadism that is, to a greater or lesser measure, in all of us" (p. 64).

Olson, *The Theory of Comedy* (1968), does not deny laughing as a part of the comic experience but attacks most preceding theorists for attending to only one of the three elements that all need to be brought into comic theory: what is laughed at, who is laughing, and the relation between the object laughed at and the subject who laughs (p. 5). Hence there is "no completely unexceptionable theory of laughter . . ." (p. 7). Analyses of the laughable do not take into account different perspectives (pp. 7–8). There are many variables in the laugher; hence the troubles in the Platonic and Hobbesian views (p. 8). Olson observes that there are many noncomic sources of laughter (p. 10); hence laughter "is only a symptom, and not a very reliable one, for it indicates contrary conditions . . ." (p. 11). He proposes that we need a neutral term like "laughter emotion" (p. 11). The "laughter emotion" is "a relaxation . . . of concern due to a manifest absurdity of the grounds for concern" (p. 16).

Kaul, *The Action of English Comedy* (1970), discusses and opposes various laughter theories of comedy (pp. 14–17). He alludes to critics who have "relied . . . on the authority of Kant, Freud, or Bergson, and thus anchored their theories in the one idea of laughter," and finds various followers of Kant's *Critique of Judgment*, II.54, "pompous" (pp. 14, 15). The difficulty with "laughter theory" is that it "invalidates the whole idea of comic *action*," of the "sustained action or preparation" which Kaul believes essential to comic effect (pp. 16, 17).

McCollom, *The Divine Average* (1971), notes the variations within laughter and aspects of laughter theories (pp. 32–33).

Martin, *The Triumph of Wit* (1974), devotes his first chapter to "The Dangers of

Laughter," an unusual subject among these volumes. Martin summarizes the seventeenth-and eighteenth-century suspicions of, and derogatory attitudes to, laughter, which had considerable influence in the nineteenth century well into the Victorian period.

Rodway, *English Comedy* (1975), objects to the bad effects of "identifying [comedy] with laughter" (p. 11).

APPENDIX 6. SATIRE AND COMEDY

Some critics treat satire as a part or a form of comedy; some sharply distinguish the two modes. The citations that follow exhibit some representative positions.

Nicoll, *An Introduction to Dramatic Theory* (1931): "Pure comedy largely grows out of the acceptance of social conventions. . . . Satire lashes the customs of society as well as the eccentricities of individuals" (p. 175).

Drew, *Discovering Drama* (1937), implicitly distinguishes between satire and comedy by distinguishing, in the general realm of "critical" comedy, between the "explicit," which derides "follies or abuses," and the "implicit," which acts by "revealing human nature as it is." But the potential distinction is blurred when she refers to Jonson and Shaw as the English masters of "direct satiric comedy" (p. 148). Thus she tends to make her main categories "satirical comedy" and "escapist comedy."

Feibleman, *In Praise of Comedy* (1939), in effect turns all comedy into satire with a virtually programmatic commitment to revolution. Comedy: "The derogation of what-is in favour of what-ought-to-be" (p. 146). Derogation proceeds by "direct ridicule of the categories of actuality (such as are found in current customs and institutions)" or "by confusing the categories of actuality as an indication of their ultimate unimportance . . ." (p. 179). "Thus comedy is an antidote to error. It is a restorer of proportions, and signals a return from extreme adherence to actual programmes, . . . Thus indirectly comedy voices the demand for more logical programs [*sic*]" (p. 181). "Comedy leads to dissatisfaction and the overthrow of all reigning theories and practices. . . . It thus works against current customs and institutions; hence its inherently revolutionary nature" (p. 200). "Thus the comedian is a reformer who is often ignorant of the fact himself . . ." (p. 222). The weight of many such passages is mildly contradicted, as if Feibleman were momentarily forgetting their implications, when he makes a qualitative list of types of comedy and puts satire near the bottom, thus: "Joy—Divine Comedy—Humour—Irony—Satire—Sarcasm—Wit—Scorn" (p. 205). Aside from logical problems in the list, the low placement of Wit—even below Sarcasm!—is surprising.

Potts, *Comedy* (1948): "Comedy accepts life and human nature. . . . Satire, on the other hand, does not accept; it rejects and aims at destruction; . . . I conclude that comedy, as well as tragedy, is not only in a different class from satire, but in a higher class; and that when a satirist develops into a comic writer his mind has become more mature and his work more truthful" (p. 155). Comedy must be distinguished not only from tragedy "but also—more difficult—from satire and farce . . ." (p. 66). Potts stresses Congreve's "good nature," which he says is not appreciated today. "It is the more important because good nature is really essential to the comic mode; without it comedy sinks to the level of satire, and with it a satirist can rise to the level of comedy" (p. 99).

Cook, *The Dark Voyage and the Golden Mean* (1949): "Whereas comedy laughs joyously over the norms of its contemporary society, satire laughs sardonically at those norms; to satire the times are out of joint. It sees the failure and corruption of the present as abnormal, judged implicitly against a norm of success and health, in the past of a golden age or in the imagined future" (pp. 48–49). Cook says that Feibleman "represents comedy as satiric criticism of the present limited historical order and as campaign for the unlimited ideal logical order of the future" (p. 49).

Swabey, *Comic Laughter* (1961): ". . . the satirist, tied to this world and with his indignant undertone, never reaches the freest ranges or loftiest heights of the artistic imagination" (p. 61). "Nevertheless satire is probably the most socially effective form of the comic, with the greatest utility as a practical instrument for the destruction of evils" (p. 62). "For in satire we generally remain aloof, at once mocking and deploring man's weaknesses, yet *looking at him from the outside*, whereas in humor we delight and sorrow *with* him, sharing, sympathizing, comprehending his frailty and tribulations" (p. 63). "Undeniably, a chief function of laughter is to help sweep the world free of shams . . ." (p. 247). But then she goes on to find in comic laughter, also, a rather hopeful and zestful participation in common life.

Amur, *The Concept of Comedy* (1963): "And the satirical, though often found in Comedy, must be clearly distinguished from the Comic. . . . In satire, there is a deliberate intensification of the emotions of hatred and contempt and a complete absence of kindliness. . . . The satirical . . . will be inimical to the spirit of Comedy if it is allowed to dominate the entire mood" (pp. 28–29). *Volpone* and *The Plain Dealer* "should be thought of as satirical plays rather than as comedies" (p. 29). "The dissociation of the Comic Spirit from satire—personal or general—has been one of the most important features of its evolution" (p. 30). "Moral indignation of a fierce and uncontrolled type is not compatible with the spirit of Comedy" (p. 31).

Schilling, *The Comic Spirit* (1965), implicitly distinguishes satire and comedy. An observer of all the flaws and misdeeds of men "may be indifferent, contemptuous, amused, or indignant, refusing to absolve mankind for its weak failure to be what it should be. Or he may think of himself as sharing like other men in the weakness that his intelligence perceives, and so end in a mood of tolerance—his laughter tempered by sympathy" (p. 11).

Merchant, *Comedy* (1972), approves A. E. Dyson's idea that "satire judges man against an ideal, while comedy sets him against a norm. This proposes a fundamental distinction, for an ideal is by its nature difficult of realization by fallible man, while a norm is humanity's resting-point. The two modes then of satire and comedy would seem to oppose bitter glee and compassionate laughter, destructive judgement and an urbane certainty of redemption . . ." (p. 42). Merchant notes that Ben Jonson can do both in one play.

Appendix 7. Secondary Surveys

Some writers on comedy pay little attention to earlier writings; others selectively or assiduously recognize predecessors, whether to record, repeat, recommend, revise, or reprove. These latter may provide surveys of some use. Obviously each critic is viewing predecessors in the light of his own code or creed. Granted that each uses his own perspective rather than a divine total perspective, the surveys listed below may serve as helpful, if partial, introductory guides to one area or another of *materia comica*.

Feibleman, *In Praise of Comedy* (1939), devotes two chapters—"Some Classical Theories of Comedy" (pp. 74–122) and "Criticism of Modern Theories of Comedy" (pp. 123–67)—to perhaps the most systematic critical review of other theories to be found in this set of volumes. He always uses his prorealist, antinominalist criterion, thus making more frequent adverse judgments of post-Renaissance theorists. In the earlier chapter he comments on classical theorists, and then Tzetzes, Vico, Hobbes, Gottsched, J. E. Schlegel, Kant, Spencer, Schopenhauer, Hazlitt, Meredith, and C. C. Everett. In the chapter on more recent critics he finds error more prevalent, but also occasionally a hopeful realistic tendency or, as he says of Freud, an "insight . . . better than his doctrine" (p. 157). The theorists discussed are Bergson, Croce, Carritt, Jankélévitch, Eastman, Leacock, Menon, Seward,Gregory, Freud (and Lipps), Dumas, Bechterev, Crile, Zuver, and Graves.

Cook, *The Dark Voyage and the Golden Mean* (1949), makes some notations on Freud on wit, Kant on laughter, and Bergson on comedy (pp. 40–47).

Monro, *Argument of Laughter* (1951), matches Feibleman in the fullness of his discussions of preceding theorists on humor and laughter, to whom he devotes a number of chapters, and whom he characteristically treats in terms of both their strong and their weak points (pp. 89–231). He organizes his discussions of others according to their adherence to one or another of the four main types of humor-theories that he believes exhaust the field: theories based on superiority, on incongruity, on release from restraint, on ambivalence.

Goodman, *The Structure of Literature* (1954), presents and explicates many Aristotelian dicta. He makes some points about the criticisms of Kant, Freud, and Bergson (pp. 80–81).

William K. Wimsatt, Jr., ed., *English Stage Comedy*, English Institute Essays 1954 (New York: Columbia University Press, 1955), opens the volume with an "Introduction: The Criticism of Comedy" (pp. 3–21). In this he makes a very compact survey of different perspectives on comedy and of some of the users of each perspective. Laughter theories: Potts, Johnson, Eastman, Hobbes, Plato, Shaftesbury, Freud, Albert Rapp (pp. 3–8). Theories of the laughable, especially those based on incongruity: Kant, Schopenhauer, Koestler (pp. 8–10). Theories with a "social and moral direction": Aristotle, some neoclassical theorists, German Romantics, Meredith, Potts (pp. 10–11). Myth and ritual: Frye, Cook (pp. 11–12). Relation between laugher and laughed-at: Bergson, Molière, Fielding, Swift, Jean Paul, F. Schlegel,Kierkegaard, Emerson, Meredith (pp. 12–17).

William K. Wimsatt, Jr., and Cleanth Brooks, *Literary Criticism: A Short History* (New York: Alfred A. Knopf, 1957), allude only incidentally to problems of comedy but often combine excellent short summaries of others' views with brief balanced comments of their own. Chapter 3 contains a compact outline of classical theory and practice of comedy, and of contrasts between tragedy and comedy (pp. 45–51). Chapter 11 touches on Dryden's theory of comedy and on the developments in comedy from the Jacobean period to the

Restoration (pp. 201–4); on Dryden's views of satire, and certain neoclassic relations between satire and comedy (pp. 207–10); and on "the rather severe and ethically serious theory of comedy to be traced from Aristotle to Meredith" (pp. 210–13). Chapter 17 includes comments on German Romantic views on comedy, humor, and irony (pp. 378–80). Chapter 25, "Tragedy and Comedy," deals with various nineteenth- and twentieth-century critics and relates some of them to eighteenth-century critics (pp. 555–82). It includes discussions of certain relationships between Nietzsche on tragedy and Bergson on comedy (pp. 567 ff.); of pre-Freudian theories of laughter (pp. 570–72); of Freud (pp. 572–75); and of Eastman's and Koestler's attacks on Freud (pp. 575–79). They say Koestler's is better.

Swabey, *Comic Laughter* (1961), applies her criteria to various predecessors and explains her differences with them, often at considerable length: Freud (pp. 70 ff., 213 ff.), Kant (pp. 104 ff.), Bergson (pp. 142 ff., 222 ff.), Schopenhauer (pp. 164 ff.), Spencer, Darwin, Hobbes, and Bain on laughter (pp. 199 ff.). Swabey is at ease in philosophical discourse and explains the positions of other theorists amply and unquarrelsomely.

Amur, *The Concept of Comedy* (1963), is committed to noticing the opinions of virtually everyone who has ever written on comedy, from classical thinkers to nineteenth-century philosophers and the very large crop of modern critics. In that sense his work provides an unusually ample introduction to comedy. His bibliography is inclusive.

Olson, *The Theory of Comedy* (1968), in addition to his running commentary on Aristotle, surveys a considerable number of theories of laughter, especially those of classical and nineteenth-century thinkers, and a few from the seventeenth and eighteenth centuries (pp. 5 ff.). He is one of the few to mention Baudelaire.

Styan, *The Dark Comedy* (1968), gives a rather sketchy survey of theories of comedy (Hazlitt, Meredith, Bergson, Freud), taking a dim view of most of them (pp. 40–42).

Kaul, *The Action of English Comedy* (1970), comments on various laughter theories (Kant, Bergson, Freud) (pp. 14–17), surveys other writings on comedy, especially Northrop Frye's essay in its two forms (pp. 18–23), and discusses Schopenhauer's incongruity theory (pp. 39 ff.).

McCollom, *The Divine Average* (1971), comments on theories of laughter (pp. 32–33), theories that seem to render comedy "pessimistic" (pp. 33–34), and psychoanalytical interpretations of humor (pp. 34–35).

Merchant, *Comedy* (1972), makes an early remark that, in view of the preceding notations in this appendix, seems much to the point: ". . . it has been so fashionable during the past fifty years to begin with the psychological basis of comedy—to cite Sigmund Freud on laughter and Henri Bergson on 'le mode renversé'—that it seems as well to clear this obstacle before pursuing a more profitable course" (p. 7). Adding Grotjahn to these names, Merchant insists on "the inadequacy of a psychological theory when it is transferred to the realm of art and its criticism" (p. 10; cf. pp. 7 ff.). Merchant provides an extensive bibliography with brief annotations (pp. 83–86). The bibliography has a historical side: it lists works on earlier periods of English comedy, on Greek drama, and on French comedy.

Martin, *The Triumph of Wit* (1974), writes a brief history of adverse views of laughter (pp. 1–16), of superiority and incongruity theories of comedy (pp. 17–24), and of conflicting ideas of wit and humor (pp. 25–46). All these chapters deal with pre-nineteenth-century forebears and nineteenth-century applications. Chapter 4 (pp. 47–66) is most unusual in that it summarizes "Phrenological Formulations" with respect to laughter, humor, etc. Chapter 5 (pp. 67–81) discusses the views of Sydney Smith, Leigh Hunt, and Thackeray, and Chapter 6 (pp. 82–100), those of George Eliot, Leslie Stephen, and George Meredith, who is credited with effecting the ultimate change in comic theory during the period.

APPENDIX 8. TRAGEDY AND COMEDY

Many students of comedy approach their subject by using tragedy as a direction-finder. Whether or not they use the sparse hints in Aristotle, they may define comedy by differentiating it from tragedy. On the other hand they may find lines of connection between the two—resemblances or affinities latent beneath the contrasting appearances that for the general mind render tragedy and comedy distinct genres. Those who view tragedy and comedy as siblings or twins, if not even a Janus-faced single identity, frequently quote Christopher Fry's "I know that when I set about writing a comedy the idea presents itself to me first of all as a tragedy. . . . If the characters were not qualified for tragedy there would be no comedy, and to some extent I have to cross the one before I can light on the other." Some critics seem also to have been moved by another Fry statement which is less quoted: "I have come, you may think, to the verge of saying that comedy is greater than tragedy. On the verge I stand and go no further." These statements are in the essay "Comedy," reprinted in *Comedy: Meaning and Form*, ed. Robert W. Corrigan (pp. 15–17).

The following notes and quotations reveal the kinds of attitude in recent circulation.

Drew, *Discovering Drama* (1937), rather nicely disposes of some of the usual distinctions between the two (pp. 138–39, 168–69). "The essential difference . . . is that Comedy is a sociable thing and that Tragedy is a solitary thing . . ." (p. 138). There is a difference between "one kind of total response" and "another kind of total response . . . in comedy temporal values prevail, and in tragedy eternal" (p. 169).

Feibleman, *In Praise of Comedy* (1939): If comedy is "the indirect affirmation of the logical order by means of the derogation of the limited orders of actuality," tragedy is "the direct affirmation of the formal logical order by means of the approval of the positive content of actuality" (p. 198). "Comedy is an intellectual affair, and deals chiefly with logic. Tragedy is an emotional affair, and deals chiefly with value" (p. 199). "Since comedy deals with the limitations of actual situations and tragedy with their positive content, comedy must ridicule and tragedy must endorse" (p. 199). "Comedy is . . . a more revolutionary affair than tragedy. . . . Thus tragedy leads to a state of contentment with the actual world . . ." (p. 200). "Comedy and tragedy emerge from the same ontological problem: the relation of the logical to the historical order" (p. 203).

Ronald Peacock, *The Poet in the Theatre* (New York: Harcourt, Brace, 1946), wants to "reaffirm the closeness of tragedy and comedy . . ." (p. 152). Tragedy and comedy "both . . . spring from the tension between our imperfect life and our ideal aspirations. They exist together in their dependence on the contradictions of life. They are parallel expressions, in different keys, of our ideas of what is good" (p. 153). They have "reference to good and evil. They are initiated by a moral experience" (p. 154). They "refer . . . to the same thing: the illusive image of our humanity. . . . But as long as there is imperfection these forms will flourish side by side as they have always done . . ." (p. 158).

Potts, *Comedy* (1948), defines comedy as a *"mode of thought,"* since its "character depends on the attitude of the writer to life" (p. 10). Comedy "depends on the eye of the beholder, not on the character of the object he has in view, [for] nothing in nature is categorically comic . . ." (p. 45). "There are only two literary modes of thought: tragedy and comedy" (p. 10). Tragedy and comedy are "strictly parallel," and "I propose to treat tragedy and comedy as distinct and mutually exclusive modes" (p. 11). Tragedy is "an expression of the natural pride of man," whereas comedy is "an expression of the natural modesty of man" (p. 114). The two modes are "natural activities of man, not invented by anyone but arising out of the quality of the human mind" (p. 14). "Tragic characters are isolated; and they tend to be either superhuman or subhuman. . . . To be comic, on the other hand, a character must be seen as one unit in a society composed of other similar units . . ." (p. 115). "There are at least two kinds of plot: the tragic plot, in *time*, and the comic plot, in *space*" (p. 140). This is the summation of an idea approached in an earlier statement: "The pattern we want in comedy is . . . a grouping of characters rather than a march of events" (p. 130).

‧ Cook, *The Dark Voyage and the Golden Mean* (1949), proceeds basically, as already noted in Appendix 1, by a systematic contrast of the tragic and the comic. Cook outlines a series of dichotomies that are variously logical, cultural, aesthetic, psychological, epistemological, and even metaphysical. "In the light of this duality, there are two basic ways of regarding life; in art this is the great generic duality, comedy versus tragedy" (p. 28). An example of Cook's rather gnomic formulations: tragedy involves the "wonderful-as-supreme probable" (p. 50), and comedy, the "search for the wonderful in probable terms" (p. 51). However, he concludes with a formal outline of "antinomic" elements, of which the following are the ones of most evident literary applicability (the tabular form is necessary to make the oppositions clear):

Tragedy	*Comedy*
Ethics	Manners
Individual man	Social man as the member of a family and generation
History of the soul	Experience in social life
Death, good, evil	Politics, sex, search for the wonderful in probable terms . . .
Good-evil	Conformity-expulsion
All in terms of soul	Denial of soul
Superhuman	Subhuman (beast, machine)

[pp. 50-51]

Swabey, *Comic Laughter* (1961): ". . . whereas the comic primarily confronts simply logical contradictions, the tragic confronts a moral predicament. . . . [The tragic character] stands at the crossroads compelled to choose his path, without knowing unambiguously which is right but sure that whichever he takes involves suffering and loss" (p. 182).

Bentley, *The Life of the Drama* (1964), regards "misery as the basis of comedy and gaiety as an ever-recurring transcendence. Seen in this way, comedy, like tragedy, is a way of trying to cope with despair, mental suffering, guilt, and anxiety" (p. 301). "The tragic poet writes from a sense of crisis. . . . The comic poet is less apt to write out of a particular crisis than from that steady ache of misery which in human life is even more common than crisis and so a more insistent problem" (p. 303). "Comedy is very often about theft, exactly as tragedy is very often about murder. . . . The motor forces are hatred [in tragedy] and greed [in comedy]" (p. 305). "Both tragedy and comedy are about human weakness, but both, in the end, testify to human strength. . . . Like tragedy, comedy can achieve a transcendence over misery, an aesthetic transcendence (of art over life), and a transcending emotion (awe in tragedy, joy in comedy)" (p. 308). "Finally, tragedy and comedy have the same heuristic intent: self-knowledge" (p. 309).

Blistein, *Comedy in Action* (1964), twits critics who glibly "tell us that tragedy and comedy are the same thing . . ." (p. xii). He proposes this: ". . . while the tragic character as well as the audience is essentially primitive, the comic character is essentially civil" (p. 18).

Hoy, *The Hyacinth Room* (1964): "The protagonists of tragedy and comedy alike are deficient in their knowledge of human limitations, . . . in self-knowledge. The tragic protagonist's lack of self-knowledge typically leads to destruction. The comic protagonist's lack of self-knowledge leads ideally to a fine enlightenment from which he cannot but benefit" (p. 6). "The sense of all such contradictions, disparities, and anomalies . . . is familiar. . . . They are the co-ordinates by means of which the tragic, the comic, and the tragicomic modes are defined . . ." (p. 7). "When [this issue] is joined in tragedy, their opposition is found to be unalterable and final. When it is joined in comedy, discordant elements are reconciled in a spirit of wise tolerance" (p. 8). In "serious drama, comic or tragic, we are confronted with what is, at bottom, a single truth about the human condition" (p. 11). Hoy quotes Kierkegaard, *Concluding Unscientific Postscript:* " 'The tragic and the comic are the same, in so far as both are based on contradiction; but *the tragic is the suffering contradiction, the comical, the painless contradiction*. . . . The comic apprehension evokes the contradiction or makes it manifest by having in mind the way out. The tragic apprehension sees the contradiction and despairs of a way out' " (p. 67).

Vos, *The Drama of Comedy* (1966): "Tragedy attempts to comprehend the mystery [of incongruities in the world]; comedy simply accepts it" (p. 79).

Kerr, *Tragedy and Comedy* (1967), sounds like Fry (whom he later quotes) when he says that he had to "come at comedy through tragedy or to stand silent before this perpetual ambiguity" (p. 17). More markedly than others on this side of the fence, he stresses the interrelationship and even the interdependence of the two genres. When the absolutes implied by tragedy are missing, comedy has harder going. In Chapter 2 (pp. 19 ff.) he argues that tragedy was prior to and a source of comedy. In Chapters 3 and 4 he develops a somewhat paradoxical position that tragic endings contain or imply a certain "joy" (this from Nietzsche) (p. 56) and that comic endings are in effect antihappiness (pp. 78–79). "Comedy, even at its lowest, is utterly dependent upon the existence, and the sometime success, of the tragic aspiration" (p. 188). "Comedy wholly loosed from tragedy is, perversely, comedy bastardized" (p. 212). "It would not seem . . . that comedy could long survive the reported death of tragedy or maintain itself in any very fit condition during one of tragedy's cyclical silences" (p. 266). Kerr is not entirely sure that tragedy is dead (pp. 273 ff.); he thinks we may be coming around from feeling defeated and determined and may be recovering a sense of freedom and responsibility and hence even of the arrogance required in tragedy (pp. 299 ff.). Existentialist thought may be a move in this direction (pp. 303 ff.). "It is necessary to stress the fact that comedy is at its most vigorous when tragedy is at its most vigorous" (p. 309). When tragedy goes, the result is black comedy, which "derives from the complete absence of any tragic aspiration. . . . Black comedy acknowledges the disappearance of affirmation altogether . . ." (p. 317). Comedy is now taking over the burden of both traditional comedy and tragedy. ". . . comedy has preserved our *seriousness* . . ." (p. 325). "With tragedy lost to us as a working form, we lack an adequate vessel for our seriousness" (p. 328).

Olson, *The Theory of Comedy* (1968): With his reliance on Aristotle's *Poetics*, Olson of course regularly crosses back and forth between the tragic and the comic, but he makes only one or two formal contrasts. "Tragedy endows with worth; comedy takes the worth away" (p. 36). "Tragedy and comedy are contraries . . . in that the former sets something before us as supremely serious, and evokes our extremest concern, while the latter disavows all cause for concern . . ." (p. 39).

Merchant, *Comedy* (1972), has a strong sense of the tendency toward generic overlap and even merger, of "the inevitable intersection of comedy and tragedy" (p. 12), of "the profound difficulty of demarcation between the tragic and the comic temper" (p. 40). "So near does the art of comedy steer to the matter of tragedy" (p. 52). In one detail he speaks like Kerr: "With the 'death of tragedy' in our day has come the emasculation of comedy . . ." (p. 61).

Rodway, *English Comedy* (1975): "Tragedy, then, solves a psychological dilemma in the audience, the key lying in *sacrifice*, the heart of the tragedy. . . . The heroes of tragedy are morally ambiguous" (p. 20). "Where tragedy is primarily an expression of man's individuality and greatness, and only secondarily . . . of his social nature, comedy is the reverse. Mainly the expression of man as a social being, it is commonly concerned with his littleness and is critical of it" (p. 21). "In one word, good comedy tends to be civilising; good tragedy, exalting. The one, so to say, expresses man as cultivator; the other, man as warrior. . . . Tragedy emphasises inflexible courage needed to face a *remorseless* Fate; comedy emphasises flexibility to get by it, round it, or on with it" (p. 22). Comedy is "the product of a purposive genial attitude" and "it is further distinguished from tragedy by its gregarious quality. The tragic hero is invested with his isolation; though it may cause his downfall, it does not reduce his stature. In comedy, such extreme individualism is seen as eccentric or abnormal" (pp. 30–31).

APPENDIX 9. THE WORLD AS COMIC ARENA

"The world," my own term for the realm that comedy deals with, is rarely used by other critics, but the idea denoted by the word is implied in a number of observations that treat "society" or "social life" as the comic scene.

Nicoll, *An Introduction to Dramatic Theory* (1931), lists special or eccentric characters treated comically and sums up that "all these are set over against a world of normal society figures. A world of Poloniuses would not be laughable, nor would a world of Malaprops" (p. 45). "The fundamental assumption of comedy is that it does not deal with isolated individualities" (p. 134).

Drew, *Discovering Drama* (1937): *"Comedy is always rooted in the social order.* It deals with the relationship of individuals to society, and of society to individuals [with reciprocal criticism]" (p. 169). "Comedy may concern itself only with the immediate field of society . . . or it may expand into the contemplation of human nature in general . . . but its final standards are . . . always *social*, . . . Comedy does not move into the realm of abstract justice, but anchors itself in this world with its imperfect but easier emotional and ethical judgments" (p. 170).

Potts, *Comedy* (1948): Much as we value our "separateness," "we need also to merge it in the life of the world into which we were born, to mix with other people, to adjust our own wills and even our characters to the *milieu* in which by choice or necessity we live and to the general laws of nature" (p. 18). The writer of comedy "is trying to present a social point of view; to measure human conduct against a norm rather than an ideal" (p. 45). A major subject of comedy is "men and women in society" (p. 58). Potts's definition: "Society . . . stands for an idea rather than a particular set of persons. It stands for coherence; for a common body of opinions and standards and a disposition to co-operate" (p. 60).

Cook, *The Dark Voyage and the Golden Mean* (1949), lists among identifying elements of comedy, "Manners, Social man as the member of a family and generation, Experience in social life" (p. 50).

Swabey, *Comic Laughter* (1961): "In comedy a duality of feeling appears in our attitude toward the 'rules of the game,' an impulse sometimes of obedience and sometimes of transgression. This two-fold sentiment in social life, which is sometimes a partisan of the code, and sometimes on the side of the rebel or violator, has much to do, in our opinion, with man's unfolding sensitivity to the comic" (p. 223). "That the comic as a specific term has reference to the general mind of society, to the aggregate of men in interaction, . . . is widely recognized" (p. 33).

Vos, *The Drama of Comedy* (1966): The comic protagonist "is subordinate to the social ethos, the society is redeemed in the man, and the society is to be 'the redeemed form of man.' . . . Comedy assumes that society must be made to work, that men must somehow learn to live together. . . . The tendency of comedy is to include as many people as possible in its final society" (p. 100).

McCollom, *The Divine Average* (1971): Comedy is "concerned not with perilous moral choices made in isolation from others but with the steps or leaps taken, the adjustments made, the routines rehearsed, and the chances encountered in an endless variety of social settings from family to committee room to carnival" (p. vii).

Rodway, *English Comedy* (1975): "The rituals from which comedy sprang seem to have aimed at just such an integration with self and society . . ." (p. 26). "During phases of satisfactory social integration we should expect the best comedy . . . to be mainly *conserving*. . . . Similarly, during the hardening phases, we are likely to find the best comedy *innovating* . . ." (p. 27). "Generally speaking, Shakespeare seems to promote integration with nature, Jonson with society. In the one a *sharing* is offered, in the other a *warning*" (p. 98).

Notes

Prologue

1. Quotations are from Eugène Ionesco, *Plays*, trans. Donald Watson (9 vols.; London: John Calder, 1958–73), 5:96–106.

Chapter 1. Some Ways into the World of Comedy

1. For various critical comments on the relation between, or the distinction between, tragedy and comedy, see Appendix 8. Several critics, most notably Walter Kerr, think that the health of comedy in any age is dependent upon the health of tragedy in that age.

2. This point, in one form or another, is often made by critics. See Appendix 9.

3. There is a vast amount of theorizing about the causes of laughter and the relation of laughter to comedy. See Appendix 5.

4. For brief sketches of various ideas about comedy—formal theories, assertions, intuitions, obiter dicta—see Appendix 1. For a partial guide to critics' observations on the positions of previous critics, see Appendix 7.

5. Cf. Bummidge in Act II of Saul Bellow, *The Last Analysis* (rev., 1965): "An old gag. She's full of them. They're really sadistic threats in comic form" (Compass Book; New York: Viking Press, 1966, p. 76). Cf. Anthony M. Ludovici; *The Secret of Laughter* (London: Constable, 1932).

6. For the Aristotelian tradition in the criticism of comedy, see Appendix 3.

7. Georges Feydeau, *Four Farces*, translated and with an introduction by Norman R. Shapiro (Chicago and London: University of Chicago Press, 1970), Introduction, p. xlix. Shapiro goes on, however, to indicate the natural limits of such pleasure: it is modified in proportion to the degree of identification with the character that the dramatist permits, or forces, the reader to have. That is, the fuller the character, the less easily we manage the

separation necessary for a feeling of superiority. These terms are my own, not Shapiro's. Baudelaire's essay, "On the Essence of Laughter, and, in General, on the Comic in the Plastic Arts," trans. Jonathan Mayne, is reprinted in *Comedy: Meaning and Form*, ed. Robert W. Corrigan (San Francisco: Chandler, 1965), pp. 448–65. It is of course a commonplace that superiority theories of laughter derive from Thomas Hobbes.

8. This view, as well as the related ideas that I have sketched in Section IV, is treated in too many ways by too many critics to make a census of them a manageable affair. Several key names in the life-fertility-springtime field are those of Henri Bergson, Susanne Langer, and Northrop Frye. For representative passages from each see Corrigan, *Comedy: Meaning and Form*, pp. 471–77, 119–40, 141–62.

9. Martin Esslin, *The Theatre of the Absurd* (rev. ed.; Anchor Book; Garden City, N.Y.: Doubleday, 1969), p. 5.

10. Henri Peyre has nicely caught the egotism of self-pity latent in absurdist thought: "the most blatant form of anthropomorphism: complaining that the world does not suit man's conveniences" (*French Novelists of Today* [New York: Oxford University Press, 1967], p. 369).

11. This point is implicit in Friedrich Duerrenmatt's remark to an American interviewer: "I am against the expression, 'The world is absurd.' I say only that the world is paradox" (Violet Ketels, "Friedrich Duerrenmatt at Temple University," *Journal of Modern Literature*, 1 {1970}: 98). In literature, paradox has been present for a very long time: cf. the blind Tiresias in *Oedipus Rex*.

12. These points are in *Philebus*, 48–49. See *The Dialogues of Plato*, trans. B. Jowett, (4th ed., 4 vols.; Oxford: Clarendon Press, 1953), 3:606–8. Plato also speaks about the mixture of emotions experienced in comedy. He attacks "all personal satire" and "sees dangers in an unseasonable employment of comedy and in an excess of laughter." See J. W. H. Atkins, *Literary Criticism in Antiquity: A Sketch of Its Development* (1934; rpt., 2 vols.; London: Methuen, 1952), 1:57.

13. For some examples of incongruity theory, see Appendix 4.

Chapter 2. The World as Comic Realm

1. Emil Roy, *British Drama since Shaw* (Carbondale and Edwardsville: Southern Illinois University Press, 1972), pp. 31–32.

2. When plays are available in various editions, I identify quotations by act, scene (if there are scene divisions), and line numbers (if these are indicated). Ordinarily I give page numbers only if I am using some special edition or translation.

3. Raymond Williams sees in this episode no more than "the steering of the estate into the right hands" (*The Country and the City* [New York: Oxford University Press, 1973], p. 53). Good critic as Williams can be, he is prevented by his system from seeing in *The Way of the World* anything but the operation of property economics. In his view, even the nice people in Restoration comedy "usually reveal themselves . . . as endowed. . . . This, in the most real sense, is the way of the world" (p. 53). Hence he cannot acknowledge that economic competence is simply a given in comedy and that the dramatic essence is the quality of life—petty or magnanimous, gross or gracious—settled for or achieved by different personalities in the realm of "competence."

4. For other formulations of this view see Appendix 9.

5. For somewhat similar statements on society as the comic scene, and on social standards as normative, see Thomas McFarland, *Shakespeare's Pastoral Comedy* (Chapel Hill: University of North Carolina Press, 1972), pp. 4–11. McFarland also refers to other critics with comparable views.

6. Walter Clemons , "Anthony Burgess: Pushing On," *New York Times Book Review*, November 29, 1970, p. 2. Burgess came up with this definition in answer to a question after he had given a public lecture.

7. Cf. McFarland, *Shakespeare's Pastoral Comedy*, pp. 16–18.

8. In the hands of different theorists the relationship between satire and comedy may be one of identity (Feibleman), of consanguinity, of habitual association, or of fundamental opposition. For samples of different opinions on this matter see Appendix 6.

9. Appendix 2 reveals the frequent, if mainly incidental, occurrence of the idea in comic theory. See also Appendix 1.C. Walter Allen remarks that Trollope and Jane Austen both write about a "graduated social order," and he adds, "Trollope may on occasion mildly satirize it, but he accepts it as fully as Jane Austen does, and he is probably the last English novelist to do so" (*The English Novel: A Short Critical History* [New York: E. P. Dutton, 1954], p. 235). The combination of "mildly satirize" and "accept" gives a good clue to the comic attitude, be the subject a kind of social order or some other aspect of society. It seems fair, however, to describe Henry Green's attitude as one of acceptance, though at times of a world painful enough to make the comedy verge on black. Ivy Compton-Burnett wavers between writing black comedy and using the world as a target.

10. This is a program note for the production of *Kean* in London in 1971. Hauser was the translator and director of *Kean*. The original drama about the actor was written by Alexandre Dumas in 1836. This was reworked by Jean-Paul Sartre in 1953 under the title, *Kean, ou désordre et génie*.

11. Max Frisch, *Three Plays*, trans. James L. Rosenberg (New York: Hill and Wang, 1967), p. 72. A cuckolded husband, Don Balthazar Lopez, speaks with a wider truth than he supposes when he assures Don Juan that even killing Lopez "will afford you no escape from this world" (p. 58). The first step toward the acceptance of the world is the recognition of its inescapability.

12. Thomas McFarland argues, however, that pastoral comedy is an "alliance [which] realizes what neither mode [i.e., pastoral and comedy] could adequately achieve by itself: the representation of paradise" (*Shakespeare's Pastoral Comedy*, p. 37).

13. The effect is fully discussed in my *Tragedy and Melodrama: Versions of Experience* (Seattle and London: University of Washington Press, 1968), pp. 7–18, 97, and in Chapter 2 of my *The Iceman, the Arsonist, and the Troubled Agent: Tragedy and Melodrama on the Modern Stage* (Seattle: University of Washington Press, and London: Allen and Unwin, 1973), pp. 22–62.

14. For more detailed discussion of the variations of "wholeness" (in contrast with dividedness) in tragedy and other forms, see my *Tragedy and Melodrama*, pp. 16–17, 79, 84–86, 97–100.

15. Cf. E. M. W. Tillyard in "The Novel as Literary Kind," *Essays and Studies*, n.s. 9 (1956): 81–82: "Comedy, in its purer sense and excluding for instance farce or melodrama, has partly to do with man's recognition that he owes something to society; with his conviction of such principles as that normal young men who forswear female society are acting foolishly and are not likely to keep their vows, that shrews ought to be disciplined, that swindlers or egoists can't suck the blood of society for ever, that even a most superior man risks becoming an outcast if he is too proud to recognize the standard of the ordinary middling person."

Chapter 3. Attitudes to the World: Challenge, Flight, Conciliation

1. For different ways of viewing the relationship between satire and comedy, see Appendix 6 and Appendix 1.C.

2. Cf. Appendix 5 and Appendix 1.C.

3. Max Frisch, *The Firebugs: A Learning-Play without a Lesson*, trans. Mordecai Gorelik (New York: Hill and Wang, 1963), p. 83 (scene viii).

4. There is considerable relevance in John Sisk's statement: "In the meantime the Papa Doc Duvaliers and Charles Mansons caricature our yearnings for a magical worldview, no less than the B. F. Skinners caricature our Enlightenment dream of a benevolent rational community." See his "Roszak's Pagan Gospel," *Worldview*, 15 (December 1972): 40.

5. A more complex and ironic version of the theme appears in Peter Luke's *Hadrian VII* (1967), a dramatization of the work by Frederick W. Rolfe (Baron Corvo).

6. Cf. my *The Iceman, the Arsonist, and the Troubled Agent: Tragedy and Melodrama on the Modern Stage* (Seattle: University of Washington Press, and London: Allen and Unwin, 1973), pp. 206–9.

7. Cf. my *Tragedy and Melodrama: Versions of Experience* (Seattle and London: University of Washington Press, 1968), p. 53n.

8. This is in the anonymous 1912 translation for the Athenian Society of London as it appears in Aristophanes, *The Eleven Comedies* (New York: Liveright Publishing Corporation, 1943), 2:36. Moses Hadas translated more recently, "To cure the city of its disease, inveterate and chronic— / That is an assignment grave, too demanding for poetry comic" (*The Complete Plays of Aristophanes*, ed. Moses Hadas [New York: Bantam Books, 1962], p. 162).

9. G. Wilson Knight, *The Golden Labyrinth: A Study of British Drama* (New York: W. W. Norton and Co., 1962), p. 14. However, the word *moral* is sometimes applied to the "superiority" theories of laughter that stem from Hobbes. Cf. the notes on D. H. Monro's *Argument of Laughter* in Appendix 6.

10. Quotations are from Christopher Fry, *Venus Observed* (London and New York: Oxford University Press, 1950).

11. See Appendix 8.

12. John P. Sisk, "War Fictions," *Commentary*, 56 (August 1973): 60.

13. J. W. von Goethe, *Faust: A Tragedy, Part One*, trans. Alice Raphael (New York: Rinehart and Co., 1955), p. 41 (sc. ii). In Bayard Taylor's translation: "Thousands were done to death from poison of my giving; / And I must hear, by all the living, / The shameless murderers praised at last!"

14. Molière, *The Misanthrope*, trans. Richard Wilbur (New York: Harcourt, Brace, 1954), p. 96 (IV.i).

15. Marquis Childs, "The Political Outlook," *Yale Review*, 36 (September 1946): 5–6.

16. Norman and Jeanne MacKenzie, *H. G. Wells: A Biography* (New York: Simon and Schuster, 1973), p. 241.

Chapter 4. Melodrama and Comedy: Rival Claimants to the World

1. The truth of the truism is vigorously contested by Robert B. Hume in "Goldsmith and Sheridan and the Supposed Revolution of 'Laughing' against 'Sentimental' Comedy," *Studies in Change and Revolution: Aspects of English Intellectual History, 1604–1800*, ed. Paul J. Korshin (Menston, Eng.: Scolar Press, 1972), pp. 237–76.

2. Various phrases sprinkled through G. Wilson Knight's comprehensive chapter on the Victorian age in his *The Golden Labyrinth: A Study of British Drama* (New York: W. W. Norton and Co., 1962) tell us what the situation was: ". . . virtue and villainy are in sharp contrast, virtue usually triumphant" (p. 240); "other such dramas of social challenge at the more popular theatres," "these sociological criticisms," "implicit criticism of a system," "the black-and-white morality in general favour" (p. 241); "satire on wealth,

snobbery and false friends," "many-pointed satire against rich seducers, town fashions, marriage for money or rank, city finance" (p. 243); "commentary on the falsities of the age" (p. 247); "The usual melodramatic elements of simplicity and distress against blackmailing villains" (p. 248); "living alone by the sea and refusing to return to 'the hollow lying world' and its 'den of thieves'" (p. 250); "Poetic dramas too showed a strong moral tone" (p. 251); "advanced social thinking" (p. 254); "various attempts to interpenetrate society with virtue," "Can we align goodness with politics?" (p. 255); etc.

3. Ibid., p. 223.

4. However, there is a very shrewd adverse analysis of Alceste in Lionel Gossman's *Men and Masks: A Study of Molière* (Baltimore: Johns Hopkins Press, 1963), pp. 248 ff. "Alceste is the very type of the modern intellectual and in large measure of Western man in general, isolated, resentful, embittered, affecting to despise society, but in reality adoring it and suffering because it does not recognize his unique and immeasurable value" (p. 249). "Alceste . . . reveals his enslavement to the world in the very act of asserting his independence of it. In reality it is not Alceste who is indifferent to the world; it is the world that is indifferent to Alceste" (p. 266).

5. Molière, *The Misanthrope*, trans. Richard Wilbur (New York: Harcourt, Brace, 1954), p. 13 (I.i).

6. Quotations are from the translation by Winifred Smith as it appears in *Masters of Modern Drama*, ed. Haskell M. Block and Robert G. Shedd (New York: Random House, 1962), pp. 701–29. *Electra* is a very complex play, crowded by figural and thematic excursions; I do not deal with the many aspects of it that do not bear directly on the issue of genre.

Chapter 5. Make Jokes, Not War

1. August Strindberg, *Three Plays*, trans. Peter Watts (Baltimore: Penguin Books, 1958).

2. He did, however, use the term *comedy* in an announcement of the play which he wrote for a newspaper. See Ernest J. Simmons, *Chekhov: A Biography* (London: Jonathan Cape, 1963), p. 135.

3. Quotations are from *Chekhov: The Major Plays*, trans. Ann Dunnigan and Foreword by Robert Brustein (Signet Classic; New York: New American Library, 1964).

4. Ivanov does not quite hang together as a recognizable human being, doubtless because Chekhov based him on a historical type—a disillusioned intellectual of the 1880s—whom he could not visualize in representative suprahistorical terms. See Simmons, *Chekhov*, pp. 138, 175.

5. Quotations are from Peter Nichols, *A Day in the Death of Joe Egg* (London: Faber and Faber, 1967).

6. *The Penguin Book of Sick Verse*, ed. George MacBeth (Harmondsworth, Eng.: Penguin Books, 1963). The sectional headings show the range of the field: "Illness," "Mental Breakdown," "Visions of Doom," "World-Weariness," "Corpse-Love," "Lovesickness," "Cruelty," "Sick Jokes." The inclusiveness and the tonal range, however, are such that "Verses about Sickness and Death" would be a more accurate title.

7. Quotations are from Joe Orton, *Loot* (New York: Grove Press, 1967).

8. Trans. Henry Reed (London: Faber and Faber, 1969).

9. Quotations are from Peter Shaffer, *The White Liars, Black Comedy: Two Plays* (London: Hamish Hamilton, 1968).

10. The identity theme is treated in a different way by David Parker in "Oscar Wilde's Great Farce: *The Importance of Being Earnest*," *Modern Language Quarterly*, 35

(1974): 173–86. Parker trivializes the play by calling it a "farce," but then makes it a very heavy affair—an anticipation of Sartrean Nothingness.

11. Quotations are from the translation by Arthur Livingston in William Smith Clark II, ed., *Chief Patterns of World Drama: Aeschylus to Anderson* (Boston: Houghton Mifflin, 1946), pp. 965–1005.

12. The comments are based on the London, 1971, production of the Sartre play as translated and directed by Frank Hauser.

13. Quotations are from the translation by Charles Malamuth and Eugene Lyons as reprinted in *Modern Continental Dramas*, ed. Harlan Hatcher (New York: Harcourt, Brace, 1941), pp. 697–738.

14. Quotations are from the text as it appears in *Elizabethan and Stuart Plays*, ed. Charles R. Baskervill, Virgil B. Heltzel, and Arthur H. Nethercot (New York: Henry Holt and Co., 1934), pp. 1281–1315.

15. Witgood of Lucre, I.i.10–15, IV.ii.108; the Hoard brothers, of or to Lucre, I.i.150 ff., I.iii.52–53; Lucre, of himself, IV.ii.61 ff.; Walkadine Hoard, of himself, IV.iv.364–65.

16. Quotations are from Christopher Fry, *Venus Observed* (London and New York: Oxford University Press, 1950).

17. Quotations are from Christopher Fry, *The Dark Is Light Enough* (London and New York: Oxford University Press, 1954). The theological grounds of Fry's view of comedy are discussed by William V. Spanos in *The Christian Tradition in Modern British Verse Drama: The Poetics of Sacramental Time* (New Brunswick, N.J.: Rutgers University Press, 1967), pp. 304–24.

18. "Comedy," *Tulane Drama Review*, 4 (1960): 78.

19. Hans Karl's embodiment of certain philosophic ideas of Hofmannsthal is discussed in the Introduction to Hugo von Hofmannsthal, *Selected Plays and Libretti*, ed. Michael Hamburger (London: Routledge and Kegan Paul, 1963), pp. lxii–lxxii. Quotations are from Willa Muir's translation in this volume, pp. 635–823.

Chapter 6. Infinite Variety

1. I have found the word only in one work, D. H. Monro's *Argument of Laughter* (1951; rpt., Notre Dame, Ind.: University of Notre Dame Press, 1963). Monro opts for "the linking of disparates: the importing into one sphere, of ideas which belong in another" as "a good formula for humour" (p. 238). But he is speaking about the make-up of humor, not the action of comedy.

2. All Shakespeare references are to *The Complete Plays and Poems of William Shakespeare*, ed. William Allen Neilson and Charles Jarvis Hill (Boston: Houghton Mifflin, 1942).

3. Quotations are from *The Complete Plays of Aristophanes*, ed. Moses Hadas (New York: Bantam Books, 1962), the translation by R. W. Webb, p. 395.

4. Ibid., pp. 405–11.

5. Ibid. (the Moses Hadas translation), pp. 103 ff.

6. Ibid. (the B. B. Rogers translation), pp. 331 ff.

7. See Act III, scene v, in the translation by Paul Nixon in the Loeb Classical Library (New York: G. P. Putnam's Sons, and London: William Heinemann, 1916). The Nixon act-and-scene arrangement differs from that of another translator, Charles E. Bennett (1945).

8. Act III, lines 252–80, in the translation by Morris H. Morgan in *Chief Patterns of World Drama*, ed. William Smith Clark II (Boston: Houghton Mifflin, 1946), p. 171.

9. For a tracing of the theme see James L. Sanderson, "Patience in *The Comedy of Errors*," *Texas Studies in Literature and Language*, 16 (1975): 603–18.

10. III.v in the translation by Richard Wilbur (New York: Harcourt Brace Jovanovich, 1971), pp. 83–84. There are similar passages in IV.ii (p. 90) and V.iv (p. 129).

11. For a study of the type see Alexander Leggatt, *Citizen Comedy in the Age of Shakespeare* (Toronto: University of Toronto Press, 1973).

12. Quoted from Peter Nichols, *The National Health or Nurse Norton's Affair* (London: Faber and Faber, 1970).

13. Carl Zuckmayer, *A Part of Myself*, trans. Richard and Clara Winston (New York: Harcourt Brace Jovanovich, 1970), p. 315.

14. The English adapter is John Mortimer; his phrase appeared in his "A Note on the Play" in the program for the Old Vic production in London in 1971. Zuckmayer's full statement was that, in dramatizing a real-life event of some years before, he wanted to tell it "like a fairy tale, though in the tone of a comedy . . . to give it a timeless truthfulness beyond the immediate occasion" (*A Part of Myself*, p. 312). In another place he calls the play a "tragicomedy" (*Second Wind*, trans. Elizabeth Reynolds Hapgood [New York: Doubleday, Doran, 1940], p. 250).

15. Quotations are from Carl Zuckmayer, *The Captain of Köpenick: A Modern Fairy Tale*, trans. David Portman (London: Geoffrey Bles, 1932).

16. This was in a letter to Zuckmayer (*A Part of Myself*, p. 315).

17. Quotations are from *Chekhov: The Major Plays*, trans. Ann Dunnigan (Signet Classic; New York: New American Library, 1964), pp. 233–312.

18. Quotations are from the translation by Willa Muir in Hugo von Hofmannsthal, *Selected Plays and Libretti*, ed. and intro. by Michael Hamburger (London: Routledge and Kegan Paul, 1963), pp. 635–823. W. E. Yates, editor of *Der Schwierige* (Cambridge: Cambridge University Press, 1966), devotes part of his Introduction to the apparently untranslatable subtleties of language in the play.

19. Quotations are from the text in *Seven Plays of Maxim Gorky*, trans. Alexander Bakshy in collaboration with Paul S. Nathan (New Haven, Conn.: Yale University Press, 1945).

20. Morgan translation in Clark, *Chief Patterns of World Drama*, p. 171. The Latin is the familiar *quot homines, tot sententiae*.

21. L. J. Potts, *Comedy* (London: Hutchinson's University Library, 1948), pp. 130, 140.

22. Quotations are from the version in Ivan Turgenev, *Three Famous Plays*, trans. Constance Garnett (London: Gerald Duckworth and Co., and New York: Charles Scribner's Sons, 1951), pp. 3–127. Rakitin's words may reflect some of Turgenev's frustrations with the opera singer, Pauline Garcia (Mme. Viardot), though their relationship was to last forty years. See David Garnett's Introduction to *Three Famous Plays*, pp. vii–ix.

23. This is in his Introduction to Emlyn Williams' adaptation of the play (London: William Heinemann, 1943), p. xi. Redgrave calls the ending of the play "glorious, gay, and yet autumnal" (p. x).

Epilogue

1. Margaret Kennedy, *The Outlaws on Parnassus* (New York: Viking Press, 1960), pp. 102–3.

2. Quoted in M. Gilbert Porter, *Whence the Power? The Artistry and Humanity of Saul Bellow* (Columbia: University of Missouri Press, 1974), pp. 9–10.

3. György Lukács, *Soul and Form*, trans. Anna Bostock (Cambridge: Massachusetts

Institute of Technology Press, 1974), p. 130. The passage quoted is in a 1909 essay on Sterne.

4. J. A. Bryant, Jr., *"The Merchant of Venice* and the Common Flaw," *Sewanee Review*, 81 (1973): 606–22. The quoted passages are on pp. 621 and 622. Cf. Cyrus Hoy: "Pure comedy represents a clear-eyed recognition and acceptance of the incongruous nature of man and of human experience . . ." ("Comic Verities," *Sewanee Review*, 83 [1975]: 694). See Appendix 2.

5. Cf. Robert B. Heilman, "Humanistic Education as Comedy: A Funambulist's Analogy," *Southern Review*, n.s. 8 (1972): 548–71.

6. Thomas Mann, *Germany and the Germans* (Washington, D.C.: Library of Congress, 1945), p. 12.

7. Philip K. Jason, ed., *Anaïs Nin Reader* (Chicago: Swallow, 1973), p. 65. Something of the comic spirit is implicit in Voltaire's "Peace is preferable even to truth" (Richard A. Brooks, ed. and trans., *The Selected Letters of Voltaire* [New York: New York University Press, 1973], p. 89) and in C. P. Cavafy's definition of "the first characteristic of the artist": "peace of soul and great surrender in the face of things which stir indignation and the rebukes of common men" (quoted by George Seferis, *A Poet's Journal: Days of 1945–51*, trans. Athan Anagnostopoulos [Cambridge, Mass.: Harvard-Belknap, 1974], pp. 146–47).

8. Edward Shils, "Ideology and Civility," in *"The Intellectuals and the Powers" and Other Essays* (Chicago and London: University of Chicago Press, 1972), p. 60. Other page numbers are indicated in the text.

9. Elmer M. Blistein, *Comedy in Action* (Durham, N.C.: Duke University Press, 1964), pp. 120 ff., 127.

10. Quoted in Walter Clemons, "Anthony Burgess: Pushing On," *New York Times Book Review*, November 29, 1970, p. 2.

11. *"The Merchant of Venice* and the Common Flaw," p. 622.

12. *Comedy in Action*, p. 18.

13. Allan Rodway, *English Comedy: Its Role and Nature from Chaucer to the Present Day* (Berkeley and Los Angeles: University of California Press, 1975), p. 22.

14. *"The Intellectuals and the Powers" and Other Essays*, p. 60, n. 24.

15. Cf. William Willeford's phrase: ". . . one of the dominant concerns of comedy of most kinds in most times and places: the concern that the world and society continue" (*The Fool and His Scepter: A Study in Clowns and Jesters and Their Audience* [Evanston, Ill.: Northwestern University Press, 1969], p. 174). Denis Donoghue quotes John Crowe Ransom's observation that "the function of a code of manners is to make us capable of something better than the stupidity of an appetitive or economic life" (*Thieves of Fire* [New York: Oxford University Press, 1974], p. 83).

16. Ronald Peacock, *The Poet in the Theatre* (New York: Harcourt, Brace, 1946), p. 151.

17. Ibid., p. 153.

18. Quoted by Frank Tuohy, *Yeats* (New York: Macmillan, 1976), p. 31.

Index

[287]

Black-Eyed Susans

Black-Eyed Susans

Julia Heaberlin

MICHAEL JOSEPH
an imprint of
PENGUIN BOOKS

MICHAEL JOSEPH

UK | USA | Canada | Ireland | Australia
India | New Zealand | South Africa

First published in the United States by Ballantine Books, an imprint of Random House,
a division of Random House LLC, a Penguin Random House Company, 2015
First published in Great Britain by Michael Joseph, 2015
001

Book design by Dana Leigh Blanchette
Printed in Great Britain by Clays Ltd, St Ives plc

A CIP catalogue record for this book is available from the British Library

HARDBACK ISBN: 978–0–718–18133–8

www.greenpenguin.co.uk

MIX
Paper from
responsible sources
FSC® C018179

Penguin Random House is committed to a
sustainable future for our business, our readers
and our planet. This book is made from Forest
Stewardship Council® certified paper.

For Sam, my game changer

Prologue

Thirty-two hours of my life are missing.

My best friend, Lydia, tells me to imagine those hours like old clothes in the back of a dark closet. Shut my eyes. Open the door. Move things around. Search.

The things I do remember, I'd rather not. Four freckles. Eyes that aren't black but blue, wide open, two inches from mine. Insects gnawing into a smooth, soft cheek. The grit of the earth in my teeth. Those parts, I remember.

It's my seventeenth birthday, and the candles on my cake are burning.

The little flames are waving at me to hurry up. I'm thinking about the Black-Eyed Susans, lying in freezing metal drawers. How I scrub and scrub but can't wash away their smell no matter how many showers I take.

Be happy.

Make a wish.

I paste on a smile, and focus. Everyone in this room loves me and wants me home.

Hopeful for the same old Tessie.

Never let me remember.

I close my eyes and blow.

Tessa, present day

For better or worse, I am walking the crooked path to my childhood.

The house sits topsy-turvy on the crest of a hill, like a kid built it out of blocks and toilet paper rolls. The chimney tilts in a comical direction, and turrets shoot off each side like missiles about to take off. I used to sleep inside one of them on summer nights and pretend I was rocketing through space.

More than my little brother liked, I had climbed out one of the windows onto the tiled roof and inched my scrappy knees toward the widow's peak, grabbing sharp gargoyle ears and window ledges for balance. At the top, I leaned against the curlicued railing to survey the flat, endless Texas landscape and the stars of my kingdom. I played my piccolo to the night birds. The air rustled my thin white cotton nightgown like I was a strange dove alit on the top of a castle. It sounds like a fairy tale, and it was.

My grandfather made his home in this crazy storybook house in the country, but he built it for my brother, Bobby, and me. It wasn't a huge place, but I still have no idea how he could afford it. He presented each of us with a turret, a place where we could hide out from the world whenever we wanted to sneak away. It was his grand gesture, our personal Disney World, to make up for the fact that our mother had died.

Granny tried to get rid of the place shortly after Granddaddy died, but the house didn't sell till years later, when she was lying in the ground between him and their daughter. Nobody wanted it. It was weird, people said. Cursed. Their ugly words made it so.

After I was found, the house had been pasted in all the papers, all over TV. The local newspapers dubbed it Grim's Castle. I never knew if that was a typo. Texans spell things different. For instance, we don't always add the *ly*.

People whispered that my grandfather must have had something to do with my disappearance, with the murder of all the Black-Eyed Susans, because of his freaky house. *"Shades of Michael Jackson and his Neverland Ranch,"* they muttered, even after the state sent a man to Death Row a little over a year later for the crimes. These were the same people who had driven up to the front door every Christmas so their kids could gawk at the lit-up gingerbread house and grab a candy cane from the basket on the front porch.

I press the bell. It no longer plays *Ride of the Valkyries*. I don't know what to expect, so I am a little surprised when the older couple that open the door look perfectly suited to living here. The plump worn-down hausfrau with the kerchief on her head, the sharp nose, and the dust rag in her hand reminds me of the old woman in the shoe.

I stutter out my request. There's an immediate glint of recognition by the woman, a slight softening of her mouth. She locates the small crescent-moon scar under my eye. The woman's eyes say *poor little girl,* even though it's been eighteen years, and I now have a girl of my own.

"I'm Bessie Wermuth," she says. "And this is my husband, Herb. Come in, dear." Herb is scowling and leaning on his cane. Suspicious, I can tell. I don't blame him. I am a stranger, even though he knows exactly who I am. Everyone in a five-hundred-mile radius does. I am the Cartwright girl, dumped once upon a time with a strangled college student and a stack of human bones out past Highway 10, in an abandoned patch of field near the Jenkins property.

6

I am the star of screaming tabloid headlines and campfire ghost stories.

I am one of the four Black-Eyed Susans. The *lucky* one.

It will only take a few minutes, I promise. Mr. Wermuth frowns, but Mrs. Wermuth says, *Yes, of course.* It is clear that she makes the decisions about all of the important things, like the height of the grass and what to do with a redheaded, kissed-by-evil waif on their doorstep, asking to be let in.

"We won't be able to go down there with you," the man grumbles as he opens the door wider.

"Neither of us have been down there too much since we moved in," Mrs. Wermuth says hurriedly. "Maybe once a year. It's damp. And there's a broken step. A busted hip could do either of us in. Break one little thing at this age, and you're at the Pearly Gates in thirty days or less. If you don't want to die, don't step foot inside a hospital after you turn sixty-five."

As she makes this grim pronouncement, I am frozen in the great room, flooded with memories, searching for things no longer there. The totem pole that Bobby and I sawed and carved one summer, completely unsupervised, with only one trip to the emergency room. Granddaddy's painting of a tiny mouse riding a handkerchief sailboat in a wicked, boiling ocean.

Now a Thomas Kinkade hangs in its place. The room is home to two flowered couches and a dizzying display of knickknacks, crowded on shelves and tucked in shadow boxes. German beer steins and candlesticks, a *Little Women* doll set, crystal butterflies and frogs, at least fifty delicately etched English teacups, a porcelain clown with a single black tear rolling down. All of them, I suspect, wondering how in the hell they ended up in the same neighborhood.

The ticking is soothing. Ten antique clocks line one wall, two with twitching cat tails keeping perfect time with each other.

I can understand why Mrs. Wermuth chose our house. In her way, she is one of us.

"Here we go," she says. I follow her obediently, navigating a passageway that snakes off the living room. I used to be able to take its turns in the pitch dark on my roller skates. She is flipping light switches as we go, and I suddenly feel like I am walking to the chamber of my death.

"TV says the execution is in a couple of months." I jump. This is exactly where my mind is traveling. The scratchy male voice behind me is Mr. Wermuth's, full of cigarette smoke.

I pause, swallowing the knot in my throat as I wait for him to ask whether I plan to sit front row and watch my attacker suck in his last breath. Instead, he pats my shoulder awkwardly. "I wouldn't go. Don't give him another damn second."

I am wrong about Herb. It wouldn't be the first time I've been wrong, or the last.

My head knocks into an abrupt curve in the wall because I'm still turned toward Herb. "I'm fine," I tell Mrs. Wermuth quickly. She lifts her hand but hesitates to touch my stinging cheek, because it is just a little too close to the scar, the permanent mark from a garnet ring dangling off a skeletal finger. A gift from a Susan who didn't want me to forget her, ever. I push Mrs. Wermuth's hand away gently. "I forgot that turn was coming up so soon."

"Crazy damn house," Herb says under his breath. "What in the hell is wrong with living in St. Pete?" He doesn't seem to expect an answer. The spot on my cheek begins to complain and my scar echoes, a tiny *ping, ping, ping*.

The hallway has settled into a straight line. At the end, an ordinary door. Mrs. Wermuth pulls out a skeleton key from her apron pocket and twists it in the lock easily. There used to be twenty-five of those keys, all exactly the same, which could open any door in the place. An odd bit of practicality from my grandfather.

A chilly draft rushes at us. I smell things both dying and growing. I have my first moment of real doubt since I left home an hour ago. Mrs. Wermuth reaches up and yanks on a piece of kite string dancing above her head. The bare, dusty lightbulb flickers on.

"Take this." Mr. Wermuth prods me with the small Maglite from

8

his pocket. "I carry it around for reading. You know where the main light switch is?"

"Yes," I say automatically. "Right at the bottom."

"Watch the sixteenth step," Mrs. Wermuth warns. "Some critter chewed a hole in it. I always count when I go down. You take as long as you like. I think I'll make all of us a cup of tea and you can tell a bit of the history of the house after. We'd both find that fascinating. Right, Herb?" Herb grunts. He's thinking of driving a little white ball two hundred yards into Florida's deep blue sea.

I hesitate on the second step, and turn my head, unsure. If anyone shuts this door, I won't be found for a hundred years. I've never had any doubt that death is still eager to catch up with a certain sixteen-year-old girl.

Mrs. Wermuth offers a tiny, silly wave. "I hope you find what you are looking for. It must be important."

If this is an opening, I don't take it.

I descend noisily, like a kid, jumping over step sixteen. At the bottom, I pull another dangling string, instantly washing the room with a harsh fluorescent glow.

It lights an empty tomb. This used to be a place where things were born, where easels stood with half-finished paintings, and strange, frightening tools hung on pegboards, where a curtained darkroom off to the side waited to bring photos to life, and dress mannequins held parties in the corners. Bobby and I would swear we had seen them move more than once.

A stack of old chests held ridiculous antique dress-up hats wrapped in tissue paper and my grandmother's wedding dress with exactly 3,002 seed pearls and my grandfather's World War II uniform with the brown spot on the sleeve that Bobby and I were sure was blood. My grandfather was a welder, a farmer, a historian, an artist, an Eagle Scout leader, a morgue photographer, a rifleman, a woodworker, a Republican, a yellow dog Democrat. A poet. He could never make up his mind, which is exactly what people say about me.

He ordered us never to come down here alone, and he never knew we did. But the temptation was too great. We were especially fascinated with a forbidden, dusty black album that held Granddaddy's crime scene photographs from his brief career with the county morgue. A wide-eyed housewife with her brains splattered across her linoleum kitchen floor. A drowned, naked judge pulled to shore by his dog.

I stare at the mold greedily traveling up the brick walls on every side. The black lichen flourishing in a large crack zigzagging across the filthy concrete floor.

No one has loved this place since Granddaddy died. I quickly cross over to the far corner, sliding between the wall and the coal furnace that years ago had been abandoned as a bad idea. Something travels lightly across my ankle. A scorpion, a roach. I don't flinch. Worse things have crawled across my face.

Behind the furnace, it is harder to see. I sweep the light down the wall until I find the grimy brick with the red heart, painted there to fool my brother. He had spied on me one day when I was exploring my options. I run my finger lightly around the edges of the heart three times.

Then I count ten bricks up from the red heart, and five bricks over. Too high for little Bobby to reach. I jam the screwdriver from my pocket into the crumbling mortar, and begin to pry. The first brick topples out, and clatters onto the floor. I work at three other bricks, tugging them out one at a time.

I flash the light into the hole.

Stringy cobwebs, like spin art. At the back, a gray, square lump.

Waiting, for seventeen years, in the crypt I made for it.

Tessie, 1995

"Tessie. Are you listening?"

He is asking stupid questions, like the others.

I glance up from the magazine, open in my lap, that I had conveniently found beside me on the couch. "I don't see the point."

I flip a page, just to irritate him. Of course he knows I'm not reading.

"Then why are you here?"

I let the air hang with thick silence. Silence is my only instrument of control in this parade of therapy sessions. Then I say, "You know why. I am here because my father wants me to be here." *Because I hated all the others. Because Daddy is so sad, and I can't stand it.* "My brother says I've changed." *Too much information. You'd think I'd learn.*

His chair legs squeak on the hardwood floor, as he shifts positions. Ready to pounce. "Do *you* think you've changed?"

So *obvious*. Disgusted, I flip back to the magazine. The pages are cold and slick and stiff. They smell of cloying perfume. It's the kind of magazine that I suspect is filled with bony, angry girls. I wonder: *Is that what this man sees when he stares at me?* I'd lost twenty pounds in the last year. Most of my track star muscle tone, gone. My right foot is wrapped in a new leaden cast, from the third surgery.

Bitterness rises in my lungs like hot steam. I suck in a deep breath. My goal is to feel nothing.

"OK," he says. "Dumb question." I know that he's watching me intently. "How about this one: Why did you pick me this time?"

I toss the magazine down. I try to remember that he is making an exception, probably doing the district attorney a favor. He rarely treats teen-age girls.

"You signed a legal document that said you will not prescribe drugs, that you will not ever, ever publish anything about our sessions or use me for research without my knowledge, that you will not tell a living soul you are treating the surviving Black-Eyed Susan. You told me you won't use hypnosis."

"Do you trust that I will not do any of those things?"

"No," I snap back. "But at least I'll be a millionaire if you do."

"We have fifteen minutes left," he says. "We can use the time however you like."

"Great." I pick up the magazine full of bony, angry girls.

Tessa, present day

Two hours after I leave Granddaddy's, William James Hastings III arrives at my house, a 1920s bungalow in Fort Worth with somber black shutters and not a single curve or frill. A jungle of color and life thrives behind my front door, but outside, I choose anonymity.

I've never met the man with the baronial name settling in on my couch. He can't be older than twenty-eight, and he is at least 6'3", with long, loose arms and big hands. His knees bang up against the coffee table. William James Hastings III reminds me more of a professional pitcher in his prime than a lawyer, like his body's awkwardness would disappear the second he picked up a ball. Boyish. Cute. Big nose that makes him just short of handsome. He has brought along a woman in a tailored white jacket, white-collared shirt, and black pants. The type who cares only vaguely about fashion, as professional utility. Short, natural blond hair. Ring-free fingers. Flat, clipped, unpolished nails. Her only adornment is a glittering gold chain with an expensive-looking charm, a familiar squiggly doodle, but I don't have time to think about what it means. She's a cop, maybe, although that doesn't make sense.

The gray lump, still covered in dust and ancient spider threads, sits between us on the coffee table.

"I'm Bill," he says. "Not William. And definitely not Willie." He smiles. I wonder if he's used this line on a jury. I think he needs a better one. "Tessa, as I said on the phone, we're thrilled that you called. Surprised, but thrilled. I hope you don't mind that Dr. Seger—Joanna—tagged along. We don't have any time to waste. Joanna is the forensic scientist excavating the bones of the . . . Susans tomorrow. She'd like to take a quick sample of your saliva. For DNA. Because of the issues we face with lost evidence and junk science, she wants to do the swab herself. That is, if you're really serious. Angie never thought—"

I clear my throat. "I'm serious." I feel a sudden pang for Angela Rothschild. The tidy silver-haired woman hounded me for the past six years, insisting that Terrell Darcy Goodwin was an innocent man. Picking at each doubt until I was no longer sure.

Angie was a saint, a bulldog, a little bit of a martyr. She'd spent the last half of her life and most of her parents' inheritance freeing prisoners who'd been bullied by the state of Texas into wrongful convictions. More than 1,500 convicted rapists and murderers begged for her services every year, so Angie had to be choosy. She told me that playing God with those calls and letters was the only thing that ever made her consider quitting. I'd been to her office once, the first time she contacted me. It was housed in an old church basement located on an unpleasant side of Dallas known best for its high fatality rate for cops. If her clients couldn't see the light of day or catch a quick Starbucks, she said, then neither could she. Her company in that basement was a coffeepot, three more attorneys who also worked other paying jobs, and as many law students as would sign on.

Angie sat in the same spot on my couch nine months ago, in jeans and scuffed black cowboy boots, with one of Terrell's letters in her hand. She begged me to read it. She had begged me to do a lot of things, like give one of her expert gurus a shot at retrieving my memory. Now she was dead of a heart attack, found facedown in a pile of documents about Goodwin's case. The reporter who wrote her obituary found that poetic. My guilt in the week since she died has been almost unbearable. Angie, I realized too late, was one of my tethers. One of the few who never gave up on me.

"Is this . . . what you have for us?" Bill stares at the filthy plastic grocery bag from Granddaddy's basement like it is stuffed with gold. It has left a trail of pebbly mortar across the glass, right beside a pink hair band twisted with a strand of my daughter Charlie's auburn hair.

"You said on the phone that you had to go . . . find it," he says. "That you'd told Angie about this . . . project . . . but you weren't sure where it was."

It isn't really a question, and I don't answer.

His eyes wander the living room, strewn with the detritus of an artist and a teen-ager. "I'd like to set up a meeting at the office in a few days. After I've . . . examined it. You and I will have to go over all of the old ground for the appeal." For such a large guy, there is a gentleness about him. I wonder about his courtroom style, if gentleness is his weapon.

"Ready for the swab?" Dr. Seger interrupts abruptly, all business, already stretching on latex gloves. Maybe worried that I'll change my mind.

"Sure." We both stand up. She tickles the inside of my cheek and seals microscopic bits of me in a tube. I know she plans to add my DNA to the collection provided by three other Susans, two of whom still go by the more formal name of Jane Doe. I feel heat emanating from her. Anticipation.

I return my attention to the bag on the table, and Bill. "This was kind of an experiment suggested by one of my psychiatrists. It might be more valuable for what isn't there than what is." In other words, I didn't draw a black man who looked like Terrell Darcy Goodwin.

My voice is calm, but my heart is lurching. I am giving Tessie to this man. I hope it is not a mistake.

"Angie . . . she would be so grateful. Is grateful." Bill crooks a finger up, the Michelangelo kind of gesture that travels up to the sky. I find this comforting: a man who is bombarded by people blocking his path every day—half-decent people clinging stubbornly to their lies and deadly mistakes—and yet he still believes in God. Or, at least, still believes in something.

Dr. Seger's phone buzzes in her pocket. She glances at the screen. "I've got to take this. One of my Ph.D. students. I'll meet you in the car, Bill. Good job, girl. You're doing the right thing." *Gurrl*. A slight twang. Oklahoma, maybe. I smile automatically.

"Right behind you, Jo." Bill is moving deliberately, shutting his briefcase, gingerly picking up the bag, in no apparent hurry. His hands grow still when she shuts the door. "You've just met greatness. Joanna is a mitochondrial DNA genius. She can work goddamn miracles with degraded bones. She rushed to 9/11 and didn't leave for four years. Made history, helping identify thousands of victims out of charred bits. Lived at the YMCA at first. Took communal showers with the homeless. Worked fourteen-hour days. She didn't have to, it wasn't her job, but whenever she could, she sat down and explained the science to grieving families so they could be as sure as she was. She learned a smattering of Spanish so she could try to talk to the families of the Mexican dishwashers and waiters who worked in restaurants in the North Tower. She is one of the best forensic scientists on the planet, who happens to be one of the kindest human beings I've ever met, and she is giving Terrell a chance. I want you to understand the kind of people on our side. Tell me, Tessa, why are you? Why are you suddenly on our side?"

A slight edge has crept into his voice. He is gently telling me not to screw them.

"There are several reasons," I say unsteadily. "I can show you one of them."

"Tessa, I want to know everything."

"It's better if you see it."

I lead him down our narrow hall without speaking, past Charlie's messy purple womb, usually pulsing with music, and throw open the door at the end. This wasn't in my plan, not today anyway.

Bill looms like a giant in my bedroom, his head knocking into the antique chandelier dangling with sea glass that Charlie and I scavenged last summer on the gray beaches of Galveston. He ducks away and brushes against the curve of my breast by accident. Apologizes. Embarrassed. For a second, I see this stranger's legs tangled in my sheets. I can't remember a time that I let a man in here.

I watch painfully as Bill absorbs intimate details about me: the cartoonish portrait of Granddaddy's house, gold and silver jewelry littered across my dresser, the close-up of Charlie staring out of lavender eyes, a neat pile of freshly laundered white lace panties on the chair, which I wish to God were tucked in a drawer.

He is already edging himself backward, toward the door, clearly wondering what the hell he has gotten himself into. Whether he has pinned his hopes for poor Terrell Darcy Goodwin on a crazy woman who has led him straight to her bedroom. Bill's expression makes me want to laugh out loud, even though I am not above entertaining a fantasy about an all-American guy with two degrees, when my type runs the opposite direction.

Even though what I'm about to show him keeps me up at night, reading the same paragraph of *Anna Karenina* over and over, listening to every creak of the house and finger of wind, every barefoot midnight step of my daughter, every sweet sleep sound that floats out of her mouth and down the hall.

"Don't worry." I force lightness into my voice. "I like my men rich and less altruistic. And you know . . . old enough to grow facial hair. Come over here. Please."

"Cute." But I can hear relief. He makes it in two strides. His eyes follow my finger, out the window.

I am not pointing to the sky, but to the dirt, where a nest of black-eyed Susans is still half-alive under the windowsill, teasing me with beady black eyes.

"It is February," I say quietly. "Black-eyed Susans only bloom like this in summer." I pause for this to sink in. "They were planted three days ago, on my birthday. Someone grew them especially for me, and put them under the window where I sleep."

The abandoned field on the Jenkins property was licked to death by fire about two years before the Black-Eyed Susans were dumped there. A reckless match tossed by a lost car on a lonely dirt road cost a destitute old farmer his entire wheat crop and set the stage for the thousands and thousands of yellow flowers that covered the field like a giant, rumpled quilt.

The fire also carved out our grave, an uneven, loping ditch. Black-eyed Susans sprung up and decorated it brazenly long before we arrived. The Susans are a greedy plant, often the first to thrive in scorched, devastated earth. Pretty, but competitive, like cheerleaders. They live to crowd out the others.

One lit match, one careless toss, and our nicknames were embedded in serial killer lore forever.

Bill, still in my bedroom, has shot Joanna a lengthy text, maybe because he doesn't want to answer her questions on the phone in front of me. We meet her outside my window in time to watch her dip a vial into the black speckled dirt. The squiggly charm on her necklace, glinting in the sun, brushes a petal as she bends over. I still can't recall the symbol's meaning. Religious, maybe. Ancient.

"He or she used something besides the dirt in the ground," Joanna said. "Probably a common brand of potting soil, and seeds that can be picked up at Lowe's. But you never know. You should call the cops."

"And tell them someone is planting pretty flowers?" I don't want to sound sarcastic, but there it is.

"It's trespassing," Bill says. "Harassment. You know, this doesn't have to be the work of the killer. It could be any crazy who reads the papers." It is unspoken, but I know. He is uncertain of my mental state. He hopes I have more than this patch of flowers under my window to bolster a judge's belief in Terrell. A little part of him wonders whether I planted the flowers myself.

How much do I tell him?

I suck in a breath. "Every time I call the cops, it ends up on the Internet. We get calls and letters and Facebook crazies. Presents on the doorstep. Cookies. Bags of dog poop. Cookies *made* of dog poop. At least I hope it's just dog poop. Any attention makes my daughter's life at school a living hell. After a few years of beautiful peace, the execution is stirring everything up again." Exactly why, for years, I told Angie no and no and *no*. Whatever doubts crept in, I had to push away. In the end, I understood Angie, and Angie understood me. *I will find another way,* she had assured me.

But things were different now. Angie was dead.

He'd stood under my window.

I brush away something whispery threading its way through my hair. I vaguely wonder whether it is a traveler from Granddaddy's basement. I remember sticking my hand blindly into that musty hole a few hours ago, and turn my anger up a notch. "The look on your faces right now? That mixture of pity and uneasiness and misplaced understanding that I still need to be treated like the traumatized sixteen-year-old girl I used to be? I've been getting that look since I can remember. That's how long I've been protecting myself, and so far, so good. I'm *happy* now. I am not that girl anymore." I wrap my long brown sweater around me a little more tightly even though the late winter sun is a warm stroke across my face. "My daughter will be home any minute, and I'd rather she doesn't meet the two of you until I've explained a few things. She doesn't know yet that I called you. I want to keep her life as normal as possible."

"Tessa." Joanna ventures a step toward me and stops. "I get it."

There is such a terrible weight in her voice. *I get it.* Bombs dropping *one two three* to the bottom of the ocean.

I scan her face. Tiny lines etched by other people's sorrow. Blue-green eyes that have flashed on more horror than I could ever fathom. Smelled it. Touched it, *breathed* it, as it rained down in ashes from the sky.

"Do you?" My voice is soft. "I hope so. Because I am going to be there when you excavate those two graves."

My daddy paid for their coffins.

Joanna is rubbing the charm between her fingers, like it is a holy cross.

I suddenly realize that, in her world, it is.

She is wearing a double helix made of gold.

The twisted ladder of life.

A strand of DNA.

Tessie, 1995

One week later. Tuesday, 10 A.M. sharp. I am back on the doctor's plump couch, with company. Oscar rubs his wet nose against my hand reassuringly, then settles in on the floor beside me, alert. He's been mine since last week, and I will go nowhere without him. Not that anyone argues. Oscar, sweet and protective, makes them hopeful.

"Tessie, the trial is in three months. Ninety days away. My most important job right now is to prepare you emotionally. I know the defense attorney, and he's excellent. He's even better when he truly believes he holds the life of an innocent man in his hands, which he does. Do you understand what that means? He will not take it easy on you."

This time, right down to business.

My hands are folded primly in my lap. I'm wearing a short, blue-plaid pleated skirt, white lacy stockings, and black patent-leather boots. I've never been a prim girl, despite the reddish-gold hair and freckles my wonderfully corny grandfather claimed were fairy dust. Not then, not now. My best friend, Lydia, dressed me today. She burrowed into my messy drawers and closet, because she couldn't stand the fact that I no longer make any effort to match. Lydia is one of the few friends who isn't giving up on me. She is currently taking her fashion cues from the movie *Clueless,* but I haven't seen it.

"OK," I say. This is, after all, one of two reasons I am sitting here. I am afraid. Ever since they snatched Terrell Darcy Goodwin away from his Denny's Grand Slam breakfast in Ohio eleven months ago and told me I would need to testify, I have counted the days like terrible pills. Today, we are eighty-seven days away, not ninety, but I do not bother to correct him.

"I remember nothing." I am sticking with this.

"I'm sure the prosecutor has told you that doesn't matter. You're living, breathing evidence. Innocent girl vs. unspeakable monster. So let's just begin with what you do remember. Tessie? *Tessie?* What are you thinking right now, this second? Spit it out . . . don't look away, OK?"

I crane my neck around slowly, gazing at him out of two mossy gray pools of nothingness.

"I remember a crow trying to peck out my eyes," I say flatly. "Tell me. What exactly is the point of looking, when you know I can't see you?"

Tessa, present day

Technically, this is their third grave. The two Susans being exhumed tonight in St. Mary's Cemetery in Fort Worth were his older kills. Dug up from their first hiding place and tossed in that field with me like chicken bones. Four of us in all, dumped in the same trip. I was thrown on top with a girl named Merry Sullivan, who the coroner determined had been dead for more than a day. I overheard Granddaddy mutter to my father, "The devil was cleaning out his closets."

It is midnight, and I am at least three hundred feet away, under a tree. I have darted under the police tape that marks off the site. I wonder who the hell they think is walking a cemetery at this time of night but ghosts. Well, I guess I am.

They've erected a white tent over the two graves, and it glows with pale light, like a paper lantern. There are far more people here than I expected. Bill, of course. I recognize the district attorney from his picture in the paper. There's a balding man beside him in an ill-fitting suit. At least five policemen, and another five human beings dressed like aliens in Tyvek suits, wandering in and out of the tent. I know that the medical examiner is among them. Careers ride on this one.

Did the reporter who wrote Angie's obituary know that his words would pry loose the rusty lever of justice? Create a small public outcry in a state that executes men monthly? Change a judge's mind about exhuming the bones and considering a new trial? Convince me once and for all to dial the phone?

The man in the suit suddenly pivots. I catch the flash of a priest's collar before I duck behind the tree. My eyes sting for a second, struck by this furtive operation and the supreme effort to treat these girls with dignity and respect when no one has a clue who they are, when there is not a reporter in sight.

The girls rising out of the earth tonight were nothing *but* bones when they were transported to that old wheat field eighteen years ago. I was barely alive. They say that Merry had been dead at least thirty hours. By the time the cops got to us, Merry was pretty well scavenged. I tried to protect her, but at some point in the night I passed out. Sometimes, I can still hear the animated conversation of the field rats. I can't tell anybody who loves me these things. It's better if they think I don't remember.

The doctors say my heart saved me. I was born with a heart genetically on the slow side to begin with. Add the fact that I was in peak running condition as one of the nation's top high-school hurdlers. On a normal day, doing homework, eating a hamburger, or painting my nails, my pulse clicked along at a steady thirty-seven beats a minute and crawled as low as twenty-nine at night when I slept. The average heart rate for a teen-ager is about seventy. Daddy had a habit of waking up at two every morning and checking to see if I was breathing, even though a famous Houston cardiologist had told him to relax. For sure, my heart was a bit of a phenomenon, as was my speed. People whispered about the Olympics. Called me the Little Fireball because of my hair and my temper when I ran a bad time or a girl nudged me off a hurdle.

While I fought for life in that grave, the doctors say my heart wound down to around eighteen. An EMT at the scene even mistook me for dead.

The district attorney told the jury that I surprised the Black-Eyed Susan killer, not the other way around. Set off a panic in him, prompted him to get rid of the evidence. That the large bruise on Terrell Darcy Goodwin's gut in the blown-up exhibit photograph, blue and green and yellow tie-dye, was my artwork. People appreciate pretty fantasies like this, where there is a feisty hero, even when there is no factual basis for it.

A dark van is slowly backing up to the tent. O. J. Simpson got off the same year I testified, and he massacred his wife and left his blood behind on her gate. There was no solid DNA evidence against Terrell Darcy Goodwin, except a tattered jacket mired in the mud a mile away with his blood type on the right cuff. The spot of blood was so tiny and degraded they couldn't tackle DNA, still fairly new in criminal court. It was enough for me to hold on to back then, but not anymore. I pray that Joanna will work her high priestess magic, and we will finally know who these two girls are. I'm counting on them to lead all of us to peace.

I turn to go, and my toe catches the edge of something. I pitch forward, instantly breathless, palms out, onto an old broken gravestone. The roots have bullied the marker until it toppled over and broke in half.

Did anyone hear? I glance around quickly. The tent is half-down. Someone is laughing. Shadows moving, none of them my way. I push myself up, hands stinging, brushing off the death and grit clinging to my jeans. I tug my cell phone out of my back pocket, and it casts its friendly light when I press the button. I shine it over the gravestone. A red smear from my hands marks the sleeping lamb guarding over Christina Driskill.

Christina entered the world, and escaped it, on the same day. March 3, 1872.

My mind burrows into the rocky dirt, fighting its way to the small wooden box that rests under my feet, tilted, cracked open, strangled by roots.

I'm thinking of Lydia.

Tessie, 1995

"Do you cry often?" First question. Gentle.

"No," I say. So much for Lydia's beauty fix of sticking two frozen spoons under my eyes after my little jags.

"Tessie, I want you to tell me the very last thing you saw, before you went blind." No lingering on my puffy face. Taking up right where we left off last time. *Smart tactic*, I think grudgingly. He actually used the word *blind,* which no one else would dare say to my face except Lydia, who also told me three days ago to get up and wash my hair because it looked like stale cotton candy.

This doctor has already figured out that a warm-up act with me was a complete waste of time.

I saw my mother's face. Beautiful, kind, loving. That's the last perfectly clear image that hung before me, except that my mother has been dead since I was eight, and my eyes were wide open. My mother's face, and then nothing but a shimmering gray ocean. I often think it was kind of God to introduce me to blindness that way.

I clear my throat, determined to say something in today's session, to appear more cooperative, so he will tell Daddy that I am making progress. Daddy, who takes off from his job every Tuesday morning to bring me here. For whatever reason, I don't think this doctor will lie to him, like most of the others. The way this doctor asks his questions is not the same. Neither are my answers, and I'm not sure why.

"There were a bunch of cards on the windowsill in my hospital room," I say casually. "One of them had a picture of a pig on the front. Wearing a bow tie and a top hat. It said, 'I hope you squeal better soon.' The pig—that's the last thing I saw."

"An unfortunate choice of wording on the card."

"Ya think?"

"Did anything else bother you about that greeting card?"

"No one could read the signature." An illegible squiggle, like a wire spring.

"So you didn't know who it was from."

"A lot of strangers sent cards from all over. And flowers and stuffed animals. There were so many, my father asked them to be sent on to the children's cancer floor." Eventually, the FBI got a clue and swept everything to a lab. I later worried about what they might have ripped out of a dying kid's hands in return for not a scrap of useful evidence.

The pig held a daisy in his pink hoof. I had left that part out. At sixteen, drugged up in a hospital bed and scared out of my mind, I didn't know the difference between a yellow daisy and a black-eyed Susan.

My cast is itching like crazy, and I reach into the slim gap between my calf and the cast with two fingers. Can't get to the spot on my ankle. Oscar licks my leg with a sandpaper tongue, trying to help.

"OK, maybe that card was the trigger," the doctor says. "Maybe not. It's a start. Here's my thinking. We're going to talk about your conversion disorder before we move on to preparing you for court. In the interest of time, there was hope by . . . others . . . that I could work around it. But it is in the way."

Ya think?

"As far as I'm concerned, time stands still in this room." He's telling me *no pressure*. That we're sailing together in my gray ocean, and I control the wind. This is the first lie I know he's told me.

Conversion disorder. The nice, fancy name for it.

Freud called it hysterical blindness.

All those expensive tests and nothing physically wrong.

All in her head.

Poor thing doesn't want to see the world.

She will never be the same.

Why do people think I can't hear them?

I tune back in to his voice. I've decided he sounds like Tommy Lee Jones in *The Fugitive*. Rough Texas drawl. Smart as hell, and knows it.

". . . it's not that uncommon in young females who have endured a trauma like this. What is uncommon is that it's lasted this long. Eleven months."

Three hundred and twenty-six days, *doctor*. But I don't correct him.

A slight squeak as he shifts in his chair, and Oscar rises up protectively. "There are exceptions," he says. "I once treated a boy, a virtuoso pianist, who had practiced eight hours a day since he was five. He woke up one morning and his hands were frozen. Paralyzed. Couldn't even hold a glass of milk. Doctors couldn't find a cause. He began to wiggle his fingers exactly two years later, to the day."

The doctor's voice is closer. At my side. Oscar bangs my arm with his nose, to let me know. The doctor is sliding something thin and cool and smooth into my hand. "Try this," he says.

A pencil. I grasp it. Dig it deep into the side of my cast. Feel intense, gratifying relief. A slight breeze as the doctor moves away, maybe the flap of his jacket. I'm certain he looks nothing like Tommy Lee Jones. But I can picture Oscar. White as fresh snow. Blue eyes that see everything. Red collar. Sharp little teeth if you bother me.

"Does this piano player know that you talk about him to other patients?" I ask. I can't help myself. The sarcasm is a horsewhip I can't put away. But on our third Tuesday morning together, I have to admit this doctor is starting to get to me. I'm feeling the first pinch of guilt. Like I need to try harder.

28

"As a matter of fact, yes. I was interviewed for a Cliburn documentary about him. The point is: I believe you will see again."

"I'm not worried." I blurt it out.

"That is often a symptom of conversion disorder. A lack of caring about whether you'll ever go back to normal. But, in your case, I don't think that's true."

His first direct confrontation. He waits silently. I feel my temper flare.

"I know the real reason why you made an exception to see me." My voice cracks a little when I want it to sound defiant. "What you have in common with my father. I know you had a daughter who disappeared."

Tessa, present day

Angie's utilitarian metal desk looks exactly the way I remember, buried in mountains of paper and file folders. Shoved into a corner of an expansive, open basement room at St. Stephen's, the stone-and-brick Catholic church that sits defiantly in the 2nd Avenue and Hatcher Street corridor of hell. Smack in the center of a Dallas neighborhood that made a Top 25 FBI list for most dangerous in the nation.

It is high Texas noon outside, but not in here. In here, it is gloomy and timeless, colored by the stains of a violent history, when this church was abandoned for eight years and this room was used as an execution factory for drug dealers.

The first and only time I'd been here, Angie told me that the hopeful young priest who rented her the space whitewashed the walls four times himself. The indentations and bullet holes in the walls, he told her, were going to be permanent, like the nails in the cross. Never forget.

Her desk lamp is the single thing glowing, casting faint light on the unframed print tacked above it. *The Stoning of Saint Stephen*. Rembrandt's first known work, painted at nineteen. I had learned about the chiaroscuro technique in another basement, with my grandfather bent over his easel. Strong lights and heavy shadows.

Rembrandt was a master of it. He made sure the brilliance of heaven was opening up for Saint Stephen, the first Christian martyr, murdered by a mob because evil people told lies about him. Three priests huddle in the upper corner. Watching him die. Doing nothing.

I wonder which came first to the basement: this print or Angie, who decided Saint Stephen's fate was a most appropriate marker for her desk. The edges of the print are soft and furry. It is attached to the pockmarked wall by three scratched yellow thumbtacks and one red one. A small rip on the left side has been repaired with Scotch tape.

Two inches away is another vision of heaven. A drawing on lined notebook paper. Five stick figures with lopsided butterfly wings illuminated by a bright orange sunburst. A child's crooked print tumbles across the sky: ANGIE'S ANGELS.

I learned in Angie's obituary that this drawing was a long-ago gift from the six-year-old daughter of Dominicus Steele, an apprentice plumber accused of raping an SMU coed outside a Fort Worth bar in the '80s. Dominicus was identified by the victim and two of her sorority sisters.

That night, he'd flirted with the victim up close. He was big and black, and a good dancer. The white college girls loved him until they decided he was the guy in the gray hooded sweatshirt running away from their drunk, crumpled friend in the alley. Dominicus was freed by DNA extracted from semen stored for twelve years in an evidence storage unit. Dominicus's mother was the first to speak to reporters in terms of "Angie's Angels," and her sweet little moniker stuck.

I'd never describe Angie as an angel. She did whatever she had to. She was a very good liar when she needed to be. I know, because she had lied for Charlie and me.

I take a step, and the hollow sound of my boot echoes on the cheap yellow linoleum that covers up God knows what. The four other desks that are scattered around the floor, in similar states of paper chaos, are also empty. *Where is everybody?*

There's a blue door on the far side of the room that's impossible to miss. I venture over. Knock lightly. Nothing. Maybe I should just hunker down in Angie's chair for a while. Swerve it around on the cranky roller wheels she complained about and stare into Rembrandt's heaven. Ponder the role of the martyr.

Instead, I twist the knob and open the door a crack. Knock again. Hear animated voices. Push the door all the way. A long conference table. Blazing overhead lights. Bill's startled face. Another woman, jumping out of her chair abruptly, knocking over her cup of coffee.

My eyes, traveling down the table, follow the river of amber liquid.

Head thrumming.

Copies of drawings, stretched edge to edge across the scratched surface.

Tessie's drawings.

The real ones. And the ones that aren't.

I am staring at the score, 12–28, scrawled in white chalk on a blackboard. A lopsided Little League game, maybe, or a bad day for the Dallas Cowboys. It is clear from the chart's wording that these are the twelve men who have been freed over the years by Angie and her rotating legal crew, and the twenty-eight who have not.

The woman who tipped over the coffee, introduced to me as a third-year University of Texas law student named Sheila Dunning, has left us. William quickly swept up the copies of my drawings, tucked them out of the way, and set a fresh mug of hot coffee in front of me. He's apologized multiple times, and I've said over and over, *It's OK, it's OK, I have to see those drawings again sometime* and *I should have knocked louder.*

Sometimes I long for the Tessie in me, who would have just spit out the unvarnished, angry truth: *You're a jerk. You knew I was coming. You knew I hadn't looked at these since I dug them out of a wall.*

"Thanks for driving all the way down here." He slides into a chair beside me and slaps a new yellow legal pad on the table. He is wearing jeans, Nikes, and a slightly pilled green pullover sweater that is too short for his frame, the curse of a broad-shouldered man. "Are you still in the mood to do this?"

"Why wouldn't I be?" Tessie, retorting. Still in there, after all.

"We don't have to talk here. In this room." He gazes at me intently. "This is our war room. Generally off limits to clients."

My eyes linger over the walls. Beside the chalkboard, enlarged snapshots of five men. Current cases, I assume. Four of the men are African-American. A young Terrell Darcy Goodwin stars in the center photograph. His arm is tossed around a guy in a red-and-gray high school baseball uniform, a little brother, maybe. Same good looks, wide-spaced eyes, chiseled cheekbones, café latte skin.

On the opposite wall: Crime scenes. Gaping mouths. Blank eyes. Confused limbs. I don't linger.

I flick my head around to a giant erase board that is scribbled with some sort of timeline.

I see my name. Merry's.

I open my mouth to speak and find his eyes glued to my crossed legs and the patch of bare white thigh above my black boots. I keep meaning to let out the hem of this skirt. I scoot my legs under the table. He resumes a professional mask.

"I'm not a client." I swallow a sip of bitter liquid, read the words on the side of the mug. *Lawyers Get You Off.*

William follows my eyes. Rolls his. "Most of our cups are dirty. Could use a good washing out." Joking. Letting the other moment, the curiosity about what's under my skirt, pass.

"I'm fine in here, William."

"Bill," he reminds me. "Only people over seventy get to call me William."

"Did the exhumation Tuesday go as planned?" I ask. "They kept it quiet. It didn't even make the papers."

"You should know the answer to that."

"You saw me by the tree."

"That hair of yours is hard to miss, even in the dark."

So *he's* a liar, too. My hair is down today, long, curling loosely past my shoulders. Still the same burnt color as the sixteen-year-old me. Two nights ago, at the cemetery, it was tucked up tight in my daughter Charlie's black baseball cap.

"You tricked me," I say. "Nice."

I shift uncomfortably in the chair. I'm talking to a lawyer, one I haven't paid a cent to keep my confidences. Sure, he could be the boy next door with those doe-y brown eyes and clean-cut hair and ears that stick out a little and enormous hands that could cover a grapefruit. The funny best friend of the guy you really want, until you realize . . . oh, *shit*.

He grins. "You look like my little sister does right before she slaps me. In answer to your question, a forensic anthropologist is getting a look at the bones first. Then Jo and her people step in. She would like both of us to watch her techs work the Black-Eyed Susan case next week. Asked me to invite you personally. Kind of as a peace offering since she ordered you not to be present at the exhumation. She really did feel bad about it."

I shiver slightly. There's no vent, no visible source of heat in here. My father used to say that February in Texas is a cold, bitter lady. March is when she loses her virginity.

"Bones are processed every Monday morning," he continues. "Jo had to pull some strings to push the Susans to the head of the line. I can pick you up, if you like. The lab's about twenty minutes from your place."

"No worry this time about contamination?" This had been Joanna's concern about me officially attending the exhuming of the bodies. She didn't want even the slightest hint of broken protocol.

"We'll be watching the process through a glass window. The new lab is set up as a teaching facility. State-of-the-art. Bones are flown in from all over the world. So are students and scientists who want to see Jo's techniques firsthand." He smiles tightly and picks up his pen. "Want to get started? I've got to be somewhere by two. For my job that pays the bills." A corporate mediator, whatever the hell that is, according to his law firm's website. I wonder where he is hiding his suit.

"Yep. Go ahead." Spoken much more casually than I felt.

"Your testimony in '95. Has anything changed? Have you remembered anything else in the last seventeen years about the attack or your attacker?"

"No." I say it firmly. *I am willing to help,* I remind myself, *but only to a point.* I have two teen-agers to protect, the one I was and the one who sleeps in that purple room.

"Just to be sure, I'm going to ask a few specifics anyway, OK?"

I nod.

"Can you describe the face of your attacker?"

"No."

"Do you remember where you met up with him?"

"No."

"Do you have any memory of being dumped in that field?"

"No."

"Do you ever remember seeing our client—Terrell Goodwin— before the day you testified?"

"No. Not to my knowledge."

"*No* is a nice simple answer," he says. "If that's the truth."

"It is. The truth."

"Do you remember a single thing that happened in those hours you were missing?"

"No."

"The last thing you remember is buying . . . tampons . . . at Walgreens?"

"And a Snickers bar. Yes." The wrapper was found in the grave.

"You've heard your 911 call that night but do not recall making it?"

"Right. Yes."

"Tessa, I have to ask again. Is there any way you will change your mind and undergo light hypnosis? See if there's anything you can remember from those lost hours? Or examine the drawings you gave me with an expert? If we jog something, anything, loose it might help us get a new hearing in front of the judge."

"Absolutely no to hypnosis." I say it quietly. "I've read enough about it to know that I can be directed to false memories. But examining my drawings from therapy? Yes. I think so. I have no idea whether it will help."

"Great. Great. I have someone in mind. Someone who has worked with me in the past. I think you'll like her." I almost laugh. If he only knew how many times I'd heard that.

He lays his pen at a perfect 90-degree angle. Twirls it. Stops it. Twirls it. William knows how to use a big, fat pause. I'm beginning to see that he might be a very clever boy in court.

"There's a reason you're sitting here, Tessa. Something you aren't saying. I really need to know what it is. Because based on those answers, you might still think Terrell Darcy Goodwin is guilty as hell."

I couldn't sleep last night wondering exactly how I'd answer this question. "I feel like I hurt . . . Terrell . . . on the stand." *Slow,* I tell myself. "That I was manipulated by a lot of people. For years. Angie eventually satisfied me that there is no convincing physical evidence against him. And I showed you the black-eyed Susans. Under my window." *Still keeping tabs.*

"Yes." His lips have stretched into a tight line. "But a judge will write off those flowers to your imagination, or just a random lunatic. He might infer that you did it yourself. Are you prepared for that?"

"Is that what you think? That I'm making it up?"

His gaze is direct, unbothered. Irritating as hell. Maybe *William* doesn't deserve to know all of it. He certainly isn't asking the right question.

I'm beginning to think he planned for me to stumble into this room all along. Slam me back into the past. Poke something sharp into my uncooperative brain.

"My drawings aren't your magic bullet," I say abruptly. "Don't pin your hopes on an angry girl with a paintbrush."

Tessie, 1995

Thursday. Only two days after our last meeting.

The doctor cut the Tuesday session short by twenty minutes, shortly after my outburst. He called twenty-four hours later to re-schedule. I don't know whether he was angry about me bringing up his daughter, or just unprepared to hear it. If I've learned anything about psychiatrists in the last year, it's that they don't like surprises from the guests. They want to be the one to scatter the path of stale bread crumbs, even if it leads into a dense forest where you can't see at all.

"Good morning, Tessa." *Formal*. "You caught me off guard the other day. To be honest, I wasn't sure how to handle it. For you, or me."

"I almost didn't come back today. Or ever." Not really true. For the first time in months, I feel like I own a small shred of power. I blow the bangs out of my eyes. Lydia took me to the mall for a new haircut yesterday. *Cut, cut, cut,* I insisted. I could almost hear my hair fall, soft and sad, to the floor. I wanted to change myself. Look more like a boy. My best friend appraised me critically when it was over. Informed me that I achieved the opposite. Short hair made me prettier, she said. Emphasized my small straight nose that I should thank the Lord Jesus for every day. Drew my eyes out like flying saucers in a big Texas sky. Lydia was practicing her similes for the SAT. She'd announced the very first time we linked arms in second grade that she was going to Princeton. I thought Princeton was a small town filled with eligible princes.

I think the doctor is pacing. Traveling the room. Oscar is not alerting me. He's sleepy, maybe because he got his shots an hour ago. My latest worry is that Daddy considers Oscar a first step to a See-ing Eye dog, and faithful, untrained Oscar will be sent away.

"I'm not surprised you feel that way." His voice is behind me. "I should have been straight from the beginning. About my daughter. Even though she has nothing to do with why I took your case." *His second lie.* "It was a very long time ago."

It bothers me, his voice bouncing at me from different places, a game of dodge ball in the dark.

I count two seconds before his chair creaks gently. Not a heavy man, not a skinny one. "Did your father tell you about my daugh-ter?"

"No."

"Did you . . . overhear something, then?" His question is almost timid. Like something an insecure normal person would ask. But this is pretty uncharted territory for him, I guess.

"I overhear things all the time," I evade. "I guess my other senses are super-enlightened now." This last part is not actually true at all. All my senses have gone haywire. Granny's recipe for fried green beans with bacon dressing tastes like soggy cigarettes; my sweet lit-tle brother's voice is like Aunt Hilda's fake red fingernails scraping glass. I suddenly cry along to country music, which I always secretly thought was for dumb people.

I'm not telling this doctor any of that yet. Let him think I'm sud-denly hyperaware. I'm not about to rat out Lydia, who has read me every word of every story on Terrell Darcy Goodwin and the Black-Eyed Susan investigation that she can get her hands on. Researched every shrink who has tried to tunnel into my brain.

All I know is that when I am lying on Lydia's pink down comforter, with Alanis Morissette moaning, and my best friend reading animatedly from her stack of library printouts . . . those are the minutes and hours that I feel the safest. Lydia is the only one who still treats me exactly the same.

She's relying on some innate seventeen-year-old certainty that I might die if I live in a silent cocoon, curled up and fragile. That handling me with care is not going to make me better.

For some reason, I think this doctor might be the second person to understand. He lost a daughter. He's got to be a close personal friend with pain. I hold out hope for that.

Tessa, present day

I snap off one more picture with my iPhone. Three images in all. I should have done it five days ago, before their stems bowed and their eyes stared dejectedly at the ground.

I've told only Angie the whole story, I think. *Now she's dead.*

I am not fooled by the fainting Susans under my windowsill. I know that each of the thirty-four eyes hoards enough seeds to carpet my whole yard, come spring. I slide on my gardening gloves and pick up the can of herbicide I've retrieved from the garage. I wonder whether he likes to watch this part of the process. I've learned that poison is the best method. Not since I was seventeen have I torn up the Susans by their roots.

A breeze flutters, scattering the spray. I taste it, bitter and metallic.

If I don't hurry, I'm going to be late to pick up Charlie. I smother on one last cancerous coat. I strip off my gloves, leave them with the spray can, run to grab the keys off the kitchen counter, hop in the Jeep, and drive the ten minutes to the freshman gym. Home of the Fighting Colts. Chattering, texting girls stream onto the sidewalk, in ponytails and obscenely tight mandatory red gym shorts that mothers should officially complain about but don't.

The backseat door pops open, startling me, like it does every time. "Hi, Mom." Charlie tosses in a blue Nike duffle that always holds smelly surprises and a backpack of books that lands like a chunk of concrete. She jumps in and slams the door.

Smooth, angelic face. Sexy legs. Tight muscles not mature enough to fight back. Innocent, and not. I don't want to be aware of these things, but I've trained myself to see her as he might.

"My laptop sucks," she says.

"How was school? Practice?"

"I'm starved. Really, Mom. I couldn't print my homework last night. I had to use your computer."

This beautiful girl, the love of my life, the one I missed all day long, is already firing up my nerves.

"McDonald's?" I ask.

"Surrrrre."

I've stopped feeling guilty about the after-practice drive-through runs. It doesn't keep my daughter from devouring a healthy full-course dinner two hours later. Charlie eats at least four times a day and remains a tall, slender rail. She has my old runner's appetite and red hair and her father's mood-changing eyes. Purplish is happy; gray is tired. Black is thoroughly pissed off.

Not for the first time, I wish that Charlie's father weren't thousands of miles away on an Army base in Afghanistan. I wish he weren't just a serious fling fifteen years ago that went awry a month before I realized I was pregnant. Not that Charlie seems to care a whit that we never married. Lt. Col. Lucas Cox sends money like clockwork and stays in constant touch. I think a Skype session with Charlie is on tap for tonight.

"We will talk about the computer later, OK?"

No answer. She's texting, I'm sure. I pull out from the curb and decide to let her decompress from the eight fluorescent-lighted hours she has spent constructing triangular prisms and deconstructing Charlotte Brontë. After Charlie abandoned *Jane Eyre* on the couch last night for Facebook, I noticed that the heroine gazing off the cover was sporting a new mustache and devil horns. *She's so whiny,* Charlie whined this morning, while stuffing her mouth with bacon.

A few minutes later, we roll up to the drive-through.

"What do you want?" I ask her.

"Uhhhh."

"Charlie, stop with the phone. You need to order."

"OK." Cheerful. "I would like a Big Mac, and a MacBook Pro."

"Very funny."

Truth is, I love this about her—the cocky sense of humor and confidence, her ability to make me laugh out loud when I don't want to. I wait until I think Charlie is about halfway through her Big Mac to start The Conversation. In the Jeep, just us, there is always more of a chance my words will end up in her brain.

"I've changed my mind and decided to get involved in the Terrell Goodwin execution," I say. "I've spoken with the new attorney on the case. A famous forensic scientist is going to reexamine the evidence. She swabbed my DNA this week."

A short silence. "That's good, Mom. You need to be absolutely sure. You've been worrying about this a lot lately. People are getting released on DNA stuff all the time now. Our science teacher told us that Dallas has freed more innocent people from Death Row than almost every other state. People just think we kill everybody." I hear her crumple up the hamburger wrapper.

"Don't toss that on the floor," I say automatically. To myself, I think: *Is that because we have more innocent people on Death Row?*

"And Angie," Charlie adds. "She was nice. She was, like, totally convinced. And she said that none of it was your fault."

"I'll be in the news again." Meaning, Charlie won't be immune.

"I've been through it before. My friends will take care of me. I got this, Mom."

The naivete of it almost makes me want to cry. At the same time, it is hard to believe that Charlie is three years younger than I was when I testified. She seems so much more *prepared*.

I pull into our driveway and switch off the ignition. Charlie is rustling to get her stuff, but I don't turn around. "Never, *ever* get in a car with someone you don't know. Never walk alone. Don't talk to reporters." My voice sounds sharper than I'd like in the tiny, closed-up space. "If I'm not home, turn the security system on as soon as you close the door."

It's ridiculous to deliver these worn-out instructions for the thousandth time, but I'd become too complacent. I have vowed ever since Angie's wake to know where Charlie is every single second. A few days ago, I turned down a freelance design project in Los Angeles to build a staircase out of old cars and recycled glass. It would have carried our finances for the next two years.

"*Mom.*" She packs as much teen-age patronization in those three letters as will fit. "I *got* this."

Before I can respond, she's tumbling out of the car, loaded up like a soldier entering battle, jogging to the front door with her house key in hand. She's in the house in seconds. Prepared, like I taught her. *Innocent, and not.*

The question that neither of us ever asks out loud: *But if not him, then who?*

I follow her slowly, fiddling with my phone. I almost trip over the duffle she dumped in the foyer, think about calling out to her, stop myself. I head to the small desk in the living room where my laptop sits, call up the email I just sent to my own address, download, hit print. Listening to it regurgitate a couple of feet away, I think Charlie's right—our house needs a more efficient grasp on technology.

The printer spits out three grainy pictures of wilting flowers. Charlie's door is already closed when I pass by.

A few seconds later, I am on my tiptoes, pulling from the top shelf of my bedroom closet the shoebox boldly marked, *Tax Documents.*

The killer has planted black-eyed Susans for me six times. It didn't matter where I was living. He likes to keep me guessing. I'm sure about this now.

He waited so long between plantings sometimes that, before

Angie, I was able to convince myself on most days that the right killer sat in jail. That the first black-eyed Susans were the work of a random stalker, and the other times the whims of the wind.

This box, made for ASICS running shoes, size 7, marked *Tax Documents,* contains the photographs I snapped every time anyway. Just in case.

I set the box on the bed and lift the lid. Right on top, the one taken with my granddaddy's old Polaroid Instant camera.

That first time, right after the trial, I had thought either I was crazy or that black-eyed Susans had suddenly sprung up in October under the live oak in our back yard because of a bizarre weather pattern. Except the ground looked disturbed. I dug up the wildflowers by myself a little frantically with an old kitchen spoon.

I didn't want to tell anybody because life in my house was returning to some semblance of normal. I was done with therapy. Terrell Darcy Goodwin sat in jail. My dad was dating for the first time.

The spoon struck another surprise in the dirt that day—something hard, orange, and plastic. An old prescription bottle. The label ripped off. Childproof cap.

Charlie has turned up her music. It strains through the wall, but can't drown out the words on a scrap of paper curled up in a little orange bottle.

Oh Susan, Susan, lovely dear
My vows shall ever true remain
Let me kiss off that falling tear
I never want to hurt you again
But if you tell, I will make
Lydia
A Susan, too

Tessie, 1995

After he leaves the office, my fingers brush over three stubby charcoal crayons; the cool metal coil binding a drawing pad; a Dixie cup of water; a few brushes, a narrow paint box with a squeaky hinge. The doctor has repeated the order of the paint colors four times, left to right. Black, blue, red, green, yellow, white.

As if what colors I choose will make a significant difference. I am already thinking of swirling the colors to make purple and gray, orange and aqua. The colors of bruises, and sunsets.

This is not the first time I have drawn blind. Right after Mom died, Granddaddy was constantly trying to distract me from grief.

We sat at his old cedar picnic table. He punched a No. 2 pencil through the center of a paper plate, a de facto umbrella, so that I could grasp the pencil but not watch my hand draw. "Making pictures in your head is primal," he said. "You don't need your eyes to do it. Start with the edges."

I remember the faint blue flower border that etched the paper plate, that my fingers were sticky with sweat and chocolate, but not what I drew that day.

"Memories aren't like compost," the doctor had said, as he guided me over to his desk. "They don't decay."

I knew exactly what he wanted out of this little exercise. The priority was not to cure my blindness. He wanted to know why my ankle shattered into pieces, what implement etched the pink half-moon that hung under my eye. He wanted me to draw *a face*.

He didn't say any of this, but I knew.

"There's infinite storage space up here." He tapped my head. "You simply have to dig into every box."

One more self-help bite from him before he shut the door, and I would have screamed.

I can hear my father outside the door, droning blurry words, like a dull pencil. Oscar has settled into the cave under the desk, his head resting on my cast. Pressure, but nice pressure, like my mother's hand on my back. The doctor's voice floats through the door. They are talking about box scores, like the world is running along just fine.

My head is blank when the charcoal begins to rub insistently against the paper.

The click of the door opening startles me, and I jump, and Oscar jumps, and my pad slides and clunks to the floor. I have no idea how much time has passed, which is new, because ever since I went blind, I can guess the time of day within five minutes. Lydia attributes it to a primitive internal clock, like the one that reminds hibernating animals to wake up in the black isolation of their caves and venture back into the world.

I smell him, the same Tommy cologne that Bobby always liberally sprays on himself at Dillard's. My doctor wears Tommy Hilfiger, sounds like Tommy Lee Jones. Everything Tommy.

"Just checking to see how it's going," he says.

He is at my side, reaching down, picking up the pad from the floor, placing it gently on the desk in front of me. My drawings, except for the one on the pad, are ripped out and scattered across his desk. My head pounds, and I press a finger into my right temple like there's a pause button.

"May I?" he asks, which is ridiculous because I'm certain his eyes are already greedily scanning. He picks up a sheet, puts it down, picks up another.

The air is thick with the heat of his disappointment; he's a teacher with a second-rate student who he has hoped will surprise him.

"It's just the first time," he says. Awkward silence. "You didn't use any paint." A hint of reproach?

He stiffens. Leans in closer, tickling my shoulder, turning my pad, which was apparently upside down. "Who is this?"

"I'm not done."

"Tessie, who *is* this?"

I had scrubbed the charcoal against the page until it was black. I had dug into his desk drawer for the No. 2 pencil eraser that I used to swirl a chaotic nest of hair around her head. My fingernail carefully scratched out big eyes, delicate cheekbones and nose, full lips rounded into a frightened O.

I thought about *the edges.* No neck anchored her in the blackness. She floated in outer space, a silent, screaming constellation. I had drawn a face, but not the one he wanted.

"It's your daughter." Why I felt the urge to torture him, I do not know. I could have said it was Lydia. Or my mother. Or me. But I didn't.

I feel a slight whoosh of air as he abruptly draws back. I wonder whether he wants to strike me. Oscar is whining way back in his throat.

"It looks nothing like her." There is a slight crack in his voice. A picture forms in my head of a perfect black egg with a white hairline fracture.

I know that his reply is inappropriate, even silly. I am a skilled artist at seventeen, but this drawing is surely distorted, even childish. *Of course* it looks nothing like her. I've never met her. *I'm blind.*

He's a doctor. He shouldn't allow me to make any of this personal for him.

When did I become capable of such cruelty?

47

Tessa, present day

I'm thinking of Lydia as I shove a digger deep into the loose soil under my windowsill, pulling out the poisoned Susans, stacking them in a neat, weedy pile beside me. The metal of the digger is stained with traces of bloody rust, but the shiny part glints in the light filtering out the screen of my bedroom window.

The yellow curtains blow white in the moonlight, billowing and retracting. While I'd waited for Charlie to conk out, I plopped on the couch, flipped on *Jimmy Kimmel Live,* and scratched out a list on the back of a grocery slip, as if that somehow made the contents more harmless.

I wanted to see them neatly written down. Every single place I'd found a patch of black-eyed Susans in the years since the trial. The big question, which I already knew the answer to: *Should I go back to each one of them alone? With Bill? With Joanna? Wouldn't it just waste their time, make them think I was even crazier than they already did?*

It seemed highly unlikely that I'd be able to find things he might have buried for me in the ground all these years later, or that I'd hit the right spot to dig, even with the photographs. Rain gushes, the earth moves.

Now, down on my hands and knees in the inky night, sifting my hand through the dirt, I wonder if I am wrong. I find an errant screw dropped from a worker's hand when the windows were replaced two years ago. A scrap of paper. The stubborn roots of a vine that appeared like a white bone.

Lydia always knew what to do in these situations. She was the one with the scientific and logical mind, able to shove aside emotion and examine everything with the clinical detachment I didn't possess. The summer we were eight, she stayed inside the lines of her coloring books, while I tried to invent a new color by melting crayons together on the sidewalk in the brutal Texas sun.

In elementary school, I liked to run against the wind for the battle of it; Lydia waited for me cross-legged on a blanket, reading something way too old for her. *The Great Gatsby. Hamlet. 1984.* Afterward, as I lay panting on the ground, she pressed cool fingers to my wrist and counted the beats of my pulse.

I knew that I would not die on Lydia's watch. She's the one who whispered in my ear while I stared at a waxy yellow version of my mother in the casket. *She is not in there.* She was unusually drawn to death, from the beginning.

When we were assigned a world history project on "a fascinating moment in British history," two-thirds of Mrs. Baker's freshman class wrote about the Beatles. I carefully etched a replica of the medieval London Bridge and pondered the miracle of God that kept the shops and houses crammed on top from crashing into the mighty Thames.

Lydia chose a river of evil so black and swirling you couldn't see the bottom. Mrs. Baker asked her to read her report out loud to the class, probably because she knew it would keep us awake at our desks.

I'll never forget Lydia's chilling delivery of her opening lines, stolen from the coroner's report.

The body was lying naked in the middle of the bed, the shoulders flat but the axis of the body inclined to the left side of the bed. The head was turned on the left cheek.

While most of her classmates were contemplating whether "I Am the Walrus" was just one big John Lennon acid trip, Lydia had buried herself in the story of Jack the Ripper's final victim.

Mary Kelly met her grisly death at the 26 Dorset Street boardinghouse, room 13. She was 5'7", twenty-five years old, a buxom prostitute, and owed twenty-seven shillings on her rent.

She was heard singing in her room hours before she died.

It doesn't take a memory expert to figure out why I remember such details so many years later and very little about the medieval London Bridge. Lydia had turned on a British accent during her presentation. At one point, her fist thumped her chest three times in a dramatization of the first knife strikes.

Silly. *Creepy.*

To write that report, Lydia had immersed herself for two weekends in the Texas Christian University library, reading dissertations and nineteenth-century medical reports and essays from self-proclaimed "Ripperologists." She tucked it in a plastic binder and told me to flip to the last page before she was supposed to turn it in.

I was gripped by horror porn: a black-and-white photograph of Mary Kelly lying in her flophouse bed, her insides ripped out. I never knew where Lydia found this, in the days before Google. Only that Lydia was always a relentless digger.

Why am I thinking about this now? I rub my hand across my forehead, wiping away sweat, leaving crumbs of dirt. I'm back in the kitchen, my foot on the trashcan pedal, dropping my collection into the trash. And then it hits me.

I had dismissed the scrap of paper because it didn't bear a sadistic poem. Now I'm picking it out of the bin, examining it more closely. It *could* be part of a candy bar wrapper. *Was it the kind of candy bar I bought at Walgreens the night I disappeared? The kind I bought every Tuesday for Roosevelt?*

Roosevelt was a fixture on my Wednesday running route, nicknamed because at straight-up noon every single day, he stood on top of an old red bucket and spouted the entirety of FDR's first inaugural speech.

By the time I flew by on Wednesdays after school, he was always long done with his diatribe. We had worked out a routine. I tossed a Snickers bar, his favorite, into the air without slowing my pace. He never failed to catch it and shoot me a big, toothy grin. It became a ritual of good luck during track season and a pact I kept up when summer started. I never lost a race after meeting Roosevelt.

And so it was decided. Every Tuesday night, I bought a Snickers bar. I didn't buy two or three or four at a time. I didn't buy them on Mondays or Saturdays. I bought one every Tuesday night, and he caught it on Wednesday afternoon, and I won and won and won.

But in those missing hours, I apparently did something I would never, ever consider doing. I ate his candy bar. There were traces of it in my vomit at the hospital.

I was committed to my ritual with Roosevelt. To winning. Did I eat the candy bar that night because I thought that I would never run a race again?

I grab a plastic snack bag out of the pantry shelf and seal the wrapper inside. *Did he touch this? Did he stand under my window, snacking?* My cell phone rings out from the living room couch, disturbing the silence that is everywhere except my chest.

Hastings, William.

"It's late, Bill." No hello.

"The day got away from me," he says. "I just want to be sure you remember to be at the UNT lab tomorrow by 9:45, fifteen minutes before the techs start the process on the bones."

How could I forget? I want to shout it at him, but instead say: "I'm driving myself." This has to be the reason he called. He seems determined to pick me up.

Bill lets a couple of seconds elapse. "Joanna wouldn't tell me what over the phone, but she says the forensic anthropologist has already found something."

Tessie, 1995

"How is the drawing at home going?" He asks this before my butt hits the cushion.

"I forgot to bring any of them with me." A lie. The drawings, nine new ones, are right where I want them—in a red Macy's shirt box in my closet labeled *Xtra Tampons,* sure to dissuade my nosy little brother.

The phone on his desk suddenly buzzes. The emergency buzz, one of my favorite sounds in the world because it sucks minutes away from me.

"I'm sorry, Tessie," he says. "Excuse me for just a moment. I've just checked in a patient at the hospital and was expecting a few questions from the nurse."

The doctor's voice travels over from the other side of the room. I can make out a few words. *Elavil. Klonopin.* Shouldn't he be doing this privately? I'm really trying hard not to hear because I don't want to imagine a person like me on the other end and get emotionally involved. So I focus on other things, like trying to match the doctor's lazy drawl with Lydia's description of him.

It was Lydia's idea. Yesterday, with my blessing, she had hopped the bus to the TCU campus and sneaked into one of the doctor's late afternoon summer classes: *Anastasia Meets Agatha Christie: Exploring the Gray Matter About Amnesia.*

When she told me the class title, I cringed a little. Too gimmicky. But then, I was looking for reasons to be critical.

If Lydia stuck on the big rounded plastic frames she wore when her contacts itched, she could easily disappear into a crowd of college students. Lydia's father told her once that she was one of those people born thirty, and repeated it often, which Lydia carried around like a mortal wound. Me, well . . . I can't tell Lydia but I feel a little uncomfortable around her dad these days.

Through our formative years, Mr. Bell concocted a kick-ass chili recipe, and hauled us to the shooting range, and whipped us around Lake Texoma in the unsinkable *Molly* every Labor Day and July 4th. But he was moody and known to strike out. And, since I turned fourteen, his eyes sometimes hesitated in the wrong places. Maybe he was just being more honest than most men greeted with puberty in bloom. Probably better to know, I reasoned, and wear longer shorts at her house.

Last night, after her successful day of spying and some of my dad's leftover Frito pie, Lydia had been in especially good spirits. "Did you know that Agatha Christie went missing for eleven days in 1926 and no one had a clue where she was?" she had asked me breathlessly, from the corner of my bed.

I had her pictured in the usual position: legs pretzeled into an easy lotus, her pink-flowered Doc Martens lost somewhere on the floor, a hot pink scrunchy holding up a mountain of black hair. Pink was Lydia's color.

A recap of the day's events in the O.J. trial buzzed in our ears as background. It was impossible to get away from it. Daddy didn't like a TV perched on top of my dresser, certainly didn't like a bloody soundtrack, but he had relented instantly when I told him the constant noise made me feel less alone. That I wasn't really listening to it.

It was only a half-lie. I found something soothing about Marcia Clark's methodical voice. How could anyone *not* believe her?

"Agatha kissed her daughter goodnight and disappeared," Lydia had continued. "They thought she maybe drowned herself in this pond called the Silent Pool because that's where they found her wrecked car."

"The Silent Pool?" I was skeptical. It was how anyone sane had to be with Lydia at least part of the time.

"*Really.* You can read it yourself." She thrust a piece of paper at me. If it had been anyone else, this would have seemed like a mean poke. But it was Lydia. My vision was less gray when she was around. Lighter, like I was splayed flat on the tickly grass, staring up into late summer dusk. I let my fingers grasp her tangible proof that Agatha Christie lived out a page in her novels, as if it were important.

"Anyway, that's where they found her car," Lydia repeated. "The other thought was that her a-hole of a cheating husband killed her and abandoned the car there. While all of this was going on, Sir Arthur Conan Doyle even took one of her gloves to a medium to try to figure out where she'd gone. It was on the front of *The New York Times.*" More rustling of paper. "But she showed up. It turned out she had *amnesia. For eleven days.*"

"This was the focus of his lecture?" It was comforting, and somehow not.

"Uh-huh. I was intrigued by the class title, so I stopped off at the library before. When I got to class, your *doctor* was talking about the etiology of the fugue state and how it's related to dissociative amnesia."

It would be very hard to live in Lydia's head. I imagined it blindingly bright and chaotic, like an exploding star. Both sides of her brain constantly at war. Because brilliant, steady Lydia was an addict when it came to murder and celebrities. The O.J. trial, her LSD. Any inane detail got her high. Like the other night, giggling about how O. J. Simpson had asked the cops for a glass of *orange juice* after the Bronco chase, followed up by ten minutes of her railing about the jury not getting the concept of restriction fragment length polymorphism.

"So what happened to her?" Trying to shuttle things along because I was curious, but wanting to know whether my doctor appeared to be a manipulative asshole.

"She was found in a spa hotel under an assumed name. She claimed not to recognize pictures of herself in the newspaper. Some doctors said she was suicidal, in a psychogenic trance. That's like a fugue state, *thus* the title of your doctor's class."

"I'd rather think of her as a nice old lady writing cozy mysteries by the fire."

"I know. It's kind of like finding out that Edna St. Vincent Millay slept around and was a morphine addict. Ednas and Agathas should be true to their names."

I'd laughed, something close to the way I used to, and imagined it drifting under the bedroom door, smoothing out a tight wrinkle in my father's face.

"A mystery novelist with a cheating husband, gone missing. Sounds like a publicity stunt."

"Some people might say that about you," my best friend retorted. A rare slip, for her. It had hit its mark, a sharp pain to the right side of my stomach.

"Sorry, Tessie, it just came out. Of course that's not true, *either*. He's the kind of professor you could get a real crush on, you know, because he has that *brain*. He's not a fake." She sat silently for a second. "I like him. I think you can trust him. Don't you?"

Smacked again. Fifteen hours later, back on the doctor's couch, I'm fully absorbing the repercussions of this turn of events. Now, Lydia, my objective, loyal friend, would give my doctor the benefit of the doubt. I wondered if she'd been crazy enough to raise her hand. Ask a question. *Get noticed*. I should have thought this through.

The doctor has just excused himself and left the room. The longer he's gone, the darker it gets. You wouldn't think it would make any difference when you're blind, but it does. The air-conditioning is noisily blowing through the vents, but it's harder and harder to breathe. I've drawn my knees up tight and crossed my arms around them. My tongue tastes like a dead trout. There is growing dread that no one will find me and pull me out in time. That I will suffocate in here.

Is this one of your tests, doctor?

The second I decide I can't take it any longer, he strides into the room. His chair creaks with his weight as he settles in. I fight the surge of gratefulness. *You came back.*

"That took longer than I thought. We can make up the time in our next session. We have about a half-hour left. I'd like to talk about your mother this week, if that's OK."

"That's not why I'm here." My response is quick. "I went over and over that years ago. Lots of people have mothers who die." A fog drools at the corners of my vision. Frenetic pricks of light everywhere, like a swarm of frightened fireflies. New guests in my head. I wonder if this means I am about to faint. *How would I know the difference?* My lips contort, and I almost giggle.

"So you shouldn't mind talking about it," he says reasonably. "Catch me up. Where were you the day she died?" *Like you don't already know. Like there isn't a big fat file on your desk that you don't even have to bother to hide from a blind girl.*

My ankle throbs and sends a message to the crescent scar on my face and to the three-inch pink line drawn carefully under my left collarbone. *Can he not see how upset I am? That he should back off?*

The pieces of his face spin around, stubborn, refusing to lock in place. Gray-blue eyes, brown hair, wire-rim glasses. Not at all like Tommy Lee Jones, Lydia had said. Still, no picture falling together for me. No way to draw him blind.

This is the worst session yet, and we are just getting started.

"I was playing in the tree house," I tell him, while the fireflies do their panicked dance.

Tessa, present day

The first Susan has arrived, bundled in white cloth, like she is dressed for a holy baptism. The woman holding her is covered in head-to-toe white, too, her mouth and nose masked, so that all I can see are brown eyes. They look kind.

She unbinds the cloth and raises Susan carefully up to the window. Most of the small group gathered in the hall on the other side eagerly raise their iPhones. Susan is bathed in brief flashes, like a movie star.

Her skull is a horror show. Her eyes are holes going to the bottom of the ocean. Most of the lower half of her jaw, gone. A few rotten teeth hanging like stalactites in an abandoned cave. It is the emptiness, those two gaping, awful holes that remind me she was once human. That she could once stare back.

Remember? Her hollow, toothless voice bubbles up in my ear. An unspent grenade erupts in my chest. It's a shock, but it shouldn't be. The Susans had been silent for more than a year this time. It had been foolish to think they were gone.

Not now. I imagine my hand clamped over her mouth. I screech out "The Star-Spangled Banner" in my head.

Bombs bursting in air. Jo is squeezing my arm.

"Sorry I'm late." I gulp in her quirky normalness. White lab coat, khaki pants, purple Nikes, plastic badge hanging off a skull-and-crossbone-printed lanyard around her neck. A whiff of something chemical, but not unpleasant.

Deep breath. I'm on this side of the glass. This side of hell.

She nods casually to the group. Besides Bill and me, four other people are cleared for this event: three Ph.D. students—one from Oxford, two from the University of North Texas—and a beautiful, unbottled blond scientist from Sweden named Britta.

We'd spent the last fifteen minutes together, strangers pretending we weren't about to observe death at its most sadistic. The students' eyes flicked to me with interest, but no one was asking questions.

Before Jo arrived, we had settled on discussing the three places in Dallas and Fort Worth that Britta should not miss seeing before returning home to her Stockholm lab in two weeks: the Amon Carter for its muscled bronze Russells and Remingtons, and for the beautiful black boy in the newspaper hat; the Kimbell for the silvery light cascading on buxom masterpieces and for the ill-fated young man in the company of wicked sixteenth-century cardsharps; the Sixth Floor Museum, where Oswald angled his rifle, and a wild-eyed conspiracy theorist defiantly roamed the sidewalk, saying, *Nope, not like that.*

As Britta eyes Bill, I am thinking it is more likely she will end up in his bed. I'd gotten a curt smile from him this morning.

"Stephen King researched part of his Kennedy time-travel opus at the Sixth Floor Museum archives," Bill is telling them.

"Great book," Jo says. "King's a genius. But he never really got Texas. And I'm saying that as an Oklahoman. Hi, Bill. Tessa. Sarita. John and Gretchen. Britta, glad you could make it today. Looks like they are just getting started."

The skull is now facing us, leering from its spot on the counter. The woman in white is still unwrapping puzzle pieces. A long, pearly leg bone, and then another in much worse shape, like a tree branch snapped off in winter.

"Tammy's in charge today," Jo says. "Running the room." The

two exchange a brief wave. Four other women dressed in sterile suits are taking their places in the lab in front of clear glass hoods. The fluorescent light is brutal, and cold.

"Looking into a serial killer's refrigerator," Bill mutters in my ear.

Jo glances our way, but I can't tell if she heard. "Each forensic analyst has a specific job," she explains. "Margaret will cut a small piece out of the bone. Toneesha will clean it with bleach, ethanol, and water. Jen will pulverize it to a fine powder, from which we extract the DNA. Bessie's only role is to spray down the surfaces as we go, to keep things as sterile as possible. It's protocol. Always."

Her eyes are focused on the activity behind the window. Jo's in her element. Brilliant, without ego. Empathetic, without cynicism.

I am thinking that Jo remembers every single person by name on both sides of the glass. I am thinking, she could be talking about how to refine sugar.

"Never forget protocol." Suddenly stern. "Never get sloppy. Somebody accused me of that once. Worst time of my life."

She doesn't extrapolate. So far, no talk of the actual case—who these bones represent, why they are special.

"We like the skull and the denser bones, particularly femurs," she continues. "Gives us the longest string of mitochondrial DNA and the best chance at retrieving information on our way to finding out who they are. We're lucky we've got these three specimens, considering the bones have been scavenged and moved at least once."

The skull is being tucked under one of the hoods. The buzzing of the saw drifts through glass, like it is floating down the street on a lazy Saturday.

When the first Susan returns to the counter, a new one-inch-square hole glares out of the top of her head.

One more degradation in an endless string of them.

I'm sorry, I say silently. But there is no toothless, hollow answer in my head.

The Dremel saw drills a leg bone while the piece of skull is scrubbed raw in the second station. The technicians have forgotten us, slipping into a comfortable rhythm. I don't know what I was expecting, but not this surreal, matter-of-fact routine.

"It must be especially exciting to work on the Black-Eyed Susans," Sarita says brightly. The student from Oxford. Her voice is British, clipped. Her black heels are too high. "It must be an honor for these techs. These must be your best."

I can feel Jo's body go taut as if it is my own. "To them," she says. "And to me, this case . . . these bones . . . are no different than any other bone entrusted to us. Each one represents the same thing. A family, waiting."

Admonished. All of us.

"Why are there three bones?" Bill shifts the conversation abruptly. "For two unidentified skeletons? I thought you only tried one bone from a victim at a time."

"Now, there's the question I've been waiting for." Still an edge to Jo's voice. "The girls' skeletons were ransacked by critters over time. Moved by their killer at least once. The old case file documents foreign soil along with the red clay mixture in that field. So, of course, not every bone was there. Our forensic anthropologist laid out what was exhumed from the two caskets, and counted. He counted three right femurs."

I hear someone suck in a strangled breath. It takes a second to realize it's me.

"Three skeletons, not two," Bill whispers, as if I can't do the math.

Five Susans in all, not four. One dead girl named Merry, three gnawed-on nobodies, and me. Another member of my tribe. Another family, waiting.

I'm the one, a Susan says conspiratorially. *I'm the one with the answers.*

Jo shoots me an odd look, even though I know I am the only one who can hear.

Tessie, 1995

I wonder what he is looking at first.

The girl without a mouth. The girl with a red blindfold. The spider's web with the trapped swallowtail. The faceless runner on the beach. The roaring bear, my personal favorite. I'd worked hard on the teeth.

"Did you remember to bring your drawings today?" he had asked first thing.

Anything was preferable to talking about the day of my mother's death. Last time, he might as well have taken a hot poker and stuck it in my belly button.

And what did he learn? That I heard nothing. Saw nothing. That all I remember is a vague image of blood, but that was dead wrong, because the police told me there was no blood. All of it seemed so freakin' off point. Another way to clutter up my head.

So, yes, I brought drawings today. As soon as he asked, I handed Doc a white cardboard poster-mailing tube. It once held the *Pulp Fiction* poster now hanging over Lydia's bed. Lydia had rolled up my drawings carefully after our three-hour session sprawled on the rough Berber of her bedroom floor surrounded by a kindergarten chaos of paper and crayons and markers.

She didn't like my idea when I sprang it on her two days ago, but

I begged. More than anyone else, she understood my fear—that someone else would find out my secrets before I did.

So she'd ridden the bus back to the TCU library. Skimmed *The Clinical Application of Projective Drawings. The Childhood Hand That Disturbs*. And, because she was Lydia: *L'Imagination dans la Folie,* which translates to *Imagination in Madness,* some random tome that studied the drawings of insane people in 1846. She had educated me on the principle of the House-Tree-Person test. House, how I see my family. Tree, how I see my world. Person, how I see myself.

When it was all over, the black crayon worn to a flat nub, I thought we'd faked it pretty well. Lydia was even inspired to draw a picture herself, which she described to me as an army of giant black-and-yellow flowers with angry faces.

The doctor is sitting directly across from me, not saying a word. I can hear the crisp rustle of paper as he flips from one sheet to the next.

The silence has to be something they teach all these manipulative bastards.

Finally, he clears his throat. "Technically excellent, especially since you have no vision. But, mostly, cliché." No emotion in his words, just a statement of fact.

My scars begin to thrum. Thank God, I didn't give him my real drawings.

"This is why I don't like you." I speak stiffly.

"I didn't know you didn't like me."

"You don't *know*? You're like all of the others. You don't give a flip."

"I give a flip, Tessie. I care very much about what happens to you. So much that I'm not going to lie to you. You obviously spent some time on these drawings. You are a very smart, talented girl. The thing is, I don't believe them. The angry animal. The girl who has no voice. The idea of running along the ocean's abyss. These Jackson Pollock black and red swirls. They're all just a little too pretty. Too pat. There is no single emotion that connects these drawings to one another. They stand alone. That isn't how trauma works. Whatever emotions you are feeling right now . . . they connect everything."

His chair creaks as he leans over, placing a sheet in front of me. "Except for this one. This one is different."

"Am I supposed to guess?" Trying to be sarcastic. Trying to figure out how he saw through me so fast. Which drawing he found meaningful.

"Can you?" he asks. "Guess?"

"Are you really going to make me play this game?" I grip Oscar's leash like a lifeline, letting it bite into my flesh. Oscar obediently clambers up. "I'm going home."

"You can go home anytime you like. But I think you want to know."

My stillness says everything.

"Tell me." I barely croak it out, suffused with rage.

"The field of strangled flowers. Leering. The little girl cowering. It's terrifying. Messy. *Real*."

Lydia's drawing. She'd spent two hours on it while singing along to Alanis. *Got a plastic smile on a plastic face.*

Lydia used to laugh about the fact that she couldn't even draw Snoopy.

She hadn't told me about the little girl. I wanted to see.

I dropped the leash and scooted myself to the edge of the cushion, words rushing up my throat before I could stop them.

"What would you say if I told you that the main thing I've been drawing . . ." I suck in a breath. "Is a curtain. Over and over, until I want to crawl out of my skin?"

"I'd say, it's a start."

A slightly higher pitch to his voice. Is it hope?

Tessa, present day

I jiggle the key into the first of two locks on the front door. My mind is dwelling on pristine white laboratories and trees made of brittle bones and the fraction of statistical hope that one of the three tiny pieces of dead girl will lead somewhere. All the way home, there was blessed silence from the Susans. While the lock refuses to cooperate, a shadow clobbers into mine, making me gasp.

"What are you so damn jumpy for, Sue?"

Euphemia Outler, right-hand neighbor. Known to me as Effie, to Charlie as *Miss* Effie (despite a marriage or two) and to a few mean boys on the block as Miss Effing Crazy. She is an ex–science professor, a self-employed suburban spy, and an early dementia patient who regularly calls me Sue—not because of my past, but because it is her only daughter's name, the one who lives in New Jersey, who had decided when her mother turned eighty, *What the hell, out of sight, out of mind.*

"Hey, you snuck up on me," I say. "How's it going today?"

In her right hand, Effie proffers a small, oblong item wrapped in aluminum foil so crinkled that it could have been reused since the Depression. In her left hand, a vase of flowers, in the tight professional array of a florist. None of the flowers are yellow and black. On her head, the floppy blue-checked sun hat that Charlie and I bought from a beach vendor in Galveston four summers ago as a gift. Effie's eyes, still those of a provocative teen, peer out of a face toughened by sun.

"I made you some banana bread. Threw some bulgur in it. And I brought in these flowers for you this morning. I saw the guy plop them on your front porch. Thought the wind might blow 'em over. Plus, I've got a problem to discuss with you."

"That was so nice. Thank you." I twist the second lock. The deadbolt is a little cranky, too. *Need to take care of that. Maybe add a third lock.* I shove open the door and Effie tramples after me in her battered green Crocs without invitation.

"Let me stick these groceries away." I avert my eyes from the flowers. "Go ahead and put the flowers and bread here on the counter, and then you can tell me about your . . . problem. I have iced tea in the fridge. Charlie brewed it last night. Caffeine, sugar, mint, lemon—the works. Charlie stole the mint from your garden after dark."

"I put bulgur in the bread because I know Charlie especially likes it. And I'll take that tea."

I am pretty sure my daughter has no idea what bulgur is, but this is likely a step up from last week's offering of oatmeal and carob cookies that Charlie cheerfully likened to eating cow manure.

Effie fancies herself as something of a chef. The problem is, she thinks like a scientist. For instance, deciding it would be a good idea to boil fresh pumpkin for pumpkin pie rather than using a time-tested can of Libby's puree. Chunks and pumpkin strings and *a lot* of canned whipped cream are what I will remember about last year's Thanksgiving dinner. But that's OK: Most Thanksgivings just flow into a dull, pleasant river, and Charlie and I will laugh about that one forever.

"*The New York Times* called bulgur 'a wheat to remember,'" Effie informs me. "They try to make everything so damn profound. I'd stop reading the paper if it weren't for the science section and if I didn't think the crossword puzzles were reviving my dead brain cells.

What the hell do they know? Dead isn't necessarily dead. Do you think *they* know a four-letter word for Levantine coffee cup?" *They* generally referred to her neurologist.

"Zarf," I say automatically.

"Well, you're the damn exception to a damn lot of things." She wanders from the black granite bar that divides the tiny kitchen from the living room and surveys the industrial Bernina sewing machine on the dining room table, draped like a bride in white tulle. "What's this week's project? Something else for one of those damn rich ladies?"

I kick the refrigerator door shut. "For one of those damn rich ladies' little girls. A tutu. For competition. Tulle underpinning, lavender appliqué. Swarovski crystals."

"Fancy-pantsy. I bet she's paying you a fortune."

In fact, she isn't paying me a fortune, because it's a sad fact that most damn rich ladies no longer appreciate the cost of things made by exacting, artful hands. Not when everything can be purchased from China with the click of a mouse.

"It's a little side job," I say. "The costume designer for a Boston ballet company has asked me to dress the leads for its spring production. I want to make sure I know what I'm doing before I say yes."

"They'd be lucky to have you. You're getting quite global. I thought you were leaving this week to design a staircase for that crazy actor fellow in California, the one who farts through his movies. Doesn't he want it made out of an old Camaro or some damn thing? And wasn't Charlie's soldier daddy flying in to stay with her while you were gone? The one who promised to patch that spot on my roof. What's his name? Lucifer?"

"Lucas. That California job's on hold for now." No explanation, because my past is never discussed. Effie knows about that part of me, or she doesn't. I have no idea and want to keep it like that. Either way, it isn't *important* to her.

I can always tell by the way someone looks at me the first time, like I'm a distressing piece of modern art. As an added piece of luck for me, Effie had mostly cut the newspaper out of her life because it made her think the world was "going to damn hell in a damn rocket ship."

That didn't mean she canceled her subscription. During the four years we'd lived in this house, she had dropped *The New York Times* on our stoop with random regularity, unread, minus the puzzle. No iPad crosswords for Effie, despite Charlie's best efforts. Effie was certain the device was controlling her, instead of the other way around.

I nudge her over to the couch. "Sit. What's the problem?"

"Aren't you going to open the card on those flowers? What's the occasion? Belated birthday?" Her eyes are lit with curiosity.

"No occasion I'm aware of. Did you say you saw who left them?" I drop the question as casually as I can. Flowers always punched a little panic button, because anyone who liked me well enough to send them, wouldn't.

"Cute fellow in a Lilybud's Florist outfit. His shorts hung off his bottom. Gave me an eyeful."

Effie could have seen that bottom today. Or yesterday. Or a month ago. *Time* is a dull, pleasant river for Miss Effie.

I tap her on the shoulder; I'd need to pick up Charlie from volleyball practice soon and she would be craving something besides bulgur-infused banana bread. "So what's the problem?" I repeat. "Shoot."

"There's a digger snatcher." She waves a small garden trowel, which I hadn't noticed until now. "I'm going to take it up with the neighborhood watch."

"Digger . . . snatcher?"

"I just drove to Walmart to buy this one—$2.99 plus tax. Been going on for six months. I buy a digger, and it disappears. I can't keep buying diggers. Do you know where your digger is? I'm thinking of taking a block digger survey."

"Um." I have to think about whether I want to answer. "Behind the house. I think I left it there when I was . . . doing a little weed-ing." Stuck upright in the ground, like a grave marker.

"I'm warning you, you might as well be leaving out a crisp $100 bill."

"I'll keep an eye out. Do you have a place . . . you regularly put your digger?" I ask this cautiously, knowing that organization is a sensitive topic for Effie.

Things in her house have a way of dancing around: a *Scientific American* on genetic engineering stashed in the freezer, the extra house key taped to the bottom of the butter dish, a bottle of Stoli vodka crammed under the bathroom sink with the rusty can of Comet from 1972.

"Well, back to sorting my seedpods." Effie stands. "The grubs ate my beans something terrible last year. I'm going to try putting out a bowl of beer for them this year. I'm sure that's pure bunk but it seems like a happier way to go than me stomping their guts out. I wouldn't mind drowning in a bowl of beer when it's my time."

I laugh. Reach over and give her a hug. "Thanks for making my life . . . normal," I say.

"Honey, I'm a sweaty mess." She meekly returns my hug. "Most people think I'm pretty weird." *Most people* generally meant her daughter.

"Well, I can relate. What kind of person builds staircases for fart-ing actors?" *What kind of person suppresses the flutter in her chest every time the sun goes behind a cloud, afraid she's going blind? Or when she opens a jar of peanut butter? When someone yells "Susan!" across a playground?*

On her way to the door, Effie pauses. "Can you send Charlie over in about a half-hour to help me and my hysterical society lady friend move some stuff? I mean, historical. Although she *is* a bit hysterical. These ladies need to get their heads out of their damn bustles, if you get my drift."

"Of course." I grin. "I'll tell Charlie."

From the stoop, I watch her navigate across the thick carpet of golden brown Bermuda, disappearing into her overgrown front garden until all that's visible is her hat bobbing like a bluebird above a mound of fountain grass.

For sixty-one years, Effie has occupied the frilly yellow house next door, a Queen Anne cottage that, like our 1920s Arts and Crafts bungalow, sits in the middle of Fort Worth's famous historical Fairmount District. Effie can't remember the exact number of paint colors she's slapped on her spindlework and fish scale shingles over time, but she dates things by saying, *When the house was lilac,* or *When the house was in its awful brown period.* Effie still pulls her Cadillac boat out of the garage to attend the neighborhood monthly historic preservation meeting. She revels in dragging Charlie, one eyeball at a time, away from her iPhone and assaulting her with neighborhood history. The trolley once rumbled down our street, which is why it is wider than most of the others. Over on Hemphill, there used to be a fantastical mansion with a life-size windmill on top, until it mysteriously burned to the ground.

When the phone inevitably reasserts its magnetic force on Charlie, Effie just brings out the hard stuff: tales about Butch Cassidy and the Sundance Kid, who lived in Hell's Half Acre only three miles from here, or the creepy, boarded-up pig tunnels that run under the city. "That's how Judas goats got their name," Effie asserts. "By herding pigs to slaughter to spare themselves. Back when, goats herded as many as ten thousand pigs a day through Fort Worth's underground tunnels to their miserable fates in the Stockyards. Like New Yorkers in the subway."

Generally, when it came down to Effie vs. Twitter, Effie won. "Kids need a sense of place," she liked to admonish me. "A sense that they all aren't living and talking in outer space."

Back in the kitchen, I firmly root myself in the uncomfortable present, on the one kitchen stool that obediently twirls little half-circles. I sip my tea and stare at the card on the flowers. It begs to be opened. I reach over, tug it off its plastic holder, lift the tiny flap, and pull out a flat cardboard square decorated with a cartoon spray of balloons.

I miss you.
Love, Lydia

The card slips from my hand onto the counter. The corner begins melting into the ring of sweat left by my iced-tea glass. Lydia's name blurs into a purple stain. Not the handwriting I remembered, but maybe it isn't hers. Maybe it is the florist's.

Why would Lydia casually send me flowers? Wouldn't she understand that I'm still in mortal daily combat with them? That I'm hanging on to the bitter shreds of our fight after the trial? We hadn't talked for seventeen years, since her family up and left without a word. The flowers seem like a taunt.

I yank the arrangement out of the vase, splashing my jeans in the process, and slide open the glass door to the back yard. Within seconds, pink Gerbers and purple orchids are scattered on top of the funeral pyre of my compost. I carry the vase to the recycling bin sitting empty outside the two-car garage that backs up along our fence line. Bemoan that Charlie should have taken in the recycling bin two days ago.

No reason to panic and think my monster sent these and signed Lydia's name. I open the gate to the slim ribbon of grass that is our side yard. SpongeBob's squeaky voice wafts from an open window next door. That means the babysitter is inside, not the fussy lawyer parents with matching Tesla sedans.

I learned a long time ago to pay attention to what is usual, and what is not.

To retrieve an encyclopedia from the smallest sound.

I round the corner. No one has planted any more black-eyed Susans under my bedroom windowsill. The ground is smoothed flat and swirled, like a pan of chocolate cake batter. The thing is, I hadn't done any smoothing or swirling.

And my digger is gone.

Tessie, 1995

"If you had three wishes, what would they be?" he repeats.

His latest game.

The curtain had gotten us nowhere last time. I had no clue why I was drawing it. I had told him that it was an ordinary curtain. Still, like there was no breeze. When I didn't bring in my drawings today, he didn't bring it up. He noted my boundaries, unlike the others, but he's irritating me in whole new ways. For instance, now insisting I show up for his little interrogations twice a week.

"Really?" I ask. "Let me see. Do you want me to say that I wish my mother would come down from her puffy cloud and give me a hug? That I wish I wasn't living in some kind of Edgar Allan Poe poem? That I wish my three-year-old cousin would stop snapping his fingers in my face to see if he can magically make me see? That I wish my father would yell at the TV again? I need a whole lot more wishes than three. How about this: I wish I weren't *answering this stupid question.*"

"Why do you want your father to yell at the TV?" A trace of amusement in his voice. I relax a little. He isn't mad.

"It was his favorite thing. Yelling at Bobby Witt when he makes one of his wild throws. Or walks somebody. Now Dad just sits there like a zombie when the Rangers play."

"And do you think that's your fault?"

The answer to this is too freakin' obvious.

I wish I'd never met Roosevelt, so I wouldn't have needed to buy a Snickers bar, so I wouldn't have been walking out of that drugstore at 8:03 P.M. on June 21, 1994. I wish I never cared about winning, winning, winning.

"It's interesting that you bring up Poe." Already moving on.

I'd bite on that one. "Why?"

"Because most people on that couch who've endured a psychic trauma compare their experiences to something in more current pop culture. Horror movies. Crime shows. I get a lot of Stephen King. And John Paul. When did you start reading Poe?"

I shrug. "After my grandfather died. I inherited a lot of his books. My best friend and I got into them for a while. We read *Moby-Dick* that summer, too. So don't go there, OK? It doesn't mean anything. I was a happy person before this happened. Don't focus on things that don't mean anything."

"Poe was mired in his lifelong fear of premature burial," he persists. "The reanimation of the dead. His mother died when he was young. Don't you think that could be more than coincidence?"

A hammer is pounding my brain. *How did he know?* Just when I thought he was an idiot, he surprised me. He was always going somewhere.

"Do you want to tell me about it?" he asks.

Oscar picks that moment to readjust himself. He licks my bare knee on the way back down. Aunt Hilda yells at him idiotically all the time, "No lick! No LICK!" but I love his slobber. And right now, it is like he is saying, *Go ahead, take a chance with this one. I want you to throw the Frisbee to me someday.*

"The college girl from East Texas . . . Merry or Meredith or whatever." I speak haltingly. "She was alive when they dumped us in that grave. She *talked* to me. I remember her both ways. Dead and alive." With eyes like blue diamonds and with eyes like cloudy sea glass. Maggots hanging out in the corners, twitchy pieces of rice.

He doesn't answer immediately. I realize this is not at all what he was expecting.

"And the police have told you that's not possible," he says slowly. "That she was already dead when you were in that grave. That she'd likely been dead for hours before you were dumped."

How carefully my doctor had read everything about this case.

"Yes. But she was *alive* in the field. She was nice. I could feel her breath in my face. She sang. And she was in the church choir, remember?" Begging him to believe me, and I am only telling him the least crazy part. "She told me her mother's name. She told me all of their mothers' names."

I wish I remembered them.

Tessa, present day

I am waiting for the morning bomb to go off. Or not. I have made coffee and buttered a piece of bulgur-banana bread, listened to Charlie blast music in the shower, loosely sketched an appliqué design for the tutu, thought about how lucky I am.

Because, make no mistake, I am terrifically lucky. If I ever forget, the Susans remind me, in chorus. And the bread isn't half-bad.

"Mom!" Charlie's shriek carries easily from inside her room. "Where's my blue jersey?"

I find Charlie in her underwear, hair slapping around like wet red string. She is tossing her room, a rabbit's nest of dirty clothes.

"Which jersey?" I ask patiently. She owns two practice uniforms and four game uniforms. The uniforms were "required to play," cost $435, and three of them looked exactly alike to me.

"Blue, blue, blue, didn't you hear me? If I don't have it for the scrimmage, Coach will make me run. He might make the whole team run because of me." Coach. No last name necessary. Like God.

"Yesterday, he threw Katlyn out of practice for forgetting her red socks. She was so *embarrassed*. And it was just because her mom washed them and accidentally stuck them in her brother's baseball basket. He's on a team called the *Red* Sox. Duh."

I pull something blue out of the tangle of clothes on the floor. "Is this it?"

Charlie is now spread-eagled and lying faceup on her unmade bed, deciding whether the world is ending. She cranes her neck slightly in my direction. I note that her backpack is open on the desk, unpacked, biology homework still flayed out. The digital clock on her dresser says nineteen minutes to go before my friend Sasha and her daughter pick her up for school.

"Mom! No! It's the one with the *white* number and that cool edging at the bottom. The *practice* jersey."

"Yes, I should have read your mind. Have you looked in the washer? Dryer? Floor of the car?"

"Why does this have to happen to *me*?" Still staring at the ceiling. Not moving. I could say, *I'm done. Good luck.* Walk out. When I shouted that very same question of the world at the tender age of sixteen, "Coach" would have seemed like a wasp to swat. Hard to believe I'd only been two years older than Charlie is now.

The very best thing about landing in that grave? Perspective.

So I peer through this morning's prism: a science test looming in second period, an a-hole of a coach who probably could have used more childhood therapy than I got, and a telltale tampon under my foot.

I consider the clawed tiger on the bed, the one wearing the zebra-printed sports bra—the same tiger that every Sunday night transforms into the girl who voluntarily walks next door to help sort Miss Effie's medicine into her days-of-the-week pill container. The one who pretended her ankle hurt one day last week so the backup setter on her volleyball team would get to play on her birthday.

"It was a really kind gesture," I had told her that night when she explained why she did not need the ice pack. "But I'm not sure it was such a good idea."

Charlie had performed her usual eye roll. "Mom, you can't let the wrong stuff happen all the time. There is no way Coach would have ever let her play. And she set three points right after that. She's just as good as me. I'm just two inches taller."

I can't count the times that Charlie has offered me her bits of tempered wisdom along with a little frightening Texas grammar.

"Dry your hair, get dressed, pack up," I order. "You have a little over fifteen minutes. I'll find the jersey."

"What if you don't?" But her legs are in motion, swinging over the side of the bed.

Eight minutes later, I find the jersey behind her hamper. White number 10 on the back, nearly invisible edging along the bottom. Strong odor of sweat and deodorant. Apparently, she'd made a half-hearted effort to put it where it belonged. No wonder we hadn't found it.

I stick it in her duffle by the front door and check for red socks. Two short honks chirp from outside.

Charlie appears. "Did you find it?"

"Yep." She looks so perfect to me that it hurts. Damp curls that hadn't been sacrificed to a Chi Ultra flat iron springing up like tiny flames. Lip gloss only, so the freckles are out. Jeans, plain white T-shirt, the St. Michael charm that she never takes off nestled in her throat. Her father mailed it last Christmas from overseas, a design from James Avery, the kingpin of tasteful Christian fashion accessories. He started selling his stuff out of a two-car garage in the Texas Hill Country in 1954. Now, six decades later, his jewelry is both holy and pricey.

But for Charlie, this piece of metal out of a Kerrville factory isn't a status symbol. It is a talisman, a sign that her daddy, in the guise of a sword-carrying saint around her neck, will keep her safe. Keep all of us safe. Lucas had worn the good luck charm as long as I'd known him, a gift from his own mother the first time he went to war.

"You're good to go," I say. "You look especially pretty. Good luck on your test."

She slings the duffle over her shoulder and glances over my breakfast offerings on the table by the door.

"Nice try, but not takin' the booger bread." She slips the granola bar and the banana into the side pocket of her backpack. Another toot of the horn. Effie will be peering out her living room window at this point.

"This day *sucks*." Charlie spins out the door, leaving the air charged and a chaotic trail from the bathroom floor to her room.

I catch the slamming screen in time to toss a wave to Sasha, whose face is hidden by the harsh glint of sun off the windshield of the familiar blue minivan. The glass is black, impenetrable. I can't tell if she is waving back.

That doesn't mean I need to run out and check that she isn't bleeding on the ground, out of sight, behind the live oak, tossed out of the vehicle while she waited patiently for Charlie. That a stranger, with all of Effie's stolen diggers stacked in the trunk, isn't necessarily behind the wheel, about to drive my fire-breathing angel off to hell.

I shut the door and lean back against smooth, cool wood. Breathe in deep. Hope that other, more normal moms harbor similar out-of-control thoughts about their children's safety.

I wrap up the rejected slice of Effie's bread, generously lathered in strawberry cream cheese, and stick it in the refrigerator. Lunch, maybe. Wash up my coffee cup and set it to drain.

For the next ten minutes, the erratic whirring of the sewing machine breaks the silence. My foot, pressing the pedal. Fingers manipulating satin. Stop. Start. Stop. Start. The background noise of my childhood before Mama died.

Not the scrape of saw against bone.

My mind is not traveling in a row of tiny perfect stitches. It is skipping, out of order, to the places he has planted black-eyed Susans. My eyes close for a second and the stitches derail and zigzag like a train off track.

The list I'd made a couple of days ago is taped to the bottom of the vegetable drawer. Shades of Miss Effie.

In forty-five minutes, I am pressing the pedal of my Jeep.

———

Long after Lydia and I broke apart, I had returned to this place. Again and again. Maybe hoping a little bit that she would, too.

Until I stopped.

It is different, and the same. The ducks sail on the shivering glass. Aimless. Waiting for the day's first crust of bread to hit the pond.

My car is slung, alone, by the side of the road. Lydia and I had usually ridden the bus here, from Hemphill to West Seventh.

My feet are soundless on the earth. About here is when they used to pick up speed, ready for takeoff.

Lydia was always talking, laughing, talking while we traveled this path. Telling me what library book she'd dragged along with her dad's soft old green hunting blanket and an already lukewarm can of Diet Dr Pepper.

The Unbearable Lightness of Being.

Diana: Her True Story.

There's a slight breeze rustling things. Half of the leaves on the hackberries and pecans are still trying to make up their minds. Is it winter or not? When Lydia and I walked here, the trees were leafy and thick. They blocked the blazing sun like a tight football huddle, casting a dark, intimate comfort that I wonder if only a Southerner can understand.

Anybody watching would think I was up to no good. If it were two hours later, when bread crusts were flying through the air, parents would tug their children away from the strange lady walking around with the rusty shovel. They might even press the non-emergency police number tucked in their contacts that they'd never used before.

On days like these, I wondered if they'd be right. Whether just two or three brain cells were deciding if I was eligible to join the woman by the tracks who lived in a tent crafted of black garbage bags and old broom handles.

This is why I brought no one with me. Not Jo, who would make no mistakes as she sealed the evidence. Not Bill, who would be worried we should have brought Jo. I am sane, and I am not, and I don't want anyone to know.

What was that Poe quote that Lydia liked so much? *I became insane with long intervals of horrible sanity.*

The ducks and the pond are well behind me now. I hear the rush of the ocean. Of course, it is not the ocean. It's just what Lydia and I closed our eyes and pretended. The only nearby route to the ocean is the Trinity River, which threads by the park on the other side and flows on for hundreds of miles, all the way to Galveston. *La Santisima Trinidad*—The Most Holy Trinity. Christened by Alonso de León in 1690.

Sense of place, Effie says.

I begin to count the pillars. One, two, three, four. Five. The ocean is above me now. I keep striding, toward a red cow in a purple dunce hat. He's new.

It takes a second to realize that he's a unicorn, not a stupid cow. The mermaid who keeps him company a few feet away has red hair that flows like mine and Charlie's. Her bright green tail floats in a sea of fish with upturned mouths that wouldn't think of biting. Peace, love, understanding.

None of this hopeful art was here all those years ago, when Lydia laid out her blanket under pillar No. 5 of the Lancaster Bridge. Now childlike graffiti covers every single concrete pier of the bridge as far as I can see. The pillars used to be splotched with ugly green paint and strangled with the kind of weedy vines that seem to need nothing to live.

The rush and rumble of traffic overhead.

The knowledge of a secret underground world.

The thrilling fear that all that throbbing chaos could crash down on you at any second, but probably wouldn't.

The worry about what might lurch out of the big thicket of woods nearby.

The same, the same, the same. The same.

I survey the parched dirt floor beneath the behemoth steel and concrete structure. Still unforgiving. Hard and bare. But he didn't plant the black-eyed Susans under the bridge at pillar No. 5, where I used to meet up with Lydia after my runs on the twisty running trails. He planted them *here*—a few feet away, under a large cedar elm at the edge of the woods. They appeared at a time of year when black-eyed Susans flourish, so I couldn't be sure. I just never came back after I found them. I was twenty-four, and Lydia and I had been estranged for seven years.

A slight rustle behind me. I jerk around. A man has emerged from behind the pillar. I grip the shovel, suddenly a weapon.

But he is not a man. He is tall and lanky, but no more than four-teen. Pale skin, slouchy jeans, faded Jack Johnson T-shirt. A black mini-backpack slung over his shoulder. There's a phone with a des-ert camouflage case clipped at his waist and what I'm pretty sure is a metal detector in his right hand.

"Shouldn't you be in school?" I blurt out.

"I'm home-schooled. What are you doing? You can't take plants out of here. It's still the park. You can only clip their leaves."

"Shouldn't you be home, then? Being schooled? I'm not sure your mother would like you along this side of the park." My nerves, no longer on high alert.

"I'm on a scavenger hunt. It's National Botany Celebration Day. Or something. My mom is over at the pond with my sister. Teaching her the wonders of duck vision. They see, like, four times farther than us or something."

His mother is close by. A *home-schooling* mother who probably has used the non-emergency police number in her phone many, many times. I have no desire to attract her attention.

There is no evidence of gathered botany anywhere on his person. "I didn't realize that botanists use metal detectors these days," I say.

"Funny." He surveys me while chewing a nail. "That's a really old shovel."

He isn't going away.

"What are you doing?" he repeats.

"I'm looking for something that . . . somebody might have left for me when I was younger. I would never steal plants on National Botany Day."

A mistake. Too friendly. Too truthful. The first light of curiosity in his eyes. He has pushed aside a brown tail of hair so I can see them. He is a nice-looking kid. Cute, even, if he adjusted the angle of his mouth a little more.

"Want me to help? Is there metal in it? A ring or something? I can run my wand. You wouldn't believe the stuff I've found in this park." He is already at my side, practically stepping on my feet, eager, the red light on his device blinking. Before I realize it, he is casually running the detector along my leg. Then the other one. Now he is roving up, toward my waist.

"Hey. Stop that." I jump backward.

"Sorry. Just wanted to be sure you weren't carrying. Knife, gun. You'd be surprised who I've met up with around here."

"What's your name?" I ask. My heart is beating hard, but I'm pretty sure his gadget did not roam high enough to disturb the metal device in my chest.

I'm beginning to wonder about the mother story. About the home-schooling.

"My name's Carl," he says lazily. "What's yours?"

"Sue," I lie.

He takes this brief exchange of names as a sign of collusion. With a professional air, he runs the detector over the area where there is the evidence of my feet trampling the weeds.

"Here?" he asks.

"About. I was going to dig in a two-foot area." *How do I get out of this? If I leave, he is sure to search on his own.*

"Whatever you're looking for . . . did an old boyfriend leave it?"

I shiver. "No. Not a boyfriend."

"The alarm ain't firing. There's nothing here." He sounds disappointed. "You want me to dig for you anyway?"

Great. I have become the highlight of National Botany Celebration Day.

"No. I need the exercise. But thank you."

He leans against a tree, texting. I can only hope it is not about me. In a few minutes, he wanders off without saying goodbye.

A half-hour later, I have hacked through the ancient piping of tree roots and dug a square hole about half the size of a baby crib, and a foot deep.

Carl is right.

There's nothing here.

I can't help but wonder whether he is watching. Not Carl. My monster.

On my knees, I rush to push the crumbly black earth back in place. It now looks like an animal's grave.

My phone chirps, a silly sound, but my heart lurches anyway.

A text. Charlie.

Sorry I was grouchy Mommy ☺

Charlie has passed her biology test.

I tuck the phone into my pocket and step into the deep shadows under the bridge. I think of the two girls who listened to the drone of traffic and imagined an ocean. Girls who had nothing more important to do than argue whether *Jurassic Park* could really happen and extol the virtues of Sonic drive-ins because they have hands-down the best ice for chewing. All of that, of course, before one of them ended up in a hole and the other one tried to pull her out.

Time to move on.

When I reach the pond, I see a mother kneeling beside a small child with a pink beret. The girl is pointing at a pair of ducks beak to beak in a staring contest.

Her delighted laugh trickles across the pond, rippling the water as it pulls more ducks her way. I see an old crazy quilt spread out behind her. A blue Igloo cooler.

What I don't see is Carl.

Tessie, 1995

He's jabbering.

Blah, blah. Jabber, jabber.

Apparently, it isn't that unusual to experience something paranormal after an *event*.

Other people talk to the dead, too. No big deal. He doesn't say it out loud, but I'm a *cliché*.

"The paranormal experience can happen during the event," he is saying. "Or afterward." *The event. Like it is a royal wedding or the UT–OU football game.* "The victims who survive sometimes believe that a person who died in the event is still speaking to them." If he says *event* one more time, I am going to scream. The only thing holding me back is Oscar. He is sleeping, and I don't want to freak him out.

"A patient of mine watched her best friend die in a tubing accident. It was especially traumatic because she never saw her surface the water. They didn't find her body. She was convinced her friend was controlling things in her life from heaven. Ordinary things. Like whether it would rain on her. People in circumstances similar to yours suddenly see ghosts in broad daylight. Predict the future. They believe in omens, so much so that some of them can't leave their houses."

Circumstances similar to mine? Is he saying that with a straight face? Surely, he is smirking. And, surely, it isn't a good idea right now to hold my head underwater with tangled fishing lines and human-eating tree stumps and silky, streaming strands of another girl's hair. Lydia's dad always warns us about what lies beneath the murky surface of the lake. Makes us wear scratchy nylon lifejackets in 103-degree heat no matter how much we sweat and whine.

"That's crazy," I say. "The rain thing. I'm not crazy. It happened. I mean I know *it happened*. She spoke to me."

I wait for him to say it. *I believe you think it happened, Tessie.* Emphasis on *believe*. Emphasis on *think*.

He doesn't say it. "Did you think she was alive or dead when she spoke to you?"

"Alive. Dead. I don't know." I hesitate, deciding how far to go. "I remember her eyes as really blue, but the paper said they were brown. But then, in my dreams they sometimes change colors."

"Do you dream often?"

"A little." *Not* going there.

"Tell me exactly what Meredith said to you."

"Merry. Her mother calls her Merry."

"OK, Merry, then. What's the first thing Merry said to you in the grave?"

"She said she was hungry." My mouth suddenly tastes like stale peanuts. I run my tongue over my teeth, trying not to gag.

"Did you give her something to eat?"

"That isn't important. I don't remember."

Oh my God, it's like I brushed my teeth with peanut butter. I feel like throwing up. I picture the space around me. If I throw up sideways, I spray the leather couch. Head down, it hits Oscar. Straight across, no holds barred, the doctor gets it.

"Merry was upset that her mother would be worried about her. So she told me her mother's name. Dawna. With an *a* and a *w*. I remember, like, being frantic about getting to Merry's mother. I wanted more than anything to climb out of there so I could tell her mom that she was safe. But I couldn't move. My head, legs, arms. It was like a truck was crushing my chest."

I didn't know whether Merry was alive, and I was dead.

"The thing is, I know how to spell her mother's name." I'm insistent. "*D-a-w-n-a,* not *D-o-n-n-a.* So it must have happened. Otherwise, how would I know?"

"I have to ask you this, Tessie. You mentioned the paper. Has someone been reading you the newspaper reports?"

I don't answer. It would get Lydia in a lot of trouble with Dad. With the lawyers, too, probably, who want me to testify "untainted" by media chatter. I overheard one of the assistants say, "If we have to, we can make this blind thing work in our favor."

I don't want anyone to take Lydia away.

"It is possible that you transposed time," the doctor says. "That you know the detail of her mother's name, how it was spelled, but found it out afterward."

"Is that common, too?" Sarcastic.

"Not *un*common."

He's checking off all the little crazy boxes, and I'm making a hundred.

The toe of my boot is furiously knocking against the table leg. My foot slips and accidentally kicks Oscar, who lets out a cry. I think that nothing in the past month has felt as awful as this tiny hurt sound from Oscar. I lean down and bury my face in his fur. *So sorry, so sorry.* Oscar immediately slaps his tongue on my arm, the first thing he can reach.

"My Very Energetic Mother Just Served Us Nine Pizzas." I murmur this into Oscar's warm body again and again, calming Oscar. Calming myself.

"Tessie." Concern. Not smirking now. He thinks he's pushed me too far. I titter, and it sounds loony. It's weird, because I really feel pretty good today. I just feel bad about kicking Oscar.

I raise my head, and Oscar resettles himself across my feet. His busy tail whacks like a broom against my leg. He's fine. We're fine.

"It's a mnemonic device," I say. "For remembering the planetary order."

"I don't understand."

"Mercury, Venus, Earth, Mars . . . My Very Energetic Mother . . ."

"I get that. But what does it have to do with Merry?" He's sounding really worried.

"Merry thought we should come up with a code to help me remember the names of the mothers of the other Susans. So I could find them later. Tell them that their girls were OK, too."

"And it had something to do . . . with the planets?"

"No," I say impatiently. "I was repeating the planet thing in the grave, trying to, you know, stay sane. Not black out. Everything was kind of spinning. I could see the stars and stuff." The moon, a tiny, thin smile. *Don't give up.* "Anyway, it made Merry think of the idea for a mnemonic device so I wouldn't forget the names of the other mothers. So I wouldn't forget. *N-U-S*, a letter for each mother. Nasty Used Snot. Or something. I remember *snot* was part of it. But I flipped the letters around and made a real word. *SUN*."

I've shocked him into silence again.

"And the other mothers' names? What are they?"

"I don't remember. Yet." It pains me to say this out loud. "Just the three letters. Just *SUN*. But I'm working on it." Determined. I run through names every night in bed. The *U*'s are the hardest. *Ursula? Uni?* I will not let Merry down. I will find the mother of every single Susan.

The doctor is twisting his mind around this.

I'm not such a cliché anymore.

"There were the bones of two other girls in the grave, not three," he says finally, as if logic has anything to do with this.

Tessa, present day

The three of us barely fit in the famous Dr. Joanna Seger's office. It isn't at all what I expect for a rock star scientist. The large window showcases a lovely view of the Fort Worth skyline, but Jo faces the door, welcoming the living. Her desk, a modern black chunk that almost swallows the whole space, is littered with forensic journals and paper. It reminds me of Angie's desktop in the church basement. The kind of desktop where passion is screwing organization and nobody's making the bed.

The signature piece rising out of the chaos: a Goliath computer running $100,000 worth of software. The HD screen displays a roller coaster of lime green and black bar codes. It's the rare spot of color except for the grinning Mexican death masks and the skeleton bride leering off a shelf like a grisly Barbie. The Mexicans, bless them, have always had a less squeamish, more realistic view of death. I'm guessing Jo can relate.

I'm afraid to peer too closely at what looks like a heart suspended in a glass box, because I'm pretty sure it is a heart suspended in a glass box. Preserved, somehow, with a putty hue. Its dull sheen reminds me of my trip to Dallas with Charlie to tour the Body Worlds exhibit, where dead humans are plasticized in polymer so we can gawk at our complex inner beauty. Charlie fought nightmares for a week after learning that this multi-million-dollar road show might be using corpses of prisoners executed in China.

I'm certain, certain, certain I do not want to know where this heart came from, either.

Lots of commendation plaques on the wall. Is that President Bush's signature?

Bill is scrolling through the email on his phone, ignoring me. He has pushed his chair so far back to accommodate his legs that he is almost in the doorway. My own knees are crammed against the desk, probably turning pink under my cotton skirt.

This is Jo's show, and we are waiting.

She is notched into her little cranny on the other side of the desk with her ear to the phone. She had the chance to say, "Sit, please," before it buzzed. "Uh-huh," she is saying now, after several minutes of listening. "Great. Let me know when you've finished up."

"Very good news," Jo announces as she replaces the receiver. "We have successfully extracted mitochondrial DNA from the bones of two of the girls. The femurs. We didn't have luck with the skull. We're going to have to try again, probably with a femur this time, although it was seriously degraded. We'll keep going at it. We won't give up. We'll find the right bone." She hesitates. "We've also decided we're going to pull DNA from some other bones. Just to be sure there weren't additional mistakes."

I can't think about this. More girls. The Susan cacophony in my head is loud enough.

I can, however, appreciate Jo's tenacity. My iPad has been very busy since I witnessed the bone cutting. This high-tech forensic lab might be a well-kept secret in Fort Worth, but not to crime fighters around the world. The building protrudes off Camp Bowie like a silver ship hull, with a cache of grim treasure: baby teeth and skulls and hip bones and jawbones that have traveled across state lines and oceans hoping for a last shot at being identified. This lab gets results when no one else does.

"That's great, Jo." There is weary relief in Bill's voice.

His tone reminds me that he is pushing a truck of bricks uphill every day with one hand and dragging me behind him with the other. This morning, I'd reluctantly agreed to ride along to meet the "expert" who is poring over my teen-age drawings. The detour to Jo's office was a last-minute surprise, and welcome. I could breathe freely for a few more minutes before I started inspecting the swirls in a curtain for a face. That is, I could breathe if my eyes stopped wandering to that heart in a box.

"That was my boss on the phone," Jo continues. "As we speak, the DNA of those two girls is being input into the national missing persons database. I don't want to get your hopes up. It's a useless hunt, obviously, if the families of the victims haven't also placed their DNA into the system for a match. The database wasn't even around when these girls went missing. Their families have to be ones who haven't given up hope, who are still bugging police and on their knees praying every night. You two are most definitely not on a movie set with Angelina Jolie, and please don't forget it."

I wonder how many times she has repeated this. Hundreds. Thousands.

Her left hand is doodling a drawing on the edge of a magazine. A DNA strand. It has tiny shoes. I think it is jogging. Or dancing.

"Six weeks until D-Day," Bill says. "But I've had less at this point with other cases and landed on top. Tell everybody thanks for persevering. Any detail about those girls' identities could provide more reasonable doubt. I want to pile it on at the hearing."

Jo's hand pauses. "Tessa, do you know anything about the forensic use of mitochondrial DNA? I'd like you to understand what we do here."

"A little," I say. "It comes only from the maternal side. Mother. Grandmother. I . . . read . . . that you were able to use it to identify the bones of one of John Wayne Gacy's victims thirty years later."

"Not me specifically, but this lab, yes. William Bundy. Otherwise known as Victim No. 19, because he was the nineteenth victim pulled from the crawl space under Gacy's house in Chicago. That was a very good day for his family. And science."

John Wayne Gacy. Put to death by lethal injection in 1994, a month and a half before my attack.

Jo's pen is moving again. Dancing DNA guy now has a partner. With high heels. Jo sticks the pen behind her ear. "Let me give you the twenty-five-cent science lesson I deliver to my sixth-grade tour groups. There are two kinds of DNA in our cells: nuclear and mito-chondrial. Nuclear DNA was the kind used way back in the O.J. trial, and, by the way, if you have a scintilla of doubt, they had him dead to rights. But that was a fresh crime scene. For older bones, we have come to depend on mitochondrial DNA, which hangs around longer. It is tougher to extract, but we're getting better all the time. You're exactly right: It remains identical in ancestors for decades. Which makes it perfect for cold cases, like this one. And *really* cold cases, like, say, the Romanovs, where forensic work finally disproved the myth that Princess Anastasia escaped from that cellar where her family was slaughtered. Science was able to prove that anyone who claimed to be her, or descended from her, was a liar. Another great case. It rewrites history."

I nod. I know plenty about Anastasia. Lydia had been fascinated with all of the romantic conspiracy theories—the ten women who claimed to be the only surviving daughter of Nicholas II and Empress Alexandra, who were executed with their children by the Bol-sheviks, like dogs. I'd also watched the convoluted, sanitized, entirely imagined, happily-ever-after Disney version of *Anastasia* while baby-sitting my six-year-old cousin, Ella. "Are you a princess, too?" Ella had asked when it was over. "Weren't you the girl who forgot?"

Bill moves restlessly. Impatient. "What about the hair, Jo?"

"Still in process. A little more red tape than we thought before we got the police to turn it over. Separate evidence box."

"The hair?" I ask. "What hair?"

"Do you really still not know the details of the case?" Bill asks impatiently. "The hair is one of two pieces of physical evidence used to convict Terrell. They found it on the muddy jacket on the farm road." Muddy jacket. Bloody glove. Suddenly I was back in O.J. Land.

"I've made it a point not to read much about the case," I say stiffly. His frustration with me hurts. "It was a long time ago. I was only in that courtroom when I testified. I don't remember a hair."

Jo is examining me carefully, her pen stilled. "The hair was red."
My hair.

"It was brought up at the last minute at trial. The prosecution expert examined it under a microscope and testified that it belonged to you. He was just one hundred percent damn *sure* it came off your head. It was the kind of junk science used back then. It is impossible to match a hair to a specific person by looking at it under a microscope. The only way is through DNA analysis. Which we are now doing."

Yet . . . only 2 percent of the population has red hair. My grandmother had drilled that into me. First, after she caught me hacking off my orange locks with scissors at age four and then again six years later when I tried to dye it gold by squeezing thirteen lemons over my head and sitting like a piece of salmon in the Texas sun.

Red hair was something else that made me lucky. *Special.*

"I know about the jacket, of course," I say steadily. "I know about the ID from the person who saw . . . Terrell . . . hitchhiking by the field. I just didn't know about the hair." *Or I forgot.*

Bill stands abruptly. "Maybe you also *don't know* that seventy percent of wrongful convictions overturned on DNA involve eyewitness misidentification. That the jacket found on the road was a size too small for Terrell. And the red hair on the jacket? It was stick straight. If your school pictures are any indication, you looked like you were growing Flamin' Hot Cheetos curls. It could have been a poodle hair, for Christ's sake."

Poodles *have* curly hair. And I don't think red poodles exist. Although Aunt Hilda once dyed hers blue.

But I understand his anger. The need to lay it on.

I know what he's thinking, although he isn't saying it out loud. The real reason Terrell Darcy Goodwin lost the last seventeen years of his life isn't because of a red hair or a jacket tossed carelessly by the side of the road or a woman who thought she could see in the dark while she was whizzing by in her Mercedes.

The real reason Terrell Darcy Goodwin sits on Death Row is because of the Black-Eyed Susan who testified, scared out of her mind.

Tessa, present day

I could have lived very happily with the idea of never, ever again. Never again plunking down on a therapist's couch. Never again thinking about my manipulative drawings of the girl running in the sand and the girl without the mouth. Never again fighting this sick feeling that the other person in the room wants to take a paring knife and slowly carve out my secrets.

Dr. Nancy Giles almost immediately ushered Bill out the door, politely telling him he would be in the way. Actually it wasn't all that polite. The fact that she is a beautiful gazelle-like creature probably took the edge off. Bill grumbled about being banned in such a little-boy manner that it made me think the two of them had known each other intimately for a long time, although he failed to mention it on the ride over.

My grandfather once told me that God puts pieces in the wrong places to keep us busy solving puzzles, and in the perfect places so that we never forget there is a God. At the time, we were standing on a re-mote stretch of Big Bend that was like a strange and wondrous moon.

Dr. Giles's face may be the human equivalent, a glorious land-scape of its own. Velvet brown skin with eyes dropped in like glitter-ing lakes. Her nose, lips, cheekbones—all chiseled by a very talented angel. She understands her beauty and keeps things simple. Hair cropped into a bob. A well-cut blue suit with a skirt that strikes her mid-knee. Gold strings dangle from her ears, with a single large antique pearl at the end of each that dances every time she moves her head. I guess her age to be creeping toward seventy.

Her office, though, is like the favorite fat uncle who wears loud shirts and offers up a slightly smashed Twinkie from his pocket. Walls the color of egg yolk. A red velour couch, with a stuffed elephant plunked in the corner for a pillow. Two comfy plaid chairs. Low-slung shelves shooting out a riot of color, crammed with picture books and Harry Potter and Lemony Snicket, American Girl dolls of every ethnicity, trucks and plastic tools and Mr. and Mrs. Potato Head. A table topped with a tray of markers and crayons. An iMac at i-am-a-Child level. A refrigerator door riddled with the graffiti of children's awkward, happy signatures. Off to the side, a basket loaded with snacks both forbidden and polyunsaturated, and no mother to smack your hand.

My eyes linger on the framed prints—not your usual doc-in-a-box muted abstractions. Instead, Chagall's magical, musical animals and the loveliest blue ever imagined. Magritte's steam engine shooting out of a fireplace, and his giant green apple, and men in bowler hats floating up like Mary Poppins.

Perfect, I think. If anything is surreal, it is childhood.

"My usual customer is a little younger." Dr. Giles says it with good humor. She has misinterpreted my roving eyes, still on the hunt for my own grim artwork. I tell my nerves to shut up, but they don't. My sweaty hands are probably stickier than the five-year-old who skipped out of the room with a dripping green Popsicle right before I stepped in.

"I'm not sure we can accomplish exactly what William wants, are you?" She has placed herself on the other side of the couch, crossing one knee over the other, her skirt inching up slightly.

Relaxed. Informal.

Or purposeful. Rehearsed.

"William has always set near-impossible goals, even when he was a boy," she continues. "The older I get, and the more horrors I've seen, my goals have become . . . less specific. More flexible. More patient. I like to think that is because I am wiser, not tired."

"And yet . . . he brought me to you," I say. "With a deadline. For very specific reasons."

"And yet he brought you to me." Her lips curve up again. I realize how easily that smile could melt a child, but I am no longer a child.

"So your plan is *not* for us to look at my drawings together."

"Do we need them? This is going to disappoint William, but I don't think you wrote the killer's name in the waves in the ocean. Do you?"

"No." I clear my throat. "I do not." I wasn't sure whether this was true. One of the first things I did the night after my sight returned was to examine every swirl of the brush. Just in case. *Who knows what the unconscious mind will paint?* Lydia had asked rather dramatically.

"I find that drawings after a trauma like yours are often widely misinterpreted." Dr. Giles reaches for the stuffed elephant tucked behind her, which is preventing her from leaning back. "There is a lot attached to the use of color, and the vigor of the pen. But a child may use blood red in his drawing simply because it's his favorite color. The drawing only represents the feeling on that day, at that very moment in time. We all hate our parents on some days, right? A scratchy, angry version of a father doesn't mean he is an abuser, and I'll never testify to things like that. So I use the drawing technique, but mostly as a way to allow young patients to get out their emotions so they don't eat away at them. It is much, much harder to say the words. I'm sure I don't have to tell you that."

"Dr. Giles . . ."

"Please. Nancy."

"Nancy, then. Not to be rude . . . but why exactly did you take Bill up on this request? If you don't believe there is really anything there to talk about." *Does she know that more than half of my drawings are faked? Do I need to tell her?*

Jo's chilling, detached lesson on bones, that damn heart in a box, the pink elephant perched beside us who knows way too much about the terrible, terrible things people do—it's about all the reality I can take today.

In an hour and a half, I will be planted in the stands at Charlie's volleyball game, surrounded by weary moms who will scream their throats raw, where the most important thing isn't worrying about the Middle East's urgent signs of Armageddon, or the 150 million orphans in the world, or glaciers melting, or the fate of all the innocent men on Death Row.

It will be whether a ball touches the ground.

Afterward, I will pull a bag of carrot sticks out of the refrigerator, throw four Ham & Cheese Hot Pockets in the microwave, one for me and three for Charlie, toss in a load of clothes, and attach white gauze to lavender silk. These are the pricks of light that have kept me mostly sane, mostly happy, day after day.

"Don't misunderstand me," Nancy is saying. "I'm not at all sure your drawings are meaningless. Your case is . . . complicated. I very much appreciate your permission to view the doctors' notes on your sessions. It was helpful, although the notes from your last doctor were a little sparse. You were blind when you created many of those pictures, correct? Your doctor at the time clearly thought you were faking most of them." So she knows. Good. "He also believed that the two of you explored every avenue when it came to figuring out the drawings of the curtain. The drawings that were, essentially, the ones that you declared spontaneous and genuine."

She glances down at the beeper vibrating at her waist, checks the number, silences it. "So there are many reasons to discount the drawings. At least that was your doctor's assessment. Would you agree?"

"Yes." My throat is dry. *Where was this going?* And a random thought, *Should I have ever asked to see the doctor's notes?*

A Susan quickly chimes: *You don't want to know what he said.*

"Of course, it's always a little hard to know exactly what we are faking," Dr. Giles continues. "The subconscious is busy. The truth tends to creep through. I am, of course, drawn to the curtain. It reminded me of a famous case history that I thought would be worthwhile to share. It's ironic, or a sign if you believe in those, but the girl's name in this other case history is also Tessa. Her name has probably been changed and her story is far different, of course. She was a young girl who had been sexually abused in her home but was far too traumatized to name her abuser. The young girl drew a cutaway picture of her two-story house, so her therapist could see inside. She drew a number of beds on the top floor. The child said the beds were for all the many people living in the house. She drew a living room downstairs, and a kitchen with an oversized teakettle. But instead of asking the girl about the beds, the therapist asked the girl about the teakettle and why it was important. The girl told her that every morning, each member of the house would pour hot water out of that kettle for instant coffee as they left for school or work. So, using the teakettle, the therapist took the little girl through that awful day of the abuse. Tessa remembered, one at a time, who had used the teakettle that morning before leaving the house. The one person remaining, who didn't use it, is the one who stayed alone in the house with her. The abuser. The girl was then able to tell the story of what happened to her."

Against my will, this woman has mesmerized me.

"I can't know for sure," she says gently. "But I believe your ordinary object could be a similarly powerful tool. It belongs somewhere. We need to look around that place. If you like, we can try some exercises."

My head pounds. I want to say yes, but I'm not sure I can. Nothing, *nothing,* is ever what I expect.

She accurately interprets my silence. "Not today. But maybe soon?"

"Yes, yes. Soon."

"May I give you a homework assignment? I would like you to draw the curtain again from memory. Then call me. I'll make time." She pats my knee. "Excuse me for a minute."

She walks toward the closed door at the back of the room. I notice a slight arthritic limp. As the door cracks open, I glimpse her personal refuge—warm light and a large antique desk.

She is back quickly, proffering a business card. Nothing else in her hands. She is not returning my drawings—at least, not today. No cheating.

"I scribbled my cell number on the bottom," she says. "I did have one more question before you go, if that's OK."

"Sure."

"The drawing of the field. The giant flowers leering like monsters over the two girls."

Girls. Plural. *Two.*

"It means nothing," I say. "I didn't draw it. A friend of mine did. We drew together. She was in on my . . . deception. My partner in crime." I laugh awkwardly.

Nancy shoots me a strange look. "Is your friend OK?"

It seems like an unusual question. So many, many years have passed. Why does it matter?

"I haven't seen her since we were seniors in high school. She left town before we graduated, right after the trial." *She just disappeared.*

"That must have been hard." Every word is careful. "To lose a good friend so soon after the trauma."

"Yes." For more reasons than I want to explain. I am inching toward the door. Lydia is not a place I will go. Not today.

Yet Dr. Giles won't let me leave, not yet.

"Tessa, I believe the girl who drew that scene, your friend Lydia, was genuinely terrified."

"You said there were . . . two girls in that picture. I always thought there was one girl. Bleeding." A tiny, tiny red tornado.

"At first, so did I," she says. "The shapes are not distinct. But if you look closely, you can see four hands. Two heads. I believe one of the girls is a protector, crouching over the other one. I don't think that is blood from the attack of the flower monsters. I think the protector has red hair."

Tessie, 1995

It is hard, pretending not to see. It has been two days. I know that I can't keep it up very long, especially with my dad. I need some time to observe, to analyze body language. To know what everyone is really feeling about me when they think I'm not looking.

The doctor scribbles away at his desk, a scritch-scratching sound that makes me want to scream.

He glances up with a concerned frown to see if I might have changed my mind about talking. Or my pose. Arms crossed, staring straight ahead. I had marched in the room at our appointed time and told him that I was done. Done, done, *done*.

We had a *deal*, I'd reminded him.

No freakin' way was I doing hypnosis, where I float along like a dizzy bluebird and tell him secret things. I set out my rules from *the beginning*, and if it was so easy to erase this one from his mind, what else might he do? Offer up a happy cocktail? I'd read *Prozac Nation*. That girl was sad. So messed up. She wasn't me.

I didn't want to be like her, or Randy, the guy with the locker next to mine, wearing an Alice in Chains T-shirt every day, popping Xanax between classes and sleeping through high school. I had heard that his mother has breast cancer. I don't want to ask, but I am always sure to smile at him when we meet at the lockers. I get it.

Randy sent me a cute card at the hospital with a thermometer sticking out of a cat's mouth. He wrote inside, *Sometimes life is so unkind*. I wonder how long it took him to find that lyric. Alanis is plastered inside my locker, so he had to know. He probably couldn't find any Alice in Chains tunes that wouldn't tell me to go kill myself or something.

Lydia had caught on right away. Tiny clues. My Bible on the dresser opened to Isaiah instead of Matthew. The TV ever so slightly more angled toward my spot on the bed. The pink-and-green T-shirt that matched the leggings, and the brown and peach Maybelline eye shadow that I hadn't put on for a year. It wasn't just one thing, she said. It was all of them.

There were surprises, everywhere. My face in the bathroom mirror, for one. Everything about me, more angular. My nose juts out like the notch on my grandfather's old sundial. The half-moon scar under my eye is fading, more pink than red, less noticeable. Dad tentatively suggested a few weeks ago that we could talk to a plastic surgeon if I wanted, but the idea of lying there like Sleeping Beauty while a man with a knife stands over me . . . not ever gonna happen. I would rather people stare.

Oscar is even whiter than I imagined, although maybe that's just because everything seems a little blinding at the moment. He's the first thing I saw at the end of my bed the morning I opened my eyes for real—a pile of dove feathers with a head. I had called out his name softly. When his tongue slapped my nose, I knew for sure I wasn't dreaming.

There was no drama to my sudden transformation. I went to sleep, I woke up, and I could see again. The world had crept back into sharp and excruciating focus.

The doctor's still at it with the scritch-scratching at the desk. I twitch my eyes over to the clock on the wall. Nine minutes left. Oscar's sleeping at my feet, but his ears are flicking around. Maybe an evil squirrel dream. I kick off my sneaker and run my foot back and forth across his warm back.

The doctor notices my movement, hesitates, and puts down his pen. He makes his way slowly over to the chair across from me. I think again what an excellent job Lydia had done of describing him.

"Tessie, I want to tell you how sorry I am," he begins. "I didn't honor our agreement. I pushed you. It is everything a good therapist should *not* do, regardless of the circumstances."

I greet him with silence but keep my gaze locked over his shoulder. Tears, barely under the surface.

Because there are things I'd still rather not see. My brother's face after my dad talked to him quietly last night about his grades, which used to be straight A's. The medical insurance forms scattered all over the table like someone lost at poker and tossed the deck. The sad, bare state of the refrigerator, weeds choking the cracks in the driveway, tight lines curved around my father's mouth.

All of this, because of me.

I need to keep trying. I want to get better. I can see. Isn't that better?

Didn't this man asking for forgiveness right now probably have something to do with that? Shouldn't I let him score that victory? Don't we all make mistakes?

"What else can I say, Tessie, that might begin to restore your trust in me?"

I think he knows that I can see.

"You can tell me about your daughter," I say. "The one you lost."

Tessa, present day

The tutu is finished.

I steam it gently, even though it doesn't really need it. Charlie makes fun of me and my Rowenta IS6300 Garment Steamer. But Rowenta has probably been my best and most faithful therapist. She pops out of the closet about once a month and never asks a single question. She's mindless. Magic. I borrow her wand and all of the wrinkles disappear. Results are instant, and certain.

Except for today.

Today, a mobile spins in my head, dangled by an unseen hand. I'm transfixed by the pictures whizzing by. Lydia's face is on one. Terrell's is on another. They dance among yellow flowers and black eyes and rusty shovels and plastic hearts. All of them, strung together with brittle bone.

It has been two days since Dr. Nancy Giles of Vanderbilt/Oxford/Harvard interpreted Lydia's drawing, right after she had announced in no uncertain terms that she didn't put too much stock in Freudian crap.

Dr. Giles thinks something was wrong with *Lydia*. That Lydia perceived *me* as the protector. Which can't be. I never told anyone about the poem he left me in the ground by the live oak. Lydia drew the picture *before* the poem. I would have died without Lydia back then, not the other way around.

I need to see this drawing again, dammit. Why didn't Dr. Giles offer to show it to me? Did she think I was a liar? That I knew something I wasn't telling? As always, as soon as I left a therapist's office, the doubts wriggled out like slimy worms.

I miss you. That's what Lydia wrote on the flowers delivered to my home after all those years of silence. Unless she wasn't the one who sent them. What if they *are* from my monster? What if my silence killed her? What if, because I *didn't* warn her, he carried out the poetic threat so coyly buried by my tree house? *If you tell, I will make Lydia a Susan, too.* What if my denial and stupidity sacrificed both Terrell and her?

Terrell. I think about him all the time now. I wonder if he hates me, if his arms are thick from push-ups on concrete, if he has already thought about his last meal, just in case. Then I remember, he can't ask for a last meal. One of the guys who chained James Byrd Jr. to a pickup and dragged him to death ruined that for everybody. He requested two chicken-fried steaks, a pound of barbecue, a triple-patty bacon cheeseburger, a meat-lover's pizza, an omelet, a bowl of okra, a pint of Blue Bell, peanut-butter fudge with crushed peanuts, and three root beers. It was delivered before his execution. And then he didn't eat it. Texas said, no more.

I can rattle off this menu ordered by a racist freak, but can't remember the day my world blew apart. I can't remember a single thing that will save Terrell.

I glance out to my studio window, glinting at the top of the two-story garage in the corner of the back yard. I should go up there. Shut the blinds. Pull out my pencils and paints, and draw the curtain. Begin my homework.

The garage was renovated from crumbling disaster two years ago. Effie gave the plan her historical stamp of approval. Blue window boxes and straggly red geraniums for her, Internet and a security system connected to the house for me.

Cheerful. Safe.

The bottom level, which once housed the previous owner's blue 1954 Dodge, is jammed with my table saw and biscuit joiner, router and drills, nail gun and orbital sander, vacuum press and welder. The tools that curve cabinet doors like sand dunes and solder master staircases into a dizzy spiral. Machines that make my muscles ache and reassure me that I can take on a man, or a monster.

The top level was designed just for me. My space. For the quieter arts. It seemed so important—a real home for my drawing table, easels, paints, paintbrushes, and sewing machines. I splurged on a Pottery Barn couch and a Breville tea maker and a Pella picture window so that I could spy into the upper floors of our live oak.

The week after the nail pounding stopped, as I sat and sipped tea bathed in the studio's white, clean, new-smell glory, I realized that I didn't want *my* space. I didn't want isolation, or to miss Charlie's burst through the door after school. So I stuck with the living room. The studio turned into the place my little brother, Bobby, hangs out to write when he visits from his home in Los Angeles twice a year and where Charlie goes on the occasion when every word out of my mouth sets her nerves on fire. *I don't know why, Mom. It's not what you're saying. It's just that you're talking.*

This is the reason that the living room is piled with brocade fabric and designer dress patterns and bead carousels that mingle with Charlie's flip-flops and textbooks and misplaced earrings and itsy-bitsy "seahorse" rubber bands for braces. Why my daughter and I have an unspoken agreement not to speak about the state of the living room, unless it involves ants and crumbs. We clean it together every other Sunday night. It's a happy place, where we create and argue and refine our love.

The studio is crowded. My ghosts moved in right away, when I did, after the last stroke of linen white on the walls. The Susans feel free to talk as loudly as they want, sometimes arguing like silly girls at a sleepover.

I should climb the steps. Greet them with civility.

Draw the curtain. Find out whether it swings from a window in the mansion in my head where the Susans sleep. *Let them help.*

But I can't. Not yet. I have to dig.

I'm staring into a gaping hole again. This time, a swimming pool, empty except for a chocolate slurry of leaves and rainwater.

Feeling ridiculous. Disappointed. And cold. I pull up the hood of Charlie's Army sweatshirt. It's 5:27. I haven't stood in this place since Charlie and I lived here when she was two. Charlie has already texted the word *hungry* while I was driving the wrong direction on I-30 with a red pickup on my tail, and twenty minutes after that, *home,* and five minutes after that, *cool tutu,* and one minute after that *um?????*

I tried calling back, but no answer. Now the phone in my pocket is buzzing. The sun is dropping lower every second, a big orange ball going somewhere else to play. The apartment windows wink fire with the fading light, so I can't see in. I hope no one is staring down at the hooded figure in the shadows armed with a shovel.

"Why aren't you at Anna's?" I blurt into the phone, instead of *hello*. "You are supposed to be at Anna's." As if that would make it so.

"Her mom got sick," Charlie says. "Her dad picked us up. I told him it was OK to bring me home. Where are you? Why didn't you answer my texts?"

"I just tried to call you. I was driving. I got lost. Now I'm on . . . a job. In Dallas. Did you lock the doors?"

"Mom. Food."

"Order a pizza from Sweet Mama's. There's money in the envelope under the phone. Ask if Paul can deliver it. And look through the peephole before you answer to make sure it's him. And lock the door when he leaves and punch in the code."

"What's the number?"

"Charlie. You know the security code."

"Not *that* number. The number for Sweet Mama's."

This from the girl who last night Googled that Simon Cowell was the young assistant who polished Jack Nicholson's axe in *The Shining*.

"Charlie, really? I'll be on my way home soon. I'm late because . . . I thought I'd remember the way."

"Why are you whispering?"

"Pizza, Charlie. Peephole. Don't forget." But Charlie has already hung up.

She'll be fine. Was that me, or a Susan? Which of us would know better?

"Hey." A man with a weed eater is quickly approaching from the other side of the house. *Busted.* I lean the shovel against a tree, too late. Even at this distance, something about the way he carries himself stirs a memory.

"This is private property!" he shouts. "What do you think you're doing here with that shovel at dinnertime?" A drawl mixed with a threat and a reprimand about proper mealtime etiquette. A perfect Texas cocktail.

Because I'm scared of the dark. Because I think there are plenty of people with itchy fingers in this neighborhood who have a gun tucked in a drawer. I know I did.

"I used to live here," I say.

"The shovel? What's that for?"

I've suddenly figured out who he is, and I'm a little astonished. The handyman. The very same one who worked here more than a decade ago, who swore every day he was quitting. As I recall, he was a distant cousin of the grouchy woman who owned the place, a converted Victorian in East Dallas advertised as *a four-plex with character.* Translated: ornate crown molding that dropped white crumbs in my hair like dandruff, windows requiring Hercules to open them, and hot showers lasting two and a half minutes if I was lucky enough to beat the exercise freak on the first floor who woke up at 5 A.M.

The windows were why I took the place. No one crawling up and in. That, and the listing's promise of *Girls Only*.

"When did the owner take out the parking spaces and dig this swimming pool?" I ask. "Marvin? Is it Marvin?"

"You remember old Marvin, do ya? Most of the girls do. Pool went in about three years ago. It used to be a gravel lot with numbered signs where everybody had a spot. But then, you'd know that. Now everybody complains they have to fight it out in the street. And Gertie has stopped filling the pool. Says it's not worth the money and that Marvin don't keep the leaves out. Old Marvin's doing the best he can. When did you say you lived here?"

"Ten years ago. Or so." Vague. I'd forgotten his habit of addressing himself in the third person. It partly explains why he never found another job.

"Ah, the good old days, when these whiney college brats didn't call Marvin at 2 A.M. about how their Apples ain't connectin' to the Universe."

I shove the laugh back down in my throat and don't correct him. I pull the hood off so I can see better, and instantly realize the mistake. I toss my hair, trying to cover the side of my face with the scar. The toss is enough for Marvin to take renewed interest in me even though I'm in roomy black sweats and running shoes and not wearing a stitch of makeup. It must have been a slow day for him at the Girls Only House, which is the real reason I'm guessing he stays.

"I'm curious," I say hesitantly. "Did they find anything when they dug up the pool?"

"Ya mean like a dead body? Whoa, you should see your face. No bodies, sweetheart. Are you missing one?"

"No. No. Of course not."

Marvin is shaking his head. "You're just like those damn kids. Or maybe you're a scout for one of those ghost shows?"

"What kids?"

"The sorority that rents the apartment right up there on the left-hand corner every fall, thinking it is haunted. Use it to scare the shit out of their pledges. Drape skeletons dressed in see-through nighties out the window. Invite their rich frat boys and serve black-eyed-pea dip and trashcan punch, the stuff they vomit up on the front porch for me to clean up. Gertie started charging a premium to rent that apartment. But do you think she pays Marvin more? Nope. Marvin just has to suck it up and clean it up."

"Why do they think . . . there are ghosts?" As soon as the question rolls off my tongue, I regret it. *You know the answer.*

"Because of the girl who lived there a long time ago. The one who got away from the Black-Eyed Susan killer. We didn't even know it was her until a year and a half after she moved in. She was nice enough. Worked at a little design firm downtown. She complained a few times that we wouldn't let her gate up the staircase for her little girl. Gertie said it would take away the old house charm."

Suddenly, his face freezes.

"Jesus, you're that girl, ain't ya? You're the Susan that lived up there."

"My name isn't Susan."

"Shoulda known soon as I saw your red hair. Crap, no one is gonna believe this. Can Marvin take a picture? You're for real, right? Not a ghost?" For a second, he seems to be truly considering this.

Before I can think, the phone is out of his pocket, the button pressed. I am recorded, with flash, for all time, into infinity, about to be passed from phone to Facebook to Twitter to Instagram— Marvin's Universe and beyond.

"Great," he says to himself, peering at his phone. "Got the shovel in the background."

If my monster didn't know already, he will soon.

I am on the hunt.

A light blares from every window as I swing into our driveway around 7. Not a sign that Charlie is scared, I remind myself, just her habit of flipping lights on as she goes and never bothering to turn them off.

I spoke with Charlie about half an hour ago. A pizza with Canadian bacon and black olives had, indeed, been delivered, eaten, and deemed "solid." Everything seemed so normal on the other end of the line. Far, far removed from my disturbing encounter with Marvin. So much so that I had stopped at Tom Thumb to fill Charlie's texted list of special requests for her lunch: yelo cheez, BF (nt honey) ham, Mrs. B's white brd, grapes, hummus, pretz, mini Os.

"I'm home," I yell, kicking the door closed behind me. The security system is switched on. Check. Charlie had even cleaned up the pizza box from the coffee table in front of the TV, where I assumed she'd been sneaking in a Netflix rerun of something on my waffle-y *I don't really like you to watch shows like that* list.

But no Charlie. No backpack. The TV, warm. I pass through the living room and set the bag of groceries on the counter with my keys.

"Charlie?" Probably in her room, living inside Bose headphones while reluctantly tramping around nineteenth-century England with Jane Austen.

I knock, because Aunt Hilda never did. No answer. I crack her door. Shove it wide open. Bed unmade. *Pride and Prejudice* operating as a coaster for a water bottle. Clothes strewn everywhere. Her underwear drawer dumped on the bed. A streak of mud across the floor.

Pretty much as she left it this morning. But no Charlie.

The rest of the house sweep takes about a minute, plenty of time for sickening waves of panic to roll in. I thrust open the sliding glass doors to the back yard, yelling her name. She's not in the hammock along the back fence line, jerry-rigged from the thick trunk of the live oak to an ancient horse post that Effie had saved from a carpenter's axe. The studio windows gleam black above me; the garage doors are shut tight.

My phone. I need my phone.

I rush back inside and fumble for it in my purse. Clumsily punch in the new security code that I had to choose after the software update yesterday. Locked out. *Shit, shit, shit.* Try the four numbers one more time, slowly. Promise myself that I will never, ever update my phone again. Hit the icon.

And there it is, my one-word, God-sent reprieve.

@ Effie's

In seconds, I am banging wildly on Effie's door. It seems to take forever for her to answer it. She's cloaked in a long white nightgown with lace that strangles her neck. Gray hair, sprung from its usual braided bun, rains down to her waist. I'd peg her as a runaway from Pemberley if she were clutching a candle instead of the largest laminated periodic table I've ever seen.

"What in heaven's name is wrong?" Effie asks.

Be patient, be patient, be patient.

"Is Charlie here?" Breathless.

"Of course she is." Effie steps aside, and there's my girl, the most beautiful sight in the world, cross-legged on the floor by the coffee table, scribbling in a notebook. I pick up every detail: hair fanned out around her face like red turkey feathers, swept up by a chip clip; the volleyball shorts she's still wearing even though it's 50 degrees outside; the fuzzy pink pig slippers; the chipped gold glitter fingernail polish. Her lips are moving, exaggerated, like a silent film star. *Save me.*

"I was sitting a bit on the front porch swing and I saw a man roaming around our yards," Effie begins.

Pizza guy, Charlie is mouthing now. Her eyes are rolling and Effie's still chattering while all my brain can do is pound out, *He doesn't have her.*

". . . I thought about how your car was gone but the lights in the house were on. Got me concerned. I called and Charlie answered and I went right over and got her. I was just helping her with a little early chemistry prep for next year."

learned about Rebecca. *He was a freaking sadist,* she announced, while everyone seated near us stared at my little moon scar.

Rebecca was a single paragraph in the feature story summing up my doctor's life, which makes me unbelievably sad. My guess? He told the reporter that the subject of his daughter's disappearance was off the table.

He certainly made it clear it was off the table for us at our last session. A nice long silence followed my question about Rebecca. So I announced I liked the print of *The Reaper* hanging over his desk. "My grandfather went through a Winslow Homer wheat period," I said. And, oh yeah, I'm not blind anymore.

I couldn't tell if he was faking his surprise. The doctor appeared genuinely thrilled about what he declared a "major, major break-through." He had fiddled around with a silly old-fashioned eye test that involved a pencil and my nose. Asked me to close my eyes and describe his face in the greatest detail possible.

He reassured me again that even though he wouldn't discuss it with me, his daughter had absolutely nothing to do with the Black-Eyed Susan case. I had never asked that, but even if she does, I'm not at all sure at this point I want to know.

It's hard not to be a little happy. I've gained three pounds in five days. My dad and brother squeezed me so hard in a three-way hug when they found out I could see again that I thought my heart would burst in my chest. Aunt Hilda hustled over a three-layer German chocolate cake, gooey with her famous coconut pecan frosting, and I'm pretty sure it was the best thing I've ever eaten.

Last night, a brand-new hardback copy of *The Horse Whisperer* appeared on my bedside table, in a house where it is unheard of not to wait until a book comes out in paperback.

The trial is fifty-two days away. That means twelve more sessions or so, if I count a couple extra to wrap things up after the trial. The end is near. I really don't want to drag distractions, like Rebecca, into things. It was kind of a mean thing for me to bring up.

Unfortunately, Rebecca is now Lydia's latest obsession, and she's on a mission to hunt down more about her in other newspapers. Whatever she finds, I tell her, will be meaningless. *Rebecca was pretty, with a lot of friends. She was such a nice girl* and *It was such a nice family* and blah, blah, blah. I don't want to sound cold, but there it is.

I know, because I've read every possible exaggeration about my life since I became a Black-Eyed Susan. My mother died under "suspicious" circumstances and my grandfather built a creepy house and I am practically perfect. The truth? My mother was struck by a rare stroke, my grandmother was the crazier one, and I am not and never will be a heroine out of a fairy tale. Even though they were all victims first, too. Snow White poisoned. Cinderella enslaved. Rapunzel locked up. Tessie, dumped with bones.

Some monster's twisted fantasy.

Bet the doctor would like me to talk about that, I think, as he settles into his chair.

He smiles. "Fire away, Tessie."

Last week, he had agreed to let me lead in this session. He also promised he wouldn't tell my dad I'd faked blindness for a little bit. A promise kept so far. I wondered if he bargained with all of his patients. If this was *appropriate*.

It doesn't matter. Today I am prepared to offer him something real.

"I'm afraid every time the lights dim . . . that I am going blind again," I say. "Like when my family went to Olive Garden and some waitress turned the lights down for dinner mood or whatever. Or when my brother shut the living room blinds behind me so he could see the TV better."

"When this happens, instead of thinking you are going blind again, why don't you just tell yourself emphatically that you aren't?"

"Seriously?" Ay yi yi. My dad was paying for this?

"Because you *want* to see, Tessie. It's not like a little goblin is sitting inside your head manning a light switch. You are in control. Statistically, the chances of this ever happening again are almost nil."

OK, kind of useful. At least encouraging. Even though chances of this happening to me were almost nil to begin with.

"What else is going on in there?" He taps his skull with a finger.

"I'm worried . . . about O. J. Simpson."

"What exactly are you worried about?"

"That he might fool the jury and get off." I don't tell him that Lydia had soaked one of her own red leather gloves in V8 juice, dried it in the sun, and demonstrated how she could spread her hand wide and get the same effect as O.J.

The doctor crosses one long leg over the other. He's much more of a conservative dresser than I'd imagined. Starched white shirt, black dress pants with a stand-up crease, loosened blue tie with tiny red diamonds, black shoes grinning with polish. No wedding ring.

"I think the chances of that happening are also practically zero," he says. "You are simply worried that your own attacker will be set free. I'd advise you not to watch any of the O.J. coverage and ratchet things up in your head."

Aunt Hilda offered this same advice for free, and tempered it by handing me a plate of fried okra fresh out of her skillet while snapping off my TV.

"Tessie, today is supposed to be all your show, but we need to divert for a second. The prosecutor called right before you arrived. He wants to meet one-on-one with you before the trial. I could ask to sit in on the interviews if you'd feel more comfortable. He's thinking about conducting the first interview next Tuesday. We can even do it in our regular session if you like."

He uncrosses his leg and leans toward me. My stomach wads itself into a hard ball, a roly-poly beetle protecting itself.

"Getting your sight back is huge. Meeting the prosecutor and getting over your fear of the trial is a logical next step. It might even help . . . jog your memory. Think of your brain as a sieve or a colander, with only the tiniest, safest bits getting through at first."

I'm barely listening to his psycho mumbo-jumbo about kitchen gadgets.

Seven days away.

"I hope you don't mind that I told him the good news," he says.

"Of course not," I lie.

I'm thinking about the little bag, packed and ready for months, wedged into the far back corner of my closet.

Wondering if it's too late to run.

Tessa, present day

Charlie and I are playing an old game on the front porch swing. Rain drills steadily on the roof.

We're pretending to be tiny dolls rocking to and fro. A little girl is pushing our swing with her finger. She's locked up her big yellow cat, so he can't paw at us. She's baking a tiny plastic cake for us in the oven, and she's made all the beds and arranged all the tiny dishes in the cabinet. She's used a toothbrush to sweep the carpet. There are no monsters in the closet, because there are no closets.

For just this moment, everything is perfect. Nothing can get to us. We are in the dollhouse.

My daughter's head is warm in my lap. She lies sideways on the front porch swing with me, her knees bent because she isn't three years old anymore with room to spare. I've covered her bare legs with my jacket for when the wind shifts and spits at us between the brick columns.

She wiggles into a more comfortable position and turns her face up to me. Her violet eyes are rimmed with black eyeliner, which makes them even bigger and lovelier, but so much more cynical. Two silver studs are punched in each ear, one slightly smaller than the other.

The eye makeup can be washed off; the extra holes will close up.

I try not to get too worked up about these things. She'd just point out the tattoo on my right hip, a butterfly among the scars.

When Charlie's braces come off in three months, that's when I'll worry. "Mom, you seemed a little crazy last night at Miss Effie's. Like, I know you were worried, but still. I'd never seen you like that. Is it because you're afraid you can't stop that guy from getting executed?"

"Partly." I fiddle with a lock of her hair, and she allows it. "Charlie, we've never talked much about what happened to me."

"You never want to." A statement, not a reproach.

"I've just never wanted you to be a part of it." Never wanted her innocence disturbed with more than the straight facts, and a sanitized version of those.

"So you still think about . . . those girls?" Tentative. "I dreamed about one of them once. Merry. She had a cool name. Someone taped a *People* magazine story to my bike a while back. It was about her mom. She said she wants a front row seat to Terrell Goodwin's execution. Have you decided for sure he didn't do it?"

I will myself to stay put instead of leaping up, to keep my foot pushing firmly and steadily against the concrete floor. A stranger left Charlie a gift. A Susan crept from my head into hers. Worse, she is just telling me about this *now*. I don't want to think that Charlie carries these secrets around because she is afraid to bring them up, and yet I know that is exactly why.

"Yes," I say. "Of course I think about those girls. About how they died, and who hurts for them. Especially right now. The forensic scientist I told you about has extracted DNA from the girls' bones. It's a long shot, and involves a lot of luck, but if their families are still looking, maybe we can find out who they are."

"You would still be looking for me. You would never give up."

I blink back tears. "Never, *never*. Honey, do you mind telling me what your dream was about? The one with Su—Merry?"

"We took a walk on this island. She never said anything. It was nice. Not scary."

Thank you, Merry.

"So you're sure Terrell's innocent?" she asks again.

"Yes, I'm pretty sure. The physical evidence isn't there." I leave out the seventeen-year trail of black-eyed Susans. The voices in my head, amplifying my doubts.

"Whoever the real killer is, he's not coming back, Mom." She says it earnestly. "He was smart enough not to get caught the first time. He isn't going to risk it. And if he was *going* to do anything, it would have happened years ago. Maybe he's in prison for another crime. I've heard that happens all the time."

My daughter's clearly given this a lot of thought. How could I be so stupid to think her teen-age brain wasn't as wired as Lydia's and mine? I don't tell her one of Jo's shocking statistics—that of 300 active serial killers roaming the United States, most of them will never be caught.

"Listen to me, Charlie. More than anything, I want to give you a normal life. I don't want you to live in fear, but I need you to be very careful right now, until we know what's happening to . . . Terrell. My job is to protect you, and you need to give in and let me for a while."

Charlie pushes herself up. "We're, like, more normal than half the people I know. Melissa Childers's mom drove the cheerleaders around one Saturday night and they stuck raw chicken inside mailboxes of these girls they don't like. Like, her mom's mug shot is on Facebook. And Anna's mom didn't get sick the other night when she was supposed to pick us up. She was drunk. Anna says she puts vodka in that Big Gulp Diet Coke in her car cup holder. Kids know things, Mom. You can't hide stuff." A rare, unfettered stream of information.

"I'm not going to ride with Anna's mom anymore," Charlie announces.

The swing. Hypnotic. *Keep talking.*

Her phone starts to blare a song I don't recognize. Instantly, Charlie stretches for it.

"Can I spend the night with Marley?"

She's already edging off the swing, away from me.

"I love this place. Nothing like Saturday night at the Flying Fish." Jo is lifting a giant frosty schooner of beer to her lips. She's sporting old Levi's and a red Oklahoma Sooners T-shirt and the gold DNA charm at her neck that goes with everything.

Bill has just returned from the counter with a basket of fried oysters and hush puppies for us to share. He's loose, in old jeans, more relaxed than I've ever seen him. His shirt is untucked. He needs a haircut. He scoots across a giant schooner of St. Pauli Girl for me. His fingers linger longer than they need to, which I decide to chalk up to the beer. This schooner is going to make my drive home a little tricky.

"One size fits all." He grins and slips in beside Jo on the opposite side of the booth, right below a crowded bulletin board with a photograph of a guy brandishing a fish on steroids.

"Is that for real?" I point at the sea monster, about as long as Charlie.

"It's the Liar's Wall." Bill pops a hush puppy in his mouth without turning around. "I've been pushing for one of those in the DA's office for years."

"That's really not fair," Jo says, frowning. "For example, for at least ten years, Dallas County has been a machine at exonerating more people through DNA than just about anyone else." An echo of Charlie.

"Ah, Jo, you're always getting mired in optimism," Bill says. "If I get Terrell a new hearing, then we'll talk."

The restaurant's picnic tables and booths are loud and packed. A line snakes by us on the way to the counter, a cowboy- and baseball-hat crowd with a Texas fetish for crispy crusts on everything. The state's collective orgasm occurs at the state fair, where even Nutella, Twinkies, and butter get dunked in the fryers.

Almost as soon as Charlie bounced out the door for her sleepover, Bill had texted, asking if I'd join the two of them here for a beer. He didn't say why.

So I hesitated, but not for long. It was either that or a sleepover with the Susans and a bottle of merlot while the thunder rumbled and lightning transformed every tree and bush into a human silhouette. I yanked my rainy day frizz into a ponytail, threw on an old jean jacket, and shot over here in my Jeep, windshield wipers slashing all the way.

Bill and Jo were at least one beer in and engaged in a heated exchange about the Sooners' quarterback when I showed up looking like I'd been making out under a waterfall. Jo tossed me the roll of paper towels on the table to dry my head and wipe off a mascara smudge she pointed out under my left eye. The conversation drifted not toward Terrell but to one of Jo's new cases, the bones of a three- or four-year-old girl that had been discovered in a field in Ohio, and then to me.

"What is it, exactly, that you do for a living?" Bill asks.

"I'm not sure there's a name for it. I'm a . . . problem solver, I guess. People imagine something they've never seen before, and I make it. It can be little, like designing a wedding crown embedded with jewels from a grandmother's ring, or big, like a floating staircase I built for a hotel in Santa Fe. *Sunday Morning* did a piece on the staircase in a series on female craftswomen, which has really helped. The host was classy enough not to mention the Black-Eyed Susan . . . thing. I can pick and choose now. Charge more."

"Is that your favorite thing you've built so far? The staircase?"

"No. Hands-down my favorite thing is the pumpkin catapult for Charlie's Field Day competition last year. We beat the school's record by sixty feet." I take another drag on my beer. "My father had a minor in physics and taught me a few things." I should have eaten more than two crackers with pimiento cheese for lunch. Bill is looking more boyish than usual in a soft gray T-shirt that clings to taut muscle. I wonder whether he and Swedish Girl have hit it off officially yet.

I decide to shift the spotlight off of me, where it always feels too hot and too bright. I debate whether to ask if they're getting me drunk to deliver bad news. My eyes linger on Jo. She could be anybody tonight—a housekeeper, a bank teller, a first-grade teacher. Her daily relationship with horror is well hidden under that Sooners T-shirt and clear blue eyes that indicate she sleeps pretty well. No one would ever pick her out as the scientist who stood in the middle of hell, running mathematical equations in her head, while the Twin Towers smoked.

"Jo, how do you keep doing what you do . . . day after day?" I ask. "Not letting it affect you."

She sets down her beer. "My gift from God is that I can look at the grotesque and not be grossed out by it. The finger. The guts. But I'm not going to tell you that I don't go home and think about the semen on the Little Mermaid nightgown. Or the bullet in the jaw of the POW that didn't kill the guy. How he must have been tortured. I wonder things like, 'Did this young mother live through the airplane crash or did she die right away?' I think about who these people are. When I stop doing that, it's the day I should quit this job."

The last part sounded a little drunk and also like the most sincere thing I'd ever heard.

"This is the only thing I'm good at," she says. "I'm a forensic scientist. It's all I know."

"You are just too damn nice." Bill clinks her mug with his. "I spend most days wanting to punch someone in the face."

She grins and toasts the air. "I'm from Oklahoma. We're the nicest people in the world. And we also love to punch people in the face. And, now and then, I have a day like today."

"If you hadn't noticed, Jo and I are celebrating," Bill tells me. "We just wanted to give you a chance to catch up first."

"And?" I ask. Jo gives him a nod, the OK sign.

"We got a match on one of the DNA samples."

His words aren't registering. He can't be talking about the Susans. Not this soon.

"We've made an ID on one of the Black-Eyed Susans through the national missing persons database," Jo confirms matter-of-factly. "One of the femur extractions."

"Are you OK, Tessie?" Bill's face is twisted in concern. I don't know if he's realized what he's done. Called me Tessie. This time his hand covers mine and doesn't let go. It stirs yet another feeling I'm not prepared for at the moment. I snatch my fingers away and tuck a wet strand of hair behind my ear.

"I'm . . . fine. Sorry. It's just a shock. After all this time. After everything you said about statistics, I just didn't expect it. Who . . . is she?" *I need to hear her name.*

"Hannah," Jo says. "Hannah Stein. Twenty years old. She disappeared from her job as a waitress in Georgetown twenty-five years ago. Her younger brother's a Houston cop now. We got lucky. He insisted that his family enter DNA into the CODIS database a few months ago after he took a required course on missing persons investigations. Hannah's mito-DNA is a match to Rachel and Sharon Stein. Her mom and her sister. Remember, mitochondrial DNA is one hundred percent from the maternal side."

"If I can prove Terrell was nowhere near Georgetown the day she disappeared . . . well, it will help." Bill's voice carries a triumphant note.

"There's one thing." Jo's eyes rest on me carefully. "The mother wants you to be there."

"Be where?" This Susan is no longer a pile of teeth and bones and a disembodied voice in my head. Her name is Hannah. She's a shadow darting out into the lightning, about to let me see her face.

"The mother is driving in from Austin with her son so we can formally give the family the ID. She specifically asked to meet you. She always suspected a cousin of theirs had something to do with Hannah's disappearance. She . . . we . . . the cops . . . want to know if you recognize him."

"The thing is," Bill says. "He's dead."

Tessie, 1995

Two of them show up in the doctor's office. A man and a woman.

The man is the prosecutor. Mr. Vega. Short, compact, around forty. Firm handshake, direct eye contact. Lots of Italian machismo. He reminds me of the football coach who hurled half our school into the gym during an impromptu tornado last year. He walks down the hall, and you know it.

The woman could pass for a high school senior. She seems like she'd be way more at home in something less uptight than whatever Ann Taylor thing she has on. I'm on the couch, and she's sitting where the doctor usually does, tapping her left heel, nervous, like maybe I'm her first big case. She says she's here as a child advocacy therapist, but I'm pretty sure she is mostly a chaperone to make sure I don't accuse the prosecutor of anything creepy.

I'm feeling remarkably who-cares about all of it, because I took two Benadryl an hour ago. This is generally not my thing, but Lydia suggested it when she heard I was meeting the prosecutor for the first time. She pokes down a couple when her parents light off into one of their three-day screaming matches. Once more, Lydia has made the right call. The air is tense and thick, but I'm drifting through it in a cushy bubble.

The doctor isn't happy. First, I haven't begged him to stay. It just doesn't seem to matter much at the moment and would require some energy on my part to make happen. Mr. Vega most definitely wants him out of the room. I am impressed that he has so quickly manipulated the doctor all the way to the doorway of his own office, because the doctor's no slouch in the manipulator department himself.

They are talking in low, urgent tones that carry. The woman, Benita, and I can overhear every word. It's awkward. I can tell she isn't sure what to do, because she's already told me we don't have to talk. I feel sorry for her.

"I like your hair," I say, because I do. It's black with a few shiny red streaks. I wonder if she does it herself.

"I like your boots," she says.

It's not like we still aren't listening to every word they're saying.

"Don't ask her any questions that begin with why," the doctor is instructing the lawyer.

"Just give us about thirty minutes, sir. You have nothing to worry about." This is the kind of "sir" that Mr. Vega probably also uses with judges and hostile witnesses. I've seen enough of Christopher Darden and Johnnie Cochran at this point.

I feel kind of sorry for the doctor now, too, being tossed out of his own space.

The Benadryl is making me so freaking *nice*.

While this tussle is going on at the door, I decide to give Benita her first test. She's already announced that she's here just for me and to ask her anything. Or ask her nothing. It's entirely up to me. Of course, I've heard this so many times at this point I could vomit. It must be, like, Chapter One in the dysfunctional witness/victim textbook.

"Why is there a problem with asking me questions with the word *why*?" I ask her.

She glances at the prosecutor, who isn't paying attention to us at all. I'm sure she's worried about delivering inside information to a teen-age subject. Probably not addressed in the textbook at all.

"Because it implies that you are to blame," she answers. "You know, like 'Why did you do such and such?' Or 'Why do you think this happened to you?' Mr. Vega would not ask you a why question. You are not to blame for anything."

This interests me. I try to remember if the doctor has ever asked me a why question and decide he hasn't. It never occurred to me that there is doctoring going on by omission, which is bothersome, and a whole new thing to worry about.

The door shuts with a crisp click, and the doctor is on the other side of it. The prosecutor rolls over the doctor's desk chair, facing me intently.

"OK, Tessie. Sorry about that. I am not at all interested in discussing the case today, so you can relax if that's on your mind. We probably won't discuss it next time, either." He nods at Benita. "Neither of us believes that it's a good idea to ask you questions about something this traumatic and deeply personal when *we* have no relationship whatsoever with you yet. So first, we'll get to know each other. I also want to assure you that I am completely prepared to go into court with your memory exactly as it is."

This is not the impression I have from the doctor at all. He's a seesaw, for sure, but always subtly pushing. Sometimes I think he is purposely trying to confuse me.

Now I have to wonder who is telling the truth. It makes my head hurt. I decide to turn the tables and ask Mr. Vega a question. He's clearly a control freak, too.

The Benadryl has set me free. I just don't *care*.

"*Why,*" I ask, "are you so sure this man is guilty?"

Tessa, present day

I'm staring at the stupid plastic heart again, half-expecting it to start beating.

It's just Jo and me. I'm the first to arrive even though it took two frantic hours to decide the appropriate outfit to wear to meet Hannah's grieving mother, who probably hopes part of her dead daughter is now living inside me. Of course, it turns out that she *is* living in me, but I don't want to tell her that. It also turns out that the proper outfit for this event is a crocheted sweater, brown leather skirt, boots, and my mother's dangling pearls, which I have never hooked around my neck before today.

"The heart is cool, huh?" Jo pulls it off the shelf, snaps open the box, and hands it to me like it is a rubber dog toy. It *feels* like a rubber dog toy. My instinct to take it was automatic, as is the one to fling it across the room. I hand it back gingerly.

"Is it real?"

"Yes. Preserved through plastination. I did it myself."

So I wasn't wrong about that part. Still, I can't believe that Jo, my hero, my good guy, is being so cavalier.

"Want to hear the story?" She glances at her watch. This is apparently her idea of a good way to distract me for the next ten minutes.

I shake my head, but her head is bent down while she's placing the heart back in its little customized stand. "My grandmother and I were driving to my aunt's the night before Thanksgiving on a dark county road in Oklahoma. The deer darted out before I could slam on the brakes."

A deer. OK. Feeling better.

"It was a nasty clunk," she continues. "My grandmother and I were both OK. But I wanted to make sure the deer was dead before we drove off. I wasn't going to leave him on the side of the road dying. But when I got to him, it was pretty clear the car did the job. Before I could decide what to do with the deer, three different pick-ups had pulled over to the side of the road. Three good ole boys passing by, and all three of them want to take the deer off my hands. I notice one of them has a sharp knife hanging off his belt."

A distressing turn of events. The heart, back to being a question mark.

"I told the guy with the knife that I'd choose him to keep the deer if he let me borrow his knife. So he hands over the knife and I cut out the deer's heart."

Grimm's fairy tale, Oklahoma-style. I'm nauseated and relieved at the same time.

"Did these truckers . . . have any idea you are a forensic scientist?" I interject. "Did they know why you wanted the heart?" *Did you know why you wanted the heart?*

"I don't remember if it came up. They were focused on deer meat."

"And you brought the heart . . . back to your grandmother in the car and put it . . . where?"

"A cooler."

"And you brought it to . . . Thanksgiving?" I didn't ask if the pumpkin pie and Cool Whip had to make room.

"My aunt was pretty distressed when she ran out to welcome us and saw the bashed-in hood and blood all over me. We had a good laugh about it."

There's something else niggling at me. "How were you going to kill the deer if he was alive?"

"I didn't know. Maybe strangle him with my shoelace. No matter what, he was going to be dead when I left him."

This is the Jo I know. And another one I didn't.

There's a knock on the door, and a student in a lab coat pokes her head in.

"Dr. Jo, the cops are here. I put them in the conference room. The front desk is sending up the family now. Bill called to say that the Stein family has officially rejected his request to be there but wanted to be sure you and Tessa knew the mother is bringing a psychic along with them."

None of this appears to ruffle Jo in the least. After all, left alone on a black Oklahoma road with her grandmother, three hulking strangers, and a knife, all she's thinking about is cutting out the heart of a deer.

"You ready?" Jo asks me.

Two detectives, one brother cop, one mother, one psychic—all waiting in grim silence around a conference table in a claustrophobic room whose only adornments are a stained coffeepot, a stack of Styrofoam cups, and a brown box of Kleenex that sits untouched in the middle of the table. The fresh-paint smell is so strong it stings my throat. Except for the brother, painfully young and official in full dress uniform, I couldn't in a million years distinguish who was who. No weepy red eyes. No crystal balls or flowing peasant shirts. No other uniforms or badges.

A man in Wrangler's and a tie immediately stands to shake Jo's hand, as does a woman around fifty, with the most motherly, kind face in the room. Detective No. 1 and Detective No. 2.

I drop into a chair, wishing to be anywhere else on earth.

I turn my attention to the woman across from me, who immediately reaches over to cover my hands. Her hair is stiff with hair spray, and aggravated with bold blond streaks. Her eyes are the bluest I've ever seen. Rachel Stein, I assume. Except I can tell from a frown on Detective No. 2's face that she isn't.

"Ma'am, we've asked that you not participate in this meeting unless asked to. You are here strictly as a courtesy to the family."

She draws her hands back reluctantly and winks, as if we are on the same team. I am repulsed. I want back whatever she thinks she has snatched out of me with her moist psychic paw.

The detective is droning out introductions while my eyes are now fixed, by process of elimination, on Hannah's mother—a pale, sharp-faced woman in her sixties. Jo had told me she was a middle school English teacher. She has that no-nonsense air about her. Except she brought a psychic.

For a split second, as our eyes meet, I glimpse horror, as if I'd just crawled out of her daughter's grave, like a mud monster.

The Steins have already met the coroner this morning to receive the official identification. Jo's job is strictly to help them believe it beyond a doubt. She is explaining the basics of mitochondrial DNA, the careful lab work, the mind-blowing genetic probabilities, within half a percent, that this is her daughter. It takes about ten minutes.

"Mrs. Stein, your daughter has been handled with the greatest of care," Jo says. "I am terribly sorry this has happened to your family."

"Thank you. I appreciate your time with us. I believe this is Hannah." She directs her gaze to the police. It is obvious she is having a hard time looking at me.

"Tessa." Detective No. 2, the woman, is speaking. I heard her name but I can't remember it. "Can I call you Tessa?"

"Of course." It comes out scratchy, and I clear my throat.

"Since there is some . . . speculation . . . in the media about whether the right man was convicted for their daughter's death, the Steins are curious if you can pick out a photo of a relative who took an unusual interest in their daughter. A suspect at the time. He is no longer alive, so you don't need to be afraid of any kind of retaliation. They are simply seeking peace of mind. No one wants the wrong man executed." She says this without rancor, but I wonder what's really in her head.

I suddenly want Bill to be here. I want him to smother my hand with his again. "That's fine."

"You remind me of my daughter," Mrs. Stein says. "Not the red hair, of course. But you give off that same . . . free spirit."

The detective slides two sheets of mug shots flat in front of me. The brother, up until now a silent, poker-straight soldier, leans in. It occurs to me that he wasn't even born when his sister disappeared. He was the recovery baby.

"He was an awful person," Mrs. Stein tells me brokenly. The twelve men on the table swim before me. Bald, white, middle-aged.

"I believe God sent that deer in front of his car." The brother's first words are a cold, hard slap. "Put him in a coma so we could yank the plug. So I didn't have to shoot the bastard myself."

I'm bewildered. Seriously? A deer? I want to meet Jo's eyes but don't. Too much deer metaphor for one day. Too much coincidence. Too much anger and certainty about God's wrath, when sometimes everything is just pointless.

"I'm sorry," I say finally. "I just don't know. There is so much I don't remember." At the same time, I realize that I am remembering *something*. Fabric. A pattern. I know where I've seen it before, but I don't know what it means.

Impulsively, I reach my hands out to the psychic.

"Do you mind?" I ask the female detective.

"Not if you don't." Bemused.

Mrs. Stein is nodding animatedly, a doll brought to life. Her son is casting me a look of scathing disappointment.

I know I have to do this, whatever I believe. For Hannah. For her mom, eaten by grief. For her brother, who is probably a cop for all the wrong reasons. For her father, who is conspicuously absent.

"Something is coming back to me." This is exquisitely true. "There's a curtain. Can you help me see behind it?"

The psychic's sweaty grip tightens. Her nails bite into my flesh. I feel like I'm being consumed by a slobbery shark.

"Of course." Her eyes glisten like shards of ice, the first thing that reassures people she is special and a window to the netherworld.

"It's a black man," she says.

I remove my hands carefully and turn to Hannah's mother. Rachel Stein's eyes are not glistening. They are a boggy, open sinkhole, and I don't want to stumble.

"Mrs. Stein, I lay in that grave with your daughter. Hannah will forever be a part of me, like we share the same DNA. Her monster is my monster. So please believe me when I say I know exactly what she would tell you right now. She would tell you she loves you. And she would tell you this woman will only hurt you. She's a liar."

Tessie, 1995

"Are you ready to nail a killer, Tessie?"

Mr. Vega is prowling, from desk to window to couch. "Because you need to be mentally tough. The defense attorney is going to try to screw with your head. I want to make sure you're prepared for his little circus tricks."

The doctor catches my eye and nods encouragement. He managed not to get kicked out of the room today. Mr. Vega and Benita have met with me two more times in the last week, once at a bowling alley and another time at a Starbucks. Mr. Vega introduced me to Mocha Frappuccinos and grilled jalapeños on hot dogs. He asked me *why* I like to run and *why* I like to draw and *why* I hated the Yankees so much. I went along with the "getting to know me" sessions because it was a lot less painful than hanging out on the couch with the doctor. Like Dad said, they were all just doing their jobs.

Things turned for me sometime during disco bowling on lane 16, while the lights flashed psychedelic and pins thundered and Sister Sledge got down. Mr. Vega and I were locked in a bowling duel. Benita was keeping score and yelling some crazy Spanish cheer from her high school days. Mr. Vega wasn't cutting me any slack, even though I had to get my surgeon's permission to temporarily strip off the boot brace to play. The man about to prosecute my monster threw a spare/strike/spare to win the game, even when I faked a limp at the end.

So maybe he was manipulative and maybe he was genuine and maybe he was a little of both. Regardless, when I sat down on the couch today to officially prepare for the trial, I was in the game—no longer on Mr. Vega's team simply because there was no way out. I wanted to win.

"I know every play this guy has." Mr. Vega is still roving the room, like he's already in court.

"He likes to get kids on the yes-no train," he continues. "Remember, the less narrative your answers, the less the jury can feel your pain. He will ask you a series of questions, where the answer is positively 'yes.' So you will answer, yes, yes, yes, yes, yes. Then he will slip in a question that is absolutely a 'no' answer, but you'll be on the train, in the 'yes' rhythm. You'll say 'yes' and when you are immediately flustered and change to 'no,' he'll ask whether you are confused. And so it begins."

I nod. This seems easy enough to handle.

"He will throw dates and numbers at you until your head spins. Whenever you are confused, ask him to explain himself again. Every. Single. Time. This makes him look more like a bully." He steps toward me, and his face goes slack.

"If four times six equals twenty-four and twice that is forty-eight, what is fifty times that plus six?"

I stare at him, disbelieving. Begin to multiply.

He jams his finger in the air. "Fast, Tessie. Answer."

"I can't."

"OK. That feeling right now, numb and slightly panicky? That's it. That's how it's going to feel. Times four." He is on the prowl again. I'm glad that Oscar isn't here. He'd be going nuts. "This will be the toughest part. He will insinuate you are hiding things. *Why is it that you can remember buying tampons on the day of the attack but not this man's face? Why did you have a relationship with a crazy homeless man? Why did you run alone every day?*"

"I run too fast for most of my friends to keep up," I protest. "And Roosevelt isn't that crazy."

"Uh-uh, Tessie. Don't just *react*. *Think* about the question. *I always ran in the daylight hours on two routes approved by my father. Roosevelt has been sitting on the same corner for ten years, and is good friends with everyone, including the local cops.* Matter-of-fact. Don't let him get to you. You did nothing wrong."

"Will he really bring up the . . . tampons?"

"I would bet on it. It's another way to make you uncomfortable. A subtle move that the jury won't notice. The tampons are a fact of life for them. For you, a teen-age girl, they are intimate and embarrassing. Believe me, Dick has no boundaries even when it comes to child victims of sexual abuse."

His eyes are laser-focused on me again.

"Why did you get suspended from two track meets last year?"

The doctor shifts positions. He wants to interfere. Mr. Vega senses it and holds up his hand in his direction, a halt signal. He keeps his eyes trained on me.

Is this the Vega who is pretending, or the real one? Either way, this question really ticks me off. Anger always starts as a little tingle in the roots of my hair, and then spreads like spilled hot water.

"A girl on another track team pushed my friend Denise off a hurdle in a regional meet so she could win in the prelims. If you were watching, and you're not a hurdler, you wouldn't have noticed. But there are certain moves, and I know them. So I walked over to her after the race and told her that I knew she cheated. She shoved me to the ground. When the track officials ran over, she told them I'd shoved her first. We were both suspended for two meets."

I straighten up. Level my gaze at him, and just him. Let him know I am mad, but under control. "It was totally worth it," I say. "Because everyone will be watching her now. She won't try it again."

Nobody speaks. I wonder if they believe me. Everyone else who knows me did. Lydia even wrote an indignant letter to the UIL board. She signed it *Sincerely, Ms. Lydia Frances Bell.*

"Perfect," Mr. Vega says. "Narrative. Calm. Perfect." He takes a few steps and places his hand on my shoulder.

The hand on my shoulder—it feels good. Still, it is so hard to know whether I like this man, or whether I just like what he is giving back to me. Power. The thing that my monster snatched away and threw in the gutter at Walgreens.

Mr. Vega removes his hand. Picks up his briefcase, on the floor next to Benita. "A short session, but I think we're done for the day. Benita's going to show you the courtroom at some point. I recommend sitting in every seat. The jury's. The judge's—my personal favorite. I want to wait until closer to the trial to go over your own testimony. We'll see whether you and the doc get any further in that time."

All of them rise, except for me. I stay planted on the couch. "Twenty-four hundred and six."

Mr. Vega stops at the door.

"That's my girl," he says. "You'll always get to the right answer if you slow down and think about it."

Tessa, present day

Of course, it's been banging me in the head, ever since I learned her name.

Rachel Stein, Hannah's mother, does not have a first name that begins with *S* or *U* or *N*. She does not fit neatly into the mnemonic device that I've put aside like a crossword puzzle I always planned to finish later. *S-U-N*. The letters that Merry provided while we chatted in the grave, to help me remember the names of all of the mothers and hunt them down.

Ever since the discovery of a third set of bones, I've been thinking that maybe my conversation with Merry wasn't a hallucination. There *were* the bones of three other girls in that grave, not two, just like Merry told me. That couldn't be a coincidence, right?

And yet. The black-and-white, driver's license, DNA certainty of Rachel Stein's name makes me wonder whether I was nuts back then, and just as nuts now. I actually had to restrain myself from peppering Mrs. Stein with questions: *Is Rachel your nickname? Your middle name? Did you change your name?*

I couldn't mess with her head anymore—trade the psychic's crazy for my crazy. Hannah's mother drifted out of that hollow conference room as a more haggard spirit than when she entered. *Closure is a myth,* Jo told me afterward. *But there is value in knowing.* Mrs.

Stein's son had to carefully prop up his mother as they exited. She moved like she was a hundred years old.

Hannah's brother and I made an unspoken pact that he would drop-kick the psychic to her altered universe. She was fuming and tripping at their heels on the way out. As soon as he had heard the word *liar* come out of my mouth, his head popped up and he shot me the most grateful look I'd ever received. As for the psychic . . . well, if I'm not cursed already, I'm sure she finished the job. My scars tingled for an hour afterward.

My Very Energetic Mother Just Served Us Nine Pizzas.

Ever since I left that room, I can't get this string of words out of my head. I imagine Merry punching a button on a jukebox, over and over. Each punch a little firmer, more frustrated. *Remember.*

My boots clunk out a rhythm as I climb the staircase. One step. *My.* Two steps. *Very.* Three steps. *Energetic.* Four steps. *Mother.* At the top, I throw open the door to my studio. Warm, stale air rushes out. I shove the picture window wide open and drink in air that is like an ice-cold tequila shot. A brave blue jay stares me down from his perch on a branch, and I blink first.

I pick up a few pages off the dusty hardwood, remnants of one of Bobby's projects the last time he stayed for a weekend. My sweet, half-doomed little brother. Now he writes for movies that end in numerals and tries to heal himself with holotropic breath-work and a sexy production assistant with a nose ring. He left for college in California and basically never returned except for short visits and funerals, which is probably what I should have done. He even chopped his last name to Wright.

I draw hearts in the dust on my drawing table, until my finger is black. I pick a white tea from the selection in the cabinet and plug in the teakettle. Listen to its friendly hiss. Decide that the old honey in the cabinet smells a little like beer and watch two sugar cubes dissolve to sand in my mug instead. Merry gives the jukebox one last punch with her finger and disappears.

I have always loved this room. I just didn't want to share it with the Susans. Today it seems that I don't have to. I wipe off the drawing table with a paper towel and clip on a piece of paper with a sharp snap that scares the bird into an irritated flutter. I begin to loosely sketch the folds of fabric, a soft sound, like a rat under the floor. I'm in a hurry so I can get to the intricate, important work. A pattern had emerged in my head while I was staring at Mrs. Stein's simple cotton blouse. At breasts that sagged with the weight of middle age.

Surprise. I am sketching flowers and it doesn't bother me. An hour floats by. Then another. There are so many, many petals, and a leafy vine that meanders, connecting them all, like a demented family tree. I fill a Dixie cup with water and open up my watercolor box. Blue, pink, and green.

These flowers are not black-eyed Susans.

And these folds of fabric are not a curtain. They were never a curtain.

I'm drawing my mother's apron. You can't see me, but I am underneath, hiding my face. I can feel the cloth tickle my nose and cheeks. It is dark under here, but enough light sifts through the thin cotton that I am not scared. The warm cushion of my mother's body is at my back.

I can't see what is on the other side.

It reminds me of being blind.

Dr. Giles is holding my painting gingerly edge to edge because it isn't completely dry.

It's closing time. All the toys and books in the room are tidied up. A couple of table lamps are glowing, but the overhead lighting is flipped off. The elephant is tucked in for the night in a doll bed, the blanket pulled up to his ears.

"So what do you think?" I ask. "Is the apron the curtain? Does the curtain have nothing to do with me being dumped in that grave? Is it meaningless?" I'm feeling guilty about sounding so urgent.

"Nothing is meaningless," she says. "The apron probably represents comfort to you. It would not be a surprise for you to connect some element of your first trauma—the death of your mother—to the other one. Tessa, the most important thing is for you to eliminate the unknown, which is frightening. If you came here and told me you could see the killer behind the curtain, like the Wizard of Oz, well . . . that isn't what you really expected, is it?"

Yes. That is exactly what I expected. I grew up in Oz.

I don't tell her that, though. Or say that this painting of my mother's apron leaves me as unsettled as the blank curtain I drew a hundred times.

Tessie, 1995

"How do you like Mr. Vega and Benita?"

Is it my imagination or does the doctor sound a little jealous?

"He's nice," I say carefully. "They're both very nice." Adults make things so complicated. Am I supposed to like the doctor better than them? Is this some kind of contest?

"If you have any questions or concerns, you can let me know. Al Vega can come on a little strong."

And you don't? "I'm good right now. But I will for sure if I do." Lately, this need to reassure him has been taking the place of my desire to annoy the hell out of him. "I do have a question about . . . something else, though."

Lydia says it's ridiculous that I'm carrying this fear around and letting it devour me, although she also thinks what's happening *is kind of cool.* "It isn't just Merry who has spoken to me."

"What do you mean?" the doctor asks. "Who else is speaking to you?"

"The other Susans . . . talk to me sometimes. The ones in the grave. Not all the time. I don't think it's a big deal. Lydia just thought I should bring it up."

"Lydia seems like an extremely sensitive friend."

"Yes."

"Well, let's start this way. What's the first thing you remember one of the other . . . Susans . . . saying to you?"

"It was in the hospital. When I first woke up. One of them told me the strawberry Jell-O sucked. And it did. It was sugar-free."

"And what else?"

"Mostly warnings. Be careful. Like that." *We told you not to touch the pig-and-daisy card.*

"When they speak, do you think they are trying to control you? Or make you do things you don't want to?"

"No. Of course not. I think, like, they want to help. And I promised to help them. Sort of a pact." It sounds absolutely insane when I say it out loud. I am rocked by the sudden terror he might convince my father to toss me in a loony bin. I am 100 percent certain that Lydia was wrong about her advice this time.

"So you talk back to them?"

"No. Not usually. I just hear them." *Careful.*

"And they never suggest that you harm yourself?"

"Are you kidding? What the crap are you talking about? Do you think I'm suicidal? Possessed?" I waggle my fingers on either side of my head, like horns.

"Sorry, Tessie. I have to ask the question."

"I have never once thought about killing myself." Defensive. And a lie. "I have thought about killing *him*."

"Normal," he says. "I'd like to do it myself." This does not seem at all like something a psychiatrist should say. I don't want to feel warm and gushy about him right now. I want a freaking answer.

"So . . . the voices. Do you think I'm . . . schizophrenic? Maybe borderline?" It occurs to me that I'm opting to be schizophrenic rather than possessed by demons. Lydia absolutely refused to help me research anything about schizophrenia. Whatever knowledge I had about it up to that point was gleaned from Stephen King.

So Oscar and I ventured to the local library on our own. The eighty-five-year-old volunteer who can barely see was on duty so I thought it was safe to ask for her help. She didn't recognize the Cartwright Girl, which is what old people call me instead of a Black-Eyed Susan.

After fifteen minutes, while the checkout line stacked up eight deep, she brought over *An Existential Study in Sanity and Madness, One Flew Over the Cuckoo's Nest,* and a Harlequin romance titled *Kate of Outpatients,* all published in the 1960s. The gist of the one by the existential psychologist was to let crazy people be crazy and stop bothering them. I reshelved it and *Cuckoo* and checked out *Kate of Outpatients.* Lydia and I are taking turns doing dramatic readings from it.

The doctor's gaze is surprisingly kind and steady but he lets the silence stretch. Probably trying to figure out how to deliver the bad news to the poor little girl who's soon going to be rocking and drooling in a room full of checker players.

"You are not a schizophrenic, Tessie. I know there is a set of psychiatrists out there who always think that voices indicate mental illness. There are an equal number of us who don't. Lots of people hear voices. When a spouse or child dies, the people left sometimes talk to them on and off all day, and hear them respond. For the rest of their lives. It doesn't make them dysfunctional. In fact, many of them claim these conversations make their lives better and *more* productive."

I love this man. *I love this man.* He is not going to lock me up.

"The Susans don't make my life better," I say. "I think they are ghosts."

"As we discussed previously, the paranormal is a normal *temporary* response."

He isn't getting it. "How do I get rid of them?" *I don't want to make them mad.*

"How do you think you could get rid of them?"

In this case, my answer is immediate. "By sending the killer to prison."

"You are well on the way to doing that."

"And by finding out who the Susans are. Giving them real names."

"What if that is not possible?"

"Then I don't know if they'll ever leave me."

"Tessie, did your mother ever talk to you after she died? Like the Susans do?"

"No. Never."

"I ask only because you have endured two terrible traumas for someone so young. Your mother's death and the horror of that grave. Part of me thinks you are still grieving for your mother. Tell me, do you remember what you did at the wake?"

My mother *again*. I shrug. "We ate food people brought over and then my little brother and I played basketball on the driveway." *I let him win. We played H-O-R-S-E. The score was ten games to two.*

"Children often play the day of the funeral as if it's any other day. It's deceptive. They grieve far longer and more deeply than adults."

"I don't think so." I remembered the awful sounds of my dad and aunt weeping, like someone was peeling off my skin.

"Adults grieve harder in the beginning, but they move through it. Kids can get stuck in one stage . . . anger or denial . . . for years. It might be at the root of your symptoms—the memory loss, the blindness, the Susans, the code that you made up in the grave—"

"I'm not stuck," I interrupt. "Merry and I didn't *make up* a code in the grave. And I don't want to talk about my mother. She's gone. My problem is strictly with ghosts."

Tessa, present day

It is only thirteen blocks from where I live now.

Lydia's old house.

It might as well be a hundred miles. I'm standing in front of her childhood home for the first time in years. It is the second place he left black-eyed Susans, and the first time I turned and ran.

Lydia always described her house as a shotgun wedding cake, a two-story beige box with a last-minute white piping of scalloped trim. A lot has changed since our childhood. The icing is crumbling. What used to be a perfectly tended green square of lawn is now black dirt choked by hoodlum weeds. No more wooden stake poked in the ground with WELCOME Y'ALL and a painted yellow sunflower. Lydia told me that her dad ripped the sign out of the ground before I came home from the hospital.

"Hey." I didn't hear his car pull up, but Bill is suddenly striding toward me, lankier and taller than I remember. Maybe it's because his long legs are extending out of black Nike shorts and expensive athletic shoes. Everything about him is damp—hair, face, neck, arms. A triangle of sweat stains the front of a crimson Harvard T-shirt, so beloved that a few rips don't matter. He finally got a haircut but it's too short for his big ears. I want him to go the hell away. And stay.

"I said not to come," I protest. "I thought you were playing basketball." I'd regretted my impulsive phone call the second Bill answered. He was out of breath. I wondered whether I had interrupted acrobatic sex with a fellow do-gooding lawyer. He claimed he was playing a pickup game.

"All but over. My fellow law pals and I were getting creamed by a bunch of high-schoolers. Your call was a welcome distraction on the way to my parents' house in Westover Hills, where I've unfortunately committed to dinner. Unless you'd like to invite me over. Or accompany me. So you said you had something to tell me. What's up?"

I promptly burst into tears.

I'm unprepared for this, and by the look on his face, so is Bill. And, yet, the river is flowing like it hasn't since my father died so swiftly four years ago of pancreatic cancer. He hugs me awkwardly, because what's he going to do, which makes me sob harder.

"Oh, hell," he says. "I'm too sweaty for this. Here, let's sit."

He guides me to a sitting position on the curb and curls his arm around my shoulders. The brace of solid muscle, his *kindness,* is waking up every hormone in my body. I need to pull out of this embrace immediately. *No complications.* Instead, my head falls sideways like a rock onto his chest and my shoulders heave.

"Uh, I don't really recommend that you put your nose in that . . . underarm," he says. But once he realizes how fully committed I am, he pulls me tighter.

After a few seconds, I lift my head slightly and let out a choke. "Hold on. I'm under control."

"Yes, you definitely have things under control." He pushes my head back down but not before I catch something hungry on his face that isn't do-gooding at all.

I raise my chin again. Our lips are two inches apart.

He pulls back. "You're red all over. Like a plum."

I giggle and hiccup at the same time. I'm a giggling, hiccuping plum. I tug my skirt down. He averts his eyes and gestures to the house behind us, the one whose address he had plugged into his GPS at my behest only twenty minutes ago. "What's up with this house? Who lives here?" It is an abrupt, purposeful shift.

God, I'm pitiful. I stand up.

"You, um, need to wipe your nose."

Utter, *utter* humiliation. I use my sweater because at this point, it doesn't matter. I suck in a deep breath as a test. It doesn't trigger another tsunami. "Hear me out for a second first," I say stiffly. "I think the Black-Eyed Susan killer has been leaving me flowers for years. Not just the other night at my house."

"What? How *many* other places?"

"Six. If you include under my bedroom window."

"Are you sure . . ."

"That they aren't just growing up in places like God intended and I'm a lunatic? Of course not. That is why I said, I *think*. The first time, I was only seventeen. It was right after Terrell's conviction. The killer left me a poem buried in an old prescription bottle. I found it when I dug up a little patch of black-eyed Susans, in the back yard of the house over there." I point four houses down, at a yellow two-story on the opposite side of the street. "My childhood home. He planted the flowers by my tree house three days after the trial ended." I watch for the awareness to set in. "That's right, *after* Terrell was locked up."

"Go on."

"The . . . person who left it twisted a warning into a poem called 'Black-Eyed Susan' written by an eighteenth-century poet named John Gay. The poem indicated that Lydia would die if I didn't keep my mouth shut." Bill's face is blank. I don't know whether it's because he doesn't know who the hell John Gay is, or whether he is trying to contain his fury.

"I didn't figure out who John Gay was until about ten years ago. He was most famous for *The Beggar's Opera*. Have you heard of it? Captain Macheath? Polly Peachum? No? Well, more to the point, he also wrote a ballad about a black-eyed girl named Susan sending her lover off to sea. There's some romantic theory that this is how the flower got its name . . ."

I begin to recite softly, as a mower revs up in a nearby back yard.

"Oh Susan, Susan, lovely dear
My vows shall ever true remain
Let me kiss off that falling tear
I never want to hurt you again
But if you tell, I will make Lydia
A Susan, too."

"Jesus, Tessa. What did your father say?"

"I never told him. You're the first person I have ever told, other than Angie. I just couldn't . . . worry my father anymore."

"And Lydia?"

"We weren't speaking."

Bill looks at me curiously.

"I told Angie right before she died," I continue. "She was concerned for Charlie and me. At the end, she was considering leaving me completely out of things."

"Why . . ."

"Why didn't she tell you? Because she was protecting me. I think she was wrong, though. I can't live with knowing I might be part of killing an innocent man. It wasn't a hard decision at seventeen. The trial was over. I wanted everything to go back to normal. I figured it could be just another sick individual who was obsessed with the case. There were plenty of those. Which meant Terrell could still be guilty as hell. The prosecutor, Al Vega, was *sure*. And Lydia . . . I was furious with her, but I certainly didn't want her life in danger."

"Hold on, OK?"

Bill leaps up and jogs to his car, a small black BMW, three little letters that I think turn normally nice human beings into road demons. He disappears inside his fancy womb for so long, I wonder whether he is listening to Bach and contemplating whether to flip on the ignition and screech off. When he finally emerges, he holds a pen and pad in his left hand. He plops back down on the curb. He's already written some notes, and I glimpse a few of the words.

John Gay. 1995.

"Keep going," he orders.

"Lately, I've revisited a couple of the places I *think* he left flowers . . . on my own. In no particular order."

"Whoa. Stop right there. You've been returning to these places. Why in the hell are you doing that?"

"I know, I know. Crazy. You see, after the first time, I never dug to see if he buried something else for me. It was like I couldn't give him the satisfaction. I couldn't let myself believe that much. I thought it could be some kid's idea of a joke. Or a random freak. We were all over the newspaper, even Lydia." She always pointed out her name to me. She was thrilled when she made *The New York Times* as *Miss Cartwright's neighbor and confidante.*

"I survived on denial," I continue. "And, yes, I realize it's insane to think anything would still be there. And yet, what if? I just thought if I did find something, it might help . . . Terrell."

And I promised the Susans.

"You're digging? Alone? Have you found anything?"

"Nothing. It's a relief, and it isn't."

"Why are we here, if your old house is there?"

"This is Lydia's house. Well, it used to be. I found black-eyed Susans here, too, a few weeks after the trial."

How much should I explain? I'd shown up at the door on a Friday afternoon with a cardboard box of her stuff. I was enacting a ritual goodbye, after our friendship imploded at the end of the trial. She hadn't been at school for a week and a half. The box held two videotapes, *The Last of the Mohicans* and *Cape Fear,* the backup makeup bag she always left in my bathroom, her Mickey Mouse pajamas.

But the house was asleep at three in the afternoon, which was unusual. No cars. The living room shades were drawn for the first time ever. I could have dumped the box and run. Instead, I unlocked the back gate. Curious. When I glimpsed the small sea of yellow flowers, I was even angrier at Lydia, and I hadn't thought that possible. *How could she let them grow?* I couldn't get out of there fast enough. Two weeks later, a For Sale sign went up, and the Bells were gone, like no one was worth a goodbye.

"Let her go," my father had advised.

"I was in the back yard returning something to Lydia and saw them," I tell Bill. I place my fingers at my temples and rub in concentric circles. "It's OK if you think this is stupid. Let's go. I'm sorry I bothered you."

He stands and yanks me up. Then he surprises me. "We're here. Might as well check it out."

We knock three times before a pasty woman with short, frustrated black hair opens the door about six inches. She surveys us like we are Texas liberals and stabs a finger at the sign under the mailbox attached to the porch siding, a slight variation on a familiar plaque to ward off solicitors: WE'RE PISS POOR. WE DON'T VOTE. WE'VE FOUND JESUS. OUR GUN IS LOADED.

Bill ignores her warnings and sticks out his hand. "Hello, ma'am, I'm William Hastings. My friend Tessa here used to have a very good friend who lived in your house. Tessa has fond childhood memories of playing in the back yard. Would you mind if she took a quick look back there for old times' sake?"

The door opens a little wider, but it's clearly not an invitation. She swivels to shove her foot at a fat yellow cat that can't make up its mind about going out. I'm guessing she's around forty-five, wearing tight jean shorts that are the size she wore two sizes ago. She is carting around a lumpy rear end on skinny legs, and I'm figuring the legs are what she's gauging her weight by as she sits on her ass and sucks down another beer.

No shoes. Band-Aids are wrapped around her big toes. Her breasts are generous flat pancakes, encased in a tank top. A tattoo of red roses snakes from her left shoulder to her elbow. The tattoo clearly required a lot of both time and clenching of teeth.

"Yeah, I mind." The woman ignores Bill's outstretched hand. She's staring at the scar under my eye. I perceive a fleeting flash of respect in her eyes. She's probably thinking *bar fight*.

"I'm curious, Mrs. . . . ?"

"Gibson. Not that it's any of your damn business."

Bill flashes his courthouse badge.

"I'm just curious, Mrs. Gibson, at 5216 Della Court, if you were a no-show to jury duty in the last five years. I have a few friends in the courthouse who would be happy to look that up for us."

"Son of a bitch," she fumes. "Five minutes. That's it. Go around the side by the gate and be sure to shut it when you go. I have a dog." She spits out the last four words like a threat and slams the door.

"Nice move," I say.

"It's not my first Mrs. Gibson."

The same old chain link fence is standing guard around back, although several degrees rustier. The horseshoe catch on the side gate requires a good thump from Bill to lift. I think about how Lydia's dad oiled it religiously.

It is a small, crunched yard with too many plastic buildings. A fake-shingled shed is shoved into the right corner, the "fancy" version with a flower box that was forgotten a long time ago. A filthy white doghouse with a red roof is plopped on the slab of concrete posing as a back porch.

A picnic table used to sit directly under a red oak tree that is now a four-foot stump topped by a statue of a bald eagle with outspread wings. The grass is long and tickly. It creeps up my leg, like a rambling daddy longlegs. Maybe it is. I almost trip over a toy plastic fire truck transformed into a weed planter.

Bill's foot lands in an enormous pile of soft dog poop, and he lets out a loud *"Shit."*

We halt, and stare more intently at the doghouse. It's big enough for a two-year-old child to sleep in. Bill whistles. A dog starts a serious racket somewhere inside the house, and I wonder if Mrs. Gibson is loading her shotgun.

"OK, where?" Bill's tone indicates he may be losing some faith in my treasure hunt. Once again, I regret involving him.

I point to the left side of the yard, at the very back. The weeds are a wild and shaggy carpet, but you can still make out the small hill that Mr. Bell used to call the Grassy Knoll. Lydia had inherited that need to nickname things.

Bill follows behind me, dragging his left shoe, trying to scrape off dog poop as he goes. I stop abruptly, lean over, and begin to yank at weeds.

"What the hell are you doing?" He glances back to the house. My weeding efforts have revealed a small metal door planted sideways into the rise of the tiny hill.

The rusty padlock that holds it closed would probably fall apart with a swift kick. I'm tempted.

"It's an old storm cellar from the '30s when the house was built. I don't recall Lydia's family ever using it. Mrs. Bell thought they were better off in the bathtub during tornado warnings than hanging out with poisonous spiders and beetles in a black hole."

"Where were the flowers?"

"Planted across the top. There's always been a layer of dirt above the concrete. Used to be grass."

"You didn't bring a shovel," Bill says, almost to himself. He's trying to fit the pieces together, and I'm holding back the big one. "You think he buried something for you . . . in the storm cellar?"

An image of Charlie flashes into my mind, crammed on a bus with shrieking volleyball girls, headed to Waco.

I'm missing her game for this.

"Yes." I place two fingers on my wrist and feel my racing pulse, because Lydia always did. "Last night, I dreamed that Lydia is down there. That the flowers marked her grave."

Tessie, 1995

"Do you ever have nightmares?"

The doctor's demeanor today, all stiff and formal, suggests he has renewed purpose. I imagine him stabbing at a random page in his Book of Tricks right before I arrived. It is probably thick as a loaf of bread, with crackled yellow pages, a worn red velvet cover, and thousands of useless magic spells.

"Let me think," I say. I've added this cheerful line to my arsenal of *sure* and *sounds good,* part of my campaign to get off this couch as soon as possible.

I *could* tell him that last night's dream wasn't exactly a nightmare, as my nightmares go, and that his daughter, Rebecca, was the guest star. I was camped out in the grave with the Susans, per usual. Rebecca peered down at us, pale and pretty, in one of my mother's flowered church dresses. She fell to her knees and extended a hand. Her hair, wound in these goofy old-fashioned ringlets, tickled my cheek. Her fingers, when they reached me, were white-hot. I woke up, my arm on fire, choking for air.

I could tell him, but I won't. It seems unkind to bring it up, and I am working on being kinder.

"I dream a lot about the grave." This is the first time I've admitted this. It also happens to be true. "The dream is always exactly the same until the end."

"Are you in the grave? Or hovering above it?"

"For most of the dream, I'm lying in it, waiting."

"Until someone rescues you?"

"No one ever rescues us."

"What do you hear?"

A truck engine. Thunder. Bones crackling like firewood. Someone cursing.

"It depends on the ending," I say.

"If you don't mind, tell me about the different endings."

"It is pouring rain, and we drown in muddy water. Or snow falls until it covers our faces like a baby blanket, and we can't see." *Or breathe.* I swig out of the glass of water his secretary always leaves for me. It tastes a little like the lake smells.

"And to be clear . . . *we* means . . . Merry and . . . the bones."

"It means the Susans."

"Are there . . . other endings besides those?"

"A farmer doesn't see us and shovels dirt into the hole with his tractor plow. Someone lights a match and drops it inside. A huge black bear decides the hole is the perfect place to hibernate and lies down on top of us. That's one of the nicer endings. All of us just go to sleep. He snores. Anyway, you get the idea."

"Anything else?"

"Well, sometimes he comes back and finishes the job. Buries us for real." *With bags and bags of manure.*

"He . . . meaning the killer?"

I don't answer, because once again, it seems obvious.

"Do you ever see a face?" he asks.

Come on, doesn't he think I would have said if I saw his face? Still, I think about his question. Rebecca's is the only face I've ever seen in this recurring event. She was lovely in her first appearance last night. Big, innocent eyes, dark corkscrew curls, skin like ivory silk.

She looked very much like Lillian Gish, probably because Lydia and I had just rented *Birth of a Nation.*

Lydia says that Lillian Gish loved to play tortured characters, *as a rebellious counter to her devastating beauty.* Lydia knows this because her dad has a huge crush on this actress, even though Lillian Gish is quite dead. She said her dad especially likes the finale of *Way Down East,* where Lillian floats unconscious on an ice floe toward a seething waterfall, while her long hair dangles in the water like a snake. Right after she told me, Lydia said she shouldn't have. That it might provoke more nightmares while I was *in this state.*

It ticked me off. She hardly ever says things like that. It makes me worry. Am I looking in more of a state than usual? Isn't she noticing I'm more cheerful? Aren't I getting better?

Either way, it probably isn't *relevant* to tell the doctor about his daughter showing up in my dream as a silent movie queen, wearing my mother's clothes. It was certainly weird and random, like just about everything else.

"No," I say. "I don't see his face."

Tessa, present day

Once again, I'm in the shadows. Watching.

My body is tucked under the eaves, pressed against the cold, dirty siding, hopefully out of camera range for the television van camped by the curb out front.

I'm trying to steady my nerves by picturing Lydia's yard the way it used to be: green, neat, and shady with two giant clay pots of red and white impatiens on each of the front corners of the flat concrete porch. Always red and white, like the Christmas lights that Mr. Bell strung along the front roofline that every single year ended ten bulbs short on one side. It was tradition for my father to comment on it whenever we drove by.

Lucy and Ethel used to live back here. Mr. Bell's hunting dogs. When he wasn't around to call them off, their excited claws left little white streaks on my calves. The old boat was usually up on blocks in the back corner, perpetually waiting for July 4th. Lydia and I used to throw off the tarp when Mr. Bell wasn't home so we could do our homework and work on our leg tans at the same time.

But there's a circus assembling here today. And I'm responsible for it. My gut cramps. Bill and Jo are staking their reputations on me.

It took three days for Bill to retrieve the judge's permission to dig at Lydia's house and another twenty-four hours to set the time for

2 P.M., which is exactly fourteen minutes from now. The district attorney was surprisingly cooperative, probably because the police are getting killed in the media. A local newspaper editorial criticized the county for "an embarrassing lack of Texas frontier justice in not identifying the bones of the Black-Eyed Susans and returning them to their families."

It wasn't a particularly well-written or researched opinion, just fiery, something Southern journalists are good at pulling out of the air on a slow day. But it had worked a little magic on Judge Harold Waters, who still reads newspapers and has presided over the Black-Eyed Susan case from the beginning. He scribbled his signature and handed it down from his perch on top of his favorite cutting horse, Sal.

I barely remember Waters during the trial, just that Al Vega was worried he was too wishy-washy on the death penalty. A few years ago, I saw the judge on CNN giving an eyewitness account of a UFO hovering over Stephenville "like a twenty-four-hour Super Walmart in the sky."

"Could have been a worse draw," Bill had told me.

And so here we are, because of my dream about Lydia, and a judge who believes in flying saucers.

Two uniformed cops are squaring off the back yard with yellow crime tape. Jo is standing on top of the Grassy Knoll with the same female detective who attended the meeting with Hannah's family. A SMU geology professor is rolling by with a high-tech ground-penetrating radar device on wheels that will never in a million years fit through the door to the cellar. It barely fit through the gate. His grim face says he's figured this out.

Jo has told me that GPR is still more theoretical than practical when searching for old bones underground, but she and Bill decided it couldn't hurt to add to the melodrama. The DA agreed. He'll make hay out of it either way.

The professor is the acknowledged local expert in the complicated task of reading GPR imagery. Still, the ground is not a womb, and Jo tells me he will not be able to discern a skeletal face. He'll be searching for evidence of soil disturbances that would suggest someone dug a grave once upon a time. He might be able to make out a human shape, but it's doubtful. He's mostly part of the show.

The yard is now buzzing with conversations, an impromptu lawn party that's starting to gel. Bill is schmoozing the pretty assistant district attorney assigned to witness this latest crazy turn of events. Her real face is buried under a Southern coat of makeup. I'm calculating the distance between them. Two feet, now one.

Mr. and Mrs. Gibson are propped up in lawn chairs in their Sunday best Dallas Cowboys T-shirts, smoking like fiends, the only two people who appear to be enjoying themselves. One of them has mowed the weeds for the occasion.

The professor is suddenly making a beeline for them. He shakes their hands. From his wild gesticulating, I've deduced that the professor wants to run his device over both the front and back yards. The Gibsons are vigorously nodding yes.

Are they imagining movie rights? Is that what prompted Mrs. Gibson to wash her hair and stick on flip-flops and fresh toe Band-Aids? Is she hoping to add a plaque under her No Soliciting sign that declares this house a historical landmark, like Lizzie Borden's?

The gate clanks behind me, and the back yard suddenly snaps to attention. Four more people are striding in. Two cops in jeans, hoisting shovels and a metal detector. Two women in CSI protective gear with an unlit lantern and a large camera. Their arrival signals that my tortured wait is almost over.

Across the yard, one of the uniformed cops is already cutting through the lock on the storm cellar. He yanks on the door and it gives way easily. He leaps back and slaps a hand over his nose and mouth, as does every person within ten feet of the door. Even Jo, who told me that on the site of the 9/11 tragedy, she smelled things she will never forget.

Now everything is going too fast. One of the crime scene investigators is busily handing out masks. One of the cops in jeans disappears into the hole like an agile snake. The shovel and lantern are handed down to him. Next, a CSI disappears. The space must be tiny, because everyone else remains aboveground. Eager. Chattering into the hole.

Mr. Bell would never let us open that door. *It's nasty down there, girls.*

Empty plastic evidence bags are dropped into the cellar. In fifteen minutes, two of the bags return to the surface, bulging. They are set alongside the back fence.

The CSI pokes her head out from the hole and she beckons for the cop with the metal detector. *In case there is jewelry?* I could tell them that Lydia always wore her grandmother's thin gold wedding band with the pinprick red ruby. I wonder for the hundredth time in four days why the cops couldn't find any of the Bell family in a search of public records. It's as if they sailed off the face of the earth.

Jo is offering her hand to the CSI, covered with muck and filth, climbing up through the door. The cop with the metal detector descends to take her place. The Gibsons are munching potato chips and passing a plastic tub of ranch dip back and forth. The geologist is methodically rolling his device over the grounds like a wheelbarrow, pausing every now and then to read his screen.

A circus.

Another evidence bag is handed up from the hole. And another and another. All of them are set along the back fence line with the others. In the end, eight black bags, like the bodies of lumpy spiders, their legs ripped off. Finally, both cops emerge, black from the knees down, tearing off latex gloves. The group huddles for a short conversation.

Jo turns and searches the yard until her eyes land on me. She walks toward me, her face twisted with concern, the longest twenty yards of my life.

How could I have left Lydia down there for so long? Why did I not figure this out sooner?

Jo's hand is heavy on my shoulder. "We didn't find anything,

Tessa. We're going to go a little deeper, but they've already dug three feet and struck clay and limestone. It would have taken the killer forever to dig through it. Seems very unlikely that he did."

"What . . . is in the bags?"

"Someone used the place as a root cellar. It was trashed with broken jars and rotting fruits and vegetables. And a couple of now-dead moles that burrowed in somehow for a last supper. There was plenty of moisture to keep it rancid. Cracks in the concrete."

"I'm so sorry . . . that I wasted everyone's time."

Nothing inside me feels that sorry. *Lydia could be alive.* Those flowers might really be from her. I feel a rising tide of unexpected joy.

"We'll still sift through the contents of those bags, back in the lab. We always knew this was a shot in the dark. Literally. And I like to leave no stone unturned. Or any cliché unturned." Trying to make me smile.

Behind her, the professor has wheeled his device right below the gaping mouth of the cellar. A small crowd is gathering, including the Gibsons, who've ducked under the crime tape. Someone in the center of the circle gives a shout. The uniforms are pushing everyone back to make room for the cops and their shovels.

The crime scene investigators are talking to the professor like he's an umpire about to make a critical decision. They turn to the cops and direct how wide to make the hole.

The men nod, and carefully crack the earth.

Tessie, 1995

The doctor is telling me a story about when he was twelve.

I'm sure there's going to be a point, but I wish he'd get to it. Lately, he's been a little all over the place.

I'm annoyed by that smudge on his glasses, by Lydia flushing all of my Benadryl down the toilet last night. *I'm sorry,* she said, but it seemed to be about much more than swirling away those pink pills. Something is going on with Lydia. For the last two weeks, she's been late instead of exactly on time and sometimes cancels on me altogether. She makes vague excuses, her cheeks flush and she rakes her teeth across the pink lip gloss on her bottom lip. She is a terrible liar. Eventually, Lydia will tell me what is wrong, so I don't bug her.

Of course, two sentences into the doctor's tale, I'm wondering if *he's* lying. He says he was a chubby boy and yet he's got all that wiry muscle under the shirt with the collar that stands like a pinned white butterfly. I bumped up against his arm once. It was immovable, concrete, a runner's leg extending from his shoulder.

"I'd come home every day after school to an empty house," he is saying.

I'm suddenly scared for the boy in an empty house even though he's sitting across from me alive and well with no visible scars.

"Tessie, do you want me to continue? Is this story bothering you?"

"Um, no. Go ahead."

"In the winter, the house was always dark and cold. So the first thing I did after I unlocked the door, before I put down my books or took off my coat, was walk to the thermostat and turn up the heat. To this day, the thump of the furnace, the smell of heat coming on . . . is the smell of loneliness. Tessie, are you listening?"

"Yes. I'm just trying to figure out your lesson here. I thought you were about to tell me something terrible happened to you." I'm disappointed. Relieved. Vaguely intrigued.

It occurs to me that I love all of the smells associated with heat. Fireplace smoke drifting my way on a chilly night run, barbecue coals declaring it Saturday afternoon. Sizzling pork chop grease, Banana Boat sunscreen, hot towels tumbled in our old Kenmore dryer. Especially after Mama died, I couldn't get hot enough. I flipped my electric blanket on high so much that it streaked a black scorch mark on the blue fabric and Daddy took it away. I still stretch out by the heating vent in the floor of Mama's walk-in closet and read. I'm not sure I would have survived the last year if I couldn't slam the screen door behind me, sprawl on the back porch lounger, and let the brutal sun fry every black thought to ashes.

"Smell is the sense that is most instantly connected with memory. Do you know anything about Marcel Proust?"

"Am I failing this test if I say no?" I can't wait to tell Lydia that the doctor is pulling a depressed French philosopher with a handlebar mustache out of his bag. It's a big step up. Lydia christened my last therapist Chicken Little after the woman suggested I read *Chicken Soup for the Soul*.

"This isn't a test. There is no way to fail in this room, Tessie." His tone is plodding, predictable—and, I realize, a little tired. "One of Proust's characters recalls an entire event from his childhood after smelling a tea-soaked biscuit. Science has been chasing this theory ever since—that smell retrieves deep memories. The olfactory bulb rests near, and instantly communicates with, the part of our brain that holds the past."

"So this *is* a test. You are telling me I can retrieve my memory through smell."

"Maybe. Are there any smells that . . . bother you since the event?"

Peanut butter, peanut butter, *peanut butter.* My dad interrogated Bobby and me last week about why an almost-full jar of Jif was in the trash. Bobby didn't tell on me.

The muscles in my thighs and legs suddenly cramp.

"Tessie, what's happening?"

I can't breathe. I have drawn my knees up to my chin. My fingers are in my ears.

"Why can't I remember? *Why can't I remember?*"

His arm is around me. He's saying something. My head falls onto his shoulder. I feel him stiffen slightly, and then relax. His body is warm, a hot water bottle, like Daddy's. I do not know or care if this is appropriate behavior for a therapist.

He is heat.

Tessa, present day

I spend forty-five minutes in the shower, but it doesn't help. I pace the house. Open the refrigerator, swig out of the orange juice bottle, slam the door shut. Pick up my phone on the counter. Consider calling Charlie. Bill. Jo. Stop myself.

Punch around on Facebook. Stick my daughter's old iPod into the speakers, and turn it way, way up so that Kelly Clarkson full vibrato is massaging my brain. Rearrange the kitchen canisters, the magazines, the mail, Charlie's scattered papers and notebooks. Fold and refold a leftover piece of satin on the floor. Obsess over neat, exacting edges in a house where things usually roll around at the whims of a churlish tide.

I want, *need* to know the contents of the box unearthed seven hours ago near Lydia's storm cellar. From my vantage point under the eaves, I couldn't tell anything other than it was metal, about twelve inches square, and easy for a CSI to carefully lift out with blue-latex-covered hands. At that point, the cops began the process of clearing the back yard of extraneous people like me. In the rising clatter of voices, Jo didn't even look my way. Bill and the assistant DA had reappeared and stood together off to the side of the hole, arms crossed, observing.

The knock at the door, three short raps, snaps me to attention. I glance down to see whether I'm decent. The answer is no. Bare legs and feet. The only thing covering me is one of Lucas's old camouflage Army T-shirts that hits about four inches below a patch of lace that Victoria's Secret calls underwear. No bra. I grab a pair of shorts out of the pile of clean clothes on the couch and hurriedly hop into them, one leg at a time.

Two more urgent raps.

The shorts are Charlie's, and they ride high under the T-shirt so that it still appears that I'm wearing nothing. But, good enough.

I thrust my eye up to the peephole. Bill.

He is perfectly framed in the oval, as if he is standing in a tiny, tiny picture from another era. His hair is wet and slicked back. I can almost smell the soap.

I know he is not here to talk about Lydia. We almost kissed on that curb. This silent debate has been going on between us ever since he brushed his head on the Galveston sea glass dangling from the ceiling in my bedroom.

I open the door. He's wearing faded Levi's, and an easy, tentative smile that is going to get me in trouble tonight. I cannot stop staring at his mouth. He's carrying a bottle of wine in each hand. One red, one white. Considerate, because he doesn't know my preference, which is neither. On a night like this, I'm a beer girl all the way. The heat in the few feet between us is unmistakable now, flushing my skin. Pretenses, denials, the fact that I'm a mom of fourteen years and he's probably still getting carded—all of it undeniably stripped away after I fell apart in his arms. Bill has barely said an unnecessary word to me since.

At this moment, we are the same people we were before we sat down on that curb, and two very different ones.

"This isn't a good idea," I say.

"No," he says, and I open the door wider.

I have three important rules when it comes to sex.

I have to be in a committed relationship.

It cannot happen in my house, in my bed.

It must be dark.

Bill abandons the wine bottles on the hall table and kicks the door closed without saying anything. He pushes me back against the wall. His body is still chilled with night air, but his fingers and lips on my skin are like drifting flames. My arms are up around his neck, and I'm pressing my body into his, craning my neck up. I have not felt this certain I should be alive in a very long time. It's making me slightly woozy.

He cradles my chin in one hand. His gaze is long enough and deliberate enough to assure me that he knows exactly what he's doing. I think, *If I look away now, if I stop this, it will still be OK, almost like it never happened.* But he bends to kiss me again, and I am lost. I want this intimate dance in my hallway to go on forever. His hands have slipped under my T-shirt and are sliding up my back.

I don't protest when he lifts me and carries me down the hall. I wrap my legs around his waist and keep my mouth on his.

In my room, he sets me down gently. His head brushes the glass again, setting off a trickle of muted music. He strips off my shirt. His shirt. Pulls me down onto my soft, messy sheets. We are instantly coiled, like people who have made love to each other hundreds of times. I close my eyes and swirl to the bottom of the river.

"Tessa, you beautiful girl," he groans, his breath on my neck. "You drive me crazy."

Crazy.

Maybe another one of his lines. Perhaps a last-ditch plea for one of us to come to our senses.

I pull away slightly, but not enough that he can see the scar near my collarbone. He's been too busy so far to notice. I'm always so careful about this. Never too drunk on love or lust to forget. My hand reaches for the switch on the lamp by my bed, and stops. The bulb has cast his face in half-glow, half-shadow. Every cliché pops into my head. Light and dark, life and death, true and false, comedy and tragedy, good and evil, yin and yang.

Golden boy lawyer and girl marked by the devil.

I use one hand to tug at the pins holding up my hair. I know exactly what I'm doing, too. There is a look on his face that I will never forget, that I will hold on to forever, no matter what happens after tonight.

No matter whether we fail Terrell.

No matter whether my monster eats us both alive.

I reach over, and snap off the light.

This is the one rule I will not break tonight.

Sex is the only time I worship the dark.

"This one?" he asks. His finger is tracing the faint line on my ankle, and I shiver.

"From surgery. You know that I broke my ankle . . . that night. Please, come up here." I tug at his hair, and he ignores me.

"And this?" He's smothering the tiny butterfly above my right hip bone with the tip of his finger.

"An impulse right before the trial," I say. I'm suddenly flooded with the memory of the exquisite pain of the needle. When I encounter people smothered in tattoos, chattering eagerly about the next one, I understand the addiction.

I only ask to be free. The butterflies are free.

Lydia's voice is ringing in my head. She quoted that line from *Bleak House* to a tattoo artist at a carnival on the state fairgrounds. Lydia was lying facedown on a fresh towel on a metal cot. The flap of the tent was closed, making it an oven. Lydia's jeans were unbuttoned and slightly pulled down over the curve of her smooth white hip. I'd gone first, oddly brave. The wings of my tattoo were stinging, even more as I watched this stranger carve out Lydia's identical twin butterfly.

Bill's fingers are urging me back to the present. He is inching his way up my body slowly, exploring, as if he is clinically gathering evidence for court. It is the first sign in the last hour and a half that my brain is working.

My hair is covering the three-inch line above my left collarbone. He pushes it aside. He *knows*.

"Tell me about this one," he says.

It is the scar I am the most ashamed of. It *feels* like my monster's work as much as if he'd inked it himself. In reality, he drew none of my scars with his own hand. "The ER doctors panicked a little the night I was . . . found. Everybody did. The EMT carried me in the emergency room door in his arms, screaming. Later, my cardiologist was furious. He said I would have needed a pacemaker eventually but not that night. Not that soon. They used wires that would be tough to extract so they left it in." My body stiffens slightly as he nuzzles my neck. This can't be a surprise to him. "*Poor little pacemaker girl*. Al Vega rammed it home on the stand. Don't you remember from the transcript?"

"Yes, but I wanted to hear it from you."

So Bill *is* on the clock. The love spell is settling like dull party glitter.

"Should we call Jo and ask what was in the box at Lydia's?" Changing the subject. Trying not to sound hurt.

"Trust me, she'll call. Try not to think about it.

"What about Charlie's father?" he asks abruptly. "Is he in the picture? I like to know when there's competition."

His question sounds an off note for me. "Lucas would say no one could compete. He's generally quite full of himself. He's a soldier. His ego keeps him alive." I touch Bill's cheek. "We haven't been together for years. Not like this."

Bill and I are uncomfortably working backward. It's wrong. This is why I generally follow my sensible rules for sex. I'm leaning over to grab for the T-shirt on the floor when it occurs to me that I should adopt another rule: Never wear the Army shirt of one man while making love to another.

"Don't leave," Bill says softly. "I'll shut up. Stay with me." He's yanking me down again, spooning his warm body against my back and tossing the comforter over us. I can't resist the heat.

Sleep isn't coming.

I nestle into Bill's back. Close my eyes and drift.

I'm back in the tent, watching Lydia's butterfly get its wings. The tattoo artist isn't that old. Maybe twenty-five. She's wearing a red, white, and blue halter top that shows a lot of skin. Her back is laced with old white scars, probably from a belt.

A four-word tattoo is flushed defiantly against the damaged canvas.

I am still here.

Tessie, 1995

"Tessie, are you listening?"

Always with the *listening.*

My lips are glued to the pin-striped straw of a Dairy Queen Dr Pepper. The leaves brushing the office window have turned a brilliant red in the last week. I've never seen a tree so lit up in August, like Monet has picked it out and struck a match to it. I figure God is using this tree as a reminder to be grateful that I'm not still blind. But he's a fickle God or I wouldn't have gone blind in the first place.

I rub at a smudge of mascara sweat stinging my eye. Lydia has been obsessed with trying new cosmetics lately, while I am busy trying to be the blur that no one notices. She had experimented on me until she perfected the blend to hide my half-moon scar—Maybelline Fair Stick 10 combined with a tube of something puke green and Cover Girl Neutralizer 730. She wrote all of this down for me, including the order in which I was to apply it, and then she made up herself in my bathroom mirror. She looked amazing when she finished. My dad once said, not meanly, that if Lydia didn't open her mouth, every boy in school would be after her. While she added a layer of clear mascara and smacked on pink lip gloss, she told me all about Erica Jong and the zipless fuck. It is the first time I ever heard her use the f-word and it was like she'd fired a shot that killed our remaining childhood.

"Sex with a stranger," she had explained. "No remorse. No guilt." More and more, I feel like I'm the wheel spinning in the mud, while Lydia's foot is on the gas.

The doctor interrupts my train of thought. "Tessie, what's with you today? What are you thinking about?"

Zipless fucks. Scar recipes.

"I'm hot. Kind of bored."

"OK, how about this. What is the emotion you have felt most of the time since you were here two days ago?" *Since you hugged me on the couch and acted like a person?*

"I don't know." I squirm. I hate this odd habit of his—starting an intimate conversation while standing five feet away.

"I think you feel guilt. Almost all of the time. Ever since the event. We keep skirting around it."

I suck slowly out of my Styrofoam cup and stare at him. *The event.* Yep, still drives me crazy when he says it.

"Why would I feel guilty?"

"Because you believe you could have prevented what happened to you. Maybe even what happened to Merry."

"I was sixteen years old. An athlete. I don't know exactly what happened, but I'm sure I could have prevented this if I'd been paying attention. It's not like I'm a two-year-old who could be tossed in a car like a pillow."

He finally sits down across from me. "You've hit right on the problem, Tessie. You aren't two or four or ten, Tessie. You are a teen-ager, so you think you're pretty smart. More perceptive than adults, even. Your father. Your teachers. Me. In fact, I hate to tell you, but this is the smartest you will ever feel in your whole life." Lydia hates the no-socks loafer look on men, and right now, so do I. I stare at his pearly ankle with the bone jutting out and think about how we are just a bunch of ugly parts. I feel so many conflicting emotions about this man. About males in general right now. If he really wanted to get anywhere, he'd ask about *that*.

"Rebecca thought she was smarter, too," he says.

His daughter's name hits the humid air like a grenade. I'm not bored anymore, if that was his intent.

"There is a reason you feel the need to blame yourself," he continues. "From all accounts, you were a very careful girl. If you accept the blame—decide you took a rare misstep—you can reassure yourself this was not a random event. If you blame yourself, you can believe that you are still in control of your universe. You're not. You never will be."

"And what about you?" I ask. "I bet you still think your daughter is alive, when she's decomposing in the muck of a river or being snacked on by coyotes. Let me enlighten *you*. Rebecca is dead."

Tessa, present day

The sunrise is painting the bedroom pink. The best time of day for talking to angels and taking photographs, according to my grandfather. For admiring clouds that drift like feathers off a flamingo, according to Sir Arthur Conan Doyle.

For shoving midnight monsters to the back of the closet.

Bill is sliding a long, skinny leg into his jeans. His back is bare, broad, wired with muscle. It's been a long time since I woke up on a Saturday morning with someone in my bed who wasn't furry or sick. I'm trying to identify the emotion in my gut. Scared, maybe. Hopeful?

Charlie isn't due back on the bus for another couple of hours but she's delivered a series of texts that dinged through a third, lazy round of lovemaking. I'm propped up against the headboard and am thumbing through them, the sheet modestly pulled up to my chest.

Third place ☹. Coach got ejected. ☺

Forgot need tub of blue hair gel for bio lab Monday. Soooorry.

What's for dinner?

Bill's cell phone rings on the bedside table while I'm thinking about where to buy a tub of blue hair gel without returning to 1965. I pick up his phone and toss it over but not before I see the caller ID.

Bone Doc.

My throw across the tumbled comforter falls short, but Bill leans in, catches the phone anyway. Winks.

I remember the first time a man winked at me. Lydia was blowing out eleven candles, one to grow on, while I watched her father's eye open and shut under the ragged brow that never quite filled in after an auto shop accident.

Bone Doc. Jo calling, to divulge the secrets of the box? For hours, even with the distraction of Bill's tongue, my mind has been prying the lid open and slamming it shut.

The box is filled with sand, silky enough to run through my fingers like a waterfall.

It is crammed with girls' jawbones, grinning wickedly at every angle.

It holds a package tied up with glittering black tinsel made of Lydia's hair.

"Hey." Bill speaks low into the phone and glances back at me. He listens without interrupting for at least a minute. "Uh-huh. I can reach Tessa."

He's zipping up his jeans at this point, balancing the phone between his ear and shoulder.

The doctor had taught me in our sessions that I could have waited five years to sleep with this man, and never really known him. The doc was speaking generally, of course. He believed that a person's most profound flaws or virtues emerge in great crisis, or they remain buried forever. I remember leaving his office that day thinking it was sad that ordinary, dull people die all the time without ever knowing they are heroes. All because a girl didn't go under in the lake right in front of them, or a neighbor's house didn't catch fire.

"Be there in about an hour," Bill is saying.

Five of us are stuffed into the tiny room, all looking like we'd come off a sleepless night.

Jo, in running shorts and a well-worn T-shirt that says *Pray for Moore, OK*. Bill, wearing the same clothes as the night before. Alice Finkel, the flirtatious assistant district attorney, hiding under a face made up with Mary Kay precision, so desperately interested in Bill that it hurts to watch. Lt. Ellen Myron, in Wrangler's, a gun strapped to her hip.

I concentrate on the three plastic evidence bags, lying in a neat row.

My fingers itch to rip them open and get this grim party rolling. Lieutenant Myron clears her throat.

"Tessa," Lieutenant Myron says, "there were three items recovered from the box exhumed in the back yard of Lydia Bell's childhood home. We're hoping you can identify the items."

"There were no . . . bones inside?" I ask. *Just tell me, dammit. Tell me you found a piece of Lydia.*

"No. Nothing like that." Lieutenant Myron flips over one of the bags. I recognize the small book immediately. Gold, frayed cover. A design of yellow flowers with green shoots trickling up toward the title. *Poe's Stories and Poems.*

"Can I pick it up?" I ask.

"No. Don't touch. I'll do it."

"That's Lydia's," I confirm. "I was with her when she bought it. Her dad drove us into Archer City to Larry McMurtry's bookstores."

Why would Lydia bury this book? After my kidnapping, she probably scourged her room of anything with a yellow flower on it. But Lydia wouldn't be able to completely part with a treasured book. She'd romanticize it like this, in a time capsule to dig up later.

Except she never came back.

Lieutenant Myron sets the book aside and dangles another bag from her thumb and forefinger. "What about this?"

I swallow hard and peer closer. "A key? I don't even recognize the random keys in my own junk drawer."

"So that's a no?"

"That's a no."

"Worth asking."

Lieutenant Myron reaches for the third bag. She holds it up, six inches from my eyes.

The room is waiting for me.

Tick, tick, tick.

Can everyone hear that? I don't know if it's my pacemaker, which never makes a sound, or the deer heart trapped in that box.

At ten, I could recite every word of "The Tell-Tale Heart." Lydia was better at it, of course. Once, she hid a loud clock under my pillow.

"Tessa?" Bill grips my shoulders. I'm swaying. The ticking is louder. His watch, *dammit,* near my ear. *Tick, tick.* I push his arm away.

"I thought this was lost." It's the voice of a seething teen-ager. "She must have taken it."

"Who took it?" The lieutenant's voice is sharp.

"Lydia. Lydia took it."

Tessa, 1995

The doctor is already seated in his chair right by the couch. He doesn't bother to stand up and greet me. I can't tell by his expression if he is still angry after last week, when I spewed that acid about his daughter being eaten by coyotes. He certainly hadn't objected when I just got up and stalked out.

I throw my purse on the floor, flop back on the couch, and cross my legs, hiking the skirt so he can see to China. He's not the slightest bit interested. I could be his eighty-year-old aunt. My face burns hot and angry, but I don't know why. I twist the ring on my finger, wishing it were his neck.

"Your mother," he says smoothly. "You found her on the day she died."

Payback for conjuring his daughter. He's wielding his sharpest knife today. It opens up a place where I store the exquisite pain of missing her. I want to scream, to shatter that pleasant, professional mask that he snaps on with an invisible rubber band. Sometimes I wonder if I died in that hole. If this room is hell's purgatory, and everything else—Daddy, Bobby, Lydia, O.J. the Monster—is part of a dream when the devil lets me sleep. If this judge in a pin-striped shirt is deciding whether to throw me in a locked attic with a bunch of cackling Susans or set me free to haunt our killer for eternity.

"I'm leaving." I say this yet remain planted on the couch. "I'm done with your dumb games."

"That's your decision, Tessie."

I was in the tree house.

She had called my name from the kitchen window. I thought she wanted me to help with the dishes. She always made a mess. Grease and flour everywhere. Crusted pans. Dirty bowls in the sink. Daddy said it was the price for biscuits that crumbled in your mouth, fudge frosting, fried okra scramble with potatoes and tomatoes that we ate like popcorn, cold, as leftovers.

I was in the tree house. But I ignored her.

"You found her on the kitchen floor."

My heart bangs against my chest.

"You were eight years old."

Her face is blue.

"She died of a stroke," he says.

I pull up the skirt of her apron. Cover her face.

"Are you angry that she isn't here? That she left you?"

I was in the tree house.

I didn't come when she called.

The guilt is roaming free now. Almost unbearable.

"Yes," I breathe out.

Tessa, present day

The object in the third plastic evidence bag on Jo's desk is tiny, probably never of importance to anyone but me and its first owner, a little girl in a frilly petticoat who is long dead and buried.

When I was fifteen, I found the ring in the bottom of a basket of junk in an antiques store in the Stockyards. It was so caked with filth that I didn't see the inset pearl, like a microscopic spider's egg, until I got it home. The ring fit perfectly on my pinky. The owner of the store told me it was a Victorian child's ring from the 1800s, probably gold-filled, which is why she said she could give it to me for $35, but certainly not the $10 I suggested. Lydia countered to the woman that she wouldn't have known the ring existed if we hadn't wandered in. "Tessie could have just stuck it in her pocket," Lydia spewed indignantly, at which point I slid an extra $25 of my Christmas money across the counter and dragged my best friend out the door.

Halfway down the block, Lydia decided that I had purchased the ring against the will of the universe and wanted me to return it. *It's bad luck to wear the jewelry of a dead stranger. Who knows what kind of terrible things happened to the girl who wore it? In Victorian times, children were raised by cruel nannies and saw their parents once a day by appointment. Winston Churchill said he could count the number of times he'd been hugged by his mother.*

By the time we arrived at the bus stop, Lydia was even more insistent, to a higher degree of craziness than usual. She made the leap from the grubby little object on my pinky to the Hope Diamond. *It grew in the ground for 1.1 billion years before it exploded out of the earth and then cursed almost everyone who touched it. Marie Antoinette got her head chopped off and her princess friend was hacked to death with axes and pikes. It even hexed the innocent mailman who delivered it to the Smithsonian. His family died, his leg got crushed, and his house burned down.*

Say what you want about Lydia Frances Bell and her ridiculous chatter, she said things I never forgot. If she were standing here, she'd be alternately dismayed and thrilled to be starring in the kind of morbid tale she devoured and repeated over and over.

The lieutenant is holding the ring so the pearl faces me like a blind eye. Everyone is being courteously silent. The weight of their expectations is suffocating.

"Yes, that was mine," I affirm. "It went missing right before I testified at the trial. Lydia thought the ring was bad luck and wanted me to stop wearing it."

"Why did she think it was bad luck?"

Pearls bring tears. Suicides and insanity, murders and carriage crashes.

"She didn't believe you should wear the jewelry of dead people unless it belonged to someone you once knew. History was important to her." *And she was right,* a Susan chimes in my ear.

It's true—the ring was on my finger when he threw me in that hole. Everything else I wore that night—my favorite black leggings, Dad's Michigan T-shirt, the cross necklace that Aunt Hilda gave me at my confirmation—disappeared. The ER doctors cut off every bit of it and handed it over to the police.

The night nurse was the first to notice the ring while checking my IV, a couple of hours after my pacemaker surgery. I could feel her wriggling it off, her fingers floating like feathers across mine. *Shhhhh.* When I woke up, there was a pinched, untanned circle where the ring had been. A month later, at home, I discovered that someone had tucked a hospital Bible into a pocket in my suitcase. When I opened it up, an envelope was taped to Psalm 23, the ring tucked inside.

The first thing I think when I hear the thump is that Charlie has tumbled out of her crib. It takes an instant of consciousness to realize that Charlie has not slept in a crib in thirteen years. She's tangled in the covers beside me, red hair splayed on the aqua pillowcase like she's floating in an ocean. It's coming back to me now: our late-night marathon of *The Walking Dead*, popcorn, and cheddar cheese chips. The antidote to identifying inexplicable objects dug out of your best friend's back yard.

I'd shut off the TV in my bedroom around 1 A.M. That could have been thirty minutes or four hours ago. It's pitch black outside the window. I reach over to touch Charlie's bare shoulder to be sure I'm not dreaming. It feels velvety and cool, but I don't make the usual move to cover her up.

A low hum of chatter, as the Susans gather in my head to confer. I feel for the phone in the bed, where it usually sleeps beside me: 3:33. Charlie's breath is even, and I decide not to wake her. Not yet.

I hear it again. The leaden sound of something dropping, like the lid of a trunk. It's outside, toward Charlie's room, but definitely not in the house. I slip over to my closet. Drop to my knees to grope around the shoe rack that hangs over the door. Second row up, fourth pocket over. My fingers tighten around my .22. For three years after the trial, this pistol was tucked in my size 2 waistband. I considered a bigger weapon, but I didn't want anyone to see the bulge against my bony hip. Especially not my dad. Lucas secretly taught me to shoot when we weren't sneaking around accidentally making Charlie. He insisted on one thing when he pressed the .22 into my hand for the first time: Go to the gun range like it's a church, at least fifty-two times a year.

I've always hoped it's OK to shoot more than you pray, because that's how it's turned out. Lucas has urged me to trade up for the last ten years, but I can't imagine any gun but this one in my hand.

I shake Charlie's shoulder and she groans. "*Not* morning."

"I hear something outside," I whisper. "Put your slippers on. And this." I toss over a sweatshirt, hanging out of my hamper.

"For real?"

"For real. Get *up*."

"Why aren't you calling the police?" The sound is muffled, as she tugs the hoodie over her face.

"Because I don't want us to be on the evening news."

"Is that your gun? Mom."

"Please, Charlie, just do what I say. We're going to slip out the back door."

"That makes no sense. The . . . thing is *out there*. Isn't this why we have an alarm system so freaking sensitive that it goes off every time I turn up Vampire Weekend? Shouldn't we at least look out the window and make sure it's not the garbage truck?"

It's at times like this that I wish I had a daughter who wasn't so wrapped in the confident armor of her beauty and intelligence and athletic grace. Instead, she is just like the Before Tessie. Both insisted strange noises outside the window were teen-age boys with soap and eggs, not monsters with rusty shovels and guns. Most of the time, they were right.

"Charlie, I just need you to do what I say. Follow me."

Another thump. Now tapping.

"OK, I heard that. Weird." Charlie is quickening her steps behind me as we navigate the darkened hall and living room. The shades are drawn as usual, but I don't want to flip on any lights.

"Follow our fire drill plan," I say. "Go to Miss Effie's. Bang on her back door. Call her house if she doesn't answer. Here's my phone. If I'm not there in five minutes, dial 911."

"Keep it. I already have my phone. What are you going to do?"

"Don't worry, Charlie. Just go." *Run.*

I push her out the back door, into utter blackness. The last thing

I see is the fleeting deer flash of her pink-and-white polka-dot pajama bottoms between the pine trees that border our properties.

I creep toward the front yard, using my photinia bushes as a shield. The thumping hasn't stopped, just moved inside me, to my chest. The gun is cocked in my hand. I want to be done with him. Tonight. *Forever.* I peer through a branch.

What the hell? Four gray squares are stuck in the middle of my yard like a row of gravestones. A small shadow hovers beside one of them, bathed in faint light. *A time-traveling Victorian girl searching for her ring?* I blink hard to make her go away. Instead, the shadow rises. The ghost child transforms into a man with a flashlight and a shiny gray nylon sweatshirt.

"Hey!" My reckless scream rips the air.

I make out a Nike swoosh, black hair, a wiry beard, before the man flips off his flashlight and runs.

If he's running, dammit, so am I. Across the yard, down the street. Feet pounding. He's too fast to be my monster. Young legs. Marathon legs. I am still fast, but not this fast. The slippers flop on my heels.

All of a sudden, he slows. Maybe he's stepped in one of our historic potholes. He's taking aim. I raise the .22 in warning just as he presses a car remote, triggering the taillights of a parked sedan. In seconds, a car door slams and he's screeching off. I can't make out the license plate.

I turn back. It's not a cemetery in my yard. I'm staring at crude plywood signs. Hate shimmers off them.

BLACK-EYED BITCH

THOU SHALT NOT KILL

REPENT!!

TERRELL'S BLOOD, YOU'RE HANDS

Just one of the crazies.
I'm not relieved.

I have the sudden, certain feeling I'm being watched.

Charlie.

The house next door, still dark.

My feet tear up the ground to Effie's. I bang hard enough on the front door that something inside clatters to the floor. There's no answer.

I kick off my slippers on the porch and race to the back. I'm thinking of my monster, standing under my windowsill. Of my daughter, in her polka-dot pajamas.

I hurl my fist at Effie's back door. More strangling silence. I survey the back yard, open my mouth again to scream Charlie's name but nothing comes out.

My frantic gaze lands on Effie's rickety garden shed in the back. In seconds, I am yanking open the door, ripping it half off its rusty hinges. Charlie is crouched in the corner by two bags of compost. The phone is pressed to her cheek, half-illuminating her face.

"Mom!" She is in my arms in seconds. A car has screeched to the curb. And another. Siren lights are filtering through the bushes.

A large shape is walking toward us, blinding us with his flashlight.

"I'm a police officer. Did one of you make a 911 call?"

"Yes, I'm Charlie. This is my mom. We're OK."

I nod, unable to speak. Gruff conversation floats from the front yard.

The policeman's light continues to travel over us. When he's apparently satisfied we aren't hurt or dangerous, he turns it on the shed.

The light trickles like water into the corners, up and down the walls.

He sees nothing out of the ordinary because he thinks what he's seeing is perfectly ordinary.

I'm seeing, but not understanding. I just know it's not ordinary.

Row after row of garden diggers.

They hang neatly in every square inch of space.

Tessie, 1995

"Do you believe in the devil, Tessie?"

Great. Like I don't get enough of this from Aunt Hilda.

"I mean it in a very metaphorical sense. I want to talk about the Black-Eyed Susan killer today. I think it would help when you're testifying to understand him a little better. That he's flesh and blood. Not mythic. Not Bluebeard. Not a troll under the bridge."

My heart beats a little faster. My hand reflexively moves over the lump above my left breast, the metal chunk under my skin that keeps my heart beating at a minimum of sixty beats a minute. I run a nervous finger on the straight three-inch scar. Lydia is already looking for a bikini with a strap that will cover it up.

"We don't know anything about the creep," I say stiffly. "We never will. He isn't talking. His family says he's normal." I don't ever say his name out loud. *Terrell Darcy Goodwin.*

"I treated a serial killer once," he says. "He was the smartest, most calculating person in the room. Could charm a million dollars out of an old lady, and did. He blended in, and stood out. He liked to get to know his victims and use that knowledge to scare them out of their minds."

"The pig-and-daisy card at the hospital." Out of nowhere.

"Do you think he sent that to you?" he asks.

"Yes. I think it made me go blind."

"That's good, Tessie. Excellent progress. Whether he sent it or not, it was a trigger for you. You control your mind, Tessie. Never forget it."

I'm nodding. I'm flushing a little, embarrassed by his compliment.

"My patient understood right and wrong, he just didn't care," he continues. "He studied carefully how to behave. He was able to simulate empathy because he regularly sat in hospital waiting rooms and observed it. He spent a year selling suits at Brooks Brothers to figure out how to dress and speak. He used the newspaper to manufacture biographies about himself as he moved around. But serial killers make mistakes. This guy did. He carried the remains of his victims in the trunk of his car because he couldn't help himself. The point is, they don't think they are human, but they are."

"I still don't get . . . the why."

"No one really knows. Maybe we will never know. For a while, doctors used to think it had something to do with phrenology. How many bumps you had on your skull. My patient turned out to be a cliché. He blamed his mother."

"Because . . ."

"We're getting a little off track here."

"Were you trying to cure this guy?" I pester him. *Or were you trying to figure out if he is the one who took your daughter?*

"Yes, against all odds, against all the rules of psychiatry, I was trying to see if that was possible. But it didn't turn out well. He is a psychopath, Tessie. He is perfectly happy the way he is."

Tessa, present day

Jo has asked me to meet her at Trinity Park, near one of the running trails, about a half-mile away from the duck pond. It seems a little strange. Too close to the bridge. Too much of a coincidence. Did someone besides a home-schooled juvenile delinquent see me digging? Is Bill reporting everything I say to Jo?

The Susans are quiet this morning. It happens that way sometimes, when my paranoia roils into such hurricane force that they can't catch their breath.

My body hasn't stopped jangling since Saturday night when I clutched my gun and pointed it toward the ghostly shape on the front lawn. On Sunday, I tried to rebound and put my daughter's life back in a normal place. I called Bill and told him to please not show up again on my doorstep with alcoholic beverages. That it was a mistake, that we had let overwrought emotion sweep us into the bed, that Swedish Scientist Girl and Assistant DA Girl would be more apt partners for him.

There was sturdy silence before he said: "We didn't touch the wine. And you're pretty apt."

Later, Charlie and I had swept the aisles at Walmart in search of blue hair gel, peppercorns, licorice, and lima beans for her 3-D re-creation of an animal cell. She chattered about turning Fruit Roll-

Ups into a Golgi body. I listened to soothing snatches of nearby conversation that floated in the fluorescent light like a country western song. *My brother just lost his house* in frozen foods and *God will find a way* by the potato chips and *Daddy's going to kill him* in front of the boxed wine. Soothing, because it seems like very few people at Walmart are pretending that things are OK, or that the world is going to end just because they *aren't* OK. I wheeled my cart through this stew of misfortune and daily kicks-in-the-ass and plain old tenacity. No one at Walmart cared a whit who I was. I arrived home with ten potatoes for $1.99 and churned out my mother's recipe for corn chowder. All of this effort at ordinary seemed to work: Charlie slipped under her fluffy comforter at the end of the night, full of starch and bacon bits and her belief that our bad guy was just a coward of a sign-maker with bad grammar.

Now it's Monday morning, and I want to say no to meeting up with Jo, but I can't. As soon as Charlie leaves for school, I strap on ASICS and yank my hair into a ponytail, every movement angry. I woke up with a deep, persistent need to run, to sweat out every bit of poison. Running is the one thing that always works. I can still manage four miles before my ankle begins to ache, and then two more miles to spite him. But, first, Jo.

The south side of the park is almost deserted when I swing the Jeep beside a shiny silver BMW. It's the only other car in this lot, which serves a small picnic area. I glance inside the BMW as I slam my door shut. A Taco Bell bag and an empty Dr Pepper can are tossed on the floor. A handful of change is mingled in the console with a movie ticket stub. Innocent enough. As I circle behind the car, heading for the path, I glance down at the BMW's license plate: *DNA 4N6*.

OK, so definitely Jo's car. I say it out loud, "*DNA 4N6*."

4N6? I try again. *DNA Foreign Sex*. Um, probably not, but it's taking my mind off the gun riding at my hip and what things a bone doc might store in the trunk of her car.

On the horizon, a straight black line. The predicted cold front and 30-degree temperature drop by nightfall. A sixtyish woman in pink fast-walks past me, pumping her arms, hurrying away from it. I stop at a homeless man curled into a fetal position, asleep on a concrete picnic table near a shopping cart crammed with useful trash. I stick a $10 bill deep into the empty coffee cup he's clutching. He doesn't move.

I do that whenever I can. For Roosevelt. I made Lydia go visit Roosevelt on his street corner after they found me, because I knew he'd be worried. I never got to say goodbye myself. He was found dead leaning against a tree, like he fell asleep there, a week before the trial.

DNA 4N6. Four-en-six. *Forensics!* I'm an idiot.

I pick up the pace once I see Jo, who is right where she said she'd be—under a landmark live oak rumored to have once been a hanging tree. She's cross-legged on a bench, sipping out of a green neoprene water bottle with a red biohazard sticker. Her black North Face windbreaker bears a *CSI Texas* logo. I'm figuring the bottle and the jacket are high-end graft from a forensic science conference.

"Thanks for meeting me here." She unfolds her lean legs and pats the bench for me to sit beside her. "I worked in the lab all weekend and needed some air. I heard about what happened at your house. Have the police caught him?"

"No. I didn't get a good look. There's an anti-death-penalty newsletter that mentions me on a regular basis, so the cops are checking that email list. The editor posted my street address in her last blog that ranted about Terrell's case. I'm not hopeful, though. I've been through this before."

"It's odd and scary . . . that these people would target you." She doesn't say it, but I know what she's thinking. *The victim.*

I shrug, used to it. "The trial was a trigger for a lot of anger. And the jury foreman was very public in saying the case turned on my testimony." *Even though I was just painting in the scenery.*

She nods sympathetically. I don't really want to talk about what happened Saturday night. It's bad enough that it's rolling on an endless loop in my head: Charlie crouching in the shed under a compulsive array of garden diggers. The police, at my insistence, breaking down Effie's back door. She had drifted off in her La-Z-Boy wearing noise-canceling headphones that she'd ordered off eBay. "You know, to maybe quiet the voices," she had told me conspiratorially while a policeman searched her house. For a brief second, I thought she was also hinting at the ones in my own head, but her eyes had been darting around like a feral cat. It seems most likely that Miss Effie's digger snatcher lives under her own roof. So I didn't tell the cops, and I hadn't yet figured out how to bring it up to Effie.

"I thought maybe you could use some good news," Jo says. "The red hair on the jacket found near the field? The mitochondrial DNA analysis proves there is a 99.75 percent chance it didn't come off your head. And there is no evidence of Terrell's DNA on the jacket itself."

"Is it enough to get Terrell a new trial?" I wonder if she's told Bill.

"Maybe. Maybe not. There's a relatively new law in Texas that allows prisoners to successfully appeal a case when scientific technology can shed light on old evidence. But I talked to Bill this morning. He's been through this wringer before with Death Row clients and he's pretty adamant that a single red hair and a sloppy expert who used junk science aren't going to be enough to convince an appeals court to overturn anything. He wants to throw more than that at the judge. Unfortunately, Terrell only has his mom and sister as alibis for the time Hannah Stein disappeared. And the cops have been unable to draw a line between Merry Sullivan and Hannah. Of course, the cops aren't exactly on Terrell's side—they are mostly focused on getting the girls identified for the families and getting the media off their backs every time the anniversary rolls around. Working at the behest of the district attorney who wants a little TV time. Did you happen to catch his press conference on Hannah?" I can tell she's not expecting an answer. "Ferreting out the real killer . . . well, that would just be a bonus for *us*."

The bitterness from her surprises me. "Sorry." She grimaces. "I'm usually the one assuming everyone's doing the best they can. I wish Bill and Angie had pulled me in much sooner." Her face turns more pensive. "I'm trying something else in an effort to identify the other two girls. I just don't know if there's time to do it."

Despite my resolve to pull back from the case, I feel that relentless tug in my gut. *I'm the one with the answers,* a Susan had insisted that day in the lab. Was it the Susan who belonged to the chattering skull? Or the new girl, lost and found in the pile of bones?

"A forensic geologist I know in Galveston is examining the bone evidence," Jo continues. "He might—a big might—be able to narrow down the area or areas where they lived. Then we could check out the cases of missing girls in those places."

"I've seen websites where you can send in a sample of your DNA and they will decipher your ancestry. Is this anything like that?"

"It is nothing, *nothing* like that. My geologist will use isotope analysis to examine the elements in her bone and try to match it to a region. It's a tool kind of in its infancy stages when it comes to forensic identification. It was first used on a boy whose torso was found floating in the Thames over a decade ago. Scientists were able to trace his origin to Nigeria."

"And it helped them identify the boy? Catch his killer?"

"No. Not yet. It's a process. When you're trying out new technology, each case is a single step on a million-mile road." Her voice is softening. "We are so much a part of the earth, Tessa. Of the ancient past. We store strontium isotopes in our bones, in the same ratio as in the rocks and soil and water and plants and animals where we live. Animals eat the plants and drink the water. Humans eat the animals and plants. The strontium is passed along, all stored in our bones in the same ratio unique to the region." The simplicity of her explanations always astounds me, and I think what a good professor she must be. "The problem is, it's a big world. And there is a relatively small database at this point when it comes to identifying geological regions. It's another long shot."

Jo has fallen silent. It still isn't clear exactly why she's asked me to the park.

"Tell me again how you deal with all of the dead ends," I finally say. "There's just so much futility. Don't you ever think you can't take it anymore?"

"I could ask you the same."

"But you *choose* this."

"I'd say it chose me. I've known since I was fourteen this is what I was supposed to do. That's why, when a kid tells me he's going to be a third baseman for the Yankees, I don't doubt him. Did you ever hear about the Girl Scout Murders in Oklahoma?"

"No," I say, although it stirs a vague memory. Lydia would know.

"Every scientist has a cold case that pulls at them for years. This Girl Scout case is mine. I was in high school when three Girl Scouts were pulled out of their tent in the middle of the night on a campout near Tulsa. They were raped and murdered and left out for show. A local man—who'd been a popular high school football player—was accused, tried, and declared not guilty. DNA evidence was collected at the time, but there was zero technology to examine it. And before you ask, the evidence is now too degraded to be useful. I've used my connections to see every single crime scene photo and read every single word on the police reports and forensic testing. The point is, if I could beam myself back to 1977, I could give those parents some answers. And it's all because scientists in labs keep trying to do futile things. My work is as much in the future as the present."

"I understand," I say. "It's possible there won't be answers in my case. For years. Why exactly did you ask me to the park? Just to up-date me?" It comes out rudely, which I didn't intend. I'm just so tired.

"No. I wanted to say . . . to make sure that you know that you can always come to me. I don't want you to ever feel alone."

She's really saying, *Don't dig without me. Not at this park. Not anywhere.*

"Tessa, have you ever thought that maybe I need you, too? That I'm not as tough as you think I am?"

The first whisper of the cold front is stirring the trees.

"Lori, Doris, Michele," she says softly. "The names of the dead Girl Scouts. *My Susans.*"

Tessie, 1995

"I'm thinking of not testifying."

It sounded way more defiant when I practiced in front of the mirror this morning with the toothbrush in my hand and aqua bubbles drizzling out of the corner of my mouth.

I'm NOT testifying, Mr. Vega.

There. That's better.

I open my mouth again to say it more emphatically but the district attorney is on his tiger prowl around the office, not the slightest bit interested in what I *think*. The doc is bent over his desk with a pile of folders, certainly listening to every word. He's the master of staying still.

"Did you hear me? I don't think I have anything of value to add. I *don't* have anything to add." I'm stammering.

Benita offers a sympathetic smile that pretty much says I'm doomed. Both she and Mr. Vega are here to review my testimony. This is the first time they want to rehearse the gory details. They've waited this long because Mr. Vega wants me to sound as spontaneous as possible. The trial is less than two weeks away, so that's pretty spontaneous.

"Tessie, I know this is hard," Mr. Vega says. "What we need to do is put the jury in that grave with you. Even if you don't remember details about the killer, you add context. You make it real. For instance, what did it smell like when you were lying there?"

My gag reflex is so strong that even he, the calloused prosecutor, reacts. I'm sure he did this on purpose, calibrating how this melodrama would play to the jury. I still think he's the good guy. I've just changed my mind. I don't want to testify for him. Cannot, *will not,* sit across from my monster.

"OK, we'll come back to that. Close your eyes. You're in the grave. Turn your head to the left. What do you see?"

I reluctantly turn my head, and there she is. "Merry."

"Is she dead?"

I open my eyes and cast them to the doctor for help, but he's busily tapping away on his computer at his desk. *Do I lie? Or tell the prosecutor that dead Merry talked to me? Surely, that would hurt the case.*

If I testify. Which I won't.

"I don't know whether she's dead." *The truth.* "Her lips are bluish gray . . . but some girls wear blue lipstick. It's Goth." I don't know why I said that. Nothing about clarinet-playing, churchgoing Merry was Goth, except when she was lying next to me in a grave like a prop for a horror movie.

"What else?"

"Her eyes are open." *Things were eating her, except when they weren't.*

"What do you smell?"

I swallow hard. "Something spoiled."

"Is it hard to breathe?"

"It's like . . . breathing in a port-a-potty."

"Are you cold? Hot? As best you can, narrative answers."

"Sweating. My ankle hurts. I wonder if he chopped off my foot. I want to look but every time I lift my head up, things kind of explode in my head, you know? I'm scared I will faint."

"Do you call out?"

"I can't. There's dirt in my throat."

"Keep your eyes closed. Turn your head to the right. What do you see?"

It hurts to turn my head. But it's easier to breathe. "I see . . . bones. My Pink Lemonade Lip Smacker. The lid is off. I don't know where it is. A Snickers bar. A quarter. From 1978. Three pennies."

The photograph in my head suddenly animates. Ants crawl in a delirious, sugar-fired frenzy on my lip gloss. A hand stretches out for the Snickers bar. I know it's my hand because it's sprinkled with pink freckles and the nails are short, trimmed, painted neatly blue with Hard Candy Sky polish. The color almost matches Merry's lips. I taste blood and dirt, peanut butter and bile, when I rip open the wrapper with my teeth. The bones of the other Susans chatter encouragement. *Keep up your strength. Stay strong.*

"I remember eating the Snickers bar," I say. "I didn't want to." *But the Susans insisted.*

"I don't remember you mentioning some of this before. Are you recalling other details? Anything about him? His face? Hair color? Anything?" I can't tell by Mr. Vega's voice if he thinks this would be good or bad.

Why is this stuff coming back now? No one tells me to, but I shut my eyes again. Turn my face up to the night sky, except there are no stars. The sun is shining. I'm out of the grave. I'm somewhere else, in a light-filled space with Merry and the Susans. Merry sleeps, while the others are whispering, chattering excitedly, making a plan. One of them is bending over me. A ring dangles off her skeleton finger, but the stone is missing. She takes the gold prongs and carves a half-moon on my cheek, and it doesn't hurt at all. There is no blood.

Get him, she says. *Never forget us.*

I know this isn't real, although the lab found my blood type, not Merry's, on the prongs of the ring locked on a Susan's finger bone. They figure, with utmost logic, that I fell on it when I was dumped into the hole.

I have to stop this before I tumble into that hole again and can't ever climb out.

"I'm not testifying. Not for you. Or them."

Mr. Vega tilts his head, ready to fire his next question.

"You heard Tessie." The doctor has raised his head from the desk. "This session is over."

Tessa, present day

I watched until Jo vanished on the path and I was sure she was not coming back. I jogged past the sleeping homeless man curled with his back to the refrigerating wind. Fumbled my way into the Jeep. Locked it. Folded myself forward against the steering wheel and stunned myself by bursting into tears. Here's what kindness and sympathy and an offer of partnership do to me.

I have driven to this office on autopilot, the last place I would have pictured myself this morning. The room is small, white-walled, and slightly chilly. A nervous woman in her thirties sits across from me, eager to start a conversation as soon as I stop pretending to read this magazine and finally make eye contact.

"It's hard, isn't it? When your kid is hurting? My kid is in there right now." The woman needs something from me. I reluctantly lift my gaze and watch her take it all in. My eyes, red and swollen. The scar. I nod with agreement and empathy, hope that will be it, and return to the headline: *Is it wrong to pay kids to eat their veggies?*

"Dr. Giles is terrific . . . if you're here for a first consult for your kid." She's not going to give up. "Lily's been going to her for six months. I highly recommend her."

I carefully close the magazine and tuck it back into the neat arc of reading material on the coffee table. "I'm the kid," I say.

The woman's face twists in confusion.

The girl who must be Lily pops out of the closed door, wearing a dizzying array of crayon-esque colors. The right side of her head is attached to a giant sparkly bow. Even with all the effort at distraction, I am drawn to the plain brown innocent eyes.

And the smile. I know that smile because I've worn it, the one that pulls at thirteen muscles and strikes a match for all the other smiles in the room and makes you appear perfectly normal and happy. Except I know Lily's terrified.

Dr. Giles isn't far behind Lily and, to her credit, does not act the slightest bit surprised to see me.

"Give me just a second, Tessa, OK? I'll have about twenty minutes before my next appointment."

"Yes. Certainly." I feel the flush of heat in my face. This isn't like me, to burst in on people, busy people, without warning. I remind myself that I have not yet paid her a cent.

Dr. Giles reaches out a hand to Lily's mother. "Mrs. Tanger, we had an especially good morning. And, Lily, you're going to draw me a picture for next time?" The little girl nods solemnly, and the doctor's eyes meet her mother's in a silent exchange. It's like watching my father's face all over again. *Hope, worry, hope, worry, hope, worry.*

Dr. Giles ushers me into the warm jungle of her office. I drop into one of her cushy chairs. I haven't rehearsed what I'm going to say. I think that seeing Lily has sucked the selfish, hot anger out of me, but I'm wrong. My hands are suddenly shaking.

"I want closure." Each word, staccato. A demand, as if Dr. Giles is somehow to blame.

"Closure doesn't exist," she responds smoothly. "Just . . . awareness. That you can't ever go back. That you know a truth about life's randomness that most other people don't."

She leans forward in her chair. "Maybe you still need to forgive him. I'm sure you've heard this before. Forgiveness is not for him. It is for you." She might as well be raking her nails on the chalkboard behind her. It's bugging me, the faint ghost of a stick figure still lingering there, half-erased. The happy sun. The flower with a center eye.

"I can't ever imagine forgiving him." My eyes are still glued to the flower on the chalkboard. I want to take the eraser and scrub away until everything is black. Make it clean.

"Then let's say that there is a way for you to get closure. How do you see that happening? What if he . . . what do you call him?"

"My monster." My voice is so low, ashamed, that I wonder if she can hear me. *What grown-up, not-crazy woman still talks about monsters?*

"OK. What if your monster opened the door right now and walked right in? Sat down. Confessed everything. You could see his face. Know his name, where he grew up, if his mother loved him, if his dad beat him, whether he was popular in high school, whether he loved his dog or killed his dog. Imagine he sat in that chair right over there, three feet away, and answered *every single one of your questions.* Would it really make any difference? Is there any answer that could satisfy you? Make you feel better?"

I stare at the chair.

The gun feels like a steel cookie cutter against my skin. I itch to fire it dead center into the fabric. Watch the white stuffing explode.

I don't want to have a conversation with my monster. I just want him dead.

Tessie, 1995

"I'm nervous." Benita's voice is vibrating.

This is an *emergency* session. They've sent Benita in alone to do the dirty work. It's been less than twenty-four hours since I announced that I would not be testifying.

She's wearing no eye makeup, which is a sure sign something is very wrong. She's just as pretty, but now she looks like the hot girl in middle school instead of the hot girl in high school. All I know is, I don't want to be the thing that makes Benita scared. She's been nothing but sweet and kind to me. Like, even her name means *blessed*.

Benita halts abruptly by the window. "I'm supposed to convince you to testify. Mr. Vega and your doctor think we have some sort of young female bond. To be honest, I'm not sure what you should do. I'm thinking about going into my uncle's cabinet-making business."

Wow. What a backfire.

"They want me to ask you what your worst fear is." She plops in the doctor's chair and meets my eyes for the first time. "They told me to sit *here*. Then I'm supposed to convince you that you will never live to regret testifying no matter how hard it is. So if you can tell me what you are most afraid of by going to court, that would be great. So they at least think I tried."

Tears are brimming in her soft eyes. I'm thinking it's not the first time she's cried this morning. I want to get up and hug her but that might break another ethical code and she's already smashed a few in this room.

"I hear that this defense attorney rips into people until there is nothing left but scraps." I speak slowly. "That's a quote my friend Lydia read about Richard Lincoln in the paper. And she overheard her dad tell her mom that everybody calls him Dick the Dick. He might get the jury to think I deserved this. Or that I'm making stuff up."

"The defense attorney is an asshole," Benita agrees. She is holding a finger horizontally under each eye, so the tears don't spill.

Without looking at the box, I grab a Kleenex and hand it over. The box is always waiting for me on the little table by my elbow, never an inch out of place. "And I don't want to be in the room with . . . the guy who did this," I continue. "With him staring at me the whole time. I can't imagine anything worse. I don't want him to feel any power over me ever again."

She dabs at her eyes. "Neither would I. It seems terrifying."

"My dad will be there. I don't want to lay out all the details, you know? Thinking about it, *talking* about it, makes me want to throw up. Like, I can see myself throwing up in the witness chair."

She takes a deep breath. "I worked on this terrible case during an internship last year. A twelve-year-old girl had been molested by a sixty-five-year-old aunt who couldn't get out of a wheelchair. It was a mess. Her own family was divided about believing the girl."

She reluctantly shifts her eyes back to me. "See, you are already wondering yourself. Mr. Vega was the prosecutor. He's brilliant. He had her talk about the details of maneuvering around the wheelchair during . . . the acts. No one doubted her when she got out of that witness chair."

"So the jury convicted her aunt?"

"Yes. Texas is vicious with child molesters. She'll die in prison."

"Was the girl glad she testified?"

"I don't know. She was pretty ripped up afterward." Benita offers me a weak smile. "I'm thinking selling cabinets would be a lot simpler, you know? They open. They close."

"Yeah," I say. "But you're good at this."

Tessa, present day

"Why does Obama need to know my damn waistline?"

Effie, in Texas Rangers pajama pants and a pale pink silk blouse with ruffles, is trotting across the lawn, shouting, waving a piece of paper. Charlie and I have just arrived home after an early after-school dinner at the Ol' South Pancake House. Some days, I wonder how long Effie stares out her window before we show up in our driveway, and if that time has any meaning for her. I'm really hoping it doesn't.

I'm sure it's been a long day of trying to remember for both of us. I'm not sure I'm up for Effie. My head hurts despite a confectioners'-sugar fix. She meets us on the porch, breathless, while her finger punches away at the typewritten letter. "It says right here that he wants me to tell him my weight, waistline, and whether I like to drink and smoke. It's not like we're courting. Although I do like a whiskey on the rocks and a smoke with a handsome black man every good now and then." A skim of green eye shadow, two rosy circles of blush, and the large fake pearl clips in her ears are dead giveaways that Effie has made it out of the house today. The pearl clips pop out of the drawer for church every Sunday, but the glittering eyelids mean she's been jousting with the ladies of the historical society. Effie regularly declares them "way too fix-y."

I prop the door open for Effie. Charlie follows while carefully balancing a clear plastic box loaded with a sea of blue hair gel and precisely arranged food products.

Effie sniffs the air deliberately.

"It's my 3-D animal cell project," Charlie tells her. "Starting to rot."

"Well, set it on the counter here and let's take a look." *Animal cell* and *3-D* take the stink out of it for Effie, who lifts the edge of the Saran Wrap cover with enthusiasm. Charlie snatches the offending letter out of Effie's other hand.

"Miss Effie, this letter is from your insurance company." Charlie begins to skim. "They're going to give you $100 off your deductible and a $25 Amazon card if you fill out this form and they approve your numbers. They also want your cholesterol."

"Damn spies, all of them." She pokes a finger into the blue cesspool. "Put *1984* on your reading list, Charlie dear. The man was a soothsayer. My waist used to be nineteen inches. Maybe I'll write that in their little chart. And then I'll call the cops and sue for sexual harassment when they send somebody around with a tape measure." Her finger continues to poke away in the box. "Hair gel for cytoplasm. Clever girl. What grade did you make on this project?"

"A minus. Which is like, really good for this teacher. The average in her class for this project over her twenty-six-year career is a C plus."

"Well, I'd say that's the sign of a bad teacher. What was the minus for?"

"The nucleus. I used a clear plastic Christmas ornament from Hobby Lobby."

"And the nuclear membrane isn't rigid. Hmm. Gotta hand that one to her, I suppose."

"Should I dump this in the compost, Mom? The jar said the hair gel is all-natural."

"It seems like more of a biological weapon at this point. I will let you and our neighborhood scientist make the call. I'm going to change into some sweats." And swig down a couple of aspirin.

I navigate the hall in the dark and flip on my bedroom light. There is a man, sleeping on my bed. Face turned away. And yet his reaction time is still better than mine. I'm looking down, fumbling for the gun in my waistband, and he's already leapt the six feet across the bed, shoved a hand over my mouth, and stifled my scream.

I struggle against him. His other arm is pressing my back against a brutal chest. *Charlie is in the house.*

"Shh. OK?"

I stop squirming. Nod. He releases his grip and I flip away, stumbling. I find myself staring furiously at Charlie's father.

"Jesus, Lucas," I hiss. "You scared me. Where in the hell did you come from? Why can't you knock on the door like a normal person?"

He shuts the door. "I'm sorry. I meant to text as soon as I got here. It was a twenty-nine-hour journey that involved turbulence and an Army pilot who enjoyed it a little too much. The cab dropped me off a couple of hours ago. Your bed was very comfy. I went right to sleep. Might have left some sand in your sheets." His face is closer to mine than necessary. "You smell like strawberry crepes." For a second, I remember what it was like to be wrapped in a burrito of solid Army muscle. And then I feel another little ping for Bill. He'd texted twice today. *How's your day?* About two hours later: *Come on, butterfly girl, talk to me.*

"Why, again, are you here?" Trying to hold my ground in every way.

"I had a disturbing Skype session with Charlie. After your night with a domestic terrorist."

"Oh." I sit on the end of the bed. She hadn't mentioned telling her dad, but why wouldn't she?

Lucas plops beside me and tosses his arm around my shoulders. "I figured I might be needed, but you'd be afraid to ask. Also, I'm trying to be respectful of your parental boundaries. If you don't think I should be here, I'll go. Charlie doesn't have to know. I can slip out the way I came in."

"Which I assume is through the front door."

"Well, yeah. You're paranoid about everything but your security code. You should change it more than once every five years."

"No."

"No what?"

"No, I don't want you to sneak out. Charlie should know you're here." *That you'll come for her.*

I knew Lucas. It didn't matter what had just rolled sweetly off his tongue—he wasn't about to go quietly after traversing an ocean for his daughter.

He has dropped his hand to my waist. Distracting. He lifts up the bottom edge of my shirt, lets his finger drift, and tugs out the .22. "You could use a little practice on your quick draw. You shouldn't carry a gun if you can't get it out of your pants."

I try to summon up a retort and fail.

"How about a little refresher tomorrow?" he asks.

My head is no longer pounding. If I still believed in them, I'd say this man was a godsend.

Lucas had never once judged my sanity, or told me no.

He slips the gun into my hand. "Put it up."

"I need a favor tomorrow morning," I say.

"Which involves?"

"Digging."

My bedroom is dark, except for the glow of the iPad. I'm propped against a stack of pillows. A full glass of wine is within reaching distance on the nightstand. Lucas is sprawled snoring on the couch, the contents of his duffle spilled out on the living room floor. Charlie is texting under her covers. The evening's competitive father-daughter game of Assassin's Creed was a little too instructional for my comfort. I was relieved when Lucas snapped off the video game about half an hour ago and tucked his teen-ager into bed for the first time in months. She pretended to be too old for tucking in, but we all knew better.

The dark is friendly, for once. The man on our sofa has sifted all of the bad things from the night and stuffed them under his pillow.

Still, I'm not at rest. I'm determined to take a little trip into the past.

I hold the picture in my hand closer to the light, which makes her eyes dance. A trail of Spanish lace spills down her hair and across her shoulders. A tiny locket nestles in her throat. A modern girl transformed into a beautiful antique bride.

I had clipped Benita's wedding picture out of the newspaper a very long time ago, about two summers after the trial. It contains only the most basic information. In the photo, Benita is beaming up at a very white man with a very white name. The bride's parents are listed as Mr. and Mrs. Martin Alvarez and the groom's as Mr. and Mrs. Joseph Smith Sr.

OK, Benita aka Ms. Joe Smith. I type *Benita Smith* into the iPad search bar and click on *Images*. The first twenty-five faces do not belong to my Benita Smith. The twenty-sixth picture is a red Mercedes, and the next is a shopping mall Christmas tree followed by a pearl bracelet and a baby's foot. Farther down, a kitchen pantry with bright red rooster door handles. In case she really did go into her uncle's cabinet business, I click to that page. No luck. I skip through endless, useless Benita Smith story links before I head to Facebook to search for Benita *Alvarez* Smith. Nothing. I delete her maiden name, and the Facebook screen rolls up hundreds of Benita Smiths.

Part of me doesn't want to work too hard at this. *Would she really know something that could help Terrell? Did she overhear something? Suspect something?*

I had let Benita drift out of my life seventeen years ago. There has to be a good reason for that, right? We had met for coffee every Tuesday afternoon for a few months after I testified. The last time, she dropped all official pretenses. She entered the café in tight black jeans and a *Remember Selena* T-shirt, with her six-year-old sister in tow. *Texas Monthly* had made Selena its tragic cover girl that month instead of me, so I was still feeling the naive bliss of being old news.

Not long after Terrell was convicted, Selena's killer had been sentenced and locked up in Gatesville. She was confined twenty-three hours a day to a tiny cell because of death threats. The Tejano music fans behind bars wanted Yolanda Saldivar to die for her sins. While Benita and I had whispered about that, her sister carefully strung plastic beads onto a shoelace. She had tied the bracelet to my wrist like a purple-and-yellow worm.

I doubt that Benita Alvarez looms boldly in the official records of the Black-Eyed Susans case. If her name is mentioned at all, Bill and Angie would have glanced right over it. She was never interviewed by the media. She didn't testify and only attended the trial on the two days that I took the stand. She was a minor player to everyone but me, drowned out by the thunder of Al Vega—or *Alfonso* as he calls himself now. Mr. Vega, 100 percent Italian, picked up the *fonso* to court the Hispanic vote when he ran his first successful race for Texas Attorney General.

When a Terrell Darcy Goodwin question is sprung on him, Mr. Vega declares *in no uncertain terms* that he would not try the case any differently today. He sent a birthday card to me when I turned eighteen, and a sympathy card when my father died. On both, he scrawled his name and wrote underneath: *I will always be there for you.* The cynic in me wonders if those words are just part of his regular signature to victims he wrestled into the witness chair. But Tessie? Tessie believes she could pick up the phone and he'd be at her front door in seconds.

I clear the search bar. Hesitate, just for a second. Type. Most of my teen-age angst about my doctor is gone. I'm staring at links to an array of bombastic papers he's written for online blogs and psychiatric journals. There's a new one since I last searched: "The Colbert Love Affair: Why We See Ourselves in an Imaginary French Conservative Narcissist."

I clear the search bar and type another name, even more reluctantly. Click on the link at the top for the very first time.

I'm staring at the weekly blog of Richard Lincoln aka Dick the Dick, instantly regretting that I just provided him with a hit, even the tiniest bit of incentive to carry on. Today's post: "Gasping for air." It's hard to look away now that I've come this far. Angie always wanted me to talk to him. Thought it might bump something loose. *He's a changed man.*

I can barely stomach the bio, so I skim. *Richard Lincoln, crusader. Nationally renowned death penalty lawyer. Author of* The New York Times *best-selling book,* My Black Eye.

My Black Eye. His confessional, a year after the trial. Whenever I'm in a bookstore, I turn the cover around, even though I've heard that he donates half the profits to the children of prisoners. Because why doesn't he donate all of them?

There's a YouTube video link beside his blog, which my fingers click without my brain's permission. At once, his voice is jarring the silent house, rising and falling like a preacher's, still a saw against my skin. I hurry my finger to turn him down. He's an upright cockroach roving an anonymous stage. *Lincoln-esque,* is how his fans describe him. *I failed Terrell,* he's saying. *I destroyed that girl. The Black-Eyed Susan case was the turning point of my life.*

I can't listen to any more.

He didn't just destroy me. He destroyed my grandparents. The police and Dick the Dick worked in odd concert in that regard. The police ransacked their castle and drove off with my grandfather's beloved truck as evidence. Nobody in Texas took a man's truck unless he was guilty as hell, so even his best and most stalwart farmer friends wondered. It didn't matter that the police said "whoops" months before the trial. Dick the Dick still hammered away in court. A tabloid screamed, *Could Grampa be the killer?* No, I can't offer *Dick* forgiveness despite the fact that, in the last thirteen years, Richard Lincoln has used DNA evidence to free three innocent men from Texas's Death Row. I pull the cover over the iPad. Nudge a couple of extra pillows to the floor. Slip deeper into sheets rough with sand from a war zone. Squeeze my eyes shut. Imagine the doctor lounging in pajamas covered with ducks in front of a *Colbert* rerun. Hope that Benita's life is strung like a party with purple and yellow beads.

I'm floating at the edge of consciousness when Lydia finds a tiny wormhole.

It's not like I haven't dragged the Internet for her a hundred times. Nothing. Not about her or Mr. and Mrs. Bell. It's like they are tiptoeing around in invisible ink while everyone else is galloping in screaming neon. The Bells *were* odd. They had little family, and made very few deep connections in town. Both sets of Lydia's grandparents were dead. I retain vague memories of a distant cousin of Mrs. Bell's who sent a poinsettia at Christmas. But how could a family simply vanish? How could nobody really care?

Over the years, I've imagined all sorts of outrageous plotlines about their fate. Maybe my monster killed them because Lydia knew something. She was always clipping out articles about the Black-Eyed Susan case and pasting them in a scrapbook she didn't think I knew about. Scribbling notes in the margins in her cramped, intelligent hand. My monster didn't turn the storm cellar into a family mausoleum, but he could have scattered their bones across the West Texas desert.

Or their bodies could be lying miles and miles under the sea with ocean garbage. The whole family could have bounced off on a spontaneous vacation and sunk to the bottom of the Bermuda Triangle in a wayward craft piloted by Mr. Bell. He was always forgetting to buy a boating permit. They could have slipped, undocumented, under the waves.

My most logical theory was witness protection. Someone had to plant the For Sale sign. Mr. Bell dealt in recycled auto parts with Mexican mafia types in the salvage yards. He rushed off in the middle of the night all the time to meet them. Lydia had shown me his drawer full of hundred-dollar bills.

I do know this. If another family on the block had quietly slipped out of town right after the trial, and Lydia was the one speculating, she'd suggest that the father was the Black-Eyed Susan killer. His wife and daughter were in on it. They were spooked by my survival and now travel from town to town, changing their names as they go, killing girls.

That's exactly the kind of story Lydia would have made up when we were under the blanket with our flashlights, and she was scaring the crap out of me.

Tessie, 1995

October third, nineteen hundred and ninety-five, 1 P.M.

O.J. was set free an hour ago, which makes me sick to my stomach.

In mere minutes, if I don't screw this up, I will be, too.

This is my last session. The doctor is recommending a follow-up every six months for the next two years, and, *of course,* I should call before then if I'm ever feeling any distress. He's taking a sabbatical in China, so he won't be around, but he will recommend someone *perfect for me.* In fact, he already has someone in mind. There's a little transfer paperwork to fill out, but he'll take care of that before he leaves. *How lucky,* he says, *that the trial only lasted a month.* That the jury took only one day to reach a verdict.

Everyone is beaming. The doctor. My dad. I'm beaming back because otherwise I might explode. *Almost free, almost free, almost free.*

"I want to say again how brave you were to testify," the doctor says. "You held your own. The bottom line: Because of you, a killer is on Death Row."

"Yes. It's a relief." A lie. The only thing that's a relief is the news that my doctor is moving to China.

He's sitting there, so smug. I can't let him get away with it. I won't forgive myself.

"Dad, can you just give us one second alone to say goodbye?"

"Sure. Of course." He plants a kiss on my head. Shakes the doctor's hand.

Dad doesn't pull the door shut hard enough when he leaves, so the doc gets up to close the two-inch gap. *Click.* Doctor-client confidentiality and all.

"Why wouldn't you ever talk about Rebecca?" I ask, before he sits down.

"Tessie, it's very painful. Surely you can understand that. And it would have been unprofessional of me to do so. I shouldn't have even said what I did. You need to let this go. It can't be a part of our professional relationship."

"Which is ending. Right now."

"Yes, but that doesn't matter. You are still my patient until you walk out that door."

"I saw you with her."

"You're really beginning to worry me, Tessie." And, in fact, his face does look worried. "You were right. My daughter is most likely dead. She isn't . . . talking to you, is she? Like the Susans?"

"I'm not talking about your daughter."

"Then I have no idea what you mean," he says.

I don't say it out loud, because what's the point?

We both know he's lying.

"See you around," I say.

PART II

Countdown

"According to the *L.A. Times,* Attorney General
John Ashcroft wants to take 'a harder stance' on
the death penalty. What's a harder stance on the
death penalty? We're already killing the guy. How
do you take a harder stance on the death penalty?
What, are you going to tickle him first? Give him
itching powder? Put a thumbtack on the electric
chair?"—Jay Leno

—Tessa, listening to *The Tonight Show* in bed, 2004

September 1995

MR. VEGA: I know that this has been a very difficult day of testifying, Tessie. I appreciate your willingness to speak for all of the victims and I know the jury does, too. I have just one more question for now. What was the worst part of lying in that grave?

MS. CARTWRIGHT: Knowing that if I gave up and died, my father and little brother would have to live without knowing what happened. That they would think things were more horrible than they were. I wanted to tell them that it wasn't that bad.

MR. VEGA: You were lying near-comatose with a shattered ankle in a grave with a dead girl and the bones of other victims—and you wanted to tell your family that it wasn't that bad?

MS. CARTWRIGHT: Well, it was bad. But imagining what happened for the rest of your life is worse. You know, letting your mind fill all that in, like, a million different ways. That's what I thought about a lot . . . how they'd have to do that. When the rescuers came, I was, like, so relieved that I could tell my dad it wasn't that bad.

29 days until the execution

In a month, Terrell's coffin, black and shiny as a new Mustang, will be hitched on a wagon to the back of a John Deere tractor. He will sink into the ground with the bodies of thousands of rapists and killers rotting in the Captain Joe Byrd Cemetery. Most of these men lived violently on the surface but they are interred on a pretty little hill in East Texas summoned out of Walt Whitman's dreams. These were men officially unclaimed in death. In Terrell's case, people claim him, *love* him—they just don't have the money to bury him. The state of Texas will do that with $2,000 of taxpayer money and surprising grace.

Inmates will rumble that tractor. They will be his pallbearers and bow their heads. They will chisel out his stone. Stencil on his inmate number. Maybe misspell his name.

They will use a shovel like the one in my hand.

My stomach churns for Terrell as I stare at the patch of black earth that my grandfather used to till behind his fairy tale house. At the very place where, twelve years ago on a hot July day, I found a suspicious patch of black-eyed Susans. It is the last place I'd ever want to dig for a gift from my monster, and so that's what I've done. Left it for last. My stomach boiled in a sick stew that day, too.

I was twenty-two. Aunt Hilda and I had banged a For Sale sign onto the front lawn a few hours earlier. Granny had died eight months before. She was buried beside her daughter and husband in a small country cemetery, eight miles down the road from their fantastical house.

That day, I'd gone outside to breathe after opening a drawer in Granny's jewelry box and sucking in a powerful hit of her church perfume. Charlie was almost three, and she'd slammed the screen door to the back porch ahead of me a few minutes earlier. When I opened the door, my beaming daughter stood several feet from the bottom of the steps, hands behind her back. She thrust out the handful of black-eyed Susans that she was strangling in her sweaty fist. Behind her, a hundred feet away, their sisters danced in flouncy yellow skirts—pretty little bullies hanging out near a row of sickly beans and a bonsai-like fig tree.

I poured a pot of boiling water into their eyes while Charlie stared from the porch. When my aunt called out from the house and asked what I was doing, I told her I was getting rid of a vicious pile of fire ants, which was just a bonus. *Don't want Charlie to get stung.* A few ants were already carting the dead away on their backs.

I'm jolted back to the present as Herb Wermuth lets the screen door slam behind him. It echoes like a tinny symbol. More than a decade later, it's his castle, not my grandfather's. He's gone inside, abandoning Lucas and me with little instruction to the devious winter sun and the garden that he says his wife, Bessie, chews up with a tiller twice a year. *Good luck finding anything.* Herb has made it clear he couldn't care less where we are digging as long as it is not for a dead body and the media isn't involved. He did ask us to try to get our business done before his wife returned in a couple of hours from a session with her new personal trainer.

At first, when we showed up on his front porch, Herb hadn't been so accommodating. "I listen to the news," he'd said grimly. "After all this time, you're not sure they got the right killer. You're working with his lawyer." His eyes had raked over the shovel hanging from my hand. "Do you actually think one of his girls is buried out back?"

"No, no, of course not." I had rushed to reassure him while hiding my revulsion at the use of the pronoun. *His.* Like the monster owns us. Owns me. "The cops would be here if that was the case. As I said, I've just always thought that it was possible that the mon . . . killer buried . . . something for me in the garden."

Herb couldn't hide it on his face—he believes, like most people around here, that the Cartwright girl had never been right in the head again.

"You've got to promise," he insisted. "No media. I got rid of some tabloid photographer yesterday asking to snap a picture of the room where the Black-Eyed Susan slept. And some guy called the other day from *Texas Monthly* wanting permission to get a portrait of you in front of the house. Said you hadn't called him back. It's so bad I'm taking Bessie to a condo in Florida until this execution thing passes over."

"No media." Lucas had responded firmly. "Tessa only needs to ease her mind." Patronizing. It sent a trickle of annoyance up my neck, but it did the trick for Herb. He even retrieved a shiny new shovel out of the garage for Lucas.

So Herb has left us to it. Except Lucas and I haven't budged since the screen door ricocheted on its hinges a minute ago. Instead of investigating the garden, Lucas is casting watchful eyes up the walls and windows of my grandfather's mythical house. He has never been here before, even though it's just an hour's drive from Fort Worth. By the time Lucas and I were wrestling in the backseats of cars, my grandfather was half-blind and permanently propped in bed.

It is comforting to know that Lucas is so focused. Protecting me from my monster, even if he has always believed, no matter what I say, that the monster is mostly confined to my head.

The house has cast a cool, dark arm across my shoulders. I know this house like it is my own body, and it knows me. Every hidden crevice, every crooked tooth, every false front. Every clever trick from my grandfather's imagination.

I start a little when Lucas steps beside me, armed with his shovel and ready to go.

The Susan times her warning to my first squishy step into the soil.

Maybe he did bury one of our sisters here.

If it weren't for the fig tree standing there like an arthritic crone, I wouldn't know where to dig. The garden is twice as large as when my grandmother grew her precise rows of Early Girl tomatoes and Kentucky Wonder beans and orange habanero peppers, which she turned to jelly that ran on my tongue like lava. This morning, other than the fig tree climbing out of it, the plot is a flat brown rectangle.

I used to stand in this garden and pretend. The blackbirds stringing across the sky were really wicked witches on brooms. The distant fringes of wheat were the blond bangs of a sleeping giant. The black, mountainous clouds on the horizon were the magical kind that could twirl me to Oz. The exceptions were brutal summer days when there was no movement. No color. Nothingness so infinite and dull it made my heart ache. Before the monster, I would always rather be scared than bored.

"This is a very open area, Tessa," Lucas observes. "Anyone who looked out a window on the west side of the house could have seen him plant the flowers. That's pretty brazen for a guy you think has managed to fool everybody into thinking he doesn't exist." He shades his eyes to look up. "Is that a naked woman up there on the roof? Never mind. It is."

"She's a replica of *The Little Mermaid* statue that gazes over the harbor in Copenhagen," I say. "The Hans Christian Andersen one—not the Disney version."

"I get that. Definitely not G-rated."

"My grandfather cast it himself. He had to rent a crane to lift it up there." I take three carefully measured steps north from the fig tree. "About here," I say.

Lucas thrusts the glistening metal of Herb's shovel with crisp,

223

clean determination into the dirt. My own rusty shovel is leaning against a tree. I've brought a stack of newspapers, an old metal sieve from the kitchen, and a pair of work gloves. I plunk myself down and begin to sift through the first chunks of overturned soil. I hear Jo's voice in my head insisting that *this isn't the way*.

I glance up, and for a second, see a little Charlie on the porch. I blink, and she's gone.

It isn't long before Lucas has stripped off his shirt. I keep sifting, averting my eyes from the muscles rippling across his back.

"Tell me a story," he says.

"Really? Now?" A black bug is skittering down my jeans. I blink, and it's gone.

"Sure," Lucas says. "I miss your stories. Tell me all about the girl up there on the roof with the nice boobs."

I pull out a rough piece of old metal. Think about how many layers to leave out of a multi-layered fable. Lucas has a short attention span. I know that he is just trying to distract me.

"A long time ago, a mermaid fell madly in love with a prince she rescued from the sea. But they were from different worlds."

"I'm already sensing an unhappy ending. She looks lonely up there."

"The prince didn't know it was the mermaid who rescued him." I pause from breaking apart a large chunk of soil. "She had kissed him and laid him on the beach, unconscious, and swum back out to sea. But she desperately wanted to be with him. So she swallowed a witch's potion that burned away her beautiful singing voice but in return carved out two human legs. The witch told the mermaid that she would be the most graceful dancer on earth, yet every single step would feel like she was walking on knives. The mermaid didn't care. She sought out the prince and danced for him, mute, unable to speak her love. He was mesmerized. So she danced and danced for him, even though it was excruciating."

"This is a horrible story."

"There's lovely imagery when it's read aloud. It loses a lot in my

retelling." I raise my eyes to the window in the turret of my old bedroom. The partly drawn shade makes it appear like a half-closed eye.
I imagine the muffled sound of my grandfather reciting on the other
side of the stained glass. *An ocean as blue as the prettiest cornflower.
Icebergs like pearls. The sky, a bell of glass.*

"And did this a-hole of a prince love her back?" Lucas asks.

"No. Which means the mermaid was cursed to die unless she
stabbed the prince and let his blood drip on her feet, fusing her legs
back into fins."

At this point, I stop. Lucas has already produced an impressive
hole the circumference of a small plastic swimming pool and about
as deep. I'm way behind on sifting through his piles of earth. All I
have to show for my efforts are a stack of rocks, the ribbon of rusted
metal, and two plastic pansy markers.

Lucas drops the shovel and falls to his knees beside me. "Need
some help?" he asks. I know him well enough to translate. He thinks
this is futile. My heart isn't really in it, either.

I hear the creak of a door opening, punctuated by a noisy slam.
Bessie Wermuth is trotting our way in fire-engine-red workout gear
that clings to two narrow inner tubes of fat around her waist. She's
carrying tall yellow Tupperware cups chunked with ice and amber
liquid.

"Good morning, Tessa." She beams. "So nice to see you and . . .
your friend."

"I'm Lucas, ma'am. Let me help you with those glasses." He
picks one and swallows a quarter of it in the first swig. "Delicious
tea. Thank you."

Bessie's eyes are fastened on Lucas's snake tattoo, which starts
around his belly button and disappears into his jeans.

"Have you found anything yet?" She raises her eyes from Lucas's
belt buckle.

"A few fossils, a plastic plant marker, a rusty piece of metal."

Bessie barely acknowledges my stash. "I wanted to tell you about
my box. Herb said he didn't tell you about my box."

"Your box?" A curl of uneasiness.

"It's a bunch of junk, really," she says. "I've even labeled it, *Stuff Nobody Wants But Mom*. You know, so my kids don't have to add it to the crap they're cleaning out when we die. There might be something in there you're interested in, though."

The sweat under my arms is icy. *What is wrong with me? It's just Stuff Nobody Wants.*

"I'm going inside to get it," she says. "I couldn't carry the box and the tea. Meet me at the picnic table."

"Are you all right? You don't look right." Lucas pulls me up. "We need a little break anyway."

"Yes. Fine." I don't say what I'm thinking—that I have a bad feeling about Bessie and her relentless tilling. We walk thirty yards and plant ourselves on the bench of an old picnic table slopped carelessly with green paint.

Lucas nods toward the house. "Here she comes."

Bessie is hauling an old U-Haul box across the yard, breathing with furious intention. Lucas jumps up and meets her halfway, relieving her of the box. He sets it in front of me, but I don't reach. I'm mesmerized by Bessie's large bold print, which says exactly what she declared it did, thereby assuring that this will be the one box her grieving, surely sentimental kids will never throw away no matter what.

"This holds all the odds and ends I've found on the outdoor property since we moved in." Bessie pops open flaps. "Useless archaeology, really. Except the old bottles. I got those on the kitchen windowsill. But if it comes out of the earth and isn't wriggling or biting me, I keep it in here. I don't organize it by year or location. It's all dumped together. So I have no idea what came out of the garden and what got kicked up by the mower."

Lucas is bending over the box, pawing through it.

"Just dump it," Bessie says. "Can't hurt anything. Then Tessa can see, too."

Before I can prepare, the contents are rolling recklessly across the *table.* *Wire springs and rusty nails, an old, half-crushed yellow-and-red-striped Dr Pepper can, and a blue Matchbox car with no wheels.* A tiny tin for Bayer aspirin, a chewed dog bone, a large white rock streaked with gold, a broken arrowhead, fossils of cephalopods that once skulked around with tentacles and eyes like cameras.

Lucas is fingering through pieces of broken red glass. He's pushed aside a tiny brown object with a point.

"This is a tooth," he says.

"That's what I thought!" Bessie exclaims. "Herb told me it was a candy corn."

But I'm staring at something that lies all alone at the edge of the table.

"I think that was Lydia's." The words catch in my throat.

"Spooky." Bessie picks up the little pink barrette, frowns at it. I pull off my gloves and take it with unsteady fingers.

"What do you think it means?" she wants to know. "Do you figure it's a clue?" Bessie isn't breathing fast because she's old, or because Lucas is a sweaty god. Bessie is a junkie. She's probably devoured everything ever written on the Black-Eyed Susans. *How could I not have seen this?* She bought my grandfather's house when no one else would. She apparently knows exactly who Lydia is without explanation.

Lucas has placed his hand on my shoulder. "We'll borrow the tooth and the . . . hair thing, if that's OK," he tells Bessie.

"Of course, of course. Whatever Herb and I can do."

I rub my finger absently over the yellow smiley face etched into the plastic. *This means nothing,* I scold myself. It was probably tugged out of Lydia's hair by a cornstalk during a game of hide-and-seek back when we thought monsters were imaginary.

And yet. The pink barrette with the smiley face. The Victorian ring, the Poe book, the key. *Why do I feel like Lydia is the one playing a game with me, planned cunningly in advance?*

Lucas scans my face, and there's no discussion of whether to sift through the rest of the dirt.

I look up. On the roof, the flash of two girls. One with fiery red hair. I blink, and they're gone.

Lydia's barrette is wrapped in a tissue in my purse. The tooth is in Lucas's pocket. About fifteen miles down the road, Lucas clears his throat and breaks the silence. "Are you going to tell me what happened to that mermaid chick?"

My passenger window swims with blue and brown. The Texas sky, a bell of glass; the rolling farmland, once buried under an unfathomable sea. *Sun so powerful that the mermaid was often obliged to dive under the water to cool her burning face.*

I still my grandfather's voice. Place my hands on burning cheeks. Turn to Lucas's profile, a rock to cling to.

"The mermaid can't bring herself to murder the prince," I say. "She throws herself into the sea, sacrificing herself, and dissolves into sea foam. But a miracle happens—her spirit floats above the water. She has transformed into a daughter of the air. She can now earn her immortal soul and go to live with God."

Daughters of the air. Like us, like us, like us, breathe the Susans.

"The Baptist in your grandfather must have loved that one," Lucas says.

"Not really. Baptists believe you can't earn heaven. The only way to save yourself is to repent. Then you're good to go, even if you turn sweet mermaids to sea foam."

Or girls to bones.

September 1995

MR. LINCOLN: Tessie, do you love your grandfather?

MS. CARTWRIGHT: Yes. Of course.

MR. LINCOLN: It would be very hard to think something terrible about him, right?

MR. VEGA: Objection.

JUDGE WATERS: I'll give you a little leeway here, Mr. Lincoln, but not much.

MR. LINCOLN: Did the police search your grandfather's house the day after you were found?

MS. CARTWRIGHT: Yes. But he let them.

MR. LINCOLN: Did they take anything away?

MS. CARTWRIGHT: Some of his art. A shovel. His truck. But they gave it all back.

MR. LINCOLN: And the shovel had just been washed, correct?

MS. CARTWRIGHT: Yes, my grandmother had run the hose over it the day before.

MR. LINCOLN: Where is your grandfather today?

MS. CARTWRIGHT: He's home with my grandmother. He's sick. He had a stroke.

MR. LINCOLN: He had a stroke about two weeks after you were found, right?

MS. CARTWRIGHT: Yes. He was very upset about . . . me. He wanted to hunt down whoever did this and kill him. He said the death penalty wasn't good enough.

MR. LINCOLN: He told you that?

MS. CARTWRIGHT: I overheard him talking to my aunt.

MR. LINCOLN: Interesting.

MS. CARTWRIGHT: No one thought I could hear while I was blind.

MR. LINCOLN: I'd like to get to your episode of blindness a little later. Did you ever think your grandfather was odd?

MR. VEGA: Objection. Tessie's grandfather isn't on trial here.

MR. LINCOLN: Judge, I'm almost done with this line of questioning.

JUDGE WATERS: You can answer the question, Ms. Cartwright.

MS. CARTWRIGHT: *I'm not sure what he means.*

MR. LINCOLN: Your grandfather painted some grisly images, didn't he?

MS. CARTWRIGHT: I mean, yes, when he was imitating Salvador Dalí or Picasso or something. He was an artist. He experimented all the time.

MR. LINCOLN: Did he ever tell you scary stories?

MS. CARTWRIGHT: He read fairy tales to me when I was little.

MR. LINCOLN: The Robber Bridegroom who kidnaps a girl, chops her up, and turns her to stew? The Girl Without Hands, whose own father cuts them off?

MR. VEGA: Oh, come on, your honor.

MS. CARTWRIGHT: Her hands grow back. Seven years later, her hands grow back.

26 days until the execution

I wonder if Jo is in a freezing lab scraping enamel off a tooth that looks like a candy corn while I fold and stack clothes still warm from the dryer. If Terrell is sitting on his rock hard cot, composing his last words, drinking water that tastes like raw turnips, while I sip my $12 pinot and decide to throw out Charlie's pink socks with the hole in the left heel. If Lydia is out there somewhere laughing at me, or missing me, or up in heaven pestering dead authors while her body rots in a place only my monster knows about. I wonder if the tooth from the ground at Granddaddy's could be hers.

For three days, I debated about whether to turn the tooth over to Jo. I couldn't explain to Lucas why I waited. It made perfect sense to try every unlikely thing, to hold nothing back unless what I really wanted was *not to know.* Jo had met us in the parking lot of the North Texas Health Science Center a few hours ago. She was still wearing white shoe covers from the lab. She had listened in taut silence to my rambling about drowning Black-Eyed Susans in boiling water and a box of useless objects that no one cared about but Bessie. I didn't mention Lydia's pink barrette with the smiley face. Jo accepted the tooth from Lucas. Said little in return.

I wonder if Jo will forgive me for not bringing her with us, although it doesn't seem all that important right now. Nothing does.

Numbness grips me, a slow-acting poison that drugs the Susans to sleep and yet still allows my hands to build perfectly tidy little towers of clothes. Clothes that have mingled intimately in the washer—Lucas's Army underwear, Charlie's flannel pajamas with the pink cotton-candy sheep, my neon running shorts.

Lucas is slugging a beer at the end of the couch, watching CNN and rolling his briefs into tiny eggrolls, Army Ranger-style, then aiming and tossing them at my head, my butt, whatever is a good target. We're pretending to be just fine while the clock ticks the seconds off my sanity. Because after Terrell dies, then what?

Keep folding. The doorbell rings, and Lucas is up, opening the door. Probably Effie dropping off a food bomb. I glance at my watch: 4:22 P.M.—a couple of hours before I have to pick up Charlie from practice.

"Is Tessa home?" A nerve, plucked like a guitar string, as soon as I hear his voice.

Lucas's feet are planted deliberately, blocking my view of the door. "And this would be regarding what?" The drawl pulls out every bit of the West Texas in him. In slow motion, I see Lucas's left hand, the support hand, casually rise and rest on his upper chest. The fingers on his right hand, clinching. The ready position for the fastest way to yank a gun out of your pants. He'd demonstrated for me in the back yard not an hour before.

"Lucas!" I jolt myself away from the couch, toppling three of the piles. "This is Bill, the lawyer I've told you about who is handling Terrell's appeal. Angie's friend." All I can see beyond Lucas is the tip of a Boston Red Sox cap. I'm behind Lucas, pushing uselessly against hard muscle. I feel around his waist for a gun that isn't there. His movements a few seconds ago, just the reflex of a wary man. I realize that while Bill can't see my face, he has a perfect view of my hand curled intimately near Lucas's crotch.

Old resentment flushes heat into my face. This macho idiocy from Lucas is the primary reason we were drawn to each other when I was a scared, hormonal eighteen-year-old, and the primary reason we broke up. He descended from a generation of men who sent hearts skittering in terror with the one-two clunk of their boots. Who lived life like everyone was about to quick-draw. Lucas leaps eagerly at cat screeches, car backfires, knocks on the door. He's a good man and a terrific soldier, the best, but as an everyday life partner, he electrocutes the roots of every hair on my skin.

"Lucas, *move*." I shove a little harder.

Lucas steps aside slightly so I can wriggle beside him.

"Bill, Lucas," I say. "Lucas, Bill."

Bill sticks out a hand. Lucas ignores it. "Hello there, Bill. I've been wanting to meet you. I've been wanting to ask how involving Tessa at this very late date is a good thing. Don't you think it's time to step away? Ride off in your BMW out there? Give Tessa and my daughter the peace they deserve?"

For a moment, I'm speechless. I had no idea Lucas was pulsing with this kind of anger. We were melting down, every one of us. I step firmly onto the porch. "Lucas. Butt out of this, OK? Whatever I'm doing, it's my call. Bill isn't forcing me."

I shut the door in Lucas's face, not for the first time. "You can wipe off that expression, Bill." Not exactly what I meant to say. Not, *I miss you.*

"So that's your soldier?" Bill asks.

"If you mean Charlie's father, yes."

"He's living here?"

"On a short leave. Long story, but Charlie was scared after that night of the . . . vandal. She Skyped Lucas about it and shortly after that he showed up on my doorstep. He has an understanding boss and was overdue for a leave to visit Charlie anyway. I didn't invite him, but I'm not sorry he came. He's on . . . the couch."

"That doesn't seem like a very long story." Bill's voice is cool. "If you're still in love with him, just say so."

My arms are crossed tight against my thin sweater. I have no interest in inviting Bill inside and refereeing between the two of them.

"This isn't a conversation . . . we need to have," I say. "You and me . . . we can't be a thing. We slept together for the wrong reasons. It's not like me to do something that impulsive. *I'm not that girl.*"

"You didn't answer the question." I meet his eyes. Flinch. The intensity is almost unbearable. Lucas had never looked at me like that. Lucas was all hands and instinct.

"I'm not in love with Lucas. He's a good guy. You just caught him at a bad moment." Already I'm wondering if Bill's laser gaze is for real, or if it's method acting with an on/off switch. Useful for withering a witness, or stripping a girl down to her scars.

Lydia had always sworn no one could reach her vagina with his eyes but Paul Newman, "Even though he's ancient." She hadn't met Bill. I wouldn't *want* her to meet Bill. To tarnish this, whatever *this* is.

Why am I thinking about Lydia right now?

Bill plunks himself down in the swing, clearly not going anywhere. I reluctantly position myself on the other end. For the first time, I notice a large manila envelope about two inches thick, in his hand.

"What's that?" I ask.

"I brought you something. Have you ever read any of your testimony from the trial?"

"It never occurred to me." A lie. I'd thought about it plenty. The jury ogling me like I was an alien and the sketch artist scratching long, swift pencil strokes for my hair. My father, sitting in the front row of a packed room, petrified for me, and Terrell, in a cheap blue tie with gold stripes, keeping his eyes glued to a blank piece of notebook paper in front of him, the one for his notes. He never once looked at me or took a note. The jury interpreted it as guilt.

So did I.

"I've pulled out a few sections for you," Bill says.

"Why?"

"Because you feel such guilt about your testimony." Bill halts the swing abruptly. He taps the envelope that now rests between us. "Please read this. It might help. You are not the reason Terrell sits in prison."

I cross my arms tighter. "Maybe you're just thinking that the more I take myself back there, the more I might remember something that would help Terrell."

"Is there something wrong with that?"

My heart begins to pound, hating this. "No. Of course not."

He pushes himself up and the swing bounces and jerks in protest. "Jo told me about the tooth. I wish you'd let us know you were going to your grandfather's. I wish you weren't so intent on shutting me out. Are you planning to dig somewhere else?" He's stilling the swing with his hand while I get up.

"No. It was the last place. Is Jo . . . mad?"

"You'd have to ask her."

He's moving away, bristling with frustration. At life. At me. I grab the envelope off the swing and follow him to the steps. "Tell me the truth. Is there any hope at all for Terrell?"

He starts to step off the porch before swiveling halfway around, almost knocking me back. I am already there, only inches away. "There are a few more appeals to file," he says. "I'm driving to Huntsville to see him for the last time next week."

I grip his arm. "The last time? That doesn't sound good. Will you tell Terrell . . . that I'm still trying very hard to remember?"

Bill's eyes are glued to my fingernails gripping his sweatshirt, always unpolished and cut short, still crumbed with dirt from my grandfather's garden. "Why don't you tell him yourself?"

"You can't be serious! I'd be one of the last people he'd want to see."

Bill removes my hand deliberately. He might as well have shoved me down.

"It isn't my idea," he says. "It's his."

"Doesn't Terrell . . . hate me?"

"Terrell is not a hater, Tessa. Not bitter. He's one of the most remarkable men I've ever met. He believes you have it the worst. For a long time, he said he could hear your weeping at night over the other sounds of Death Row. He says a prayer for you before he goes to sleep. He's told me not to push you."

Terrell has heard me crying on Death Row. I'm keeping him awake. I'm an echo in his head, like the Susans are in mine.

"Why in the hell didn't you tell me this before?"

"There's no human touch. Can you imagine that? Twenty-three hours a day in a tiny cage with a narrow slot for food. A tiny Plexiglas window that's so high he has to ball up his mattress and stand on it to see out, for a fuzzy view of nothing. One hour a day to briskly walk around another small cage for exercise. Every second to think about dying. You know what he says is the worst part? More than the sounds of men screaming, or trying to choke themselves, or arguing over imaginary chess games, or incessantly tapping typewriters? The smell. The stench of fear and hopelessness oozing from five hundred men. Terrell never takes deep breaths on Death Row. He thinks he might suffocate or go insane if he does. I can't swig a deep breath without thinking of Terrell. Why didn't I tell you before, Tessa? Because you have enough to carry around."

He taps the envelope I'm holding. "Read this."

He doesn't wave goodbye as he backs out of the driveway.

When I walk inside, Lucas is facing the door, leaning against the back of the couch, dragging on his beer. Waiting. "What's wrong?" He's already restacked the piles of clothes that toppled over, a Lucas-style apology. "What did he want?"

"Nothing important. I think I'm going to take a nap before I pick up Charlie."

"You're sleeping with him." A statement, not a question.

"I'm going to take a nap." I brush past him toward the hall.

"He could be using you, Tess."

I close my bedroom door and slide down its back to the floor. Lucas is still calling after me. Tears prick at the corners of my eyes.

I run my nail under the flap of the envelope and pull out the tidy stack of court documents.

Bill might not think Tessie's guilty. But I know she is.

September 1995

MR. LINCOLN: Tessie, would you say that you played unusual games as a child?

MS. CARTWRIGHT: I'm not sure what you mean.

MR. LINCOLN: Let me put it this way. You have a pretty big imagination, right?

MS. CARTWRIGHT: I guess so. Yes.

MR. LINCOLN: Did you ever play a game called Anne Boleyn?

MS. CARTWRIGHT: Yes.

MR. LINCOLN: Did you ever play a game called Amelia Earhart?

MS. CARTWRIGHT: Yes.

MR. LINCOLN: Did you ever play a game called Marie Antoinette? Did you lay your head on a tree stump and let someone pretend to lop off your head?

MR. VEGA: Your honor, once more, Mr. Lincoln's questioning is simply designed to distract the jury from anything meaningful and from the man who sits in that chair on trial.

MR. LINCOLN: On the contrary, your honor, I'm trying to help the jury understand the environment where Tessa grew up. I find that very meaningful.

MR. VEGA: In that case, let me enter into the record that Tessa also played checkers, dolls, tea party, thumb wars, and Red Rover.

JUDGE WATERS: Mr. Vega, sit down. You're bugging me. I'll let you know when you're bugging me, Mr. Lincoln, but you're close.

MR. LINCOLN: Thank you, your honor. Tessa, would you like a drink of water before we continue?

MS. CARTWRIGHT: No.

MR. LINCOLN: Did you ever play Buried Treasure?

MS. CARTWRIGHT: Yes.

MR. LINCOLN: Did you ever play Jack the Ripper?

MR. VEGA: Your honor . . .

MS. CARTWRIGHT: Yes. No. We started the game but I didn't like it.

MR. LINCOLN: We, meaning you and your best friend, Lydia Bell, whom you mentioned earlier?

MS. CARTWRIGHT: Yes. And my brother. And other kids in the neighborhood who were around. It was a super-hot day. A bunch of us were bored. But none of the girls wanted to be the victims after one of the boys brought out a ketchup bottle. Maybe it was Lydia. We decided to do a Kool-Aid stand instead.

MR. VEGA: Your honor, I used to dissect live tadpoles by the river when I was six.

What does that say about me? I'd like to remind him and the jury that Tessa is the victim here. It's been a very long day for this witness already.

MR. LINCOLN: Mr. Vega, I have a really good answer for your tadpole question. But right now, I just want to note that Tessie's childhood involved games about violent deaths, missing people, and buried objects. That art imitated life long before she was found in the grave. Why is that?

MR. VEGA: Jesus Christ, you are actually testifying. Are you calling what happened to Tessa "art"? Are you suggesting it was some kind of divine karma? You're a son of a bitch.

JUDGE WATERS: Up here, boys.

"I don't think you're crazy. Evil sneaks up on little cat feet. *It sits looking over harbor and city on silent haunches.* I know that ain't the way the poem goes. It's supposed to be fog on little cat feet. Fog. Evil. It works either way. You usually can't see the headlights comin' at you until it's too late."

I blink away the image of this giant on a cot reciting a Carl Sandburg poem, trying not to listen to men scratching up the walls like cats.

"When I first saw you," Terrell is saying, "you were sitting in the box in that pretty blue dress, shaking so hard I thought you might shatter to pieces. I saw my daughters sitting there."

"That's why you didn't look at me," I say slowly. There had been such debating back and forth over The Blue Dress. Everyone had an opinion. Mr. Vega, Benita, the doctor, Lydia, even Aunt Hilda. The lace was itchy, but I never told anybody. When I testified, I had to casually flick my hand at my neck and my shoulders to make sure I wasn't really crawling with bugs. The Blue Dress was nothing Tessie would ever wear in real life. *The hem should hit her just slightly above the knees so the jury can see the brace on her ankle. Not too sexy. She's going to wear the brace, right? Can we gather in the waist to emphasize that she's still pretty much skin and bones? The color makes her look a little bit yellow, but I think that's good.*

"I wasn't going to make it worse for you." Terrell's voice brings me back. He's grinning. "I'm a pretty ugly man."

A guard rattles the cage at Terrell's back. "Gotta go, Terrell. Closing early."

"A man's going down tonight," Terrell tells me matter-of-factly. "The Row's always extra-tense when a man's going down. This is the second time this month." Terrell is rising while he speaks into the receiver. His broad body fills the window, softer and rounder than I expected. "It took real guts for you to come here, Tessie. I know you're tied up about this. Remember what I said. When I die, let it go."

My stomach dances with sudden panic. *This is it.*

The words are boiling up in a desperate rush. "I'm going to testify again if they'll give you a hearing. Bill is a terrific lawyer. He really believes there is . . . some hope. Especially now, with the DNA results on the red hair. It's not mine, of course." I pull a copper strand over my ear.

Terrell knows every bit of this already. Bill has already spent an hour with him. He's nearby, finishing up the habeas appeal on his laptop. All the other things Bill hoped might come through to bolster the appeal haven't.

"Yeah, Billy's a good boy. Never met a more Lord-guided man who doesn't believe one inch in the Lord. I've still got a little time to change his mind." Terrell winks. "Take care of yourself, Tessie. Let it go." And he hangs up.

I'm frozen to the plastic chair. It seems like everything has been neatly decided with that final click of the receiver. Terrell's fate. Mine.

He leans over and touches a finger to the glass in a direct line with my moon scar. It begins to throb. A Susan, tapping. *He's too good to be true, too good to be true.*

His mouth is moving. I'm panicking. I can't hear through the glass.

He repeats it a second time, carefully forming the words.

"You know who it is."

Bill didn't want to bring me here tonight, but I insisted. We are only a few hundred yards from the infamous Death House unit known as "The Walls," where Terrell informed me just hours earlier that a man was going down. The Walls is a quaint, stately old building too tired to sigh. It's been witnessing death by rope and electricity, gunfire and poison, for more than a century.

Next door, there's a small white frame house with a neatly covered barbecue grill on the front porch. Embracing the other side, a church.

Terrell is lying in his cell a few miles away in the Wynne Unit on

Death Row, about to put away his reading. Bill has told me that even with lockdown and lights out, Terrell will know before we do if tonight's execution has been carried out.

When I ask how that can be, he shrugs. The prisoners have their ways.

Tiny ice pellets crackle on my jacket. I pull up my hood. We won't be allowed inside. We are merely voyeurs.

I've breathed in the dust of my premature grave, but I've never felt anything as oppressive as the weight of this air. It's as if a dying factory threw up death, spewing plumes of grief and misery, hope and inevitability. The hope is what makes it seethe. I wonder how far I'd have to run to get away from this toxic cloud. Where its filmy edges end. Two blocks from the death chamber? A mile? If I peered down from space, would it be smothering the whole town?

Huntsville is a mythical place that I had all wrong. In my mind, Huntsville was a single house of horrors. A giant slab of concrete in the middle of nowhere where the state of Texas locks up Things that deserve to die. Where stuff happens that you don't ever, ever need to know about unless it's on a big screen with Tom Hanks.

That's what Lydia's father, a big fan of Tom Hanks and the revengeful philosophy of Deuteronomy, always told us.

I was badly misinformed. Huntsville is not just one badass prison but seven scattered around the area. The death house that looms in front of us in the waning light doesn't sit in the middle of nowhere.

It's a 150-year-old redbrick building with a clock tower where time has literally stopped. It's located two blocks off the quaint courthouse square, in the middle of town. People are downing chicken-fried steak and strawberry cake right now at the city's best restaurant, within easy eyesight of The Walls.

The cops are casually roping off the front of the prison with crime scene tape. We are within shouting distance of a windowless corner of the building, where the execution will take place.

I'm trying not to let Bill know how bothered I am by all of this matter-of-fact efficiency. It started right away, when Bill easily slid his car into a spot at the side of the brick prison wall and shouted up to the guard on the roof to ask if it was OK to park there. She shouted back, "Sure," like it was a middle school basketball game.

The Fors and the Againsts are obediently positioning themselves on opposite sides of the building, with four hundred yards between them, fighters in a ring who will never meet.

So civilized. So uncivilized. *So casual.*

A few Texas Rangers stand idly by, watching the small but slowly gathering crowd. No one appears concerned there will be trouble. Two Spanish television crews are setting up for live shots, while the rest of the press corps is composed of dark heads in a lit building across from the prison. A group of Mexican women are kneeling beside a blown-up portrait of the condemned, singing in Spanish. Two-thirds of the anti-death-penalty crowd is Mexican. The other third is mostly white, old, resigned, and quiet.

Tonight, a Mexican national is going to be executed for pumping three bullets into the head of a Houston cop. And then, in nineteen days, it's Terrell. And then a guy who hit his pizza delivery girl in the head with a baseball bat, and then a man who participated in the gang rape and murder of a mentally challenged girl on a lonely road. And on and on.

Every few minutes or so, Blue Knights are rounding the corners on their Harleys. They are former police officers avenging their own, who would maybe like to push the syringe themselves. I watch them position themselves on the far side of the prison, the pro side, near the execution chamber. The police and guards have sprung to life, and are directing them to park a little farther away.

"Are you sure you want to be here?" Bill asks one more time. We are hovering in a little bit of no-man's-land, in between both camps. "I'm not sure there's a point."

Of course there's a point. The point is, I don't know what I believe. I just know what I want to believe.

I don't say it, though. The less emotion, the better. We agreed to an uneasy détente as soon as I called and asked him to please take me with him to Huntsville to meet Terrell. I promised I wouldn't flake out. My eyes drift across the street to a man holding a battery-operated Christmas candle. He's leaning against a railing backed up to a gas station billboard that tells newly sprung prisoners to cash their checks *here*. He's comfortably packaged between two women with the peaceful countenance of nuns, and two men, all riding past sixty.

Bill follows my gaze. "That's Dennis. He never misses. Sometimes, he's the only guy out here."

"I thought there would be more people. Where are all the people who scream on Facebook?"

"On the couch. Screaming."

"When will it start?"

"The execution?" He glances at his watch. "It's eight now. Probably in about fifteen minutes. Usually, it's set for six and it's done by seven. There was a delay tonight while the federal court was debating a last-minute appeal that the condemned was mentally deficient." He gestures back across the street. "Dennis and that core group of four over there show up more as a vigil than protest. I mean, at this point, the writing's on the wall. Dennis is the one who always stays until the bitter end, even on the rare occasion when appeals go on until midnight. He waits until the family of the executed walks out. Wants them to know someone is out here for them."

I picture it—a skinny old Santa, his Christmas candle, a lonely corner by a Stop sign, and the night.

"The woman with the bullhorn is Gloria." He redirects my attention to the sign-wielding protesters in the street, who are oddly silent. No chanting. "She's a fixture, too. She pretty much believes everyone on Death Row is innocent. Of course, most of them are guilty as hell. She's much beloved for dedication, however. She'll start counting it down soon."

"Where are the families now?"

"The family of the victim, if any of them want to be there, is already inside the prison. The family of the prisoner is in the building across the street. I've heard Gutierrez has asked his mother not to watch. Whoever *is* witnessing for him will walk across with a few reporters as soon as all appeals have expired. That's the high sign." He is directing my eyes under the clock tower, where there are steps that lead up and inside.

A young television reporter in a brand-new blue suit and a bright lavender camera-ready tie has appeared to my right. He's thrusting his microphone into the face of a woman carrying a sign that declares the governor is a serial killer. The camera casts eerie light on both of their faces.

The protester's shoulders are hunched in an arthritic mountain. She's traveling on red cowboy boots anyway. She drawls her answers to the reporter a little cynically, as if she's seen a hundred of him. *Yes, the lights of the whole town used to dim for a second every time a prisoner was electrocuted. Yes, this is a typical crowd. Yes, Karla Faye Tucker was the biggest zoo, being a woman. Someone on the square even advertised "Killer Prices."*

The reporter cuts her off abruptly.

Bill nudges my shoulder. Gloria has raised the bullhorn to her lips.

Shadows are moving across the street. Ice keeps shooting out of the sky.

The air suddenly vibrates with the roar of a hundred angry tigers, so loud and so fierce that it rattles my brain, the balls of my feet, the pit of my stomach.

The thunderous noise drowns out Gloria shouting into her bullhorn and the hymn of the women, whose mouths continue to open and close like hungry birds.

The Blue Knights are revving their motorcycles in unison, so he can hear.

Kill him.

September 1995

MR. VEGA: Will you please state your full name for the record?

MR. BOYD: Ural Russell Boyd. People call me You-All. Ever since I played basketball in high school. The cheerleaders turned it into one of their yells.

MR. VEGA: How would you like me to address you today?

MR. BOYD: You-All's fine. I'm a little nervous.

MR. VEGA: No need to be nervous. You're doing just fine. You own four hundred acres of land approximately fifteen miles northwest of Fort Worth, correct?

MR. BOYD: Yes, sir. In my family for sixty years. But everybody still calls it the Jenkins property.

MR. VEGA: Will you please tell us what happened on the morning of June 23, 1994?

MR. BOYD: Yes, sir. My hound dog went missing. We were supposed to go bird hunting that morning real early. When I couldn't find him, I set out with Ramona.

MR. LINCOLN: Ramona is . . . ?

MR. BOYD: My daughter's horse. Ramona was the most in the mood for a ride that morning.

MR. LINCOLN: And what happened after that?

MR. BOYD: Almost right away I heard Harley start to howl near the west pasture. I thought maybe he met a copperhead. I've had some problems with copperheads.

MR. VEGA: You followed his howl?

MR. BOYD: Yes, sir. Once he started he wouldn't stop. I think he felt the vibration of Ramona's hooves and could feel us coming. He's a real smart dog.

MR. LINCOLN: Approximately what time was this?

MR. BOYD: About 4:30 A.M.

MR. LINCOLN: How long did it take to find Harley?

MR. BOYD: Ten minutes. It was dark. He was at the far corner of the property, about a half-mile off the highway. He was keeping watch.

MR. VEGA: What was he keeping watch over?

MR. BOYD: Two dead girls. I didn't know that the one girl was alive. She didn't look alive.

MR. VEGA: Will you please describe to the jury exactly what you saw when you came upon the grave?

MR. BOYD: First, I flashed my light on Harley. He was flat down in a bunch of flowers in a ditch. He didn't move. I didn't see the hand at first because his nose was lying on it. I knew it was a girl's hand because of the blue fingernail polish. Sir, I'd like to take a minute.

MR. VEGA: Certainly.

MR. BOYD: (inaudible)

MR. VEGA: Take all the time you need.

MR. BOYD: It was a bad moment. My daughter picks those flowers all the time. I hadn't checked her bed before I left the house.

18 days until the execution

While Bill and I waited for Manuel Abel Gutierrez to die, a light freezing rain had transformed the highway home into a ribbon of glistening ice. It's the kind of storm that Yankees make fun of on Facebook with a picture of a spilled cup of ice on the sidewalk that shuts down schools or a cartoon that depicts massive car pileups with one culprit snowflake. It would be funny, if a tenth of an inch of ice in Texas wasn't deadly.

Bill had announced six minutes onto I-45 that he wasn't about to skate the four-hour trek back, and swung the car around. So here we are, locked in a Victorian ice castle two blocks from the death chamber and its dissipating cloud. We were lucky that Mrs. Munson, the eighty-seven-year-old B&B proprietor, picked up her phone at 11:26 P.M. Every other hotel that lined the highway was booked solid, their parking lots crammed with cars frosted like petits fours.

Bill is running the water in his bathroom. The sound rushes through the wall and under the one-inch gap beneath the connecting door. Mrs. Munson had called up to us three times as we climbed the stairs to say that the whole house was replumbed and wired with central heat, as if we might not understand the $300 price tag per room. I bounce lightly on the bed, running my fingers over the path of tiny stitches of red and yellow tulip quilt. I want to tell Mrs. Munson that her accommodations are worth every penny.

Lydia would love this room with the cheery lemon walls and the grim faces of dead people staring off the dresser. The iron lamp with a gold-fringed shade that glows like a tiny fire. The ice chips clicking against the window, chattering teeth.

She would lie on this bed and construct a doomed romance for the gauzy antique wedding dress that hangs like a ghost in the half-open wardrobe, and a more terrifying tale about the door to another dimension that hides in the shadows behind it. Maybe she'd combine the stories into one. This night would race ahead, a splendid, radiant adventure. We would be girls again, before monsters and devastating words, our imaginations locked together.

There's a short knock on the connecting door.

"Come on in, Bill," I say immediately.

Bill hesitates on the threshold, dressed in jeans and a T-shirt that must have been hidden under his button-down. "I found toothbrushes in a cabinet in my bathroom. Want one?" I slide off the bed and walk over.

"Thanks." I pick blue over yellow. "I could use a glass of wine, too. Maybe a shot of tequila."

"I don't think that's stocked in the bathroom cabinet. I'm getting a bottle of water from the little fridge in the hall. Want one?"

"Sure."

He disappears into his room before I can tell him to use my door to the outside hall. We are being so very polite. Earlier tonight, before we headed to the execution, Bill had punched a button on his computer and officially filed Terrell's habeas corpus appeal with the federal court. It emphasizes the "junk science" DNA results on the red hair, the overwhelming statistics on faulty witness ID, and a statement from me, the living victim who thinks the real Black-Eyed Susan killer might still be stalking her and is willing to testify to it.

No mention of mysterious black-eyed Susan plantings or a buried book of Poe in Lydia's back yard or a tooth in an old U-Haul box.

I have wished, more than once, that I had kept the sick piece of poetry I found under my tree house instead of ripping it to shreds and throwing away the pill bottle it came in. It might have been impossible to retrieve DNA or fingerprints from the paper or plastic all these years later, but it was tangible proof that I wasn't making it up.

Bill's habeas petition is far short of what he wanted to file at this point, but he is hoping it is enough for the judge to grant a hearing. He's hoping that Jo will shake more loose from the bones in the meantime.

"Here you go," Bill says. "I see you've got cable TV, too. It's just a little hard to see around these tree trunk bedposts. Did you reach Lucas?"

"It's all good. He's got it covered. Charlie's asleep."

"Can I sit down for a second?"

"Sure."

He pulls the straight-back chair from beside the dresser and sits on a needlepointed seat of roses. I reassume my position on the corner of the bed.

"You asked the other day if there's hope," Bill says. "After today . . . I just think it's better if I'm honest. I think it is likely that Terrell is going to die. He's on a runaway train. I know today was tough. Meeting Terrell. The execution. It doesn't matter how you feel about the death penalty. I was all for the death penalty five years ago and it's just as fucking grim either way."

I'm stunned by this admission. I had never imagined him with a single doubt.

"Two things happened for me to change my mind. The duh lawyer moment when I realized that you're never going to find a rich white guy on that gurney. And the Angie moment. She made me get to know a couple of guys on Death Row. Guilty ones, like a guy who broke in to a back yard high on meth and shot an elderly woman sitting in the garden in her wheelchair, so he could run inside and steal her purse. Angie didn't think I could do this job to her satisfaction until I understood that it wasn't just about proving innocence. That I needed to be all in. To understand that men on Death Row were human beings who did horrible things but that didn't mean *they* were horrible things. The men that I've met who are sitting on Death Row are not the same men who committed those crimes. They are sober. Born again. Repentant. Or bat-shit crazy." He eases back in the chair. "Occasionally, but not often, innocent."

I wonder how long he's been holding in this speech and why he chose tonight to give it. "I don't know where I am on the death penalty," I say. "I'm just . . . not . . . there." *I have promises to keep.*

"And Terrell?"

"I can't talk about Terrell."

He nods. "I'll let you get some sleep."

As soon as he shuts the door between us, I'm desperate to wash away everything about this day. I enter a bathroom both bygone and modernly appointed, strip off all of my clothes, and lay them on the counter. I dread putting them on in the morning. They're tainted by death. But I'd brought nothing else in my backpack—just a couple of PowerBars, a water bottle, a spool of silk thread and needles for an experiment in lace-making. And, at the last minute, I'd tossed the testimony inside, mostly in case Bill asked if I'd read it. I hadn't. I'd opened the envelope, pulled out the papers, and stuck them right back in.

I push aside the shower curtain and crank the knob. The hot water responds, silky, hot, and immediate. I wash everything three times before stepping onto slick white subway tile and reluctantly tugging on the day's underwear and a white cotton tank that had been my ineffective effort at winter layering. I towel-dry my hair into a frenzy of curls, too exhausted to use the expensive ceramic blow dryer on the counter.

I slip into chilly sheets, shivering, trying not to think about the grieving mother who raced to a morgue tonight. Who hoped, for the first time in years, to touch the body of her son, a killer, while it was still warm.

At 4:02 A.M., my eyes pop open. I'm gasping for breath as if someone just snatched a pillow from my face.

Lydia.

Cool light streams through the windows. The winter storm, asleep. My mind, racing.

To Charlie, safe at home, tangled in her comforter. I picture her breathing softly, in and out, and I breathe in rhythm with her. To Lydia, holding the paper bag to my face after a race, telling me to *breathe*, and I do. In and out.

Lydia, Lydia, Lydia. She's invaded this room. The old Lydia, who checked my pulse, and the other one, who is scratching to get out of Bill's envelope in my backpack.

Did I just miss the clues? Or are all of us just one betrayal, even one sentence, away from never speaking to each other again? I always, always defended my best friend. Even Granddaddy, a fan of her rabid imagination, wasn't completely sure.

He asked once: "What do you see in Lydia?"

"She's like no one else," I had replied, a little defensively. "And loyal."

She changed in the month before the trial. The old Lydia made fun of the push-up Wonderbra. She stuck her hands under her breasts, arranged them into little mountains and mocked the Eva Herzigova billboards. *Look me in the eyes and tell me that you love me.* She cocked her knee, planted her hands on her hips, thrust out her chest, and drawled: *Who cares if it's a bad hair day?*

The new Lydia *bought* a Wonderbra and strapped it on. She complained that all high school boys wanted was a blank slate to draw their pencil on. Her grades dipped into the A minuses. She renounced Dr Peppers and Sonic cheese tots, and worst of all, she stopped her incessant, encyclopedic chatter. I knew I should press her, but I was trapped in my own head.

Old Lydia kept all of my secrets.

New Lydia told my secrets to the world.

I'm standing over his bed. The covers are a rumpled drift, like snow is falling through the ceiling. Bill is facing the other way. His body, rising and falling, slow and steady.

It isn't like me to do this, I think, as I shed my T-shirt and it falls soundlessly to the floor. I don't play games. I'm not impulsive. *I'm not that girl.* I lift up the quilt and slide in. Press my bare skin against the heat of his back. His breathing stills. He waits pregnant seconds before turning over to face me. He's left a few inches of distance between us.

"Hey," he says. It's too dark to read his expression.

This was a mistake, I think. He's already mentally moved on. He's reaching out now to push me away.

Instead, his finger travels my cheek, the side without the scar. I'm suddenly aware that my face is wet.

"You OK?" His voice, husky. He's being chivalrous, offering me a last chance to escape, even as I make a naked present of myself in his bed.

"I'm not that kind of girl." I lean in. Drift my tongue along his ear.

"Thank God," he replies, and tugs me to him.

A bird's distress call slices the silence and jars me awake. It's a high-pitched plea from a branch by the window. *Why is my world frozen? Where did everybody go?*

I crawl out of bed, away from the delicious heat of Bill's body. His breathing, rhythmic.

I shut the connecting door, back on my side of it. I relive the intimacy of what just happened. Things I didn't do unless I was in love. *How can I ever be sure his attraction is to me, and not the shiny glitter of Black-Eyed Susan?*

My red North Face jacket drips like blood off the closet doorknob. A fresh white orchid is stuck all alone in a slim vase, even though no one knew I was coming. A young woman in the antique frame on the dresser gazes at me coolly as if I have no place in her room.

She's just a girl in this picture, about Charlie's age. A thick, migraine-inducing braid is roped around her head. I imagine her with loosened braids and a little of Charlie's MAC eye makeup. I pick up the picture and flip it over.

Mary Jane Whitford, born May 6, 1918, died March 16, 1934, when a convict roaming the sugarcane fields stepped in front of her carriage and startled the horses.

A tourist attraction. Like me.

It makes sense that Lydia would come to me here, in this room, embroidered like a doily in the dark fabric of this town. Where I'm reminded by a pretty girl in braids that we don't get to choose.

I almost died three hours ago on I-45, halfway between Huntsville and Corsicana. What an ironic end that would have been—the lone survivor of the Black-Eyed Susan killer taken out by an eighteen-wheeler packed with baked goods. A truck driver a hundred feet in front of our car had skidded on a patch of ice into a perfect jackknife. If skidding were an Olympic sport, he'd win. All I could think for six seconds, while Bill and I hurled toward a picture of a giant pink confetti-sprinkled donut, was, *Is it all going to come down to this?*

Instead, it came down to me completely rethinking BMWs. Their drivers act superior for a reason.

Lucas is opening my front door before I can, a good thing because I don't remember the new security code he insisted on, and a bad thing because Bill is still in the driveway making sure I get inside safely. I turn to wave but Bill is already backing the BMW onto the street. I hope he believed me when I said I wasn't sleeping with Lucas.

Breakfast at the B&B was a little awkward. Bill sat across from me, at a table formally appointed with fragile crystal and an array of silverware, while Mrs. Munson sat at the head of the table and chattered on about how prisoners carved the intricate detail on the cupboard behind us. It was impossible to resist the work of art placed in front of us by Mrs. Munson's daughter, a Dutch baby pancake with a strawberry fan on top and a spritz of powdered sugar.

Maybe Bill was upset that he woke up alone in bed. Later, in the car, we each seemed to be waiting for the other to bring up those thirty intimate minutes. It almost seemed like a dream conjured by a house that missed the noise and meaning of its old life—the people who wed on its lawn, gave birth in its beds, lay dead in their coffins in the front parlor. Except I can still feel his handprints on my skin.

After Bill avoided the near-accident, the silence in the car grew even more awkward. As if Bill was exhausted from saving lives.

Because I'm distracted by such boy-girl worries, still wearing death like a coat, still delirious not to *be* a Dutch baby pancake, it takes a second to register the expression on Lucas's face.

"Welcome home." He seems uneasy. He's pulling the backpack off my shoulder as I walk the few steps into the living room.

"What's wrong?" I ask.

"Someone leaked your . . . feeling . . . that the Black-Eyed Susan killer has planted flowers for you over the years. A few quack experts on TV are chiming in on your mental state. There's a shadowy picture going around of a woman with a shovel at the old Victorian house where you used to live. It's supposed to be you. Well, it *is* you. But it's hard to tell."

"When did you find this out?"

"Why don't you sit down?"

"I've been sitting for hours."

Lucas examines my face carefully. "Charlie texted me. It's all over Twitter and Instagram."

"Shit. Shit, shit, *shit*."

He hesitates. "I had to turn off the ringer on the phone. Why do you even have a landline?"

"Is it OK if we don't talk about this right now? It doesn't really matter, does it? Terrell's going to die. It's impossible to protect Charlie." I've moved over to the kitchen island, where Lucas has stacked the mail. He's behind me, rubbing my shoulders. Kind. Concerned. But not helping. His fingers are grinding the death that clings to these clothes into my skin.

I try to be casual as I move away. "What's this?" I'm fingering an opened cardboard box. A new paperback lies next to it on the counter.

"That came in the mail yesterday. Charlie opened the box because she thought it was *Catch-22* and wanted to get going on it for an English class. She says she asked you to order it a week ago?"

"I forgot. I didn't order *Catch-22*. Or any other books."

"Your name is on the address label." He turns the box over so I can see.

"Where's the receipt?" I'm staring at the book cover. A filmy image of half-spirit, half-girl rising out of a rocky sea. *Beautiful Ghost* by Rose Mylett.

Rose Mylett. The name stirs something unpleasant at the back of my brain.

Lucas reaches inside the box. "Here's the receipt. It looks like it was a gift. There's a message. *Hope you enjoy.* Nothing else."

Hope you enjoy. Ordinary words that crawl like three spiders up my back.

"Are you OK?" he asks.

"Sure," I say dully. "It's just a book. A gift. I need to get these clothes off."

"One more thing. Your friend Jo dropped by for a second. You need to give her a call. That geochemist friend of hers is coming to town, the one who's been working on the Susan bones. She wants you to meet him. Oh, and that tooth from your grandfather's yard? It's from a coyote."

Twenty minutes until Charlie gets home from school. A little longer before Lucas returns from his hunt for *Catch-22* and coffee with a "new friend"—Lucas code for "female."

There's no time to dry my hair. I wrap the belt of my robe more tightly around my waist, ransack Charlie's drawer for some fuzzy socks, and plant myself on her unmade bed with my laptop. It had found a happy home in her sheets during my absence.

I am suffused with manic energy, pulsed back to life by the shower and the certainty that Rose Mylett means something. Her name is an insistent drill in my skull, more important than me, as the Grim Reaperette, skipping across Twitter right now, or calling Jo to hear about more hopeless efforts to pull names from dust. Those bones are stubborn.

I get an immediate hit. The first Rose Mylett that pops up isn't a true crime writer. The image on my screen isn't of an airbrushed author trying to look smart and beautiful and ten years younger.

This Rose Mylett is very dead. Murdered in 1888. A purported victim of Jack the Ripper. A prostitute also known as Catherine, Drunk Lizzie, and Fair Alice. She was wearing a lilac apron, a red flannel petticoat, and blue-and-red-striped socks when she was found with the imprint of a string around her neck.

For a second, I'm fourteen again, in the second row, smearing on Pink Lemonade Lip Smacker, listening to Lydia's Jack the Ripper report that instilled nightmares in half of our class.

My fingers are still working in the present. They skip to the next page and, four links down, find *Rose Mylett, author, Beautiful Ghost, What Elizabeth Bates is trying to tell us about her murder fifty years later.* Yep, the same book as the one sitting on my kitchen counter. I read the plot summary quickly. This crime rings no bells whatsoever—the tale of a young English royal who vanished off the rugged coast of North Devon on her honeymoon—184 reviews, 4.6 stars. Published five years ago in the U.K. That .4 off of perfect would eat at Lydia. There's no author bio. No other book by Rose Mylett. The site does politely suggest, "If you like this author, you might also like these books by Annie Farmer and Elizabeth Stride." I Google quickly even though I already know. Two more Ripper victims. Clever, clever Lydia.

This has to be Lydia, right? Sending me flowers. Mail-ordering a book for my reading pleasure.

Still walking the earth after all. Still sticking her nose in evil. Stealing her pseudonyms off of pitiful dead whores. Making money off of excruciating sorrow. For some ungodly reason, she's messing with me.

Why are you suddenly back, Lydia?

I snap the laptop shut.

My daughter is coming home.

For a few precious moments, I bask in the Bohemian essence of Charlie: the black chalkboard wall she painted herself last summer, now scribbled with Stephen Colbert quotes and skilled graffiti from her friends; her collection of moon-and-stars ornaments that hang on fishing line thumbtacked to the ceiling; the array of candles in various stages of melted life on the windowsill. The trophies she's stuffed into the top shelf of her closet because they are "braggy."

I'm hurriedly spilling detergent into the washing machine when I hear the click of the key in the lock.

"Mom?"

"In the laundry room!" I yell back. Three clunks. Her backpack, hitting the floor. One shoe off, and then the other. *Good sounds.*

Charlie wriggles her arms around me from behind just as I'm about to drop the lid on clothes that will probably never feel clean again.

"Why is it so freaking cold outside?" she asks. Not *Why are you*

such a freak? The kind of mom who ends up on Twitter? I pull Charlie's arms tighter.

"I missed you," Charlie says. "What are we eating?" She releases
me from our backward hug. I decide to throw some extra Biz into
the washer.

"I missed you, too. I'm thinking of making eggala."

"Awesome." Eggala, short for egg a la goldenrod, our go-to comfort food. Hard-boiled egg whites chopped into a white sauce, slath-
ered over white toast, sprinkled with powdery yolk. Lots of salt and
pepper. Dr Pepper on the side. Aunt Hilda made it once a week for
me when I was blind.

"I'm sorry about . . . today," I say.

"No big deal. My friends don't believe it. They are starting a
campaign against it. Make some bacon, OK? Hey, don't start the
washer. I've got a ton of volleyball clothes. People forgot shi—stuff
all week and Coach kept making us run. *Everything* stinks. Plus,
some guy's mom is *losing it* because he has this scabby thing going
on with his foot. These people in Star Wars suits cleaned all the
locker rooms and now every person in school smells like Lysol. Well,
the guys smell like Lysol *and* Axe."

"Hmm, not good." I shut the lid. "Don't worry, I'll wash another
load of your clothes after this."

"But there's hardly anything in there," she protests. "I'll go get
the rest of it right now. I can't forget anything tomorrow. The team
can't *take* any more running."

She's already stripped off her clothes. She's standing there in her
bra, panties, and knee-high socks, the cheerful, melodramatic all-
American girl. Fourteen years ago, she was the adorable pink package with red fuzz sent to a teen-age girl named Tessie so she'd agree
to stay on the earth.

"That's OK." I shut the washer lid firmly. "I don't want these
clothes to bleed on yours."

I'm lying and telling the truth.

I'm in my pajamas when I remember to call Jo. She picks up on the first ring.

"Tessa?" she asks eagerly.

"I'm so sorry I didn't call sooner."

"It's OK. I talked to Bill. He told me about your trip. Ice and sorrow and no tequila. Sounds grueling. Can you drop by my office tomorrow?"

"Yes. Sure." My response is immediate even though all I really want is to lock the front door and never come out.

"I wanted to give you a heads-up before we meet because this will be part of his presentation." Jo is rushing the words. "I've held something back from you because it just seemed . . . like a little too much. You know? A week and a half ago, one of my Ph.D. students was finishing up cataloging the remains of the Susans from the two caskets we exhumed. There was a lot of detritus, as you might imagine. Dirt, clay, dust, bits of bone. I just wanted to make sure every last piece of it was recorded after we figured out the original coroner missed that there was a third right femur. In fact, we're looking back at some of the other cold cases he worked and have found other mistakes."

"Just spit it out, Jo," I say.

"My student had a hunch about a tiny piece of cartilage. I confirmed that hunch. The cartilage came from a fetus. One of the two unidentified girls was pregnant with a baby girl. We just tested the baby's DNA against Terrell's. There's a 99.6 percent chance he isn't the father. We're throwing the baby's DNA into criminal databases. Maybe we'll get a hit. A new lead."

Of course Terrell isn't a match.

I'm counting in my head. Six girls in that grave. Merry and me. Hannah makes three. Two more unidentified sets of bones. And now a little girl. One of them is buzzing awake in my head, reminding me, just in case I forgot.

I'm the one with the answers.

September 1995

MR. VEGA: Tessie, can you tell us a little about Black-Eyed Susan glitter?

MS. CARTWRIGHT: It's hard to explain. My friend Lydia came up with the name for it.

MR. VEGA: Just do your best. Maybe you could start by telling us about the time you stood outside in the middle of a bad storm and your father couldn't get you to come in.

MS. CARTWRIGHT: I was thinking that if I stood out there long enough the rain would wash out all the Black-Eyed Susan glitter.

MR. VEGA: Can you see this glitter?

MS. CARTWRIGHT: No.

MR. VEGA: And when did you first notice it?

MS. CARTWRIGHT: The day I got home from the hospital. Again, I can't see it. For a while, I decided it was in my conditioner. In the

Ivory soap. In the detergent we put in the washer. I decided that's why I could never get it out.

MR. VEGA: Do you have glitter on you now?

MS. CARTWRIGHT: Just a little. The worst time, it was in the Parmesan cheese I put on my spaghetti. I threw up all night.

17 days until the execution

There are no Susan bones on Jo's conference table. Just that lonely brown Kleenex box. My heart feels like someone hammered a nail into it.

I was worried I would be late for Jo's meeting, but it's apparent as I open the door to the conference room that everyone else is even later. The room is empty except for the table and chairs, unless you count the requiem of pain that Hannah's mother and brother left behind. If there were a black light to reveal grief and anger, it would surely be streaked in graffiti, Dalí-like, on these walls. Not only sucked from Hannah's family, but all of the others who sat here waiting for their loved ones to be reduced to the stubborn rules of science.

The door clicks shut behind me. The fluorescent glare feels like it's restricting the flow of blood to my head. I slide into the chair where Hannah's brother sat at attention in his dress blues not so long ago and, for a few minutes, try not to think.

The door opens, and all of them spill into the conference room at once. Bill; Lieutenant Myron; Jo; and her Russian friend, Dr. Igor Aristov, the genius from Galveston.

"Igor, as in Igor Stravinsky," Jo had told me last night on the phone, knowing that I was, of course, imagining the hunchbacked Frankenstein one and not the one who composed *The Rite of Spring.*

This Igor, though, is not hunched, or wearing a black hood, or creeping me out with white golf ball eyes. He is tall and fit, wearing khakis and a red Polo. His eyes are warm and hazel. Fine wrinkles run out of the corner of his eyes and stop short. There are the tiniest shreds of gray at his temples.

He immediately crosses the room to take my hand first. "You must be Tessa. It is a pleasure." His accent is thick as paste, and most women would want him to say their names over and to never let go of their hands. Not me. I'm only in this room as a conciliatory gesture to Jo. I don't want to hear Igor's maybes and ifs. Unless this lab genius is about to pull a miracle out of his ass, I need to listen to Bill. I need to come to terms with Terrell's fate.

Lieutenant Myron is the first to slide into a chair. I wonder if I look as raw as she does. "Everybody, sit," Jo says. "We're going to make this as quick as possible. Ellen had a rough night."

"A cop and his bride of six months," Lieutenant Myron explains. "He fired a shot into her face for every month of marriage. Go ahead, Jo."

Jo nods. Her hands are agitated with no place to go. I've never seen her this visibly on edge. "Usually," she says, "I will send Igor samples of powder from the bones and he emails his findings to me. But that's white paper between two scientists. I want the three of you to hear everything straight from his mouth just in case some detail tickles your brain." She is careful not to look at me. It is obvious I am the one whose brain needs the most tickling.

Igor has settled himself at the head of the table. "I am a geochemist. A forensic geologist. Do any of you understand the basics of isotope analysis?

"I will keep it as simple as possible," Igor continues, without waiting for an answer. "I will refer to each case as Susan One and Susan Two. I received samples from the femur of Susan One and from the skull and teeth of Susan Two. I also received a scraping from a fetus that belongs to Susan Two. I was able to determine that one of the women lived much of her life in Tennessee, and the other was most certainly from Mexico."

"What?" Bill's surprise pops the tension in the room. "How can you possibly know that?"

Igor shifts a level gaze to Bill. "Your bones absorb the distinct chemical markers in the soil where you live. Some of it has retained the same ratio of elements—oxygen, lead, zinc, et cetera—for hundreds of thousands of years, all the way back to when rivers and mountains formed. And then there are more modern markers. It's easy to tell that Susan One is American, not European, because America and Europe used different refinery sources for leaded gas."

"We're soaking crap from the air into our bones?" Lieutenant Myron is pressing forward, suddenly engaged. "Regardless, we don't use leaded gas for cars anymore."

"It doesn't matter," he replies patiently. "The residue from leaded gas, even though it's been banned for years, still clings to our soil and soaks into our bones. Susan One's markers also indicate that for a significant portion of her life she lived near a specific set of mines, probably near Knoxville, Tennessee. I can't tell you how long exactly. Or specifically where she died. I might have been able to if I had a rib bone. Ribs are constantly growing and remodeling and absorbing the environment. We can usually use them to guess at a victim's residency for the last eight to ten years of life. And, of course, a lot of the bones were lost, so the grave only provided random puzzle pieces."

"Mexico. Tennessee." Bill's eyes are trained on Lieutenant Myron. "Your killer could be a traveler. Terrell was a homebody."

"He's not *my* killer." Lieutenant Myron's sarcasm gets zero reaction from Bill, who continues tapping notes into his phone.

"Come on, guys, let him talk," Jo says.

"It doesn't bother me," Igor says. "It's thrilling to be out of the lab, frankly. To meet you, especially, Tessa. I rarely meet any victims. It makes my science . . . alive. And this case is particularly interesting. I was able to discern even more from Susan Two and her unborn fetus. Susan Two's bones reflect a corn-based diet and the elements of volcanic soil. If I could hazard a guess, I'd say she was born in or near Mexico City. I concur with Jo that she was in her early twenties when she died."

"What else?" Bill asks.

Igor lays his palms flat on the table. "There was only one skull in that grave, which belonged to Susan Two. I asked Jo to send me scrapings of very specific teeth because the teeth can give us a time-line." His voice, so far in college lecture mode, has picked up a little excitement. "It's fascinating, really, what this science reveals. As children, we put things in our mouths. The teeth enamel absorbs the dust. The first molar forms when a person is three, and freezes the isotope signal for that period of time. So I can say that Susan Two's first molar tells us she was living in Mexico as a toddler. The incisors close at age six to seven. The chemical markers in one of her incisors indicate she was still living in Mexico. The third molar's signal shuts down in the teen-age years. For Susan Two, still Mexico. After that, I don't know. Sometime in her late teens or early twenties, she moved, or was kidnapped."

"This is remarkable." Lieutenant Myron glances around the table. "Isn't this remarkable?" I can't tell whether she is genuinely engaged or giddy from lack of sleep and a steady diet of savagery.

"How are you certain she left Mexico alive?" Bill asks. "We know the bones were moved at least once because they didn't originate in that field of flowers where Tessa was dumped." He flicks a look up at me, as if remembering I'm in the room. "Sorry, Tessa. My point is, maybe her bones were simply moved across the border."

"Her baby tells that part of the story," Igor says quickly. "This young woman lived in Texas for at least the last few months leading up to her death. I know this because fetal bones are the most current marker we can get. They were still developing and therefore still ab-sorbing the current environment at the time of death."

Lieutenant Myron shoves fingers through her uprooted hair. "If she was an illegal immigrant, or kidnapped, that makes our job nearly impossible. Her family wouldn't want to reveal its illegal status and certainly wouldn't stick their DNA in a database. If they thought a drug cartel grabbed their daughter, there's even less of a chance—they wouldn't want to piss them off. Those guys hang headless bodies from bridges. The family would need to protect their other daughters if they have them."

Jo nods her head in agreement. "She's right. I've worked on some of the bones of girls and women who have been murdered and buried in the desert near Juarez. Talked to the families. They're scared shitless. There are hundreds of girls in that desert. More every year."

"I can only share my science." Igor shrugs. "And, frankly, I drummed up a lot more than is usual in cold cases like this. This is a fairly new strategy in forensic science. We are lucky these women lived in places where we have established soil databases. My dream is that we can map out a good portion of the geological world in the next decade, but it's spotty as hell at the moment."

Bill's face is inscrutable, but I know what he's thinking. It's too late for this. Someday, science may give the Susans back their names, but not in time for Terrell.

It's Lieutenant Myron who jumps up, newly animated. She walks over and gives Bill a playful punch in the shoulder. "Cheer up. You're one of those Texans who believes in evolution, aren't you?" She turns to the rest of us.

"We'll get busy with missing person and newspaper databases," she says. "In an hour, we'll be looking for missing girls in their late teens or early twenties from Tennessee and Mexico that fit our time frames. I'm most hopeful on the Tennessee angle. Good job, Dr. Frankenstein. This is something real. Y'all think I don't care? I care. I just like real."

She wouldn't want to be in my head. I'm wondering why none of the Susans speak to me in Spanish.

———

I enter the house quietly and see my Death Row clothes folded and stacked neatly in a kitchen chair. I wonder if Charlie or Lucas alienated them from the others; it's a toss-up as to which one sees through me better.

Charlie's volleyball clothes are piled on the coffee table. A vacuum cleaner has swallowed up the popcorn crumbs in front of the couch. Lucas has been taking care of the mundane, important details of my life while I've been trying to fathom how we are so deeply connected to the earth and wind that it is cooked into our bones.

I have no problem believing Dr. Igor. It wasn't exactly science, but there was a period when I believed that if someone brushed my shoulder by accident or shook my hand that black-eyed Susan pollen would rub off like a sticky curse. People had thought I was obsessive-compulsive because I ignored outstretched hands. I was just protecting them.

I'm a big girl now. I offer strangers the firm grip of my grandfather and swallow my daughter in a hug twice a day and let friends take a sip from my Route 44 Sonic iced tea, all without breaking out in a sweat. That doesn't mean *Black-Eyed Susan* isn't still who I am. It's a brand. Like *schizophrenic. Fat. ADD.*

Lucas rises briefly from the couch, then falls back down when he sees me. He's already asleep again, a soldier grabbing zzz's while he can, so I don't call out for Charlie. She's probably in her room doing her complicated dance. Jane Austen, calculus, Snapchat. Repeat.

It's at moments like these that I find it hard to explain to myself and to Charlie why Lucas and I don't work as a permanent team. How many lieutenant colonels would fold girls' underwear? I smell potato soup gurgling in the Crockpot because that is about the sum total of Lucas's dinner repertoire. Potatoes, onions, milk, salt, pepper, butter. Bacon bits, for Charlie. If pressed, he can also kick out a pretty mean bologna and mustard sandwich.

Normal always tries to cuddle up with me but I tend to push it away. My mother was making brownies one second and then she was dead on the kitchen floor. That is my baseline for normal. After that, it's a very jagged graph.

I set my purse on the kitchen counter. *Beautiful Ghost* has been shoved off to the side with some unopened mail. I want to read it, and I can't bear to touch it. It will hold answers about Lydia I can't fathom knowing, or I'll prick my finger on its paper and fall into a cursed sleep. My fingers absently examine the foil-wrapped brick on the counter, which wasn't there this morning. The scrawl on the masking tape label declares it to be *Effie's Carob Fig Bread Surprise*. Almost all of Effie's recipes have the word *Surprise* tacked to the end, and if they don't, they should.

I wonder if her daughter is next door right now trying to politely chew and swallow. As I pulled in the driveway, I noted the Ford Focus with New Jersey plates parked at Effie's. She had told me last week in excited tones that her daughter was venturing down South for a visit. I discounted it, thinking she was confused with the time that Sue made that false promise a year ago, or even three years ago. I don't know what her arrival means after years of staying away, but I hope it's good for Effie. Maybe Sue got a peek of the digger snatcher who lives in Effie's brain, too. He's a first-class thief all right, just not the kind Effie thinks. The sight of all those diggers lined up in a row still sends a chill through me.

I toss an afghan over Lucas and decide to check on Charlie. Her bedroom door is shut tight. I knock. No response. I knock again a little harder before turning the knob. The white lights strung around the ceiling are twinkling, a sign she was planning to be camped out here for a while. But no Charlie.

A slight noise on the other side of the wall, in my room. A sniffle? Is she sick? Seeking comfort in my bed while I'm off on a field trip with the Susans? Guilt washes over me. Lucas should have called to let me know. Maybe the flu shot didn't take, or her allergies are acting up, or Coach scratched her fragile teen-age heart with an off-hand remark.

No. Not sick. Charlie's cross-legged on my bed like Lydia used to be, her curls falling forward, intent on what she's reading. There's a frenzy of paper everywhere, littering the bed, the old antique rug on the floor. My backpack rests against the pillow behind her. It's unzipped for the first time since I returned from Huntsville. I want to scream *No,* but it's way too late.

Charlie's cheeks are slick with tears. "I was looking for a highlighter."

She holds up a piece of paper.

I know in that instant that our relationship will never be the same.

"Is this why you won't eat Snickers bars?" she asks.

Before I can utter a word, Lucas is there. He's holding out my phone, which I'd left on the kitchen counter with my purse.

"It's Jo. She says that you have to come back to her office. Immediately."

September 1995

MR. LINCOLN: Lydia . . . I can call you Lydia, right?

MS. BELL: Yes.

MR. LINCOLN: Exactly how long have you known Tessa Cartwright?

MS. BELL: Since second grade. Our desks were in alphabetical order. Tessie's aunt used to say that God made out that seating chart.

MR. LINCOLN: And you've been best friends since? For ten years?

MS. BELL: Yes.

MR. LINCOLN: So when Tessie went missing you must have been terrified?

MS. BELL: I had a really bad feeling right away. We had like a secret way of letting each other know we were OK. We'd call the other one and let the phone ring twice. And then we'd wait five minutes and let the phone ring twice again. It was kind of a silly thing we did when we were little. But I stayed home and waited.

MR. LINCOLN: Tessie didn't call? And you never left the house?

MS. BELL: No. Well, I left for about ten minutes to check her tree house.

MR. LINCOLN: Check the tree house for . . . Tessa?

MS. BELL: We used to leave notes in this little crack.

MR. LINCOLN: And there was no note?

MS. BELL: No note.

MR. LINCOLN: Were your father and mother home during this period of waiting while Tessa was missing?

MS. BELL: Yes. My mom was. My dad had some emergency at work. A car's engine exploded or something. He came home later.

MR. LINCOLN: Yes, we'll get back to that. In an earlier deposition, you mentioned that you have had nightmares since Tessa's attack. Is that right?

MS. BELL: Yes. But not as terrible as Tessie's.

MR. LINCOLN: Can you describe some of yours?

MS. BELL: There's really just one. I get it practically every night. I'm standing on the bottom of the lake. It's cliché. Freud wouldn't be too interested, you know?

MR. LINCOLN: Is Tessie in this dream?

MS. BELL: No. I can see my face but it's not my face. My father is reaching his hand down from his boat. He was always freaked one of us was going to go under. Anyway, his college ring falls into the water and starts sinking. He was always freaked about that happening, too, and never wore it on the boat. He went to Ohio State for a year. He's really proud of that. He loves that ring. He bought it at some garage sale.

MR. LINCOLN: I know this is hard but try to keep your answers just a bit simpler, OK? Tell me this: Was Tessa ever afraid of your father?

16 days until the execution

This time, I'm not the first one there. It's a little past midnight. The Kleenex box on the conference room table has been disturbed. Moved to the very far edge of the table. Jo is pulling on latex gloves. She'd told me on the phone that I needed to drive over, *now,* but I couldn't leave Charlie in a paper bed of my testimony. We had to talk. Charlie is a little Tessie, sometimes. Too quick to reassure adults that she's OK.

Jo wouldn't tell me *why* I had to come. It was maddening. *Drive carefully,* she urged. Once I unwrapped myself from Charlie, I drove at warp speed, through two red light cameras, wondering what waited for me. My monster in handcuffs. More Susan skeletons grinning in ugly glee.

There is one other person in the room. A young girl by the window who is very much alive. A silky black ponytail trails down her back. She is gazing out the window at silvery trees, lit by pale moonlight, on the lawn of the Modern Art Museum across the street. Two stainless steel trees, their branches intricately, tediously soldered, pulling toward each other as if by magnetic force. That is how I feel about this girl, as if she can't turn toward me fast enough. When she does, I have an immediate impression of familiarity. Of longing.

"This young woman is Aurora Leigh," Jo says. "She says she is Lydia Bell's daughter."

It's not like it wouldn't have been my first guess. The hair is darker, the skin even more ivory, but the eyes, full of dreamy blue intelligence, unmistakable.

And her name. Aurora Leigh. The epic heroine of Lydia's favorite poem.

"Hello, Aurora," I say. I'm trying to tamp down the words being silently pelted at Aurora by the Susans. *Liar,* screams one. *Imposter.*

Jo is drumming her fingers on the table, drawing my attention back. "Aurora went to the police station first. They called Lieutenant Myron, who is off duty. She told the front desk to call me."

"I was making a scene." Aurora plops into the nearest chair and drops a handful of crumpled tissue onto the table. Her nose is shiny and red and pierced by a tiny silver ring. Her lovely eyes are bloodshot. "I'm sorry. I'm calmer now."

"You sit, too, Tessa." She turns to Aurora. "Do you want me to explain?" She touches Aurora's shoulder, and she flinches.

"No," says Aurora. "That's OK. I'll do it. I'm OK. Really. I just wanted someone to listen to me. You listened." She turns to me with eagerness. "I saw a story on Fox about the box that was dug up. It's my mom's stuff. It belongs to me."

"But I explained to Aurora that it is still evidence," Jo says. "That she can maybe get it back later."

"I don't want it later. I want to see it now." Matter-of-fact and petulant at the same time. Reminds me of Charlie. This girl couldn't be more than two years older. Sixteen. Seventeen, at most.

"I didn't know Lydia had a daughter." My voice sounds surprisingly calm. "Where is your mother right now?"

"I've never met her." Aurora's words are an assault. Accusatory, even.

Jo forms her face into a professional mask. "Aurora tells me she has lived with her grandparents since she was born. Mr. and Mrs. Bell. Although Aurora says she just learned that they changed their last name. They told her that her mother was dead and they had no idea who her father was. She had no reason to doubt them. Then her grandmother died. Her grandfather had a stroke last year and was moved to a full-term care facility. Aurora has been living with a foster family in Florida. I've already called them to let them know she's OK."

"So . . ." I begin.

"So a lawyer cleaned out her grandparents' safe deposit box a month ago. Birth certificates. Tax documents. It's all there in Aurora's bag." She points to a stuffed, pink-flowered tote.

"They lied to me. Every single day, they lied to me. I'm not Aurora Leigh Green. I'm Aurora Leigh Bell." Aurora pulls out another Kleenex. "I was saving money for a private investigator. I was Googling around in the meantime. It freaked me out when Lydia Bell's name came up a couple of times. You know, in those Black-Eyed Susan stories. But I didn't know if it was the same Lydia Bell. I didn't want it to be. And then I saw that story about the police digging at my grandparents' old house. They said their real names on the air. So I knew. I couldn't wait anymore. I stole some money out of my foster mom's purse for the bus." Tears are lurking again. "She's going to kill me. She probably won't take me back. She's not that bad really."

"She's just happy that you're OK, Aurora. Remember, I talked to her and she told you not to worry." Jo, reassuring. "Aurora is worried that her mother was a victim of the Black-Eyed Susan killer and that's the reason her grandparents went into hiding. I told her there is absolutely no evidence that she was. I explained that you could tell her the most about her mother. What she was like. Who she was dating."

I open my mouth, and close it.

As far as I knew, Lydia only made it as far as third base one time, with our school's star third baseman. Lydia reveled in the literalness of it. She even told me she was considering similar conquests with the first and second basemen. It made me ache for her. When it came to Lydia, boys just wanted a cheap thrill: to meet a beautiful, crazy girl in the dark and hope she didn't bring an axe.

Aurora's face is twisting with impatience. Here she is, defiant, flesh and blood evidence that I never dreamed existed. I feel ineptly unable to answer without hurting her. Aurora's eyes are incandescent holes despite the harsh light of the conference room. Even with the nose ring and a scowl, she's a stunning replica of her mother.

"Jo, why are you gloved?" I ask.

"I was about to swab Aurora's DNA. I told her I can't give her the evidence, but I can run her DNA through all of the databases."

"So that maybe she can find my father. That was blank on my birth certificate." Aurora is so hopeful. Innocent. "Maybe he didn't know about me."

"How old are you?" I ask.

"Sixteen."

So Lydia was pregnant when she hurtled out of town. The picture is a little clearer. Why the Bells might flee. Mrs. Bell believed brides should bring their hymens to the altar intact. Sperms and eggs instantly make microscopic people. A pregnant daughter would be the ultimate humiliation in her world. Abortion, not an option. But changing their names?

"Jo says you were best friends." Lydia's daughter is begging me. For anything.

Aurora's arrival seems a little too pat.

She might be telling the truth. Or she might be a pawn of her mother's.

"She was loyal," I lie. "Like no one else."

September 1995

MS. BELL: No. Tessie is not afraid of my dad. He could be a little mean after a few beers but he never bothered Tessie. She was so tough sometimes. Stood up for everybody. One time I told her that I could never handle it if I'd been the one to wake up in that grave. Don't get me wrong. She's messed up. Or maybe she's just mortal now like the rest of us. But I'd be totally nuts. And you know what she said? She said, that's why it happened to me and not you. Not to make me feel guilty or anything, or be martyr-y, just because she really can't stand to see anybody else hurt. You need to know something . . . Tessie is the best.

MR. LINCOLN: Again, try to keep your answers short and confine them to my questions. I'm sure Mr. Vega has told you this, too.

MR. VEGA: I'm not objecting.

MR. LINCOLN: Lydia, let me ask you this. Are you ever afraid of your dad?

MS. BELL: Only sometimes. When he drinks. But he's getting help for that now.

MR. LINCOLN: Lydia, your dream sounds pretty scary to me. At the bottom of a lake with no one coming to your rescue.

MS. BELL: I never said that no one comes to the rescue. My dad always dives in after me.

MR. LINCOLN: Interesting that you never mentioned that ending when I took your deposition. How can you be sure your father wasn't going for that college ring he loved so much?

MR. VEGA: OK, your honor, now I'm objecting.

12 days until the execution

"Reconstructing memory doesn't work this way," Dr. Giles says. "It's not a magic act. And I'm not the expert on light hypnosis. I've told you that."

I'm staring down the same empty velour chair as last time, the one where Dr. Giles suggested I picture my monster and give him a pop quiz. There's a frizzy blond Barbie nestled in the corner, her arms confirming a touchdown. "So tell me how it works," I beg.

"Some therapists use the imagery of a rope or ladder. Or tell you to watch a painful event from above, as a voyeur. There's a famous quote—that traumatic memory is a series of still snapshots or a silent movie and the role of therapy is to find the music and words."

"So, let's find the music," I say. "*And* the pictures. I pick . . . watching from above. Let's make my movie."

I don't tell her about Aurora, who is safely back in Florida with her foster mom.

I don't tell her that I'm giving Lydia the starring role today. She always wanted it, and I was always snatching it away. I was the little girl with the dead mommy. I was the Black-Eyed Susan.

I'm hoping Lydia will appear in that chair and tell me something I don't know. She usually does.

"If you really want to try hypnosis, I'll recommend another therapist. I'm not on board here. This is not what I do. I thought you understood this."

"I don't want another therapist."

My forehead begins to sweat. I'm hanging from the ceiling, a bat in the dark.

There I am. In the back of the parking lot. Tying my Adidas shoe with the pink laces that were in my Christmas stocking. Glancing up. There's Merry, gagged with something, pressing her face against a backseat window of a blue van. Me, running. Clinging to a sticky pay phone. Praying the silhouette turning the ignition in the van didn't see me. Sudden, excruciating pain in my ankle. Concrete slamming up. His face, looming. Strong arms, lifting me. Black.

"Tessa. Are you seeing something?"

Not now. I can't stop the movie to talk. I want more. I close my eyes into a light so bright it burns. There's Lydia, dancing with the Susans. Pushing them off the floor. Voguing to Madonna in my kitchen. Brushing my hair until my scalp tingles. Imitating Coach Winkle's sex talk: *Every time you think about doing it, I want a picture of my head to pop up. I'll be saying: "Genital warts, genital warts!"*

Images, smashing into my brain. Lydia's drawing of the red-haired girl and the angry flowers. Mr. Bell, drunk. The dogs yipping and spinning in crazy circles. Mrs. Bell crying. Lydia and I pedaling our bikes to my house with our bodies slung low and forward, feet churning as fast as they can. Mr. Bell's Ford Mustang breathing like a nasty dragon in the driveway while we hide in the flower garden. My father talking to him in calm tones on the porch. Sending him away. It was one night, and a hundred nights.

Me, the protector. A sob catches in my throat.

Cut. New scene. Here comes the doctor. Right on cue. I've seen this part of the movie before. There's Lydia. And over there, under that tree, are Oscar and me. Such a pretty campus to take a walk. If I'd let Oscar tug me the other way, I never would have seen them.

The camera weaves in close. I can almost read the titles of the library books crammed in Lydia's arms. Lydia, the pretend college girl. Yammering up at the doctor in her usual, earnest frenzy. The doctor, hurried, trying to be polite, looking like he wants nothing more than to get away.

September 1995

MR. LINCOLN: Your honor, permission to treat the witness as hostile. I've been patient but I'm in the home stretch here. This witness has skirted around my last five questions.

JUDGE WATERS: Mr. Lincoln, I see nothing hostile about a hundred-pound girl wearing glasses unless it's that her IQ is larger than yours.

MR. LINCOLN: Objection . . . to you . . . your honor.

JUDGE WATERS: Ms. Bell. You need to answer. Did Tessie lie about anything related to this case?

MS. BELL: Yes, your honor.

MR. LINCOLN: OK, let's go over this one more time. Tessie lied about the drawings?

MS. BELL: Yes.

MR. LINCOLN: And she lied about when she could see again?

MS. BELL: Yes.

MR. LINCOLN: And before the attack, she lied about where she was going running?

MS. BELL: Yes. Sometimes.

MR. LINCOLN: And your father also lied about where he was going sometimes?

MR. VEGA: Your honor, objection.

9 days until the execution

A little more than a week before Terrell is scheduled to die, and I'm cleaning out Effie's freezer.

The judge rejected Terrell's habeas corpus appeal five hours ago, news leached to the bottom of my stomach. Bill delivered the announcement by phone. I could barely listen after I heard the word *rejected*. Something about how the judge felt it was *a tough call* but there was *no convincing evidence* that Terrell was innocent and the jury got it wrong.

It's not like the police aren't still plugging away with Igor's new theories. They've turned up sixty-eight names, all females in their late teens to early twenties from Mexico and Tennessee who went missing in the mid-to-late '80s—Jo's best estimate on the age of the bones.

The problem is, that list of sixty-eight translates to hundreds of searches for family members who have moved or died or who don't answer their phones or who simply won't give up their DNA to help identify the Susans. At least fifteen people contacted by the police are family members still listed as suspects in some of those cases. Some of them are probably killers, just not the one we're looking for. Eleven girls on the list turned out to be runaways found alive but never removed from the missing persons database. It's a slog that could take months or years, all of it surmised from an ancient code from the earth. It seems impossible. I can't even figure out the best way to scrape purple Popsicle juice out of Effie's freezer.

"Effie, keep or toss?" I know the answer—it's been my mantra for the last hour—but I'm asking anyway. I'm holding up a plastic bag that contains the battered paperback copy of *Lonesome Dove*. Gus McCrae and Pea Eye Parker had been freezing to death for years behind several foil-wrapped items furry with ice crystals. Those have solidly hit the trashcan outside without Effie's knowledge.

"Keep," Effie admonishes me. "Certainly. *Lonesome Dove* is my favorite book of all time. I put it in there so I'd know where it was." I'm never sure with Effie if these explanations are truth or cover-up.

Two days after Terrell is scheduled to die, Effie is moving to live with her daughter in New Jersey. I can barely breathe thinking about the absence of Effie's spirit in this house, but here I am, helping my friend load her life into boxes. At least that was the plan.

So far, she has not relinquished her hold on anything, including four iron skillets that are almost exactly alike except for the stories fried into their black history. In one, Effie made her husband's favorite Blueberry Surprise pancakes on the day he died. The skillet with the slightly rusted handle belonged to her mother. Effie almost came to blows over it post-funeral with a sister *who can't cook a lick*. The other two leave the best, crispest *almost burnt* crust on okra and cornbread, and *you always have to have two pans of okra*.

Effie is rather elegantly sprawled on the kitchen floor in a pair of old red silk pajamas, looking like an old Hollywood diva, if that's possible sitting on yellowed black-and-white linoleum surrounded by sixty years of pots and pans. The kitchen, like the rest of the house, is a wreck. She has spent the last three days yanking every single thing out of the cabinets, shelves, and closets and tossing it onto the beds, the floor, the tables, any available open space. The effect is that of a tornado hitting an antiques store.

"Sue, you're awfully quiet. Is it that damn Terrell Goodwin business?"

My fork stops its scraping. My head emerges from the freezer. Effie called me Sue, her daughter's name, while asking me the most pointed question of our relationship.

"Don't look so surprised. My mind's not that far gone, hon. I thought you might finally bring it up after the police broke down my door that night and ripped off my earphones. But you didn't, and that's fine. It's not even a smidgen of who you are, honey. Who you are—well, I'm going to miss who you are something terrible. And Charlie. I want to see that girl grow up. She's going to teach me to do that Sky-hype thing. Did I tell you that Sue's fiancé and I had a real good talk last night? He's fifth-generation New Jersey Italian. He told me it's always been an honor and privilege in his family to take care of the old. At least that's what I think he said. I couldn't understand half the conversation. I thought he had a speech impediment for the first fifteen minutes."

I laugh because I've listened to Effie rattle off fluent French in her East Texas drawl, and it wasn't as pretty as a Hoboken accent. It's a slightly uneasy laugh, because I'm not interested in any heartfelt, tell-all goodbye with Effie. I'm going to leave her dreams alone. I don't want her to see my eyes dilate into black holes or for her to walk endless fields of yellow flowers that hold the scent of death. I don't want her to wake up still smelling it.

I'm relieved when my phone begins to buzz somewhere near a counter of jumbled spices. I dig it out from under yellowed directions for a Sunbeam Percolator and a recipe for Doc's Gay Salad. I have no memory of placing my phone under anything; it's like the kitchen is turning into some form of kudzu and growing over itself.

Jo's name is on the screen. An instant sense of dread, pickled with hope.

"Hello," I say.

"Hi, Tessa. Bill told me he let you know about the judge's ruling. Sucks."

"Yes, he called." I want to say more, but there's Effie.

"I'm a little worried about Bill. He looks like he hasn't slept for days. I've never seen him quite like this with a case. I think it's all tied up in his grief for Angie. Like he can't let her down."

If I start to feel something for Bill or Terrell right now, I will feel everything. I already sense the hot well building behind my eyes.

"There's another reason I'm calling," Jo continues. "The cops got the guy who stuck those signs in your yard. He was caught vandalizing the lawn of a Catholic priest in Boerne. I thought you might want to get a restraining order. He's free on bond. His name is Jared Lester. He'll probably end up with a severe fine and community service instead of jail time."

"OK. Thanks. I'll think about it." *I'll think about not purposely pissing him off right now.*

"One more thing. He claims, rather proudly, that he planted the black-eyed Susans under your windowsill several weeks ago. I've checked, and the potting soil in his garage has the same basic signature as what I sampled from your yard that day. I don't think he's lying. He brought it up voluntarily in the police interview. Here's the deal. He's only twenty-three." Meaning, not my monster. I do the math. He was five when I was tossed in that grave.

Effie's eying my throat, where my pulse drums. One of my tears drops onto the yellowed coffeepot instructions with the cartoon percolator with a Mr. Kool-Aid face. I begin to methodically stand the spices into efficient lines.

How long has Jo known? Long enough that the police have caught this man, interviewed him, and set his bail. Long enough to run tests on potting soil.

I should give Jo a break, of course. As she ran that test, she had to know the outcome couldn't reassure me that much.

My monster is still out there.

This time, the door opens, and it's me on the other side wanting in.

I search his face, and my heart cracks.

I silently beg him to see all of me. The Black-Eyed Susan who talks to dead people, and the artist with the half-moon scar who tortures paint and thread to make sure beauty exists somewhere inside her. The mother who named her daughter Charlie after her father's favorite Texas knuckleball pitcher, and the runner who has never stopped running.

"You look like hell," I say.

"What are you doing here?" As he says this, Bill is pulling me across the threshold into his arms.

We haven't spoken much or texted in the last several days. Bill doesn't appear to have showered for most of them. I don't mind. He smells alive. His chin scrapes my cheek like sandpaper. Our lips connect and, for a very long time, that's all there is.

"This is a bad idea," he says, breaking us apart.

"That's my line."

"Seriously. I'm running on fumes. Let me get you a beer and we'll talk."

"I'm so sorry about Terrell," I say, following him inside. "Sorry for everything." My words, inadequate.

"Yes. Me, too." His voice is grim.

"I didn't mean to be so short on the phone. I was just . . . shocked."

He shrugs. "Next stop, U.S. Court of Appeals. A bunch of buffoons with rubber stamps. The habeas appeal was our real shot. Have a seat and I'll be back with your beer."

He disappears through an archway, leaving me to glean what I can from the first encounter with his living space. I scour the art on the walls the way other people surreptitiously peer at bookshelves and CD collections. Or used to anyway. A few decent modern prints with reds, greens, and golds. Nothing that provides insight into Bill's soul, and if it does, I don't want that to pop my bubble.

I pick out a buttery white leather chair and wonder a little too late if I'd gotten a nice young law intern named Kayley into trouble by bullying her for Bill's home address. When I showed up in Angie's basement, Kayley dripped as much exhaustion as Bill. I wore her down with my red eyes, driver's license, and a rambling dissertation on Saint Stephen, still being stoned to death over Angie's shrine of a desk. Kayley spent much of the dissertation time trying not to gape at my scar, openly impressed that she was meeting the myth.

All of which led me to this 1960s-era converted garage, which I'm sure is worth about $600,000 plus. It nests in the winding waterways and trees of Turtle Creek, a famous, wealthy old Dallas neighborhood where Indians used to camp. I love the play of light on hardwoods, the gracious white brick fireplace with a grate covered in ash, even the concentric coffee rings near the open laptop on the coffee table. The art, not so much. It matches these pillows.

Bill appears with two St. Pauli Girls in his hands. I want to think this means he took note of my favorite beer and stocked it.

"In case you're wondering," he says, gesturing with his beer, "I'm a squatter. My dad enjoys flipping town homes after retirement, which I guess is better than playing baccarat at Choctaw. My mother decorates. So I'm just here making it look lived in until it sells." He takes a swig and settles on the couch directly across from me.

"I have to confess," he says. "Kayley called to warn me you were coming."

"So you could get your gun out." I smile.

"Well, it wouldn't be the first time," he says.

I switch the subject back to Terrell. "How many times have you won a reprieve in a death penalty case?"

"A reprieve? Five or six. That's the real goal most of the time. To extend life as long as possible, because if you're sitting on Death Row in Texas, you are most likely going to die on that gurney. I've only worked one case with a Capra-esque ending. Angie was the lead. I don't do this full time. But you know that."

"That one time . . . you must have been . . . elated," I say.

"*Elated* isn't exactly the right word. It doesn't change that the victim died a horrible death. There's a family out there who might always feel like we set a killer free. So I'd say, more like very, very,

very relieved. Angie insisted we did our high-fiving in private." Bill pats the side of the couch. "Come here. You're too far away."

I get up very slowly. He pulls me down into his arms and drags a kiss along my mouth. "Lie down."

"I thought this wasn't a good idea."

"This is a very good idea. We're going to sleep."

The fierce pounding rocks both of us upright and fully awake.

Bill jumps from the couch, leaving me gracelessly sprawled against the pillows. He's already peering through the peephole before my feet touch the floor. In a second, I'm beside him. "Go into the kitchen," he orders, "if you want to keep us a secret."

I don't budge, and he turns the knob.

I'm blinded by lime green. A ski jacket meant to stand out to rescue helicopters on a snowy slope. Jo's head is sticking out of it. She pushes her way into the room like she's been here before.

She's quickly figuring out what my presence means. "Tessa? Why . . . ?" She shakes her head. "Oh, never mind. It doesn't matter. You should know, too."

"Know what?" I'm awkwardly smoothing my hair.

"About Aurora."

"Is something wrong? Is she hurt?" *Or dead?*

"No, no. It's her DNA. We found a match. It's bizarre."

"Come on, Jo. What's up?" Bill, impatient. Watching my face.

"We have a DNA match from Aurora to the fetal bone from the Black-Eyed Susan grave. They shared the same father. They would have been half-sisters."

"A DNA match to . . . Lydia's daughter?" Bill is asking the incredulous words while I'm trying to catch up. To let go of the picture of Lydia and a high school boy in a naked tangle.

Lydia slept with the killer. Or she was raped.

I'm the one with the answers, a Susan whispers.

Bill's phone begins to bleat. He pulls it out of his pocket, annoyed, and glances at the screen. His face is suddenly locked down.

"I have to take this." He points a finger at Jo and me. "Hold off saying more until I'm off the phone."

Jo guides me by my elbow back to the couch. The Susans are whispering very low, like the wind humming through that tiny hole in my tree house.

That night, the Susans come to me in my sleep. They are frenzied, running around, a blur of youthful limbs and bright swirling skirts, more alive than I've ever seen them. They are searching for my monster in every nook and cranny as if their mansion in my head is about to explode. As if it is for the very last time.

They are shouting and cursing at each other, at me.

Wake up, Tessie! they are shrieking. *Lydia knows something!* They are spreading out like Army men. Opening and slamming closet doors, tearing off bedcovers, dusting cobwebs off chandeliers, ripping weeds out of the garden. Merry, sweet Merry, is falling to her knees to beg God's mercy.

A Susan calls out. *Over here! I've found the monster!* She's telling me to *hurry, hurry, hurry* because she can't hold him down for long.

I teeter on the edge of consciousness. The Susan is planted on top of him, her red skirt swirled over his body like blood. She is using every last bit of strength to twist his neck around so that I can see. A worm is gyrating out of his mouth. His face is caked with mud.

I wake up sobbing.

My monster is still wearing a mask. And Lydia knows exactly who he is.

September 1995

MR. LINCOLN: I think we're all done, Ms. Bell. Thank you for your testimony. I'm sorry it's been a difficult day for you.

MS. BELL: It wasn't difficult. I have one more thing. It's about Tessie's journal.

MR. LINCOLN: I wasn't aware she had a journal.

MR. VEGA: Objection. I know nothing about this journal. It is not in evidence, your honor, and I don't see its relevance.

JUDGE WATERS: Mr. Lincoln?

MR. LINCOLN: I'm thinking.

JUDGE WATERS: Well, while you're thinking, I'm going to ask the witness a few questions.

MR. VEGA: Objection. I believe you are overstepping a little here, your honor. We only have this witness's word that it exists.

MR. LINCOLN: I believe I have to object as well, your honor. I'm walking a ledge just like Mr. Vega here, not knowing its contents.

JUDGE WATERS: Thank you for your united interest in pursuing the truth, gentlemen. Look at me, Ms. Bell. I need you to speak very generally. Did you bring up the journal because you think there is something in it pertinent to this trial?

MS. BELL: Most of it was running times, personal stuff. Sometimes she'd read to me from it. A fairy tale she made up. Or show me a little sketch she did. Or . . .

JUDGE WATERS: Hold on, Ms. Bell. Did Ms. Cartwright let you read her journal?

MS. BELL: Not exactly. When she was acting funny, I would, though. And I'd go through her purse or drawers to make sure she wasn't hoarding Benadryl and stuff. That's what best friends do.

JUDGE WATERS: Ms. Bell, I need you to answer my question with a yes or a no. Do you believe there is something in the journal that is pertinent to this trial?

MS. BELL: That's hard to say but, you know, like, I wonder. I never read the whole thing. I skimmed. We used to do our journals together. It was one of our things.

JUDGE WATERS: Do you know where Tessie's journal is?

MS. BELL: Yes.

JUDGE WATERS: And where is that?

MS. BELL: I gave it to her psychiatrist.

JUDGE WATERS: And why did you do that?

MS. BELL: Because it had a picture she drew when she was blind of a red-haired mermaid jumping off her grandfather's roof. You know, killing herself.

PART III

Tessa and Lydia

Flowers are restful to look at. They have neither
emotions nor conflicts.

**—Lydia, age 15, reading the words of Sigmund Freud
while lounging on her father's boat, 1993**

Tessa, present day

Effie is standing on my front porch holding a lumpy brown package. Her flimsy robe is billowing out behind her. The neighborhood is dead asleep, except for us and a few streetlights. Before she knocked, I was wide awake trying to read *The Goldfinch* but thinking about Terrell.

Three days left.

"I forgot to give you this earlier." Effie plops the package into my arms. "I saw some girl in a purple dress drop it off. Or maybe it was a handsome man in a suit. Anyway, I saw it on your front porch this afternoon. Or yesterday. Or maybe a week ago. I thought I should bring it in for you."

"Thank you," I say, distracted.

Tessie scrawled on the front. No stamp. No return address. It feels squishy, with something stiff in the middle.

Don't open it. A Susan, warning me.

I cast my eyes past Effie, onto the dark lawn. I survey the lumps of bushes crouching between our property lines. The shadows dancing to a tuneless rhythm on the driveway.

Charlie is at a sleepover. Lucas is on an overnight date. Bill is at the Days Inn in Huntsville because Terrell begged him.

Effie is already floating back across the yard.

303

Lydia, age 16

43 HOURS AFTER THE ATTACK

This is not my best friend.

This is a thing, with a Bozo the Clown wig and a slack face and tubes running everywhere like an insane water park except the water is yellow and red.

I'm holding Tessie's hand and squeezing it, timing every squeeze by my watch, because her Aunt Hilda told me to. *About every minute,* she said. *We want her to know we're here.* I'm trying not to squeeze the part of her hand where the bandage is turning a little pink. I overheard a nurse say Tessie's fingernails were ripped out, like she was trying to claw her way out of a grave. They had to pick yellow flower petals out of the gash in her head.

"It can take like eighteen months for toenails to grow back," I say loudly, because Aunt Hilda said to keep talking because *we don't know what she can hear* and because I'd already reassured Tessie that her fingernails will only take six months.

As soon as I heard Tessie was missing, I threw up. After twelve hours, I knew for sure something evil got her. I started writing what I'd say at the funeral. I wrote how I wouldn't ever again feel her fingers braiding my hair or see her draw a lovely thing in about thirty seconds or watch her face go animal when she runs. People would have cried when they heard it.

I was going to quote Chaucer and Jesus and promise I'd devote my entire life to looking for her killer. I was going to stand at that pulpit in the Baptist church and throw out a warning to the killer in case he was listening because killers usually are. Instead of saying *Peace be with you,* people were going to flip around in their pews and give each other jumpy stares and wonder from now on what exactly was living next door to them. There's a knife in every kitchen drawer, pillows on every bed, anti-freeze in every garage. Weapons everywhere, people, and we're ready to blow. That would be my message.

Tessie thinks humans are basically good. I don't. I'm dying to ask if she thinks evil is an aberration now, but I don't want her to think I'm rubbing it in.

The monitor over the bed is screeching for the hundredth time, and I jump, but Tessie doesn't move. I feel like my hand is squeezing a piece of mozzarella cheese. It hits me full blast for like the tenth time that she'll never be the same. There's a bandage on her face that's hiding something. She might not be pretty anymore, or funny, or get all my literary references, or be the only person on earth who doesn't think I'm a total ghoul. Even my dad calls me Morticia sometimes.

The beeping *won't stop.* I punch the call button *again.* A nurse swings open the door, asking me if an adult is coming back in soon. Like *I'm* a problem.

I don't want to be dispatched to the waiting room again. There are a million people in there. And Tessie's track coach was driving me crazy. Repeating how lucky it is that the *calvary* got to Tessie in time. *Calvary is where Jesus died on the cross, you moron.* I tell the story to Tessie again, even though I already did a few minutes ago.

Tessie's eyelids flutter. Except her Aunt Hilda warned me her eyes do that regularly. It doesn't mean she's waking up.

I picked out Tessie in second grade, the instant I sat down at the desk next to hers.

I squeeze her hand. "It's OK to come back. I won't let him get you."

Tessa, present day

I close the door. Finger in the security code.

Turn around and almost stop breathing.

Merry's face is pressed into the mirror's reflection on the wall.

She's trapped on the other side of the glass, just like the night she pressed her face against the car window in the drugstore parking lot. How much effort it must have taken for her to throw herself up from the backseat, half-dead, half-drugged, gagged with a blue scarf, one last-ditch effort to hope that someone like me would happen along to rescue her. Of all the Susans in my head, Merry's the least needy, the least accusing. The most guilty.

It's OK, I say softly, walking toward her. *It is not your fault. I'm the one who's sorry. I should have saved you.*

By the time I press my palm flat against the glass, Merry's already gone, replaced by a pale woman with messy red hair, green eyes, and a gold squiggly charm in the hollow of her throat. My breath fogs the mirror, and I disappear, too.

Merry has shown up twice before. She appeared in the doctor's office window when I was seventeen, five days after I got my sight back. Four years ago, she sang "I'll Fly Away" in the back row of the church choir at my father's funeral.

I walk over to the kitchen drawer, pull out a knife, and slice it across the package.

The Susans, a rising hum in my head.

Lydia, age 16

I'm pounding on the door and yelling Tessie's name.

She's locked me out. I'm stuck in her stupid pink fairy tale bedroom that was fine *when we were ten*. I woke up and she wasn't in bed and now I can't get the door to the terrace open. I *told* her I didn't want her out there alone tonight because she's blind and it's dangerous and I've been left in charge. But, really, it's because I think she might jump off her grandfather's roof.

Today was another Sad Day. She's had twenty-six in a row. I mark a smiley face on my calendar every day she smiles *once*. No one else is marking smiley faces on a calendar and yet if Tessie kills herself tonight, it will be the fault of Lydia Frances Bell.

Lydia was never a good influence. Lydia's morbid. Lydia might have given Tessie a little push.

I put my ear on the door. Still alive. She's playing something dirge-y on her flute. It takes a lot of breath to blow a flute. I wouldn't want to stand too close and get a whiff. She hasn't brushed her teeth for six days. No one but me is counting *that* number, either. One life lesson of the Tessie thing is that it's harder to love people when they smell. Of course, there are a lot of good parts, too. It's cool to be called her *fairy tale friend* by *People* magazine. And I feel a secret, tickly thrill all the time now, the same as when I'm staring into the ocean and thinking about how deep and black it goes, and what lurks on the bottom. I *like* walking around inside a terrible novel, *living* it, getting up every day to write a new page, even if people always see Tessie as the main character.

The door is budging a little, so I bang my hip into it a little harder. It was her grandparents' stupid idea, not mine, to bring her to their castle for the weekend. Of course, they crashed at 9:30 and are half-deaf.

Surely she wouldn't jump because of that Frida Kahlo remark I made at dinner. Her grandmother had given me a dirty look. I mean, it was her grandfather who brought it up.

He was telling Tessie about how Frida Kahlo had painted in bed after the terrible bus accident when she was eighteen that left her frozen in a body cast. Frida's mother made this special easel for her bed. So Tessie's grandfather asked her if she'd like him to make something like it for her. He was trying to inspire her, but it seems to me the lesson there is that a random bus accident screwed up Frida Kahlo pretty much for life, just like Tessie's going to be. And all I *said* was that it was a good thing Kahlo killed herself because she was literally painting herself to death. I thought it was funny. Like, how many Frida Kahlo faces can the world take?

The door suddenly gives way, and I stumble onto the terrace. She's sitting on the ledge with her back to me, wearing her grandfather's extra-large white Hanes T-shirt, looking like Casper the Friendly Ghost. She forgot her nightgown on our little overnight trip, so she borrowed the shirt out of her grandfather's drawer.

There are much better ways to kill yourself, I am thinking. *And I wouldn't wear that.*

Maybe I should let her jump. It just pops in my head.

If she did, she'd probably just end up in a wheelchair because she's just that lucky. Or unlucky. It's such a freaky line. All this hard work to bring her back to life when I'm pretty sure she wishes she'd gone to sleep in that grave and never woken up.

I'm really, really pissed off tonight. More than usual. I'm *crying*. I'm not sure how long I can keep this up. All those stories in the newspaper, and yet the ugly, real story is never told.

She's still playing the stupid flute. It makes *me* want to jump.

"Please get off the ledge," I choke out. *"Please."*

Tessa, present day

1:54 A.M.

I reach into the package and tug out a plastic bag.
    A shirt is inside.
    Crusted with blood.
    I recognize it.

Lydia, age 17

I could draw *twenty* smiley faces in my calendar today.

My mom just brought us freezing cans of Coke with straws, and Chips Ahoy on a plate. She said it was good to hear us laughing so much again. I locked the door after that. It was Tessie's idea to draw these fake pictures for her new doctor, a big shocker, because it's more like the kind of thing *I* would come up with. Tessie was never a big liar but I've never had a problem if it's a means to an end. She told me she's not ready to let this new doctor peer into her soul. The soul thing was just her mimicking the doctor she got stuck with right before this one. That idiot told her she could cure her blindness if she jumped off the high dive and opened her eyes underwater. I've never seen Tessie's dad so mad as when I told him. *He might as well be suggesting she kill herself!*

Tessie's wearing these white nerdy pajamas with lace that her Aunt Hilda gave her. If she could see, she wouldn't be caught dead in them. But she can't, and it's kind of sweet. They make her look all innocent, like the world isn't ending.

"Do you have the black marker?" Tessie's asking.

"Yes." I perfect a grimace on a flower and hand it over.

For once, I'm not embarrassed to draw in the same room as Tessie. She had to go blind for that to happen. Everything she draws is always so *perfect*. I like this picture. I definitely draw better when Tessie's no competition.

Still, I'm thinking this picture's a little *literal*. A field of monster flowers. A girl cowering. It needs *drama*.

I add another girl right on top of the other one. Scratch in some red. Are the girls fighting to the death? Is one killing the other? Are the poor little flowers actually just worried and trying to make it stop?

Ha-ha. Let him wonder.

Tessa, present day

2:03 A.M.

My eyes are glued to the brown stain on the pink shirt. My shirt. She borrowed it from me a very long time ago and never returned it.

It's a lot of blood.

Not for the first time, I'm numbly contemplating the idea of Lydia, murdered.

Lydia was fond of ketchup, I remind myself. Of corn syrup and red dye, manipulation and guessing games.

There's something else in the package.

A college-ruled notebook. I recognize it, too. There used to be a whole box of them.

A date is scribbled on the front of this one. And a name.

The *L* curls up on the end, like a cat's tail. I'd seen her write that *L* a hundred times.

My hand hovers between the notebook and my cell phone.

Deciding how to play.

Lydia, age 17

"I'm Lydia Frances Bell," I introduce myself, wishing I hadn't added the *Frances*. Or used the *Lydia*, which I never felt was my true name. I'm more of an Audriana or Violetta or Dahlia. I should have given him a fake name. Tessie would say it was stupid to introduce myself to him in the first place. She'd be mad. I told her I was just going to sit in her doctor's class one time to observe and not even raise my hand. I've come twice since then. Tessie is driving me freaking crazy. Last night, she nearly tore my head off when I made myself a peanut butter sandwich and brought it to her room. I mean, get over it. It's a *sandwich*.

Today is the first time I signed up for his office hours. I feel as fully prepared as I can be. I've researched everything I can about him. I've read his lecture series *From Marilyn Monroe to Eva Braun: History's Most Powerful Bimbos*. I *devoured* the case study of that girl who survived being buried alive by her stepdad, which got everyone all into him being Tessie's therapist when his name appeared on the list of candidates. He's been a visiting professor at *three* Ivy League schools. He *never* teaches anything with 101 in the title. I couldn't find much personal, so that was a bummer, and *nothing*

315

about his missing daughter, but I'm sure he's a private man and is totally devoted to his life's work.

"I'm so glad you dropped by, Lydia," he's saying. "I've seen you sitting in the front row." His smile is a draught of sunshine. He makes me *think* in Keats.

I lay down my *copious* notes on his last lecture, about the dark triad of personality, so he can see right away what a good student I am. He asks me whether I agree with Machiavelli that we are not helpless at the hands of bad luck. It was apparently a rhetorical question, because he's still talking. I love the sound of his voice rolling over all those four-syllable words. I feel like he is having sex with my brain.

I have ten brilliant questions all set to impress him, and I haven't asked a single one.

He has rolled his chair over from behind the desk. His knee is pressing against my leg in this delicious pleasure-pain thing. I can barely *think* with his knee on mine and yet he acts like it's not even there.

I know I need to tell him I'm the Lydia who is Tessie's best friend, but not when he's looking at me like that.

Next time.

Tessa, present day

2:24 A.M.

I'm whipping through the pages. They're brutal. Nicking me, stabbing me, kicking me in the gut. Blowing me a few kisses. Love and resentment, all mixed up.

A whole other Lydia going on when I was sixteen years old. A picture behind a picture. I flash back to that night on the terrace when I thought we dredged up everything. Every unspoken pebble of anger. Every benign tumor that had been growing since our friendship began—the tumors that live under the skin of every relationship until the unforgivable moment that changes their chemistry forever.

I was wrong. There was so much more.

I'm trying to reconcile the girl in this notebook with the one who gave me back my breath with a brown paper bag. Who hugged me all night when my mother died, and braided my hair when I was blind. Who read me breathless poetry. Who wrote notes in Edgar Allan Poe's favorite cipher, with invisible ink made from lemon juice, and stuck them in a crack in my tree house for me to find the next day. So I could hold her words up to the sun.

I feel sick.

The phone rings. I jump up, knocking over a bottle of water.

Lydia's ink begins to blur.

I blot frantically at the pages.

The phone shrills again. Insistent.

I stare at the Caller ID.

Outler, Euphemia.

At least a quarter of the pages left. I don't know how Lydia's story ends. Or how quickly my time with the journal will be up. I have to figure, very, very soon.

I pick up the receiver.

"Sue? Sue?" Full-on Effie panic.

She lowers her voice.

I think the damn digger snatcher is here.

Lydia, age 17

Tessie is *screaming* at me.

You gave my diary to the doctor? You rifle through my things?

"I had to give jurors the full picture." Good grief, she is freaking *out*. I thought she'd get it. "I gave him the diary to *protect* you. I testified to all that stuff to help convict Terrell."

"Yeah, right. You had to tell them I didn't bathe? That you found lice in my hair? That I stole painkillers out of Aunt Hilda's medicine cabinet?"

"I'm sorry I said the boys call you Suzy Scarface. That was a very unfortunate headline."

"Do they really call me that, Lydia?" Tessie looks like she's about to cry. But I can't give in. She always wants things both ways.

"You testified for *you*," Tessie is saying. "So *you* could be a star."

We're standing on her grandfather's terrace like we have a million times before. She's shaking, she's so freaking mad at me. But, like, I'm getting madder by the second, too. *Doesn't she understand everything I've done for her?* She's yelling, and I'm yelling right back, the catfight of the century. Finally, she doesn't have a comeback. There's just silence and black night and us, breathing hard.

"I saw you with the doctor." Her tone creeps me out.

"What are you talking about?" Of course, I *know* what she's talking about. *But which time? How much does she know?* I take a stab. "You mean the time I gave him your diary?"

"I guess. I was walking Oscar at the college. What did you think you were doing, Lydia? *Get out.*"

Her grandmother is suddenly at my back, clawing my shoulder, wheezing a little, because she had to climb all those stairs. She never liked me much. "Girls—"

"Get out, Lydia," Tessie sobs. *"Getoutgetoutgetout."*

Tessa, present day

2:29 A.M.

I'm crossing the yard, running. Barefoot. It feels like a dream. A starry night above my head. A sweet, drifting perfume, nauseating.

Shadows hang off every tree, ready to smother me. I focus on the light trickling out of Effie's kitchen window. On the cold steel in my hand. On the idea of Effie, alone with a monster. The one eating her brain, the one who turned girls to bones, the one who used to brush my hair and secretly despise my weakness. Maybe all three.

Waiting for me. Using Effie as bait.

What is that on the ground? I bend and brush my fingers on the grass. Confetti. It litters a path between my house and Effie's. I rub the bits of paper between my fingers. Watch the pieces tumble and float downward like brilliant abstract thoughts.

It isn't confetti.

The grass is littered with black-eyed Susans.

Someone has ripped off their body parts and left me a trail.

I'm gasping, sucking at air that is evaporating.

Van Gogh's sky is spinning above me.

My head is exploding with images, and settles on one.

He has finally wiped the mud off his face.

My monster. The Black-Eyed Susan killer.

He's clean, and shaved. Smiling.

The Susans yip with joy. *That's him that's him that's him!*

I can feel his arm trapped around my shoulder. Smell the cologne on his suit coat.

Hear his lazy, reassuring drawl.

If you had three wishes, Tessie, what would they be?

Lydia, age 17

3 DAYS AFTER THE TRIAL

We made love twice. He's already on the edge of the bed.

"I'm going to take a shower, sweetheart," he says. "Then I'm going to have to run. So pack up, OK?"

Sweetheart. Like I'm a 1940s thing on the side. How about getting a little more mythological? Calling me Eurydice? Or Isolde? I'm thinking that Lydia Frances Bell deserves better right now than scratchy sheets and *pack up* and *sweetheart*.

The shower is already running.

I slip naked out of bed, shivering. He always keeps it freezing in his apartment. He doesn't like the noise of the furnace coming on and off. *Whatever*. I grab his shirt off the floor and slip my arms into it. Flap the long sleeves like a bird. It's his last day at school before his China sabbatical. He says Tessie doesn't ever need to know we slept together, which is, like, *huge*. I'm thinking she'll get over the testimony stuff. I give her a month.

These packing boxes are freaking everywhere.

Maybe I'll explore. Find a memento he won't miss.

I stick my hands in the pockets of his old man suits. I wish he'd let me dress him. His shirts are way too starchy. They scratch my

323

neck. I thumb through a stack of textbooks that would bore the crap out of me. I rove around in his boxer shorts drawer. Ordinary, ordinary, ordinary.

The shower's still running.

I open and shut more empty drawers. Check out the freezer.

Thumb through a pile of mail. Geez, even Tessie leaves me better surprises.

I almost didn't bother to open the cabinet under the kitchen sink.

That's where I found them.

Straggly yellow flowers with black eyes, sitting in the dark.

Tessa, present day

I'm kneeling. Staring at a petal stuck to my hand. Pulsing with rage.

At him. At myself, for knowing all along but being too afraid to see.

At Lydia.

I don't know how much time has passed. Seconds? Minutes? The light still glows steadily from Effie's kitchen.

You control your mind, Tessie. The doctor. In my head. Leering. Mocking.

I will myself to stand.

Petals are everywhere, glued to my knees, to the soles of my bare feet.

I reach down to brush them off.

They are not petals.

They are tiny, twisted scraps of Kleenex. Fragments of tissue that have disintegrated in the washer. The ones constantly nesting in the pockets of Effie's robes and sweaters.

This is Effie's trail. It leads to her front door, miles away from the grave where Tessie went to sleep.

Except Tessie is waking up. The old Tessie, who outran boys,

325

who beat a plodding heart, who risked scabs and bones and scars, *who did not lose* because her dead mother cheered her across the finish line.

I see Tessie crouched on a track in blinding sunlight. Heat rises in visible waves. Her eyes are down. To finish first, she will spend the least amount of time possible in the air, over the hurdles.

Her fingertips are poised on gritty dirt.

Mine are twisting Effie's doorknob.

Both of us, ready for the gun to go off.

Lydia, age 17

10 DAYS AFTER THE TRIAL

He's like a serial killer Mr. Darcy, offering me his hand so that I can step into the boat bobbing away off the ratty dock. We took this wiggly little path down from the cabin to get here. His idea, the rental cabin. Our special goodbye night, he says, before he takes off for China or wherever he's really going. This place is remote as hell. I wonder if he brought other girls here. Or does he choose a new spot every time? Everything's black. The water, the sky, the forest of trees behind us. And what about that tarp in the bottom of the boat? Does he really think that Lydia Bell is this stupid? Of course, I'm stepping into a boat with a serial killer but that's what you have to do when there's no real evidence and you're the very last hope.

"Careful," he warns as I step down. "Want to drive?" While I sit, he's yanking the outboard string, having a little trouble getting it all revved up. I could offer advice but I don't.

"No, thanks," I say. "I'd be scared. I'm just going to sit back and look at the moon if I can find it. I have a flashlight. Maybe I'll read to you." I wave the book in my hand, *The Ultimate Book of Love Poems: Browning to Yeats,* even though I have a photographic memory and I've read this book a billion times.

"I didn't know anything was capable of scaring you," he teases. *Hmm*, I'm thinking, *the scared thing might have been too much*.

"You're going to love it out here on the lake in the dark," he's saying. "Just your style. Wait to read until we get to a good spot. I'll cut the motor and we can drift a little. Drink a little wine."

He's about two miles out, slowing the boat down, when I flick on my flashlight, open the book, and begin. " 'You love me. You love me *not*.' "

The words get lost in the noise of the engine.

"What?" Impatient. "I told you not to read yet."

I go silent, which is hard.

He kills the motor in the middle of the lake.

I'm prepared, of course. Ten questions are typed out in my head, numbered one under the other. I shut the book.

Question No. 1: "Did you kill those girls?"

"What girls, sweetie?"

"Did you think I wouldn't love you anymore? That I would tell?"

"Lydia. Stop."

"Did you know who I was that very first day in your office? That I was Tessie's best friend?" I want him to say *no*. I want him to *explain*.

It's hard to see his face in the dark. His body remains perfectly relaxed. "Sweetheart, of course I knew. I know everything about you and Tessie. You are fucked-up little girls."

I'm watching his hands, fiddling with a coiled rope.

It's official. Lydia Frances Bell loved a serial killer.

My heart is pounding pretty hard, which is to be expected. I keep my eyes on the rope. "Where are you really going on that plane?"

"Surely your big brain has better questions than this, Lydia. But to answer . . . I'm not sure yet."

"I have ten questions total."

"Fire away."

"Do you really have a daughter named Rebecca?"

"I do not." He's grinning.

"No family? No friends?"

"Unnecessary, don't you think?"

"My other three questions don't matter."

My fingers curl around Daddy's gun in my coat pocket.

"I'm pregnant," I say.

The gun, now aimed at his chest.

Blood drooling out of his shoulder instead.

I didn't even hear it go off. A gunshot on the lake sounds like the sky is cracking. Like it might rain shards of glass. That's what Tessie used to say.

I steady my hand.

"Wait, sweetheart." He's pleading with me. "We can work this out. You and I, we're the same."

Tessa, present day

2:44 A.M.

The foyer, dark.

"Effie?" I call out.

"In the kitchen, Sue." Her voice traveling over from the next room. Lilting. Her panic erased. I smell something burnt.

I wonder if it's gunpowder. If my neighbor has shot her digger snatcher dead with that little pearl-handled revolver she keeps loaded in her bedside table against my wishes.

You can do this. For Charlie.

I round the corner.

It is an ordinary tableau.

And a chilling one.

Lydia, a very alive, *blond* Lydia, seated at the table.

Effie, beaming and placing a blue-flowered china plate in front of her.

"There you are!" Effie enthuses. "False alarm! It wasn't the digger snatcher after all. It was just Liz here. Which is a real treat."

Lydia, smiling. Not buried in an anonymous grave. Not broken. Not sorry. A part of everything.

Her lips are slashed with bright red. I see the tiny, tiny black birthmark on her upper lip that one boy teased her was a tick. She'd held her hand over her mouth for a week.

Her left leg is crossed over the right knee at a slightly odd angle. She used to sit just like that one summer to hide a mark from her dad's belt buckle. It became a habit she couldn't break.

I knew her habits. I knew secrets that made her howl. I could tear her to shreds.

Lydia watches me carefully. Still not saying a word.

My gun clatters to the floor.

I don't move. Because that was my move.

"You dropped something, honey," Effie is saying. "Aren't you going to pick it up? You might remember me talking about Liz. She's the researcher from the national historical society who visits me now and again. She stored some of her boxes of Fort Worth research in my shed not that long ago. She visits societies all over the nation!"

I remember. *Boxes, taped tightly shut. Charlie, helping Effie and a strange woman lug them to the shed.*

"Liz came over tonight to get something she needs out of them, and didn't want to wake me," Effie continues. "I told her it was best not to skulk around here in Texas. She spends most of her time in more civilized places like Washington and London, isn't that right?"

Lydia, this *dyed,* smiling, nodding Lydia, has been insinuating herself into Effie's life. Pretending to be someone she isn't. Spying, like she always did. *Watching me. Watching Charlie. Delivering her diary to my doorstep. Returning my shirt, soaked in red. Playing her little games.*

"Where is he?" I hiss at Lydia.

It was Lydia who always told me not to say the doctor's name out loud. *Seize control. Limit his power.*

"The digger snatcher isn't here, honey." Effie, trying to clear things up. "Like I mentioned, it was Liz in the back yard. We were just discussing that little Mudgett man from Chicago who tried to build one of his murder castles downtown. Liz knows *everything* about old Fort Worth. I agree with her that a plaque should be erected on that lot where he planned his slaughterhouse for girls."

"I'm sure she knows all about serial killers." I can't tear my eyes off her. The brilliant, familiar eyes. Expensive tortoiseshell glasses. Hair tied up in a chic, messy knot. A chunky Breitling leather watch hugging her wrist. A plain wide band of hammered silver on her right hand.

"He's dead, Tessie." The first words Lydia has uttered to me in seventeen years. Her voice, triumphant. "I killed him."

"Of course he's dead," Effie prattles. "Mr. Mudgett died in prison in 1896. He was hanged at Moyamensing, Liz. You just told me a second ago that he twitched for fifteen minutes."

Lydia, age 17

I press the trigger four times.

Simple as that for a fucked-up Texas girl.

I crawl over him to the wheel.

It takes eleven minutes to whip around the lake in the dark and find Dumbo. My marker. The large tree on the west shore with a single branch that curves up like an elephant's trunk.

This is the creepiest spot in the lake. Dead Man's Triangle. Good fishing, but if people go under here, they often don't pop back up. I've driven a boat around this lake since I could see over the front and my father was a drunk, which means pretty much since the day I was born. Daddy and I had our best times on this lake. I gutted the fish without throwing up, and he swilled vodka out of Coke cans and always did.

My mind is *so quiet*. Like, quieter than it's ever been. It's weird. I stop the motor. Drift for a second. Better get back to business. It isn't that hard to push him out of the boat. *Plop.* He sinks in less than a minute. I don't feel a thing, watching him go under. I toss in the old book I found under his kitchen sink with the black-eyed Susans and the Cascade. *Rebecca* by Daphne du Maurier. Blood had soaked the brittle binding, or I would have kept it. That book was my No. 8, 9, and 10 questions, but he was about to lasso me with that freaking rope.

It takes no time to motor back, yank up the tarp in the boat, and collect all our stuff around the cabin. *Be out by 11 A.M.*, the notice on the back of the door instructs me. *Make sure the boat is properly docked. Leave the cabin key on the table.*

My teeth are chattering and my hands and feet are numb when I stick his key in the ignition, but I'm feeling pretty good about myself. I drive around to the Lake Texoma State Park camping area and dump the tarp and his suitcase in two giant garbage bins on either end.

I'm halfway to the rental place to return his car when I run out of gas.

Tessie, present day

2:52 A.M.

My monster's dead.

My best friend's alive, folding a white napkin into a tidy point.

So why do I feel this terrifying urge to run?

To scream at Effie.

Run.

Lydia, age 17

I thought Daddy was going to kill me. He had to pick me up at a Whataburger in Sherman. I had walked four miles. There was blood on my face and clothes. I told the woman behind the counter that it was a burst packet of ketchup when I asked if I could use the phone. Daddy is smarter than that.

He broke me just like he always does. I was so tired. I could barely move. He didn't have to threaten much. I wish I could have called Tessie.

Daddy said a lot of things on the way home. *You have no proof he was the killer. Under no circumstances will you have an abortion. Jesus Christ, Lydia. Jesus Christ.*

I overheard him make a call to two of his salvage yard pals. He was paying them to gas up the doctor's rental car and return it.

No matter how hard I try, I can't get warm.

It seems like a million years ago that I stood behind a shed and watched him bury flowers under Tessie's tree house.

Now my parents are on the couch making a plan and I'm out here in my back yard doing a little burying of my own. I'm calling it the little box of Bad Things. The key to the cabin that I forgot to leave on the counter. Tessie's ring that I stole and stuck in a corner of my jewelry box because it was bad luck for her. My favorite Edgar Allan Poe book, because I thought I heard it ticking tonight on the shelf and I wasn't going to live with that the rest of my life. I'm not *ever* going to be crazy like Tessie.

Tessa, present day

She's crazy. *Lydia is crazy.*

When should I have known? As soon as she sat down beside me in second grade with her red glitter pencils sharpened like ice picks?

She's prattling now, like Lydia always does when she tells the truth, about Keats and the sky cracking over the lake and how *the last thing I saw of him was a bald spot like a big mosquito bite* and then *black, black, black.*

The doctor. My monster. Her lover.

At the bottom of the lake. The one where I taught Charlie to slalom. She probably skied right over him.

He was always dead.

Relief, flooding me. Realization, rocking me to hell.

I'm the one who kept my monster alive.

My best friend let that happen. Let me suffer. Let Terrell pay for what he did not do.

Lydia, a greedy flower. More like a black-eyed Susan than any of the girls in that grave. Controlling. Thriving in devastated soil.

"I watched him plant black-eyed Susans under your tree house four hours after we made love for the last time," Lydia is saying smoothly. "I found them in little plastic pots under his cabinet and then I followed him and watched him dig the hole. You don't have to hit *me* over the head." She giggles.

He will never touch my daughter, I'm thinking.

He is bones.

Lydia loved him.

"You look strange, dear," Effie says. "Tired. You should sit."

"The flowers . . . ?" I stutter at Lydia.

"Yes?" Impatient. Waiting for something.

Gratitude. Lydia's waiting for gratitude. I strain against a flood of anger and disbelief. She held my sanity hostage for seventeen years and would like to be thanked for it. I feel a rabid urge to slap her, to tear at her shiny fake hair, to scream *why* until Effie's old house shakes on its foundation.

Lydia is already restless, and I need to be sure. "Lydia," I start again. "If he's dead . . . who kept planting black-eyed Susans for me all these years?"

Her eyes steady on mine. "Are you accusing me? How should I know? They're just *flowers,* Tessie. Are you still freaked out by a PB and J, too?"

"Liz's job has not a thing to do with planting," Effie interjects. "It's Marjory Schwab over at the garden society who's in charge of wildflowers. And it's Blanche something who provides the sandwiches. Or maybe her name is Gladys. And it's Liz, not Lydia, dear."

"It's OK, Effie," I say.

Lydia dabs a napkin at her lips. More pretend. She hasn't taken a bite of whatever Effie lump is on the plate in front of her. "I know you're mad, Tessie. But perfect murders don't just *happen.* Timing is everything. It was very O.J. of me to keep my shirt, don't you think?"

"That's . . . *his* blood on the shirt," I say slowly. "The night you killed him."

"Did you not finish the journal?" she demands. "I gave you forty-five minutes."

My mind is shutting her out. Focusing like a laser on the one thing that is still important. That can still be fixed. *Terrell*.

The doctor's blood on the pink shirt. The fetus in the grave. Aurora's DNA.

All connected. Science that could help free Terrell. If Lydia is telling the truth, the blood on that shirt links them all. The doctor not only fathered Lydia's daughter, but the child of a murdered Black-Eyed Susan.

"Aren't you going to ask me why I'm here?" Lydia sounds plaintive, just like she did at ten and twelve and sixteen. "I have three years of research about the doctor out there in the shed. Colleges he taught at. Girls who disappeared while he was there. Circumstantial, but it ties up pretty nicely. And we'll get them to drag the lake, of course. And I'll let them interview me but I'll be too devastated to share *everything*." She's giddy with her Lydia-ness. "I showed up *for a reason*, Tessie. The last-minute stay will be a fantastic way to end my new book. Even if they kill him, I'm a hero for trying. The book's all about the *other* surviving Black-Eyed Susan. *Me*. I tell it like a modern feminist fairy tale. You'll love it. The point being, the monster gets it in the ass."

"I'm beginning to think you are not with the historical society," Effie says.

Lydia is sticking her fork into a piece of Effie's cake. It's almost to her lips.

I don't stop her.

For the first time in a long time, I feel hope. Like a cool wind has whistled my head clean.

The monster, 1995

October third, nineteen hundred and ninety-five, 1 P.M.

Cheers to O.J., who just walked out of court a free man.

It's our final session. Tessie's got that telltale flush in her cheeks. She's upset.

Her itty-bitty scar stands out on her tan like a new moon in a sky of freckles. No makeup covering it up today. I like that. A sign of restored confidence. The nuclear emerald eyes are sharp and focused. That glorious copper hair is pulled back flat against her skull like she's about to run a race. The muscles in her face are taut and purposeful, not a limp bag hanging off bone like the first day she walked in here. She's still biting her nails but she's painted them carefully with a lovely lavender polish.

I want to tell her so many things.

How I intended to tear her apart, but it was much, much more thrilling to put her back together.

How Rebecca was both a flippant lie I told a lazy reporter and a metaphor for everything. Rebecca is the ghost who kept me company on the worst night of my life. She is every wife and daughter I will never have and every special girl who sat down in my class, lifted her eyes, and did not glimpse her fate.

I want to tell Tessie that sometimes—many times—I am sorry.

341

I want to finish that story I started about the sad boy who walked to a lonely house after school and turned on the heat.

Tessie had been worried about that boy, I could tell. When she's sad, her face always crinkles prettily, like origami.

That boy's mother always left a horrible surprise for him to find while she was at work. A dead baby bird on his pillow. A live water moccasin in the toilet. A cat turd in the Twinkies box. Gags, she called them.

The Saturday night that he put twenty crushed pills into his mother's cheap red wine, she fell asleep on page 136 of Rebecca. *Daphne du Maurier. She pronounced it* doomayer, *like the fat clod she was.*

He had plumped up her pillow, flipped on the air conditioner to high in the middle of winter, and read the whole book before he called the police and told them she'd been suicidal for months.

"I saw you with her." Tessie is taunting me.

I want to put my hand on Tessie's knee to stop its jackhammering.

I want to place that well-thumbed book in her hand.

I want to tell her that red flowers, not yellow ones, had a special meaning for Rebecca.

I want to tell her that very soon, I'm going to run my finger over the butterfly tattoo on her hip. The one just like Lydia's.

EPILOGUE

Imagination, of course, can open any door—turn the key and let terror walk right in.

—Lydia, age 16, reading *In Cold Blood* under the bridge in Trinity Park, waiting for Tessie to finish her run, ten days before the attack, 1994

Tessa

One at a time, the pieces have come forward, like shy girls stepping up to dance.

Lydia admitted to a cold-blooded killing and to a relationship with the doctor, but never to planting the black-eyed Susans in her back yard or at my old apartment or nestled by my grandmother's dead tomato vines or under the bridge that roared like an ocean.

If that's true, the doctor planted flowers exactly once, the first time. The wind and a death penalty nut were responsible for the rest. I allowed a diabolical gardener to live in my head for more than a decade. Like the Brothers Grimm, I ascribed power to an ordinary, innocent object. Oh, the hell that can be wrought from a hand mirror. A single pea. A one-eyed flower.

I remembered the T-shirt Merry was wearing, one morning while I watched Charlie eat Frosted Cheerios out of a yellow cereal bowl that used to be my mother's. *Welcome to CAMP SUNSHINE,* the shirt read, except the dirt and the blood obliterated everything but the *SUN. S-U-N.* My desperate mnemonic device naming the mothers of those girls was just a brain chip gone haywire. *A survival tool,* Dr. Giles says.

Dr. Giles tries to convince me every other session that the Susans in my head weren't real. I'll never believe her. The Susans are about as real as it gets. I used to lie awake at night imagining my mind as my grandfather's house, with passageways and dark rooms seeking a candle and Susans sleeping and waking in all of the many beds. Now the moon is pouring like melted butter through those windows. The floors are swept. The beds are made. The closets emptied.

The Susans have flown from my head, but only because I kept my promises. That was my grandfather's one survival tip if I ever found myself trapped in a fairy tale. Keep your promises. Bad things happen if you don't.

The bones of the two other Susans in that grave have been officially identified as Carmen Rivera, a Mexican foreign exchange student at University of Texas, and Grace Neely, a cognitive studies major at Vanderbilt. The earth's code turned out to be remarkably accurate. Eight other unidentified girls in morgues in three states have been linked to Lydia's meticulous research.

To my relief, Benita Alvarez Smith does not peer out of any picture lineup except the one in her church's directory. Lucas tracked her down for me. She's a happily married mother of two in Laredo who's meeting me for coffee when she's in Fort Worth next month to visit her parents.

The best part, of course, is Terrell. Lydia's encyclopedic research set Terrell free. That, and the DNA match between her shirt and the fetus, created enough reasonable doubt for a state court to halt the execution and release Terrell six weeks later. I was worried that three days wouldn't be enough time to brake the Texas death train. Bill declared that, on Death Row, three days is an eternity.

So now Terrell is tearing out hearts on talk shows, reassuring people about a purposeful life, God, forgiveness, all the things that should not fall out of the mouth of a man who was the innocent victim of a racist system. Off camera, Terrell confines himself to one room, keeps the shades drawn, sleeps best on the couch, so far unable to wean himself from claustrophobia.

He's also collecting $1 million in compensation from the state of Texas and a guaranteed $80,000 annuity every year for life. Who knew that the state that executed the most people also was the most generous in compensating for its errors?

Charlie and I miss Effie. She Skypes us in pink plastic curlers, mails food bricks without regard to the cost of postage, keeps up the good fight with her gremlins. The new owners next door painted her house a non-historical Notre Dame blue and gold. The three tiny human terrors they brought with them have ripped out every bit of Effie's landscaping. Charlie politely refuses to babysit for a standing offer of $20 an hour.

Jo continues her battle with a never-ending supply of monsters, throwing on her white lab coat every day and grinding up the bones of the lost. We've become running buddies, and more. The night before Lydia's grand appearance, she had dropped by. She unfastened her gold DNA charm necklace and looped it around my neck like an amulet of protection.

I spend a lot more time than I'd like to admit thinking about Lydia Frances Bell aka Elizabeth Stride aka Rose Mylett. She makes her home in England, where she lives with her two cats, Pippin and Zelda. At least that's what it says in the bio on the back of her *New York Times* bestseller, *The Secret Susan*. Charlie is reading Lydia's book on the sly. *Let her do it*, Dr. Giles insists.

Charlie and Aurora text regularly. They started following each other on Facebook after the media coverage that threw all of us into a boiling soup for two months. *Aurora's had a sucky life, and I haven't*, Charlie tells me, as if defending the relationship. *She wants to be a nurse. Her foster parents just bought her an old yellow Bug. She's still hoping her mom will pick up the phone and call.*

Their relationship makes me happy, and uneasy.

My gaze is stretching as far as it can over the sloshing, murky Gulf. I'm thinking about how to paint it. With dark, reckless abstract strokes? With a brilliant Jesus sky resurrecting everything that lives under the surface?

Jesus isn't a sunburst today. There was a shark attack an hour ago, so there are only a few spots of brave color in the water. It's cloudy. The water is leaden and impenetrable, like it often is in Galveston even when the sun is shining. The sand is littered with seaweed that makes it feel like you are walking barefoot on a thousand snakes.

My daughter and I return to this rickety rental house for a week every summer anyway. The hard, chunky sand is perfect for castle building. The sunsets are worth every second of still watching. At night, you can plunk down on the seawall and count the fish jumping out of the water in the moonlight. It's an island, ugly and beautiful, with a history as deep and dark and quirky as ours.

For the first time, we tentatively invited company. Bill may drop by this weekend. I'm on the deck, watching Charlie run along the water's edge with her friend Anna, whose mom has been whisked to a three-month rehab for her Big Gulp Diet Coke and vodka habit. No one passing by would guess that anything tugs at either of these teen-agers. They are kicking at the surf, laughing, their chatter mixing it up with the seagulls.

Reminding me of two other girls.

Before Lydia hopped a plane, she told the police a serpentine and wholly convincing tale about the night she took out the Black-Eyed Susan killer. Self-defense. Rape. Manipulation by her parents. The police have never considered filing charges. When they stumbled across the same online psychological journal pieces I did, written under the doctor's name, Lydia freely admitted penning them herself. "It made me feel less like his victim to use his name," she told them. "I can't explain it." So they even let her off the hook for that.

Anti-death-penalty advocates are still trying to goad Terrell into suing her. The female talk show hosts who chatter in silly tribal circles don't like that Lydia cashed in. Domestic violence groups remain staunchly behind her. She was a teen-age girl sexually manipulated by a killer. *Either that,* I think, *or the other way around.* Much has been made about the doctor's cleverness. The risks he took to thwart the process. His ability to fool a district attorney and a devoted father. The way he snaked onto a list of doctor candidates so I'd choose him myself.

I lock my rage in a place I go less and less often. I use the tricks he taught me. When I do let him crawl into my head, he is very much alive. Sitting under that Winslow Homer painting with his legs stretched out, waiting for me. Slithering in the dark along the lake bottom. They've dragged parts of Lake Texoma with high tech equipment three times now, unearthing the skulls of a fifty-something unidentified woman and a two-year-old boy who went under last fall, but not the remains of a monster.

Of course, it makes me wonder.

If almost every word out of Lydia's mouth was a lie.

If her pockets are full of seeds.

If Lydia and I are really finished.

Just in case, I hold on to a final weapon. Her diary. I've curled her notebook into my old hidey-hole in the wall of my grandfather's basement. I won't hesitate to pry open that tomb if I need to. Bring all of her darkness and vanity up to the light. Let Lydia's own words vanquish her. Strip her back down to the pale, weird little girl no one wanted to play with but me.

I do go to sleep certain about one thing.

Wherever Lydia is, alone with her pen or lying on soft sands or stretched out in a field of flowers, the Susans are quietly building their new mansion in her head, brick by brick.

THE END

Look, you shoot off a guy's head with his pants down, believe me, Texas ain't the place you want to get caught.

—Lydia and Tessie, 14, watching *Thelma and Louise*, hanging out the back of a pickup at the Brazos Drive-in, 1992

Acknowledgments

This book took an army of kind, brilliant human beings—scientists, therapists, and legal experts—who generously advised me about cutting-edge DNA science, the impact of psychic trauma on teenagers, and the slow path to a Texas execution.

Mitochondrial DNA whiz and Oklahoma girl **Rhonda Roby** consulted on *Black-Eyed Susans* over text, phone, email, and beer. She also shared her profound experiences identifying victims of serial killers, the Vietnam War, Pinochet, plane crashes, and 9/11. She stood with some of the best scientists in the world at Ground Zero in the days after the attack, and spent years getting answers for families. Her personality, expertise, and humanity are woven throughout this book. And that crazy deer story? It's true. Rhonda now works a dream job as a professor at the J. Craig Venter Institute.

The University of North Texas Center for Human Identification in Fort Worth is represented with a little fictional license, but not much. Its mission, under **Arthur Eisenberg**, is beyond imagining—to put names to unidentified bones when no one else can. Law enforcement agencies from all over the world send their coldest cases here. And, yes, UNTCHI did identify one of the unidentified victims of serial killer John Wayne Gacy thirty-three years after his remains were dug out of a crawl space under a Chicago house.

George Dimitrov Kamenov, a geochemist at the University of Florida, opened my mind to the miracle of isotope analysis and its current use in solving crimes and identifying old bones. He made me understand, more than anyone ever has, that we *are* the earth. George also inspired one of my favorite twists.

Nancy Giles, a longtime children's therapist, provided intricate detail about how both good and bad therapists operate and a reading list of psychiatric textbooks (*Shattered Assumptions, Too Scared to Cry, Trauma and Recovery*) that changed the course of this book. I was also aided by her son, Robert Giles III, an expert with the Child Assistance Program in the Judge Advocate General's Corps for the U.S. Navy, and his wife, Kelly Giles, a therapist who has dedicated a good portion of her life to treating abused children. Nancy's husband, Bob Giles, a two-time Pulitzer Prize–winning editor and former boss of mine, believed in me early in my journalism career. He's a big reason why I eventually had the crazy confidence to write a book.

David Dow, a renowned Texas death penalty attorney, jumped right into the imaginary plot of my book and told me how he'd handle the case. What I didn't expect is that he'd end up feeding the philosophical core of one of my characters. His memoir, *The Autobiography of an Execution,* is unforgettable, and I highly recommend it no matter how you feel about the death penalty.

One of David's former Death Row clients, Anthony Graves, took time out of a precious day of freedom to chat with me on the phone and share his experiences as an innocent man behind bars. He spent eighteen years in prison, falsely accused of killing a family of six. Now free, he operates with a spiritual confidence that makes most of us puny by comparison. Check out his tireless advocacy at www .anthonybelieves.com.

Dennis Longmire, a professor at Sam Houston State University, has shown up for years as a steadfast regular at Texas executions. He holds a battery-operated Christmas candle. One chilly night in front of the Texas Death House, he and other regulars explained the matter-of-fact reality of executions to me. John Moritz, a former

Fort Worth Star-Telegram reporter who witnessed more than a dozen executions, provided additional detail.

The mother-daughter team of **Mary and Mary Clegg,** who run the Whistler bed and breakfast just blocks away from the infamous Walls Unit, revealed the softer side of Huntsville, Texas. I took a little fictional license with the ghosts of their beautiful ancestral home, but they did serve me the most delicious Dutch baby pancake I ever ate. Anyone who stops in Huntsville, don't miss the Marys.

I'd also like to note an article by **Cathy A. Malchiodi** about the use of art intervention with traumatized children. She detailed the case of little "Tessa" and a dollhouse, which I've included as an anecdote in this book.

Laura Gaydosh Combs led me to information on fetal bones.

Black-Eyed Susans is fiction, but it was important to me that the forensic science, the role of therapy in psychic trauma, and the legal path of Texas executions be rooted in truth. If there are any mistakes or flights of fancy, they are mine.

I'd also like to thank:

Christopher Kelly, a phenomenal friend and writer who is a critic when I need one and a shoulder to cry on when I don't.

Kirstin Herrera, the only pal I know who would take me up on a grim invitation to stand outside the Texas death chamber on the night of an execution.

Christina Kowal, for handing me the Big Mac line from the backseat and for inhabiting part of Charlie. Also her mom, dear cuz **Melissa.**

Sam Kaskovich, my son, for drawing mustaches on Jane Eyre, thinking trophies are braggy, and operating with such faith and kindness. This book is passionately dedicated to him.

Kay Schnurman, who makes magic out of thread and steel and was the inspiration for Tessa's artistic side.

Chuck and Sue Heaberlin, my parents, who must wonder why all this dark stuff jumps from my head to paper, but are proud of me anyway.

At Random House, a village: **Kate Miciak,** my editor, a bulldog and a poet who executes the best line edits on the planet; **Jennifer Hershey,** an early champion of *Black-Eyed Susans;* **Libby McGuire; Rachel Kind** and her foreign rights team; my rockin' publicist, **Lindsey Kennedy.** And the people who save me from my errors and turn a book into a beautiful package: production editor **Loren Noveck,** copy editor **Pam Feinstein,** production manager **Angela McNally,** text designer **Dana Leigh Blanchette,** and cover designers **Lee Motley** and **Belina Huey.**

Also, **Kathy Harris** for an early copy edit.

Maxine Hitchcock at Michael Joseph/Penguin UK, for her enthusiastic support of this book and my career.

Danielle Perez. I won't forget. Thank you.

Steve Kaskovich, my husband, therapist, and early reader. The luckiest day of my life was when he threw those Mardi Gras beads across a newsroom and then asked me out until I said yes.

Garland E. Wilson, artist, morgue photographer, singer, and storyteller. He was the best grandfather a girl could have. I miss your creepy basement.

And, finally and most emphatically of all, my agent, **Pam Ahearn,** who was there at every twist and turn of these pages. She never stopped believing in this book or in me. I will be forever grateful.